eBook and Digital Learning Tools

for

By the People

Brief Fourth Edition

JAMES A. MORONE
ROGAN KERSH

Carefully scratch off the silver coating with a coin to see your personal redemption code.

88031018-SH95-8BPV

This code can be used only once and cannot be shared!

If the code has been scratched off when you receive it, the code may not be valid. Once the code has been scratched off, this access card cannot be returned to the publisher. You may buy access at **www.oup.com/us/morone**.

The code on this card is valid for 2 years from the date of first purchase. Complete terms and conditions are available at **https://oup-arc.com**.

Access length: 6 months from redemption of the code.

OXFORD
UNIVERSITY PRESS

Directions for accessing your eBook and Digital Learning Tools

VIA THE OUP SITE

Visit **www.oup.com/us/morone**

↓

Select the edition you are using and the student resources for that edition.

↓

Click the link to upgrade your access to the student resources.

↓

Follow the on-screen instructions.

↓

Enter your personal redemption code when prompted on the checkout screen.

VIA YOUR SCHOOL'S LEARNING MANAGEMENT SYSTEM

Log in to your instructor's course.

↓

When you click a link to a protected resource, you will be prompted to register for access.

↓

Follow the on-screen instructions.

↓

Enter your personal redemption code when prompted on the checkout screen.

For assistance with code redemption or registration, please contact customer support at **arc.support@oup.com**.

BY THE PEOPLE

DEBATING AMERICAN GOVERNMENT

BY THE PEOPLE

DEBATING AMERICAN GOVERNMENT | BRIEF FOURTH EDITION

JAMES A. MORONE
Brown University
ROGAN KERSH
Wake Forest University

NEW YORK OXFORD
OXFORD UNIVERSITY PRESS

Oxford University Press is a department of the University of Oxford. It furthers the University's objective of excellence in research, scholarship, and education by publishing worldwide. Oxford is a registered trade mark of Oxford University Press in the UK and certain other countries.

Published in the United States of America by Oxford University Press
198 Madison Avenue, New York, NY 10016, United States of America.

Library of Congress Cataloging-in-Publication Data

Names: Morone, James A., 1951- author. | Kersh, Rogan, author.
Title: By the people : debating American government / James A. Morone, Brown
    University, Rogan Kersh, Wake Forest University.
Description: Brief Fourth Edition. | New York : Oxford University Press,
    [2018] | Includes bibliographical references and index.
Identifiers: LCCN 2018049759| ISBN 9780190928728 (Paperback) |
ISBN 9780190928759 (Looseleaf) | ISBN 9780190928735 (ebook) |
Subjects: LCSH: United States. Constitution. | United States—Politics and
    government—Textbooks.
Classification: LCC JK276 .M67 2019 | DDC 320.473—dc23
LC record available at https://lccn.loc.gov/2018049759

9 8 7 6 5 4 3 2 1
Printed by LSC Communications, Inc., United States of America

Many teachers and colleagues inspired us. We dedicate this book to four who changed our lives. Their passion for learning and teaching set the standard we aim for every day—and on every page that follows.

Richard O'Donnell

Murray Dry

Jim Barefield

Rogers Smith

By the People comes from the Gettysburg Address. Standing on the battlefield at Gettysburg, President Abraham Lincoln delivered what may be the most memorable presidential address in American history—defining American government as a government "of the people, by the people, for the people." Here is the full address.

Four score and seven years ago our fathers brought forth on this continent, a new nation, conceived in liberty, and dedicated to the proposition that all men are created equal.

Now we are engaged in a great civil war, testing whether that nation, or any nation so conceived and so dedicated, can long endure. We are met on a great battle-field of that war. We have come to dedicate a portion of that field, as a final resting place for those who here gave their lives that that nation might live. It is altogether fitting and proper that we should do this.

But, in a larger sense, we can not dedicate—we can not consecrate—we can not hallow—this ground. The brave men, living and dead, who struggled here, have consecrated it, far above our poor power to add or detract. The world will little note, nor long remember what we say here, but it can never forget what they did here. It is for us the living, rather, to be dedicated here to the unfinished work which they who fought here have thus far so nobly advanced. It is rather for us to be here dedicated to the great task remaining before us—that from these honored dead we take increased devotion to that cause for which they gave the last full measure of devotion—that we here highly resolve that these dead shall not have died in vain—that this nation, under God, shall have a new birth of freedom—and that government of the people, by the people, for the people, shall not perish from the earth.

Brief Contents

Contents

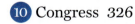

About the Authors

JAMES MORONE (BA, Middlebury College, MA and PhD, University of Chicago) is the John Hazen White Professor of Political Science and Public Policy at Brown University and five-time winner of the Hazeltine Citation for outstanding teacher of the year. Dr. Morone, an award-winning author, has published ten books, including *The Heart of Power* (2009, a "New York Times Notable Book"), *Hellfire Nation* (2003, nominated for a Pulitzer Prize), and *The Democratic Wish* (1990, winner of the American Political Science Association's Kammerer Award for the best book on American politics). He has written over 150 articles and essays, and has commented on politics in the *New York Times*, the *London Review of Books*, and the *American Prospect*. Dr. Morone has been elected to the National Academy of Medicine and the National Academy of Social Insurance. He has served as president of the politics and history section of the American Political Science Association and the New England Political Science Association. He also has served on the board of editors for eight scholarly journals.

ROGAN KERSH (BA, Wake Forest University, MA and PhD, Yale University) is provost and professor of political science at Wake Forest University. A leading scholar in American political science, Dr. Kersh is best known for his work on health reform, obesity politics, and interest groups/lobbying. As a political science faculty member at Syracuse from 1996 to 2006, he won three different teaching awards; from 2006 to 2012, as associate dean of New York University's Wagner School of Public Service, he won both the Wagner and NYU's teaching awards, as well as the Martin Luther King, Jr. Award for scholarship, teaching, and university service. Dr. Kersh has published two books and more than 50 academic articles and has provided commentary on U.S. politics for dozens of different media outlets including CNN, *Newsweek*, and the *New York Times*. He was president of the American Political Science Association's organized section on health politics and policy in 2011–2012 and is an elected fellow of the National Academy of Public Administration.

Preface

AT FIRST, THEY CAME IN SMALL numbers: one child, two children, a few huddled together. Then a surge: In the spring and summer of 2014, tens of thousands of unaccompanied minors crossed the Mexican border into the United States. The exhausted children—mostly from Honduras, Guatemala, and El Salvador—faced poverty and violence at home. Together, this was a humanitarian tragedy. But it was also a political problem.

Conservative critics of the Barack Obama administration slammed the White House for not acting sooner to stem the tide and for being "soft on immigration." Donald Trump launched his long-shot presidential bid, a year later, with a tough attack on undocumented migrants. From the left, another set of voices condemned the president for not providing services to children whose families were so desperate they would send them alone across dangerous ground to an uncertain destiny. Whatever course the administration took, it faced angry rebukes.

As partisans traded insults and pundits criticized the government's mistakes, something remarkable happened: Americans of all backgrounds—urban and rural, churched and secular, liberal and conservative—came together to help the children. College students and local residents joined to hand out medical kits and food packets. Lawyers flew in to offer free legal assistance in securing asylum. Church leaders created makeshift shelters and organized short-term housing among the congregants. One bishop in San Antonio, Texas, said the crisis had deepened his prayer life. This is a classic story that runs right through American history: People pull together in the face of troubled times.

Help or Clash?

That's the United States in a nutshell. People pitch in. This is a nation of joiners and helpers and activists. It always has been. Visitors in the nineteenth century were astonished by the nation's civic spirit. To this day Americans form book groups, organize car washes to raise money for good causes, stack sandbags during floods, send checks to the Red Cross, support the military, and insist that the government help those who need help. "We are inevitably our brother's keeper because we are our brother's brother," wrote Martin Luther King. "Whatever affects one directly affects all indirectly."[1]

But that's only one side of the story. Stream a news show and what do you see? Fights! A few years ago, one of us (Jim) was about to go on a news show to discuss the fallout after singer Janet Jackson inadvertently (and very briefly) went X-rated during the Super Bowl halftime show. Jim was scheduled alongside another commentator who was very agitated about Jackson's behavior and believed that it signaled the decline of America. Jim told the producer that, after exploring our different views, it would be great if we could find some common ground. No way, retorted the producer, who explained her ideal closing shot: You'll be shouting over each other on a split screen while the host coolly ends the segment by saying, "We'll have to leave it there for now, but feelings run high and we'll be hearing a lot more on this topic." Unfortunately, searching for common ground does not draw an audience like people screaming onscreen.

The producer was demonstrating another side of America: rugged individualists who push their own views and self-interests. Individualism is also an all-American story. Its origins lie in a frontier culture that expected everyone to watch out for themselves. This is the America that resents anyone—especially the government—telling people what to do.

Which is the real America? They both are. Sometimes this is a land of cooperation, sometimes a nation of competition. American politics, as you'll see, reflects both views.

By the People?

This brief edition of *By the People* was created for those who want a shorter, streamlined, and less expensive version of the more comprehensive edition.

---

[1] *Where Do We Go from Here: Chaos or Community?* (New York: Harper & Row, 1967) 181.

Although we have condensed the longer book's story of American government—there is less history and policy here—we think we have preserved the book's essential features, engagements, insights, and tone.

We picked the book's title—*By the People*—because Lincoln's phrase raises the deepest question in American politics: Who has the power? Or to put it more pointedly, do the people rule in this day and age? Democracy is a constant struggle; it is an aspiration, a wish, a quest. In every chapter we'll ask how well Americans are living up to Lincoln's ideal. Does the new media (Chapter 7) or the contemporary Congress (Chapter 10) or the bureaucracy (Chapter 12) or state government (Chapter 3) support or subvert government by the people? We'll present the details—and let you decide whether we should press for reform or leave things alone.

We'll be straight with you: We won't pretend there was a golden age in some imaginary past. After all, the United States has been home to political machines that enthusiastically stole votes, maintains an Electoral College designed to distort the people's vote for president, and governs through an elaborate system of checks and balances that blunts the popular will. (Again, you'll soon see two sides to each of these features of American government.) At the same time, you'll read about bold popular movements and unexpected electoral surges that changed the face of the nation. In many ways, these are the most exciting moments in American history. They spring up at unexpected times, inspiring ordinary people to achieve great things. Does Donald Trump's election signify such a surge? Or are the protest movements that have sprung up the larger agent of change? Read on and you'll be able to answer those questions—and many more.

Who Are We?

Here's Jim's very first political memory: My parents were watching TV, and as soon as I walked into the room I could see that my mother was trying hard not to cry. "What's going on?" I asked my parents nervously. My dad—a proud Republican who had fought in World War II—said, "Well, the U.S. had a racial problem, but that man there, he's going to get us past it." "That man there" was Martin Luther King Jr., giving one of the most famous speeches in American history: "I have a dream," said King, that "my four little children will one day live in a country where they will not be judged by the color of their skin but by the content of their character." My mother had been born in Poland and her near tears reflected pride in her new nation—and the uplifting aspirations of that August day.

Both of us grew up thinking about the dream—and about the nation that dreams it. America is constantly changing, constantly new. In every chapter we'll ask the same question: Who are we? We'll explore a lot of different answers.

Four themes are especially important in this book. **Race** touches everything in the United States, from the Constitution (Chapter 2) to the political parties (Chapter 9). The nation rose up out of both freedom and slavery; race quickly became one of the great crucibles of American liberty. Likewise, **immigration** includes some of history's saddest passages involving the mistreatment of recent arrivals. And yet we are a nation of immigrants that continues to welcome the world's "huddled masses yearning to breathe free"—the famous words long associated with the Statue of Liberty. More than a fifth of all the emigrants around the globe come to the United States every year. Race and immigration are tied up in another powerful topic: **gender and sexuality**. From women in Congress to same-sex marriage, from teen pregnancy to abortion, we'll show how negotiating an answer to "Who are we?" always puts an emphasis on questions of gender and sexuality. Finally, we're especially interested in **American generations**, and more specifically the attitudes and contributions of today's young people, the millennial generation. If you're one of them, the future belongs to you. This book is an owner's manual for the government that you're going to inherit. We'll have much to say about you as we go along.

The most important thing about all these categories is not their history, or the ways they've influenced voting behavior, or how the courts treat them—although we'll cover all those topics. Rather, what matters most about American politics are the opportunities to get involved. As you'll see, groups and individuals can and do make a difference in a nation that is always evolving. We hope our book inspires you to actively participate in making the American future.

How Government Works

We won't oversell the role of individuals. People's ability to advance political change is always shaped by the way the government is organized and operates. From the very start, this book emphasizes the unusual structure of American government.

Begin with a Constitution full of checks and balances, add a multilayered federalism, develop a chaotic public administration (President Franklin Roosevelt cheerfully called the uproar a three-ring circus), spin off functions to the private sector (especially during wars), complexify Congress (thirty-one different committees and subcommittees tried to claim jurisdiction over just one national health insurance proposal), and inject state and federal courts into every cranny of the system. Then throw the entire apparatus open to any interest group that shows up. The twenty-first century adds a 24/7 news cycle with commentary all the time and from every angle.

Turn to foreign policy, where high principles contend with tough-minded realism in a fractious world. When the most formidable military in human history is mustered into action, watch presidential power expand so rapidly that it sets off international debates about whether the great republic is morphing into an empire.

In Short

As you read this book, you'll repeatedly encounter four questions:

- *Who governs?* This is the question of democracy and power—or, as we phrased it earlier: Is this government by the people? And if and where it falls short, how might we refresh our democracy?

- *How does American politics work?* Our job is to make you think like a political scientist. What does that involve? You'll learn in the next chapter—and throughout the book.

- *What does government do?* You can't answer the first two questions if you don't know what the courts or the White House or Congress or interest groups actually do—and how they do it.

- *Who are we?* Americans endlessly debate America's identity. We are students, businesspeople, Hispanics, seniors, Texans, environmentalists, gays, Republicans, Democrats, Christians, Muslims, military families—and the list goes on. Sometimes it adds up to one united people; at other times we're left to wonder how to get along. Either way, American politics rises up from—and shapes—a cacophony of identities and interests.

Changes to the Fourth Edition

In this new edition, we have:

- Analyzed recent seismic events, especially involving the Trump administration, that have shaken up U.S. institutions, ideas, and interests.

- Supplied new and updated statistics and figures in each chapter, tracking both long- and short-run political trends.

- Analyzed the mixed results of the 2018 midterm elections.

- Traced the erosion of civil discourse and expanding polarization within American society, made manifest in moments such as the controversial Supreme Court nomination of Justice Brett Kavanaugh and related #metoo movement.

- Directly encouraged readers to plunge into the great pageant of American government, in part through posing queries inviting them to take a side on vital issues.

- Tackled the issue of "fake news" and related charges of media bias.

- Updated immigration coverage, including a new section to cover the rights of non-citizens in the United States.

- Provided students with the background needed to understand contentious policies surrounding trade wars, free trade, and trade agreements.

- Called attention to the important role of the federal bureaucracy in underserved, rural areas in a new chapter opening vignette.

- Added a new evaluation of how federalism has evolved during the Obama and Trump administrations.

- Expanded coverage of the LGBTQ civil rights movement.

- Added a new What Do YOU Think? feature about appointing bureaucrats to address the issue and concern regarding a "deep state."

- Incorporated updated data on millennial trends in party affiliation, attitudes, and changing styles of participation.

- Revised By the Numbers features to focus on a theme within the chapter and ask fundamental questions related to that theme.

- Updated infodata features so that the first question always asks students to quantitatively analyze the visual, and the second question asks students to apply that information to consider a related issue.

- Systematically balanced examples from left and right, to take into account new political sensitivities in our highly partisan age.

Getting Involved

By the People is a new approach to courses in American government. The book displays U.S. politics and government in all its glory, messiness, and power. Like every textbook, this one informs our readers. But, as we hope you can already see, we don't describe government (or ideas about government) as inert and fixed. What's exciting about American politics, like the nation itself, is how fast it changes. And the constant, endless arguments about what it is and what it should be next. Our aim is to get you engaged—whether you already love politics, are a complete newcomer to government, or whether you are a newcomer to the United States itself. In the pages that follow, we'll bring American government to life. Get ready to start a great debate . . . about your future.

One final word: We've been working out the story line for this book throughout our teaching careers. We've taught everything from very large lectures to small seminars. Like all teachers, we've learned through trial and error. We've worked hard to pack this book with the stories, questions, and features that our own students have found effective. That spirit—the lessons we've learned in the classroom—animates everything that follows.

Teaching and Learning Support

Oxford University Press (OUP) offers instructors and students a comprehensive teaching and learning package of support materials for adopters of *By the People, 4e.*

Ancillary Resource Center

The Ancillary Resource Center (ARC) at www.oup.com/us/Morone is a convenient destination for all teaching and learning resources that accompany this book. Accessed online through individual user accounts, the ARC provides instructors with up-to-date ancillaries while guaranteeing the security of grade-significant resources. In addition, it allows OUP to keep users informed when new content becomes available. The ARC for *By the People: Debating American Government, 4e* contains a variety of materials to aid in teaching:

Instructor's Resource Manual with Test Item File—The Instructor's Resource Manual includes chapter objectives, detailed chapter outlines, lecture suggestions and activities, discussion questions, video resources, and web resources. The Test Item File includes more than 2,500 test questions including multiple-choice, short-answer, and essay questions.

Computerized Test Bank—The computerized test bank that accompanies this text is designed for both novice and advanced users. It enables instructors to create and edit questions, create randomized quizzes and tests with an easy-to-use drag-and-drop tool, publish quizzes and tests to online courses, and print quizzes and tests for paper-based assessments.

PowerPoint-Based Slides—Each chapter has two slide decks to support your lectures. One deck includes the chapter outline and content; the other includes only the artwork included in the text.

CNN and other video resources—Offering recent clips on timely topics, clips are approximately 5 to 10 minutes in length providing a great way to launch your lectures about key concepts with real-world issues and examples.

Digital Learning Tools

www.oup.com/us/Morone

By the People: Debating American Government, 4e comes with an extensive array of digital learning tools to ensure your students get the most out of your course. Approximately 45 homework assignments—totaling over 12 hours of assignable materials—organized by chapter, with autograded assessments have been developed exclusively to support OUP's *By the People* text. These activities have been extensively reviewed by users of similar digital content in their classrooms. Several assignment types provide your students with various activities that teach core concepts, allow students to develop data literacy around important contemporary topics and issues, and to role play as decision makers to engage with problems that simulate real-world political challenges. The activities are optimized to work on any mobile device or computer. For users of learning management systems, results can be recorded to the gradebooks in one of several currently supported systems. Access to these activities are provided free with purchase of a new print or electronic textbook. These and additional study tools are available at www.oup.com/us/Morone, through links embedded in the enhanced eBook, and within course cartridges. Each activity is described below:

Interactive Media Activities are simulations of real-world events, problems, and challenges developed to connect text and classroom topics to everyday life. Designed to be assigned as homework, each activity takes approximately 15 to 20 minutes to complete and produces unique results for each student. Students are placed into the role of a political actor or decision maker, get to experience how various aspects of politics works, and see the trade-offs required to produce meaningful policies and outcomes. Topics include the following:

- Individualism versus Solidarity
- Passing Immigration Reform
- Electing Cheryl Martin
- Building the USS Relief
- Intervening in Bhutan
- The Fight Against Warrantless Wiretapping
- Balancing the Budget
- Redistricting in "Texachusetts"
- Saving the Electric Car
- Election Reform
- Fact Checking the Media

- Passing the Thirteenth Amendment
- Negotiating with China
- *NEW*—Healthcare and Federalism
- *NEW*—The Changing Face of Affirmative Action
- *NEW*—Surveys, Bias, and Fake News
- *NEW*—Free Speech on Campus
- *NEW*—The People Versus the Pipeline

Media Tutorials: These animated videos are designed to teach key concepts taught in the course, as well as address important contemporary issues. Each tutorial runs 2 to 4 minutes in length and ends with an assessment for students to test what they know. Topics include the following:

- The Constitution: A Brief Tour
- Civil Rights: How Does the Fourteenth Amendment Ensure Equal Rights for All Citizens?

- Federalism: What Does It Mean to Incorporate the Bill of Rights?
- Political Participation: What Affects Voter Turnout?

- Media: How Is the News Shaped by Agenda Setting, Framing, and Profit Bias?
- Interest Groups: What Is a Political Action Committee (PAC), and What Makes Some PACs Super PACs?
- Congress: Why Do We Hate Congress but Keep Electing the Same Representatives?
- The Judiciary: How Do Judges Interpret the Constitution?
- Polling: How Do We Know What People Know?

- Campaigns and Elections: How Does Gerrymandering Work?
- *NEW*—Democracy Versus Republic
- *NEW*—Freedom of Religion
- *NEW*—Executive Orders
- *NEW*—Political Culture Across States
- *NEW*—Party Organization
- *NEW*—Bureaucracies
- *NEW*—Discretionary and Mandatory Spending

NEW—**Issue Navigators:** These new features offer students an interactive way to explore data related to major issues in American politics today, and allow students to reflect on the sources of their own views and opinions. Each activity will improve your students' abilities to think through their political opinions by using compelling and vetted information to raise the level of classroom debate. Students will analyze several data sources and positions for each topic. They'll then get to answer questions that indicate their own beliefs and values on these issues, and compare them to national polling data. The exercises include assessments around the data to ensure students can interpret the data presented and understand what it means. Issues include the following:

- Climate Change
- Immigration
- Gerrymandering/Redistricting
- Gun Control
- Free Trade and Tariffs
- Healthcare Reform
- Social Security
- Tax Reform

Enhanced eBook: The enhanced eBook provides students with a versatile, accessible, online version of the textbook, with all of the above resources integrated on the appropriate pages via clickable icons that connect to each study tool. The eBook reader also provides functionality that will help students be more effective in their study time—for instance, bookmarking, highlighting, note taking, and search tools. Every new copy of the print text includes access to the eBook. The eBook is also available for separate purchase, either online or through campus bookstores.

Online Study Tools: Many additional online study tools are available at www.oup.com/us/Morone for the student's self-paced learning and assessment. For each chapter, these include interactive flashcards, chapter review PowerPoint slides, key term quizzes, chapter quizzes, chapter exams, short-answer and essay tests, videos, web activities, and web links.

Learning Management System Integration: OUP offers the ability to integrate OUP content into currently supported versions of Canvas, D2L, or Blackboard. Contact your local rep or visit oup-arc.com/integration for more information.

Format Choices

Oxford University Press offers cost-saving alternatives to meet the needs of all students. This text is offered in a loose-leaf format at a 30 percent discount off the list price of the text; and in an eBook format, through Redshelf for a 50 percent discount. You also can customize our textbooks to create the course material you want for your class. For more information, please contact your Oxford University Press representative, call 800.280.0280, or visit us online at www.oup.com/us/Morone.

Packaging Options

Adopters of *By the People* can package *any* Oxford University Press book with the text for a 20 percent savings off the total package price. See our many trade and scholarly offerings at www.oup.com, then contact your local OUP sales representative to request a package ISBN. Below are additional suggestions to package with the text:

STAY CURRENT

For an additional $10, package Emenaker and Morone's *Current Debates in American Government*, Second Edition!

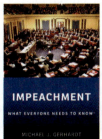

GET SPECIALIZED

Package with a *What Everyone Needs to Know* paperback **for only $5!** Written by leading experts, each volume in this acclaimed series offers a balanced and authoritative primer on complex issues and countries.

WRITE AND RESEARCH BETTER

Package with *Writing in Political Science* **for only $5** or *Research and Writing Guide for Political Science* for free!

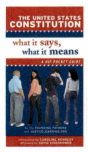

KNOW YOUR RIGHTS

Package with *The United States Constitution: What It Says, What It Means* **for free!**

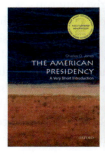 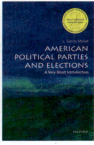

BECOME AN EXPERT IN NO TIME

Package one of Oxford's *Very Short Introductions* **for free!**

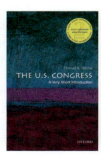 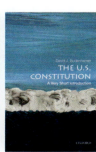

Acknowledgments

One particular goal we had with this edition was to ensure that our presentation of this subject was as balanced and unbiased as possible, given the political climate today. In order to achieve this, we sought the council and advice of David C. W. Parker from Montana State University. His expertise on Congress, and especially the Conservative Republican agenda, both before and after Trump was elected, helped us to present and celebrate the multiplicity of political perspectives in U.S. politics today. David read every word, and saved us from errors of fact and judgment alike. We are very thankful for his contributions which were thoughtful and considerable and which made the book all the better.

When he signed us up to write this book, publisher John Challice looked us each in the eye and said, "You know, this is going to be so much work—you're going to be married to us." He was right. Yes, it was a lot of work. And yes, the Oxford team has been like a family that carried us through the process.

There would be no book without Jennifer Carpenter, our extraordinary editor. She guided us through the process with enormous skill. Along the way, Jen earned the highest praise authors can give their editor: She cared about the book as much as we did. Our development editor, Naomi Friedman, helped us so much she ought to be considered a coauthor—she suggested, edited, cut, and cheered. Development manager Thom Holmes gracefully turned our messy manuscript into a tight narrative bursting with special features. Assistant editor Alison Ball guided the art program and tracked down every picture in the following pages. Senior production editor Barbara Mathieu and production manager Phil Scott coordinated an amazing production process; we broke the publishing record for the number of times two authors wrote, "Good point!" in the margins of an edited manuscript. Judy Ann Levine did a fine copy edit on an impossible schedule. Art director Michele Laseau did the beautiful design. We are especially grateful to marketing manager Tony Mathias for getting this book into your hands. To all of you in our immediate Oxford family: Thank you! Thank you!

We had an even more important team at our side—our families and our friends. Over the course of this book's initial conception and subsequent writing, Rogan moved from Syracuse University's Maxwell School to New York University's Wagner School, with a sabbatical leave at Yale along the way—and then, just as we were finishing the first edition, to Wake Forest University. Colleagues in all four places were unfailingly generous with ideas and comments; thanks especially to Suzanne Mettler, Jeff Stonecash, David Mayhew, Ellen Schall, Shanna Rose, and Shankar Prasad. Because we strive throughout to get both the political science and the practical politics right, a group of experienced and reflective inside-the-Beltway friends cheerfully and patiently provided insight into their world: Bill Antholis, Matt Bennett, Laura Schiller, Erik Fatemi, Tom Dobbins, Dan Maffei, Bob Shrum, Marylouise Oates, and Don and Darrel Jodrey. Grateful thanks to them as well as a wonderful set of current and former students, many now working in government and politics.

By the People's long journey to completion grew infinitely more enjoyable once Sara Pesek joined me for the trip—through this book and everywhere else, from Australia to Ze Café in midtown New York City. Sara's insights into public policy made for the liveliest newlyweds' conversations (if you're a politics junkie) imaginable; my biggest bouquet of thanks to her for that rarest of gifts: a loving, fully joined partnership.

Jim offers warm thanks to my colleagues at Brown who form a wonderful community of scholars and teachers—always ready for coffee, lunch, or wine and a conversation about political science. Extra thanks to Peter Andreas, Mark Blyth, Corey Brettschneider, Ross Cheit, Elisabeth Fauquert, Alex Gourevitch, Rebecca Henderson, Bonnie Honig, Sharon Krause, Rick Locke, Susan Moffitt, Rich Snyder, Wendy Schiller, and Ashu Varshney. And my wonderful students sampled every idea in this book. They are my constant teachers. Grateful thanks to Ryan Emenaker, Dan Carrigg, Kevin McGravey, Ferris Lupino, Rachel Meade, Meghan Wilson, Aaron Weinstein, Brandon Welch, and Cadence Willse.

My brothers, Joe and Peter Morone—and their families—are lifelong companions always ready with a cheerful take on the state of politics and the world. Special thanks to Lindsay, Ann, Joe, James (now a rising political scientist at Penn), Noreen, and Maegan Morone. My mother, Stasia, kept reminding me to enjoy the journey—and that there might be more to life than *By the People*. And the memory of my dad was a constant visitor as I read, and thought, and wrote.

The revisions for this edition were joyfully interrupted by Jim's wedding. If you detect a smile between the lines, it's because we were celebrating my new family. Rebecca Henderson leapt into my life filling it with talk and ideas and dreams (and much more). And Harry, my wonderful son, takes me hiking and talks me through high ridges that I couldn't imagine trying without him. If this edition reads happier than the last—it's the spirit of Harry and Rebecca on the pages.

Manuscript Reviewers

We have greatly benefited from the perceptive comments and suggestions of the many talented scholars and instructors who reviewed the manuscript of *By the People*. They went far beyond the call of duty in sharing thoughts and making corrections. Their insight and suggestions contributed immensely to the work.

Fourth Edition

Alex Acs
Ohio State University

John Robert Altick
The Citadel

Patricia Andrews
West Valley College

Matthew Bergbower
Indiana State University

Linda M. Bos
Mount Mary University

Diana Cohen
Central Connecticut State University

William J. Corbett
New Mexico State University

Nelson C. Dometrius
Texas Tech University

Bruce Farcau
University of Central Florida, Valencia College

Richard Groper
California State University Los Angeles

Jan Hardt
University of Central Oklahoma

Soren Jordan
Auburn University

Philip Klinkner
Hamilton College

Eric Lopez
University of Texas at Tyler

Arlene Sanders
Delta State University

Carly Schmitt
Indiana State University

Cynthia Stavrianos
Gonzaga University

Chunmei Yoe
Southeastern Oklahoma State University

Third Edition

Bryan T. Calvin
Tarrant County College, Northwest

John Carnes
Lone Star College–Kingwood

Rosalind Blanco Cook
Tulane University

Paul B. Davis
Truckee Meadows Community College

Michael Dichio
Fort Lewis College

Dawn Eaton
San Jacinto College South

Kathleen Ferraiolo
James Madison University

Ingrid Haas
University of Nebraska–Lincoln

James Hite
Portland State University

Jeneen Hobby
Cleveland State University

Michael Hoover
Seminole State College

Daniel Hummel
Idaho State University

Nina Kasniunas
Goucher College

Nicholas LaRowe
University of Southern Indiana

Brad Lockerbie
East Carolina University

A. Lanethea Mathews-Schultz
Muhlenberg College

Don Mirjanian
College of Southern Nevada

Carolyn Myers
Southwestern Illinois College

Hong Min Park
University of Wisconsin–Milwaukee

Marjorie K. Nanian
Schoolcraft College

Coyle Neal
Southwest Baptist University

Paul Parker
Truman State University

Jane Rainey
Eastern Kentucky University

Joseph Romance
Fort Hays State University

Michael Romano
Georgia Southern University

Jennifer Sacco
Quinnipiac University

Eric Schwartz
Hagerstown Community College

Daniel Lavon Spinks
Stephen F. Austin State University

Jeffrey M. Stonecash
Syracuse University

Kathleen Tipler
University of Oklahoma

Carl Wege
Social Sciences College of Coastal Georgia

Geoffrey Willbanks
Tyler Junior College

Second Edition

Nathan Blank
Casper College, University of Wyoming, Kentucky Community & Technical College System

Nichole Boutte-Heiniluoma
Jarvis Christian College

Blake Farrar
Texas State University

Jennifer Felmley
Santa Fe Community College

Paul Foote
Eastern Kentucky University

Jeneen Hobby
Cleveland State University

Gary Johnson
Weber State University

Steven Nawara
Valdosta State University

Geoffrey Peterson
University of Wisconsin–Eau Claire

Ronald C. Schurin
University of Connecticut

John Shively
Longview Community College

Toni-Michelle C. Travis
George Mason University

First Edition

Brian A. Bearry
University of Texas at Dallas

Emily Bentley
Savannah State University

R. M. Bittick
Sam Houston State University

Wendell S. Broadwell Jr.
Georgia Perimeter College

Allison Bunnell
Fitchburg State University

Frank P. Cannatelli
Southern Connecticut State University

Jason P. Casellas
University of Texas at Austin

Stefanie Chambers
Trinity College, Hartford, Connecticut

Suzanne Chod
Pennsylvania State University

Michael Cobb
North Carolina State University

McKinzie Craig
Texas A&M University

Michael Crespin
University of Georgia

Amanda DiPaolo
Middle Tennessee State University

Stewart Dippel
University of the Ozarks

Jasmine Farrier
University of Louisville

Michaela Fazecas
University of Central Florida

Joseph J. Foy
University of Wisconsin–Parkside

Megan Francis
Pepperdine University

Rodd Freitag
University of Wisconsin–Eau Claire

Joseph Gardner
Northern Arizona University

David Goldberg
College of DuPage

Frederick Gordon
Columbus State University

Jeff Harmon
University of Texas at San Antonio

Jeneen Hobby
Cleveland State University

Mark S. Jendrysik
University of North Dakota

Brian Kessel
Columbia College

Christopher L. Kukk
Western Connecticut State University

Sujith Kumar
University of Central Arkansas

Lisa Langenbach
Middle Tennessee State University

William W. Laverty
University of Michigan–Flint

Jeffrey Lazarus
Georgia State University

Angela K. Lewis
University of Alabama at Birmingham

Gregg Lindskog
Temple University

Brent A. Lucas
North Carolina State University

Thomas R. Marshall
University of Texas at Arlington

A. Lanethea Mathews
Muhlenberg College

Vaughn May
Belmont University

Lauri McNown
University of Colorado at Boulder

Christina A. Medina
New Mexico State University

Patrick R. Miller
University of Cincinnati

Michael K. Moore
University of Texas at Arlington

Roger Morton
California State University, Long Beach

Yamini Munipalli
Florida State College at Jacksonville

Gary Mucciaroni
Temple University

Jason Mycoff
University of Delaware

Steven Nawara
Valdosta State University

Anthony Neal
Buffalo State College

Mark Nicol
Saginaw Valley State University

Stephen A. Nuño
Northern Arizona University

Michael Parkin
Oberlin College

Richard Pious
Barnard College

Elizabeth A. Prough
Eastern Michigan University

Wesley B. Renfro
St. John Fisher College

John F. Roche, III
Palomar College

Amanda M. Rosen
Webster University

Anjali Sahay
Gannon University

Joanna Vecchiarelli Scott
Eastern Michigan University

Samuel Shelton
Troy University

Majid Shirali
University of Nevada, Las Vegas

Joyce Stickney Smith
Hillsborough Community College, Ybor Campus

Mitchel A. Sollenberger
University of Michigan–Dearborn

Chris Soper
Pepperdine University

Barry L. Tadlock
Ohio University

Edwin A. Taylor III
Missouri Western State University

Delaina Toothman
Texas State University

Jan P. Vermeer
Nebraska Wesleyan University

Jennifer E. Walsh
Azusa Pacific University

Donn Worgs
Towson University

Larry L. Wright
Florida A&M University

Shoua Yang
St. Cloud State University

Mike Yawn
Sam Houston State University

Melanie C. Young
University of Nevada, Las Vegas

Khodr M. Zaarour
Shaw University

Marketing Reviewers

Oxford University Press would also like to acknowledge the contribution of additional scholars and instructors who class tested and provided their assessment of the completed manuscript, using this work with hundreds of students in classrooms across the nation.

Second Edition

Ted Anagnoson
University of California, Santa Barbara

Steven Bayne
Century College

Joshua Berkenpas
Western Michigan University

Jeff Bloodworth
Gannon University

Theodore C. Brown
Virginia State University

Kim Casey
Northwest Missouri State University

Jay Cerrato
Bronx Community College

Ericka Christensen
Washington State University

Kevin Davis
North Central Texas College—Corinth

Dennis Driggers
California State University, Fresno

Paul Gottemoller
Del Mar College

Sara Gubala
Lamar University

Dan Guerrant
Middle Georgia College

Timothy Kersey
Kennesaw State University

Michael Latner
California Polytechnic State University

Maruice Mangum
Texas Southern University

Donna Merrell
Kennesaw State University

Patrick Moore
Richland College

Martha Musgrove
Tarrant County College—Southeast Campus

Michael Petersen
Utah State University

Mikhail Rybalko
Texas Tech University

Joanna Sabo
Monroe County Community College

Hayden Smith
Washington State University

First Edition

Gayle Alberda
Owens Community College

Herrick Arnold
Orange Coast College

Alex L. Avila
Mesa Community College

John Barnes
University of Southern California

Charles Barrilleaux
Florida State University

Ronald Bee
Cuyamaca College

Michael Berkman
Pennsylvania State University

Angelina M. Cavallo
San Jacinto College

Adam Chamberlain
Coastal Carolina University

Matt Childers
University of Georgia

Benjamin Christ
Harrisburg Area Community College

Diana Cohen
Central Connecticut State University

Paul M. Collins
University of North Texas

William Corbett
New Mexico State University

Mark Ellickson
Missouri State University

Deborah Ferrell-Lynn
University of Central Oklahoma

Paul Foote
Eastern Kentucky University

Peter L. Francia
East Carolina University

Rodd Freitag
University of Wisconsin–Eau Claire

Fred Gordon
Columbus State University

John I. Hanley
Syracuse University

Jeff Hilmer
Northern Arizona University

Jeneen Hobby
Cleveland State University

Ronald J. Hrebenar
University of Utah

Mark Jendrysik
University of North Dakota

Aubrey Jewett
University of Central Florida

Gary Johnson
Weber State University

Michelle Keck
The University of Texas at Brownsville

William Kelly
Auburn University

John Klemanski
Oakland University

Richard Krupa
Harper College

Christine Lipsmeyer
Texas A&M University

Brent Lucas
North Carolina State University

Margaret MacKenzie
San Jacinto College

Jason McDaniel
San Francisco State University

John Mercurio
San Diego State University

Melissa Merry
University of Louisville

Roger Morton
California State University, Long Beach

Gary Mucciaroni
Temple University

Adam J. Newmark
Appalachian State University

Randall Newnham
Pennsylvania State University

Roger Nichols
Southwestern College

Anthony J. Nownes
University of Tennessee, Knoxville

Anthony O'Regan
Los Angeles Valley College

Kenneth O'Reilly
Milwaukee Area Technical College

Sunday P. Obazuaye
Cerritos College

Amanda M. Olejarski
Shippensburg University

Kevin Parsneau
Minnesota State University

Michelle Pautz
University of Dayton

Martin J. Plax
Cleveland State University

Sherri Replogle
Illinois State University

Kim Rice
Western Illinois University

Ray Sandoval
Dallas County Community College
District

Laura Schneider
Grand Valley State University

Scot Schraufnagel
Northern Illinois University

Ronnee Schreiber
San Diego State University

Ronald Schurin
University of Connecticut

Jeffrey M. Stonecash
Syracuse University

Katrina Taylor
Northern Arizona University

Ryan Lee Teten
University of Louisiana

John P. Todsen
Drake University

Delaina Toothman
University of Maine

Dan Urman
Northeastern University

Ronald W. Vardy
University of Houston

Adam L. Warber
Clemson University

Gerald Watkins
Kentucky Community & Technical
College System

Patrick Wohlfarth
University of Maryland, College Park

Wayne L. Wolf
South Suburban College

Jeff Worsham
West Virginia University

Finally, thanks to you for picking up this book. We hope you enjoy reading it as much as we did writing.

Jim Morone and Rogan Kersh

BY THE PEOPLE

DEBATING AMERICAN GOVERNMENT

Ideas That Shape American Politics

ARMY CAPTAIN RUSSELL BURGOS hunkered down in his bunker as mortars ripped through the night. A year ago he had been a political science professor; now he was fighting in Iraq. Burgos's unit was operating in an area where the fighting was fiercest. "A mortar attack in the middle of the night," he mused, "is an odd place to reconsider a course syllabus." But that is exactly what he found himself doing. Experiencing war made him see politics in new ways.[1]

As shells fell on the American base, Burgos realized that his classes had been missing something: the study of ideas. All around him, men and women were fighting and dying over ideas—ideas such as freedom, democracy, equality, power, and faith in God. Strangely enough, Burgos wrote later, ideas had barely come up in his own political science classes. Yet ideas helped explain why the United States launched the war, how it fought the war, and how it explained the war to both friends and enemies.

Who are we? Our ideas tell us—and they tell the world. The United States is a nation built on ideas. You will see ideas at work in every chapter of this book, for they touch every feature of government and politics. As you read about these concepts—and as you continue through this book—think about other important ideas that should be added to the list alongside the seven we discuss in this chapter. If you come up with a compelling example, we may quote you in the next edition.

In this chapter, you will:

- Learn about the four questions that guide this book.

- Explore the seven key ideas that shape American politics.

- Investigate the essential question: How do ideas affect politics?

Army Captain Russell Burgos hands out supplies to Iraqi children.

BY THE NUMBERS

American Ideas

Number of times the word *rights* appears in the Declaration of Independence	10
Number of times the word *rights* appears in the original Constitution	0
Number of times the word *rights* appears in amendments to the Constitution	15
Percentage of Americans who say a representative democracy, a direct democracy, rule by experts, and rule by military is a good way to govern the country, respectively	86, 67, 40, 17[2]
Percentage of total wealth in the United States owned by top 1%, top 10%, and bottom 90%, respectively	40, 78, 22[3]
Percentage of Americans who say that government should act to reduce economic inequality	65[4]
Percentage of Americans who think prayer should be allowed in public schools	57[5]

What expectations do you have of government? What ideas guide your political actions?

The Spirit of American Politics

We address four questions throughout this book to help make sense of American politics and government. By the time you finish reading, you will understand the debates sparked by each question—and you will be ready (and, we hope, eager) to join the debates.

Who Governs?

As Benjamin Franklin left the Constitutional Convention in 1787, a woman stopped him. "What kind of government have you given us?" she asked. According to legend, the wise old Franklin responded, "A republic, madam—if you can keep it." The United States organized itself around a ringing declaration of popular rule: Governments derive "their just power from the consent of the governed." In a **republic**, the people are in charge. Franklin knew, however, that popular governments are extremely difficult to "keep." All previous republics—such as Athens, Rome, and Florence—had collapsed. His point was that the people must be vigilant and active if they are to maintain control. Every American generation faces new challenges in keeping the republic.

Who governs? Do the people rule? Some of us would answer "yes—and today more than ever." After all, candidates such as Donald Trump and Bernie Sanders defied party leaders in the 2016 election. Sanders won twenty-three contests and Trump went all the way to the White House. Ordinary people can make a difference too. After a gunman murdered seventeen people at Marjory Stoneman Douglas High School in Parkland, Florida, students confronted politicians about guns and school safety and shook up an old political stalemate. Six weeks later Florida Governor Rick Scott signed bipartisan legislation introducing some gun controls. These examples suggest that our government still reflects the ideas and passions of the people.

Yet America's popular government faces a lot of paradoxes. Americans have inaugurated five presidential candidates who lost the popular vote. Think about that: More than one in every ten presidents (and two out of the last three) was not the people's choice. Congress adds another peculiar twist to popular rule. Its approval rating averaged a dismal 20 percent on November 6, 2018, when Americans went to the polls.[6] Yet nearly 93 percent of House incumbents won reelection, most of them by large majorities. The public expressed sharp disapproval—then voted to return nearly all of them to Washington for another term.

As you can see, democracy is complicated. Yes, the United States is the world's oldest democratic country. Yet a candidate who loses the popular vote wins the White House, a terribly unpopular Congress is reelected in a landslide, and unelected judges, appointed for life, can strike down the will of the people's representatives. Over the course of this book, you will see why these limits to democracy were introduced; and you will judge whether they are still a good idea, or whether they distort American democracy and remove power from the people.

Over the years, political scientists have developed theories to answer the question of where the power really lies in American politics. Four theories are especially important:

- *Pluralist theory* suggests that people influence government through the many interest groups that spring up to champion everything from fighting global warming to banning abortions. Pluralists suggest that interest groups give most people a voice.

- *Elite theory* counters that power actually rests in the hands of a small number of wealthy and powerful individuals—especially the richest Americans, corporate executives and the top government officials who cater to both.

- *Bureaucratic theory* argues that the real control lies with the millions of men and women who carry out the day-to-day operations of modern government. Bureaucratic experts establish policy regardless of popular views

Republic: A government in which citizens rule indirectly and make government decisions through their elected representatives.

- *Social movement theory* emphasizes the power citizens can wield when they organize and rise up in protest—regardless of who is in control of day-to-day politics.

These theories offer different answers to the vital question: Who rules in America? We will often return to this question—and ask you to consider which of these theories best describes power in the United States today. (And, yes, you'll be able to mix, match, and create your own.) However, before you can decide who is in charge you have to know how the political system actually works.

How Does American Politics Work?

How have our ideas about democracy and republics shaped our government?

Consider a classic definition of politics: *who gets what, when, and how.*[7] Every society has limited amounts of money, prestige, and power. Politics helps determine how we distribute them—to whom, in what amounts, under which rules. A second definition is even simpler: *Politics is how a society makes its collective decisions.* Every nation has its own way of deciding. This book explains how collective decisions are made in the United States by focusing on the four "Is": ideas, institutions, interests, and individuals.

Ideas. Powerful ideas shape American politics. As you will see later in this chapter, we stress seven essential ideas: liberty, democracy (or self-rule), individualism, limited government, the American dream, equality, and faith in God. At first glance, these ideas look simple, but as you will quickly learn, each has at least two different sides. Each idea provokes long, loud controversies.

Institutions: The organizations, norms, and rules that structure government and public action.

Institutions. When most people talk about politics, they think about individuals: President Donald Trump, senators such as Kamala Harris (D-CA) or Tim Scott (R-SC), governors like Kate Brown (D-OR) and Greg Abbott (R-TX), or commentators such as Michael Savage and Samantha Bee. Political scientists, on the other hand, stress **institutions**—*the organizations, norms, and rules that structure political action.*

Congress, the Texas legislature, the Missoula (Montana) City Council, the Supreme Court, the Department of Homeland Security, and the news media are all institutions.

Think about how institutions influence your own behavior. You may compete in a classroom by making arguments. If the debate gets heated and you shove someone, however, you are in trouble. But if you play basketball after class, things are quite the opposite. There, a little shoving is fine, but no one wants to play hoops with someone who is always arguing. Different institutions—the classroom, the gym—have different rules, and most people adopt them without a second thought. Notice how different institutional rules give different people advantages.

● *The U.S. Capitol, Washington, DC. Tourists see an impressive monument to democracy. Political scientists see an institution with complicated rules that give advantage to some individuals and groups.*

Smart students who think quickly have an advantage in one institution (the classroom), while fast, athletic students have an advantage in another (the gym). Political institutions work in the same way. The U.S. Senate, the Chicago City Council, the Nevada legislature, the state courts in Florida, the governor's office in Wisconsin, the Marine Corps, and thousands of other institutions all have their own rules and procedures. Each institution organizes behavior. Each gives an advantage to some interests over others. By the time you finish this book, you will know to ask the same question every time you encounter a political issue. Which institutions are involved, and how do they influence politics?

Interests.   For many social scientists, interests lie at the center of the story. Political action flows from individuals, groups, and nations pursuing their own self-interest.

In the chapters that follow, we explore three types of interests: interest groups pushing to influence politics, individuals aiming to maximize their own self-interest (known as **rational-choice theory**), and the ideal of a public interest shared by everyone in society.

Individuals.   This book puts special emphasis on how ordinary people influence politics and change their world. Examples range from the Civil Rights Movement to the Tea Party to students demonstrating on behalf of immigrant rights. Our hope is simple: We want to inspire you, our reader, to get involved.

Rational-choice theory:
An approach to political behavior that views individuals as rational, decisive actors who know their political interests and seek to act on them.

Test your knowledge
of civics.

What Does Government Do?

The Constitution begins with the basic functions of government, circa 1787: "Establish justice, ensure domestic tranquility, provide for the common defense, promote the general welfare, and secure the blessings of liberty." Their list—we get to the details in Chapter 2—still describes the functions of the government, even as its size has grown. We can get a more focused look at the federal government's priorities by looking at what it spends its money on. Figure 1.1 shows you the major budget categories in the $4.4 trillion annual budget.

Many people are surprised when they examine the federal budget for the first time. More than 75 percent of all federal government spending goes to just four programs: the military, Social Security (which provides income for people over the age of sixty-five, as well as for people with disabilities and other groups), Medicare (which provides healthcare for people over sixty-five), and Medicaid (which provides healthcare for lower income Americans; about half of Medicaid spending also goes to people over sixty-five). America's national government devotes most of its resources to the military and to seniors. These four add up to more than $3 trillion.

FY 2018 program spending

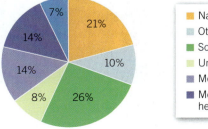

- National defense
- Others
- Social Security
- Unemployment and labor
- Medicare
- Medicaid and health
- Net interest

● **Figure 1.1** *The U.S. federal budget. What government spends. Notice the big four: Social Security, Medicare, Medicaid, and National Defense.*
Source: (Christopher Chantrill)

Tune into the budget debates and you will hear lots of noise about budgets being out of control. These programs are very popular and politicians meddle with them at their peril. Public officials often talk about cutting the budget. But unless they are cutting one of the big four programs, the cuts will not produce a lean government.

Of course, government does a lot more than spend. It sets the rules for society: Drive on the right side of the street. Stop at red lights. No tobacco for children. No rat hairs in restaurant food. No discrimination against women when hiring. No insider trading in stocks. Most people agree with these rules. Others are much more controversial. Over 600,000 people were arrested in 2017 on marijuana related charges although pot is legal in nine states. Guns are easier to get in Texas than California. Government—national, state, and local—constantly sets the rules for society.

As we go through this book, we will keep coming back to a vital question: Should government do fewer things? Or more?

Who Are We?

The United States is a nation of immigrants, a country where individuals come to reinvent themselves. The nation is always changing—the latest shift, at least according to some forecasts, will see people who consider themselves Caucasians becoming a minority of the population in the next thirty years (see Figure 1.2). All the features of American politics—ideas, the Constitution,

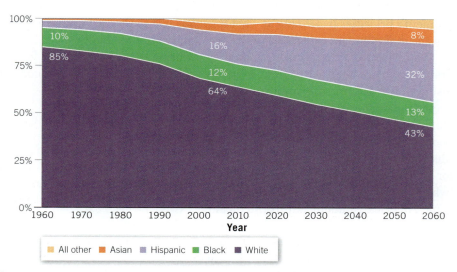

Changing Face of America

Percentage of total U.S. population by race and ethnicity, 1960–2060

● **Figure 1.2** *Race and ethnicity in America—yesterday, today, and tomorrow (U.S. Census Bureau).*

Web Activity 1.2

presidents, media personalities, bureaucrats, interest groups, and more—are part of the struggle to define and redefine the nation. American politics constantly addresses the most fundamental question about a people: Who are we? We begin every chapter of this book by showing how the topics in the chapter help explain who we are.

Who are we? The most important answer to that question is *you*. If you are a member of the so-called millennial generation (born after 1982), the future of the nation lies in your hands. To us, that is a comforting thought. Studies suggest that you are, on average, more responsible, harder-working, and more law-abiding than the generations that came before (including ours). You tend to volunteer more, donate a higher share of your income to charity, and start more entrepreneurial organizations with social impact. You may just be the generation that finally redeems the endless American quest for racial harmony and gender equality. You are also a generation at home in a rapidly changing and diverse world.[8]

As you will see throughout the book, American politics has become especially rough—full of raised voices and bitter name calling. Yet democracy thrives on tolerance. Our hope is that a new generation will take up the challenge of "keeping the republic" by expressing their own voices loudly and clearly while respecting and listening carefully to those of all others.

The Bottom Line

» We explore American government by asking four questions

» Who Governs? Does power rest with the people or with rich and powerful elites?

» How does American politics work? We emphasize four "I" factors: ideas, institutions, interests, and individuals.

» What Does Government Do?

» Who Are We? In a rapidly changing nation, the answer to this question is constantly being rewritten.

A Nation of Ideas

On July 4, 1776, American leaders issued a Declaration of Independence explaining their decision to break away from England. Its second paragraph describes the idea that animated them:

> *We hold these truths to be self-evident, that all men are created equal, that they are endowed by their Creator with certain unalienable rights, that among these are life, liberty and the pursuit of happiness.*

Most of us have heard that line so often that it has lost its force, but it is one of the most powerful ideas in history. It explains the role of government—securing each individual's rights to life, liberty, and the pursuit of happiness. The Declaration states that people form governments—"*to secure those rights.*" And, although the men and women who fought the revolution fell far short of this ideal, they left the nation an inspiring goal. Every American generation argues about how it can best achieve the Declaration's glittering promise to "secure" the rights of every citizen.

Many people believe that the United States is a unique nation, different from every other. That view is known as **American exceptionalism**. Others critique the idea and note that every nation is distinctive in some way. One thing is exceptional about the United States: Seven key ideas guide our politics. Most of them can be traced back to the Declaration of Independence.

What are the seven big ideas? Liberty, self-rule (which is often called democracy), limited government, individualism, the American dream, equality, and faith in God. These ideas touch almost everything the nation does. They are the foundation of American politics.

There is an unusual twist to these ideas. Americans rarely agree on what they mean. Each has two sides (at least) and they spark ardent disputes. To reveal the real truth about American politics, we should post signs at all the airports that say: "*Welcome to the great argument that is the USA.*"

Now let's consider the first key idea.

Liberty

As the Revolutionary War broke out, the royal governor of Virginia promised freedom to any slave who joined the British. Eighty thousand slaves ran for the British lines. Some of them fought in black units, with their motto—"liberty for the slaves"—sewn onto their uniforms.[9]

The enslaved men and women who fought for the British saw their hopes dashed when their side surrendered at the Battle of Yorktown in 1781—effectively ending the Revolutionary War. After the battle, the Redcoats, as the English soldiers were known, began to withdraw, rowing out to the warships bobbing in the harbor for their long retreat. One desperate group of slaves raced past the sentries on the wharf, dove into the sea, and swam toward the long rowboats that were ferrying the defeated British troops out to their naval vessels.

As the black men tried to clamber aboard the small boats, British troops pushed them away. Fearful that the swimmers would swamp the craft, the troops pulled out axes and hacked off the slaves' hands and fingers. And *still* they kept coming, trying to surge aboard, thrashing after their fading dream of liberty. The image is unforgettable: These men were so desperate for freedom that even as the Redcoats swung their bloody hatchets, they kept clutching for the boats that might carry them away from bondage.

American exceptionalism: The view that the United States is uniquely characterized by a distinct set of ideas such as equality, self-rule, and limited government.

JOHN HANCOCK'S DEFIANCE.

● *Ideas have consequences. John Hancock of Massachusetts defiantly signs the Declaration. According to legend, he signed it in big, bold letters so that King George III could read Hancock's name without his spectacles—and "double the reward for my head."*

"The Land of the Free"

No idea comes up more often in American history than freedom or liberty (we use the words interchangeably). The national anthem declares America "the land of the free." During the civil rights movement of the 1950s and 1960s, high school students spilled out of Baptist churches and marched toward dogs and high-pressure fire hoses, singing, "Everyone shout freedom, freedom, freedom!" The Statue of Liberty is inscribed "Give me . . . your huddled masses yearning to breathe free." A group of conservative Republicans in Congress established the Freedom Caucus in 2015.

What is **freedom**? It means that the government will protect your life, your liberty, and your property from the coercion of others (including public officials) in order to permit you to pursue the goals you define for yourself.

Freedom: The ability to pursue one's own desires without interference from others.

The Two Sides of Liberty

Everyone agrees that freedom is a basic American value. But, in practice, Americans disagree about what it means—and what governments should do to ensure it. There are two different views: negative liberty and positive liberty.[10]

The more familiar view is **negative liberty**: *Freedom is the absence of constraints.* Society's responsibility, from this perspective, is to make sure that others (especially government officials) do not interfere with individuals.

Negative liberty: Freedom from constraints or the interference of others.

The government protects your right to believe what you wish, to say what you like, and to practice any faith (or none at all). Negative liberty firmly limits government action. Public officials violate your freedom when they collect taxes from you to feed the hungry or punish you for smoking tobacco or marijuana. Negative freedom is the right to act as you want.

Positive liberty: The ability—and provision of basic necessities—to pursue one's goals.

The alternative is **positive liberty**: *the freedom to pursue one's goals.* From this perspective, individuals cannot really be free—they cannot pursue their desires—if they lack the basic necessities of life. Protecting liberty means ensuring that every citizen has food, shelter, healthcare, and educational opportunities. After all, how can people be free if they are hungry or homeless? This view requires government help give all people a real chance to achieve their desires.

President Franklin D. Roosevelt forcefully expressed this view in 1941. As the United States prepared for World War II, he proclaimed that the nation was fighting for "four freedoms": freedom of speech, freedom of worship, freedom from want, and freedom from fear. The first two—freedom of speech and religion—were traditional negative liberties: no one could interfere with these rights. However, "freedom from want" was something new, a positive liberty that involves helping people who have fallen on hard times. Roosevelt was suggesting that social welfare policies such as unemployment insurance and Social Security were part of the all-American idea of freedom. Today, positive freedom includes efforts to educate everyone, ensure they have healthcare if they need it, and help them to stop smoking. The guiding notion: Poor education, illness, or addiction makes it difficult for them to pursue their goals.

Hear President Roosevelt deliver his speech on the four freedoms.

What Do YOU Think? Negative Versus Positive Liberty

Americans often disagree about the meaning of "freedom." Is it the absence of constraints (negative liberty) or a realistic opportunity to pursue one's goals (positive liberty)?

Do you believe in negative liberty? Government should not interfere with individuals. Freedom means leaving every person alone to do what he or she wishes—without interference. As President Reagan famously said, "as government expands, liberty contracts."

Or positive liberty? Freedom simply is not a meaningful concept if you or your family are chronically hungry. A decent society must lift everyone to a basic minimum. That's what living in a democracy should be about, as President Franklin D. Roosevelt said: "True individual freedom cannot exist without economic security and independence."

Do you fall somewhere in between? Think about how you might combine these two concepts. You may find it easier to answer this question after reading about the other major ideas. If you are not ready to choose, read on—and then return to this question.

Which idea of freedom is right? That depends on your values. Beneath these two visions of liberty lie different perspectives on the good society. The negative view emphasizes personal autonomy: Taxing me violates my freedom of property. The positive view follows Roosevelt: Membership in a free society means sharing enough wealth so that everyone enjoys freedom from want. The two perspectives reflect different values, different visions of society, and different definitions of liberty.

The Idea of Freedom Is Always Changing

Once upon a time, Americans permitted slavery and racial segregation. Women lost all their legal rights the day they were married; their possessions—even their very bodies—passed into the custody of their husbands. Immigrants from China, and later from India, were denied any hope of becoming Americans no matter how long they lived in the country. The ideal of freedom moved Americans to reverse each of these prejudices.

Scholars disagree about how to interpret the results. Some see American history as a steady march toward greater liberty. Yes, they admit, American history is full of oppression. However, our faith in freedom leads oppressed groups to fight for their rights and, little by little, freedom has grown.[11]

Other thinkers warn that the outcome in the fight is never inevitable. Instead, freedom is won and lost . . . and won and lost again. Americans fought their bloody civil war to end slavery, only to watch new forms of racial segregation and oppression take hold and last almost for another century. We should never take liberty for granted.

The Bottom Line

» Liberty—or the freedom to pursue your goals—is the most often invoked American value.

» There are two different views of what liberty means. *Negative liberty* emphasizes a lack of constraints on individuals, even if those constraints are intended to help others. *Positive liberty* calls on the community to help everyone satisfy their basic needs.

» Freedom has expanded to new groups over time. Some scholars see the rise of freedom as inevitable, reflecting American ideals; others see it as a constant battle that can always go either way.

Self-Rule

As the American Revolution began, crowds gathered in the towns and cities. The people, they declared, would seize authority from royal governors (appointed by the tyrannical king) and exercise power themselves. "The mob has begun to think for itself," lamented one wealthy New Yorker. "Poor reptiles, before noon they will bite" (meaning *revolt*).[12]

Patriotic crowds ignored the skeptics. At mass meetings, the people voted for laws, enforced decrees, and even issued wedding licenses. Here is a powerful image of democracy: American people bypassing government officials and running the country themselves from the town commons. The people ruled.

That principle sounds simple. The United States is the world's longest running democracy—of course, the people rule. But from the beginning, a great debate arose about how to achieve **self-rule**. The Constitution was meant to settle the issue—but we are still arguing about its meaning, some 230 years later.

How do we achieve self-rule? Americans have long vacillated between two very different paths—a *democracy* and a *republic*.

Self-rule: The idea that legitimate government flows from the people.

One Side of Self-Rule: Democracy

Democracy involves citizen participation in making government decisions. Whether directly or through freely elected representatives, they exercised self-rule. (*Demos* is the Greek word for "the people" and *kratia* is the Greek word for "rule/power.") In early New England, citizens governed in town meetings—without relying on elected officials.

Democracy: A government in which citizens rule directly and make government decisions for themselves.

Thomas Jefferson, who drafted the Declaration of Independence and served as the third U.S. president, was the most vocal proponent of maximizing democracy. "The will of the majority," wrote Jefferson, is a "sacred principle" and "the only sure guardian of the rights of man." If the people cannot govern themselves, asked Jefferson, how can they possibly be trusted with the government of others?[13]

Referendum: An election in which citizens vote directly on an issue.

The result is a rich American legacy of taking to the streets to demonstrate, rally, and protest. Examples include demonstrations on behalf of young immigrant "Dreamers"; gun owners rallying in support of the Second Amendment; giant Earth Day demonstrations that launched the modern environmental movement; and the 1963 March on Washington, which was electrified by Martin Luther King's "I Have a Dream" speech. Some of these movements drew supporters from right across the political spectrum.

Many states institutionalize the democratic ideal by letting the public vote directly on policy issues such as crime victim rights or expanding health insurance. Voting directly is known as a **referendum** and is permitted in twenty-seven states.

● *Students take to the streets to protest the Trump administration's policies toward race and immigration.*

In addition, twenty-four states permit **initiatives**: Individuals can circulate petitions that propose a new law or Constitutional amendment.

Another Side of Self-Rule: A Republic

Most of the men who drafted the Constitution did not agree with Jefferson about democracy. The states had tried to create direct democracy right after the American Revolution. George Washington thought the result was chaos. "We have probably had too good an opinion of human nature," he grumbled. James Madison put it most famously: "Democracies have [always] been spectacles of turbulence and contention . . . as short in their lives as violent in their deaths." The problem, said Madison, was that in direct democracy, the majority often gets carried away. They push their self-interest without paying attention to the rights of the minority. Direct democracy, he concluded, offers no barrier to lynch mobs crying for blood.[14]

"If men were angels," wrote James Madison in *Federalist* No. 51, "no government would be necessary." The great challenge, he argued, was to devise government institutions that would protect individual rights even if a majority of the people were selfish and corrupt. His solution: a **republic**.

In a republic, the people rule indirectly through their elected representatives. The constitutional framers made an important contribution to the theory of self-rule. Classical democratic theory was wrong in expecting that popular government would only work if the people were virtuous. In fact, the people are often not virtuous at all. A republic tries to filter their views through elected officials.

A Mixed System

Which view of self-rule holds in the United States? Both do. We can say that the United States is a democratic republic because it includes elements of a democracy *and* a republic. There are plenty of opportunities for direct participation. At the same time, American government is organized to check the majority. The House, the Senate, the president, and the Supreme Court all put the brakes on one another. And all of them face fifty different state governments, each with its own politics, powers, and programs. American government operates through elected and unelected officials who answer (sometimes indirectly) to the public.

The sheer number of elected officials—more than five hundred thousand—reveals our hybrid form of government. There is one elected government official for every six hundred Americans. Few other nations come close to this ratio. We elect representatives, reflecting our origins as a republic, but the enormous number of opportunities to serve in elective office moves us closer to a democracy.

Although our government combines elements of both democracy and republic, the debate continues about which way we should tilt. Which stance do you prefer? Jefferson's faith in direct democracy? Or Madison's belief that people should govern through elected representatives?

Initiative: A process in which citizens propose new laws or amendments to the state constitution.

Republic: A government in which citizens rule indirectly and permit elected representatives to make decisions.

Limited Government

Back in 1691, while America was still part of Great Britain, King William III appointed Benjamin Fletcher to be governor of New York and gave him control over the New England colonies (which had been independent until then). The Connecticut legislature did not want to cede its power to Governor Fletcher and immediately selected a new commander for the local militia—a direct challenge to the new governor's authority. Fletcher sailed to Hartford, the capital of Connecticut, with a small detachment of troops. He assembled the Connecticut militia and had an officer read the royal proclamation declaring his authority over the state—and its militia.

As the officer read aloud, the Connecticut militiamen began to beat their drums in defiance. Fletcher tried to restore order by commanding his soldiers to fire their muskets in the air. In response, the commander of the Connecticut militia stepped forward, put his hand on the hilt of his sword, and issued his own warning: "If my drummers are again interrupted, I'll make sunlight shine through you. We deny and defy your authority." Outnumbered and in no mood for bloodshed, Fletcher beat a quick retreat to his vessel and sailed ignominiously back to New York City. Because the king and his ministers were more than three thousand miles away, they never heard about this little rebellion against their authority.[15]

The Origins of Limited Government

The tale of Governor Fletcher illustrates an enduring idea: Americans distrust centralized leadership and seek to limit its power. Eighty years before the Revolutionary War, Connecticut had grown used to electing its own leaders and going its own way. The people saw the king as a distant figure with no right to interfere in their affairs. The image of central government as a remote, untrustworthy authority that threatens our freedoms runs through American history.

Why did Americans develop this distrust? The answer lies in how the people secured their rights in the first place. In most nations, the central government—made up of kings or aristocrats or both—grudgingly granted their people rights such as the vote or jury trials. Sometimes the people rebelled (as in France), sometimes they negotiated with kings (England), and sometimes monarchs expanded rights to modernize their nations (Thailand). All these countries share a common experience: Kings or the central governments that replaced them were the source of rights and liberties. No wonder citizens in these nations instinctively look to the government for help in solving their problems. The United States was different. Experience taught Americans to see the central government not as a potential source of rights, but as a threat to their life, liberty, and happiness.

And Yet . . . the United States Has a Big Government

A paradox lies at the heart of this idea, limited government. People across the political spectrum demand government action. Many **conservatives** seek to use federal authority to secure the border against illegal immigration, crack down on illegal drugs, forbid abortions, or enhance homeland security.

Most **liberals** reject the idea that public officials should interfere in people's private lives. But they are all for active government when it comes to economic policy or corporate regulation. They call on the government to sponsor fast trains, regulate Wall Street, protect the environment, and offer school lunch programs (there's the freedom from want, again).

Limits on Government Action

In short, Americans often say they do not like this idea of limited government and then demand government action for causes they care about. Their calls for action generally face two hurdles: the desire to limit government and the Constitution.

When the framers designed our political system, they organized suspicion of government right into the system. The federal Constitution includes an intricate system of checks and balances on power, which we will explore in Chapter 2. The Constitution limits what Congress may do—and Americans vigorously debate exactly where those boundaries actually are.

Although it is difficult for government officials to undertake new tasks, the barriers are not insurmountable. During times of crisis, people turn to the government and demand action. Skilled leadership also can negotiate sweeping changes. And once programs go into effect, they often prove popular.

Ironically, the limits on change make it difficult to repeal new programs once they make it past all the hurdles and are up and running. For example, Social Security was passed in 1935 during the economic crisis of the Great Depression; Medicare passed in part because of a great electoral landslide in 1964. Both are now extremely popular policies; in fact, they are so popular

Conservatives: Americans who believe in reduced government spending, personal responsibility, traditional moral values, and a strong national defense. Also known as *right* or *right-wing*.

Liberals: Americans who value cultural diversity, government programs for the needy, public intervention in the economy, and individuals' right to a lifestyle based on their own social and moral positions. Also known as *left* or *left-wing*.

● *When people are suffering, even many critics of the government set their views aside to demand action. Here, a Houston SWAT officer rescues a mother and son from floodwaters.*

that they are known in Washington as "the third rails"—touch them and die (politically, of course). Americans often reject "Big Government," while demanding government action and fiercely defending the programs they like.

When Ideas Clash: Self-Rule and Limited Government

When President Trump was running for president, he promised to repeal and replace the Obama administration's healthcare legislation and to build a wall on the southern border. However, election winners always face difficulties putting their policies into effect—a result of the many limits that Americans have placed on their own government.

Notice the clash between two leading American ideas: self-rule and limited government. Self-rule says that the winning party should be able to put their policies into place. In a democracy, the majority should rule.

But another value, limited government, responds: Not so fast. We do not like government meddling in our private lives, so we designed institutions that make it very difficult for elected officials to follow through on their promises. Even a president who wins a national election by a large margin must still convince the majority in the House of Representatives and 60 percent of the Senate. (Why 60%? You'll find out in Chapter 10.)

Watch President Trump talking about a border wall.

What Do YOU Think? **Self-Rule Versus Limited Government**

Some observers think we no longer have government by the people because it is too difficult for elected officials to get things done. These reformers seek an easier path to government action. However, that prospect raises fears of a more active government. Which should we emphasize, self-rule or limited government? It's time to make your choice.

I'm with Thomas Jefferson. It should be easier for elected officials to enact the programs they promised. If they cannot do so, elections become less meaningful. When the people vote for something and their representatives fail to deliver, it fosters cynicism about the entire political process. Self-rule requires us to follow the people's mandate. If the majority does not like the results, it can express its displeasure in the next election.

I'm with James Madison. The checks and balances that make large-scale reforms difficult protect the United States from overbearing government and from sudden changes—whether rapidly expanding or cutting programs. The barriers to government action *should* be high. If the public really wants something, it will probably happen over time. Limited government is more important. Don't change the process.

Not sure? This is a formidable question. You may very well change your mind—maybe more than once—as you continue to read this book.

The clash between principles leads to an important question: How should we balance self-rule and limited government? Making it too difficult undermines majority rule. But remove the barriers and the winning party can pass all the programs it promised—until it loses in elections and the other party eliminates all those programs and pushes through the agenda that it promised.

 **The Bottom Line**

» Americans distrust their government more than people in most other democracies traditionally have. The Constitution builds that distrust into our governing rules by providing for limited government. The result is a durable status quo.

» In many other countries, politicians can usually deliver the programs they promised on the campaign trail. In the United States, winners confront multiple barriers to fulfilling their campaign promises.

» However, once programs do go into effect, they often prove popular and difficult to change.

Individualism

Political scientist John Kingdon was visiting his niece in Norway. She was expecting a baby and Professor Kingdon asked what she planned to do about her job. She casually replied that she would receive a full year's leave at 80 percent of her normal pay and that her company was required to give her job back after the leave. "Who pays for all this?" asked Professor Kingdon. "The government, of course," his niece replied. She was surprised the question had even come up. "Is it any different in the United States?" she asked innocently.[16]

As Kingdon explained, it is completely different in the United States: Advocates fought for years to pass the Family and Medical Leave Act (1993), which requires employers with more than fifty workers to allow up to twelve weeks of *unpaid* leave for pregnancy, adoption, illness, or military service. Americans generally value **individualism**: *The idea that individuals, not the society or the community or the government, are responsible for their own well-being.* We, as a society, do not pay for maternity leave. Instead, we expect private individuals and families to handle birth, or adoption, or caregiving. But that is only one part of the American story.

Individualism: The idea that individuals, not the society, are responsible for their own well-being.

Community Versus Individualism

The idea of individualism is a source of controversy in every nation. There are two ways to see any society: as a *community* or as a collection of *individuals*. Every nation includes both, but government policies can be designed to

Social democracy: The idea that government policy should ensure that all are comfortably cared for within the context of a capitalist economy.

emphasize the community or to focus on individuals. Let us take a closer look at these two principles.

Countries that emphasize the community are called **social democracies**. Social democrats believe that members of a society are responsible for one another. They view government as a source of mutual assistance. The government provides citizens with the basics: good health insurance, retirement benefits, generous unemployment packages, and—as we saw in the Norwegian case— maternity benefits.

In exchange, people pay high taxes. Almost half of a Norwegian's income goes to taxes. One effect of high taxation: It is difficult for most citizens to get very rich. At the same time, the extensive welfare state makes it far less likely that people will live in poverty. Communal societies are far more equal than individualist ones—not just in opportunity, but in outcome. Most Western European nations are social democracies.

Social democracies are based on *solidarity*, the idea that people have a tight bond and are responsible for one another. Some societies exhibit a strong sense of solidarity. In general, this sense increases during wars, economic depressions, or other crises that get everyone to pull together. Scholars have found that more homogeneous societies—where people look alike, share the same values, and practice the same religion—exhibit higher rates of solidarity than very diverse societies.

American politics includes a streak of solidarity. Martin Luther King put it eloquently: "I am inevitably my brother's keeper because I am my brother's brother."[17] However, the commitment to solidarity rises and falls in the United States. Perhaps it will strengthen again, with the rising generations?

Now let us turn to individualism. In this view, people and their families are responsible for their own welfare. The economist Milton Friedman famously wrote that "the world runs on individuals pursuing their separate interests." Leave people free to choose their interests, Friedman continued, and the public

● *Classic images of individualism and solidarity. The Republican National Convention backdrop emphasizes self-reliance and individual achievement; Bernie Sanders emphasizes community and solidarity.*

interest of the whole society will emerge.[18] Rather than taxing people and using funds to aid the less well-off, proponents of this perspective opt for low taxes and a green light for private entrepreneurs. People who work hard will get ahead, they say, and society will grow and prosper.

Individualists value the chance to get ahead more than they value a society where everyone is equal. In social democracies, government regulations aim to protect workers. In contrast, individualists oppose government controls and believe that private companies should be able to expand or contract their workforce as they see fit (as long as they hire and fire without discriminating). People should take care of one another through churches, charities, or other private means. Individualism points toward limited government, faith in economic markets, and a strong emphasis on *negative liberty*.

The Roots of American Individualism: Opportunity and Discord

Americans lean toward individualism and away from social democracy. Why? Two famous explanations look to the past. One finds the answer in golden opportunities. A second emphasizes social and racial discord.

Golden Opportunity.   For centuries, most Europeans and Asians lived as serfs or peasants working small plots of land. Powerful rulers kept them firmly in their place—there was little chance for individuals to get ahead by working hard. In early America, by contrast, there appeared to be endless land and opportunity. With hard work and a little luck, anyone (at least any white male) could earn a decent living and perhaps even a fortune. Stories about early settlers clearing their own land were later reinforced by images of rugged individuals on the western frontier. Hard workers relied on themselves—not the government.

There is a lot of myth in these stories. Frontier life was less about brave individualism and more about communities. Settlers could not build a barn, a church, or a meetinghouse without their neighbors' help. But the image of hardy individuals on the frontier remains a powerful ideal in American political culture. And there was an important truth at its core: Few societies have ever offered so many individuals as much opportunity to rise and prosper as early America did.[19]

● *Individualism in historical memory: At high noon on April 22, 1889, bugles sounded and a great mob—lined up impatiently outside the territory—surged across the Oklahoma border and snatched up as much land as they could stake out. Although the government sponsored the land giveaway, the image that has stuck is of people grabbing the land for themselves. Oklahoma still honors the scalawags that snuck in early ("sooner") and staked the best land—that's where the motto "The Sooner State" comes from.*

Social Conflict.   Another explanation for American individualism emphasizes the enormous differences within our society: The country is too big and the population too diverse to develop a sense of solidarity. What, after all, did Calvinist Yankees in New England have in common with Roman Catholics in Baltimore or Anglican planters in Virginia—much less Spanish speakers in Florida or Texas? Moreover, a nation that included four million black slaves by 1860 had a terrible divide running through its heart.

By the 1830s still another source of division had arisen. Immigrants were arriving by the tens (and later hundreds) of thousands—speaking different languages and practicing what seemed like strange customs. Each generation of immigrants added to the American cacophony. For example, Irish Catholics (who arrived in the 1830s and 1840s) appeared strange and threatening to the English Protestants who had immigrated a century earlier. Could Catholics, with their allegiance to a foreign pope, really understand or uphold American values? Fifty years later, newly arriving Italians, Poles, and Chinese seemed just as threatening to the Irish, who by then had settled in.[20] All of these divisions made solidarity far more difficult to feel than in the more stable, homogeneous populations.

Which explanation is correct? Both are on target. Unprecedented economic opportunity and vast social divisions have reinforced individualism.

Who Are We? Individualism and Solidarity

Americans are not individualists pure and simple. Rather, the two themes—individualism and solidarity—always compete in American politics. Individualism is more robust and more often in evidence, but a sense of solidarity also unites the population. Americans often pull together, as communities and as a nation. People take care of their neighbors and support government programs to improve the lives of people they do not know. The United States may have deep divisions, but it is remarkable how quickly they can disappear. A substantial majority of Americans today are children, grandchildren, or great-grandchildren of immigrants—many of whom were once regarded as strange and different.

All this raises another question to ponder: Where would you draw the line between solidarity and individualism? The answer directly relates to one of this book's central questions: *Who are we?* Take the test in "What Do You Think?" to learn where you stand on the continuum between rugged individualism and strong solidarity.

The Bottom Line

» American politics includes both individualism and solidarity.

» Different leaders, parties, groups, and individuals weigh the two values in different ways. However, compared to other nations, the United States is at the individualist end of the spectrum.

What Do YOU Think?

Individualism Versus Solidarity

Please score yourself on the following ten statements:

0 = Disagree strongly
1 = Disagree
2 = Agree
3 = Agree strongly

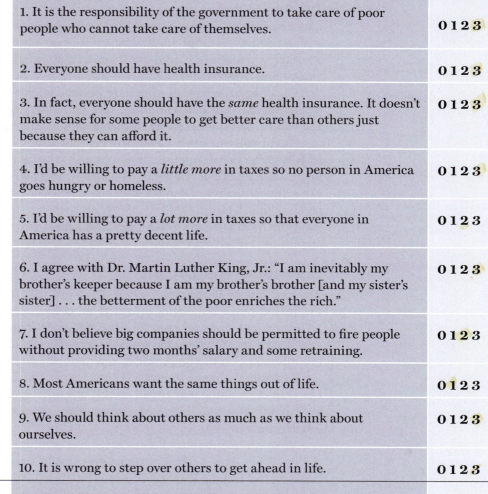

Take the test online and find out how you score.

1. It is the responsibility of the government to take care of poor people who cannot take care of themselves.	0 1 2 3
2. Everyone should have health insurance.	0 1 2 3
3. In fact, everyone should have the *same* health insurance. It doesn't make sense for some people to get better care than others just because they can afford it.	0 1 2 3
4. I'd be willing to pay a *little more* in taxes so no person in America goes hungry or homeless.	0 1 2 3
5. I'd be willing to pay a *lot more* in taxes so that everyone in America has a pretty decent life.	0 1 2 3
6. I agree with Dr. Martin Luther King, Jr.: "I am inevitably my brother's keeper because I am my brother's brother [and my sister's sister] . . . the betterment of the poor enriches the rich."	0 1 2 3
7. I don't believe big companies should be permitted to fire people without providing two months' salary and some retraining.	0 1 2 3
8. Most Americans want the same things out of life.	0 1 2 3
9. We should think about others as much as we think about ourselves.	0 1 2 3
10. It is wrong to step over others to get ahead in life.	0 1 2 3

Scoring

0–5 You are truly a rugged individualist!
5–14 You are largely an individualist.
15–20 You are a moderate who sees both sides of the issue.
20–24 You are a social democrat.
25–30 You are a true-blue believer in solidarity!

Now, speak to others who scored very differently from you.
Try to understand how and why they came to hold their views and explain why you hold your own.

🔵 The American Dream

Benjamin Franklin perfected a classic American literary form—tips for getting rich. Anyone, he assured his readers, could be successful by following a formula: be frugal ("A penny saved is a penny earned"), hardworking ("No gains without pains"), steady ("Little strokes fell great oaks"), bold ("God helps those who help themselves"), and—most important—morally upright ("Leave your vices, though ever so dear").[21]

Franklin summarized what later became known as the American dream: *If you are talented and work hard, you can achieve personal (and especially financial) success.* A popular historian, James Truslow Adams, was the first to actually call this doctrine an American dream: "a land in which life should be better and richer and fuller for everyone, with opportunity for each according to ability or achievement."[22] The idea scarcely changes across generations. "The American dream that we were all raised on is a simple but powerful one," averred President Bill Clinton, more than two centuries after Ben Franklin. "If you work hard and play by the rules, you should be given a chance to go as far as your God-given abilities will take you."[23]

Spreading the Dream

The legacy of the Revolutionary War, according to historian Gordon Wood, was the spread of the American dream to all classes. National leaders originally imagined that they were establishing a classical republic, such as Athens, in which a few outstanding men would govern the people. Instead, the Revolution established the common people as the basis of government and gave them an unprecedented chance to make their fortunes. What did the mass of people care about? "Making money and getting ahead," wrote Wood. Yes, the goal was vulgar, material, and crass. But opportunity had never been available on such a broad scale before.[24]

Enabling the dream of success remains an important part of any policy debate. Will a proposal help small business? Will it create jobs? Will it stifle entrepreneurs? Immigrants still come to the United States in large numbers—far more than to any other country—partly to pursue the dreams of success.

Challenging the Dream

As with every important idea, the American dream generates conflict. Critics raise two questions: Has the system become rigged to favor the wealthy at the expense of giving everyone a fair shot at success? And is the pursuit of wealth an undesirable value, either on its own merits or because it crowds out other important values?

Is the System Tilted Toward the Wealthy?   Some critics question whether the American dream is still open to everyone or whether it has grown biased toward the rich and powerful. Early America offered more opportunities to get ahead than perhaps any nation in history. And this remained true for many years.

Most Americans Believe There Is

"OPPORTUNITY TO GET AHEAD"

Although most people see the American dream as a viable goal, demographic groups differ in their perception of their chances of achieving it.

Most people say they have achieved the American dream – or are on their way to achieving it

Do you believe your family has achieved the American dream? (%)

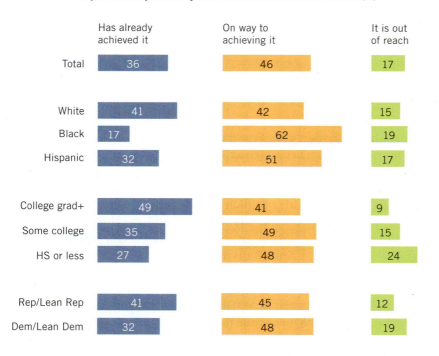

	Has already achieved it	On way to achieving it	It is out of reach
Total	36	46	17
White	41	42	15
Black	17	62	19
Hispanic	32	51	17
College grad+	49	41	9
Some college	35	49	15
HS or less	27	48	24
Rep/Lean Rep	41	45	12
Dem/Lean Dem	32	48	19

Note: Whites and blacks include only those who are not Hispanic; Hispanics are of any race. "Don't know" responses not shown.

THINK ABOUT IT

What percentage of whites, Hispanic, and African Americans believe that they have achieved or are achieving the American dream?

How does education affect a person's perception of whether the American dream is within reach?

Which of the groups do you belong to? Does your attitude align with the majority of others in your demographic group?

Source: Pew Research Center

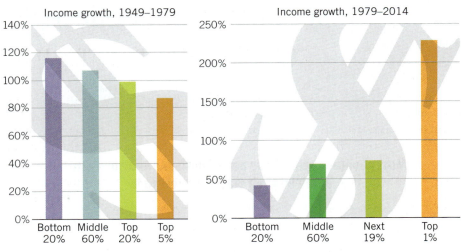

Income growth, 1949–1979

Income growth, 1979–2014

● **Figure 1.3A** *Between 1949 and 1979, those on the bottom saw their earnings grow faster than those on the top (Robert Frank, Falling Behind).*

● **Figure 1.3B** *. . . but look how that changed after 1979. Now those on the bottom have very little income growth while the wealthy have very rapid growth. Is this a bad thing? Americans disagree (Russell Sage Foundation, Chartbook of Inequality).*

During the boom years after World War II, middle-class incomes rose faster than incomes at the top. Then, starting around 1979, this trend changed. Money began to flow to the wealthiest more than to the other classes. Figures 1.3A and 1.3B compare the two periods.

Today, the wealthiest three million Americans, the top 1 percent of households, enjoy a lot more of the nation's wealth (over 40%) than the 290 million people who make up the bottom 90 percent (and control just 22.8% of the wealth). The sixty million Americans at the bottom of the charts own almost nothing—one-tenth of one percent of the national wealth. The median white family is ten times wealthier than the median black family. Inequality continues to rise, as the gap between richest and poorest widens.[25]

Many social scientists now argue that the chance of moving up—from poverty to wealth—is fading in the United States. Critics worry that the system is tilted toward insiders with good connections (known as crony capitalism) or the children of the wealthy. Both conservatives and liberals challenge the United States to live up to its promise of equality of opportunity.[26]

Does the American Dream Promote the Wrong Values? A second critique of the American dream questions the chase for wealth as a human value. Environmentalists criticize the damage caused by big houses, sprawling suburbs, gas-guzzling cars, and opulent lifestyles. Others cite the harm to old-fashioned communal ideals. "These dark days will be worth all they cost us," said President Franklin Roosevelt during the depths of the Great Depression, "if they teach us that our true destiny is . . . to minister . . . to our fellow man." Today, young American evangelicals are offering an even sharper challenge to greed and the race for success as a threat to the biblical call to service.[27]

Voices like these have questioned the pursuit of economic success to the exclusion of community and social justice. Fifteen million children—around 21 percent—live below the poverty line in the United States. Critics charge that something is amiss with the American dream if we let so many of our children live in poverty.[28]

The capitalists who celebrate wealth often have to wrestle with economic populists who would rather share it. In a 2017 poll, just 11 percent agreed that "becoming wealthy" is a key feature of the American dream; far more (77%) emphasized "freedom of choice in how to live one's life" (the "liberty" idea highlighted earlier), and 48 percent "making valuable contributions to my community" (the "solidarity" idea).[29] This trend seems especially strong among younger Americans. In a series of Harvard University studies, nearly half (between 44–48%) of eighteen- to twenty-nine-year-olds said that the American dream did not apply to their generation—a trend worth watching closely in coming years.[30]

Despite critics and challenges, Americans usually celebrate the gospel of success. The nation's politics, economics, and culture accommodate the dreams of wealth. In comparison with other wealthy nations, Americans pay less in taxes, regulate business less, take fewer vacations, and place more emphasis on getting ahead.

Compare liberties and poverty levels among nations.

The Bottom Line

» The American dream is the belief that anyone who works hard can get ahead and grow wealthy.

» Critics argue that hard work is no longer enough to achieve the dream. They make two criticisms: the poor and middle classes are falling farther behind the wealthy because of bias in the political economy, and other values are more important than wealth.

» Despite the critics, the dream remains a powerful American idea.

Equality

When Alexis de Tocqueville, a French visitor to America (and one of our favorite authors) arrived in the United States in 1831, he was amazed by the widespread equality. In one of his first letters home, he reported watching servers in a tavern sit down at the next table to eat and drink alongside the guests. Here was a society where people from all ranks shook hands, discussed politics, and chased money. Everyone seemed to be equals.

Tocqueville distilled this thought into the first sentence of his great book *Democracy in America*: "No novelty in the United States struck me more vividly . . . than the equality of condition." In a world that was still full of aristocrats and inherited privilege, American society embodied the great idea at the heart of the Declaration of Independence: "All men [and women] are created equal."[31]

Equality means that *every citizen enjoys the same privileges, status, and rights before the laws.* There are three different types of equality to consider when analyzing the concept: *social, political,* and *economic.*

Equality: All citizens enjoy the same privileges, status, and rights before the laws.

Three Types of Equality

Social equality means that all individuals enjoy the same status in society. There are no American barons or archdukes who inherit special benefits when they are born. Except for slavery, there have never been fixed social classes. Few American politicians boast of noble origins or good family lineage. On the contrary, for the past 150 years candidates have flaunted (or invented) their working-class roots. Even very wealthy politicians often claim to have humble origins (for many years, they boasted about the log cabins they supposedly grew up in). An old cliché in American politics, one with a lot of truth to it, is the saying that any little boy or girl could grow up to be the president—or a millionaire.

Social equality: All individuals enjoy the same status in society.

Political equality means that every citizen has the same political rights and opportunities. Americans enjoyed universal white, male *suffrage*—or the right to vote—much earlier than did citizens of most nations. Over time the opportunity to vote spread. Today there are lively debates about whether we still ensure everyone an equal opportunity to affect the political process.

Political equality: All citizens have the same political rights and opportunities.

Some reformers suggest, for example, that if everyone is to have the same chance to influence the political process, we should remove money from elections. Otherwise, the wealthy will have outsized influence. Others counter that individuals who are excited by candidates should be allowed to contribute to them.

The quest for political equality raises many other issues: Does everyone enjoy an equal right to a fair trial—or have the costs of going to court elevated this basic value beyond the reach of many people? Does the voting system make it too difficult for some people to register and cast their ballots? Does every citizen have an *equal opportunity* to influence the political process and are they all treated the same way before the law?

Economic equality: A situation in which there are only small differences in wealth between citizens.

Economic equality focuses on differences in wealth. For more than a century and a half, the United States stood out for its economic equality.[32] Today the nation has changed dramatically—toward inequality.

In 1970, the level of economic inequality in the United States was similar to that in most other wealthy democracies. On one measure of economic inequality, known as the Gini coefficient, the United States ranked between France and Japan. Today, in contrast, America has become far less equal than nations such as Japan, Sweden, and Germany. We are now closer to the most unequal country in the world (Lesotho) than we are to the most equal (Sweden). Should we adopt public policies that aim to limit economic inequality? Let us look more closely at this much contested issue.

● *Alice Walton, daughter of Wal-Mart founder Sam Walton, inherited over $30 billion.*

● *Should we worry about economic inequality? Should we change the rules so that the wealthy get less and poor people more?*

How Much Economic Inequality Is Too Much?

Inequality in America has reached levels not seen in almost a century. One illustration of national differences in economic inequality arises from the "salary gap." In 1965, the **median** (or typical) American chief executive officer (CEO) made twenty-six times more than a typical worker in his or her company. In Japan today the figure is roughly the same. But in the contemporary United States, the median CEO makes between three hundred and five hundred times the salary of the average employee (depending on the study). Is this a problem for the idea that "all men are created equal"?

American public policies (and public opinion) often endorse the race to wealth. People who have won great success—hedge-fund managers, basketball stars, bank executives, and breakthrough entrepreneurs—should enjoy the wealth they accumulate. On the other side, critics charge that the richest 1 percent take advantage of everyone else. Tax laws and other rules are tilted in their favor. This is an old debate that has gone back and forth throughout American history: Should we encourage or discourage the accumulation of terrific fortunes?

Median: A statistical term for the number in the middle or the case that has an equal number of examples above and below it.

Opportunity or Outcome?

Many Americans accept high levels of economic inequality, contending that these are not fatal to our hopes for an egalitarian society. That's because of an important distinction between *equal opportunity* and *equal outcome*.

Equal opportunity is the idea that every American has a similar chance in life. Each person gets one vote and the process should be transparent and open to all. In economics, it means that every individual gets a fair shot at achieving the American dream. Whether you are white or black, Anglo or Latino, male or female, rich or poor, equal opportunity means you should have a similar opportunity to influence the political process and to win economic success.

Equal opportunity: The idea that every American has the same chance to influence politics and achieve economic success.

Equal outcome: The idea that citizens should have roughly equal economic circumstances.

Assess current debates on tax reform

Equal outcome, in contrast, is the idea that a society guarantees not only opportunity but also results. Some nations reserve a minimum number of seats in the national legislature for women or specific ethnic groups. And, as we have already seen, others keep their taxes high and offer extensive social benefits, knowing that these will keep successful people from getting too far ahead of everyone else.

Today, the United States aims for equal opportunity. The winners fly in private jets; the losers may end up with nothing. But questions—and hard political choices—about equal opportunity remain. How do we give people a real chance to affect the governing process? How much education is enough to help ensure that an individual can make it in the marketplace? Do we need to provide early childhood reading programs? And what should we do about past injustice? Does the long legacy of slavery, segregation, and repressive policies toward Native Americans require our society to offer compensation to these groups? What about inheritance laws that permit some people to start life with billions and others with nothing?

These questions return us to the same policy debates we introduced during the discussion of positive and negative liberty. Should we guarantee the basics—or simply protect individual rights and let every person run the great race alone?

Concern has grown in recent years that the gap between rich and poor has grown so large that it undermines equality of opportunity. For most of the nation's history, middle class Americans had the highest average incomes in the world. However, the percentage of Americans who are middle class shrank from 61 in 1971 to 50 by 2015[33] (see Figure 1.4). Meanwhile, the very wealthy have pulled away from the rest of society. As the gap between the rich and the poor continues to widen, liberals warn that growing disparities are creating a land of a few billionaires and many hungry children with grim prospects. Conservatives respond that the effort to redistribute wealth from rich to poor discourages entrepreneurs from innovating. Expanded wealth at the top, they say, will help the many through job creation.

Over time, the United States has gone from the most equal society in the world to one that is considerably less equal than other wealthy nations. The past thirty-five years, in particular, have seen a sharp spike in inequality. American politics has come to emphasize other ideas—negative liberty, individualism, the American dream of getting ahead—over equality. Still, the United States is a dynamic and fast-changing nation. Today many Americans, both conservatives and liberals, have begun to call for renewed efforts to increase equality of opportunity. This may be one of the hottest issues in American politics today.

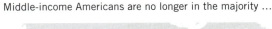

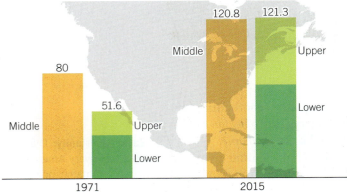

Middle-income Americans are no longer in the majority ...

80
Middle

51.6
Upper
Lower

120.8
Middle

121.3
Upper
Lower

1971   2015

Adult population by income tier (in millions)

● **Figure 1.4** *The middle class is losing ground in the United States (Pew Social Research).*

 **The Bottom Line**

» Equality means that every citizen enjoys the same privileges, status, and rights before the law.

» There are three types of equality: social, political, and economic.

» Today, America generally aims for *equal opportunity* rather than *equal outcome*, although heated discussions rage over what society must provide to ensure true equal opportunity.

Religion

In the 1630s, a large contingent of Puritans escaped European persecution and sailed to New England with an ambitious aim: to establish a biblical common-wealth that would serve as a Christian model for the rest of the world. Governor John Winthrop, in his shipboard sermon, called their settlement "a city upon a hill" and expected "the eyes of all people on us." How did they fare? If people really were watching, they soon saw unexpected complications.

For example, Quakers from Pennsylvania—whom the Puritans despised for lacking discipline—began sailing north to convert the New Englanders. If the Quakers succeeded, they would subvert the whole idea of a model Puritan soci-ety. New England's women, the ministers worried, might be especially vulner-able to Quaker heresies. The authorities banned Quakers from Massachusetts under threat of having an ear cut off (one each for the first and second offenses), their tongues pierced by hot pokers (third offense), and finally death. Quaker martyrs joyfully challenged the Puritan authorities. Four were hanged before English authorities ordered an end to the punishment.

This story reflects the importance of religion, the intense competition between sects, and a missionary fervor about saving the world. Even today, pol-iticians of every stripe repeat the idea of a "city on a hill" (although few realize that Winthrop was quoting the Sermon on the Mount in the New Testament).

Still a Religious Country

Religion plays an enduring role in American politics and society. The central-ity of religion may not surprise you. But it is a powerful example of American exceptionalism. As most nations grow wealthier, religious fervor wanes. Citizens in developed countries, from Britain and France to Japan and South Korea, tell pollsters that God is not very important in their lives. In contrast, Americans maintain high levels of religiosity. Some 87 percent of Americans say they believe in God, 53 percent belong to a church, and nearly 46 percent attend church regularly. To find higher levels you have to go to poorer nations such as India, Egypt, and Indonesia.[34] However, the percentage of Americans who

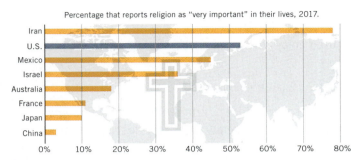

Percentage that reports religion as "very important" in their lives, 2017.

Figure 1.5 *Look how American religiosity stands out. As nations grow wealthy, religion nearly always loses its importance. The United States is the great exception (Pew Research Center).*

are religiously unaffiliated—who describe themselves as atheist, agnostic, or "nothing in particular"—appears to be growing. [35]

So Many Religions

Americans have a lot of religions to choose from. One recent survey found sixteen different Christian denominations with more than a million members each.[36] That is just the beginning. Jews number over 6.7 million, Muslims some three million, and seven other non-Christian groups have over one hundred thousand adherents each (two of the fastest growing are Wiccans and Pagans).[37] In contrast, many other nations have a single major faith, often supported by the government through tax dollars.

Why so many religions? From the start, different colonies began with distinct religious affiliations. By forbidding the federal government from boosting any official faith, the Constitution kept the field open for any new preacher with a religious idea that might attract a following. Because none can win official recognition, each religious institution is only as strong as the congregation it can muster.

This open market explains why new religions spring up all the time. But why do Americans respond? That's one of the great mysteries of American culture. In most other nations, religion declines as the society gets wealthier. The United States is the great exception—most people continue to worship (see Figure 1.5).

Religious observance is not the same throughout the United States. Texas and Georgia (proud members of the "Bible Belt") have high religiosity, Florida and Missouri are in the middle, Colorado and Wisconsin are not especially religious, and Maine is the least religious of all. Generational change is also at work.

Although millennials continue to report high rates of religious faith, an unusual number do not affiliate with any denomination. Most believe in God but not organized religions.

In surveys asking about formal religious affiliation, nearly a quarter of Americans, and more than a third of millennials, responded "none." [38]

The Politics of Religion

How is religion relevant to politics? As we will see in Chapter 2, the Constitution appears to erect a "wall of separation between church and state," as Thomas Jefferson described it. Yet America's energetic religious life—marked by great evangelical revivals—injects three different types of political issues into American politics.

First, there is the question of what exactly the Constitution forbids. May teachers lead prayers in public schools? May students in the bleachers organize prayers before football games? May judges post the Ten Commandments in a courthouse? Questions such as these spark intense debates about just where to draw the line between church and state.

Second, religious faith often inspires people to throw themselves into political issues. The civil rights movement spilled out from Baptist and Methodist churches across the South, brimming with religious rhetoric, religious symbols, and religious zeal. The opponents of racial equality—arguing for slavery and segregation—also framed their response in religious terms. In American politics, both sides often invoke God. The controversies swirling around the politics of peace, abortion, the environment, equality, same-sex marriage, and many other issues have all, to varying extents, made the same leap from pulpit to politics. Today, conservatives are more likely to take their faith into the political arena, but this has not always been true.

Third, religious fervor sometimes fosters a missionary sense in American politics. As the nation expanded westward, Americans declared their "manifest destiny"—God had given an entire continent to his chosen people. During the Cold War, American leaders constantly invoked God as a way of contrasting the United States with communist nations. Congress added "under God" to the Pledge of Allegiance (in 1954) and "In God We Trust" to paper money (1955). John Winthrop's idea—America as a model for the world—still inspires many Americans.

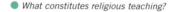

● *What constitutes religious teaching?*

 **The Bottom Line**

» Religion plays an enduring role in American politics and society. This is unusual—almost unique—among wealthy countries.

» Americans have an unusually large number of faiths to choose from, although younger people are less likely to affiliate with an organized religion.

» Religion touches politics in three ways: It injects questions about the role of religion in political life. It inspires political participation. And it fosters a missionary sense in American foreign policy.

How Do Ideas Affect Politics?

Most political scientists agree that the seven ideas of this chapter are central to American society. But how do these ideas influence our politics? There are two familiar answers. Either ideas influence our culture or they operate through our institutions. There is still another possibility to bear in mind, however: Perhaps they have a life all their own.

Ideas in American Culture

Political culture: The attitudes, beliefs, and assumptions that give order and meaning to public life.

Each nation has a unique **political culture**, constructed over the years by a people and its leaders. Anthropologist Clifford Geertz described culture as the stories a group tells about itself. Ideas such as liberty, the fear of government, individualism, and the American dream together are the foundation of American political culture. They are the stories we tell about ourselves.[39]

A culture shapes the way people think about politics and government. Culture develops slowly over time, shaped by history and experience. Colonial Americans' shared beliefs, stories, and mental habits—their culture—inspired the founding generation to develop a Constitution that limits the power of government. Why did the framers add a Bill of Rights to the Constitution? Their abiding faith in individualism. Why are there so many checks and balances in our national government? A fear of too much government, dating back to colonial times. Why do we regulate and tax less than other nations? The American dream's gospel of success. This shared culture leads men and women to fight for policies that reflect freedom or democracy; policies that reflect social-democratic solidarity are more difficult to win because they resonate more faintly through American culture. American hopes and fears often seem peculiar to people in other nations—just as their hopes and fears may not resonate in the United States.

The United States has a rich national culture that remains a perpetual work in progress. Every era and each generation experience their own exuberant debate about what the nation has been, and what it should be.[40]

Find out how political culture shapes government.

The Ideas in Political Institutions

A different perspective suggests that ideas operate through political institutions. The institutions are key to political action. James Madison explained the *institutional perspective*. Past political theory expected republican citizens to virtuously seek the public interest. But, Madison continued sardonically in the *Federalist Papers*, "enlightened statesmen will not always be at the helm."[41] The Constitution did not ask people to be virtuous; instead, it developed a government that would operate smoothly even if its citizens were greedy and their leaders corrupt. The institution—the rules and organizations built into the government— would shape popular behavior.

Many political scientists follow Madison's argument. It is our governing institutions, starting with the Constitution, that shape American politics. From an institutional perspective, the barriers to enacting new programs emerge not from a dislike

● *Ideas move politics. A member of Americans for Prosperity, a conservative group, goes door-to-door to persuade voters about the benefits of tax cuts.*

of government but from the way the government is organized. The U.S. government is slow to act, according to this view, because it is *designed* that way with multiple checks and balances on every level of government. When Americans criticize their policymakers for inaction, perhaps they miss the point: Gridlock is a consequence of the institutions we have inherited.

Culture or Institutions?

Although historians and sociologists tend to emphasize political culture, many political scientists are skeptical about its explanatory power. How, they ask, can something as static as national culture explain the fluid, fast-changing American political scene?

For example, the cultural perspective suggests that the United States has never passed national health insurance because Americans do not trust government. The institutional perspective counters that it is less a matter of popular belief and more the way the government is designed. After all, they continue, Harry Truman won the presidential election of 1948 in part by promising national health insurance. But Congress—using the checks and balances central to our national government's institutions—buried the proposal.

Proponents of culture as the primary driver of politics respond that cultural values are not meant to explain every possible political action. Events, leaders, movements, and government agencies all introduce change. But culture forms a boundary. It limits the possibilities, shapes our perceptions, and influences our reactions. Ideas, culture, and institutions all reinforce one another. Truly understanding a nation means understanding all three.

The Bottom Line

» How do the foundational ideas influence politics? Political scientists point to three different ways.

» First, ideas shape American culture, which in turn affects our politics.

» Second—and most popular among political scientists—ideas operate through political institutions. We must study those institutions to appreciate how ideas shape politics and policies.

» Third, ideas may have their own independent power.

Conclusion: Culture and Institutions, Together

Do the ideas described in this chapter add up to a political culture that shapes the attitudes of American men and women? That cultural argument seems intuitive to many people. On balance, however, most political scientists underscore the importance of institutions.

As a political science student, you can decide for yourself on the relative power of ideas and institutions as you read this book. But you do not have to choose one or the other. We believe that culture and institutions together play a role in American politics. They reinforce each other. Yes, national institutions make it difficult to pass big national programs such as universal health insurance; and yes again, opponents invoke powerful cultural norms—such as individualism and liberty—to persuade Americans that such legislation threatens their values. For us, the most interesting question is how ideas, culture, and institutions (along with interests and individuals—the four "Is" introduced earlier in this chapter) all interact to shape American politics.

Finally, ideas have a power of their own—above and beyond the culture and institutions they have helped to shape. Ideas of liberty, democracy, or the American dream can move people to act. That is exactly what Captain (and Professor) Russell Burgos was thinking as the mortars flew into his post in northern Iraq.

As you read through this book, you will constantly encounter the seven ideas we have described in this chapter. Think about which seem most important and powerful to you. And pay attention to how they appear to operate—through the culture, through institutions, with a life of their own, or (as we believe) in all these ways at different times and in different circumstances.

CHAPTER SUMMARY

Check your understanding of Chapter 1.

This book examines four key questions: Who governs? How does American politics work? What does government do? And Who are we? Seven important ideas influence American politics. Each idea has at least two different interpretations—differences that spur intense political debates.

Freedom means that the government will protect your life, liberty, and property from the coercion of others (including government) so that you can pursue the goals you define for yourself. In one view, freedom requires *positive government* action to make sure that everyone has the basics to permit them to pursue their goals. In another view, the government guarantees only *negative freedom*—the freedom to pursue your goals. You are free to succeed or to fail on your own, but there are no government guarantees about food, or homes, or healthcare.

Self-rule means that people govern themselves through clearly defined procedures such

as elections. In a democracy, citizens participate directly in making government decisions. In a republic, the people rule indirectly through their elected representatives. The American system is a combination of the two, a democratic republic.

Americans value *limited government*: They distrust government and place limits on the authority it can exercise.

Individualism means that individuals—not society or the government—are responsible for their own well-being. For those who favor community or social democracy, the public interest is best served when members of a society use government to take care of one another. Americans take both an individual and a communal view, but the individualistic view is more powerful.

The *American dream* holds that if you are talented and work hard, you will succeed and grow wealthy. Critics argue that the system is rigged or that the dream promotes the wrong values.

However, the dream remains a powerful force in American politics.

🟢 *Equality* allows each citizen to enjoy the same privileges, status, and rights before the law. Some define equality as a matter of *opportunity*—the idea that every American has an equal chance. Others promote equal *outcome*—a guarantee of results. There are three types of equality to consider: Social equality means that all individuals enjoy the same status in society. Political equality guarantees every citizen the same rights and opportunities to participate in politics. Economic equality minimizes the gap between citizens' wealth and earnings.

🟢 *Religion* plays an enduring role in American politics and society. The great question is how we limit government interference without limiting religion itself.

🟢 These seven ideas mark Americans' beliefs as a people. They can shape politics through national culture, through political institutions, and through their own influence on Americans.

Need to review key ideas in greater depth? Click here.

KEY TERMS

American exceptionalism, p. 10
Conservatives, p. 17
Democracy, p. 14
Economic equality, p. 28
Equality, p. 28
Equal opportunity, p. 29
Equal outcome, p. 30
Freedom, p. 11

Individualism, p. 19
Initiative, p. 15
Institutions, p. 6
Liberals, p. 17
Median, p. 29
Negative liberty, p. 11
Political culture, p. 34
Political equality, p. 28

Positive liberty, p. 12
Rational-choice theory, p. 7
Referendum, p. 14
Republic, p. 5
Self-rule, p. 14
Social democracy, p. 20
Social equality, p. 28

Flashcard review.

STUDY QUESTIONS

1. The second paragraph of the Declaration of Independence boldly explains why "governments are instituted among men." Why? Why are governments formed? Do you agree with that assertion about government's most basic function?

2. *Liberty* is often described as the most important American idea. Describe the two different views of liberty. Which do you think is more accurate?

3. Review the seven principal "American ideas" we have identified in this chapter. Are *new* foundational ideas bubbling up in American politics today? What examples can you imagine?

4. The Declaration of Independence asserts that all men are endowed by their creator with inalienable rights to life, liberty, and the pursuit of happiness. Over time, Americans have extended that idea to more and more people—poor people, former slaves, women. Are there groups in our society today who are *not* getting the full benefits of this ideal? How might that be changed?

5. What is the difference between a democracy and a republic? Which principle does contemporary American government reflect, or does it reflect both? If you were a Founder, which of these principles would you emphasize?

6. There are three forms of equality—social, political, and economic. Define each.

7. Describe the two approaches to economic equality: opportunity and outcome.

8. When it comes to religion, the United States is different from most wealthy societies. How? How do young people differ from previous generations in their approach to religion?

9. Ideas shape both culture and institutions. Explain.

 Go to **www.oup.com/us/Morone** to find quizzes, flash cards, simulations, tutorials, videos, and other study tools.

2 The Constitution

THE R. R. MOTON HIGH SCHOOL in Farmville,

Virginia, was a mess. The roof leaked, the heat barely worked, the classrooms were overcrowded, and the school bus kept breaking down. When it rained, students sat under umbrellas and shivered in their coats. Moton was a black school; across town, the white students were warm and dry. On April 23, 1951, a Moton junior named Barbara Johns decided to take action. She fooled the principal into leaving the school for the day and forged notes to the teachers calling an assembly. When the students had all filed into the auditorium, the sixteen-year-old stood on stage, called for a strike, and led a student march to the Prince Edward County Courthouse to protest the shabby state of the school.

As you can imagine, Barbara Johns and her fellow student protesters landed in trouble. The students and their families called a leading civil rights group, the National Association for the Advancement of Colored People (NAACP), which dispatched a team of lawyers. The lawyers explained that local governments run American schools, and there was not much the NAACP could do about the conditions at Moton High—but they could try and challenge the entire policy of racial segregation. The NAACP sued the school district, arguing that forcing African Americans into a separate school violated the United States Constitution. The Supreme Court took the case, *Davis v. School Board of Prince Edward County*, bundled it together with two similar cases, and three years after the student strike, delivered one of the most famous court decisions in American history, a ruling known as *Brown v. Board of Education*.

A sixteen-year-old took a big risk, the Supreme Court unanimously ruled that she was right, and hundreds of laws across many states were struck down for violating the Constitution. The Court ruled that segregated education facilities were inherently unequal and violated the Fourteenth Amendment of the United States Constitution, which declares: "No state shall . . . deny to any person . . . the equal protection of the laws."[1]

● *Student strikers at Moton High School, led by Barbara Johns. The protestors had an enormous impact because civil rights lawyers found a way to place their grievance in the context of the U.S. Constitution.*

In this chapter, you will:

● Discover the roots of the Constitution in early America.

● See why Americans declared independence from England and learn about their first government under the Articles of Confederation.

● Follow the arguments that shaped the Constitution and get an overview of the final document.

● Read about the debate over whether to adopt the Constitution.

● Learn how Americans have changed the Constitution—and how the Constitution has changed America.

ement
ntal principles
that governs a nation or an
organization.

Stop and think about the power Americans invest in this document written long ago. The **Constitution** is the owner's manual and rulebook for American government. It specifies how the government operates, setting out what the government may do and how to do it. If you want to learn about any feature of American politics, always check the Constitution first.

Who are we? The answer to that question is always changing, but the Constitution provides the ground rules for those changes. It organizes our political life. The Declaration of Independénce describes the ideas behind America. The Constitution takes those ideas and turns them into laws. It *institutionalizes* American ideas.

This sounds simple: The Constitution guides the government. But there is a wrinkle. It is often unclear how the Constitution applies to modern questions. After all, it is just 4,400 words written on four pages of parchment a long time ago. Many provisions can be read different ways, and the document is silent on many topics. As a result, we always have to *interpret* how the Constitution applies to a case today.

Segregation is a prime example. The Constitution does not say anything about racial segregation. Back in 1896, as states were imposing segregation on African Americans, the Supreme Court ruled (8–1) that segregation did not violate the Constitution. In 1954, the Court unanimously ruled that it did (in the case the students at Moton High initiated). Different justices in different eras read the same words in changing ways. We constantly debate exactly how to read the Constitution's words, and how to apply them to the questions we face.

The Trump administration came to Washington DC eager to introduce change—new rules for immigration, new rules for international trade, new auto emission standard , and the list goes on. Each and every change–and how it is made—has to square with the Constitution. To understand what is happening in American politics today you need a solid understanding of that document written more than 230 years ago.

Watch the commemoration of the Constitution's 200th birthday.

The Colonial Roots of the Constitution

No nation in the eighteenth century had anything like the American Constitution. Most nations wrote their governing documents much later; some countries, such as England and Israel, never wrote one at all. However, the American Constitution did not spring up out of nowhere. Many features of colonial politics propelled the new nation toward its constitution.

- First, the colonies were three thousand miles away from the king and his armies. Authorities back in England debated policies and issued orders; the American colonists frequently ignored them and did what they wished. No one back in London paid much attention. The

BY THE NUMBERS
The Constitution

Number of the 13 states that voted for the Constitution within six months	**6**
Number of states that initially voted against the Constitution	**2**
Number of delegates in New York, Virginia, and Massachusetts who could have defeated the entire Constitution by switching their votes	**18 (3% of the delegates in those states)**
Number of *proposed* amendments to the U.S. Constitution introduced in Congress since 1791	**over 11,600**
Number of *successful* amendments since 1791	**17**
Percentage of the U.S. population that can block a constitutional amendment	**3**

How easy is it to change the Constitution? How easy should it be?

English policy of ignoring colonies was known as *salutary neglect*; it permitted the colonies to develop their own political institutions. When England started interfering in colonial affairs, the Americans revolted.

- Second, beginning with the Virginia House of Burgesses in 1620, every colony elected its own legislature. As a result, the colonists had a great deal of experience with representation. New settlements demanded seats in the assemblies. New immigrants wanted the right to vote. In some places, such as New Jersey, women with property could vote. Americans grew up arguing about representation—and that prepared them for the debate over the Constitution.

- Third, plentiful land created opportunities for ordinary people. Early America was not an equal society by any means: there were aristocratic families and slaves, prosperous merchants and **indentured servants**. However, by the standards of the time, the New World was a land of extraordinary social mobility. Economic conditions helped foster a republic.

Indentured servant: A colonial American settler contracted to work for a fixed period (usually three to seven years) in exchange for food, shelter, and transportation to the New World.

Compact: A mutual agreement that provides for joint action to achieve defined goals.

Covenant: A compact invoking religious or moral authority.

- Fourth, some colonies began with mutual agreements between the settlers, known as **compacts** or **covenants**. The Pilgrims, who landed in Massachusetts in 1620, introduced the idea; before they went ashore all forty-one adult males signed a mutual agreement known as the Mayflower Compact (named after their vessel, the *Mayflower*). In most nations, the right to rule stretched back through history. In contrast, the individuals on the *Mayflower* formed a new society, based on their mutual agreement and consent. Many New England communities began with such compacts or covenants—religiously inspired forerunners of a constitution.

- Fifth, many colonists came to the New World to practice their religion in peace. Beginning in Rhode Island in 1636, a revolutionary idea began to emerge: the individual's freedom to practice religion without government interference. In some colonies, it was followed by other rights, such as freedom of speech and freedom of the press.

- Sixth, border areas in early America were violent and insecure due to brutal wars with Native Americans. The French claimed land to the north and west, the Spanish to the south and west. Colonists also constantly fought one another over their own boundaries. After the break with England, insecure borders pushed the Americans to adopt a strong central government.

Each colony governed itself in its own way. However, the six features described here—distance from English authority, representation, social mobility, covenants, individual rights, and violent borders—all propelled Americans toward the Constitution of 1787.

 **The Bottom Line**

» Colonists developed their own political institutions, including compacts that became the forerunners of the Constitution.

Why the Colonists Revolted

The roots of the American Revolution lie in a great English victory. Centuries of rivalry between England and France burst into war in 1754. Known as the French and Indian War in North America, the conflict spread through the colonies from Virginia all the way to Canada. Colonial American militias fought side by side with the British army and defeated the French in 1763. Thirteen years later the colonists declared independence and turned their muskets on the English.

Why did the Americans suddenly revolt? Because the victory over France introduced two fateful changes. First, ten thousand English troops remained in the colonies to protect the newly won land. The existence of those "Redcoats" meant that England could now enforce its policies: The days of salutary neglect were over. Second, the English had run up a crushing debt during the ten years of war and decided that their colonists should help pay for it. The Americans' reaction was explosive.

The Colonial Complaint: Representation

It was not just Britain's demand for money that provoked the colonists. Americans had grown used to making their own decisions through their elected assemblies. When the English imposed new taxes, without the approval of the colonial assemblies, they violated the idea of self-rule. The result was an unusual revolution. Most revolutionaries rise up against regimes that have long repressed them. In contrast, the Americans fought to preserve rights that they had been exercising during the many years of happy neglect.

Beneath the conflict lay a deep philosophical difference about representative democracy. The colonists considered their assemblies the legitimate voice of the people; if taxes had to be raised, they were the ones to do it. Colonial assemblies were very responsive to the voters and their daily concerns—they worried about things like building roads and surveying new lands. Political theorists call the colonial view of governance **delegate representation**: Do what the voters want.

> **Delegate representation:** Representatives follow the expressed wishes of the voters.

The British never understood this view of representation because they operated with a different one. Unlike the colonists, the English did not change their electoral districts every time the population shifted. English elected officials were expected to pursue the good of the whole nation. Your representative is not an "agent" or an "advocate," argued English statesman Edmund Burke, but a member of Parliament who must be guided by "the general good." This view is known as **trustee representation**: Do what is best for the voters regardless of what they want you to do.[2]

> **Trustee representation:** Representatives do what they regard as in the best interest of their constituents—even if constituents do not agree.

The Conflict Begins with Blood on the Frontier

After the French and Indian War, settlers poured westward (Figures 2.1 and 2.2). Native Americans fought back; they rallied around Chief Pontiac and overran colonial settlements in Virginia, Maryland, and Pennsylvania. To end the fighting, England closed the border and prohibited settlers from moving westward, past the Appalachian mountain chain. The colonists were stunned. The arbitrary boundary, announced in the Proclamation of 1763, had been drawn amid lobbying by land speculators, who could make or lose fortunes depending on whether their own land was open to settlement. The proclamation threatened the westward thrust that spelled opportunity to the restless colonists. American settlers did not care about Native American rights to land. As they saw it, a corrupt English monarchy was blocking American pioneers from settling the wide-open spaces that they had helped win from France.[3]

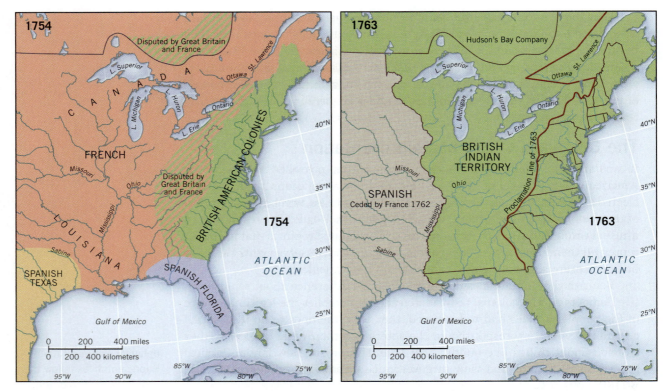

● **Figures 2.1 AND 2.2** *The colonies before (left) and after (right) the French and Indian War. Spain lost Florida but gained the land west of the Mississippi in compensation for having supported France. Napoleon would grab it back from Spain and then, after failing to quell a slave rebellion in Haiti in 1803, abandoned the New World and sold the vast lands to the United States. Note the line formed by the Proclamation of 1763 on the map on the right. England tried to forbid settlers from crossing that line.*

Mercantilism: An economic theory in which the government restrains imports and promotes exports to maintain national power and wealth. Popular in the sixteenth and eighteenth centuries.

The colonists responded in their traditional way—they ignored regulations that did not suit them. But now there was a British army in America to enforce the policies. The Proclamation of 1763 was followed by the Quartering Act (1765), which required colonial assemblies to billet British troops in empty barns and warehouses. Suddenly, the Redcoats seemed like an occupying army.

Britain also began to enforce its **mercantilist** trade policies, which meant American ships had to bypass their traditional (and lucrative) partners and do business only with English colonies at higher prices. Colonists who ignored the decree were charged with smuggling: Wealthy merchants now faced imprisonment or large fines for trading with French colonies. To make matters even worse, the English introduced taxes to help support their army of Redcoats. These widely reviled duties culminated in the Stamp Act of 1765.

The Stamp Tax and the First Hints of Independence

Stamp taxes were a common way to raise money in England, but imposing one on the colonies set off a firestorm. Parliament ignored the colonial assemblies and simply announced the new tax. Colonists responded by convening a Stamp

Act Congress that met in October 1765. Delegates from nine colonies sent a protest to the king and to Parliament. The English policies were pushing the colonists into working together.

Protests against the stamp tax spread throughout the colonies. Mobs hung, burned, and beheaded tax collectors in effigy. They attacked tax collectors' offices and homes. Across the sea, English authorities were incredulous. All they could see were ungrateful colonists who refused to pay for their own protection.[4]

The Townshend Acts Worsen the Conflict

After Parliament reluctantly lifted the stamp taxes, colonists celebrated the repeal and tensions eased—until Parliament followed up with the Townshend Acts in 1767. These acts instituted another round of new taxes; revenues were earmarked to pay a new colonial authority, the American Board of Customs, which would collect taxes independently of the colonial assemblies. An imperial bureaucracy was explicitly denying the colonists self-governance. The Townshend Acts also suspended the New York State Assembly for refusing to house and supply British troops.

New Yorkers and, later, Bostonians seethed with anger over having their legislatures dissolved. Mobs harassed the customs officials, who found it impossible to carry out their duties and called for help. A British warship arrived and officials seized a vessel owned by John Hancock, one of the resistance leaders, and charged him with smuggling. That move set off riots, bringing British troops into the city to restore order. Before long, there were almost four thousand Redcoats in a city of fifteen thousand people. The Boston mobs harassed the soldiers with taunts, rocks, and snowballs until on March 5, 1770, one detachment of Redcoats panicked and fired point-blank on the crowd.

The Boston Massacre, as the event quickly became known, left five civilians dead. The first to fall was a sailor named Crispus Attucks, the son of an African slave and a Natick Indian who had escaped slavery some twenty years earlier. Ironically, the son of two groups who would not be liberated by the revolution—an African slave and an American Indian—was the first to bleed for the cause. Paul Revere memorialized the massacre with an engraving that transformed the panicky soldiers threatened by a mob into a line of killers firing into a heroic cluster of civilians. Historian Gordon Wood described the engraving as "perhaps the most famous piece of anti-military propaganda in American history."[5]

At the start of the crisis, six years earlier, colonial leaders were respectfully petitioning the king to rescind policies. Now, blood had been shed and the colonists began to talk about rebellion.

The Boston Tea Party

The British repealed all the Townshend duties except a tariff on tea. Tea was a global industry in 1773—think of it as the eighteenth century's must-have product. But the East India Tea Company was on the verge of bankruptcy. In 1773, Parliament tried to rescue the company by granting it a monopoly over the tea trade in the New World. The colonial shippers who had long been trading tea would be shut out by this rival trading network.

● Paul Revere's engraving of the Boston Massacre. It makes the British look like cold-blooded killers—not historically accurate but powerful propaganda for independence.

First Continental Congress:
A convention of delegates from twelve of the thirteen colonies that met in 1774.

When ships with East India tea arrived, mobs in Philadelphia and New York forced them to sail away without unloading their cargo. In Boston, however, Governor Thomas Hutchinson would not permit such nonsense. He insisted that the three ships in Boston Harbor would not leave until their tea was safely delivered. On a dark December night, about fifty men, some "dressed in the Indian manner," blackened their faces and boarded one of the ships. They hefted 342 chests of tea onto the deck, bashed them open with hatchets, and dumped the contents—worth about £9,600 (between $1.5 and $2.5 million today)—into Boston Harbor.[6]

Revolution!

British leaders were furious. Past insubordination paled next to this direct economic hit on a struggling British company. They first demanded compensation; when a Boston town meeting voted that down, the English introduced what colonists dubbed the Intolerable Acts. The laws closed Boston Harbor until the tea was paid for, abolished town meetings, authorized the quartering of troops in any home in Massachusetts, and essentially put the state under military control. King George himself put it bluntly: "The colonists must either triumph or submit."

Americans refused to submit. Instead, twelve colonies sent representatives to the **First Continental Congress** in September 1774. The Congress petitioned for an end to the Intolerable Acts, called for a boycott on British goods, and asserted colonial rights to "life, liberty, and property." They agreed to meet again in May 1775.

Before the Continental Congress reconvened, fighting had begun. In April 1775, the British commander in Boston, General Thomas Gage, sent one thousand troops from Boston to seize guns and ammunition stored at Concord, Massachusetts. Armed colonists who called themselves "minutemen" blocked the way and came under British fire at Lexington and Concord. Eight were shot dead. The British found and destroyed the weapons, but their march back to Boston was horrific. Minutemen hid behind rocks and trees and sniped at them all along the way. By the time the English army limped back into the city, they had lost three hundred men.

A Long Legacy

Revolutionary images and slogans still resonate in American politics today. The "Tea Party" holds rallies around the nation. Civilians anxious about immigration call themselves "minutemen" and patrol the border with Mexico. "Militias" organize and train to defend their personal rights. And Americans from across the political spectrum aspire to live up to the Revolution's dreams of equality. The Revolution left the new United States with symbols, slogans, and an enduring political concern: <mark>arbitrary government that threatens the people's liberties.</mark> But it also raises a provocative question: Are Americans too quick to exaggerate routine disagreements by making analogies to the revolutionaries?

The Bottom Line

» For more than a century England largely ignored its American colonies. Elected assemblies governed the colonists. After the French and Indian War, the English bypassed the colonial legislatures and imposed new rules and taxes.

» These actions violated traditional colonial rights and exposed two different ideas of representation—the American concept of *delegate representation* (representatives respond to their constituents' desires) and *trustee representation* in England (representatives do what they consider best for all).

» English action also harmed colonial economic interests. The conflict very quickly escalated.

» Americans fought an unusual revolution: Rather than demanding new rights, they were trying to preserve rights and economic interests they had long been exercising.

The Declaration of Independence

The **Second Continental Congress**, which met in May 1775, faced the job of declaring independence, mobilizing an army, organizing a government, and rallying thirteen colonies very different from one another around a single cause. A year later, on July 4, 1776, the Congress voted to adopt a Declaration of Independence as a statement to the world of America's purpose. The document has two parts: a statement of principles and a list of grievances. (The full Declaration is reprinted in Appendix I.)

Second Continental Congress: A convention of delegates from the thirteen colonies that became the acting national government for the duration of the Revolutionary War.

The Principle: "We Hold These Truths . . ."

In one elegant paragraph, the Declaration of Independence distills America's political philosophy into five towering ideals:

- All people are equal.
- Their creator endowed them with rights that cannot be taken away.
- These rights include life, liberty, and the pursuit of happiness.
- People form governments to protect those rights.
- Governments derive their just powers from the consent of the governed.

These ideas were not new. Political philosophers, especially the English thinker John Locke, had used similar language. In his *Two Treatises on Government*, published more than a century earlier, Locke argued that in nature, there are no rules. Life is ruled by force and violence. To secure safety and freedom, people contract with one another, enter into civil society, and form governments that can protect one another's life, liberty, and property.

As a statement of governing ideals, the Declaration of Independence was—and to this day, still is—breathtaking. In 1776, it was also a far cry from reality. Thomas Jefferson, who drafted much of the document, was a slave owner. The Declaration essentially invites future cruelty when it refers to "merciless Indian savages." Its authors did not live up to their noble sentiments. We do not fully live up to them today. Even so, the document stands as the great statement of American idealism—something every generation can fight for.

Grievances

The second part of the Declaration lists twenty-seven grievances against King George III. These tell us what the American colonists cared about as they began the Revolution. Three complaints dominate the list:

- *Violations of the right of representation.* This complaint comes up in ten of the twenty-seven charges against England. It is by far the most intensely felt grievance.

- *A standing army not under civilian control.* In particular, British soldiers acted in peacetime without the consent of American legislatures. Five complaints are about the British military.

- *Loss of an independent court.* This violation of traditional justice comes up six times.

Today the Revolution is often boiled down to the colonists' slogan "No taxation without representation." The Declaration emphasized *representation* much more than taxation; taxes did not show up until way down the list, as grievance number seventeen ("Imposing taxes on us without our consent"). Of course, many of the acts that precipitated the Revolution—from new taxes to tighter trade rules—were economic challenges, but what reverberates through the Declaration are the rights of representation.

 **The Bottom Line**

» The Declaration of Independence asserted philosophical ideals as the basis of the new American government.

» The first part of the Declaration features five ideals that sum up the nation's political principles.

» The second part of the Declaration lists twenty-seven grievances that led to the break.

The First American Government: The Articles of Confederation

When the United States declared its independence, it linked the thirteen former colonies—now states—into a **confederation**, or *alliance of independent states.*

Independent States

The states organized their governments to reflect popular desires. They introduced annual elections and extended the right to vote. Some built benches in the assembly halls so that the public could watch their representatives in action.

Of course, the new rules still left many people out. Women had participated in the Revolutionary War, but they could not vote in most states.[7] And slavery persisted in every single state.[8]

Still, the revolutionary spirit unleashed a powerful egalitarian urge. States from Massachusetts to Virginia pondered the abolition of slavery. In some states, such as New Jersey, women with property were allowed to vote. And across the nation, state legislatures were, as historian Gordon Wood put it, "probably as equally and fairly representative of the people as any legislatures in history."[9]

The National Government

The Continental Congress approved its first constitution, called the Articles of Confederation, in November 1777. The document, which reflected Americans' recent experience with England, kept the national government weak and dependent on the states.

Central government power was placed in a Congress whose members were selected and paid for by the states. There was no chief executive (the states would implement the laws), no central authority to tax (all revenues would come from state governments), and no central power to muster an army (the states supplied the troops). Each state had a single vote in Congress. Important matters required the vote of nine states. Any changes to the Articles of Confederation required the agreement of all thirteen states. The articles created a weak central government.[10]

Some Success . . .

Americans had good reason to be proud of their new government. Power remained close to the people. The new government overcame incredible odds and, by April 1783, had defeated the most powerful military force in the world. Americans considered themselves both democratic and prosperous.[11]

Confederation: A group of independent states or nations that yield some of their powers to a national government, although each state retains a degree of sovereign authority.

● *A series of legends have grown up around Molly Pitcher, whose real name was Mary Ludwig Hays McCauley. The most famous has her stepping in to take the place of her fallen husband at the cannon during the Battle of Monmouth. The stories probably combine descriptions of many women who fought with the American army.*

The Continental Congress also won a major policy success when it stopped the squabbling among states claiming western land. Instead, the Northwest Ordinance of 1787 established a process by which individuals could buy western lands: When an area attracted a minimum number of settlers, it could apply to be a state with all the same powers and privileges as the existing states. With this act, the United States established its mechanism for western expansion.

. . . And Some Problems

But four major problems plagued the new American government.

First, Congress could not raise taxes and had no money of its own. The states were reluctant to provide funds. The Continental Congress had trouble supplying (much less paying) the army throughout the Revolutionary War. George Washington drew a lesson that would always guide his politics: *The new republic needed a vigorous national government if it was to survive.*[12]

Second, requiring unanimity made it impossible to amend the Articles. When Congress tried to fix its financial problems by levying a 5 percent tax on imported goods, twelve of the states agreed. However, Rhode Island's legislature denounced the proposal as "the yoke of tyranny fixed on all the states."[13] When loans from France and Holland came due, there was no way to pay them. Again, many leaders drew a lesson: *A vigorous national government needed a stable source of revenue.*

Third, state governments were dominated by their legislatures, which operated without any checks and balances. The result was too often bias and even chaos. Legislatures wrote (and repealed) laws to benefit individuals. They forgave debts. They seized private property. Leaders eventually reached yet another important lesson: *Different sources of government power should balance one another.*

Fourth, the weak national government had a difficult time standing up to foreign powers. Spain closed the Mississippi to American vessels. Pirates brazenly seized American ships in North Africa. National-minded Americans reached an obvious conclusion: *A weak central government left the nation vulnerable.*

One event, Shays's Rebellion, dramatized the problems of government under the Articles. Captain Daniel Shays led a rebellion that broke out in western Massachusetts in August 1786 and spread across the state. Thousands of farmers, protesting high taxes and interest rates, took up their muskets and shut down courthouses to stop foreclosures on their farms. When Governor James Bowdoin summoned the local militia to defend the Worcester courthouse, members refused;

● *Captain Daniel Shays led a rebellion to protest farm foreclosures in 1786.*

If you could go back and offer advice to American leaders in 1787, what would you tell them? Should they stick with the Articles of Confederation or write a new constitution?

Yes, stick with the Articles of Confederation.	**No, build a new central government.**	**I am divided about this.**
A strong, central government can become tyrannical—forcing the people to pay taxes or depriving them of their rights to express their beliefs, practice their religion, or own guns. More power should reside with local government, which is closer to the people. Citizen militias can defend communities without a national army to tempt leaders to intervene in foreign conflicts.	The national government under the Articles is weak and chaotic. The national government needs to be powerful enough to repel foreign threats, to oversee national development, and to facilitate trade and good relations between the states.	The Constitution will enable the United States to eventually become a wealthy and powerful nation—but it will be less democratic than the local and state governments that dominated under the Articles.

some joined the rebellion. Finally, Bowdoin hired an army and broke the rebellion. Shays's sympathizers shifted strategy: They won seats in the General Court (as they called their legislature) the following year and legislated the debt relief that the farmers had been fighting for.[14]

For many national leaders, Shays's Rebellion was the last straw. Under the Articles of Confederation, neither the national government nor an individual state was strong enough to protect public property (e.g., courthouses) or private property (the repayment of loans). Shays's Rebellion pushed the most influential men in the colonies to write a new constitution. Not everyone agreed. Many Americans thought that problems such as Shays's Rebellion were the growing pains of a more democratic government that reflected the people and their desires.

Secrecy

Spring 1787 arrived cold and blustery, delaying many of the delegates on their way to Philadelphia. James Madison from Virginia got there first, with a plan for a new

Alarmed by spreading chaos, the Continental Congress called for a national meeting in Annapolis, Maryland. Only twelve delegates from five states arrived at Mann's Tavern in Annapolis (picture above)—not enough to do official business. With Shays's Rebellion raging, the delegates requested each state to appoint representatives to meet in Philadelphia, Pennsylvania, the following May, in 1787, and so quietly authorized a convention that would write an entirely new constitution—and permanently transform the United States.

constitution. Madison was short, shy, and balding; today, we recognize him as one of America's greatest political thinkers. The next delegate from Virginia arrived with more fanfare. As George Washington approached, church bells pealed, cannons thundered, army officers donned their old uniforms to ride escort, and local citizens lined the streets and cheered. The presence of the great American hero made the convention's success more likely.

On the first day, the delegates unanimously elected George Washington to chair the convention. Then they agreed on a controversial rule: The deliberations would be completely secret. Guards were placed at the doors. Windows were shut and remained closed, even after the Philadelphia summer turned stifling. Most of what we know about the convention comes from James Madison himself, who took a seat at the front of the room and kept meticulous notes.

Was it a good idea to impose secrecy? The young republic had only recently opened up its political process to the people. Thomas Jefferson called the decision to close the convention "an abominable precedent." In a republic, he argued, the people should always know what their leaders are doing.[15]

However, the delegates wanted to speak their minds freely without worrying about how their words would appear in the newspapers. Many also believed that states would withdraw their delegation as soon as they heard that the convention was debating an entirely new constitution. Without secrecy, they might have to abandon their bold plan and simply amend the Articles of Confederation—which was, after all, what they had been asked to do.

 **The Bottom Line**

» Under the Articles of Confederation, thirteen independent states bound themselves into a confederation with a weak central government that had to rely on the states to implement its decisions.

» Although feeble, this first U.S. government was, by the standards of the time, a very democratic one.

» Delegates to the Constitutional Convention convened to fix the problems with the Articles of Confederation but chose to go much further and propose a new American government.

The Constitutional Convention

As they thought about reorganizing their new government, American leaders balanced the two political dangers they had recently encountered.

- British officials' behavior warned them that a powerful central government could strip the people of their rights.

- Experience with the Articles of Confederation warned them that a weak government could fail to protect their rights.

The delegates debated from May into September in 1787. Six major themes dominated their attention.

How Much Power to the People?

The delegates faced a dilemma. They wanted their government to answer to the public; that was why they had fought the Revolution. But too much democracy, they thought, had led to chaos; "the people," complained one delegate, "are the dupes of pretended patriots."[16] The delegates wished to represent the public through better educated, wealthier, and more experienced leaders—men like themselves.

Over the course of the convention, the delegates developed a view of representation that Madison called *filtration*, or *indirect elections*: The public would vote for men (and later women) who would, in turn, vote for public officials. The speeches during the convention's first days are a bit shocking to us today. The delegates wanted to make the public *less* involved in government than they had been in the eleven years since the United States declared its independence. The new Constitution would permit the public to vote for only one federal office—members of the House of Representatives.

The debate about public involvement did not end with the Constitution. Over time, Americans would get a more active role in their governance. Citizens would win more control over electing presidents and choose their senators directly. The "public" would also expand to include all women, African Americans, and younger Americans (eighteen- to twenty-year-olds), as we will see in future chapters.

The debate that began at the Constitutional Convention continues to this day. It animates one of the key ideas we discussed in Chapter 1: self-rule, balanced between direct democracy and indirect representation. At a still more fundamental level, the debate speaks to one of the great questions of American politics: *Who governs?*

Public involvement in government has grown dramatically over the centuries, but Madison's principle of filtration still keeps the people at arm's length from their government in many areas.

Learn about the founders.

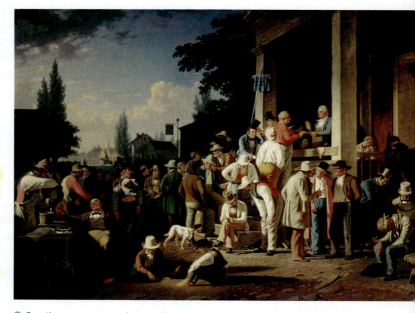

● *Over time, common men began voting in American elections. This painting shows the raucous results. Note the heavy drinking—and how this, like all early American elections, was a completely male event.*

National Government Versus State Government

The Articles of Confederation left most power with the states. Madison's plan for the new government would have shifted most governing authority to the national level.[17]

Many delegates disagreed with this dramatic change. They believed that state and local governments were closer to the people and could more accurately reflect public sentiments—precisely what Madison was trying to avoid. Some pro-states' rights delegates charged Madison and his allies with trying to "abolish the State Governments altogether." This issue led delegates from New York to walk out of the convention; Rhode Island refused to send any delegates in the first place. The convention was soon down to eleven of the thirteen states.[18]

In the end, the delegates compromised on a system that included both national and state power. The federal government took over many functions—but far fewer than Madison had originally proposed. The states kept many duties—but far fewer than states' rights advocates would have liked. This mixed system, with a stronger national government that leaves considerable power with the state governments, is called **federalism** (and we'll discuss it in Chapter 3). The debate about how to balance national government power and state power continues to the present day.

Big States Versus Small States

Another intense dispute at the Constitutional Convention revolved around a division we rarely notice today: the large, more populous states (led by Virginia and Pennsylvania) versus the smaller states (led by New Jersey and Delaware). Large states argued that representation should be based on population; small states wanted each state to have an equal voice. That debate led to two different plans, one put forward by Virginia (a big state) and the other by New Jersey (on behalf of the small states).

The Virginia Plan. Large and small states squared off as soon as Governor Edmund Randolph of Virginia presented Madison's original plan for the Constitution. A powerful speaker, Randolph addressed the delegates for four hours. The plan, which became known as the **Virginia Plan**, had five key points.

1. Congress would have two chambers, a form known as a **bicameral** legislature, with representation in both chambers based on state population.

2. Citizens would vote for members of the House of Representatives; the number of representatives would reflect the size of the state. The House of Representatives would, in turn, vote for senators from a list of candidates provided by the state legislatures. This limited the states' role and is an example of filtration, or indirect elections.

Federalism: Power divided between national and state government. Each has its own sovereignty (independent authority) and its own duties.

Virginia Plan: Madison's plan, embraced by Constitutional Convention delegates from larger states; strengthened the national government relative to state governments.

Bicameral: Having two legislative houses or chambers—such as the House and the Senate.

3. Congress would elect the president. Here the Virginia Plan suddenly turned vague and did not specify whether the president would be one man or a committee; nor did it say how long the executive would serve.

4. National courts would be established and the judges would have life tenure.

5. Congress would have broad powers to legislate in all cases where the states were "incompetent." A "council of revision" made up of the president and the Supreme Court would have the authority to nullify any state law.

Delegates who had not already been briefed by Madison were stunned. The plan would build a robust national government. Congress could "call forth the force of the union" against any state and the federal government could strike down state laws. Early votes indicated that the Virginia Plan enjoyed a small majority at the convention.

Delegates from small states protested that they would soon "be swallowed up." Each state had "its peculiar habits, usages, and manners," they insisted, and these must be protected. Under Madison's plan, three states (Virginia, Pennsylvania, and Massachusetts) would have enough members in Congress to form a majority all by themselves. Representatives from the smaller states repeatedly threatened to walk out of the convention.[19]

The New Jersey Plan. The small states pushed back with their own plan, introduced by William Paterson of New Jersey and known as the **New Jersey Plan**. Rather than construct a new national government, this plan focused on strengthening the Articles of Confederation. It had four key points:

1. Congress would have only one chamber, a form known as a **unicameral** legislature. Each state would have one vote in Congress, regardless of its size—exactly the same as in the Articles. However, congressional acts would be the supreme law of the land, making the new constitution stronger than the Articles of Confederation.

2. Congress would elect a committee to serve as the federal executive for one term only.

3. The executive committee would select a supreme court, which would be responsible for foreign policy, economic policy, and the impeachment of federal officials.

4. The national government could tax the states and would have the exclusive right to tax imports.

The New Jersey Plan left the states at the center of American government but took a step toward a stronger national government by permitting it to raise taxes and exercise more authority over interstate commerce. When the vote was called, only three states supported the New Jersey Plan.

New Jersey Plan: Put forward at the convention by the small states, it left most government authority with the state governments.

Unicameral: Having a single legislative house or chamber.

● *Louis Glanzman's recent painting of the Constitutional Convention. Washington towers over everyone at the center in a black frock coat. To his right stands James Madison. Alexander Hamilton is the red-haired man standing sixth from the right. Aged Benjamin Franklin, eighty-one years old, sits at the center of the room, chatting with Hugh Williamson, a delegate from North Carolina.*

The Connecticut Compromise. Convention delegates decisively approved the Virginia Plan's bicameral Congress with a House and a Senate. They voted for a House of Representatives based on population. Then debate turned to the Senate. If the delegates voted with the Virginia Plan—that is, the House of Representatives would vote for senators—the big states would essentially win the debate. Tempers grew short. Luther Martin, a garrulous delegate from Maryland, wrote home that the convention was on the verge of breaking up.[20]

Big states seemed to have the votes to carry seven states and win the Virginia Plan's version of Senate elections. But when the roll was called, on July 2, one big-state supporter from Maryland and two from Georgia slipped out of the convention hall. With their exits, both states shifted and the vote came out a tie: five states for the Virginia Plan, five against, and one evenly split.

To break the deadlock, the delegates formed a committee, which was tilted toward the small states. It came up with a compromise, brokered by Roger Sherman of Connecticut and known as the Connecticut Compromise. The House would be based on population; the Senate would have two representatives for each state, chosen by the state legislature. (Americans did not vote directly for their senators in all states until 1913.) Because legislation had to pass through both houses, the public and the states would each have a say. Because the delegates wanted power over taxes and spending to be in the people's hands, they required that all finance-related bills had to be introduced first in the House.

The compromise squeaked through—five states voted "yes," four "no," and one split. The big states won the House of Representatives; the small states got their way in the Senate. The compromise continues to give rural states a great deal of clout in the Senate, sparking a debate about whether small, rural states such as Vermont or Wyoming have too much power over Congress.

The President

Even the master planner James Madison arrived at the convention without a clear design for the presidency—also known as the *executive authority* because it *executes* (or puts into effect) the laws. The delegates even wavered about whether executive authority should be placed in one individual or a committee.

Committee or Individual?   Many delegates worried that a single executive would grow powerful and become, as Governor Randolph put it, "the fetus of monarchy." Madison and his allies, however, feared that the Connecticut Compromise opened the Senate door to the same petty state politics that had wrecked the Articles of Confederation. They therefore decided that the president should be one individual, independent of Congress, who could represent the public. After much back and forth, they settled on a four-year term and permitted reelections. (In 1951, the Twenty-Second Amendment limited the president to two terms.)

The Electoral College.   How would the United States choose the president? The Constitution's framers saw a problem with every option. They did not think the people had enough information or wisdom. They did not trust state legislators to put aside their own narrow concerns and think about the national interest. Delegates from big states did not want to give Congress the job now that state legislators were picking two senators from each state. What could they do? In response, they came up with the most complicated rigmarole in the Constitution: the **Electoral College**. Each state would select individuals known as *electors*—the delegates hoped they would be well-known individuals with sound judgment, who could make a wise choice for president.

How many electors would each state have? Another compromise: Each state would have the same number of electors as it had members of Congress. That meant a state's population would matter (given proportional representation in the House) but also that every state was assured of two more votes (reflecting their representation in the Senate). If no individual received a majority of electoral votes—which last happened in 1824—the House of Representatives would choose from among the five candidates with the most votes. They would vote by state, and each state would get just one vote—again, a concession to small states.

Who would elect the electors? The convention simply left this question to the states. At first, the state legislatures took the job of voting for the electors. But in the late 1820s the states ceded this right to the people (again, white men, although by then they did not need to own any property). The people voted state by state for their electors—as Americans still do (Figure 2.3). Today, all the electors in a state generally cast their votes for the candidate who won the state (although only twenty-six states legally require them to do so).

As we saw in the last chapter, the Electoral College selected five presidents (11%) who lost the popular vote, a sharp limit on popular rule. The original idea, giving the vote to men of good judgment, is now forgotten and the Electoral College enhances the power of less populated states.

> **Electoral College:** The system established by the Constitution to elect the president; each state has a group of electors (equal in size to that of its congressional delegation in the House and the Senate); today, the public in each state votes for electors who then vote for the president.

Separation of Powers

One idea that evolved during the convention was the separation of powers. Each branch of government—the president, Congress, and the judiciary—has its job to do: The delegates vested "all legislative powers" in Congress, the executive

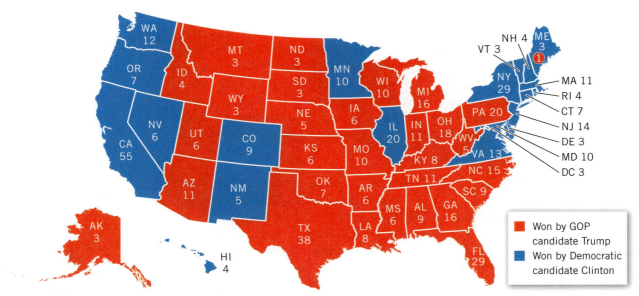

● **Figure 2.3** *Electoral College map for the 2016 presidential election. For the second time in the last five elections, the candidate who lost the popular vote became president by winning the Electoral College.*

power in the president, and the judicial power (to try cases) in the courts. The Articles of Confederation had created only a national legislature; in Britain, power was also concentrated in Parliament, their national legislature. Now, the United States would have three independent branches.

The framers added a crucial twist: checks and balances. Each power the Constitution grants to Congress, the presidency, or the courts is balanced by a "countervailing" power assigned to another branch. Each branch is involved in the others' business. In this way, as Madison later put it, one branch's ambition for power would always check the other branches' ambitions (see Figure 2.4).

For example, Congress passes legislation but needs the president to sign a bill into law. The president can veto (reject) the bill (checking Congress); Congress can override the veto by a two-thirds vote of both chambers (balancing the president).

The president is commander-in-chief, but the Constitution gives Congress the power to declare war and set the military's budget. The president negotiates treaties, but the Senate must ratify them by two-thirds vote. The president appoints cabinet officers and Supreme Court justices, but the Senate must approve (or confirm) them. Congress holds the ultimate power over all federal officers. The House can impeach (or formally accuse) the president or any other officer in the executive or judicial branch of "Treason, Bribery or other high Crimes and Misdemeanors"; the Senate looks into the accusation and decides whether to actually remove the person from office. What are "high crimes and misdemeanors"? Well, because they have never been fully defined, Congress must use its judgment.

These checks and balances are among the most distinctive features of the American Constitution. The French political philosopher Montesquieu wrote

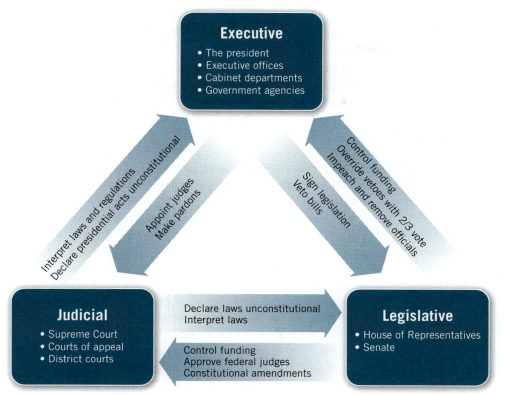

Figure 2.4 *Separation of powers—the checks on the federal level. Multiply these across state and local levels and a vital question of American politics arises: Is this chaotic and fragmented state ready to take on the world? We have been posing the question since 1787.*

an influential treatise, *The Spirit of the Laws* (published in 1748), which argued that to avoid tyranny, the executive, legislative, and judicial functions of government must be separated from one another—and never placed in a single individual or body. However, few governments have ever developed this principle as fully as the U.S. Constitution did.

Checks and balances continue to spark disagreement. Many scholars have argued that separated systems are more prone to gridlock—a paralysis of governing institutions—than other democracies. The danger of gridlock is that major issues such as climate change or the national debt become harder to address. An even greater potential danger: Are people growing so tired of stalemate they vote for leaders who are willing to ignore the constitutional limits?[21] We get into this question in Chapter 11. Has the U.S. government developed too many checks and balances to meet the challenges of the twenty-first century? Or do the Constitution's checks and balances remain in good working order, controlling power and preserving self-rule?

"A Principle of Which We Were Ashamed"

The convention rethought almost every aspect of government—except slavery. Why? For some delegates, the answer came down to self-interest. Of the fifty-five delegates, twenty-five were slave owners. George Washington brought three slaves with him to Philadelphia. In three states—Georgia, South Carolina, and Virginia—slaves made up more than one-third of the population. And the men and women in bondage were a source of wealth and power. Each time the subject of slavery came up, delegates from South Carolina and Georgia offered the convention a stark choice—protect slavery or form a union without us.

In the end, the delegates wanted a strong union more than they hated slavery. The Constitution includes three major references to slavery—without ever mentioning the word itself. Each time, the slaveholding states got what they wanted.

The Three-Fifths Compromise. Slavery was first thrust on the convention's agenda with the question of how to count slaves when allocating seats in the House of Representatives. As Table 2.1 shows, nearly four in ten of Virginia's residents were slaves. If slaves were counted as part of the population, southern states would have as many members in the House of Representatives as the northern states.

As soon as the issue came up, James Wilson of Pennsylvania sprang to his feet and offered a compromise. For the purpose of apportioning representation, Wilson proposed, let the total number of slaves count as three-fifths of the free people of a state. The strange fraction came from the Continental Congress. When it was trying to raise revenue from the states, Congress calculated each state's wealth on the basis of population. It then arbitrarily estimated that slaves would generate three-fifths as much wealth as free people.

TABLE 2.1 The Population in 1790

STATE	TOTAL POPULATION	SLAVES	PERCENTAGE ENSLAVED
Connecticut	237,655	2,648	1.1
Delaware	59,096	8,887	15.0
Georgia	82,548	29,264	34.5
Maryland	319,728	103,036	32.2
Massachusetts	378,556	0	0.0
New Hampshire	141,899	157	0.1
New Jersey	184,139	11,423	6.2
New York	340,241	21,193	6.2
North Carolina	395,005	100,783	25.5
Pennsylvania	433,611	3,707	0.9
Rhode Island	69,112	958	1.4
South Carolina	249,073	107,094	43.0
Virginia	747,550	292,627	39.1

Source: U.S. Census

This crude calculation now came back to haunt the Constitution. The delegates immediately accepted the Three-Fifths Compromise. Its actual wording is as peculiar as the rule itself.

> *Representatives . . . shall be apportioned among the several states according to their respective numbers, which shall be determined by adding the whole number of free persons, including those bound to service for a term of years [indentured servants] and excluding Indians not taxed, three fifths of all other persons.*

The Constitution never says "slave," but simply "three fifths of all other persons." In fact, a reader who did not know that the passage refers to slavery would have a hard time understanding it. Why did the Constitution's framers—who were usually so precise—write such a convoluted sentence? Because they did not want the word *slavery* to appear in the Constitution. John Dickinson, a thoughtful delegate from Delaware, put it best: The awkward wording was, he said, "an endeavor to conceal a principle of which we were ashamed."[22]

The Slave Trade.   A second question involved the slave trade. Could the federal government regulate or abolish it? Many delegates were repulsed by the idea of stealing human beings from Africa, chaining them into the hulls of ships bound for America, and selling the survivors to the highest bidder. George Mason from Virginia rose and gave the most prophetic speech of the convention: "Every master of slaves is born a petty tyrant. They bring the judgment of heaven on a country. As nations cannot be rewarded or punished in the next world they must be in this. Providence punishes national sins, by national calamities." It was a powerful speech. However, Mason himself owned more than three hundred slaves. Their worth would rise if the slave trade were abolished.

No one else at the convention was willing to follow Mason's attack. In the end, backers of a strong Constitution struck a bargain and permitted the slave trade for another twenty years, in exchange for more national power over interstate commerce and the authority to tax imports. Historian William Beeman calculated that by extending the slave trade they condemned 200,000 Africans to slavery—almost equaling the total (250,000) from the preceding 170 years.[23]

Fugitive Slaves.   Finally, in August, as the convention was winding down, delegates from the slave states proposed a fugitive slave clause—requiring the rest of the nation to assist in returning runaway slaves. This time there were no deals and barely any debate. The northern delegates simply accepted the proposal. Northern merchants, after all, benefited from the slave trade right alongside Southern planters. Every region was complicit in the tragic decision.

"The National Calamity."   Many Americans revere the document that has guided the nation for more than 225 years. However, George Mason was right when he predicted a "national calamity." Seventy-two years later, Abraham Lincoln would echo Mason as he reflected on the carnage of the Civil War (1861–1865) in his

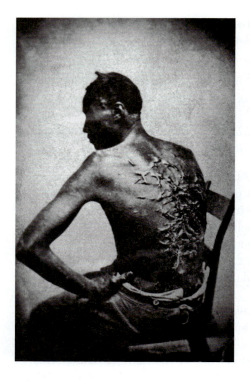

A vivid example of slavery's brutality. Fifty years after the Constitutional Convention, abolitionists rose up and denounced the Constitution as a "covenant with death and an agreement with hell" because of its slavery compromises. Advertisements for runaway slaves reported identifying marks—such as horrific scars from whipping and even branding.

second inaugural address: "God . . . gives to both North and South this terrible war as the woe due to those by whom the offense [of slavery] came."

The Constitution's slavery passages—like the Civil War that led to their repeal—remind us that the convention was the beginning of an American journey. Each generation must face the same challenges that confronted the founders. *Who are we?* Can we try to make the United States more just, more democratic, and more inclusive? The Declaration of Independence gives America its ideals: All people are created equal. The Constitution, in turn, provides the rules. Americans have struggled over the meaning of the ideals and the implementation of the rules ever since these documents were written.

The Bottom Line

» The constitutional framers balanced two dangers: government that was too strong (the king of England) versus government that was too weak (the Articles of Confederation).

» The debates focused on five central issues:

1. Should the people be directly involved in government? Most delegates believed in filtration, or indirect elections.

2. National versus state power, which came down to a standoff between larger and smaller states. Led by Madison, the big states introduced the Virginia Plan. Small states countered with the New Jersey Plan. The Connecticut Compromise offered a solution: House members were elected on the basis of population, but every state had two Senate seats.

3. The nature of the presidency.

4. How best to separate powers, answered through a system of checks and balances. For the most part, these limits on concentrated authority would continue to develop long after ratification.

5. Slavery: Pragmatic compromise overcame moral concerns. Delegates took care not to use the word *slavery* in the Constitution, but several clauses enabling the institution to grow and expand would lead to the greatest conflict in the nation's future.

An Overview of the Constitution

By September 17, after four months of deliberation, the Constitutional Convention had done its work. Thirty-nine of the original fifty-five delegates lined up to sign the document. There are only seven articles in the Constitution, each broken down into multiple sections. (Their full text appears in Appendix II.) These passages remain the institutional foundation of the American political system.

Preamble

The Constitution begins with a preamble, the most elegant sentence in the document:

> We the people of the United States, in order to form a more perfect union, establish justice, insure domestic tranquility, provide for the common defense, promote the general welfare, and secure the blessings of liberty to ourselves and our posterity, do ordain and establish this Constitution for the United States of America.

The Constitution's authority rests on "we the people." As we have seen, the Constitutional Convention produced a weak version of the people—one that permitted slavery, excluded women, and permitted "we the people" to vote for exactly one branch of Congress. The next phrase—"in order to form a more perfect union"—addresses these limitations. Americans always struggle toward that more perfect union.

The preamble offers six goals for the new government. Ask yourself how you would rate the U.S. government on each of them today (see What Do You Think?).

Article 1: Congress

Article 1, the longest in the Constitution, describes the new Congress. Section 2 of the article establishes a House of Representatives elected every two years. In 1789, the average size of a House district was around 33,000 people—today the

What does the Constitution do? Get a brief tour.

What Do YOU Think? **Have We Achieved the Constitution's Goals Today?**

Think about the goals listed in the preamble. Then give a grade to each: an "A" if you think the United States has lived up to its goals, and . . . well, we're sure you know all about grades!

Goal:	Grade Today:
Form a strong union	_____
Establish equal justice for all	_____
Insure domestic tranquility (that is, peace at home)	_____
Provide for the common defense (today, we might say homeland security)	_____
Promote the general welfare	_____
Secure liberty for ourselves and posterity	_____

size of an average district has grown to nearly 750,000 people. Representatives must be twenty-five years old and have been citizens for seven years. Section 3 establishes a Senate with two members from every state, elected every six years; they must be at least thirty years old and have been a citizen for nine years.

Section 8 is the most important passage in Article 1—and perhaps the entire Constitution. Its seventeen short paragraphs tell Congress what it may do, including the "power to lay and collect taxes," declare war, regulate interstate commerce, coin money, and raise an army.

Think about the reach of congressional authority. The largest and most expensive program that Congress oversees is Social Security, which pays monthly pensions to older people. If you read all of Section 8, you may be puzzled—nothing in it remotely justifies paying for retirement pensions. How, then, could Congress create the Social Security program? Because the very last paragraph of Section 8 empowers Congress:

> [T]o make all laws which shall be necessary and proper for carrying into execution the foregoing powers, and all other powers vested by this Constitution in the government of the United States.

That phrase, known as the *necessary and proper clause*, gives Congress—and the government—a great deal of creative leeway. What are the limits of the power granted to Congress by this clause? This is another point on which the delegates in Philadelphia disagreed. Unsurprisingly, Americans still argue about how far the necessary and proper clause stretches congressional authority.

Section 9 of Article 1 lists the things Congress may *not* do. Its second prohibition is especially important today: "the privilege of the writ of Habeas Corpus shall not be suspended unless when in cases of rebellion or invasion the public safety may require it." *Habeas corpus* means that government cannot hold prisoners without formally charging them with a crime. The U.S. government may not simply throw someone in jail without a charge.

Article 2: The President

The Constitution's second article shifts focus from the legislature to the executive branch. The president, Article 2 specifies, must be a natural-born American at least thirty-five years old and is chosen by electors for a four-year term. As we saw, each state originally decided who elects the electors—today every state has turned the power to choose electors over to the public. Very few nations use the American process for selecting the head of state.

Whereas Article 1 lists congressional do's and don'ts in detail, Article 2 says very little about presidential powers and duties. The president is commander in chief of the army and the navy. Presidents make treaties if two-thirds of the Senate approve; they appoint ambassadors, Supreme Court justices, and all other officials—again with the advice and consent of the Senate.

Although these seem like a limited set of powers, the Constitution includes another clause that has permitted an enormous expansion of presidential powers: "The executive power shall be vested in a President of the United States." What that "executive power" is, and how far it can stretch, has been debated throughout American history. President Obama, for example, facing a Congress unwilling to act on immigration reform, in 2012 unilaterally declared a "Dreamers" policy that allowed young children brought illegally into the United States to apply for work permits and avoid deportation. How could he do so? The administration claimed he was using his authority to execute the laws that govern immigration. President Trump eagerly reversed the order—although he has taken an expansive view of presidential power on other issues. Where does that leave the Dreamers? The Congress and the Supreme Court will have to weigh in.

Section 4 allows for removing a president "on impeachment for, and conviction of, treason, bribery, or other high crimes and misdemeanors." Three presidents have faced formal impeachment proceedings, although only one, Richard Nixon, resigned his office. The grounds for impeachment—what exactly is a high crime—remain highly contested. Until very recently, impeachment was rarely even mentioned; as the combat between the parties grew, beginning in the 1980s, intense partisans began to raise the prospect all the time.[24]

Article 3: The Courts

Article 3 creates the Supreme Court and authorizes Congress to organize additional courts. Alexander Hamilton called the Supreme Court "the least dangerous" branch of government, and the Constitution describes it only briefly. The justices are selected by the president, approved by the Senate, and have tenure for life—still another buffer against democratic politics. Article 3 grants the Supreme Court power over all cases "arising under this Constitution, the laws of the United States and treaties made."

The Constitution is silent on the Court's most formidable power: May it overrule an act of Congress? Or an executive declaration by the White House? Sixteen years after the Constitutional Convention, Chief Justice John Marshall, in deciding a case called *Marbury v. Madison*, ruled that the Court could strike down an act of Congress. (We review this case in detail in Chapter 13.)

Notice how the powers of each branch have evolved over time. Americans are constantly challenged to read and interpret precisely what the Constitution requires.

Article 4: Relations Between the States

Article 4 defines the relationship between the states that had so plagued the Articles of Confederation. A state may not discriminate against citizens of other states—each must give "full faith and credit" to the official acts of other states. Article 4 also guarantees every state a republican form of government.

The "full faith and credit" clause became a major issue when some states recognized same-sex marriage while others refused. After more than a decade, the Supreme Court took the issue off the table by striking down all state laws that limited marriage to a man and a woman. Now you know where they got the authority to do so: the Supreme Court's authority to judge which laws and regulations violate the rules laid down by the Constitution. (We'll discuss the case in Chapter 4.)

Article 5: Amendments

Article 5 authorizes amendments to the Constitution. The process is extremely difficult. Two-thirds of both the House and Senate must approve. Then three-fourths of the states must ratify—either through the state legislature or through state conventions. The only amendment to be ratified the second way is the Twenty-First Amendment, which in 1933 repealed the prohibition on alcohol.

Over one hundred thousand amendments have been proposed since 1791 (when the first ten amendments, or Bill of Rights, went through); only seventeen have passed. When citizens or companies disagree with a Supreme Court ruling, occasionally they try for a constitutional amendment. As you can see they very rarely succeed.

The Constitution forbids amendments on two matters: No amendment could stop the slave trade before 1808, and no state can be denied equal suffrage in the Senate (two seats) without its approval. In this way, the two fiercest debates at the convention were placed beyond the reach of future generations.

Article 6: The Law of the Land

Article 6 makes the Constitution the supreme law of the land. It also specifies that there must be no religious test for holding any federal office. Some states, however, had religious tests for holding state and local office and even for voting, up until the 1830s.

Article 7: Ratification

Article 7 announced that the Constitution would go into effect after nine states had ratified—a controversial move because the United States was still operating under the Articles of Confederation, which could be amended only by all thirteen states.

The Missing Articles

Many Americans thought that the original Constitution was missing something important. Only a handful of individual rights were mentioned in the document. It said nothing about free speech, free press, freedom of religion, jury trials, or the right to bear arms. The debate over ratifying the Constitution would quickly expose this weakness. As we will see, ratification helped introduce an important addition: the ten amendments known as the Bill of Rights.

 **The Bottom Line**

» The Constitution is a brief, elegant document with a preamble and seven articles (or major sections).

» The articles of the Constitution address (1) Congress, (2) the president, (3) the Courts, (4) relations between the states, (5) instruction for amending the Constitution, (6) an assertion that the Constitution is the supreme law of the land, and (7) a process for ratifying the Constitution.

Ratification

The new Constitution now went to the states, where ratifying conventions would vote it up or down. Most states were closely divided, but the Constitution had two big advantages. First, it offered a clear plan in a time of trouble; opponents could only say "no" and force the nation to start all over again. Second, the convention had attracted many of the most prestigious men in America, beginning with George Washington and Ben Franklin. Supporters of the Constitution were known as *Federalists*—making their opponents the *Anti-Federalists*.

The Anti-Federalists

The Anti-Federalists rooted their argument against ratification in **classical republicanism**. Popular government, in this view, should model itself on ancient republics such as Athens and Rome. Republics should be small and local, permitting maximum popular participation in public affairs. When we discussed the idea of self-rule in Chapter 1, we introduced the idea of direct democracy (celebrated by Thomas Jefferson); classical republicanism is the original version of that idea.

The Anti-Federalists were not interested in a centralized nation–state such as the European empires. They had four major criticisms of the new Constitution:

- First, it stripped political control from citizens and placed it in a powerful national government.
- Second, the president looked too much like a king.
- Third, standing armies and navies were a threat to peace and liberty. Republics relied on citizen militias—which could be mustered during wartime—to protect the people.
- Fourth, and most important, the Anti-Federalists hammered away at the Constitution's missing piece, a bill of rights.[25]

Politics also played a role in the Anti-Federalist argument. Many of the men who opposed the Constitution were powerful political figures in their own states. A national government would diminish their influence.

Many of the Anti-Federalist (and civic-republican) arguments remain alive today. Americans often criticize the federal government and cheer the idea of restoring power to state and local officials, who are closer to the people. The Anti-Federalists may have lost the debate in 1788, but their fear of federal power and their yearning to return authority to the people endures—and shapes one answer to our great question, *Who are we?*

The Federalists

The arguments in favor of the new Constitution were summarized by an editorial dream team. James Madison and Alexander Hamilton (with a little help from John Jay, who would become the first chief justice of the United States) wrote eighty-five short essays that appeared in newspapers to explain and defend the Constitution. Known as the *Federalist Papers*, these essays achieved three very different purposes. First, they are pro-Constitution editorials, even propaganda; the authors

Classical republicanism: A democratic ideal, rooted in ancient Greece and Rome, that calls on citizens to participate in public affairs, seek the public interest, shun private gain, and defer to natural leaders.

● *The ratification of the Constitution was a close call. Patrick Henry, a powerful orator, led the opponents (known as Anti-Federalists) in Virginia. Virginia was one of seven states where the vote was close.*

were fighting to get New York to approve the new Constitution, and they did not pretend to be neutral. Second, they are the single best guide to the thinking that guided the Constitution. However, we must read them carefully, always weighing the *Papers* as persuasive rhetoric on the one hand and as explanations of constitutional logic on the other. Finally, the *Federalist Papers* are brilliant theoretical essays about politics and government.

The two most famous *Federalist Papers*, no. 10 and no. 51, are reprinted in Appendix III to this book. The eighteenth-century language sounds strange to our ears, but the argument is brilliant. *Federalist* no. 10 argues, surprisingly, that a large national government can protect liberty more effectively than small local governments. Madison, the essay's author, begins by introducing the "mortal disease" that always destroys popular government. You might imagine that he was referring to tyrants like George III. Instead, he points to *factions*—groups that pursue their self-interest at the expense of others. And in the United States, said Madison, factions usually reflect economic interests. This issue still haunts American foreign policy today: Removing tyrants will not achieve stable popular government until factions are controlled.

How can we diminish the effects of factions? Not through local governments, argued Madison. In each local area, one economic interest is likely to predominate—farmers, merchants, big manufacturers, or even poor people eager to tax the rich. Because the same local group will always be in the majority, it is difficult to stop that group from taking advantage of the minority.

Madison's realistic assessment was a breakthrough in political theory. The classical view assumed that for popular government to survive, the people—that is, the voters—had to be virtuous and respect one another. Madison introduced a more modern view: expect people to pursue their own self-interest. As he wrote in *Federalist* no. 51, "if men were angels, no government would be necessary." If popular government is to survive, it must be organized to protect minorities from majorities who are going to pursue their own self-interest.

How can we do this? Move the debate to the national level, said Madison. A larger political sphere—a bigger government—will always have a great many diverse interests, arising from all the states. With so many different factions, no one interest will be able to dominate. Each faction will form a small minority of the whole and will therefore need to form alliances. As the issues change, so will the groups that are in the majority and the minority. As a result, no one faction will be able to impose its will on the minority for very long.

Madison's idea would run into trouble, however, if the same two sides face off against one another on every national issue. When that occurs, there is no need to form shifting alliances. That's what happened in the slavery debate in the 1850s.

Two Strong Arguments

To this day, both sides—Anti-Federalist and Federalist—sound persuasive. The Anti-Federalists tapped into a deep American yearning for local governments that respond directly to the people. The Federalists argued that only a national government could really protect the people's rights and turn the new nation into a great power.

A Very Close Vote

The small states got their way at the Constitutional Convention and, not surprisingly, they ratified quickly and unanimously—Delaware, New Jersey, and Georgia all signed by January 2, 1788. In Pennsylvania, some members of the assembly hid to slow down the process. Enthusiastic mobs found the reluctant members and marched them to the deliberations. The public crammed into the hall and gathered outside the building. After a month, Pennsylvania ratified the Constitution forty-six to twenty-three and Benjamin Franklin led a cheering throng through the streets to Epple's Tavern for celebratory toasts (see Table 2.2 for a summary of the voting).

TABLE 2.2 **The Final Vote for the Constitution**

STATE	DATE OF RATIFICATION	VOTE IN STATE CONVENTION
1. Delaware	December 7, 1787	Unanimous [30–0]
2. Pennsylvania	December 12, 1787	46–23
3. New Jersey	December 18, 1787	Unanimous [38–0]
4. Georgia	January 2, 1788	Unanimous [26–0]
5. Connecticut	January 9, 1788	128–40
6. Massachusetts	February 7, 1788	187–168
7. Maryland	April 28, 1788	63–11
8. South Carolina	May 23, 1788	149–73
9. New Hampshire	June 21, 1788	57–47; required two meetings
10. Virginia	June 25, 1788	89–79
11. New York	July 25, 1788	30–27
12. North Carolina	July 21, 1789 [after election of Washington]	194–77
13. Rhode Island	May 29, 1790 [first Congress in session]	34–32

Key: *Easy Ratification*   *Tough Fight*   *Originally Refused*

● *New York City celebrated ratification by cheering Alexander Hamilton—still remembered as a major intellectual force. Here, Broadway hit* Hamilton *recalls the most forceful Federalist.*

In Massachusetts, Governor John Hancock, who had been the first delegate to sign the Declaration of Independence, dramatically switched from the Anti-Federalist side—on one crucial condition. He asked that amendments protecting individual rights be introduced to the new Constitution. It was the first prominent insistence on a bill of rights. Even with the switch, Massachusetts delegates approved only narrowly, 187 to 168. Other states followed the two Massachusetts precedents: request a bill of rights and unite after the debate.

After Maryland and South Carolina voted for the Constitution, the action moved to Virginia—the largest state and the most intense contest to date. Governor William Randolph, who had presented the Virginia Plan at the convention, and George Mason, who had scorched the slave trade, both refused to sign the Constitution. After a furious debate, Virginia voted for the Constitution 89 to 79.

In New York, the new Constitution squeaked through by a 30 to 27 vote.

Not every state voted in favor. Rhode Island town meetings voted against holding a convention to debate the Constitution. Rhode Island would reluctantly join the union after George Washington had been president for two months. North Carolina initially rejected the Constitution by a lopsided vote of 184 to 83. In New Hampshire a convention met, refused to ratify, and adjourned; four months later the delegates reconvened and voted yes, and on June 21, 1788, New Hampshire became the ninth state to ratify. The Constitution would now be the law of the land.

Ratification was a very close contest. If a total of just 3 percent of the delegates across Virginia, Massachusetts, and New York had changed their vote, the Constitution would have gone down to defeat. Americans came within a whisker of rejecting the Constitution that now defines the nation and its government.

The Bottom Line

» The debate over ratifying the Constitution featured two visions of American government.

» The *Federalists* argued that only an energetic national government could protect the nation and secure liberty. The *Anti-Federalists* called instead for a modest government that left power in state and local hands.

» The state-by-state voting on ratification was very close and it was more than a year before the Constitution was approved.

» More than 230 years later, Americans are still debating the same question—how strong should the federal government be?

Changing the Constitution

Although most Anti-Federalist leaders eventually rallied to the new Constitution, they insisted on a crucial addition to the Constitution: a bill of rights.

Passing the 13th Amendment

The Bill of Rights

Today, the first ten amendments to the Constitution, known as the **Bill of Rights**, form a crucial feature of the Constitution and of American government. *These set out the rights and liberties—the protections from government— that every citizen is guaranteed.* Freedom of speech, freedom of the press, freedom of religion, the right to bear arms, and the long list of additional rights are an essential part of America's identity. Table 2.3 summarizes the amendments that make up the Bill of Rights.

Bill of Rights: The first ten amendments to the Constitution, listing the rights guaranteed to every citizen.

TABLE 2.3 **Summarizing the Bill of Rights**

1. Congress may not establish a religion or prohibit the free exercise of religion; it may not abridge freedom of speech or of the press or of the people's right to assemble and to petition government.
2. Citizens have the right to bear arms.
3. No soldier may be quartered in any house without the consent of the owner.
4. There must be no unreasonable search or seizures. Government authorities may not break into your house without a search warrant.
5. No one may be forced to testify against him- or herself (declining to do so is now known as "taking the Fifth"); no one may be deprived of life, liberty, or property without due process of law. The government may not take private property (if, for example, it wants to build a highway) without just compensation.
6. Certain rights are guaranteed in criminal trials.
7. Accused persons are guaranteed the right to trial by jury.
8. The government may not force citizens to pay excessive bails and may not impose cruel and unusual punishments.
9. Enumerating these rights does not diminish the other rights retained by the people.
10. Any powers not given to the federal government are reserved for the states and the people.

Originally, the Bill of Rights applied only to the federal government. The First Amendment reads, *"Congress shall make no law . . . abridging the free-dom of speech."* At the time, states that wanted to limit speech or set up an official religion were free to do so.

The Fourteenth Amendment, ratified after the Civil War in 1868 to protect the former slaves, commands that no *state* may deny "any person . . . the equal protection of the laws." In theory, this amendment extended the Bill of Rights to the states—meaning state governments must honor each right just as the na-tional government must do. However, the Fourteenth Amendment only kicked off a long process, known as **incorporation**: The Supreme Court applied (or "incorporated") each right to the state governments, one right at a time. That process continues down to the present day: the Supreme Court "incorporated" the right to bear arms in 2010. As a result, no state or city may violate the sec-ond amendment right to bear arms. Where exactly does this leave gun control laws? The debate continues—stay tuned!

Incorporation: The process by which the Supreme Court declares that a right in the Bill of Rights also applies to state governments.

The Seventeen Amendments

After the Bill of Rights was passed, constitutional amendments became rare events—only seventeen have passed since 1791. Successful amendments all do at least one of four things: They *extend rights*—for example, guaranteeing the right to vote to eighteen-year-olds (seven amendments extend rights). They *adjust elec-tion rules*—for example, limiting the president to two terms (eleven amendments focus on elections). They *change government operations*—for example, switching Inauguration Day from March to January (four amendments focus on govern-ment rules). Or they *affect governmental powers over individuals*—for example, prohibiting alcohol and then (fourteen years later) permitting alcohol again. Table 2.4 summarizes the seventeen amendments that have been ratified since 1791.

Apart from formal amendments, American government—and how we inter-pret the Constitution—has changed over time. We constantly debate how to ap-ply the Constitution and its amendments to current issues. May Congress limit the money corporations give political candidates? May a woman have an abor-tion? May a college campus stop people from carrying guns? May universities consider an applicant's race as part of an admissions decision? May a Christian student group pray before class? The wording of the Constitution permits differ-ent interpretations. These questions—and many more—require Americans to read the Constitution and reflect on what it tells us, more than 225 years after it was ratified. We will encounter all these questions in Chapter 4.

The Constitution Today

The political life of the American colonies prepared the way for something no nation had done before: The United States organized a new government around a Constitution, written in the people's name, and voted on by the people's rep-resentatives in every state. The document still guides American politics today. Who are we? Reading the U.S. Constitution is one important way to find out.

But there is a catch. Americans disagree about how to read the Constitution. One view, called **originalism**, or strict construction, insists that Americans

Originalism: A principle of legal interpretation that relies on the original meaning of those who wrote the Constitution.

TABLE 2.4 **Amendments to the U.S. Constitution**

AMENDMENT	DESCRIPTION	YEAR RATIFIED	RESULT
11	Required state consent for individuals suing a state in federal court	1795	Modified government operations
12	Separated votes within the Electoral College for president and vice president	1804	Shifted election rules
13	Prohibited slavery	1865	Expanded individual rights
14	Provided citizenship to former slaves and declared that states could not deny civil rights, civil liberties, or equal protection of the laws	1868	Expanded individual rights
15	Granted voting rights to members of all races	1870	Expanded individual rights
16	Permitted national income tax	1913	Expanded government powers over individuals
17	Provided for direct election of senators	1913	Shifted election rules
18	Prohibited alcohol	1919	Expanded government powers over individuals
19	Extended the vote to women	1920	Expanded individual rights
20	Changed Inauguration Day from March to January	1933	Modified government operations
21	Repealed Prohibition	1933	Adjusted government powers over individuals
22	Limited president to two terms	1951	Shifted election rules
23	Extended the vote for president to citizens in Washington, DC	1961	Expanded individual rights
24	Prohibited a poll tax [one way to keep black people from voting]	1964	Expanded individual rights
25	Established succession plan in case of president's death or disability	1967	Modified government operations
26	Extended the vote to eighteen-year-olds	1971	Expanded individual rights
27	Established that congressional pay raise couldn't go into effect until the next election	1992	Modified government operations

are bound to the literal meaning of the Constitution and its amendments, as their original authors and debaters understood them. From this perspective, the Constitution's meaning does not change with the times.

Another view was first articulated by Thomas Jefferson, who warned Americans not to view the Constitution with "sanctimonious reverence," as if it were "too sacred to be touched." The nation's founders should not be worshipped, he said, noting wryly that as one of the founders, he was all too aware of their limitations. "I know also," concluded Jefferson, "that laws and institutions must go hand in hand with the progress of the human mind."[26]

View The *10-Minute Guide to the Constitution* from Cornell University.

Amend the Constitution Today?

ON WHAT ISSUE?

In the 230 years or so since the Bill of Rights was ratified, just seventeen more amendments to the U.S. Constitution have been adopted—the most recent in 1992. Yet proposals keep coming, with more than 750 introduced in the U.S. House or Senate since 1999. Here are the most frequently proposed amendments over this period.

THINK ABOUT IT

What issues do most proposed amendments address? Which of these would you support? Why or why not?

If you could propose a constitutional amendment not on this list, what would the subject be? Protecting data privacy? Abolishing the Electoral College? Send your best idea to your senators or representative, and just maybe they'll introduce it in the next session of Congress!

Source: Pew Research Center

Balanced budget is the most frequently proposed constitutional amendment since 1999

Most common subjects of proposed amendments, 1999–2017

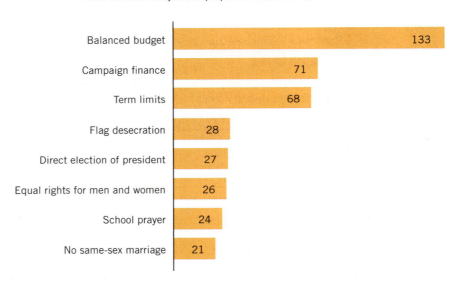

Subject	Count
Balanced budget	133
Campaign finance	71
Term limits	68
Flag desecration	28
Direct election of president	27
Equal rights for men and women	26
School prayer	24
No same-sex marriage	21

What Do YOU Think? | **How Strictly Should We Interpret the Constitution?**

After considering the two approaches to interpreting the Constitution known as originalism and pragmatism, choose a position.

I'm an originalist.	**I'm a pragmatist.**	**I'm in the middle.**
Contemporary justices should not try to substitute their judgment for that of the Constitution's framers. We cannot avoid the arbitrary use of power if we allow everyone to read the Constitution as they like. Before long, the Constitution will not mean anything at all. When the Second Amendment protects the right to bear arms, we must interpret that literally and allow individuals to purchase guns.	Times change and conditions evolve. The modern world imposes challenges (and features new technologies) that the framers could not have imagined. Failing to permit the text to evolve would turn the document into an eighteenth-century straitjacket. The founders' idea of the right to bear arms protected state militias, not individual gun owners. We should consider the historical context when we interpret the Constitution.	I believe the difference between these positions is far less stark than it appears at first glance. Even if we try very hard to get back to the document's original meaning, we always read the Constitution in light of the present. Every effort to interpret the Constitution will be guided by our own ideas and our own times.

Many scholars and politicians have followed Jefferson's advice. They see a living, breathing, changing Constitution—one that speaks to each generation a little differently. This view of an evolving Constitution is known as **pragmatism**. *We cannot help but bring our own background, ideas, and judgments to bear as we think about the meaning of the document.*

As we will see throughout this book, it is often hard to tell exactly how the Constitution applies to our times. Different people reading the document come to very different conclusions—even if they are searching for the original meaning. In the end, the difference between originalism and pragmatism may not be as large as their proponents think.

Pragmatism: A principle of legal interpretation based on the idea that the Constitution evolves and that interpretation of the Constitution must be put in the context of contemporary realities.

The Bottom Line

» The Bill of Rights comprises the first ten amendments to the Constitution, which define the rights of American citizens.

» Seventeen more amendments (of more than one hundred thousand proposals) followed over the next 215 years.

» American politics is always changing, but the Constitution still stands as the American political rulebook. However, the Constitution must be interpreted for it is often unclear what the document means and how it applies to contemporary cases.

Conclusion: Does the Constitution Still Work?

Every chapter that follows will focus on a different feature of the Constitution as it operates today—federalism, civil liberties, civil rights, Congress, the presidency, and so on. As you explore these institutions, keep asking yourself: Does the world's oldest constitution still work? Most Americans believe that it does. That is why it has lasted so long. But some disagree. Robert Dahl, a much revered political scientist, argued that the Constitution is just not democratic enough.[27] It does not include modern rights. Checks and balances are sometimes too cumbersome, making it difficult to pass needed laws—and presidents respond by gathering ever more power. Congress no longer checks the president when it comes to war. The general effect, explained Dahl, is to water down American democracy.

The debate takes us back to the very first question we asked in Chapter 1. Who governs? Do "we the people" still rule? Or has real power slipped away to the rich and powerful? These are questions that every chapter will address.

Regardless of whether you are an *originalist*, a *pragmatist*, or someone in between, you should check to see what the Constitution says every time you study another feature of American politics. Start with the Constitution and you will know the basic rules of American politics.

CHAPTER SUMMARY

Check your understanding of Chapter 2.

● The Constitution provides the ground rules for American politics. However, it is often unclear exactly how the Constitution applies to contemporary issues. We have to interpret its meaning.

● The colonial experience prepared America for thinking about a constitution. The English practice of *salutary neglect* permitted the colonies to develop their own political institutions, centered on their legislatures. Americans got used to *delegated representation* (reflecting voter sentiment), which contrasted with the British view of *trustee representation* (representing the whole nation regardless of public opinion).

● The Declaration of Independence has two parts. First, it states the American ideal: All people "are created equal" and "endowed by their creator with certain unalienable rights" including "life, liberty, and the pursuit of happiness." Second, it lists colonial grievances, emphasizing the rights of free people to elect their legislatures.

● The first American government, under the Articles of Confederation, was an alliance of independent states that maximized popular participation. This government had some great successes, but many leaders felt that it was too weak and left the United States vulnerable to foreign powers.

● The Constitutional Convention, convened to fix the problems with the first American government, focused on six broad issues: popular involvement, national versus state power, big versus small states, checks and balances, the presidency, and slavery.

● Ratification of the Constitution involved an extremely close battle between Anti-Federalists, who opposed the Constitution, and Federalists, who supported it. The first ten amendments, known as the Bill of Rights, came out of the ratification debates and were approved by the First Congress. Seventeen more amendments followed in the next 215 years. American politics has changed enormously, but the Constitution continues to stand as the basic blueprint for American political life.

Need to review key ideas in greater depth? Click here.

Flashcard review.

KEY TERMS

Bicameral, p. 54
Bill of Rights, p. 71
Classical republicanism, p. 67
Compact, p. 42
Confederation, p. 49
Constitution, p. 40
Covenant, p. 42
Delegate representation, p. 43

Electoral College, p. 57
Federalism, p. 54
First Continental Congress, p. 46
Incorporation, p. 72
Indentured servant, p. 41
Mercantilism, p. 44
New Jersey Plan, p. 55

Originalism, p. 72
Pragmatism, p. 75
Second Continental Congress, p. 47
Trustee representation, p. 43
Unicameral, p. 55
Virginia Plan, p. 54

STUDY QUESTIONS

1. Describe five ways that the colonial experience prepared the United States for a constitution.
2. Winning the French and Indian War drove two wedges between England and the colonies. What were they?
3. What is the difference between delegate representation and trustee representation? How did the difference lead to the American Revolution?
4. What are the five overarching ideas introduced by the Declaration of Independence? In your opinion, how close are we to achieving those aspirations today?
5. Describe the first government that Americans organized after they broke away from England. Where was most of the power located? What problems arose under this government? What was successful about it?
6. When it came to writing the Constitution, the delegates had to balance two fears. One emerged from the battle with England and the other from American experience under the Articles of Confederation. Describe these two fears.
7. What did Madison mean by "filtration of representatives"? List two examples of filtration in the original Constitution.
8. Describe the differences between the Virginia Plan and the New Jersey Plan. If you had to choose between them, which would you choose and why?
9. Describe what the Constitution says about the following:
   How the House of Representatives is elected.
   How the president is elected.
   How amendments can be added to the Constitution.
10. Describe the differences between the Federalists and the Anti-Federalists. Which side would you be on? Why?

Optional assignment: Choose one of the thirteen original states. Now, write a speech to be presented before its ratifying convention arguing for or against the new constitution.

Go to **www.oup.com/us/Morone** to find quizzes, flash cards, simulations, tutorials, videos, and other study tools.

Federalism and Nationalism

"NOW HE'S ASSAULTING MY DAUGHTER."

Victoria Mesa-Estrada, a Florida attorney, was alarmed. Her client had an abusive partner, and he was beginning to molest her daughter. Mesa-Estrada told the woman to go straight to local law enforcement. But the client didn't feel that she could. She is an undocumented immigrant and feared that she would be arrested by the police and deported back to Mexico—without her daughter, who had been born in the United States and is an American citizen (thanks to the Fourteenth Amendment). Victoria's client, like many of the roughly 12 million undocumented people in the United States, lives in the shadows—afraid to report a crime, visit a school, drive a seriously ill child to a hospital, seek police protection from an abusive partner, or take action against employers who refuse to pay them.[1]

In response, almost 500 cities have become "sanctuary" or "welcoming" cities—the police do not ask about legal status during routine encounters. That way, undocumented individuals can rely on the basic services and protections—police, hospitals, schools, and so on. Many Americans argue that offering sanctuary protects the basic human rights that everyone deserves.

Others oppose the idea. During his 2016 campaign, President Donald Trump turned up the heat on this issue by publicizing the case of Jose Ines Garcia Arate who was on trial, but later acquitted, for the murder of a 32 year-old woman in San Francisco—a sanctuary city.[2] Opponents worry that undocumented immigrants take jobs away from American citizens (Figure 3.1) and, by condoning unauthorized immigration, sanctuary cities compromise the rule of law. Or that the existence of undocumented immigrants divides the society, making it more difficult to win higher wages and expand social welfare policies—a fear expressed in Europe as well as in the United States.[3]

● *Dreamer Gloria Mendoza demonstrates on behalf of the Deferred Action for Childhood Arrivals (DACA), a program that grants legal status to young undocumented individuals. Immigration is a classic federalist subject, with national, state, and local governments all involved.*

In this chapter, you will:

● **Learn what federalism is.**

● **Explore the strengths of federal and state governments.**

● **Examine how federalism works—and how it has evolved.**

● **Review the contemporary conflicts that surround federalism.**

● **Explore American nationalism, the force that binds and shapes our federalist polity.**

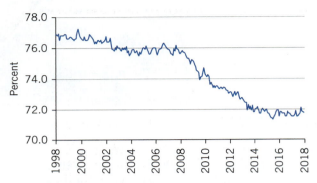

● **Figure 3.1** *Labor force participation rate among men aged 25 to 54. Experts from across the political spectrum believe there is no relationship between immigration and the "flight from work" among white men. Are they right? Or have Donald Trump and his economic nationalism struck a chord with some of the men who have exited the workforce? (Bureau of Labor Statistics)*

Watch a U.S. House debate on a refugee bill.

Assess current debates on immigration

Some states have cracked down on sanctuary cities with laws requiring local police to check the status of anyone they suspect may be undocumented. In 2018, Florida's house of representatives voted to end sanctuary practices, but the bill died in the state senate. Likewise, in Texas, state government regulations require police to follow one standard ("ask and hold") while cities such as Houston, which bear primary responsibility for public safety, rely on another ("don't ask, don't tell"). In contrast, Oregon passed a statewide sanctuary law in 2018.

The standoff is complicated by the complexities of federalism. The Constitution gives the federal government—not the cities or states—authority over immigration. The Supreme Court recently affirmed that immigration is a federal issue. However, the states and the cities have responsibility over most law enforcement; as a result, proponents of the sanctuary city movement say local officials *do* have the authority to set policy for local law enforcement—unless the state overrides them. As you can see, in the immigration debate, the lines of authority—flowing between federal, state, and local governments—have gotten all tangled up.

Who governs? All levels of American government—local, county, state, and federal. In the United States, most problems and many programs fall under multiple jurisdictions. The lines of responsibility between levels of government are often blurred and constantly renegotiated.

In Chapter 2, we traced the constitutional checks and balances between Congress, the executive, and the courts. Now we explore an even more intricate balancing act: federalism. Federalism is the relationship between different levels of government, sharing power while they squabble over who gets how much over what. This complex interplay between national and state governments stretches all the way back to the founding-era clash between Federalists (who wanted a strong national government) and Anti-Federalists (who sought more power for the states).

Who are we? A nation of divided loyalties and governments. We are from the United States *and* Texas *and* Houston, from the United States *and* Ohio *and* Columbus. The results are innovation, liberty, and confusion. Fires in southern California, an oil spill off Alaska's coast, food poisoning at Chipotle, or a mass shooting in Santa Fe, Texas, bring out local authorities, state officials, and national

BY THE NUMBERS
Federalism

Estimated number of governments in the United States	**90,056**[4]
Number of national governments (and as percentage of all government)	**1**
Number of state governments	**50 (0.1%)**
Number of county or parish governments	**3,031 (3.5%)**
Number of town or city governments	**87,025 (96.6%)**
Number of nonmilitary personnel who work for the federal government	**2.7 million**[5]
Number who work for state governments	**5.3 million**
Number who work for local governments	**13.7 million**
Percentage of Americans who say they trust their national, state, and local governments to do what is right most of the time	**19, 62, 71**[6]

What level of government—local, state, or national—touches your life?
Which governments do you interact with the most?

agencies, all scrambling to get on the same wavelength. The same goes for addressing the opioid epidemic, setting the minimum wage, protecting clean water, managing public schools, and legalizing pot. Federalism is ingrained in our Constitution, our institutions, and our national culture.

This chapter explains how federalism works. The story in a nutshell: Federalism is a source of creativity and innovation, but it makes effective and efficient governance far more difficult.

🛈 Forging Federalism

History gave early Americans two choices about how to organize their politics: a unitary government or a confederation. After trying each, the Americans invented a third approach.

Most nations in the 1780s had **unitary governments**. The national government—the king and Parliament in England, for example—made policy for the nation and local governments carried out their decrees. To this day, most nations are organized this way. Local government is an administrative extension of national government. Because Americans rebelled against Britain's unitary government, most did not want to reintroduce the same system all over again.

A second traditional form, **confederation**, leaves most power in the states or provinces while a weak central authority provides common defense or economic benefits. Today, the European Union is struggling to make a confederation work. Americans tried this system under the Articles of Confederation. As we saw in the previous chapter, it proved too weak.

At the Constitutional Convention, the delegates devised an innovative hybrid: a *federal system* in which power is divided and shared between national and state governments. The Constitution gives some decisions to the national government (declaring war, coining money); others to the states (establishing schools); and some are overlapping (raising taxes, running courts, regulating business). Over time, the shared tasks mushroomed. Because each level is independent and their powers overlap, conflict is built into the system.

To complicate matters, the United States also has independent local governments, at the town, city, and county levels. These add still more layers of elected officials, government employees, services to provide, taxes to be paid, and seats at the table when decisions are made.

On the surface, the state and local governments might seem to have a built-in advantage over the national government—the more local the government, the more the people trust it (Figure 3.2).[7] However, local governments are *not* sovereign units of the federal system. The Constitution balances authority between national and state governments; local leaders, in turn, derive their authority from the state government.

Some states grant their local governments broad powers, known as *home rule*; others jealously hold onto authority and approve or reject every local government action. When Denton, Texas, forbade fracking (an oil-extraction process that raises concerns about environmental damage), the state government stepped in and rejected the local regulations. When New York City proposed congestion pricing (charging vehicles a toll during peak hours), it was the state that decided whether they could go ahead. All the overlap and

Unitary government: A national polity governed as a single unit, with the central government exercising all or most political authority.

Confederation: A group of independent states or nations that yield some of their powers to a national government, although each state retains a degree of sovereign authority.

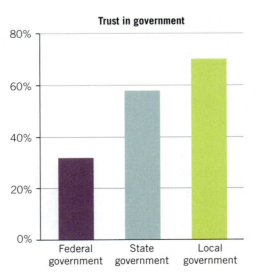

● Figure 3.2 *Trust in government gets stronger as government gets closer to the public (Gallup).*

conflict we have described between federal and state governments gets replicated—sometimes with even more intensity—between state and local governments.

The Bottom Line

» The United States rebelled against a *unitary* system and rejected a *federation* after trying one for a decade.

» The Constitutional Convention created a new hybrid form of government: a federal system of shared and overlapping powers. Power is divided and shared between national and state governments.

» American federalism is further complicated by local governments, which are reliant on state government for their authority.

Who Holds Government Authority?

Who decides whether marijuana should be legal, whether the government funds healthcare, or whether guns may be carried openly? The most important issue in federalism is who decides what. Political scientists see some advantages to leaving things up to the states—and others for making decisions on the national level.[8]

Advantages of State-Level Policy

First, proponents of state action argue that state officials are *more responsive* to citizens. The United States is a vast nation spanning states with very different problems and attitudes. Maine and Minnesota do not need to regulate water in the same way as desert states such as Arizona and Nevada. Large cities try to curb gang violence with curfews and gun buy-back programs that would not make much sense in rural areas. Citizens of Delaware expect more government services (and pay higher taxes) than people in Florida. In short, state and local government can match policies to local conditions and values without a "one-size-fits-all" national policy.

Second, states sometimes offer more *protection for individual rights.* Same-sex couples were permitted to marry in some states long before federal officials were willing to support their right to marry. Back in the nineteenth century, national officials ridiculed the idea of women voting even while women were winning voting rights in the Western states. On the other hand, states vehemently denied African Americans the right to vote, forcing supporters of racial equality to take the fight to the national level (we'll explore all these cases in Chapters 4 and 5).

● *Environmental regulations differ dramatically from state to state. Low regulation states, such as Louisiana and Texas, contrast with high regulation states like California. Americans constantly debate the virtues of local culture and control versus national standards of safety and environmental protection.*

Diffusion: The spreading of policy ideas from one city or state to others, a process typical of U.S. federalism.

Third, federalism fosters *political innovation*. Different states can experiment with new programs, trying them out on the local and state levels before they get debated on the national level. Supreme Court Justice Louis Brandeis put it famously: "A single courageous State may . . . serve as a laboratory; and try novel social and economic experiments without risk to the rest of the country."[9] Ever since, states in a federal system have been called "laboratories of democracy"—allowing us to test policy options. Throughout American history, innovations have bubbled up from the states before going national. The list includes environmental protections, worker safety, direct election of senators, child nutrition programs, alcohol prohibition, and marijuana legalization. This process of testing and spreading ideas is known as **diffusion**.[10]

Finally, a more controversial point: Some argue that federalism gives people more *choices*. Each state offers a different bundle of costs and services (Figure 3.3). Do you want government services? Move to Connecticut or Alaska. If you prefer limited government, choose the South or the Rocky Mountain west. Likewise, people who care about tough environmental standards can choose places with stringent rules like California or Oregon.[11]

This last point is disputed by advocates who point out that many Americans are not free to simply move. If a policy is a good one, they argue, all Americans deserve to enjoy it—which brings us to the advantages of national policies.

The Advantages of National Policy

First, national policy is often fairer than state or local policies. A single mother working full time for nine dollars an hour can be treated for breast cancer under New York's Medicaid program but is not eligible for any treatment at all in Texas. Health advocates charge that this discrepancy is unjust and call for uniform national policies. Likewise, environmentalists argue that every citizen should have clean air and clean water regardless of their state's history of supporting regulation (they also note that air and water pollution don't stop at state boundaries). Gun advocates point out that Ohio permits residents to openly carry firearms, New York restricts "open carry" to pistols, and Massachusetts restricts all guns. Finally, America's racial experience suggests that, at times, national decisions are required to overcome local prejudices.

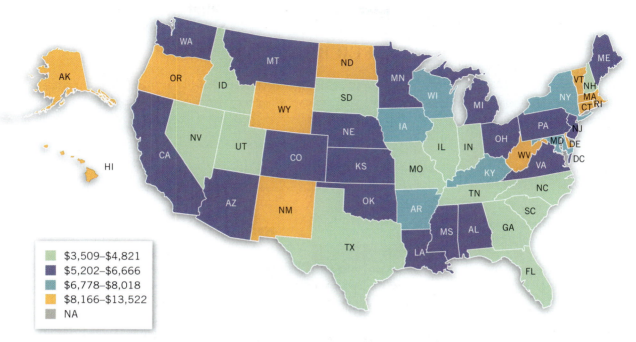

● **Figure 3.3** *Per capita state spending on healthcare. Some states spend more than others per person. Think of this as a choice between values: Some states emphasize individualism (less government spending) while others aim to implement positive freedoms (more spending). But here's the crucial question: Can Americans choose a state that reflects their own values? (The Kaiser Family Foundation).*

This desire for fairness leads critics to worry that competition between states and localities leads to a *race to the bottom.* Leave social welfare policy to the states, argue defenders of national standards, and the result is a bidding war in which each state tries to cut programs (and taxes) more than neighboring states—to attract middle-class people and new business.[12]

Second, national policies can *equalize resources across the nation.* Every time there is a crisis—Hurricane Harvey in the Gulf of Mexico, a terrorist attack, raging wildfires—all eyes turn to the U.S. government, which can bring more resources and expertise to bear on the problem than individual states can. Those resources also can make day-to-day policies work across all fifty states. That way, even poorer states can have the resources they need.

Third, national policies can *standardize best practices* across the nation. After we have tested new policies in the state "laboratories of democracy," a national policy can ensure that the lessons are spread to everyone. Minimum standards ensure that no state chooses inadequate health or education policies for its children.

Finally, leaving authority in state hands introduces *problems of coordination* among federal, state, and local agencies. All address chronic problems such as poverty, pollution, and crime. Simply getting all the first responders onto the same communication frequency has taken many years and millions of dollars. With many different agencies responding to multiple layers of authorities, using

Regulatory Policies

DIFFER BY STATE

How does your state combat the opioid epidemic? Like so many policy matters in the federalist United States, rules may differ dramatically from one state to the next. For example, states may restrict the number of days that the prescriptions can cover (without being renewed), require substance abuse disorder assessment prior to issuing a prescription, mandate that the pharmacists check ID before dispensing the opioids, and educate clinicians who prescribe these drugs.

THINK ABOUT IT

Connecticut, New York, and Massachusetts have low rates of opioid use. Which of the regulations have each of these states adopted? Based on this evidence, are the regulations successful? What can other states learn from these three states?

What regulations does your own state have to fight the opioid epidemic? Do you believe they are excessive, sufficient, or not extensive enough? Do you think it would be better if the federal government mandated these policies?

Source: Athena Health

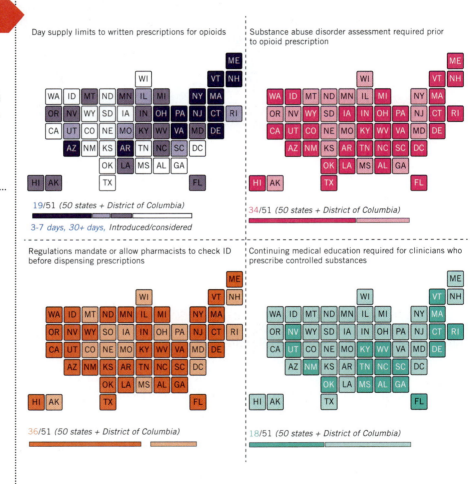

Day supply limits to written prescriptions for opioids

19/51 (50 states + District of Columbia)

3-7 days, 30+ days, Introduced/considered

Substance abuse disorder assessment required prior to opioid prescription

34/51 (50 states + District of Columbia)

Regulations mandate or allow pharmacists to check ID before dispensing prescriptions

36/51 (50 states + District of Columbia)

Continuing medical education required for clinicians who prescribe controlled substances

18/51 (50 states + District of Columbia)

different procedures, and trying to achieve slightly different goals, the result can be chaos. A patchwork of rules and regulations across the states can leave citizens and national companies bewildered about which rules apply where.

In sum, the ambiguity in federalism sets up a continual dispute. Do we leave decisions with the states because they are "closer to the people"? Or do we place them on the national level to try to promote equality and high standards across the country, even if local people resent them? For many Americans, the answer shifts with the issue.

Should federal laws criminalizing marijuana possession override state efforts to legalize it? Liberals generally say no and support local choice. Should stricter national clean-air standards override state pollution regulations and expanded national healthcare standards override state insurance regulations? Now most liberals switch sides and say yes. Conservatives also flip as issues change. These debates are built right into our federal institutions and are an integral part of our federalist system. Recognize one key institutional point: *Federalism gives advocates on both sides many different political venues in which to address problems, challenge policies, and assert rights.*

What Do YOU Think? Preserving Local Values or Promoting Consistent National Policy?

In 2014, Colorado permitted adults to buy up to an ounce of marijuana in licensed stores. Other states followed. There was just one problem: Federal laws outlaw the possession, manufacture, and sale of marijuana. Growing ninety-nine plants, now legal in Colorado, can bring lifetime imprisonment in other states. The Obama administration announced it would not prosecute legal users in Colorado—essentially setting aside the federal laws. Meanwhile, neighboring states want to uphold federal protections and cities such as Colorado Springs moved to forbid local marijuana stores, called dispensaries. In 2018, the Trump administration rescinded the Obama rule and threatened to prosecute regardless of local laws. Should we leave marijuana use to the states, or insist on a national standard?

I'm a federalist; let each state decide. Because cultures differ by state, marijuana regulation should be handled state-by-state. Socially progressive states should have the right to legalize marijuana. Other states can learn from their experiment, assess the advantages and the disadvantages, and decide what policies to adopt.

I'm a nationalist; we should have one consistent standard. The patchwork of changing laws—including within a single state—is confusing. Furthermore, the legalization of pot might negatively impact neighboring states as stoned drivers and tainted merchandise cross borders. The national government should establish a policy that is best for all Americans.

Not sure. On this, like many other policies raised in this chapter, it can be hard to come down definitively on one side.

The Bottom Line

» The most important question in federalism is where to place responsibility—on the state or national level.

» State-level policy has four advantages: It reflects local needs, enables innovations in the laboratories of democracy, protects rights, and enhances choice.

» National-level policy also has four advantages: It enhances fairness (avoiding a race to the bottom), equalizes resources, promotes national standards and best practices, and facilitates coordination.

How Federalism Works

So far this chapter's message is clear: Federalism offers endless opportunities for confusion and discord as different layers of government tussle over who has responsibility for what. However, Americans have hammered out rules that enable our federalist system to function pretty well—most of the time. These rules evolved over time and are not always clear. Even the terminology can be elusive: Americans routinely call the national government the *federal government*, a practice we follow in this chapter, although that term properly describes the whole system of shared powers stretching across national, state, and local units.

The Constitution Sets the Ground Rules

The Constitution can be read two ways. In some respects, it restricts the national government in favor of the states; in other ways, it empowers the feds.

The Constitution Empowers National Authority.   Article 1, Section 8, lists nineteen powers vested in the national government: Congress has the authority to pay debts, raise an army, punish pirates, establish a post office, handle U.S. foreign policy, and so forth. Because they are set out in black and white, scholars call these **delegated powers**—also known as *express* or *enumerated powers* (you can read them in the Constitution in Appendix II). This section of the Constitution is crisp and clear about the limited list of national government powers.

An especially important delegated power grants the national government authority over interstate commerce. How far does that authority extend? A loose reading gives Congress power over everything touched by goods shipped between states. For example, Congress used the **commerce clause** to forbid racial discrimination in restaurants—after all, their salt and sugar come from out of state. This broad reading is increasingly controversial. What do you think? Is it appropriate to use the interstate commerce power to outlaw racial discrimination?

The final clause adds ambiguity by authorizing Congress to make all laws *necessary and proper* for carrying out the delegated powers—*or any other*

Delegated powers: National government powers listed explicitly in the Constitution.

Commerce clause: The constitutional declaration empowering Congress to regulate commerce with foreign nations, between states, and with Indian tribes.

power the Constitution vests in the national government. This **necessary and proper clause** is also known as the *elastic clause* because it stretches national government authority to include anything implied in the Constitution's text. Across two centuries, the elastic clause—especially when it is combined with the interstate commerce clause—has been used to justify expanded national authority over everything from creating banks to regulating airlines to overseeing zoos. These new areas of jurisdiction are **implied powers**—powers that are implied by, but not specifically named in, the Constitution's text.

The **supremacy clause**, found near the end of the Constitution in Article 6, buttresses the delegated and implied powers. The clause declares that the national government's laws and treaties are the "supreme law of the land" and override state laws whenever the two clash—provided the power is granted to the federal government. As you might imagine, fierce debates (and plenty of court cases) turn on whether powers have actually been granted to national officials in specific areas.

Federal officials also wield a set of **inherent powers**—not explicitly named or strongly implied in the Constitution, but growing out of the very existence of a national government. For example, when the Federal Government revises the list of communicable diseases that require quarantines, it relies on its inherent powers rather than a clear constitutional claim.

The Constitution Protects State Authority. At the same time, the states have their own authority guaranteed by the Tenth Amendment—the final amendment in the Bill of Rights. This "reserves" to the states all powers not specifically granted to the national branches in Washington. Small-government advocates brandish the Tenth Amendment. Congressional conservatives in the 115th Congress proposed a Tenth Amendment Restoration Act that required a full review of every government agency to see if its existence violated the Tenth Amendment—if so, the agency would be eliminated. Though the bill failed, it illustrates a new emphasis on the Tenth Amendment.

The states' **reserved powers** include public education, public health, public morality, commerce within the state, and organizing state elections. Police, prisons, and local courts are also in each state's hands. State and local officials carry out most investigations, arrests, trials, and incarcerations—unless a federal law has been violated. The vast majority of American court cases are adjudicated in state courts, and state prisons and local jails hold 90 percent of the inmates in the United States.

The Constitution Authorizes Shared Power. Federalism is not just about tension between government levels. State and national authorities share many responsibilities, termed **concurrent powers**. Both

Necessary and proper clause: The constitutional declaration that defines Congress's authority to exercise the "necessary and proper" powers to carry out its designated functions.

Implied powers: National government powers implied by, but not specifically named in, the Constitution.

Supremacy clause: The constitutional declaration (in Article 6, Section 2) that the national government's authority prevails over any conflicting state or local government's claims, provided the power is granted to the federal government.

Inherent powers: Powers not specified or implied by the Constitution but necessary for the president or Congress to fulfil their duties.

● *Interstate conflict: New York City has strong laws regulating guns. Should it be required to honor Vermont's lenient rules?*

Reserved powers: The constitutional guarantee (in the Tenth Amendment) that the states retain government authority not explicitly granted to the national government.

Concurrent powers: Governmental authority shared by national and state governments, such as the power to tax residents.

Full faith and credit clause: The constitutional requirement (in Article 4, Section 1) that each state must recognize and uphold laws passed by any other state.

national and state governments have the power to raise taxes, build roads, construct bridges, update telecommunications networks, borrow money, and regulate business (see Figure 3.4). The next time you are stuck in traffic inching past a sign announcing new transportation construction, look it over carefully: you will usually see that the project is supported by a combination of national, state, and local funds.

Federalism also involves relations among the states. The Constitution directs each state to give **full faith and credit** to the actions of other states. For example, your driver's license, issued in your home state, is honored everywhere else in the United States.

The Constitution also sets up some definite barriers to the states. They may not launch a navy, negotiate treaties with another country, or coin their own money. The Bill of Rights—although it originally applied only to the federal government—imposes a long list of limits on government in the name of individual rights and freedoms. In short, the Constitution empowers and limits both the national and the state governments.

Emphasizing some parts of the Constitution—inherent powers, the interstate commerce clause, the necessary and proper clause, and the supremacy clause—justifies a robust national government. This reading of the Constitution enables a national government that regulates toxic spills, forbids racial discrimination, enforces airport security, and prosecutes the war on drugs. Emphasizing other clauses, such as the Tenth Amendment, yields a more modest national government that defers to the people of each state. That is the reading that leaves states alone to decide their environmental rules or regulate state universities.

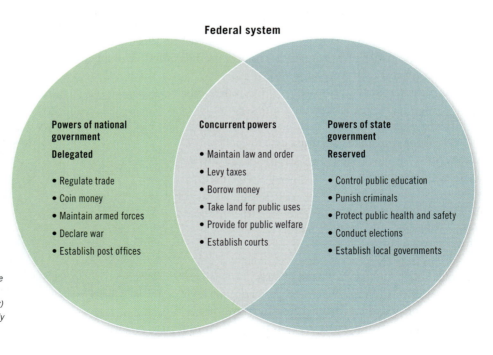

Federal system

Powers of national government
Delegated

• Regulate trade
• Coin money
• Maintain armed forces
• Declare war
• Establish post offices

Concurrent powers

• Maintain law and order
• Levy taxes
• Borrow money
• Take land for public uses
• Provide for public welfare
• Establish courts

Powers of state government
Reserved

• Control public education
• Punish criminals
• Protect public health and safety
• Conduct elections
• Establish local governments

● **Figure 3.4** *The Constitution delegates some powers to the federal government, reserves some to the states, and allocates some to both. Those joint (or concurrent) powers have stretched dramatically over the years.*

Again we return to a vital point: American government is a perpetual argument, a work in progress. The Constitution's ground rules for federalism are open to interpretation and reinterpretation. They have guided a long, often creative debate about which level of government should be doing what.

In different eras, Americans have organized federalism in different ways. The following sections explain how.

Dual Federalism (1789–1933)

For its first 150 years or so, the United States practiced **dual federalism**: state and national governments had relatively clear responsibilities. The state governments wielded at least as much authority as the federal government. American historians with an eye for metaphor describe this arrangement as "layer cake" federalism: The different levels of government—national, state, and local—fell more or less into separate layers. Each level of government was supreme within its own band of influence (see Figure 3.5).

This division of labor left the national government in charge of three major areas. First was international relations—a significant role, as the United States deployed troops overseas 165 times in its first 150 years—and that count does not include a long and bloody series of conflicts with Native American tribes.

Second, the national government developed responsibility for "internal improvements" such as transportation, a single currency, and overseeing westward expansion. In early America, it was cheaper to ship iron from London to Philadelphia than it was to move it fifty miles inland from Philadelphia. Transportation networks—roads, canals, and railroads—solved the problem of moving freight (and people). For the first eighty years, Americans did not even share a currency—hundreds of banks printed their own bills that became useless if the bank went under during one of the frequent economic panics. The Banking Acts of 1863 and 1864 finally standardized the money circulating in the United States.

Third, the federal government regulated relations and commerce between the states. This became an explosive issue when slave states demanded assistance in capturing men and women running for their freedom.

During this era, states retained control over almost everything having to do with individual citizens. The states oversaw education, marriage, professional regulation, business contracts, crime, drinking, and burial. To this day, state governments wield primary responsibility over individual behavior, although the federal government now touches most of these matters directly or indirectly.

The layer cake was never quite as clear-cut as the metaphor suggests. The national

Dual federalism: Clear division of governing authority between national and state governments.

Compare federal and state authority.

American federalism
Layer cake or marble cake?

Layer cake federalism
has a clear division of governing authority between national and state governments.

Marble cake federalism
mingles governing authority with functions overlapping across national and state governments.

● **Figure 3.5** *Different federalist styles throughout U.S. history.*

government distributed land in unsettled territories. Before the Civil War, it housed the bitter fight over slavery. In the 1870s, it used control of interstate commerce to crack down on pornography, restrict contraception, and fight abortion. In 1920, the Eighteenth Amendment forbade the transportation and sale of intoxicating liquors. State and national authorities had overlapping jurisdiction in enforcing the act[13]—and when states such as New York decided to ignore the ban on liquor, federal officials stepped in to enforce it (a 1920s version of the marijuana debate). Still, despite many exceptions, government activity remained, very roughly, separated into layers.

Cooperative Federalism (1933–1981)

During the New Deal of the 1930s, the dual arrangement collapsed. President Franklin Roosevelt (FDR) and large Democratic majorities in Congress responded to the Great Depression by passing policies that strengthened the national government's role. Roosevelt presided over a shift toward **cooperative federalism**, characterized by a far more active federal government and blurred lines of authority (Table 3.1). A new bakery metaphor emerged: the *marble cake*, in which the various ingredients—different government functions—all swirled together. In one program after another, the responsibilities of federal, state, and local governments were increasingly mingled: Funding rules, administration, implementation, and execution cut across the different layers of federalism (see Figure 3.5).

Officials in Washington provided federal funds through **grants-in-aid**—national funds accompanied by specific instructions to state and local officials about how the money could be spent. Governors and other state leaders, desperate for resources during the Depression, accepted these national grants for roads, bridges, hospitals, healthcare clinics, welfare payments for poor people with children—the list goes on. Most of the funds were accompanied by Washington rules and oversight.

Cooperative federalism: Mingled governing authority, with functions overlapping across national and state governments.

Grants-in-aid: National government funding provided to state and local governments, along with specific instructions about how the funds may be used.

● *Constructing canals, bridges, roads—and later, railroads—was a major national government responsibility in the nineteenth century (left), as was delivering the mail, a task that briefly included the Pony Express (right).*

TABLE 3.1	Comparing Dual and Cooperative Federalism

DUAL FEDERALISM	COOPERATIVE FEDERALISM
NATIONAL POWERS	
Enumerated: The national government may only wield powers specifically listed in the Constitution.	**Elastic:** The national government may wield powers "necessary and proper" to support its function.
LOCATION OF SUPREME AUTHORITY	
Separate sovereignty: National and state governments each have authority within their own spheres.	**National supremacy:** States retain important powers but are subordinate to the national government except where the Constitution strictly forbids.
KEY PRINCIPLE	
States' rights: Each state is largely free to govern its own affairs.	**Power sharing:** National and state officials work together wherever possible—also with local officials, who became more prominent after the 1930s.

After World War II, a new era of economic prosperity emerged. Many state and local officials began expressing resentment at the national meddling in their affairs. Federal dollars continued to flow, however, and even the most ardent states' rights advocates were not going to deny their constituents the national bounty.

Cooperative federalism, with Washington dominating many policy areas, lasted from the New Deal (starting in 1933) through the 1970s. Senator Everett Dirksen (R-IL) quipped in 1964 that if the trend toward increasing national power continued, only mapmakers would care about the state boundaries.[14]

New Federalism

Ronald Reagan's presidency (1981–1989) ushered in another change in American federalism, enthusiastically termed **new federalism** by its advocates. Reagan and fellow conservatives tipped the pendulum of power away from national officials, promoting more authority by state and local officials. In place of grants-in-aid, with national officials carefully specifying the rules and regulations that accompanied the funds, the Reagan administration relied more heavily on **block grants**. Block grants, first introduced in 1966, also channel federal dollars to a specific policy area, such as education or transportation or health, but leave the program's details to state and local bureaucrats.

One feature of block grants made them controversial. The grants-in-aid that marked cooperative federalism often provided unlimited funding for a specific purpose; for example, everyone who qualifies for Medicaid receives hospital coverage, and every eligible person gets food stamps. In contrast, block grants provided a fixed amount of funds for healthcare or nutrition. State and local officials do whatever they think best with the funds; however, the federal government limits its contribution, forcing state officials to make hard choices

New federalism: A version of cooperative federalism, but with less oversight by the federal government (which still provided funds) and more control on the state and local level.

Block grants: National government funding provided to state and local governments, with relatively few restrictions or requirements on spending.

"In Two Words, Yes And No"

FEDERAL BENEFITS

FEDERAL AUTHORITY

"STATES RIGHTS"

HERBLOCK
©1949 THE WASHINGTON POST CO

• *Struggles over the extent of cooperative federalism, captured in 1949—and still an issue, seventy years later.*

Progressive federalism: Modern federalism variant in which the national government sets broad goals for a program, and relies on state innovations to achieve them.

about who qualifies for the program—and who does not. Republicans have pushed hard to shift grant-in-aid programs to block grants, posing a trade-off for state officials: more authority, fewer funds.

New federalism does not restore the neat layers of dual federalism—if anything, the lines of authority are even more swirled together than ever. Perhaps you can think of this scenario as a many-flavored marble cake.

Progressive Federalism

The Obama administration, building on the George W. Bush administration, introduced **progressive federalism** in 2009: The national government sets program goals and relies on state innovations to achieve them. Note the mix of traditional Democratic approach (national goals) and Republican values (state innovation). The Obama administration deployed this approach across a host of policy areas—education, healthcare, the environment, and more.

Education. The Obama administration announced a program called Race to the Top. It encouraged states to compete for national dollars, rewarding creative education policies. By promoting *competition* among states, the administration sought to nudge states toward desired policy goals without relying on overbearing national regulations.

Healthcare. The most controversial program during the Obama administration, the Affordable Care Act (or ACA), aimed to deliver healthcare to the fifty million uninsured Americans. Congress mandated that all uninsured people buy coverage. The federal government issued rules and regulations (defining the insurance products); the states were incentivized to build insurance exchanges where individuals could shop among competing health insurance plans. If the states were not up to the task—or simply opposed to the policy—the federal government built the website that sold insurance plans in the state. In 2017, Republicans in Congress repealed the mandate but left the rest of the ACA intact.

In progressive federalism, the federal and state governments are partners, constantly negotiating over their joint program. Sometimes the debate is friendly, sometimes adversarial; it can take place in the courts, in Congress, and in the media. The key feature is that programs are defined through the intricate back and forth between federal and state officials.

Federalism Today

The Trump administration is trying to go back to new federalism: Fewer federal dollars, fewer federal regulations. The administration planned to eliminate the $3 billion block-grant program for infrastructure projects and cut or end funding for the largest social-services, health, and housing block grants. Most survived in the 2018 budget, but Democratic gains in the 2018 midterm may slow any return to new federalism.

Today, federalism has become a battlefield in partisan conflict. During the Obama administration, many states actively resisted federal policies—from enacting more muscular immigration restrictions to filing suits against Obamacare.[15] The conflict escalated right from the start of the Trump administration. When the president pulled out of the international climate change treaty known as the Paris Accord, more than 20 states and some 230 counties and large cities signed an "America's Pledge" to meet the greenhouse gas reductions in the agreement. States attorneys general (the chief legal officer in each state) have filed lawsuits against White House policies on everything from immigration policy to healthcare subsidies. During Trump's inaugural year in office (2017), 27 such lawsuits were filed. In contrast, a total of eight such suits were filed across the first years of the Reagan (1981), Clinton (1993), and Obama (2009) administrations put together.

Navigate federal and state healthcare policy.

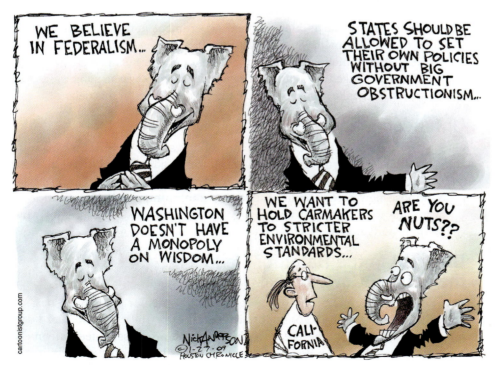

● As this cartoon humorously shows, which level of our federalist government a politician supports generally depends on the issue in question. (Nick Anderson)

Time will tell whether the Trump era has taken our hyperpolarized federalism to new levels.

The Bottom Line

» The Constitution grants the national government both delegated (or enumerated) powers and implied powers. Some features of the Constitution emphasize broad national powers (e.g., the elastic clause); others seem to emphasize state power (the Tenth Amendment).

» Successive eras of federalism have taken place: dual federalism with clearly demarcated authority; cooperative federalism with federal dominance and blurred lines; new federalism, less federal money, more state authority—now a goal of the Trump administration; and Progressive federalism with national goals and state innovations.

» Federalism reflects the increasing polarization of the country.

Issues in Federalism

Dual, cooperative, new, and progressive—successive versions of federalism point to the perpetually shifting nature of government power and accountability. Today, federalism is in unusual flux as national government authority both expands (healthcare) and contracts (marijuana control); as states make more choices in some areas (environmental regulation) and less in others (same-sex marriage); and as the parties take turns calling for more national power in some areas and less in others. Let's take a look at some of the current issues in this debate.

Unfunded Mandates

Unfunded mandate: An obligation imposed on state or local government officials by federal legislation, without sufficient federal funding support to cover the costs.

One issue in today's federalism debates charges that Washington saddles states and localities with **unfunded mandates**—federal laws or regulations state or local governments must pay for. For example, when federal regulations impose new safety requirements on commuter trains, state and local governments must buy and install the new technology—regardless of what shape their budget is in.

Drowned in the Bathtub? Reducing the Federal Government

Devolution: The transfer of authority from national to state or local government level.

The debate over federalism often reflects a particular American passion (especially strong among conservatives): the desire to reduce the size and scope of government. One pillar of the new and progressive federalism—at least in theory—has been **devolution**, or the transferring of responsibility for government programs from national to state and local authorities—and then to the private sector. Devolutionists have fought to reduce the influence of government at every level. "I don't want to abolish government," declared conservative activist Grover Norquist. "I simply want to reduce it down to the size where I can . . . drown it in the bathtub."[16] This attack on big government gets fervent support from the conservative grassroots.

In theory, Republicans prefer state and local control, while Democrats are more likely to seek Washington-based solutions. The reality is far more complicated: Both parties sometimes press for increased national authority and, at other times, defer to the states.

What happens when the states want more innovation than the federal government? When states like California passed legislation with strong environmental measures, the Republican Bush administration overruled them through **preemption**.

● Members of an armed antigovernment militia monitor the entrance to the Malheur National Wildlife Refuge Headquarters near Burns, Oregon, in 2016. The occupation of a wildlife refuge by armed protesters in Oregon reflects a decades-old dispute over land rights in the United States, where local communities have increasingly sought for more voice in the use of public land.

The Obama administration quickly reversed that policy and encouraged states to launch forceful environmental protections. Now, the Trump team is fighting California—in court, on the airwaves, and in Congress—to preempt once again. The old rule of thumb is reversed: Democrats urged strong state action; Republicans overruled it with (weaker) federal regulations.

Preemption: The invalidation of a U.S. state law that conflicts with federal law.

Relations between national, state, and local levels take a dizzying array of forms. Sometimes officials work in partnership; sometimes they are locked in combat. To keep all the tangled relationships clear, intergovernmental liaison officers work across national, state, city, and even town governments.

Federalism in the Courts

Most federalism disputes are about drawing a line where national power ends and states' authority begins. One simple explanation for major historical shifts: the party in power. The Roosevelt administration initiated a new (Democratic) era and introduced cooperative federalism. The Nixon and Reagan administrations brought Republicans to the center of power and introduced new federalism. The Democratic Obama administration introduced progressive federalism. The Trump administration aims to go back to new federalism.

The courts offer another chart to the tides of federalism. Judges have typically played a balancing role when it comes to federalism. Supreme Court decisions favored national prerogatives during the early republic, when many individual states had more power and prestige than the federal government in Washington. In a series of landmark decisions, the Supreme Court—led by Chief Justice John Marshall—protected national government powers from state incursions. In 1818, Maryland's legislature imposed a tax on the Baltimore branch of the first U.S. national bank. The bank refused to pay and the state sued the bank.

What does it mean to incorporate the Bill of Rights?

The Maryland Supreme Court ruled that the Constitution is silent about the federal power to establish a bank (it certainly is not one of the *delegated* powers), and that the bank was therefore unconstitutional. Maryland was perfectly free to tax it. In *McCulloch v. Maryland* (1819), Chief Justice Marshall, writing for a unanimous court, overruled the Maryland court and struck down the tax. Invoking the necessary and proper (or elastic) clause, he ruled that Congress could draw on "implied powers" required to operate a functional national government and that states blocking such actions—in this case, by levying a tax on the bank—violated the Constitution. [17] In these and later decisions, Marshall and many other officials in the early republic were anxious to keep dual federalism in balance. At the time, doing so meant expanding national power.

In some eras—such as the period between the 1880s and the 1930s—the courts tilted away from federal authority to states and private corporations. On the other hand, the rise of activist government during the 1930s might not have been possible if the Supreme Court had not, quite dramatically, reversed its course and accepted New Deal legislation beginning in 1937 (we'll cover the details in Chapter 13). This transition to federal power led later Courts to uphold congressional actions such as the Civil Rights Act (1964) and the Voting Rights Act (1965), which limited the ways that state and private actors could discriminate. It also led the Court to strike down many state actions; for example, they denied Texas's right to ban abortion (in *Roe v. Wade*, 1973), struck down states' "three strikes" laws that jailed people for life after three (often minor) offenses (*Johnson v. United States*, 2015), and overruled state laws that banned same-sex marriage (*Obergefell v. Hodges*, 2015).

In recent years, beginning under Chief Justice Rehnquist in the mid-1990s and gaining strength with a consistently conservative majority under Chief Justice Roberts since 2005, the Supreme Court has emphasized local and state power. In fact, the Rehnquist Court (1994–2005) struck down more acts of Congress than any previous Court in U.S. history; many of these decisions were premised on defending state power. The Roberts Court (2005 to the present) has continued this trend (Table 3.2). If history is a reliable guide, the current judicial trend will fade over time, as the pendulum of state and national power swings yet again.

The Bottom Line

» Devolution transfers responsibility back to state and local governments.

» Both parties in office take a varied approach that belies the simple expectation that Democrats seek national programs while Republicans try to devolve power to state and local authorities.

» The courts have played an important role in defining federalism.

» In recent years the Supreme Court has tended to tilt toward local and state power.

TABLE 3.2 Recent Supreme Court Decisions on Federalism

FAVORING NATIONAL GOVERNMENT
• *Arizona v. United States* (2012). Struck down key provisions in an Arizona immigration law, upholding federal-government authority to set immigration policy and laws.
• *King v. Burwell* (2015). Ruled that premium tax credits provided under the Affordable Care Act (ACA) applied in every state, though several conservative-led states had argued otherwise. Compare to the 2012 ACA case below.
• *Obergefell v. Hodges* (2015). Requires all states to issue marriage licenses to same-sex couples and to recognize same-sex marriages validly performed in other jurisdictions.
• *Cooper v. Harris* (2017). Ruled that North Carolina violated federal voting-rights laws by moving thousands of African American voters into congressional districts that had already elected African American Democrats.
• *Bond v. United States* (2011). Extended to individuals the right to challenge federal statutes on the grounds that these statutes interfered with powers reserved to the states.
• *National Federation of Independent Business v. Sebelius* (2012). This decision on the Affordable Care Act (ACA) struck down the national government's power to set standards for expanded Medicaid eligibility across the states.
• *Shelby County v. Holder* (2013). Reversed a long-standing provision in the Voting Rights Act that required states with a history of voting discrimination to obtain federal permission before making changes to their election laws.
• *United States v. Windsor* (2013). Struck down a section of the federal Defense of Marriage Act (DOMA) and declared that same-sex couples who are legally married deserve equal rights to all federal benefits that other married couples enjoy.
• *United States v. Texas* (2016). Invalidated Obama administration's executive act protecting from deportation certain unauthorized immigrants (parents of U.S. citizens, or legal permanent residents), and granting them work permits. Twenty-six states, led by Texas, challenged the White House policy.

Nationalism, American Style

Federalism trains our focus on the Constitution, how institutions evolve (layer cakes versus marble cakes), and the clash between national versus state. However, something deeper holds the entire complicated apparatus in place. It is the elusive cultural sentiment known as *nationalism*, the American public's sense of identity as Americans.

Nationalism helps maintain the federal balance by instilling loyalty to nation, state, and locality. In this section, we explore the development of American nationalism. But it can also turn inward and exclude others—as we will see when we turn to civil rights in Chapter 5. In this section, we explore the development of American nationalism—in its positive and negative variants.

The Rise of American Nationalism

In the excitement of the Revolution, former colonists from New Hampshire to Georgia celebrated the defeat of the British army. Yet after the revolution, the sense of "Americanhood" began to wane.[18]

Restored national sentiment came from an unlikely source—the Constitution became a touchstone for Americans' shared sense of belonging. Following ratification in 1789, celebrations broke out across the new nation. In Boston, a three-day festival featured a town feast for twelve thousand. North Carolina's capital Raleigh greeted the Constitution with such a cannonade that elderly residents wondered if the Revolutionary War had started again. It was the start of the nationalism that lives on to this day.

Powerful nationalism is a double-edged sword. On the one hand, a strong sense of national identity fosters mutual support and loyalty. On the other hand, the most enthusiastic nationalists are those most likely to draw strict boundaries around who counts as an American. "Help and loyalty are offered only to 'true Americans,'" writes political scientist Elizabeth Theiss-Morse, "not Americans who do not count and who are pushed to the periphery of the national group."[19]

America's Weak National Government

Americans have long exhibited a passionate nationalist sense—and ironically, this strong nationalism is linked to relatively weak governing institutions. How does a U.S. government described by many of its own citizens as "overbearing" and even "tyrannical" count as *weak*? Today, we measure the strength of central governments by looking at three main principles: size, authority, and independence.

Size. For many years, the American national government was much smaller than those in other nations. It grew in leaps during World War I, the Great Depression, World War II, the Cold War, and the Great Society of the 1960s. Each growth spurt brought protests—and efforts to cut the government back. Despite all the fears—or perhaps because of them—the U.S. government still spends less than most other wealthy nations. For example, the federal government spends far less per pupil than most other democracies. But that does not mean Americans ignore education—the federal system shifts the spending to the states and cities.

● *The Pledge of Allegiance still evokes strong nationalist sentiment among many Americans.*

Authority.   By the mid-nineteenth century, most developed nations had powerful and efficient national bureaucracies, known as the civil service. In contrast, American government engaged its citizens without a strong central administration or bureaucracy.

Communal activity stretched well beyond the government. American **civic voluntarism** projected something unusual: robust nationalist feeling, stimulating widespread individual efforts for the common good. The spirit of voluntary participation has lived on for generations, inspiring mass public involvement in everything from bowling leagues to civil rights organizations. The United States has always emphasized community participation over centralized administration. The same local spirit that helps define federalism limits the authority of national officials.[20]

> **Civic voluntarism:** Citizens voluntarily participating in public life without government involvement—for example, getting together to build a playground or clean up the litter in town.

Independence.   In a powerful centralized system, government officials can act forcefully—as long as their superiors approve. In contrast, Americans separate and divide governing power more than any other wealthy country. Federalism operates along a vertical dimension; power is shared among different levels of government—national, state, and local. At every level and within every branch and institution, there are further checks. American state legislatures, like Congress, have two chambers (Nebraska is the lone exception); all have multiple committees and subcommittees within each chamber. Each legislature faces an executive and an independent judiciary. Checks and balances at every level multiply federalism's horizontal division of power. No public official can act independently. Each needs cooperation from others.

The Bottom Line

» Americans have long felt a strong sense of nationalism. This helps bind together a large and diverse nation with a fragmented government.

» Nationalist bonds can also turn corrosive and exclusionary. "Nationalists" claiming America stands only for Anglo-Saxons or Christians or English speakers sow division.

» A weak government means that American institutions (and officials) rank relatively low on three dimensions: size, authority, and independence.

» The political results include an emphasis on citizen participation, the importance of building alliances, and a reliance on power and money.

Conclusion: Who Are We?

Federalism seems, on the surface, like a simple matter of government engineering: How do we decide who does what on the federal, state, and local levels? In reality, federalism reflects an intense philosophical debate, carved into institutional stone.

Conflicting views about power and democracy, fairness and liberty have always marked American politics. Successive eras allocated power differently. Dual federalism (the layer cake) largely kept the state and national spheres separate. The era of cooperative federalism saw the national government expand its role and mix with state and local functions (the marble cake). Today, conservatives and court decisions promote a new federalism that devolves more decisions to state and local governments—until the states pursue an agenda that clashes with theirs (for example, tough environmental regulations).

Issue after issue returns us to this question of where to locate government authority: federal, state, or local. Who should decide whether to restrict e-cigarette "vaping" by teens? Address climate change? Encourage immigrant "Dreamers" to remain in the United States? Promote educational standards? Allow—or halt—government collection of cellphone data? Protect the homeland?

Federalism is the mark of a weak national government. However, the paradox of American politics is that weak government is balanced by a powerful nation with a robust sense of national identity. That force helps bind together all the centrifugal institutions of a federal system shot through with checks and balances on every level of government.

Many critics suggest that a weak central government diminishes American capacity for the challenges of the twenty-first century. Others fear the opposite: An inexorably growing state marks the decline of American liberty. We revisit these fears throughout this book. For now, simply recognize that this debate echoes those that Federalists and Anti-Federalists were expressing in the 1780s. The conflict involves balancing the most important American values, never an easy task.

CHAPTER SUMMARY

Check your understanding of Chapter 3.

🟢 The United States separates power in multiple ways, both horizontally (across branches of government) and vertically (across national, state, and local levels).

🟢 Most other nations have more centralized unitary governments.

🟢 The American founders adopted a federalist system, in part to protect against concentrating too much power in one person or branch, but also to expand protections for individual rights, increase government's flexibility, and enable more political innovations to flourish.

🟢 Different versions of federalism are evident in U.S. history, from dual federalism (states and nation performing largely separate functions) to cooperative and new versions that involve closer partnership across government levels. Issues such as devolution and unfunded mandates mark ongoing negotiations over the terms of the elaborate arrangement of local, state, and national governing power.

🟢 We may wonder what has held the United States together despite its divided authority—especially given regional differences that culminated in civil war. An uncommonly strong sense of national identity is a large part of the answer. Americans' devotion to national unity was instrumental in building a robust nation—although nationalism has its ugly, xenophobic sides as well.

● Alongside the concept of a strong nation is an anomaly among most countries with a similarly robust national spirit: a relatively weak American national government. This less powerful set of government institutions is found across American history, in both the limited size of our federal bureaucracy and Washington's constrained capacity to act.

● An abiding commitment to separated powers, organized by the Constitution, helps explain the persistence of this weak government alongside our strong nation. Debates also have persisted about how to reform the U.S. federalist, separated-powers polity. We invite you to join the conversation.

Need to review
key ideas
in greater depth?
Click here.

KEY TERMS

Block grants, p. 93
Civic voluntarism, p. 101
Commerce clause, p. 88
Concurrent powers, p. 90
Confederation, p. 82
Cooperative federalism, p. 92
Delegated powers, p. 88
Devolution, p. 96
Diffusion, p. 84

Dual federalism, p. 91
Full faith and credit
    clause, p. 90
Grants-in-aid, p. 92
Implied powers, p.89
Inherent powers, p. 89
Necessary and proper
    clause, p. 89
New federalism, p. 93

Preemption, p. 97
Progressive federalism, p. 94
Reserved powers, p. 90
Supremacy clause, p. 89
Unfunded mandate, p. 96
Unitary government, p. 82

Flashcard review.

STUDY QUESTIONS

1. Can you imagine the United States without federalism? Suppose that a central national authority ran the country, and governors and mayors—and other subnational officials—were entirely subordinate to the national government. Describe some of the changes that would likely result. Would this shift toward a unitary state be an improvement in your view? Why or why not?

2. Define the following: Dual Federalism; Competitive Federalism; New Federalism; Progressive Federalism.

3. You're asked to advise senior members of Congress. How would you advise them to approach the issue of federalism? Should they give more or less discretion to the states?

4. Think about your own political loyalties. Are they most strongly felt for your hometown or home city, the state where you grew up (or where you live now), or the nation as a whole? What do you think accounts for your outlook? If you are not from the United States, reflect on your own sense of political identity: Is it primarily to a nation, a region, or a local place?

5. If you feel a strong sense of national pride, do you think it comes with any undesirable aspects? If you are not an especially avid American nationalist, why not? What would happen if most citizens exhibited a skeptical outlook toward the country?

6. A wide range of reforms have been suggested for improving the American system of separated powers. Are there any other changes you would make to the federalist division of power across branches and between national, state, and local governments?

 Go to **www.oup.com/us/Morone** to find quizzes, flash cards, simulations, tutorials, videos, and other study tools.

4 Civil Liberties

SIMON TAM AND HIS DANCE ROCK band named themselves "The Slants" as a way to push back against a politically correct culture that tiptoed around racism. The band members, who are Asian Americans, told interviewers that they wanted to reclaim the slur. But when they applied for a trademark, the U.S Patent and Trademark Office rejected their application because the name was "disparaging to people of Asian descent." Tam sued.

Some people agree with the copyright office, arguing that hate speech has no place in our society. Groups that have faced discrimination—for their race, ethnicity, religion, sexual orientation, gender identity, or anything else—should be protected from further insult. This issue has roiled many college campuses. If a speaker has expressed hostility or hatred toward others, say some students and faculty members, they should be stopped from speaking on campus. Across the country students have shut down events and administrators have canceled speakers.

Wait a minute, say others. The First Amendment guarantees Americans the right to free speech—to say what they wish, especially if it is unpopular and even if it is hateful. You may argue against those who speak hatefully, this side argues, but you may not take away their free speech. Allison Stanger, a political science professor who was injured when students at Middlebury College violently disrupted a right-wing speaker, put it this way: "Our constitutional democracy will depend on whether Americans can relearn how to engage civilly with one another, something that is admittedly hard to do with a bullying president as a role model."[1] Stanger, like other Americans, was reacting to the erosion of civil discourse on both sides of the political spectrum.

Two important values are clashing in this case. On the one hand, a community should treat its members with respect. On the other, free speech is the basis of a free society. Which side is right? Both are. The First Amendment to the Constitution *does* guarantee people's right to free

● *Simon Tam and the Slants. The Supreme Court ruled unanimously that the First Amendment protected the band's name—even if is hateful.*

Listen to Simon Tam and the Slants' song about their legal victory.

speech. This is the bedrock of American liberty: protecting individuals when they wish to speak out, practice their religion, or assemble to protest—even if what they say, or believe, or rally for is deeply unpopular.

When Simon Tam and the Slants ended up before the Supreme Court, the Court unanimously ruled in their favor. Even if they had been using the slur against Asians in a hateful way, the Court argued, the government was wrong to limit free speech by denying a trademark. "The proudest boast of our free speech jurisprudence," wrote the Court majority, is that we protect the freedom to express "the thought that we hate."[2] In balancing freedom of speech versus protecting communities from hate speech, the Court came down strongly in favor of free speech.

However, every right has limits. Individual protections are always balanced by community needs or by other people's rights. And the context matters. As Supreme Court Justice Oliver Wendell Holmes put it back in 1919, every action "depends upon the circumstances in which it is done. . . . The most stringent protection of free speech would not protect a man from falsely shouting "fire" in a crowded theater and causing a panic."[3]

Who are we? We are a nation always wrestling with a great trade-off—majority rule versus individual liberties. On the one hand, the United States is a democratic republic, which means the majority should get its way. On the other hand, it is a nation of rugged individualism, which tilts toward protecting individual freedom and rights. What we will see in this chapter is that in our democracy, a majority—even a very large majority—cannot violate the civil liberties of even a small minority.

The tension is exacerbated because we are (and always have been) a nation of minority groups—Irish, Italian, gay, Muslim, Seventh Day Adventist, gun owner, Hmong, transgender, African Americans, and the list goes on. When the majority feels threatened or offended, it sometimes moves to limit the minority's rights, making civil liberties all the *more* important.

Civil liberties: The limits on government that allow people to freely exercise their rights.

What are **civil liberties**? They are the limits we put on governments (and the majorities that elect them) so that individuals can exercise their personal freedoms. Americans have long embraced the figure of the brave individual, standing up for their rights. In practice, complexity abounds.

Civil Liberties

Number of rights listed in the Bill of Rights	**31**
Number of rights protecting freedom of religion	**2**
Number of rights protecting people accused of crimes	**19**
Number of years after the Bill of Rights was ratified before the Supreme Court ruled that state governments could not interfere with freedom of speech	**134**
Number of years before it ruled that states could not interfere with the right to bear arms	**219**
Number of new rights secured by constitutional amendment in the past fifty years: (the Twenty-Sixth Amendment extended the right to vote to eighteen- to twenty-year-olds)	**1**
Percentage of Americans who supported the death penalty in 1994 and today, respectively	**80, 55**[4]
Number of states that have not executed anyone since 1976	**16**[5]
Number of states that have not executed anyone since 2010	**37**
Total number executed in Texas, Virginia, Oklahoma, and Florida since 1976	**871**
Total number executed by the federal government in that period	**3**

How has our interpretation of civil liberties and the government's responsibility to protect them changed over time?

The Rise of Civil Liberties

May an anti-abortion protester shout warnings at women entering family planning clinics? May states ban violent video games? May a skinhead stand on a street corner and urge people to attack Latinos, Sikhs, or Jews? The answer to all three questions is "sometimes." We always weigh the rights of individuals against the concerns and safety of the community. Who decides? Usually, the courts do. And there is often more than one reasonable answer when the courts take up a question.[6]

Civil Rights and Civil Liberties

Civil rights: The freedom to participate in the full life of the community—to vote, use public facilities, and exercise equal economic opportunity.

Civil rights and liberties demand opposite things from government. Civil rights require government action to help secure things such as the right to vote or speak out; **civil liberties** restrict government action to protect individual rights. Until people have won their rights, the idea of protecting them is meaningless. When governments enforce civil rights for some people, they often limit the liberty of others. For example, as we will see in Chapter 5, the Civil Rights Act of 1964 outlawed segregated restaurants. That legal action freed blacks and Latinos to eat where they wished but limited the liberty of racist restaurant owners to serve only those they wanted to serve.

In practice, the two concepts are not opposites. The long battle for civil rights led to more robust civil liberties for everyone. The fight against slavery eventually led to the Fourteenth Amendment, which—as we will soon see—is the cornerstone of modern civil liberties. Without the long American struggle for civil rights, "we the people" would have many fewer civil liberties.

The Purpose of Civil Liberties

Lillian Gobtas was the seventh-grade class president in a Minersville, Pennsylvania, school in 1935. She refused to pledge allegiance to the flag because, as a Jehovah's Witness, she was taught that the pledge placed the nation ahead of God. Lillian was taunted, attacked, and expelled from school. In 1940 the Supreme Court upheld the expulsion. (To add insult to injury, a clerk misspelled her name and the case is known as *Minersville School District v. Gobitis*.) With American entry into World War II, in 1941, the sect faced prejudice, beatings, burnings, and even castration. "They're traitors," declared a sheriff in Maine, "the Supreme Court says so. Ain't you heard?"[7] This is the nightmare for civil liberties: The government failed to protect liberties—and inflamed majority hatred. Three years later, in 1943, the Court reversed itself. The Constitution protected children whose faith proscribed the pledge.

● *Legal? Sometimes! When? Read on…*

In announcing its new position, the Court made a classic statement of civil liberties: "The very purpose of a Bill of Rights was to withdraw certain subjects from the vicissitudes of political controversy, to place them beyond the reach of majorities and officials."[8]

The Slow Rise of Civil Liberties

The Bill of Rights barely touched American life in the nineteenth century because it only applied to the federal government. The First Amendment begins, "*Congress* shall make no law" prohibiting the exercise of religion or restricting speech. Well, what about the states?

In 1833, John Barron found out. Barron owned a wharf in Baltimore Harbor until the city diverted the water and left his dock high and dry. Barron sued, arguing that the city had violated the Fifth Amendment by taking his property for public use "without just compensation." The Supreme Court ruled (in *Barron v. Baltimore*) that the Fifth Amendment applied only to the federal government. The Anti-Federalists, reasoned the justices, had demanded the Bill of Rights to protect them from the federal government. Washington could not strip Barron of his property rights—but Maryland or Baltimore could. [9]

The Bill of Rights eventually reached the states thanks to the quest for civil rights. After the Civil War, Congress passed the Fourteenth Amendment (ratified in 1868) to protect the newly freed slaves. Every discussion of civil liberties turns the spotlight on one passage in the Fourteenth Amendment:

> **No state** shall . . . *deprive any person of life, liberty, or property, without due process of law; nor deny any person within its jurisdiction the equal protection of the laws. [emphasis added]*

Look again at the first two words. The amendment directly addresses the states. No state may deprive any person of life, liberty, or property, which are exactly what the Bill of Rights protects. The Fourteenth Amendment *seems* to apply the Bill of Rights to the states. In 1873, the Supreme Court disagreed: The Fourteenth Amendment applied only to freed slaves and to no one else.[10]

Over time, the Court changed its mind. In 1897, the Court returned to the issue in *Barron v. Baltimore* and ruled that state governments could not seize property without compensation. One phrase of the Fifth Amendment—"nor shall private property be taken for public use, without just compensation"—now applied to state and local government as well as to the federal government. The Supreme Court had "incorporated" the right into the Fourteenth Amendment. The Supreme Court decides, case by case, which rights apply to state governments—a process called **selective incorporation**.

In 1937, the Court formulated a principle for deciding which rights to incorporate: Is the right essential to our idea of liberty? If so, the Fourteenth Amendment's due process clause—quoted earlier—required states to respect that right and the Court then incorporated, or applied, it to the states.[11] Over time, the Court incorporated almost every phrase of the Bill of Rights, beginning with freedom of speech (in 1925), continuing with the practice of religion (1940), and moving to the right to own guns in 2010 (see Table 4.1).[12]

Selective incorporation: Extending protections from the Bill of Rights to the state governments, one right at a time.

TABLE 4.1 Incorporation of the Bill of Rights into the Fourteenth Amendment

THE BILL OF RIGHTS	YEAR	KEY CASE
I. *Free exercise of religion	1940	*Cantwell v. Connecticut*
No establishment of religion	1947	*Everson v. Board of Ed*
Free press	1931	***Near v. Minnesota*** **
Free speech	1925	***Gitlow v. New York***
Right to peaceful assembly	1937	*De Jonge v. Oregon*
Right to petition government	1963	*NAACP v. Button*
II. Right to keep and bear arms	2010	***McDonald v. Chicago***
III. No quartering of soldiers		Not incorporated
IV. No unreasonable search and seizure	1949	*Wolf v. Colorado*
No search and seizure without warrant	1961	***Mapp v. Ohio***
V. Right to grand jury indictment		Not incorporated
No double jeopardy	1969	*Benton v. Maryland*
No forced confession	1964	*Escobedo v. Illinois*
Right to remain silent	1966	***Miranda v. Arizona***
No seizure of property without compensation	1897	*Chicago Burlington and Quincy RR v. Chicago*
VI. Right to public trial	1948	*In re Oliver*
Right to speedy trial	1967	*Klopfer v. North Carolina*
Right to trial by impartial jury	1966	*Parker v. Gladden*
Right to confront witnesses	1965	*Pointer v. Texas*
Right to compel supportive witnesses to appear	1967	*Washington v. Texas*
Right to counsel in capital punishment cases	1932	***Powell v. Alabama***
Right to counsel in any criminal trial	1963	***Gideon v. Wainright***
VII. Right of jury trial in civil cases		Not incorporated
VIII. No excessive bail		Not incorporated
No cruel and unusual punishment	1962	*Robinson v. California*
IX. Rights not limited to rights listed in the first eight amendments		Not relevant to incorporation
X. Powers not delegated to the national government are reserved to the states and the people		Not relevant to incorporation

* Note how the First Amendment rights were incorporated early in the process. Most protections for those accused of crimes were applied between 1962 and 1968.
** Boldfaced cases are discussed in this chapter.

In the rest of the chapter, we examine the most important civil liberties and the issues they raise.

The Bottom Line

» The Supreme Court neatly defined civil liberties in 1943 in *West Virginia State Board of Education v. Barnette*: The Bill of Rights withdraws certain subjects from political controversy and places them beyond the reach of majorities and officials.

» The Bill of Rights did not apply to the states until the Fourteenth Amendment required that *no state* could deprive any citizen of life, liberty, or property.

» The Court applied the Bill of Rights to the states one right at a time between 1897 (no taking of property without compensation) and 2010 (the right to bear arms).

Privacy

We begin with an especially controversial civil liberty that, unlike all the others we examine, is never directly mentioned in the Constitution. Instead, the majority on the Supreme Court ruled that it is implied by the First, Third, Fourth, Fifth, and Ninth Amendments.

Penumbras and Emanations

In the mid-nineteenth century, contraceptives were widely available. Then, encouraged by the federal government in the 1870s, every state banned them—partly because of fears that immigrants would have more children than native-born Americans. Almost a century later, the director of Planned Parenthood of Connecticut defied that state's ban and dispensed condoms at a birth control clinic in New Haven. The Supreme Court heard the case (*Griswold v. Connecticut*, 1965), struck down the law, and declared a dramatic new right: the right to privacy.

How could the Court protect privacy if the Constitution does not even mention it? Justice William O. Douglas explained: The rights that are specifically mentioned in the Bill of Rights "have penumbras . . . that give them life and substance." The *penumbras*—literally, the shadows—of the First Amendment create "zones of privacy" in which people have a right to make their own choices free from government interference. So do the "emanations" from other amendments, such as the Third Amendment's ban on quartering soldiers in private homes—which, he pointed out, was designed to protect privacy. In addition, the Ninth Amendment declares that other rights exist besides the ones mentioned in the Constitution and they are also "retained by the people." Privacy is one of those rights.

The *Griswold* case itself did not stir much controversy. After all, most people thought married couples had every right to use condoms. In 1973, however, the right to privacy led to one of the most controversial Court decisions ever.

Roe v. Wade

In *Roe v. Wade* (1973) the Supreme Court drew on the right to privacy and struck down a Texas law banning abortion. The Court ruled that the right to privacy is "broad enough to encompass a woman's decision whether or not to terminate her pregnancy"—within the first three months of pregnancy (before the fetus can live outside the womb). During that first trimester, the state governments cannot *regulate* or *infringe on* a woman's right to abortion.

What Do YOU Think? Is There a Right to Privacy?

Are you ready to try your first case? How would you rule in *Griswold v. Connecticut*? Do you agree that there is "a right to privacy" in the Constitution that permitted the Court to strike down the Connecticut ban on contraceptives?

Yes. Although the Constitution does not specifically mention privacy, a modern reading of the document would conclude that privacy is a basic right that the courts should protect. In addition, the consequence—a woman's right to control her own pregnancy—is an essential part of gender equality as we understand it today.

No. We have to stick to the simple language of the Constitution itself. We disrespect and even damage the document by reading things into it. Those who opposed Connecticut's ban on contraceptives should have gone to the legislature and lobbied them to change it.

What it means. No matter how you voted, you're part of a long intellectual tradition. If you said yes, you agree with a school of thought (which we call *pragmatist*) that says the courts must be guided by the *general ideas* that underpin the Constitution. If you voted no, you're voting with *originalism*, the school of thought that limits judges to considering the original intent as explicitly stated in the Constitution's text.

Roe v. Wade changed American politics. Although it was not immediately controversial, within a decade, two very strong perspectives had emerged. People who supported the decision—known as "pro-choice"—viewed the decision as essential to gender equality because it enabled women to control when (and whether) they have children. From this perspective, *Roe* opens the door to vocations and careers for women. It protects women's health by doing away with the dangerous "back alley" abortions that desperate women sought out before *Roe* made abortions safe and legal. Democrats, for the most part, are pro-choice.

Those who oppose the decision—known as "pro-life"—believe that life begins at conception and that abortion is murder. Many religious activists took *Roe v. Wade* as a call to enter politics. The grassroots campaign to overturn the decision became a powerful force in modern conservatism. The Republican Party committed itself to overturning *Roe*.

● *Off-duty police offer Robert Sanderson's body lay covered by a yellow sheet (on right) in this 1997 bombing of an Alabama family planning clinic. Decades after the Roe decision, abortion remains the subject of fierce debate, civil disobedience—and occasional criminal acts.*

The debate added new intensity to American politics, because activists on each side felt they were fighting for the soul of the nation: on the one side, equality for women; on the other side, the life of the unborn. The intensity has helped politicize Supreme Court appointments. Each new nomination raises the same questions. What is his or her attitude toward abortion? Will it swing the Court?

Planned Parenthood v. Casey

Challenges to *Roe v. Wade* led to a string of Supreme Court decisions. In 1980, the Court accepted a congressional ban on federal funding, and in 1989, it upheld a Missouri prohibition on abortions in public hospitals. In 1992, the Court took up a Pennsylvania law that seemed to directly challenge *Roe* by imposing regulations on women seeking abortions, even in the first trimester. Many observers, on both sides of the issue, predicted that the Court would overturn *Roe v. Wade* and permit states to outlaw abortions.

Instead, in *Planned Parenthood v. Casey* (1992), the Court voted (5–4) to take a middle ground. The Court upheld a woman's right to terminate her pregnancy, as a "component of liberty." However, it rejected *Roe v. Wade*'s trimester framework, which forbade any state limitations in the first trimester. Now the Court majority allowed states to legislate "measures aimed at ensuring that

Judicial rule: A hard-and-fast boundary between what is lawful and what is not.

Judicial standard: A guiding principle that helps governments make judgment calls.

a woman's choice contemplates the consequences for the fetus." In short, the right to abort a nonviable fetus could be balanced—but not overruled—by the state's desire to protect potential life so long as state regulations did not impose "an undue burden" on the woman's choice.

The original *Roe* decision had propounded **a judicial rule**. Rules set clear boundaries between what is lawful and what is not: The states may not interfere with a woman's right to have an abortion in the first trimester. Now, *Casey* replaced the rule with a **judicial standard**. A standard establishes a more general guiding principle rather than a hard-and-fast rule. What is an "undue burden" on a woman's choice? That's a judgment call.

The debate continues. In the last three years, fifteen states passed sixty-three new restrictions on abortion while twenty-one states passed measures to protect reproductive rights. In 2016, a closely divided Supreme Court set down new rules: States may restrict access to abortion only when the medical benefits outweigh the burden imposed on a woman seeking an abortion. The controversy continues.[13]

Sex Between Consenting Adults

Does the right to privacy extend to same-sex couples? In 1986, the Supreme Court ruled it did not, upholding Georgia's antisodomy law. In 2003, the Supreme Court reversed itself (in *Lawrence v. Texas*) and extended the right of privacy to same-sex couples. In striking down a Texas antisodomy law the majority echoed the original *Griswold* decision: "Liberty protects the person from unwarranted government intrusion into . . . private places."

Clashing Principles

Discover how the Patriot Act raised privacy concerns.

The privacy cases generally reflect public opinion. By 1965, most Americans believed that couples should be permitted to use birth control. *Roe v. Wade* appeared to reflect the popular view in the early 1970s, but precipitated an enormous surge defending a right to life. Later decisions balanced the right to an abortion with state restrictions—roughly in line with majority views. It may seem a good idea that courts reflect majority opinion. But the Constitution and the Court are designed to stand up to the majority. They are supposed to protect the rights of unpopular minorities like Jehovah's Witnesses in the 1940s and gay Americans in the 1980s.

● *John Geddes Lawrence (left) and Tyron Garner (right). The police, investigating a gun disturbance complaint, broke into Lawrence's apartment—which had gay posters prominently displayed on the walls. When Lawrence began to argue, the police arrested both Garner and him for "deviant sexual intercourse." In* Lawrence v. Texas *the Supreme Court struck down the Texas antisodomy law for violating the Constitution's privacy protections.*

As we will see throughout this chapter, applying the Constitution is never simple. The United States is founded on two ideas that often clash. The story of civil liberties is the story of managing the collisions between the two core principles—the needs and desires of the majority versus the liberties of the individual.

The Bottom Line

» The Court discovered a right to privacy implicit in the shadows of the First, Third, Fourth, Fifth, and Ninth Amendments.

» The Court applied the right to privacy to strike down laws banning abortion. In *Roe v. Wade*, the court issued a *rule* prohibiting states from interfering during the first trimester.

» The Court extended privacy rights to same-sex couples by striking down antisodomy laws.

Freedom of Religion

The First Amendment begins with two commands protecting religion.

Congress shall make no law respecting an establishment of religion, or prohibiting the free exercise thereof.

The federal government may not establish an official religion—that's known as the **establishment clause**. And it may not interfere in religious practice—the **free exercise clause**.

The Establishment Clause

By the time the Constitution was written, Americans already practiced many faiths: Puritans (or Congregationalists) in Massachusetts, Quakers in Philadelphia, Baptists in Rhode Island, Anglicans in Virginia, Catholics in Maryland, and Jews in Newport, Rhode Island. The Constitution posed a threat. What if the federal government imposed a national religion? The First Amendment's establishment clause is designed to prohibit that. But what exactly did it forbid the government from doing? The debate began immediately.

President George Washington (1789–1797) called for a national day of prayer each year. Was that encouraging religion? President Thomas Jefferson (1801–1809) thought so and rejected the practice. The First Amendment, wrote Jefferson, builds "a wall of separation between church and state."[14] When the Supreme Court extended the establishment clause to the state governments in 1947, Justice Hugo Black quoted Jefferson's "wall of separation."[15] Until recently, Jefferson's metaphor guided the Court's efforts.

The problem is that "wall of separation" has never been built. The cash in American pockets is inscribed "In God We Trust"; children pledge allegiance to "one nation, under God"; Moses, holding the Ten Commandments, is carved into the Supreme Court building. Congress opens each session with a prayer (led by an official chaplain); and presidents end their speeches with "God bless America"—a sentiment no leader would invoke in England, France, or Japan.

Establishment clause: In the First Amendment, the principle that government may not establish an official religion.

Free exercise clause: In the First Amendment, the principle that government may not interfere in religious practice.

Despite the many interconnections, the courts have tried to separate church and state. The question is how?

The establishment clause is clearly designed to keep government officials from favoring one religion—or religion over non-religion. In a blockbuster case, *Engel v. Vitale* (1962), the Supreme Court ruled that New York's practice of starting the school day with a nondenominational prayer violated the establishment clause.[16]

A long string of controversial decisions followed. Each returned to the vexing question about exactly where to construct Jefferson's wall. May public schools introduce a minute of silent prayer or meditation? (No.) May graduation include a prayer? (No.) May students lead prayers at football games? (No.) Can a city or state government display the Ten Commandments? (Yes, if it does not make a religious statement). May a city put up a Christmas display? (Yes, if it includes secular as well as religious symbols—known sarcastically as the "two-reindeer" rule.) Are business owners free to refuse service to same-sex couples on religious grounds? (Yes, ruled the Supreme Court in 2018.)

In 1971, the Court established a test to guide decisions about separating church and state. In *Lemon v. Kurtzman*, the Court ruled on a Pennsylvania law that paid teachers who taught nonreligious subjects in church-affiliated (mainly Catholic) schools. The Court forbade the practice and promulgated what became known as the *Lemon test* for judging what government actions are permissible. First, the law must have a *secular* purpose. Second, its principal effect must *neither advance nor inhibit religion*. Finally, it must not *excessively entangle* government in religion. Paying the teachers in religious schools was, the Court ruled, an "excessive entanglement," and Pennsylvania could not do it.

As the Court grew more conservative, the Lemon test came under fire. Justice Scalia complained: "Like some ghoul in a late night horror movie that repeatedly sits up in its grave and shuffles abroad... *Lemon* stalks our Establishment Clause jurisprudence."[17] Today, two different perspectives have emerged. **Strict separation** still tries to separate church and state using the Lemon test. An alternative view is known as **accommodation**: Government does not violate the establishment clause so long as it does not confer an advantage on some religions over others. Accommodation is gathering momentum making establishment clause cases unpredictable. For example, in 2017, the Court ruled (7–2) that when a state offers a funding program (for instance, improving playgrounds), it cannot rule out church schools or other religious organizations (*Lutheran v. Comer*). Strict-separation adherents lamented, "Goodbye, Establishment Clause."[18]

Free Exercise of Religion

The First Amendment also prohibits government from interfering with the "free exercise" of religion. Once again, the Court's view has evolved.

The first landmark case was decided in 1963. Adell Sherbert, a Seventh-Day Adventist, refused to work on Saturday because it violated her faith. She

Strict separation: The strict principles articulated in the Lemon test for judging whether a law establishes a religion. (See "accommodation.")

Accommodation: The principle that government does not violate the establishment clause as long as it does not confer an advantage to some religions over others. (See "strict separation.")

● *Debating the establishment clause. The Supreme Court found Kentucky's display of the Ten Commandments unconstitutional by a 5–4 vote (left), but a similar display in Austin, Texas, acceptable—also 5–4 (right). What was the difference between the two? Justice Breyer, who switched his vote from "no" (Kentucky) to "yes" (Texas) explained: The Texas Commandments had stood for forty years as one of many monuments celebrating the development of the law, while the Kentucky tablets had been recently erected as an expression of religious faith.*

was fired. South Carolina rejected her claim for unemployment benefits because she refused other jobs that also required work on Saturday. Claiming that the state was infringing on her free exercise of religion, Sherbert sued the state for her unemployment benefits. In deciding the case, Justice Brennan introduced a two-part test, known as the *Sherbert* or *balancing test*. First, was the government imposing a "significant burden" on her ability to exercise her faith? Second, did the government have a "compelling interest" for imposing the burden? In this case, the Court ruled that there was a real burden on Adell Sherbert and no compelling state interest for denying her unemployment benefits.

The Sherbert test lasted until 1990, when the Court took a completely different approach. Two Oregon men participated in a Native American ritual that included taking peyote—a hallucinogen. The men were fired from their jobs at a private drug rehab center and then were denied unemployment benefits for violating Oregon drug laws. The men sued, arguing that they should be exempted from the peyote ban because it was essential to their religious practice. Under the Sherbert test, they might have won. However, the Supreme Court ruled (6–3) against the two men and, in the process, made it much more difficult to sue the government for interfering with religious expression. In *Employment Division v. Smith*, the Court asked simply if the Oregon drug law was a neutral law applied in a neutral way. Yes, the law was neutral. It was not aimed at Native American religious practice because it forbids *everyone* from smoking peyote.

The *Employment Division* case replaced the Sherbert balancing test with a *neutrality test*. The new test asks only whether the same law applies to everyone. So long as the law does not target a religious group, the Court will permit it. Obviously, this makes it much more difficult to sue on the basis of "free exercise" of religion.[19]

Religious groups—from the Catholic Church to the *Witches' Voice*—mobilized against the Court's decision. Congress passed the Religious Freedom

How do we interpret the free exercise and establishment clauses?

● Using the neutrality test, the courts struck down a Florida law that forbade the use of animal sacrifices because it specifically targeted the Cuban Santeria religion.

Restoration Act of 1993 (RFRA), which required federal and state governments to use the old Sherbert balancing test. In 1997, the Court stepped in again. It ruled that Congress lacked the constitutional authority to order the states to use the balancing test. Congress came back three years later, reaffirming its authority with the Religious Land Use and Institutionalized Persons Act; in addition, twenty-one states passed their own RFRA laws—all restoring the Sherbert balancing test. In 2015, the Supreme Court turned around and reverted to the Sherbert balancing test when a Muslim inmate sued Arkansas arguing that prison regulations denying all prisoners the right to grow beards violated his rights to practice his faith. The court ruled unanimously (in *Holt v. Hobbs*, 2015) that the state could not burden someone's exercise of religion (shave your beard, work on Saturday) without showing a compelling state reason.

What Do YOU Think?

May the Christian Youth Club Meet in School?

The Good News is a Christian youth club that wanted to meet in school after class hours. The school district said that this would amount to a public school's endorsement of Christianity. The case went to the Supreme Court. Justices Stevens (who argued against Good News) and Scalia (who supported Good News) each wrote opinions. Which opinion would you sign on to?

Justice Stevens: "Evangelical meetings designed to convert children to a particular faith . . . may introduce divisiveness and tend to separate young children into cliques that undermine the school's educational mission." The school district is right to stop the practice.

Justice Scalia: Religious expression cannot violate the establishment clause where it is (1) purely private and (2) open to all on equal terms. Milford [the school district] is discriminating against a religious group because it lets other groups meet.

Testing these views. As you consider whose side to take, consider how one would decide this case using the Lemon test (with Stevens) or the accommodation view (with Scalia). How did the court actually rule? The answer is in the endnotes.[20]

The Bottom Line

» The First Amendment has two religious clauses: The government may not *establish* a religion and it may not interfere with the free *exercise* of religions.

» The courts have ruled on establishment cases by trying to approximate Jefferson's wall separating church and state. Government action is permissible if it meets three criteria known as the Lemon test: It must *have a secular purpose, neither advance nor inhibit religion,* and *not excessively entangle* government in religion. A more recent view (known as accommodation) simply requires that government not promote one religious view over another.

» In protecting the free exercise of religion, the courts traditionally asked if the government had a compelling interest for imposing a burden.

Freedom of Speech

Now, we turn to the civil liberty the courts rank most important, freedom of speech. After its religious clauses, the First Amendment states:

> *Congress shall make no law . . . abridging the freedom of speech or of the press.*

Protecting freedom of speech.

A Preferred Position

The Supreme Court gives the First Amendment a "preferred position" among all the amendments to the Constitution. And among the liberties listed in the First Amendment (free speech, religion, press, assembly, and the right to petition government), free speech holds a "preferred position." When freedom of speech conflicts with any other right, the Court generally will "prefer" or protect speech.[21]

Why do contemporary courts put so much emphasis on the right to express opinions? Because democracy requires vigorous debate. As a result, the courts will be skeptical of any effort to curb speech, however hurtful.[22] Of course, every right has its limits. Much of the debate that surrounds the right to speech is about identifying the boundaries—the limits—of protected speech.

Political Speech

In every generation, political leaders are tempted to stop subversive talk—or harsh criticism. Just ten years after the Constitution was ratified, Congress drafted the Alien and Sedition Acts. Tensions with France were running high, and the acts made it illegal to "print, utter, or publish . . . any false, scandalous, and malicious writing" against the government. The meaning of the acts was brutally simple: criticize the government and face prosecution.

The first modern free speech cases arose during World War I. President Woodrow Wilson had signed the Espionage Act. Charles Schenck, general secretary of the Socialist Party of Philadelphia, was found guilty of violating it because his pamphlets urged men not to enlist for a war designed to pour profits into greedy Wall Street. Was his freedom of speech abrogated? Under normal circumstances it might be, wrote Justice Oliver Wendell Holmes for a unanimous Court, but this was wartime. Distributing these documents, he wrote, was like falsely shouting "fire" in a crowded theater. Holmes then formulated the most famous test for free speech: Speech is not protected if it poses "a **clear and present danger** that it will lead to 'substantive evils'" (*Schenck v. United States*, 1919).

Clear and present danger: Court doctrine that permits restrictions of free speech if officials believe that the speech will lead to prohibited action such as violence or terrorism.

In the early 1920s, many Americans were anxious about foreigners, immigrants, socialists, communists, and anarchists. The Supreme Court hardened the "clear and present danger" test by ruling that judges did not have to "weigh each and every utterance." They could simply determine whether the "natural tendency and probable effect" of the speech was to "bring about something bad or evil"—even if that danger lay in the distant future.[23]

The clear and present danger test stood for decades. Then in *Brandenburg v. Ohio* (1969), the Court complained that "puny" threats, which no one took seriously except "nervous judges," were being declared a clear and present danger. The issue arose when a Ku Klux Klan (KKK) leader, Clarence Brandenburg, organized a rally where the Klan members burned crosses, waved guns, and called for "revengeance" against Jews and African Americans. The Supreme Court struck down Brandenburg's conviction and rewrote the clear and present dangers test. The state may not interfere with speech unless the speech "incites imminent lawless action" *and* is likely to actually "produce such action."

Test Yourself: The Simpsons Versus the First Amendment—Which Do You Know Better?

Five rights are listed in the First Amendment, and there are five Simpsons. Thirty-four percent of Americans can name four of the five Simpsons. Only 1 percent of Americans can name four of the five rights.

How about you? How many First Amendment rights can you name? How many Simpsons? (Answers below.)

(Source: McCormick Tribune Freedom Museum, Chicago).

Answers: The Simpsons, from left to right: Homer, Bart, Lisa, Marge, and Maggie. First Amendment rights: Freedom of religion, speech, press, and assembly, and the right to petition government.

The result makes it very difficult to curtail political speech—even when it is highly offensive. The court protected members of Westboro Baptist church, who appeared at military funerals jeering the army, with signs such as: "Fag sin—you are going to hell." The government may limit the speech only if the bad effects—a lynching, a terrorist attack—are likely to happen immediately.[24]

Symbolic Speech

When Clarence Brandenburg burned his cross, he engaged in a form of speech known as **symbolic expression**. He was demonstrating a point of view with an act rather than as a speech. The First Amendment protects symbolic speech—again, within limits.

Symbolic expression: An act, rather than actual speech, used to demonstrate a point of view.

In 2003, the Supreme Court identified those limits when it took two cross-burning cases on the same day. One involved a KKK ceremony. The original cross burnings, after the Civil War, signaled the murder of a former slave—an emblem designed to frighten people during what amounted to a campaign of domestic terrorism. Now the Court drew a fine distinction. Individuals may burn crosses to express their views, but not to intimidate others. The KKK burned the cross as part of a ritual without directly threatening or intimidating anyone.[25] On the same day, however, the Court upheld the conviction of another cross burner. In this second case, two men had come home after a night of drinking and burned a cross on a black neighbor's lawn. Their act directly intimidated the neighbors. Even if there is no immediate (or clear and present) danger, intimidating people is not protected by the First Amendment.[26]

Burning the American flag is another unpopular symbolic expression. Forty-eight states and the federal government banned flag burning. The Supreme Court narrowly struck down the law (by a 5–4 vote).[27] Congress responded by passing legislation defending the flag. The Court overturned that, too.[28]

In 2015, the Supreme Court narrowly upheld (5–4) Texas's refusal to issue a license plate with a Confederate flag. Notice the distinction: The government may not restrict Simon Tam's (fronting the Slants) hate speech, but the Texas government may decide what it wants and does not want to "say" through license plates, monuments, or flags—all forms of state speech. Today, that issue has boiled over across the south as the region confronts its Confederate legacy. Some argue that Confederate flags and monuments commemorate those who fought for the enslavement of African Americans; others contend that they celebrate Southern heritage. The key question: When the state speaks, what should it say?[29]

Limits to Free Speech: Fighting Words

Is there any way to rein in cross burning, gay bashing, slurs against Catholics, and other forms of hateful speech? Other democracies are much tougher on hurtful speech; so are many colleges and universities. Their logic is simple:

● *Is this symbolic speech protected? A closely divided Court ruled yes (left) and no (right).*

How can you build a good community if some members feel singled out, threatened, or diminished?

Hate speech: Hostile statements based on someone's personal characteristics, such as race, ethnicity, religion, or sexual orientation.

Fighting words: Expressions inherently likely to provoke violent reaction and not necessarily protected by the First Amendment.

One legal doctrine offers a limit to **hate speech** by restricting **fighting words**. The Supreme Court defined these as "personally abusive epithets which, when addressed to the ordinary citizen, are, as a matter of common knowledge, inherently likely to provoke violent reaction."[30] The Court states the principle but has been reluctant to apply it. Reformers trying to create codes of decent language generally rely on the logic of "fighting words"—but it is not easy to restrict speech unless it threatens to lead to criminal action and does not express a specific political position.

Limited Protections: Student Speech

How about students speaking out? In the 1969 landmark *Tinker* decision, the Court announced that students "do not shed their constitutional right to freedom of speech or expression at the schoolhouse gate." That decision, however, has been qualified in a series of cases that balanced student rights with the schools' educational mission.

In 1965, John (15 years old) and Mary Beth Tinker (13) violated school rules by wearing a black armband to protest the Vietnam War. They were suspended and told to return when they were ready to abide by the school's rules. The Supreme Court overturned the suspension and established what became known as the Tinker rule: The students' right to free speech could be curtailed only if it "materially and substantially interferes with the requirements of appropriate discipline in the operation of the school."[31]

Free Speech on Campus

Around the country, many universities forbid hate speech on campus. They forbid harassment (oral, written, graphic, or physical) against any group that might face discrimination—African Americans, Latinos, LGBTQ people, military veterans, religious denominations, age groups, and others. These codes, in turn, provoke fierce opposition. Critics argue that restrictions on speech create taboo subjects and people with unpopular opinions could end up being expelled. What should campus leaders do?

Yes. Forbid hurtful speech. We must protect LGBTQ students, students of color, military veterans, and any other groups that face hatred and violence. Hate speech fractures communities and hurts people. It is frightening and painful to the targeted groups. It poses a threat to teaching and destroys the community spirit necessary for learning.

No. Forbid restrictions on speech regardless of how hurtful. Everyone has the right to an opinion—even if it is a horrible opinion. We can punish criminal behavior, but we should never punish people for simply expressing their views—especially on a college campus, where exploration of ideas is a core value.

In subsequent cases, the Court found that teachers and school officials had an obligation to teach students proper conduct and could regulate speech that was vulgar, indecent, offensive (1986), or inconsistent with the educational mission of the school (1988).[32]

School speech debates now face the digital frontier. Social media enable widespread, lightning fast broadcast of information—as well as malicious gossip, cyberbullying, and cruel rumors. By 2018, 48 states had passed laws forbidding online cyberbullying, though some civil liberties advocates critique them as restrictions on protected speech. Across the country, schools have suspended students for posts deemed inappropriate or illegal.

The First Amendment offers students—in high schools or colleges—less protection than it offers adults. School officials may regulate speech as long as they do not do so arbitrarily.

 **The Bottom Line**

» Free speech is crucial to democracy, and the Court gives it a privileged position—even against angry public opposition at flag burning, cross burning, or homophobic displays at military funerals.

» Free speech can be curtailed if it poses a "clear and present danger." Today, the Court requires the danger to be both imminent and likely to occur.

» There are limits to free speech, including fighting words and student speech.

🔒 Freedom of the Press

Freedom of the press follows most of the same rules as freedom of speech. The written word has always been essential to politics. The form changes—from pamphlets in 1770 to digital media today. Written words share the "preferred position." Broadcast media are slightly different and subject to federal regulation (as we will explore in Chapter 7).

Prior Restraint

Prior restraint: Legal effort to stop speech before it occurs—in effect, censorship.

The effort to stop speech before it occurs is known as **prior restraint**. Although the Supreme Court has permitted government officials to punish people for what they have said or printed, it has never allowed federal government agents to gag citizens before they have had their say.

In 1931, public officials in Minneapolis shut down a newspaper named the *Saturday Press*, published by an avowed racist who claimed that Jewish gangs were running the city. In *Near v. Minnesota* (1931), the Court ruled that the state could not suppress the paper, no matter how obnoxious, but it left the door open to prior restraint for national security reasons.

In another famous case, the Richard Nixon administration tried to use national security to stop the *New York Times* from publishing a rich archive of classified material, known as the Pentagon Papers, that exposed the mistakes and deceptions that led the United States into the Vietnam War. Again, the Supreme Court permitted publication (6–3) and emphasized the "heavy presumption" against prior restraint outweighed potential damage to national security.[33]

Explore current censorship issues.

The shift from print media to the Internet has made it even more difficult for courts to permit prior restraint and stop publications. In 2008, WikiLeaks, a web-based venue for anonymous whistle-blowers, published internal documents from a Swiss bank that appeared to show tax evasion and money laundering at the bank's Cayman Islands branch. The bank went to court and won a restraining order against publication of the leaked documents. Stopping a newspaper from publishing is straightforward: The court enjoins the publisher. However, because WikiLeaks operates anonymously and globally, it is almost impossible for a court to suppress the information. In the WikiLeaks case, the court tried to seal the site's American address. The documents simply appeared on mirror sites—and the controversy only drove eyeballs to the site.[34]

Then, in 2013, Edward Snowden, a contractor working for the National Security Agency (NSA), leaked a huge cache of classified documents detailing the NSA's extensive data collection. The reports, published in the *Washington Post*, revealed the NSA was collecting metadata on millions of cellphone calls and tapping data from tech companies. Both WikiLeaks and Snowden illustrate how new media renders the government helpless against the spread of embarrassing and potentially harmful electronic information. The old question was "should prior restraint be permitted?" The new question is whether it is possible at all.

Obscenity

The First Amendment does not protect obscenity. However, the courts always face the same problem: What is obscene? Justice Potter Stewart put it famously when he said simply, "I know it when I see it." Of course, different people see "it" in different things. The Court's emphasis on free speech leads it to reject aggressive regulation of obscenity.

In *Miller v. California* (1973), the Supreme Court created a three-part test for judging a work to be obscene. The **Miller test** holds that speech is not protected by the First Amendment if it has all three of these characteristics:

1. "The average person, applying contemporary community standards, would find that the work, taken as a whole, appeals to the prurient interest" (meaning that it is meant to be sexually stimulating).

2. It depicts sexual conduct in a "patently offensive way."

3. The work lacks "serious literary, artistic, political or scientific value."

> **Miller test:** Three-part test for judging whether a work is obscene (if it has all three, the work loses First Amendment protection).

The Miller test only created new questions. What does it mean to be patently offensive? Offensive to whom? How do we rely on community standards of decency when the Internet and the digital media flow across borders?

In recent years, the Court has been hostile to most efforts at banning material. It struck down a congressional effort to ban online material that showed "sexual, excretory activities or organs."

Feminist scholars have tried to change the framework of this debate. Pornography, they argue, subordinates women in the same way that hate speech demeans minorities. Nations, such as Canada, have essentially accepted this perspective. Although U.S. courts have not taken this view—and continue to protect hate speech—the feminist position continues to be an important part of the debate.[35]

Congress and most states now outlaw revenge porn in which explicit photos or videos are posted online without the subject's consent. The courts, however, have been skeptical, striking down these laws in Arizona, Vermont, and Minnesota. The Supreme Court has yet to weigh in.

The Court flatly forbids child pornography—a sharp limit to free speech. In 2008, it upheld a law, spearheaded by evangelical conservatives, forbidding material that led someone to believe it included "minors engaging in sexually explicit conduct." The case involved a man who boasted online, "Dad of toddler has 'good' [hard core] pics of her and me for swap of your

● *Almost anything goes. It is very difficult to win a libel judgment. Singer-songwriter Ciara filed a $15 million suit against her then-partner, Future, for his derogatory tweets. She soon dropped the case. Defamation suits are very difficult to win.*

toddler pics, or live cam." Even in this case, two members of the Court disagreed. They feared that the law permitted prosecution of individuals who were simply misleading buyers into thinking that the pictures were illegal. The Court is so sensitive to free speech that even in a case like this one, two justices voted to strike down the child protection law for chilling speech.[36]

Libel

There are limits to the false things one can write or say about someone. (Written falsehoods are known as *libel*; spoken falsehoods are known as *slander*.) The courts have made it very difficult for public officials or celebrities to win a libel (or slander) judgment. To do so, they must prove not just that a statement was false and that it caused them harm but also that it was made with malice or "a reckless disregard for the truth."

Today, the Court allows even outrageous claims, cartoons, spoofs, and criticism directed at public officials and celebrities. By contrast, English law is just the opposite and puts the burden of proof on the writers to prove the truth of what they have written. President Trump has repeatedly attacked the American libel laws, calling them "a sham and a disgrace." Supporters see this as part of Donald Trump's effort to shake up American politics and law, but given the Court's position on free speech, it will be very difficult to make changes.[37]

 **The Bottom Line**

» The rules for freedom of the press reflect those of free speech and strongly protect free expression.

» The courts are especially skeptical of any effort to impose prior restraint. The new media makes it almost impossible to even try.

» Obscenity is not protected by the First Amendment. The Court has spent a long time wrestling with just what counts as obscenity and now uses the three-part Miller test.

The Right to Bear Arms

The Second Amendment asserts a uniquely American right. No other national constitution includes the right to bear arms. The text in the Constitution is ambiguous:

> *A well regulated militia, being necessary to the security of a free state, the right of the people to keep and bear arms shall not be infringed.*

On one reading, this amendment simply protects colonial-era militias. On another, it guarantees the right to own weapons.

A Relic of the Revolution?

Skeptics question whether Americans have any right to bear arms at all. The Second Amendment, they say, protected state militias. Early Americans believed that only tyrants kept permanent armies. In a republic, the citizens volunteered for service in local militias that defended their communities and their nation. The Second Amendment, in this reading, is a "relic of the American Revolution" and simply forbids the national government from disarming the local militias. It does not involve a constitutional right to tote weapons. [38]

Those who favor this view generally emphasize public safety and gun control. They argue that America's high homicide rate—over 9,300 killed or wounded in mass shootings since the Sandy Hook Elementary massacre in 2012—reflects the easy availability of rapid-fire, high capacity weapons in the United States. [39]

A seller prepares weapons for a gun show. Americans disagree about whether guns should be heavily regulated, as in most advanced democracies, or whether existing regulation should be removed.

The Palladium of All Liberties?

Proponents of gun rights read the same constitutional sentence very differently. As Justice Scalia explained, the Second Amendment has two parts—a preface about militias and a clause that really matters, declaring that "the right . . . to keep and bear arms shall not be infringed." Many see the right to bear arms as the most important right of all—"the palladium of all the liberties of the republic," as one justice put it in 1833 (a palladium is something that secures). [40]

The Supreme Court has been moving decisively to defend gun rights. In 2008, the Court struck down a District of Columbia rule that restricted guns in people's homes. [41] In 2010, in *McDonald v. Chicago*, the Court finally *incorporated* the Second Amendment. For the first time, the constitutional right to bear arms applied to state and local governments.

The *McDonald* decision seemed to make it more difficult for cities and states to regulate weapons—but in the years since, most state and local restrictions have been upheld. Florida's governor, in the wake of a Parkland High School mass shooting in 2018, signed into law the most significant gun restrictions in that state in decades. [42]

Assess current debates on the Second Amendment

The Bottom Line

» Some critics see the Second Amendment as an outmoded defense of citizen militias.

» Others see it as an important individual right—perhaps even the most important right in the entire Constitution.

» In 2010, the Supreme Court incorporated the right to bear arms as an essential individual right. Since then, however, most state and local restrictions have been upheld.

Guns on Campus

CONCEALED CARRY?

The Second Amendment's ambiguous "right to bear arms" guarantee has been a source of much debate. College campuses historically have enjoyed low homicide rates.[43] However, after a shooting at Virginia Tech in 2007 left thirty-two people dead, political science major Chris Brown founded Students for Concealed Carry to lift bans on campuses. The map shows which states allow concealed carry, which ban it, and which leave it up to the campuses to decide.

THINK ABOUT IT

Which policies have most states adopted on this issue? Do you see trends among the more liberal states of the northeast or the more conservative states of the south?

Do students carrying concealed weapons make your campus safer? Or less safe? Why?

Source: National Conference of State Legislatures

Concealed weapons laws

WA, MT, ND, MN, WI, ME, VT, NH, NY, MA, CT, RI, NJ, DC (passed), MD, OR, ID, SD, IA, MI, PA, NV, WY, NE, IL, IN, OH, WV, VA, CA, UT, CO, KS, MO, KY, TN, NC, AZ, NM, OK, AR, MS, AL, GA, SC, TX, LA, FL, AK, HI

- ■ Concealed weapons banned
- ■ Campuses decide to ban or allow
- ■ Concealed weapons allowed

The Rights of the Accused

The Bill of Rights places special emphasis on protecting people accused of crimes. Four amendments (Four, Five, Six, and Eight) list thirty-one different rights for those who face criminal charges. No other issue gets as much attention. Protecting the accused involves another careful balancing act. On the one hand, the courts must restrain law enforcement and defend the constitutional freedoms that define America. On the other hand, too many curbs on law enforcement might lead to more crime. After vastly expanding the rights of the accused in the 1960s, the courts—in step with Congress, presidents of both parties, and most states—now tilt firmly toward law enforcement. However, American incarceration rates are the world's highest and especially disrupt minority communities. Even as crime rates are low, poor and minority communities face very high incarceration rates.

In this section, we examine the most important (and controversial) protections one at a time. As you read, think about the trade-offs between safe streets and civil liberties. There are solid arguments on both sides of the issue.

The Fourth Amendment: Search and Seizure

The Fourth Amendment protects people from government officials bursting into their houses:

> *The right of the people to be secure in their persons, houses, papers, and effects, against unreasonable searches and seizures, shall not be violated, and no Warrants shall issue, but upon probable cause, supported by Oath or affirmation, and particularly describing the place to be searched, and the persons or things to be seized.*

British officials in the 1770s ransacked people's homes, searching for weapons or smuggled goods. The Fourth Amendment prevents that from happening again. Justice Lewis Brandeis described it "as the right to be left alone—the . . . right most valued by civilized men."[44] The police may not enter a home unless they go before a judge and explain why they suspect that evidence of a crime can be found in a specific place. The judge determines whether there is "probable cause" to issue the warrant. It sounds simple, but there are large gray areas (see Figure 4.1).

The landmark search and seizure case began in 1957 with a tip that Dollree (Dolly) Mapp was hiding a bombing suspect in her apartment. In addition, the police suspected she had illegal gambling paraphernalia. The police knocked at her door, but she refused to let them in. They eventually broke the door down, and when she demanded to see a warrant they waved a piece of paper—not a warrant—in the air. The police searched the apartment and the basement. They never found the bombing suspect or the gambling material, but they did discover a suitcase of pornographic material—which was then illegal. Mapp was convicted on obscenity charges. The Supreme Court threw out the conviction and, in *Mapp v. Ohio* (1961, decided 6–3), devised the **exclusionary rule**:

Exclusionary rule: The ruling that evidence obtained in an illegal search may not be introduced in a trial.

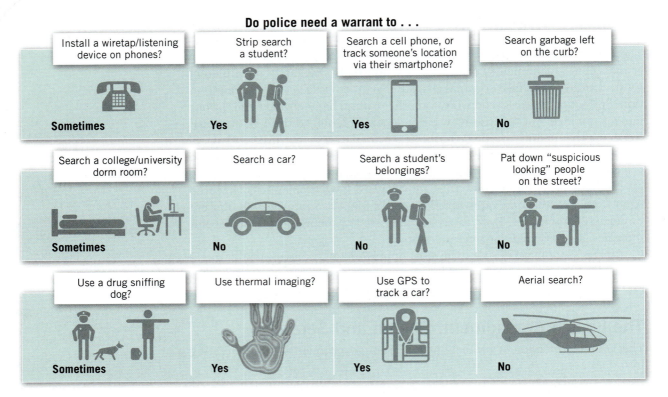

Do police need a warrant to . . .

Install a wiretap/listening device on phones?	Strip search a student?	Search a cell phone, or track someone's location via their smartphone?	Search garbage left on the curb?
Sometimes	Yes	Yes	No
Search a college/university dorm room?	Search a car?	Search a student's belongings?	Pat down "suspicious looking" people on the street?
Sometimes	No	No	No
Use a drug sniffing dog?	Use thermal imaging?	Use GPS to track a car?	Aerial search?
Sometimes	Yes	Yes	No

● **Figure 4.1** *When are search warrants required?*

Evidence obtained in an illegal search may not be introduced in a trial. Even evidence that clearly proves someone is guilty of a crime may not be used if it was improperly obtained.

Twenty years later, President Ronald Reagan (1981–1989) urged both Congress and the courts to abolish the rule. Supreme Court Chief Justice John Roberts, then a young Justice Department attorney, wrote the memos supporting Reagan's criticism. During the Reagan years, the courts began making exceptions to the exclusionary rule. For example, in 1984 police arrested Alberto Leon when they discovered a large quantity of illegal drugs in his possession. Their warrant had expired but the Supreme Court made a "good faith" exception and permitted the drugs to be introduced as evidence.[45] By 2009, Justice Roberts wrote (in a 5–4 opinion) that there was no need to exclude evidence if the police violated a suspect's Fourth Amendment rights because of "isolated negligence."[46]

In 2011, the Supreme Court crossed an important threshold. It permitted officers to break into a house without a warrant. The officers in the case knocked, identified themselves, and heard movements that sounded like the destruction of evidence of drug use. The only dissenter, Justice Ruth Bader Ginsburg, wrote that the ruling would seriously curtail the use of warrants by police. Writing for the majority, Justice Samuel Alito took a hard line. Residents who "attempt to destroy evidence have only themselves to blame."

In 2016, the Court ruled 6–3, that evidence would have to be excluded "if there were flagrant police misconduct." In short, the courts have loosened—but not eliminated—the exclusionary rule.[47]

The Fifth Amendment: Rights at Trials

The Fifth Amendment lists a long series of rights focused largely on criminal trials. Consider them one clause at a time.

> *No person shall be held to answer for a capital, or otherwise infamous crime, unless on . . . indictment of a Grand Jury.*

Before the government can prosecute, it must persuade a jury. A **grand jury** does not decide on guilt or innocence, only on whether there is enough evidence for the case to go to trial. The grand jury meets secretly and hears only from the prosecutor, so, as one New York judge once quipped, a decent prosecutor should be able to get a grand jury to "indict a ham sandwich."[48]

Grand jury: A jury that does not decide on guilt or innocence but only on whether there is enough evidence for the case to go to trial.

> *Nor shall any person be subject for the same offense to be twice put in jeopardy of life or limb.*

An individual cannot face **double jeopardy**, or be tried twice for the same offense. ("Jeopardy of life and limb" refers to the old colonial practice of punishing people by lopping off an ear or damaging other limbs.) Without this provision, the government could simply keep trying people over and over.

Despite this prohibition, individuals sometimes face multiple trials. They can be tried on different charges, tried in federal court after being acquitted in state court, and—if they are acquitted on criminal charges—they can be sued for damages. In a famous case, former football star O. J. Simpson was acquitted of murdering his wife and her companion, only to lose a civil judgment for damages to the victims' families.

Double jeopardy: The principle that an individual cannot be tried twice for the same offense.

> *Nor shall be compelled in any criminal case to be a witness against himself.*

The Constitution aimed to protect citizens from torture and coerced confessions. The liberal Warren Court tried to put teeth into this right by requiring police officers to inform suspects that they have the right to remain silent, now known as the **Miranda warnings** (*Miranda v. Arizona*, 1966). The Court ruled that any evidence acquired before the warning could not be admissible in court. The ruling created an enormous outcry. Richard Nixon used *Miranda* in the 1968 presidential campaign as evidence that the United States had grown "soft on crime." Congress tried to pass a law to get around the ruling, which the Court eventually struck down.[49]

Over the past forty years, the courts have limited the *Miranda* rights—permitting confessions made to a police officer posing as another inmate (1990), carving out an exception for public safety (1984), and limiting the rules when defendants take the stand in their own defense (1970).[50]

Miranda warnings: A set of rights that police officers are required to inform suspects of, including the right to remain silent.

The controversy subsided long ago and Miranda warnings have become "part of the national culture" as Chief Justice William Rehnquist once put it. Every TV cop show ends with the police nabbing the criminal while intoning, "You have the right to remain silent." Some defense lawyers claim, half seriously, the phrase is now so familiar that what defendants actually hear is, "We've caught you, and you're in big trouble now."

The Sixth Amendment: The Right to Counsel

The Sixth Amendment guarantees a speedy and public trial decided by an impartial jury. It includes another important provision, the right to counsel:

> *In all criminal prosecutions, the accused shall . . . have the assistance of counsel for his defense.*

The Supreme Court weighed in on the issue in an explosive case, known as the trial of the Scottsboro Boys. In 1931, nine young African American men, riding a freight train in Alabama, were accused of raping two white women. Despite evidence that the charges were false (one woman immediately recanted), angry mobs gathered, and eight of the young men were rushed through trials and condemned to death. In *Powell v. Alabama* (1932), the Court ruled that, at least in a capital case (a case that could end in the death penalty), the defendants are entitled to lawyers who must be given enough time to meet with their clients and prepare their case. The Scottsboro case was a civil rights breakthrough for another reason: None of the African Americans unfairly accused of raping a white woman was executed—though seven of the nine languished in jail for years.

In 1963, the Court expanded the right to counsel to all felony cases. Clarence Gideon, a Florida drifter, was allegedly caught breaking into a poolroom where he had stolen beer, soft drinks, and the change out of the jukebox. When he came to trial, he demanded a lawyer, but the Florida court denied the request. Gideon was convicted and sentenced to five years, but from his jail cell, working with legal texts, he scrawled an appeal. "Something astonishing . . . happened," wrote Anthony Lewis in a book on the case. "This loser's plea made it all the way to the Supreme Court." In *Gideon v. Wainwright* (1963), the Supreme Court ruled that the Sixth Amendment supported his claim and that the state must provide a lawyer to defend those who cannot afford one. With a competent lawyer, Gideon was

● The Scottsboro Boys, with their attorney Samuel Leibowitz, under guard by the state.

acquitted. Attorney General Robert Kennedy commented, "An obscure Florida convict had . . . changed . . . the whole course of American legal history."[51] A network of public defenders spread across the country.

In 2012, the Court dramatically increased the scope of the right to competent counsel by ruling that defendants have a constitutional right to effective attorneys during plea-bargain negotiations (in a 5–4 ruling). Today, almost all federal cases (97%) and most state felony charges (94%) involve a plea bargain, in which the defendant pleads guilty in exchange for a lighter sentence without actually going through a formal trial. With American courts clogged by arrest backlogs, this is one way to get the cases through the system.[52]

In practice, the right to counsel has grown increasingly difficult to maintain. The public is reluctant to spend tax revenues on lawyers who defend poor men and women accused of crimes. Public defenders face huge caseloads with small salaries—a Department of Justice study reported that legal aid attorneys handle as many as 900 felony cases per year.[53] At the state level, the caseload is also overwhelming. The forty-nine public defenders in Rhode Island handled 15,000 cases in 2017.[54] For all the problems, however, publicly funded criminal defense remains an essential—if endangered—part of civil liberty and American justice.

The Eighth Amendment: The Death Penalty

The Eighth Amendment introduces the question of capital punishment.

Cruel and unusual punishment . . . shall not be . . . inflicted.

Is execution cruel and unusual punishment? Around the world, 101 nations have abolished the death penalty—including all of Western Europe, where it is considered a violation of human rights. In contrast, the United States executed twenty-three people in 2017 and 366 in the last decade. Although the number of executions has been falling steadily, more than 2,800 men and women have been sentenced to capital punishment and are waiting on death row (Figure 4.2). Public support for the death penalty has fallen below 50 percent and is now at a 44-year low.

Proponents of the death penalty argue that some crimes are so terrible that justice demands capital punishment. It brings closure to grieving families. It may deter future murders (although there is no definitive evidence one way or the other). Moreover, they argue, some criminals are so dangerous that they should be executed to protect other prisoners, prison officials, and the general public.

Opponents respond that killing people is immoral and that no government should be given the power to "play God." Because social systems are imperfect, some, perhaps many, innocent people will be executed. The system is tilted against African Americans; blacks make up 12 percent of the population but, from year to year between a quarter and a half of those who are executed. In 2018, 41 percent of the inmates on death row were African American and another 13 percent were Latinos. Repeated studies have shown that in capital

Executions by State

States that executed in 2017-18
States that executed in the last five years
No executions in the last five years

SD (1)
NE (1)
OH (3)
VA (2)
MO (1)
TN (3)
AR (4)
AL (5)
GA (3)
TX (20)
FL (4)
AZ
DC (none)

● **Figure 4.2** *Map of executions in the United States (Death Penalty Information Center).*

cases, the race of the victim is a crucial matter—members of minority groups accused of murdering white people are the most likely to receive the death penalty.[55]

In 1972, the Supreme Court halted all executions, arguing that state laws were so vague that similar cases produced different outcomes. "The death standards are cruel and unusual," wrote Justice Potter Stewart in *Furman v. Georgia*, "the same way that being struck by lightning is cruel and unusual"—meaning that death sentences seemed to be meted out randomly. Thirty-five states drafted new capital punishment laws using *Furman* as a guide. In 1976, the Court permitted executions to go forward where state statutes included clear criteria to guide judge and jury in weighing death sentences. However, nearly three-fourths of all executions since 1976 have taken place in seven states (all in the south).[56]

Beginning in 1992, a network of law students and their professors began to use DNA evidence to review capital cases. Known as the "Innocence Project," they have documented false convictions of more than 354 inmates (161 of whom were convicted of capital crimes). All those exonerated have now been released.[57]

The Court has imposed additional limits on the death penalty. It has ruled that it is "cruel and unusual" to execute people convicted of crimes other than murder, striking down five state laws that allowed execution for child rape (2008). It has forbidden the execution of mentally ill individuals (2002) and of juvenile offenders (2005). In a much-discussed case, however, the Court ruled that lethal injections did not constitute cruel and unusual punishment despite the claim that they caused "an intolerable risk of pain" (2007).[58]

The Bottom Line

» The Bill of Rights places special emphasis on the rights of those accused of crimes. Even so, American incarceration rates are the highest in the world.

» The police may not search or seize without a warrant (with minor exceptions); they must inform suspects of their right to remain silent; the accused have a right to legal counsel. The courts have widened the legal right but it is often limited by underfunded public defenders.

» Under current interpretation, capital punishment is not considered "cruel and unusual punishment." However, the number of executions has been falling.

» Between 1962 and 1968, the Supreme Court vastly expanded the rights of the accused. Recent Court decisions have tilted the balance back toward law enforcement.

Terrorism, Non-Citizens, and Civil Liberties

After the terrorist attacks on September 11, 2001, Congress passed the **USA Patriot Act**. In the fear and emotion of the terrible moment, few criticized the legislation. The act enhanced security by removing restrictions on law enforcement. Removing restrictions, however, means limiting rights. The Patriot Act, the broader campaign against terrorism, and continued terrorism around the world have revived a long-standing national debate: How do we balance civil liberties and public safety?

USA Patriot Act: Legislation that sought to enhance national security passed in the aftermath of the September 11, 2001, attacks.

Contacts with Forbidden Groups

The federal government enhanced rules that bar Americans from offering aid to terrorist organizations. Although the law forbids aiding terrorist organizations, expressing general support for such an organization is protected speech.

Drawing the line between public safety and free speech remains hotly contested. For now, U.S. courts permit the government to prosecute web postings if they provide funding or other specialized assistance to terrorist groups. What do you think? Is there an obvious balance between protecting free speech and fighting terrorism?

Surveillance

Domestic surveillance requires a warrant. To prevent terror attacks, however, the Bush, Obama, and Trump administrations have all permitted the NSA to conduct international surveillance without a search warrant. Major controversy erupted in 2013 around the Snowden leaks described earlier in this chapter.

Snowden revealed that the NSA has been collecting bulk data—over a trillion pieces of information—on phone calls, computer searches, texts, and more. The phone data include the caller, receiver, date and time of the call, and length of the call—but not a transcript of the conversation itself. Although the revelations created an uproar and calls for reform, Congress eventually reauthorized the surveillance program for six years without major new protections.[59]

The Rights of Non-Citizens

The war on terror prompted many questions around a more general question: What are the constitutional rights of non-citizens? A long body of case law, going back to the 19th century, extends most basic Constitutional

● *Terrorist attacks, such as the San Bernardino shootings, raise the question of how to balance national security with privacy rights.*

rights to non-citizens—if someone is stopped by the police, for example, they have the same Miranda rights whether they are citizens, legal immigrants, or people without documentation. State governments may not pass laws that single out immigrants and discriminate against them.

There is one major difference, however: Immigration laws apply to non-citizens and, in that context, the procedural standards are different. There are still some rights—the right to remain silent and the right to legal counsel—but they are far more restricted.

The Trump administration's vigorous push against undocumented individuals from certain countries puts this issue in a spotlight and raises a still more complicated issue: How does the Constitution apply to immigrants not yet in the United States (standing before a customs agent at the airport, for example)? The courts will be grappling with that question for a long time to come.

 **The Bottom Line**

» The response to 9/11 and subsequent terror attacks created a new debate about the balance between civil liberties and public safety.

» With the Snowden revelations, controversy arose about the NSA data collection of phone records and Internet surveillance. Although Congress passed legislation with some limits after the revelations, in 2018, Congress reauthorized the surveillance without major new protections.

» Most Constitutional rights apply to non-citizens. However, they are also ruled by immigration laws which offer more limited rights.

🛈 Conclusion: The Dilemma of Civil Liberties

How should the government balance its duty to keep the public safe, or to uphold public moral standards, with its responsibility to protect civil liberties? This is one of the most important issues facing American democracy. If we tilt too far toward combating terrorism or outlawing practices considered socially unacceptable, Americans lose the liberties that have defined the nation since 1776. If we tilt too far the other way, the nation may be vulnerable to attacks or lose its moral core. Getting the balance right is a major challenge facing Americans today. The courts take the lead in protecting rights, but elected public officials define the policies that the courts are weighing. President Trump has been particularly outspoken on these issues. Ultimately, that puts the balance between communal needs and individual rights in the hands of the voters.

Isn't that exactly where it belongs? No. Recall the Supreme Court's judgment in 1943 when it reversed its earlier decision and protected the Jehovah's Witnesses: "The very purpose of a Bill of Rights was to withdraw certain subjects from the vicissitudes of political controversy, to place them beyond the reach of majorities and officials and to establish them as legal principles to be applied by the courts."[60] A core point of civil liberties is to protect the rights of individuals—even if it means overruling the majority of the country.

CHAPTER SUMMARY

🟢 Civil liberties are the limits we put on governing bodies (and the majorities that elect them) so that individuals can exercise their rights and freedom. Disputes are usually resolved by the courts and guided by the Bill of Rights.

🟢 The Bill of Rights did not apply to the states until the Fourteenth Amendment required that *no state* could deprive any citizen of life, liberty, or property.

🟢 The Supreme Court applied the Bill of Rights to the states one right at a time between 1897 (no taking property without compensation) and 2010 (the right to bear arms). The process is known as incorporation.

🟢 The Court discovered a right to privacy implicit (in the shadows) in the First, Third,

Fourth, Fifth, and Ninth Amendments. The Court applied the right to privacy to strike down laws banning abortion. In *Roe v. Wade* the Court issued a rule prohibiting states from interfering during the first trimester. In *Planned Parenthood v. Casey*, the Court replaced the rule (which applies in all cases) with a standard (that permits some exceptions) forbidding laws that put "an undue burden" on the right to privacy. The Court extended privacy rights to same-sex couples by striking down antisodomy laws in 2003 and bans on same-sex marriage in 2015.

🟢 The Constitution bans government from establishing (or favoring) a religion. In one view, this means separating church and state. For many years, the three-part Lemon test guided judicial decisions in cases involving religion.

Check your understanding of Chapter 4.

A more recent view requires simply that government not promote one religious view over another.

 The Constitution also forbids government from interfering with religious practice (the free exercise clause). The courts traditionally asked if the government had a compelling interest for imposing a burden—the Sherbert test. In 1990, the court shifted and required only that the government action be neutral and apply to everyone. Congress, state governments, and religious groups pushed back and the courts have, once again, returned to the traditional Sherbert test.

Need to review key ideas in greater depth? Click here.

Free speech is crucial to democracy, and the Court gives it a privileged position—even against angry public opposition to flag burning, cross burning, or homophobic displays at military funerals. Free speech can be curtailed if it poses a "clear and present danger." Today, the Court requires the danger to be both imminent and likely to occur. There are limits to free speech involving fighting words, student speech, commercial speech, and obscenity.

Some critics see the Second Amendment as an outmoded defense of citizen militias. Others see the right to bear arms as an important individual right—perhaps the most important liberty in the Constitution. In 2010, the Supreme Court ruled it an essential constitutional right.

The Bill of Rights places special emphasis on the civil liberties of those accused of crimes. Even so, American incarceration rates are the highest in the world. The police may not search or seize without a warrant, they must inform suspects of their right to remain silent, and the accused have a right to legal counsel. Under current interpretation, capital punishment is not considered "cruel and unusual punishment—but public opinion appears to be slowly changing."

Terror attacks created a new debate about the balance between civil liberties and public safety.

Most constitutional rights apply to noncitizens. However, they also are ruled by immigration laws that offer more limited rights.

KEY TERMS

Flashcard review.

Accommodation, p. 116
Civil liberties, p. 106
Civil rights, p. 108
Clear and present danger, p. 120
Double jeopardy, p. 131
Establishment clause, p. 115

Exclusionary rule, p. 129
Fighting words, p. 122
Free exercise clause, p. 115
Grand jury, p. 131
Hate speech, p. 122
Judicial rule, p. 114
Judicial standard, p. 114

Miranda warnings, p. 131
Prior restraint, p. 124
Selective incorporation, p. 109
Strict separation, p. 116
Symbolic expression, p. 121
Miller test, p. 125
USA Patriot Act, p. 135

STUDY QUESTIONS

1. What are civil liberties? How are they different from civil rights?

2. In *Barron v. Baltimore*, the Supreme Court ruled that the Fifth Amendment did not

protect a landowner if the state took his property. Why?

3. Describe how the Bill of Rights was applied to the state governments. First, describe the

constitutional amendment that directly ad-dressed the states. Then, describe the process of incorporation by which the Supreme Court applied the Bill of Rights to the states.

4. Describe how the Supreme Court declared the right to privacy. Discuss the case from a pragmatist's and an originalist's perspective. Would you vote to maintain the right to pri-vacy? Or to overrule the precedent established in the *Griswold* case? Explain your reasoning.

5. Describe the three-part Lemon test for de-termining whether a state action violates the establishment clause. The late Justice Scalia was highly critical of the Lemon test. What was his view? Do you agree with it or not? Explain why.

6. Sometimes the Court permits a racist to burn a cross. Sometimes it forbids it. Explain the reasoning in each case. Do you agree

with the Court's distinction or would you rule differently?

7. There are two interpretations of the Second Amendment right to bear arms. Describe each. Which do you support? Why?

8. The Supreme Court gives free speech a "privileged position" among the rights in the Bill of Rights. What does that mean? How does the Court justify that position?

9. Feminist scholars argue that privileging free speech in pornography cases actually under-mines free speech. What is their argument? Do you agree or disagree? Explain why.

10. How does the NSA surveillance raise ques-tions about the balance between public safety and civil liberties? How do you think about balancing civil liberties with protection against terrorism? If you had to emphasize one goal more than the other, which would you emphasize? Why?

 Go to **www.oup.com/us/Morone** to find quizzes, flash cards, simulations, tutorials, videos, and other study tools.

5

The Struggle for Civil Rights

IN AUGUST 2017, HUNDREDS of white supremacists poured into Charlottesville, Virginia, to protest the city's decision to remove a statue of Confederate General Robert E. Lee. On Friday night, holding torches, they marched across the beautiful University of Virginia campus and chanted "you will not replace us," "Jews will not replace us," "white lives matter," and "blood and soil"—a Nazi slogan. Counterprotesters greeted them with cries of "No Nazis! No KKK! No fascist USA!" and "black lives matter." Fights erupted. Police arrived, declared the assembly unlawful, and shut it down.

The next day, a larger group of white supremacists and neo-Nazis, some carrying shields, pikes, and rifles, marched toward the statue of Lee in Emancipation Park. Members of the college community, gathering in counterprotest, were shocked to face the mass bigotry. Thirty ministers locked arms in prayer at the entrance to the park in an attempt to keep the protesters out. As fights flared up amid more taunting, the police separated demonstrators and counterdemonstrators.[1]

Then a sad day turned tragic. One of the white supremacists drove his car into the crowd that had come to stand up against racism. Nineteen were injured and 32 year-old Heather Heyer lay dead.[2] Americans were stunned. President Trump sparked an uproar when he refused to condemn the Nazis, saying "there were good people on both sides." Neo-Nazi websites hailed his reaction while Republican and Democratic leaders denounced the president.[3] Suddenly, the ugliest features of America's racial past seemed to have leapt into the present.

Who are we? We are a profoundly diverse nation, founded on the idea that all people are "created equal" and "endowed" with "unalienable rights" including "life, liberty and the pursuit of happiness." We are also a nation that often fails to live up to its noble founding vision.

Civil rights are the freedom to fully participate in the life of the community—to vote in elections, to enjoy public facilities such as parks, and to take full advantage of economic opportunities such as good jobs. People face discrimination when they are denied rights and opportunities

● White supremacists and neo-Nazis marched on Charlottesville, Virginia, clashing with Antifa, a violent left-wing group, and local counterprotesters. These events shocked the nation.

In this chapter, you will:

● Explore the seven steps to winning civil rights in the United States.

● Review the African American experience that set the pattern for civil rights.

● Assess women's quest for economic and political rights.

● Examine the political experience of Hispanics, Asians, and Native Americans.

● Consider the rights of other groups, including disabled people, same-sex partners, and transgender individuals.

Civil rights: The freedom to participate in the full life of the community—to vote, use public facilities, and exercise equal economic opportunity.

because of their race, gender, ethnicity, religion, disabilities, age, or other personal characteristics. Once citizens have won their rights, public attention shifts to protecting them. We covered those protections—known as civil liberties—in Chapter 4. The long battle to win civil rights is perhaps the most powerful story in American history. It reveals the deepest truths about the United States and its values. It tells us who we are—and who we strive to be.

We can view the history of civil rights in two different ways. Some observers see a steady march toward a deeper and richer equality. Sixty years ago, white supremacists would not have faced so many counterprotesters. African Americans were still restricted from voting in many southern states, and prestigious professions were closed to them. Today African Americans are CEOs of Fortune 500 companies, head elite academic institutions—and one recently served two terms as U.S. president. Forty years ago, only one woman in American history had won a U.S. Senate seat. Today, the Senate includes 24 women, and the U.S House more than 100, both the most in history. From this perspective, the American promise marches relentlessly on.[4]

Other observers, however, warn that there is nothing inevitable about winning rights. Sometimes rights expand, sometimes they contract. Yes, Asians won full rights, but Native Americans did not. African Americans scaled the old barriers, but today they still face the daily stress of racism. They are more likely to live in poverty or face jail time. There is nothing inevitable about American equality, say proponents of this perspective, and citizens should never take it for granted.[5]

As you read this chapter, ask which view seems more accurate to you: Has the United States advanced consistently toward greater civil rights for all? Or has the progress been unsteady? Whatever your answer, continue to ask: What can and should we do to ensure fair treatment for everyone?

Watch how the nation responded to the events in Charlottesville.

Winning Rights: The Political Process

How does a group win political rights? Each civil rights campaign has its own unique history. However, the efforts usually involve the following stages—not necessarily in this order.

Seven Steps to Political Equality

1. *A group defines itself.* Discrimination usually stretches back through time and seeps into the way the powerful view others: whites ruled blacks, men took responsibility for "the weaker sex," Indians were "savages," society pitied the disabled, and psychiatrists defined

BY THE NUMBERS
Civil Rights

Number of black mayors in 1965	**0**
Number of black mayors in 2018	**at least 500**[6]
Percentage of southern students who attended integrated schools 8 years after *Brown v. Board of Education* (ruling in 1954)	**1**
Percentage of southern students who attended integrated schools 8 years after the passage of the Civil Rights Act of 1964	**91**
Percentage of white and black Americans who were poor in 1959	**18, 55**[7]
Percentage of white, black, and Hispanic Americans, respectively, who are poor today	**8.7, 21, 18**
Number of Hispanic members of Congress in 1990, 2000, 2019	**10, 18, 44**
Year the Supreme Court struck down laws forbidding marriage between blacks and whites	**1968**
Percentages of whites, blacks, Hispanics, and Asians, respectively, married to a member of a different race today	**11, 18, 27, 28**[8]
Percentage of whites, Latinos, and blacks, respectively, who report "a great deal" or "a fair amount" of confidence in the police	**61, 45, 30**[9]

How far have we come in achieving civil rights for all people? How far do we have to go?

homosexuality as an illness. In the first step toward civil rights, a group embraces its shared identity and redefines itself as a victim of discrimination. Groups usually reject their old, often demeaning labels and find a new name: Negroes, Miss, queers, and cripples became African Americans, Ms., LGBTQ individuals, and persons with disabilities.

2. *The group challenges society.* The next step involves entering the political arena and demanding rights. Civil rights campaigns often go beyond normal politics and include marches, demonstrations, creative protests (such as kneel-ins before segregated churches), and even riots.

3. *The stories change.* Civil rights always involve a contest over the stories that a society tells about a group. Why does the United States discriminate against people in the first place? Because the majority portrays them as dangerous, inferior, or helpless. Winning rights requires changing the story. As you read about efforts to secure rights—past and present—be alert to the many different stories we tell about the groups in our society.

4. *Federalism comes into play.* Civil rights politics splashes across local, state, and federal governments. Because many minority groups are concentrated in certain states and regions, discrimination often begins on the local level. Furthermore, state and local officials control many of the policies that influence civil rights: education, law enforcement, and voting rules. In other cases, states and localities first introduce reforms: Before the Nineteenth Amendment established women's suffrage nationally, women won voting rights in western states.

● *Lucretia Mott, who helped organize the Seneca Falls convention for women's rights, is attacked by an angry mob. Women who challenged their own subordination faced violence in the nineteenth century.*

5. *The executive branch often breaks the ice.* Presidents can issue executive orders (rules with the force of law that do not require congressional approval) that create opportunities and momentum for a civil rights campaign. President Truman desegregated the U.S. military in 1948 and President Obama extended protections for gender identity in 2014.

6. *Congress legislates a blockbuster.* Typically, it is Congress that passes great changes, which finally secure civil rights that echo through history. The Fourteenth Amendment to the Constitution, ratified in 1868, still dominates every effort to win rights. The Civil Rights Act of 1964 profoundly changed civil rights in the United States.

7. *It all ends up in court.* The courts are the ultimate arbiters of civil rights. Individuals and groups challenge laws they consider unjust. The courts consider what the Constitution requires of Americans and weigh the laws, rules, regulations, and private actions for what is permissible and what is not.

Notice how many moving parts there are in the reform process. We have already seen why this is so: American government is unusually fragmented, marked by overlapping actors and institutions all balancing one another. That makes it difficult to change deep social norms—such as racial or gender discrimination. Reformers have to win over many different power centers—state legislatures, Congress, governors, the judiciary, the media, and the public.

How the Courts Review Cases

Because civil rights generally end up in court, the judicial framework is important. The courts use three categories for determining whether acts violate "the equal protection of the laws" guaranteed by the Fourteenth Amendment.

Suspect Categories. Any legislation involving *race, ethnicity, religion,* or *alienage (immigration status)* faces **strict scrutiny**. The Supreme Court is primed to strike down any law that singles out a race or ethnicity or religion unless there is a strong reason for doing so. The Court will ask: Does the government have a *compelling government interest* in singling out a race or an ethnicity?

> **Strict scrutiny:** The standard by which courts judge any legislation that singles out race or ethnicity.

Quasi-Suspect Categories. In 1976, women's advocates won a special category for gender cases: Quasi-Suspect. Any legislation—federal, state, or local—that introduces sex-based categories has to rest on an *important state purpose*. This is not as strong a test as a *compelling* interest. But it is still a powerful requirement, one that can touch many aspects of politics, economics, and society. For example, in 1996 the Court ruled that excluding women from the Virginia Military Institute (VMI), a state funded school, did not serve an important state purpose. VMI had to open its doors to women cadets or forgo state funding.

How does the 14th Amendment apply to different groups?

Nonsuspect Categories. Other categories do not face special scrutiny—at least not yet. Legislation based on age, sexual orientation, gender identity, or physical handicaps simply has to have some rational connection between the legislation and a legitimate government purpose. This is the weakest test, but it can still bar discrimination. Using this test, for example, the Court ruled that there was no rational basis for a Colorado constitutional amendment that forbade any protection for gays and lesbians.[10]

This threefold division is the framework for civil rights law. As with almost everything else in American government, politics produced these categories. Groups argued, lobbied, demonstrated, and sued to win stricter scrutiny.

● *A civil rights effort helped lift the ban on women in combat in 2013. Since 2016, women can perform all combat jobs—and can join the Navy SEALs.*

The Bottom Line

» The battle for civil rights generally includes seven characteristics. The group seeking rights must define itself, challenge society, and change the way it is viewed. The contest for rights spills across federalism and all three branches of government and involves states, the executive, Congress, and the courts.

» Courts interpret charges of discrimination using three standards: suspect, quasi-suspect, and nonsuspect.

Race and Civil Rights: Revolt Against Slavery

On a hot summer day in Ferguson, Missouri, a police officer confronted a black man accused of stealing some cigarillos from a convenience store. Reports differ about what happened next but there is no doubt how it ended: Officer Darren Wilson fired twelve bullets at Michael Brown and his body lay bleeding on the street for four hours. Vigils soon turned to protests and then into a movement: "Black Lives Matter."

A stunning series of images quickly flashed before the public: Eric Garner, wrestled to the ground on Staten Island, New York, and choked to death as he gasped, "I can't breathe." In Baltimore, Maryland, police arrested Freddie Gray and chained his legs in the back of a police wagon; a week later he was dead of a severed spinal column. In Baton Rouge, Louisiana, Alton Sterling was pinned to the ground for illegally selling CDs outside a convenience store—and shot to death. As the death toll of unarmed black people swelled, the Black Lives Matter movement grew. Beneath the protests lay a profound message: 150 years after slavery, many Americans do not feel fully equal and empowered.

African Americans came to America chained in the holds of slave ships, sold at auction, separated from their families, and killed for challenging their oppressors. After emancipation, leaders of the black community were systematically murdered by the thousands. Over time, people of color faced lynching, especially if they were successful; voting restrictions that almost completely disenfranchised them in the south; discrimination in the north; and restricted access to housing, schools, hospitals, hotels, and restaurants, and the list goes on.

Yet African Americans constantly fought against bias and furnished the United States with many of its stars in science, art, literature, politics, medicine, sports, and entertainment. In fighting injustice, African Americans developed the tactics that other groups would use in their own battles for civil rights; black movements forged the laws, amendments, and judicial doctrines that opened the door to civil rights across society. The black quest for freedom included two powerful crusades, one in the nineteenth century and one in the twentieth.

The Clash over Slavery

Slaves were permitted to have churches, and in the early nineteenth century, religion offered leadership, organization, and a powerful message. By the middle of the nineteenth century, the dream of freedom had become a kind of religious faith in the slave quarters.[11] Three additional forces precipitated a national crisis over slavery: a moral crusade for abolition, economic interests, and political calculations.

Abolition.   An **abolition** movement rose up, branded slavery sinful, and demanded its immediate end. The abolitionists were unusually diverse for the time; the movement's leadership included women and people of color (most famously, Frederick Douglas). It was small and considered radical, but its writings created a furious reaction. Many Americans—in the south and the north—feared the abolitionists would incite the slaves to rebellion. Most people preferred to ignore the issue.

Economics.   As the United States spread west, every new settlement prompted the same question—would it be slave or free? Northerners opposed slavery on the frontier for moral reasons as well as economic ones—the spread of slavery threatened their opportunity to settle in western lands. Southerners, however, insisted that slavery needed to spread into new states to survive. Because the federal government controlled territories until they became states, the question—slave or free?—constantly haunted Congress.

Politics.   Every time a territory applied for statehood it called into question the political balance between slave states and free states in Congress. Because every state has two senators, an equal number of free and slave states permitted the South to defend its "peculiar institution." The slaves (who counted as three-fifths of a person for the purposes of representation, as we saw in Chapter 2) gave southern states an additional thirty-six seats in the House of Representatives.

The Senate managed to negotiate the tensions with a series of shaky compromises. The **Missouri Compromise** of 1820 drew a line through the Louisiana Territory (see Figure 5.1). All new states and territories north of the line, except Missouri would be free; everything south of the line would be open to slavery. In 1845, as Americans moved west, Congress extended the line to include Texas. In 1850, California wanted to enter the Union, but extending the old line to the coast would split the new state—half slave and half free. The solution was another compromise, the **Compromise of 1850**, which turned the decision over to residents of the territories.

Abolition: A nineteenth-century movement demanding an immediate and unconditional end to slavery.

Missouri Compromise: An agreement to open southern territories west of the Mississippi to slavery while closing northern territories to slavery.

Compromise of 1850: A complicated compromise over slavery that permitted territories to vote on whether they would be slave or free and permitted California to enter as a free state. It also included a strict fugitive slave law forcing northerners to return black men and women into bondage, which was hugely controversial for it forced people in free states to assist slaveholders.

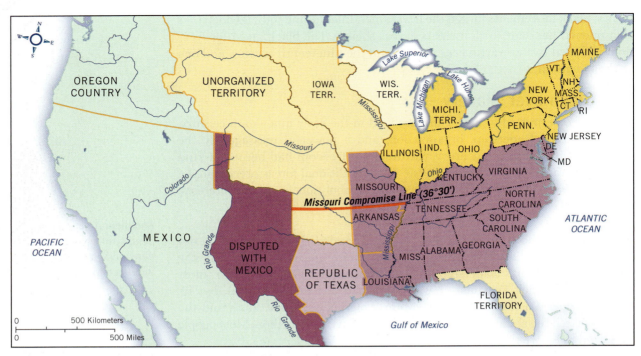

● **Figure 5.1** *The Missouri Compromise—all new American territory below the line would permit slavery; all above (except Missouri) would be free.*

Dred Scott v. Sandford

In 1857, the Supreme Court stepped in with a shattering decision that upset all the careful compromises. A slave named Dred Scott sued for freedom. He argued that he had been taken to live in a free territory before returning to Missouri and that, as a result, he should be free. Chief Justice Roger Taney ruled that he was not free because neither the territories nor the federal government had the power to limit slavery or give a black man rights. What about the Missouri Compromise? Unconstitutional, ruled Taney. Popular sovereignty? Also unconstitutional. The ***Dred Scott v. Sandford*** decision ruled that no territory could restrict slavery, much less elevate blacks to citizenship.

The decision created an uproar and three years later, in 1860, Abraham Lincoln ran for the presidency on a platform that flatly opposed the extension of slavery into any territories. When Lincoln won, southern states began withdrawing from the United States and the Civil War erupted. In the four years from 1861 to 1865, more people lost their lives than in all the other American wars combined. However, from the blood and ashes arose a second American founding.

Dred Scott v. Sandford:
A landmark Supreme Court decision holding that black men could not be citizens under the Constitution of the United States. It created a national uproar.

The Second American Founding: A New Birth of Freedom?

In his Gettysburg Address, President Lincoln announced "a new birth of freedom" and declared that the United States had been "conceived in liberty and dedicated to the proposition that all men are created equal." Lincoln expressed a view of self-government that the Declaration had not fully embraced and the Constitution had rejected: "government of the people, by the people, for the people."[12] With this simple declaration, Lincoln rewrote the American idea of freedom.

Lincoln's bold innovation was institutionalized in four documents. In 1863, Lincoln's **Emancipation Proclamation** freed the slaves—but only in areas that were still rebelling. Ironically, Lincoln freed the slaves in the states where he had no power to enforce his decree. The slaves themselves, however, bolted by the thousands toward the Union army and transformed it, as one historian wrote, into "a reluctant dragon of emancipation." When the Civil War was finally over, Congress wrote three "Civil War amendments" that gave full legal force to Lincoln's new birth of freedom.[13]

● During the Civil War some 200,000 African Americans, most of them former slaves, fought for the Union—a crucial factor in the war of attrition with terribly high casualties on both sides.

The *Thirteenth Amendment* (ratified in 1865) abolished slavery.

The *Fourteenth Amendment* (1868) made anyone born in the United States, including former slaves, a U.S. citizen. We have already seen the most crucial passage of the Fourteenth Amendment, for it is at the heart of American civil liberties (described in Chapter 4): *No state shall "deprive any person of life, liberty or property without due process of law; nor deny to any person . . . the equal protection of the laws."*

Through this language, as we saw in Chapter 4, the Fourteenth Amendment applied the federal Constitution and the Bill of Rights to the states. The key phrase—the **equal protection of the laws**—would become a core legal weapon in the battle for civil rights. It might be the single most important addition to the Constitution in the last two hundred years. It forbids any law designed to harm a group.

The *Fifteenth Amendment* (ratified in 1870) guarantees that voting rights "shall not be denied . . . on account of race, color, or previous condition of servitude." Do you notice what is not mentioned? Gender. Women had reasoned that because they were citizens, their right to vote should not be "denied or abridged," but the Supreme Court rejected this interpretation in 1875.

Freedom Fails

What happened to the former slaves? The era after the Civil War began with soaring hopes—and ended bitterly. Black families—torn apart during slavery—joyously reunited. African Americans formed communities, organized churches, voted, entered politics, and demanded respect from their former owners. Two African Americans were elected to the U.S. Senate and twenty-one to the House of Representatives. However, black empowerment

Emancipation Proclamation: An executive order issued by President Abraham Lincoln that declared the slaves in all rebel states free.

Equal protection of the laws: The landmark phrase in the Fourteenth Amendment that requires equal treatment for all citizens.

met fierce resistance. Some whites were outraged when the freedmen no longer stepped aside on the sidewalks; many whites faced economic hardship, even ruin, after war ravaged their land and their labor force disappeared.

Southern state and local governments reacted by passing *black codes*. These regulations tied blacks to the land, restricted their movements, and stripped them of rights such as voting, owning guns, or buying property. Legal restrictions were backed up by the violent Ku Klux Klan (KKK), which sought to prevent them from exercising their new rights by intimidating former slaves and killing rising black leaders.

For a time, Congress supported the former slaves. In an effort known as **Reconstruction**, it tried to rebuild the South around a vision of racial justice. Congress organized a Freedmen's Bureau to assist the former slaves. The Civil Rights Act of 1866 guaranteed African Americans the same property rights as white Americans; the Civil Rights Act of 1875 limited private racial discrimination in hotels, restaurants, and theaters.

However, dreams of racial equality began to slip away. The North, weary of the conflict, withdrew the army from the South in 1877. Congress repealed the laws that implemented the Civil War amendments; no national mechanism was left to enforce "the equal protection of the laws." In the Civil Rights Cases of 1883, the Supreme Court struck down the Civil Rights Act of 1875, ruling that Congress did not have the authority to stop private discrimination. It took eighty-nine years before the Civil Rights Act of 1964 would find a way around this ruling.[14]

By the 1890s, the state governments had gutted the Fifteenth Amendment right to vote. The *grandfather clause* forbade people from voting if their grandfathers had not voted; obviously, if your grandfather was a slave, he did not vote. Poll taxes required paying a fee that most black people could not afford. **Literacy tests** required voters to read and interpret any passage in the state constitution. These new rules did what violence and intimidation had failed to accomplish—they drove blacks out of politics. African Americans have been the only group in any democracy, noted political scientist Richard Valelly, to enter the electorate and then be cast out all over again.[15]

The white majority in the south built a system of segregation known as **Jim Crow** (named after minstrel shows in which white singers and dancers blackened their faces and pretended to be Africans). Jim Crow laws segregated the races. African Americans could not go to white schools, play in the park, visit the zoo (Thursday eventually became "black day" at many zoos), drink from the same water fountain, eat at a white restaurant, stay in a white hotel, go to a white hospital, pray in a white church, or vote. The small African American population in the north also faced racial discrimination, but it was more subtle and not built into the legal system in the same way as the Jim Crow laws.

In 1896, the Supreme Court ruled in ***Plessy v. Ferguson*** that there was nothing inherently discriminatory in requiring separate but equal facilities for black and white races. "If one race be inferior to the other socially," wrote

Reconstruction: The failed effort, pursued by northerners and southerners, to rebuild the South and establish racial equality after the Civil War.

Literacy test: A requirement that voters be literate; in reality, a way to restrict black suffrage.

Jim Crow: The system of racial segregation in the U.S. South that lasted from 1890 to 1965, and that was often violently enforced.

Plessy v. Ferguson: An 1896 Supreme Court case that permitted racial segregation.

the majority, "the Constitution of the United States cannot put them upon the same plane." In practice, the facilities were not at all equal.[16] A year later, in *Williams v. Mississippi*, the Supreme Court unanimously upheld the poll tax and literacy test, announcing that it was not convinced "that their administration was evil, only that evil was possible under them." The Court looked the other way as African Americans were driven right out of politics.[17]

The entire system of southern segregation was held in place by the raw brutality of lynching—ritualized murders of black men (and occasionally women) who had violated the codes. These murders were not crimes of mob passion but organized killings, with police directing traffic around the scene and white families posing for pictures around the victim's mutilated body. They served as a horrific way to enforce racial separation.[18] The white majority directed extraordinary fury at men and women who fell in love across the racial divide because they threatened the entire structure of segregation.[19]

How could the majority accept such repression? Once again, the white majority repeated a false story. Novels, plays, and films portrayed dangerous black men threatening white women and white culture. The story in its most blatant form provided the plot for one of the seminal works in cinematic history. *The Birth of a Nation* (1915) features lust-filled black men, backed by federal troops, menacing white women until the KKK saves the day. In one of the last triumphant scenes, the Klan disarms the skulking black men and stops them from voting. Woodrow Wilson screened the film in the White House, and it became one of the top-grossing films of all time.[20]

See clips from and analysis of The Birth of a Nation.

The Bottom Line

» The clash over slavery eventually led Lincoln to redefine the American idea of self-rule: "government of the people, by the people, for the people."

» *Institutional changes* marked the rise and fall of civil rights. Congress passed the Civil Rights Acts, and the states ratified the Thirteenth, Fourteenth, and Fifteenth Amendments.

» The Fourteenth Amendment contains the crucial legal rule for civil rights: "No state shall . . . deprive any person of . . . the equal protection of the laws."

» Later, courts struck down some civil rights laws, Congress repealed laws implementing the Civil War amendments, and the states introduced segregation, which the Supreme Court accepted.

» However, it was *culture*—the false stories that white Americans told about their fellow citizens—that clamped discrimination into place by inducing the majority to ignore the violations of black rights.

The Fight for Racial Equality

Great Migration: The vast movement of African Americans from the rural South to the urban North between 1910 and the 1960s.

De jure discrimination: Discrimination established by laws.

De facto discrimination: More subtle forms of discrimination that exist without a legal basis.

National Association for the Advancement of Colored People (NAACP): A civil rights organization formed in 1909 and dedicated to racial equality.

Beginning in the 1910s, many African Americans left the South and moved to factory jobs in the northern cities—a journey known as the **Great Migration**. By the 1950s, 40 percent of the black population lived in the North, where they faced a completely different type of racial discrimination.

Two Types of Discrimination

There are two types of discrimination. Legal discrimination—known as **de jure discrimination**—involves laws that explicitly deny civil rights. By the time the civil rights movement ended, around 1970, Americans had conquered de jure discrimination—an enormous achievement.

A second type of discrimination—known as "in fact" or **de facto discrimination**—exists without explicit laws and is more subtly embedded in society. Segregated residential neighborhoods are an example; this type of discrimination is much harder to address. The questions Americans face today is whether de facto restrictions still exist—and, if so, how much.

The Modern Civil Rights Campaign Begins

In 1909, black leaders formed the **National Association for the Advancement of Colored People**, or **NAACP**, and began fighting segregation. In 1941, they finally won the first executive order on race since Reconstruction. President Franklin Roosevelt signed an order barring racial discrimination by defense contractors and created the Fair Employment Practices Committee to ensure compliance. What pushed Roosevelt to act? Black leaders, led by A. Philip Randolph, threatened a massive protest march on Washington just as the United States was gearing up to fight the racist Nazi regime in World War II.

Over one hundred thousand black troops fought in the war only to be greeted by segregation when they returned home. They added their voices to the call for equality—and helped change the cultural image of black people. In 1948, Harry Truman desegregated the armed forces, making the military the first racially integrated federal institution in the United States.

The Courts

Brown v. Board of Education: The landmark Supreme Court case that struck down segregated schools as unconstitutional.

The NAACP also went to court and chipped away at Jim Crow laws enforcing segregation. Democratic President Franklin Roosevelt (1933–1944) appointed eight Supreme Court Justices during his twelve years in office. The result: a Court sympathetic to civil rights. In 1944 the Supreme Court struck down the all-white Democratic primary in *Smith v. Allwright*, rejecting the idea that a political party was a private organization and could discriminate if it so wished.[21] The Court struck down segregation in interstate buses, law schools, and graduate schools—and then took a monumental step.[22]

In May 1954, in ***Brown v. Board of Education***, the Court ruled that segregated schools violated the equal protection clause of the Fourteenth Amendment. In public education, ruled the Court, "the doctrine of separate but equal has no place." Separate facilities were inherently unequal.[23]

Brown was a momentous decision. The follow-up, however, was far less dramatic: Almost nothing changed. The Court did not impose a strong timetable or implementation plan. National officials did little to support *Brown*, and state and local leaders did much to oppose it. A decade after *Brown*, less than 1 percent of the schools in the South had been desegregated.

Where desegregation did occur, as in Little Rock, Arkansas, the results could be explosive. The day before schools opened in 1957, Governor Orville Faubus came out against the desegregation of Little Rock's Central High School. The Arkansas National Guard turned away the nine high school students who tried to enter the school the next day.

"Separate but equal" for George McLaurin meant a desk in the hallway. McLaurin, who was pursuing his Ph.D. at the University of Oklahoma, sued the university, and the Supreme Court ruled against segregated classes in graduate school.

The governor backed off in the face of a court order. When the students came back two weeks later, the National Guard had been replaced by what the *New York Times* called "a mob of belligerent, shrieking hysterical demonstrators" shouting racial epithets. President Dwight Eisenhower, a Republican, reluctantly dispatched the 101st Airborne to enforce the court order and desegregate Central High.

Elected officials throughout the South could not help but notice that Governor Faubus had become a local white hero and was returned to office for an unprecedented third term. Many white politicians reacted by staunchly fighting civil rights and desegregation. Without political support, even a major court decision like *Brown v. Board of Education* would neither crack segregation nor integrate the schools.

The Civil Rights Movement

What defeated segregation was not the Supreme Court or the paratroopers from the 101st Airborne, but ordinary American people who rose up and seized the moment in an organized movement that began in Montgomery, Alabama, on a December afternoon in 1955.

Rosa Parks was riding the bus home. The white section filled up and, when a white man got on board, the driver called

The civil rights movement took courage. Here, protesters sitting at a whites-only lunch counter were taunted and doused with ketchup.

Watch Martin Luther King's "I Have a Dream" speech.

out that he needed another row. Everyone in the first black row was expected to get up. Parks refused to relinquish her seat and was arrested. The local NAACP called a boycott of the Montgomery bus lines and put twenty-six-year-old Martin Luther King, Jr. in charge and a campaign of Christian nonviolence began.[24]

It took more than a year but the pattern was set: The Court had opened the legal door. Protesters then braved arrest, scorn, and violence to actually win change on the ground. In February 1960, four black college students from North Carolina A&T University sat at a white lunch counter and inspired a tactic that spread throughout the South. Within a year, seventy thousand people—black and white—had sat at segregated counters while onlookers jeered, poured ketchup on the sitters, and held cigarette lighters to the women's hair. From lunch counters, the sit-ins spread to movie theaters, parks, pools, art galleries, libraries, and churches.

In 1961, activists came up with a new tactic. Young people rented Greyhound buses and rode as **Freedom Riders** to protest segregated interstate bus lines and terminals. The first bus was pursued by a "citizens' posse" and set ablaze. Men tried to hold the doors of the burning bus shut, and the students narrowly escaped—only to be viciously beaten with bats and pipes.

Still, segregation did not yield. The stalemate was finally broken in Birmingham, Alabama. Young marchers tumbled out of churches and walked, singing and clapping, into appalling police violence. Fire hoses sent them sprawling, police dogs snapped and bit. Television blazed the images around the world. The police overreaction horrified the nation.

The Democratic Party was split between northern liberals and southern segregationists. The Kennedy administration was reluctant to embrace civil rights for it did not want to lose support from the southern Democrats. The images from Birmingham forced the issue, and the administration finally submitted strong civil rights legislation to Congress.

Freedom Riders: Black and white activists who rode buses together to protest segregation on interstate bus lines.

Free rider problem: A barrier to group or collective action arising because people who do not participate still reap the benefits.

Political scientists point to the **free rider problem**. Civil rights protesters faced dogs, beatings, even death; those on the sideline reaped the same results with no risks. Why did thousands of Americans ignore cost-benefit calculations and protest. Was it the idea of freedom? Their moral convictions? Or perhaps the shared exhilaration of fighting for something larger than themselves?

Congress and the Civil Rights Act

Congress blocked civil rights legislation—as it had done many times in the past. In May and June 1963, a great wave of protests

● *Freedom Riders narrowly escaped the burning bus—only to be beaten bloody.*

followed the Birmingham images. Media stories about demonstrations, violence, and arrests fostered a sense of crisis. The **1963 March on Washington** marked the high point of the peaceful protest movement; the entire nation watched Martin Luther King, Jr. put aside his prepared text and declare, "I have a dream."

In November 1963, President Kennedy was assassinated, and action on civil rights became, as President Lyndon Johnson would put it, a martyr's cause. The **Civil Rights Act of 1964** was powerful legislation. It forbade state and local governments from denying access to public facilities on the basis of race, color, or national origin. The law prohibited employers from discriminating on the basis of race, color, religion, sex, or national origin. It barred discrimination in private motels, hotels, theaters, and other public accommodations. There would be no more black Thursdays at city zoos. Congress relied on its constitutional authority over interstate commerce to forbid private businesses from discriminating—no more restaurants or hotels that served only whites.

Opponents sued, claiming that private businesses such as motels should be free to choose their own patrons. The Supreme Court ruled that because motels served people from other states, Congress could use its power over interstate commerce to stop owners from discriminating. Ollie's Barbecue in Birmingham, Alabama, did not have patrons from other states. However, in *Katzenbach v. McClung*, the Court ruled that it received supplies through interstate commerce and so fell under congressional jurisdiction. The era when traveling African Americans had to sleep in their cars was finally over.[25]

The Civil Rights Act also empowered the federal government to withhold funds from segregated schools. In less than a decade the number of southern schoolchildren in integrated schools jumped from almost none to more than 90 percent (see Figure 5.2).

The following year Congress passed the Voting Rights Act of 1965. This law protected the right to vote, struck down voter suppression tactics such as the literacy test, and empowered the attorney general and the U.S. District Court of Washington, DC, to weigh any proposed voting change in suspect areas for its potentially discriminatory effect. The legislation effectively secured the Fifteenth Amendment guaranteeing the right to vote. African Americans surged to the ballot boxes, and following behind black voters came black elected officials (see Table 5.1). Over time, the number of elected black officials skyrocketed—increasing 129 fold in forty years. However, African Americans, who comprise more than 12 percent of the American population, still make up only about 2 percent of all elected officials.

1963 March on Washington: A massive rally for civil rights highlighted by Martin Luther King's "I Have a Dream" speech.

Civil Rights Act of 1964: Landmark legislation that forbade discrimination on the basis of race, sex, religion, or national origin.

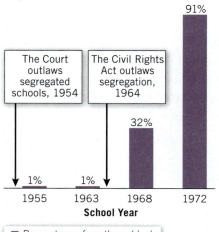

The Court outlaws segregated schools, 1954

The Civil Rights Act outlaws segregation, 1964

91%

32%

1% 1%

1955   1963   1968   1972
School Year

■ Percentage of southern black children in integrated schools

● **Figure 5.2** *The Civil Rights Act of 1964—rather than the Brown v. Board of Education Supreme Court decision in 1954—led to rapid integration of southern schools.*

TABLE 5.1 **Total Number of Black Elected Officials**

	1964	1970	1980	1990	2019
Mayors	0	81	205	314	600 (est.)
Members of Congress	5	9	19	19	52
Total black elected officials in the United States	70	1,469	4,914	7,370	More than 10,500 (est.)

Sources: Congressional Research Service; African American Mayors' Association; Joint Center for Political Studies

Black power: A slogan that emphasized pride in black heritage and separate black institutions to nurture black interests.

Learn about the KKK's failed attempt to conceal their identity.

After the relentless hostility, harassment, and violence, activists began to reject nonviolent protest and seized on **black power**—the idea that African Americans should forget integration and empower the black community to act on its own. The civil rights movement split: Many continued to follow King and his campaign of nonviolent protest. Groups such as the Black Panthers armed themselves and vowed to answer violence with violence. Still others, such as the Nation of Islam, sought separation from whites.

Eventually, years of frustration burst into urban riots—also known as insurrections. The deadliest erupted in Watts, Los Angeles, in August 1965 (34 deaths) and Detroit in July 1967 (43 deaths). Most had a local cause—often incidents involving all-white police forces. White liberals who had energetically supported civil rights began to turn away from the movement. The era of civil rights gave way to a desire for "law and order"—a slogan that presidential candidate Richard Nixon used to great effect on the campaign trail in 1968.

 **The Bottom Line**

» The NAACP won a series of cases against segregation, culminating in *Brown v. Board of Education*; however, implementation proved difficult.

» In the early 1960s, ordinary men, women, and children—black and white—organized in mass movements to turn the legal promise of the *Brown* decision into a practical reality. As the images from marches became more dramatic, surging public opinion pushed Congress to pass the Civil Rights Act of 1964 and the Voting Rights Act of 1965.

» Taken together, these institutional changes ended de jure segregation in the United States.

» The black movement set the model for future civil rights campaigns by many other groups.

🔵 The Post Civil Rights Era

After the successful challenge to *de jure* segregation, civil rights reformers faced the perplexing problems of subtle, *de facto* discrimination. Protesters can kneel in front of a segregated church, but how do they challenge dead-end jobs and shabby neighborhoods

Affirmative Action in the Workplace

In the 1960s and 1970s, a new approach emerged to assist groups that had faced discrimination. **Affirmative action** involves direct, positive steps to increase the representation (especially in schools and workplaces) of groups that have faced discrimination in the past. The strategy started with race and then grew to redress other forms of discrimination, such as those based on gender and ethnicity.

In 1971, the Supreme Court developed a doctrine called **disproportionate impact**. Companies could not hire or promote employees in ways that created "built-in headwinds for minority groups [that] are unrelated to measuring job capability." Companies who never hired women or had zero minority managers would be suspected of those "built-in headwinds."[26]

Affirmative action raises difficult issues. The goal is *equality of opportunity*—giving each person the same chance to achieve success. But some critics charge that it actually produces *equality of outcome* by reserving jobs or opportunities for individuals based on their race or gender.

Critics charged that this was unfair to white men. Americans faced a dilemma: How could they address the results of years and years of discrimination without creating cases of reverse discrimination against white males? The issue is so complicated because it mixes race and economics. Perhaps all populations that have historically been poor—rural whites as well as blacks, for example—should have some claim on affirmative action?

Affirmative action eventually created a backlash and the Supreme Court began to narrow its use. In 1986, the Court warned that such programs could be used only in cases of "severe discrimination" and should not "trammel the interests of white employees."[27] By 1995, a more conservative Court rejected the entire idea of explicitly setting aside places for racial groups.[28]

Affirmative action:
Direct steps to recruit members of previously underrepresented groups into schools and jobs.

Disproportionate Impact:
The discriminatory effect of some policies even if discrimination is not consciously intended.

🟢 *Should the University of Texas consider race as one factor in admissions? School officials argued that doing so increased diversity. These protesters, outside the Supreme Court in 2015, argued that it is reverse discrimination. In 2016, the Court narrowly (4-3) permitted the program (Fisher v. University of Texas, 2016).*

What Do YOU Think?   Higher Education and Affirmative Action

One of the most difficult problems in politics is how to make up for past injustice. What do we, as a society, owe to groups who have faced violence and discrimination for many generations? Consider higher education—the path to success in contemporary society. Which of the following positions would you support?

I favor affirmative action in college admissions. Preferential admissions for members of long-marginalized groups makes up for many generations of discrimination. And it's good for everyone by promoting diversity—drawing on people from different backgrounds makes for a stronger community and a richer educational experience. It also builds a more equal society if races, classes, and genders socially interact and learn to work together in their formative years. Over time, affirmative action in education will help a whole generation look past ascriptive categories like race, gender, and ethnicity.

I oppose affirmative action in college admissions. Past discrimination does not justify special treatment now. In *Grutter v. Bollinger* (2003), the Supreme Court implied that the correct period should last roughly three generations, or sixty years (1965–2025). Although male students comprised 58 percent of the student body in the 1970s when affirmative action went into effect, they now make up only 44 percent.[29] Furthermore, affirmative action is tantamount to reverse discrimination against hardworking individuals from overrepresented groups, such as whites and Asian Americans. Education should have only one yardstick: merit!

Affirmative Action in Education

Civil rights advocates believed that if children from different races and ethnicities went to school together, they would shed the prejudices that marked their parents and grandparents. However, because many children lived in single race neighborhoods, local schools would inevitably be segregated. One solution, known as **school busing**, aimed to achieve racial integration by driving students to other neighborhoods. Busing declined after the 1980s and observers still disagree over whether it was an idealistic often successful effort to create a new generation that could move beyond racial divisions or liberal social engineering that only whipped up racial animosity by using children to right old social wrongs.

School busing: An effort to integrate public schools by mixing students from different neighborhoods.

Apply affirmative action laws.

Another controversy arose over affirmative action programs that reserved places in universities for members of minority groups. Many schools sought to make up for past discrimination and enhance diversity across their student body. These quotas, too, created a backlash. One landmark education case focused on the medical school at the University of California at Davis, which held sixteen places in its entering class of one hundred for members of minority or economically disadvantaged groups. Allan Bakke, a white man who had been rejected by the medical school, sued, arguing that his academic scores were higher than the scores of minority applicants who had been accepted. In a 5–4 decision, *University of California v. Bakke* (1978), the Supreme Court ruled in favor of Bakke; setting a quota, as the university had done, violated the equal protection guarantee of the Fourteenth Amendment. Although the Court barred racial quotas, it accepted the use of race as a "plus" factor in the admissions process.[30] In 2016 the Court narrowly upheld the use of affirmative action in admissions decisions—ruling that the University of Texas's admission policy, which factors in diversity without setting quotas, met the standards of "strict scrutiny."[31]

The Court has painfully picked its way through the minefield of equal opportunity. Crucial questions abound: How does a nation make up for past discrimination? What is owed to people who have been mistreated for generations? For how long? And what about people who feel they are losing out today because of efforts to address past injustice? Should we put aside the terrible racial past and simply worry about all poor people? These cases are hard because there are important goals on both sides.

The Bottom Line

» To make up for past discrimination, legislatures and courts turned to affirmative action in the 1960s and 1970s. Employers and schools that had previously excluded groups now set aside places for them.

» The courts initially sponsored affirmative action programs but are increasingly skeptical of any race-based categories, including those designed to ameliorate past injustice.

Women's Rights

In the early nineteenth century, an American woman had no political rights. She could not vote, serve on a jury, or enter into a contract after marriage. Her husband controlled her property, her wages, and even her body.[32]

Suffrage

The struggle for women's rights in the United States was intertwined with the fight for racial equality. Women in the abolition movement grew frustrated by the barriers they faced—they could lecture to women but not men (because that would be "promiscuous"), they could join abolition societies but not be elected officers.[33] The first American gathering for women's suffrage, the 1848 **Seneca Falls Convention**, grew directly from the gender barriers.

In the 1870s, the women's movement gained momentum. The Women's Christian Temperance Union attacked alcohol as a cause of male violence against women. It championed voluntary motherhood (no more marital rape), suffrage for women, and decent wages. The American Woman Suffrage Association emphasized winning voting rights state by state. It broke from the edgier National American Woman Suffrage Association, which also pressed for employment rights and easier divorce (which conservatives jeered as free love).

Seneca Falls Convention: The first convention dedicated to women's rights, held in July 1848.

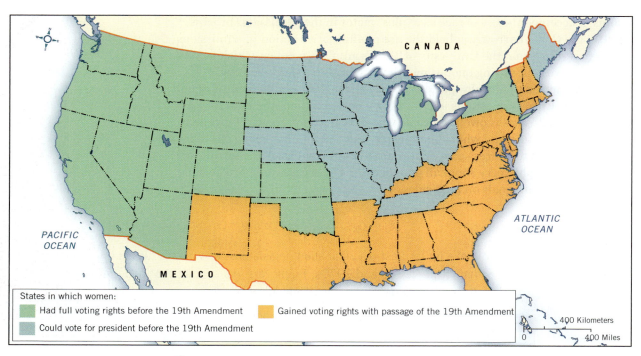

States in which women:

■ Had full voting rights before the 19th Amendment ■ Gained voting rights with passage of the 19th Amendment

■ Could vote for president before the 19th Amendment

● **Figure 5.3** *Before the Nineteenth Amendment, women had full voting rights in the West, limited rights in the Midwest, and almost none in the South and East.*

Success came first in the West, beginning with Wyoming (1869) and Utah (1870)— partially because gender roles were less settled in those territories and partially because of strong populist reform movements that swept through the West. By 1916 women voted in every state of the West and Midwest except New Mexico. In contrast, four states in the North voted to reject suffrage during the 1916 presidential election and the South remained strongly opposed for fear that women would oppose segregation (see Figure 5.3).[34]

During World War I, women took on new roles throughout the economy and increased the pressure for suffrage. Eventually, President Woodrow Wilson grudgingly supported suffrage as a "wartime measure." The Nineteenth Amendment—giving women the right to vote—cleared Congress, over stiff opposition in the Senate, and was ratified by the states in 1920. Still, Women were slow to win political office. Fifty years after suffrage, only three had been elected to the U.S. Senate for full terms and, after the 1970 election, there were just 11 women in the House of Representatives (just 2% of that chamber) Then, during the 1970s–1980s, beginning at the local level and reaching Congress in the 1990s, the number of women officeholders soared.

The Civil Rights Act of 1964

The breakthrough slipped into the Civil Rights Act of 1964. This land-mark law, as we have seen, was designed to bar racial discrimination. Congressman Howard Smith, a segregationist from Virginia, proposed adding a single word—"sex"—to the legislation with the hopes of making a mockery of the legislation and killing the bill. The House floor rang with laughter as the men in Congress debated the proposal. Smith's tactic failed and the Civil Rights Act passed, barring discrimination based on "race, color, religion, *sex* and national origin."

At the time, no one expected the gender provision in the Civil Rights Act to have the same far-reaching consequences for gender rights as *Brown v. Board of Education* had for African Americans—but it did. Like the Supreme Court decisions on race, the Civil Rights Act opened the door to gender change and the women's movement seized the opportunity.

At first, officials ignored the gender provision. The **Equal Employment Opportunity Commission** (**EEOC**), charged with monitoring compliance to the Civil Rights Act, considered it a "mischievous joke perpetrated on the floor of the House of Representatives." In response, a network of women organized the **National Organization for Women** (**NOW**), drawing directly on the tactics of the civil rights campaign—demonstrations, rallies, lobbying, and litigation.

Congress and the EEOC began to pay attention. For example, in 1972, Congress passed Federal Education Amendments that denied federal funds for programs discriminating against women (Title VI) and that required equal athletic opportunities for men and women (Title IX). Underfunded women's sports teams began getting the same treatment as the men's varsity programs.

● *The cheering fans do not realize how the Civil Rights Act changed their world.*

Equal Employment Opportunity Commission (EEOC): Federal law enforcement agency charged with monitoring compliance to the Civil Rights Act.

National Organization for Women (NOW): An organization formed in 1966 to take action for women's equality.

Equal Rights Amendment (ERA): An amendment, originally drafted by Alice Paul in 1923, passed by Congress in 1972, and ratified by thirty-five states, that declared: "Equality of rights . . . shall not be denied or abridged . . . on account of sex."

Reframing the issue: Redefining the popular perception of an issue.

Equal Rights Amendment

The politics of civil rights spilled into other areas of gender politics. Feminists had introduced an **Equal Rights Amendment** (**ERA**) in Congress every year between 1924 and 1972. The amendment was simple: "Equality of rights under the law shall not be denied . . . on account of sex." By 1972, it had become uncontroversial, and Congress easily passed it. Five years later, the ERA was just three states short of ratification. Then Phyllis Schlafly, a conservative activist, organized STOP ERA. Schlafly argued that the amendment threatened traditional family life.

"What the libbers don't understand," said Schlafly, is "that most women want to be a wife, mother, and homemaker."[35] By **reframing the issue**, Schlafly halted the ERA in its tracks. Nearly half the states have adopted sex-equality language in their state constitution, but Congress has not voted again on the issue for more than 35 years.

The Courts

Like the black civil rights leaders, women targeted the courts. Led by Ruth Bader Ginsburg (now a Supreme Court justice), advocates challenged discriminatory state laws, case by case. Because gender was a *nonsuspect category*, the courts upheld any state law as long as it had some "rational connection to a legitimate state purpose." In a series of cases, culminating in *Craig v. Boren* in 1976, the Court lifted gender into a new category of *heightened scrutiny*—not as rigorous a test as the scrutiny the courts give racial classifications, but more rigorous than the test applied to other groups. Ironically, the Court created the category—a major victory for women's rights—through a case in which men challenged an Oklahoma statute that set the drinking age for beer at eighteen for women and twenty-one for men.

The courts also applied the prohibition on gender discrimination in the Civil Rights Act to sexual harassment. In 1998, the Supreme Court expanded the protection by ruling that an employee did not have to prove a specific instance of sexual harassment if there was a hostile workplace environment—this might include sexual advances, lewd comments, or general attitudes. The Court ruled that even if employers were not aware of specific instances of harassment, they remained liable for the general culture of the workplace.

Women's advocates raised the issue of differential pay more than a century ago. Today, women working full time earn less than men—although the exact amount of the disparity is hotly disputed and varies from 80 percent to 95 percent, depending on the methodology. In a famous case, Lilly Ledbetter sued after a nineteen-year career with Goodyear Tire Company because she had been paid less than men in the same position. A jury found Goodyear guilty of pay discrimination, but the Supreme Court reversed the judgment by a 5–4 vote. The majority ruled that Ledbetter should have sued within 180 days after Goodyear set her pay, long before she knew about the salary differential. In 2009, President Obama signed equal-pay legislation—known as the Lilly Ledbetter Act—that permits an employee to sue 180 days from her last paycheck (resetting the clock each time she gets a lower paycheck).[36]

Class action: A lawsuit filed on behalf of an entire category of individuals, such as all people in public housing in a state or all the female managers of a large company.

Recent Supreme Court decisions, however, have made it more difficult to sue businesses for discrimination. In a major case, decided in 2011, the court turned down a **class action** suit brought against Walmart. The suit alleged that the company systematically discriminated against women by offering them less pay and fewer promotions. The Supreme Court ruled—once again, by a 5–4 margin—that simply showing that women received less pay was not enough to prove discrimination. Rather, the plaintiffs (the women suing) needed to demonstrate a specific company-wide policy that set lower wages for all the women involved in the class action.[37]

Progress for Women—But How Much?

There had never been a woman Supreme Court justice until Ronald Reagan named Sandra Day O'Connor in 1981; today, three of the nine justices are women. In 1964, 7 percent of American women got bachelor's degrees

TABLE 5.2 Women CEOs of *Fortune 500* Companies

Year	2000	2010	2015	2017	2018
Women CEOs	3	15	23	32	24

Source: Zameena Mejia, "Just 24 female CEOs lead the companies on the 2018 Fortune 500 – fewer than last year. May 21, 2018. CNBC.

(compared to 12% of men); in 2016, 33.7 percent of women do (now surpassing the 33.2% of men). There had never been a woman CEO of a Fortune 500 company until 1972. In 2017, the number was up to 32 and then, in 2018, fell back to 24—just 5% of the total (see Table 5.2).[38]

Gender politics raise provocative questions about social roles and power. Issues such as equality and women's rights in the workplace continue to generate conflict. The #MeToo movement burst on the scene in 2017. After years of tolerating sexual assault and harassment, women began to speak out—and a long list of male celebrities in every field was exposed for indecent behavior. The movement is both a bracing sign of progress and a harsh reminder that we still have a long way to go to reach gender equality.

 **The Bottom Line**

» When women organized to win rights in the 19th century they met with ridicule and violence.

» Women first won voting rights in the West and Midwest before finally securing the Nineteenth Amendment, guaranteeing the right to vote.

» The Civil Rights Act of 1964 bars gender discrimination. The women's movement organized to take advantage of legal changes. The law transformed American gender roles in political and professional life.

» Gender politics became especially controversial, spilling into many other issues including the #MeToo movement.

Hispanics

Hispanics, or Latinos (we use the words interchangeably), play a powerful and growing role in American politics and culture. Hispanics are the largest minority group, making up over 17 percent of the American population—up from 6.4 percent in 1980.

Latinos have long faced discrimination. They were already living in the Southwest—in Arizona, California, New Mexico, and parts of Colorado, Nevada,

● During the early twentieth century, Latinos began to organize for civil rights. This replica of a 1929 Texas restaurant sign helps to illustrate why.

Utah, and Texas—before the United States took those lands from Mexico in 1848. As white settlers poured into the new territory, the original Latino residents faced discrimination, segregation, and violence.

Today, despite enormous success in achieving the American dream, Hispanics still face challenges. They are more likely to be poor, less likely to have health insurance, and underrepresented in almost every political venue. Despite all this, Latinos have a higher life expectancy than most other American groups.

Challenging Discrimination

Latinos established the League of United Latin American Citizens (LULAC) in 1929. Like the NAACP, the organization fought segregation through lawsuits. In *Mendez v. Westminster*, decided in 1947, the court struck down Latino school segregation in Orange County, California; the case was a precursor to *Brown v. Board of Education* and involved some of the same lawyers.

During the 1960s, young Latinos turned to activism. In 1968, high school and college students called a massive student strike that reverberated through the Southwest. They pushed mainstream Latino organizations to fight more aggressively against discrimination and they challenged immigration policies that restricted movement across the Mexican border. Many young people took a slur against Mexicans, *Chicano*, and turned it into a movement they labeled **Chicanismo**—a defiant pride in their heritage and culture. At the same time, the United Farm Workers (UFW) organized migrant workers who picked crops up and down the West coast. The UFW—with its black Aztec eagle and charismatic leaders—became another symbol of Latino mobilization.

Chicanismo: A defiant movement expressing pride in Latino origins and culture in the face of discrimination.

Today, the central questions for Latino politics turn on immigration, language, and—perhaps most important—just how the very diverse Hispanic population might mobilize together for political action.

The Politics of Immigration

Despite their long American heritage, Hispanic politics is wrapped up with immigration. The United States is an immigrant nation but the door to foreigners has historically swung from wide open to shut tight. Restrictions in the 1920s limited immigration—President John Kennedy sadly noted forty years later that America no longer offered a beacon for immigrants. After his assassination, in 1965, Congress lifted the restrictions and a new era of immigration began. Today, one in eight American residents was born abroad.

Ancient Fears. Immigrants trigger fears that are repeated for every new group: They will undermine American values and culture; they will take away jobs; they will cling to their own languages, and remain loyal to their countries of origin and their supposedly un-American ideas. All this was said about the Irish back in the 1840s—and they were also persecuted for being Catholics; in 1900, one U.S. Senator justified the mob that killed 11 Italians after a jury exonerated them of a murder (since, he implied, the Italians were natural criminals).[39]

As a candidate, Donald Trump expressed hostility to some immigrants, especially emphasizing Mexico. As president, he has made limits on immigration one of his signature issues. At one private meeting, the president reportedly deplored immigration from "sh—t hole countries"—though he was referring to Haiti rather than Mexico. Senator Marco Rubio (R-FL) immediately tweeted that immigrants should be judged "on who they are, not where they come from."[40]

In 2017, more Mexicans returned home than arrived in the United States. Still, the debate continues about whether to build a border fence with Mexico (57% say no) and whether to allow undocumented immigrants who were brought to the United States as children to become citizens (75% say yes).[41]

Three Categories. Immigrants fall into three different categories.

1. Those who were born in the United States or have become *American citizens* (roughly 66 percent of the Latino population) claim the same rights as any citizen. They are in the same protected legal category as African Americans. Any law that singles them out is "suspect" and subject to strict scrutiny by the courts.

2. The U.S. government labels foreigners who have not become citizens *"resident aliens."* There are approximately 13.1 million. They may work and pay taxes, but they cannot enjoy the benefits of citizenship: They may not vote in most elections and are not eligible for many government safety-net programs such as Medicaid.

3. An estimated 11 million people are not legally authorized to be residents. Most arrived on a temporary visa, got a job or fell in love, and simply remained after their legal time in the country expired. Others slipped across the borders (310,000 were arrested in 2017). Unauthorized border crossings have plunged since the start of the Trump administration, falling some 40 percent in the first months of 2017.[42] Undocumented individuals have limited constitutional rights.

Undocumented Individuals. The debate over the rights of people who are not legally authorized to be in the United States is especially intense. Some argue that undocumented immigrants are part of the American economy and society. They live in fear of jail and deportation. As a result, many are wary of going to a hospital, visiting their children's school, or reporting crimes against them. Many Americans want to bring these individuals out of the shadows and make them eligible for driver's licenses (as 12 states currently permit) and universities (see Figure 5.4). Ultimately, they argue, the United States should give its undocumented a path to legal status.[43]

Opponents respond that undocumented individuals have broken the law and should not be rewarded. They also fear that immigrants will take jobs and depress wages. Finally, they say, undocumented immigration undermines the social cohesion—the sense of solidarity—within a society.

In 2012, President Obama signed an executive order—bypassing a deadlocked Congress—aimed at protecting over one million undocumented individuals who were brought to the United States as children. The Supreme Court blocked an extension of the program and President Trump ended it, arguing that the president did not have the legal authority to protect these "Dreamers." Instead, Trump pointed out, this was something Congress could (and should) do. The conflict goes on, in courts, in Congress, and within the administration.

Even Hispanic citizens whose families have lived on American soil for many generations may be subject to discrimination due to immigration politics. It may lead police to single out Latinos, a practice known as **racial profiling**. Hispanic immigration is a major contributor to the classic American question: *Who are we?*

Racial profiling: A law-enforcement practice of singling out people on the basis of physical features such as race or ethnicity.

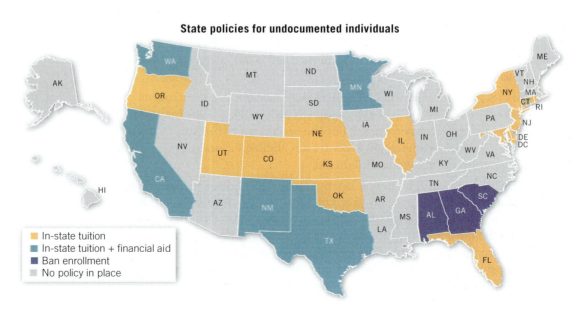

State policies for undocumented individuals

- In-state tuition
- In-state tuition + financial aid
- Ban enrollment
- No policy in place

● **Figure 5.4** *States' varied higher-education rules for undocumented students, ranging from eligibility for financial aid to forbidding enrollment. (Education Commission of the States)*

Language Controversy: Speak English!

As long ago as 1752, Benjamin Franklin worried that there were so many Germans in Philadelphia that "instead of them learning our language, we must learn theirs or live as in a foreign country." In recent decades, Spanish language use has become a major issue. In 1974, the Supreme Court ruled in *Lau v. Nichols* that equal protection required schools to assist students whose primary language was not English. Many school districts established bilingual education programs. Opponents argue that bilingual education divides the community, undermines traditional American culture, and disadvantages students who fail to learn English.

Political Mobilization

Hispanic Americans face other challenges. More than one in five live below the poverty line—two and a half times the rate for non-Hispanic whites. They have less health insurance coverage and face tensions with law enforcement.[44]

When they turn to politics to address these issues, Latinos face both barriers and advantages. The biggest barrier lies in the nature of the Hispanic community itself. In fact, *Hispanic* is a misnomer. Hispanic people come from many different places, each with its own concerns (see Figure 5.5).

For Mexican Americans, concentrated in the Southwest, the politics of immigration looms large. In contrast, Puerto Ricans, the second-largest Hispanic population, are American citizens by birth; immigration is less relevant to them. Salvadorans, now the third-largest Latino group, face the problems of more recent immigrants—poverty, social integration, and community building. Cuban Americans offer still another contrast. They have high average incomes and have traditionally voted Republican—though the youngest generation now breaks evenly between the parties.[45]

Learn about Hispanic and other civil rights groups.

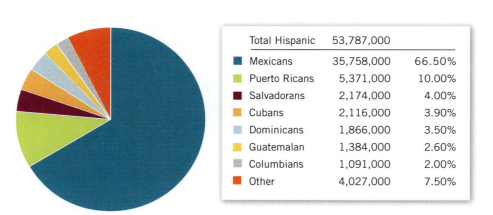

Total Hispanic	53,787,000	
Mexicans	35,758,000	66.50%
Puerto Ricans	5,371,000	10.00%
Salvadorans	2,174,000	4.00%
Cubans	2,116,000	3.90%
Dominicans	1,866,000	3.50%
Guatemalan	1,384,000	2.60%
Columbians	1,091,000	2.00%
Other	4,027,000	7.50%

● **Figure 5.5** *Countries of origin—Hispanics in America. Some two-thirds of Latinos who live in the United States were born here. This figure shows their national heritage. (U.S. Census)*

 *More than 250 years after Benjamin Franklin expressed his concern, the owner of Geno's Steaks in Philadelphia announces that people should speak English. This is a hot issue—and always has been.*

Is there a common political denominator across this diverse population? Today, a pan-Latino movement seeks to find common ground and mobilize voters around issues that transcend any one country or group. Shared political influence, if Latinos seek to exercise it, figures to be formidable: The Hispanic population has grown three times faster than the general population in the past two decades. Latino leaders note that Mexican American voters moved California decisively into the Democratic column in the past fifteen years.

In 2006, when the Republican-led Congress proposed tough new restrictions on undocumented immigrants, massive demonstrations sprang up around the United States. In the past, Latino protesters had waved Mexican flags and symbols. This time, they marched under a sea of American flags. Researchers, who were undertaking a major survey of Hispanic Americans during the time period, discovered that the protests made Hispanics feel significantly more American.[46]

The surge in demonstrations reflects the convergence of three important trends: the rapid growth of the Latino population, a sense of shared identity within that population, and an increasing identification with the American homeland. This combination may prove to be one of the most important political developments in future elections.

The Bottom Line

» Latinos, the largest immigrant group, have been the fastest growing population in the United States; the rate of increase has slowed in recent years.

» Latinos are a diverse people with different national identities, histories, cultures, and concerns.

» A key political question is whether Latinos will mobilize around shared interests and concerns. If they do, they will become an even more formidable political force.

Asian Americans

Asian Americans are the third-largest minority in the United States—after blacks and Hispanics—and, according to the Pew Research Center, are now the fastest growing.[47] Unlike Latinos, they do not share a common language;

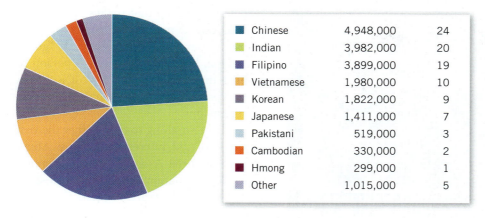

■ Chinese	4,948,000	24
■ Indian	3,982,000	20
■ Filipino	3,899,000	19
■ Vietnamese	1,980,000	10
■ Korean	1,822,000	9
■ Japanese	1,411,000	7
■ Pakistani	519,000	3
■ Cambodian	330,000	2
■ Hmong	299,000	1
■ Other	1,015,000	5

● **Figure 5.6** *Countries of origin. The national identities of about 20 million U.S. residents whose heritage is Asian. (U.S. Census)*

unlike African Americans, they do not share a common historical experience. As you can see from Figure 5.6, Asian Americans range from Indians to Vietnamese, from Filipinos to Koreans.

Asian Americans have the highest education level and the highest median personal income among American population groups. However, the statistics mask as much as they reveal because Asian Americans range from Indian Americans with high income and education levels to the Hmong from the mountains of Laos with income levels about one-third the U.S. average.

Asians have a long history of negotiating the American lines between "us and them." Congress passed the Chinese Exclusion Act (in 1882) barring Chinese immigrants and declaring Chinese people ineligible for citizenship. By 1917, Congress had extended the ban to "all natives of Asia including the whole of India." The California Alien Land Law of 1913 forbade "aliens ineligible for citizenship"—that is, Asian immigrants—from owning land. Each restriction came amid painful stereotypes. The Chinese were excluded because, as one California congressman put it, "His ancestors have bequeathed to him the most hideous immoralities."[48]

After the Japanese attack on Pearl Harbor in 1941, President Roosevelt ordered the army to round up Japanese Americans and place them in cold, flimsy, miserable internment camps. They lost their liberty, jobs, property, and bank accounts. The Supreme Court upheld the internments.

The wartime camps only marked the extreme case. Schools and neighborhoods were strictly segregated—giving rise to "Chinatowns." San Francisco established separate schools for Chinese Americans in the 1880s and maintained them until *Brown v. Board of Education.* Across the United States, Asian Americans found themselves straddling the racial binary of black and white, particularly in the Jim Crow South.[49]

Perhaps the oddest cultural twist of all is the stereotype that emerged in the 1960s. Many Asian groups were perceived as the "model minority": a

West coast white supremacy nineteenth-century style

hardworking group that makes its own way without any demands for rights or privileges. It may seem that this is a "good" stereotype, but by reducing each person to nothing more than a member of a group, stereotypes demean individuals and stoke social tensions.

Is there anything to tie together the vast populations and interests? Perhaps. About one out of three Asian Americans reports facing discrimination and slurs. A 2018–2019 lawsuit against Harvard suggests that some elite U.S. universities may be excluding Asian American candidates. An internal Harvard study found that Asian Americans have a lower chance of gaining admission than similarly qualified white, Latino, or black candidates. Is this a new form of exclusion? The courts—and U.S. population will debate that question in coming years. [50]

The Bottom Line

» Asian Americans, the third-largest minority group in the United States, are the fastest growing.

» Asian Americans have faced discrimination—including today, the image of a "model minority" that, as with any stereotype, is simplistic and hurtful.

» Asian Americans are a tremendously diverse group. The key to their political effectiveness as a group lies in finding common interests and forging ties to other groups.

Native Americans

The original natives of the United States own the saddest story about rights denied. Before the Europeans arrived, an estimated ten million American Indians lived on the land that would become the United States. As European colonists spread, they introduced deadly diseases, denied indigenous peoples' sovereignty, fought bitter wars, and slowly pushed the tribes from their ancestral lands.

The Lost Way of Life

One dark side of American expansion was "Indian removal." As settlers moved west, Indian tribes were forced from their homelands. By the time the United States stretched from coast to coast, less than a million of the ten million natives remained.

Recent historians have warned us against simply seeing Native Americans as the passive victims of American westward expansion. The Indians built their own empires and, at times, forced the white settlers to retreat. During King Philip's War (1675–1678), natives destroyed or damaged one in five Massachusetts villages. (The war is named after the Native American leader Metacomet, known to the English as "King Philip.") Between 1750 and 1850, the Comanches dominated economic and military life in the Southwest and pulled white settlers, Spanish colonies, and other tribes into what amounted to an imperial system. Some Iroquois tribes, hoping to preserve their lands, cultures, and independence, sided with the British during the American Revolution. Tecumseh (a Shawnee warrior) forged an alliance of Native American peoples across the Midwest to resist American expansion. With much blood and conflict, the federal government forced most Native American populations into reservations by the late 1800s.[51]

On the reservations, the tribes were pushed to adopt European lifestyles. The Dawes Act of 1887 divided reservation lands into individual parcels to destroy traditional ownership customs and encourage farming. Boarding schools educated and assimilated native children. By halting the transmission of cultural legacies, it was hoped that whites could "kill the Indian" and "save the man." Even Sitting Bull, famed Lakota seer and fierce opponent of white settlement, sent his son to be educated to ensure him a place in an uncertain future.[52]

Indians and the Federal Government

Native Americans have had an ambiguous legal status. In 1831, the Supreme Court ruled that Indian tribes were **"domestic dependent nations"**—essentially, a separate people but without the rights of an independent nation. Native Americans were not considered citizens and were not protected by the Constitution, until Congress passed the Indian Citizenship Act in 1924. Even today, their legal status remains ambiguous. Of a total Native American population of some two million in the continental United States, about half live on tribal reservations, which are independent jurisdictions subject to federal but not state governments. These Indians are both American citizens and members of self-governing independent lands. Another three million Alaskan natives became U.S. citizens when Alaska joined the union in 1959.

The primary connection of Native Americans on reservations to American government is bureaucratic rather than electoral. The Bureau of Indian Affairs (BIA) is responsible for Native American issues. The early placement of the bureau offers a telling symbol: It was part of the Department of War. Later, Congress moved it to the Department of the Interior, whose chief purpose is to promote and protect natural resources and public lands. Native Americans joke that BIA stands for Bossing Indians Around.

Social Problems and Politics

Native Americans face poverty rates almost double the national rates: 26.2 percent compared to 14 percent for the nation as a whole. Life on the reservations is especially difficult. Most are in rural areas with few jobs or

Domestic dependent nation: Special status that grants local sovereignty to tribal nations but does not grant them full sovereignty equivalent to independent nations.

Assimilation of Native Americans, often forced, was an official U.S. government policy well into the twentieth century. Pupils at Carlisle (PA) Indian Industrial School, c. 1900.

resources. Native Americans tend to suffer from low education levels, high infant mortality rates, and lower life expectancy.

Native Americans' civil rights politics divides, roughly, into two camps. The *ethnic minority perspective* argues that Indians should engage American democracy and mobilize for rights and equality. The alternative is the separatist *tribal movement*, which advocates withdrawing from American politics and society and revitalizing Native American culture and traditions.

The civil rights protests of the 1960s included Native American activists. Led by the American Indian Movement (AIM), tribes occupied the Bureau of Indian Affairs in Washington, DC—for six days in November 1972. They "captured" Alcatraz Island in San Francisco Bay and occupied the site of the infamous prison for nineteen months between 1969 and 1971. They seized control of the village of Wounded Knee on the Pine Ridge Indian Reservation, the site of a massacre of Indians in 1890, for seventy-one days, declared the reservation a sovereign nation, and exchanged occasional gunfire with federal marshals. During the Wounded Knee Incident, AIM brought its grievances before the United Nations General Assembly.

In recent years, some tribes have used their exemption from state laws to create highly profitable gambling businesses and resorts. The Supreme Court ruled, in 1987, that because tribes are considered sovereign entities, they are free from state prohibitions on gaming. According to the gaming industry, 233 of the nation's 565 tribes run casinos. Whether this is a positive development—for the tribes, for the communities around them, and for the United States—is a matter of hot debate.

 **The Bottom Line**

» Native Americans lost their way of life in the face of colonial settlers' diseases and armies.

» The Supreme Court gave American Indians a special status: a separate people without rights. Although they retain the special status, Native Americans became U.S. citizens in 1924.

» Native Americans support two different civil rights strategies: The ethnic minority approach argues for winning political rights and benefits. The tribal movement approach prefers to withdraw and to emphasize a separate Indian society and culture.

Groups Without Special Protection

The idea of demanding rights has spread to other groups that were not mentioned in the Civil Rights Act and have never drawn special scrutiny from the courts.

People with Disabilities

Before 1970, children in wheelchairs did not go to school, and most blind children never learned how to read. People with disabilities lived outside mainstream society. A political breakthrough came in an unnoticed provision, which liberal congressional staff slipped into an obscure bill. **Section 504** of the 1973 Rehabilitation Act borrowed language directly from the Civil Rights Act of 1964 and applied it to the disabled: "No . . . handicapped individual . . . shall, solely by reason of his handicap, be excluded from participation in, or be denied the benefits of . . . any program or activity conducted by an executive agency." Suddenly, any university receiving federal funds—and all government agencies—had to accommodate disabled people.

Section 504 gave activists a political focus. When the government was slow to issue regulations, for example, sit-ins at regional offices pushed the matter forward. Note the familiar political dynamic: Congressional staffers dreamed up a change, giving advocates a focus for action. People with handicaps and their advocates soon mobilized for widespread change on every level of government. Local health boards, planning agencies, and school officials all began hearing from the advocates. The political pattern resembles African Americans after *Brown v. Board of Education* and feminists after the Civil Rights Act: Government action provided new legal rights; the group then organized and demanded further change.

Advocates went from requesting welfare benefits to demanding civil rights. The process culminated in 1990, when Congress passed the Americans with Disabilities Act (ADA). The ADA forbade companies of twenty-five or more employees from discriminating against handicapped people. It also required companies to make "reasonable accommodations" for wide ranges of disabilities.

Unlike racial discrimination, however, a business can avoid making accommodations if it would be expensive or inconvenient to do so. Courts constantly weigh the costs and benefits. What is reasonable to require of a firm or a store or a university to accommodate special needs? Even with this delicate balancing of costs and access, the ADA created what amounts to a massive affirmative action program for people with disabilities. Public transportation, schools, shops, and businesses all must help facilitate a normal, mainstream life for people with special needs.

Sexual Orientation and Gender Identity

The movement for same-sex rights began with a riot. In June 1969, police raided a New York City gay bar named the Stonewall Inn. Traditionally, gay people had submitted to such raids. This time, the gay community broke the unwritten rules, inspired by the struggle of other groups for civil rights. The

Section 504: An obscure provision in an obscure Congressional act that required all institutions that received federal funds to accommodate people with disabilities.

Stonewall riot marks the moment that the LGBTQ community stopped apologizing and affirmed its identity. Coming out and disclosing sexual orientation became a major vehicle for raising political consciousness in the 1970s. In 1973, the American Psychiatric Association removed homosexuality from its list of mental disorders.

In the early 1980s, gay communities were devastated by a mysterious plague—AIDS. No one knew what the illness was or how it was transmitted—only that diagnosis meant death. The disease pushed gay groups into local politics. In every city, gays organized and established links to the medical community, local governments, and social service networks.

Few recent changes in American politics and culture are as dramatic as the transformation of same-sex civil rights. In 1993, newly elected Bill Clinton ran into a firestorm when he promised to open the military to gay men and women. Eighteen years later, the Obama administration ended the policy; the quiet reaction in Congress reflects the changing cultural norms.

The same arc—from fierce resistance to broad acceptance—marked same-sex marriage. Back in 2000, Vermont recognized civil unions, legal arrangements that conferred some of the same rights and duties as marriage. The state erupted in protest. What happened next was a revolution in public opinion (which we'll cover in the next chapter). Approval of same-sex marriage leapt from 35 percent in 2001 to 62 percent in 2017.[53]

Political institutions followed the revolution in public opinion. Massachusetts became the first state to permit same-sex marriage. Other states followed. In 2015, the Supreme Court, in *Obergefell v. Hodges*, narrowly (5–4) enshrined same-sex marriage as a national civil right. The majority held that both the Fourteenth Amendment's *due process clause* ("no state shall deprive any person of life, liberty or property without due process of law") and its equal protection clauses ("nor deny to any person . . . the equal protection of the laws) forbade states from discriminating among couples on the basis of sexual orientation. Notice how the amendment, put in place to benefit former slaves after the Civil War, continues to offer broad protection against discrimination. But it took activism and public opinion—led by the attitudes of younger Americans—to achieve political change. Few civil rights areas—in politics, law, or public opinion—have evolved as quickly as this one.[54]

Even so, one in four LGBTQ Americans still reports serious employment discrimination.

Twenty states have put employment protection in place that forbids employers from discriminating on the basis of sexual orientation or gender identity. The Justice Department under the Trump administration argues that the Civil Rights Act does not protect workers on the basis of sexual orientation. "Without a federal law," summarized one employment attorney, "many people could be exposed to discrimination just because they are gay."[55] An appeal court ruled against the Trump administration in 2018 and held that employers may not discriminate on the basis of sexual orientation. The issue is likely to head to the Supreme Court.[56]

Protections for Sexual Orientation and Gender Identity

HOW DO EMPLOYMENT LAWS VARY BY STATE?

In February 2018, Saints Peter and Paul Catholic School fired its first grade teacher, Jocelyn Morffi. She had just returned from her Florida Keys wedding to her same-sex partner. Morffi looked at her legal options. Miami-Dade County has an ordinance that protects against employment discrimination, but exempts religious institutions. As the map shows, some states have instituted laws to protect individuals from discrimination in the workplace; Florida and others have not.

EMPLOYMENT

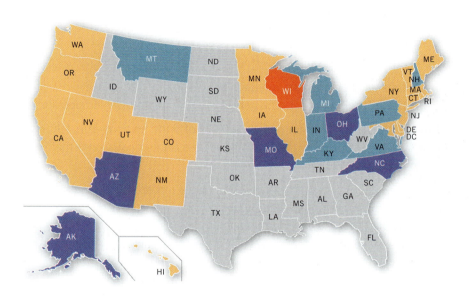

THINK ABOUT IT

How do protections vary geographically? Where are the states that grant the most protections located? Where are those that grant the least?

What protections against employment discrimination does your state provide? What protections do you think it should provide?

Source: Human Rights Campaign

The Federal Equal Employment Opportunity Commission is currently accepting complaints of sexual orientation and gender identity discrimination in employment based on Title VII's prohibition against sex discrimination.

*Transgender individuals receive protection against discrimination in Florida and New York.

*North Carolina's executive order enumerates sexual orientation and gender identity. However, this order has a bathroom carve-out for transgender employees making the executive order not fully inclusive.

Prohibit discrimination based on sexual orientation and gender identity (20 states & D.C.): California, Colorado, Connecticut, Delaware, District of Columbia, Hawaii, Illinois, Iowa, Maine, Maryland, Massachusetts, Minnesota, Nevada, New Jersey, New Mexico, New York, Oregon, Rhode Island, Utah, Vermont, Washington

Prohibit discrimination based on sexual orientation only (2 states): New Hampshire, Wisconsin

Prohibit discrimination against public employees based on sexual orientation and gender identity (6 states): Indiana, Kentucky, Michigan, Montana, Pennsylvania, Virginia

Prohibit discrimination against public employees based on sexual orientation only (5 states): Alaska, Arizona, Missouri, North Carolina, Ohio

No protections

LGBTQ individuals, in most places, still face formidable barriers to full civil rights—in employment, housing, education, and public accommodations.[57] One example illustrates the state of the debate. In February 2016 the city of Charlotte passed an ordinance prohibiting businesses, such as restaurants and stores, from discriminating against LGBTQ customers. In addition, the ordinance ensured that transgender individuals could use the restroom for the gender with which they identify. Concerned that this would open the door for sexual predators to target children in the bathroom, conservatives in the North Carolina legislature rushed through House Bill 2, which required individuals to use public bathrooms that match the biological sex on their birth certificate.[58] The law set off a major backlash. The NCAA relocated championship games scheduled to be held in the state.[59] Stung by the outcry, the state repealed the bathroom clause but continued to forbid cities from legislating protections to LGBTQ individuals. Will it stand? Public opinion data suggest that this is one area that could change rapidly, given that the younger generations across political perspectives overwhelmingly support LGBTQ rights. Stay tuned!

The Bottom Line

» People with disabilities used an obscure bureaucratic rule to mobilize, and eventually won the Americans with Disabilities Act. The goal is to mainstream disabled people.

» The gay (and lesbian) movements were born in a burst of pride and anger in 1969. Gays were the first to confront AIDS—a harrowing plague (in its early years) that pushed them into politics and community building.

» Gay, lesbian, bisexual, and transgender communities have moved toward the mainstream, driven in part by strong public opinion support from younger Americans. The Supreme Court ruled that states may not discriminate against same-sex partners when issuing marriage licenses. Still, LGBTQ Americans still face challenges in employment, education, housing, and other venues.

The Fight for Civil Rights Goes On

How close has the United States come to achieving racial equality and civil rights? A few key areas indicate how the past half-century of movements has changed America—and how far we still have to go.

Voting Rights Today

During the 2018 election, 22 states debated bills to make voting more difficult. That's on top of the 16 states that introduced restrictions for the 2016 election such as government issued voter ID, no more same-day voter registration, limited early voting, fewer polling places, and limits on students trying to cast ballots where they go to school. Proponents argued that these measures will reduce fraud. Critics respond that there are very few documented instances of voter fraud and charge that the measures were put into place to depress black, Latino, and young turnout—all groups that tend to vote Democratic. In general, Democrats have tried to make voting easier, Republicans to make it more difficult. Each party stands to gain from the changes it proposes.[60]

The Supreme Court made restricting the vote easier in 2013 when it struck down the central requirement in the Voting Rights Act of 1965. Now, southern states that had once denied African Americans the vote were no longer required to clear voting rights changes with the federal Justice Department. Chief Justice Roberts declared that the country had changed in the half-century since the rules went into place.[61]

Economic and Social Rights Today

Equality has many dimensions. Are Americans more equal when it comes to health, wealth, and social justice? Again, we find a mixed story: much progress and a long way to go.

Health. In 1950, before the civil rights movement, whites lived over 9 years (or 14%) longer than African Americans. By 2017, that racial difference had fallen to just 3.2 years (or 4%). Moreover, Asian and Hispanic Americans have a longer average life expectancy than whites (Table 5.3).

Income. Few groups in history have experienced a rise out of poverty as rapid as African Americans between 1959 (55% in poverty) and today (22% in 2017). Still, the black poverty rate remained roughly three times the white poverty rate for the entire time. The percentage of Hispanic and Native Americans who live in poverty is close to the black rate (Table 5.4). The racial differences track the enormous rise in inequality between 1970 and today.

TABLE 5.3 Average Life Expectancy, by Ethnic and Racial Group

Asian American	87.3
Hispanic	83.5
White	78.8
Native American	76.9
African American	75.6
Source: Kaiser Family Foundation	

TABLE 5.4 Percentage of People in Poverty, by Race

White	8.8
Hispanic	19.4
African American	22.0
Native American	28.3
Asian American	10.1
Source: U.S. Census	

MEN

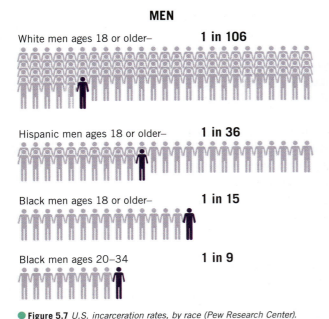

White men ages 18 or older– **1 in 106**

Hispanic men ages 18 or older– **1 in 36**

Black men ages 18 or older– **1 in 15**

Black men ages 20–34 **1 in 9**

● **Figure 5.7** *U.S. incarceration rates, by race (Pew Research Center).*

The New Jim Crow: The idea that mass incarceration of African Americans has effects comparable to legal segregation. The term is the title of a book by Michelle Alexander.

For a different perspective, turn to CEOs in the top 500 corporations. As we saw earlier, there are 24 women in that corner office. There are eleven Hispanics, nine Asian Americans, three blacks (compared to six as recently as 2012), and no Native Americans. The number in 1995 for every one of these groups: zero.

Incarceration. One final twist to the American civil rights story introduces a new alarm: African American men are seven times as likely to be in jail as whites. Latinos are three times as likely (Figure 5.7). American incarcerations are the highest in the world with 2.1 million people locked up and another 3.7 million on probation and at risk of landing back in jail for small offenses. Is this "**the new Jim Crow,**" as civil rights advocates have argued?[62]

Most observers believe that the United States has gone too far in sending people to jail—especially for minor offenses. Studies repeatedly suggest a racial bias throughout the criminal justice system. When subjects were asked to "imagine a drug user," 95 percent pictured a black person. In reality, 72 percent of users are white.[63] There are subtle forms of racial and ethnic discrimination at every stage of the criminal justice system. In 2016, a coalition of prominent liberals and conservatives began a campaign to overhaul the criminal justice system. A new front has opened in the long battle for civil rights.

 **The Bottom Line**

» Voting rights remains a source of fierce political debate today.

» When we turn to health, poverty, and criminal justice, we find a familiar story: The United States has made great progress, but the United States has a long way to go to achieve full civil rights.

Conclusion: Civil Rights . . . By the People

Race. Gender. Latinos. Asians. Immigrants. Native Americans. People with disabilities. Sexual orientation. Transgender individuals. The struggle for civil rights—in many ways, the struggle to secure American ideals—spans the nation's history and engages every generation. Each group described here fought for civil rights. No American idea is more powerful than the idea of inalienable rights; and none generates more arguments.

Government actions are crucial in winning (or losing) rights. One important lesson to draw from this chapter is the far-reaching consequences of laws and court cases. The 1964 Civil Rights Act, for example, ended de jure segregation, focused the women's movement, changed gender relations in schools and workplaces, inspired the disabilities rights movement—and its influence continues even today.

The Supreme Court has been at the center of the storm across the last half century of debates about civil rights. Liberals argue that the Court must ensure that past discrimination does not hobble future generations. Conservatives call on the judiciary to end programs that benefit some individuals (and perhaps harm others) simply because of race, gender, or any other factor.

America's civil rights movements were each extraordinary efforts to overcome centuries of injustice, targeting minority and marginalized groups of all types. But did the nation do enough to give every member of society a genuine opportunity to succeed? Has America, as Justice Roberts declared, truly "changed"?

Ultimately the power to win change lies with the people. The *Brown* decision became an enormous force for change only after the civil rights movement sprang into action. Throughout this chapter, we have seen people rise up to transform the politics of rights—marching into violence in Birmingham, prodding a reluctant government to implement the gender provisions in the Civil Rights Act of 1964, waving American flags over immigrant rights in Chicago, taking over a bureaucrat's office to hurry implementation of disability rules in Washington, and fighting for same-sex marriage when it seemed like an impossible dream. It was the people who helped shape the meaning of the legislation and court decisions. Through their passion and their activism, the people are constantly pushing the United States to live up to its founding ideals.

Each generation faces the same challenge: how to expand civil rights and build an inclusive community. That challenge is what drew the two of us to political science. The job of making a better, fairer, nation now passes to you. It is our own hope that you, the mostly young adults reading our book, will, like so many Americans in the past, lead the United States toward greater civil rights.

CHAPTER SUMMARY

Check your understanding of Chapter 5.

🟢 The battle for civil rights generally includes seven stages. A group defines itself, challenges society, and changes the cultural story. The contest for rights spills across federalism; the executive branch can break the ice; Congress is the key to deep social change; the courts are the final arbiters of rights.

🟢 The Fourteenth Amendment contains the crucial legal rule for civil rights: "No state shall . . . deprive any person of . . . the equal protection of the laws."

🟢 A great mass movement rose up in which ordinary men, women, and children turned the legal promise of the *Brown v. Board of Education* decision into a practical reality. Protests eventually led to the Civil Rights Act of 1964 and the Voting Rights Act of 1965. The black civil rights movement set the model for future civil rights campaigns by many other groups.

🟢 Legislatures and courts turned to affirmative action in the 1960s and 1970s. The courts, and the public, have become increasingly skeptical of these programs.

🟢 Women first won voting rights in the states—across the West—before securing the Nineteenth Amendment, guaranteeing the right to vote regardless of gender.

🟢 The Civil Rights Act of 1964 bars gender discrimination. The women's movement organized to take advantage of the legal changes. The results transformed American gender roles in political and professional life.

🟢 Latinos, the United States's largest immigrant group, are a diverse people with many national identities, cultures, and concerns. Will they mobilize around shared interests? If they do, they will become a formidable political force, poised to advance civil rights claims for "Dreamers" and other Hispanic Americans.

🟢 Asian Americans are the third-largest minority group in the United States and now comprise 5 percent of the population. They are also a tremendously diverse group.

🟢 Native Americans lost their way of life in the face of disease, armies, and settlers. The Supreme Court gave them a special status: a separate people without rights. Although they retain the special status, they became U.S. citizens in 1924.

🟢 People with disabilities leveraged an obscure bureaucratic rule to mobilize and eventually won the sweeping rights of the Americans with Disabilities Act.

🟢 The gay (and lesbian) movements were born in a burst of pride and anger in 1969. Gays were the first to confront AIDS—a harrowing plague that pushed them into politics, health provision, and community building.

🟢 Gay, lesbian, bisexual, transgender, and queer communities have moved into mainstream politics. Nevertheless, they still face discrimination at work, in school, and over housing.

Need to review key ideas in greater depth? Click here.

KEY TERMS

1963 March on Washington, p. 155

Abolition, p. 147

Affirmative action, p. 157

black power, p. 156

Brown v. Board of Education, p. 152

Chicanismo, p. 164

Civil rights, p. 141

Civil Rights Act of 1964, p. 155

Class action, p. 162

Compromise of 1850, p. 147

De facto discrimination, p. 152

De jure discrimination, p. 152

Disproportionate impact, p. 157

Domestic dependent nation, p. 171

Dred Scott v. Sandford, p. 148

Emancipation Proclamation, p. 149

Equal Employment Opportunity Commission (EEOC), p. 161

Equal protection of the laws, p. 149

Equal Rights Amendment (ERA), p. 161

Freedom Riders, p. 154

Free rider problem, p. 154

Great Migration, p. 152

Jim Crow, p. 150

Literacy test, p. 150

Missouri Compromise, p. 147

National Association for the Advancement of Colored People (NAACP), p. 152

National Organization for Women (NOW), p. 161

Plessy v. Ferguson, p. 150

Racial profiling, p. 166

Reconstruction, p. 150

Reframing the issue, p. 161

School busing, p. 158

Section 504, p. 173

Seneca Falls Convention, p. 159

Strict scrutiny, p. 145

the new Jim Crow, p. 178

Flashcard review.

STUDY QUESTIONS

1. Name the seven steps involved in civil rights campaigns. Give examples of three, drawing on historical material.

2. Describe the Civil War Amendments. Why was the Fourteenth Amendment so important?

3. What was Jim Crow legislation? What happened to Jim Crow practices?

4. Describe the sit-ins and Freedom Rides of the civil rights movement. What was the point?

5. Describe three effects of the Civil Rights Act of 1964.

6. What is affirmative action? *For further reflection*: Write your own Supreme Court decision. Would you accept affirmative action in your college or university? Why or why not?

7. What are undocumented immigrants? *For further reflection*: What should the United States do about undocumented individuals?

8. What is the Lilly Ledbetter Law? *For further reflection*: Why do you think President Obama chose that as the first law to sign as president?

9. Although same-sex marriage has won national acceptance in courts and public-opinion polls alike, LGBTQ people continue to face discrimination. Discuss recent examples of limits on gay or transgender citizens' civil rights and how these might be redressed.

 Go to **www.oup.com/us/Morone** to find quizzes, flash cards, simulations, tutorials, videos, and other study tools.

6 Public Opinion and Political Participation

MAUREEN DOWD, A COLUMNIST for the *New York Times*, sat in her Denver hotel room and nibbled a caramel chocolate-flavored marijuana bar. Nothing. She ate some more. Suddenly, it hit her. "I lay curled up in a hallucinatory state for the next eight hours," she told her readers, "panting" and "shaking with paranoia." The next day, she found out that the bar should have been cut into 16 pieces. To many older people, like Dowd, what Colorado had done when it legalized recreational marijuana seemed—for better or for worse—like a social revolution. After all, twenty years ago, only one in four Americans supported legalizing marijuana. Then the number began to rise. Why? Because pollsters started asking a new generation with a very different outlook (Figure 6.1).[1]

Millennials (born between the early 1980s–2000) strongly support recreational pot (71% in 2017). Even Republican millennials agree (63%). That is a far cry from the oldest cohort, where a large majority still disapproves. A new generation led the change in public opinion—and that led to new government policies. In 2018, thirty states had legalized marijuana in some form—up from zero twenty years ago. Is that the end of the story? Perhaps not. Many people still oppose the change. The Trump administration Justice Department reminds citizens that marijuana remains a federal offense and greenlights federal prosecutors who want to bring federal cases regardless of state laws. Still, with Colorado marijuana sales topping $1 billion a year, most observers think the change is here to stay.[2]

Same-sex marriage reflects a similar story. Public approval leapt up from 31 percent in 2001 to 62 percent in 2017. Again, a new generation came along with different opinions and moved the results (Figure 6.2). As we saw in the last chapter, state legislatures started approving same-sex marriage laws and, in one courtroom after another, judges ruled that banning it violated the Fourteenth Amendment's guarantee of "equal protection under the law."[3]

● *New generation, new attitudes. A marijuana festival in Colorado, one of the 30 states that had legalized the drug in some form by 2018—reflecting a major shift in public opinion.*

In this chapter, you will:

● Identify the sources of our opinions.

● Explore how public opinion is measured.

● Reflect on the role of public opinion in a democracy.

● Explore different forms of political participation across U.S. history.

● Examine why people participate.

● Identify the benefits and drawbacks of an emerging "clickocracy" as political engagement moves online.

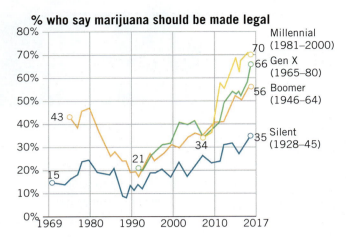

% who say marijuana should be made legal

Millennial (1981–2000) 70
Gen X (1965–80) 66
Boomer (1946–64) 56
Silent (1928–45) 35

43
21
34
15

● **Figure 6.1** *Millennials set the pace. Growing support for legal marijuana reflects a change in public opinion between generations. (Pew Research Center)*

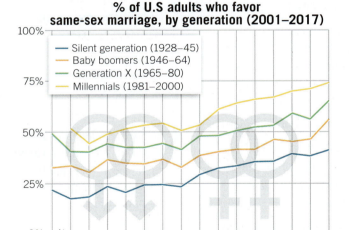

% of U.S adults who favor same-sex marriage, by generation (2001–2017)

- Silent generation (1928–45)
- Baby boomers (1946–64)
- Generation X (1965–80)
- Millennials (1981–2000)

● **Figure 6.2** *Support for same-sex marriage has risen dramatically . . . with millennials setting the pace (Pew Research Center).*

However, strong public views do not mean government action. Take global warming. Seventy-four percent of Americans believe there is solid evidence for global climate change.[4] Yet the Obama administration and a large Democratic majority in Congress failed to act back in 2009; Republicans began signing a "No Climate Tax Pledge," promising to oppose any climate change bills that required government spending. President Trump brushes aside the majority view and the scientific consensus, and calls it "a hoax." A minority—but one with very strong feelings—agrees with him. Much of this climate change denial is supported by fossil-fuel industry leaders. In the past decade, Democrats and Republicans have developed sharply different views of whether government should address climate change—making action far more difficult.[5]

Who are we? The world's oldest democracy. Public opinion takes us to the heart of self-rule. The people's views are paramount in government. Isn't this exactly the way it should be?

Not necessarily. Remember that the Constitution limits direct popular rule through the Electoral College, lifetime appointment for federal judges, the system of checks and balances, and many other institutions. American government is designed to balance public opinion and the judgment of public officials.

How officials respond is linked to who participates in our political system. When it comes to government action, who we really are rests, to a large extent, on who is willing to join in, express their views, and become part of our political system.

BY THE NUMBERS
Public Opinion and Political Participation

Percentage of millennials and the "Silent Generation" (aged sixty-five and over), respectively, who approve of marijuana legalization	**71, 35**
Percentage of these generations, respectively, who believe abortions should be legal in most cases	**62, 48**
Percentage of these generations, respectively, who would rather have a smaller government providing fewer services	**38, 64**
Percentage of baby boomers, Gen X, and millennials, respectively, who expect that Social Security will provide no benefits by the time they retire	**28, 50, 51[6]**
The authors' predicted probability that there will be no Social Security by the time the millennial generation retires	**0.001[7]**
Percentage turnout of voting-age population, U.S. presidential election, 1940, 1980, and 2016, respectively	**63, 58, 56**
Estimated number of political-themed blogs, 2001 and 2018	**500,[8] more than 100,000[9]**
Proportion of U.S. college students who report volunteering for public service, including informal volunteering such as helping neighbors, 2015	**82[10]**

How do what we think and how we participate change from generation to generation? How will this influence our political process and our policies?

Sources of Public Opinion

Public opinion is simply the sum of individual beliefs and opinions. Your views about how the United States should handle relations with North Korea, whether to cut taxes or raise the minimum wage, whether sports betting should be legal, and whether *Game of Thrones* is too violent for television—along with the views of everyone else in the country—make up public opinion. One central theme for this chapter: What role should your preferences play when public officials make policy? But before pondering that, we turn to a more basic question: Where do opinions come from?

Political Socialization

Why do white Americans trust the police more than black or Latino Americans? How come some of your friends—but not others—support a strong military? Why is one classmate a staunch Republican and another completely uninterested in politics? We call the many forces that shape our political attitudes and values **political socialization.**

> **Political socialization:** The process by which individuals acquire their political values and outlooks.

President Lyndon Johnson (LBJ) once remarked, "Tell me where a man comes from, how long he went to school, and where he worships on Sundays, and I'll tell you his political opinions."[11] LBJ, a big-talking Texan, may have exaggerated a bit. But basic life details are strong agents of socialization. And, yes, as Johnson claimed, they help predict where people stand. Let us look at some of the major sources of political socialization.

Parents and Friends. Many people absorb the political attitudes of their parents and caregivers. Mark Losey, running for a U.S. House seat, told his audiences a typical story about how he chose his party: As a child he used to go walking on his grandfather's farm. On one of those walks, recalls Losey, I asked, "'Grandpa, are we Democrats or Republicans?' My grandpa, who grew up on a farm during the height of the Great Depression, paused. 'Before Roosevelt became president, our family almost starved to death,' he replied. Grandpa Wren is still a Democrat. So am I."[12] Of course, some people—a minority—react against the attitudes they grew up hearing as children. Senator Orrin Hatch, a Utah Republican who retired in 2019 after 42 years in Congress, was raised a staunch Democrat. In college, recalls Hatch, "I learned that personal responsibility . . . was supremely better for businesses and individuals than an intrusive federal government that led to personal dependency."[13] That belief turned him into a Republican. Social networks, friends, and colleagues exert a major influence in shaping public opinion. We tend to adopt views expressed by the people around us.

Education. Education is a major agent of socialization. Many of us were influenced by our teachers going right back to kindergarten when students begin to say the Pledge of Allegiance. Those who seek graduate degrees—and most college professors—are more likely to identify as liberals than as conservatives.[14]

Gender. Gender also has a major effect on political views. Men are more likely to support nuclear power plants, fracking to extract natural gas, genetically modified foods, and testing products on animals. As you might guess from these examples, men lean Republican.

Race. As we have already seen, race plays an enormous role in American politics and history. African Americans are more likely to be regular churchgoers, more supportive of government spending on social services, and more Democratic. Hispanics tend to be socially conservative on issues such as abortion (see Figure 6.3) but liberal on government services (see Figure 6.4). They also have tended to be strongly Democratic. White Americans lean Republican.

Religion. Religion shapes public opinion on major value questions—from support for food stamps to views about abortion. White evangelicals vote strongly Republican (between 70 and 80 percent). Catholic voters tend to be split. Black Protestants, Latino Catholics, Jews, and Muslims all trend decidedly Democratic.

Life Events. As we grow up, major events shape our outlooks. The plunge into a Great Depression (in the early 1930s), the attack on Pearl Harbor (in 1941), the assassination of Martin Luther King (1963), the 9/11 terrorist attack (2001), the Great Recession of 2008—all potentially influence the young people who are just forming their political opinions. Each generation grows up with its own shared events, technologies, and expectations.

In sum, there is much truth in Lyndon Johnson's crack about understanding how a person votes. He just did not have enough variables to give a full account of political socialization. Family, friends, education, gender, race, and what you have experienced—tell us all those things and we can make a pretty good guess about where you stand politically.

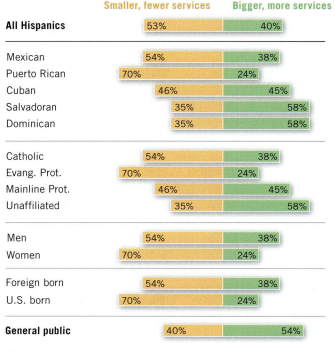

Views on abortion, by religion and nativity
% of Hispanics in each group who say abortion should be illegal in all or most cases OR legal in all or most cases

	All–mostly Illegal	All–mostly Legal
All Hispanics	53%	40%
Catholic	54%	38%
Evang. Prot.	70%	24%
Mainline Prot.	46%	45%
Unaffiliated	35%	58%
Attend worship services		
Weekly+	69%	25%
Monthly/yearly	46%	44%
Seldom/never	35%	58%
Foreign born	58%	33%
U.S. born	43%	49%
General public	40%	54%

● **Figure 6.3** *Hispanics tend to be socially conservative on issues such as abortion and religious observance . . .*

Role of government
% of Hispanics in each group who prefer smaller government with fewer services or a bigger government with more services

	Smaller, fewer services	Bigger, more services
All Hispanics	53%	40%
Mexican	54%	38%
Puerto Rican	70%	24%
Cuban	46%	45%
Salvadoran	35%	58%
Dominican	35%	58%
Catholic	54%	38%
Evang. Prot.	70%	24%
Mainline Prot.	46%	45%
Unaffiliated	35%	58%
Men	54%	38%
Women	70%	24%
Foreign born	54%	38%
U.S. born	70%	24%
General public	40%	54%

● **Figure 6.4** *. . . but liberal on the role of government. (Pew Research Center)*

Explore polls to discover how different factors influence opinion.

Party

Party preference has become an even stronger predictor of individual opinions than factors such as race and religion. Most politically active Americans register as either Democrats or Republicans and generally stay committed to their party (even if they call themselves independents, most stick to one party or the other). In recent years the differences between the parties have grown on almost every issue. "From immigration reform to food stamps to student loans," commented one respected pollster, "Republicans and Democrats inhabit different worlds."[15]

For a time, political scientists believed that elected officials were far more partisan than the public at large. Political scientist Morris Fiorina and his colleagues argued that most Americans are moderates. More recent analysis suggests decades of surging partisan division within the public.[16]

Self-Interest: Voting Our Pocketbooks

Some experts believe that economic self-interest matters most. They think people with more money will vote for lower taxes, while people with less will vote to expand social programs.

Yes, economic interests are important—but they are only one factor among many. In a book entitled *What's the Matter with Kansas?*, economist Thomas Frank pointed out that Kansas has some of the lowest average incomes in the country but votes for a congressional delegation made up exclusively of Republicans, who support cutting taxes and social programs. If they focused on their economic interest, argued Frank, they would be more likely to vote for Democrats. Recent studies in states such as Wisconsin, Mississippi, and Kentucky reach the same conclusion.[17] Yet, in general, poorer Americans are more likely to affiliate with Democrats, while wealthier Americans are equally divided between the parties (see Table 6.1). Wallets are not everything—but they explain a lot.[18]

TABLE 6.1 **Party Affiliations by Income Level**

FAMILY INCOME	REPUBLICAN	DEMOCRAT	INDEPENDENT
$150,000+	29%	29%	38%
$100,000 to $149,999	30%	30%	37%
$75,000 to $99,999	30%	29%	38%
$50,000 to $74,999	27%	30%	38%
$40,000 to $49,999	24%	33%	40%
$30,000 to $39,999	19%	33%	43%
$30,000	17%	35%	42%
Source: Pew Research Center			

Elite Influence

Stop for a moment and think about who you listen to when you make up your mind about an issue. Most people turn to friends and family. A series of studies, most notably by the political scientist John Zaller, suggested that people also look to **political elites**. People embrace signals from political leaders that are consistent with their prior beliefs.[19]

Some people look up to "experts" such as Megyn Kelly, Anderson Cooper, or other academics or media personalities. Others follow very visible public figures such as Oprah Winfrey. And politicians shape opinions: President Trump's tweets are followed by millions and powerfully influence supporters' views.

When elites compete to win over the public's views on issues, they are trying to *frame* the issue—to give the issue a particular slant. For example, when obesity became a source of widespread popular concern, many leaders joined the food industry in framing the issue as one of personal responsibility: Obesity is, they said, a problem of self-control. The simple solution: eat less, exercise more.

Others framed the problem as a "toxic food environment"—too much high-fat, low-nutrition food is available cheaply, from fast-food drive-throughs to school cafeterias. As the public health consequences of obesity became clearer, the toxic food environment perspective gained traction. The framing battle reached a fever pitch when former New York mayor Michael Bloomberg proposed banning sugary drinks larger than sixteen ounces—prompting cheers from public health advocates and fury from conservatives sounding off against the nanny state.

Political elites: Individuals who control significant wealth, status, power, or visibility and who, consequently, have significant influence over public debates.

Wars and Other Focusing Events

Americans pull together during crises. Tragedy, terrorist attacks, and the start of wars generally produce consensus—and a spike in the government's approval ratings. Nearly 90 percent of Americans backed the decision to invade Afghanistan a few weeks after the September 11, 2001, terrorist attacks on the World Trade Center and the Pentagon. Wars inspire a strong sense of "We're all in this together," but that sentiment generally evaporates, often quickly.[20]

Most dramatic events have a similar, if smaller, effect on public opinion. When a bridge collapsed in Minnesota, there was a spike in support for infrastructure spending and environmental regulation—only to see both surges fade away. However, there are exceptions. When Parkland students mobilized and spoke out for gun control, they kept the issue alive and pushed the Florida legislature into taking some action. Savvy political scientists discount the spikes in public opinion, knowing that the poll numbers generally come back down again (Figure 6.5). The key to keeping an issue alive: organizing a group that keeps on pushing even after the public has moved onto another issue—as we explore in Chapter 9.

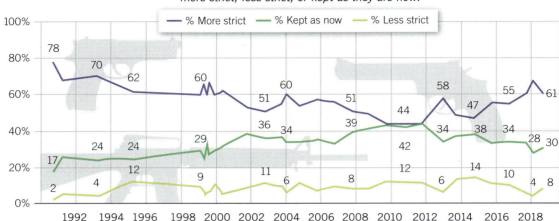

In general, do you think the laws covering the sale of firearms should be made more strict, less strict, or kept as they are now?

— % More strict   — % Kept as now   — % Less strict

● **Figure 6.5** *Percentage who approve of enhanced gun controls spikes after shootings, as happened after the December 2012 Sandy Hook Elementary School shooting and the Stoneman Douglas High School February 2018 shooting. (Gallup)*

The Bottom Line

» *Political socialization* refers to the factors that shape our political opinions: economic interest, family, friends, education, gender, race, religion, and major life events.

» Party identification has become the most reliable predictor of public opinion.

» Self-interest and political elites also influence political attitudes.

» Issue framing can shift individual and collective views.

» Dramatic events, especially wars, also have a powerful role in shaping our opinions. However, most spikes in public opinion are short lived.

How do we know what "the people" think?

Measuring Public Opinion

How do we know what the people are thinking? Professional polling firms such as Gallup, major media organizations, partisan outfits, and academic research centers all jostle to provide the most up-to-date polls. Candidates for office commission private polls; presidents and governors retain pollsters to gauge public opinion. Let's take a look at good polling, bad polling, and how to tell the difference.

Polling Bloopers

Back in 1920, a magazine named the *Literary Digest* helped introduce the idea that polls could predict presidential elections. The magazine relied on postcards sent in by subscribers. It boasted that it had never failed to predict the winner. Then, in 1936, the *Digest* forecast a lopsided defeat for incumbent President Franklin D. Roosevelt—who went on to win the biggest landslide in a century (he took every single state except Maine and Vermont). Why was *The Literary Digest* so wrong? Because its readers tended to be wealthy people who did not like Roosevelt or his policies. The biggest polling blooper of recent years? The 2016 election. Most polls gave Hillary Clinton a solid lead. Reading the polls, some experts declared her election up to 99 percent. Why were they wrong? Clinton won by 2.1 percent of the national vote—close to the consensus prediction of 3 percent. But polls were off in a few key states—throwing off predictions for the Electoral College (see Chapter 8). The lesson: polling is an inexact science and election rules (like the Electoral College) make it even more difficult to make confident predictions. But some polls are a lot better than others.[21]

Polling 101

Imagine that you are hired to conduct a survey about the next mayoral election. Where do you start? You could ask a few friends in your American government class who they plan to vote for, but that would not give you a reliable way to predict the winner. Here is how to improve your poll.

The Random Sample. Pollsters pick a random selection of individuals who reflect the entire population. All individuals should have an equal chance of being interviewed. Otherwise your results are likely to be misleading—skewed toward a subpopulation, such as the wealthy, or the young, or people who just happened to surf to your website.

Sampling frame. If your poll is to accurately reflect public views, your survey respondents must reflect the population: That means they must mirror the population's *age, education, income, race* or *ethnic group, gender,* and many other factors that reflect who will vote in the mayoral election. Asking only your classmates would bias the poll toward college-educated and young people. A good representative survey includes **demographic groups** in rough proportion to their presence in the population.

Refining the Sample. Do you want your poll to represent *all* city residents or only those who will probably vote? Choosing **likely voters** will more accurately predict the outcome of most elections—but predicting exactly who will come out on Election Day makes the pollster's job more difficult. This is where they went wrong in key states during the 2016 election.

Timing. Before you start knocking on doors or dialing numbers consider the *timing* of your survey. When do you conduct the poll? If you do it during the day, people with jobs will be away from home or unable to talk; if you conduct a telephone poll on a Friday evening, you are unlikely to find many younger residents at home—skewing your results to older people's opinions.

Listen to excerpts from Roosevelt's fiery 1936 campaign speech.

Random sample: A sample in which everyone in the population has an equal probability of being selected

Sampling frame: A designated group of people from whom a set of poll respondents is randomly selected.

Demographic group: People sharing specific factors like age, ethnicity/race, religion, or country of origin.

Likely voters: Persons identified as probable voters in an upcoming election. Often preferred by polling organizations, but difficult to specify with great accuracy.

Framing effects: The way the wording of a polling question influences a respondent.

Push poll: A form of negative campaigning that masquerades as a regular opinion survey. They usually feature unflattering information about an opponent.

IF THE ELECTION WERE
HELD TODAY, WOULD YOU:
a.) VOTE AGAINST REPUBLICANS,
b.) THROW THE CORRUPT, EVIL
    BUMS OUT, OR
c.) BANISH THE GOP
    TO EVERLASTING
    SCORN AND
    RIDICULE?...

FULLER©2006
ARTIZANS.COM

MEDIA POLL

● *Mocking bias in the polls.*

Talking POLITICS

TYPES OF POLLS

Benchmark polls. Conducted by a campaign as the race begins, these surveys provide a basis for comparison, or a "benchmark," for later polls. With a benchmark number, candidates can tell if their likelihood of winning is rising or falling.

Straw polls. Informal polls carried out by local party organizations or news outlets. They often involve actual (nonbinding) votes cast by party members. Media organizations (and the straw poll winners) report results, especially during presidential primaries.

Wording. Once you have chosen your sampling frame and have decided when to ask questions, you face an even more important question: What exactly will you ask? If this were a chat with your classmates, you might ask simply, "Who do you support in the 2020 mayoral election?" But surveys must take into account **framing effects**: The *way* pollsters ask a question often influences the response.

For example, researchers from Pew asked people to choose between a tax cut and "funding new government programs." The public overwhelmingly picked the tax cut, 60 percent to 25 percent. Then the pollsters adjusted the question and asked people to choose between a tax cut and funding for "programs on education, the environment, health care, crime fighting and military defense." Now, 69 percent opted for the government programs and only 22 percent for the tax cut. The wording made all the difference.[22] A good poll will pretest the questions to sniff out the subtle biases that creep in with different wordings.

Lies, Damn Lies, and Polls. Campaigns and advocacy groups often *want* to skew their survey results and use framing effects to their advantage. Some polls go even further and actually try to influence respondents' views. These efforts—which do not even pretend to be legitimate attempts to measure opinions—are called **push polls**. These "polls" have more impact on unsuspecting respondents because they are campaign advertisements masquerading as scientific surveys.

For example, people who answered the phone during the 2018 California primary were first asked questions about the infamous contamination of the water in Flint, Michigan, and then asked whether they supported a water fee increase in California. The pro-fee pollsters, having duly primed their respondents, then announced that 69 percent favored the increase. This, of course, was more an advertisement than a serious poll.[23]

Technology and Error. Younger Americans are especially hard to reach and survey. Can you guess why? Many young people—and 47 percent of all phone users—rely on mobile phones rather than landlines.

Sampling Error and Response Bias. Finally, you have collected the raw data from your survey respondents. Time to tell the world about your poll? Not so fast. You still need to determine your poll's **margin of sampling error**, a statistical calculation for how accurate your results are. By carefully designing their

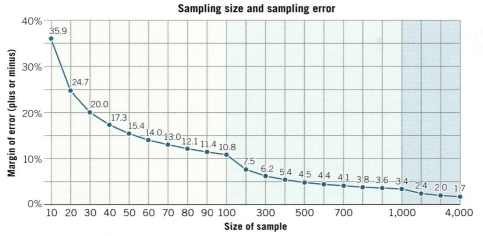

● **Figure 6.6** *Sampling errors decline with larger sample sizes. (Pew Research Center)*

polls, national surveys are able to achieve small errors with as few as 1,000 respondents (see Figure 6.6).

Pollsters also must consider **response bias** in publicizing their findings. Studies show that some respondents purposely mislead pollsters. A classic example of response bias arose when Tom Bradley, the first African American mayor of Los Angeles, ran against a white candidate, George Deukmejian, for governor of California in 1982. Bradley had a comfortable double-digit lead in opinion surveys as Election Day approached—but lost the race. Pollsters must be alert to what is now known as "the Bradley effect": the possible inclination of some survey respondents to hide their real opinions so they do not appear racist or sexist. Pollsters speculate there may have been "shy" Trump voters in 2016—people reluctant to admit they supported Trump, especially after a Hollywood Access caught the future candidate making obscene comments.

Sample size, framing effects, and margin of error: Account for all these, and you are well on your way to conducting a truly scientific public opinion survey. One important reason to understand the design of polls is to enable you to distinguish the good from the bad. Table 6.2 summarizes some of the tips.

Do Opinion Surveys Influence Us?

Might the profusion of polls also affect the decisions citizens make—including how to vote? Some evidence suggests that they may. Candidates who are leading in the polls tend to pick up support from voters who were undecided, or who weakly supported the opponent. The **bandwagon effect** in polling varies considerably from election to election. It can be exaggerated by media coverage.

Talking POLITICS

Brushfire polls. Internal surveys conducted by a campaign once election season begins. They provide details about how a candidate is performing; if things are going poorly, the campaign can work to put out the "brushfire" (swiftly burning) opposition.

Exit polls. Performed on Election Day, both by campaigns and news organizations, these surveys intercept voters as they exit the voting location. Media reporters often rely on exit polls to call results, even if ballots have not been officially counted.

Margin of sampling error: The degree of inaccuracy in any poll, arising from the fact that surveys involve a *sample* of respondents from a population, rather than every member.

Response bias: The tendency of poll respondents to misstate their views, frequently to avoid "shameful" opinions that might appear sexist or racist.

Bandwagon effect: When people join a cause because it seems popular or support a candidate who is leading in the polls.

TABLE 6.2 Tips on Reading Polls

1. *Check out the margin of error.* Then reread the poll and take it into account. A 3 percent margin of error means plus or minus 3 percent—turning a 50 percent approval rating into what is, in reality, an approval rating between 47 and 53 percent.
2. *What is the timing?* The farther away from Election Day, the less meaningful the results.
3. *The random sample is the gold standard.* If the respondents chose themselves (by deciding to take the survey), then it may be fun to read . . . but it is probably not an accurate picture of the public.
4. *What is the sample size?* Be wary of polls that interview a small number of people. For a national poll, 1,000 to 1,500 respondents are typical. If the margin of error is too large (say over 5%), then approach the poll with caution.
5. *Compare across polls.* Because every poll has biases, read a range of polls, toss out the extreme findings, and take an average of the rest.

Craft and interpret surveys to advise Congress.

Boomerang effect: The discrepancy between candidates' high poll ratings and election performance, caused by supporters' assumption that an easy win means they need not turn out.

A cousin of polling's bandwagon effect is the **boomerang effect**. Here, a candidate who has been consistently ahead in opinion surveys performs worse than expected on Election Day. The logic is that supporters see a big lead for their candidate, figure that she will win without any difficulty, and so do not bother to vote.

 **The Bottom Line**

» Scientific surveys have come a long way. Professionals now design well-specified polls—that can occasionally have unanticipated errors—as happened with the 2018 state-based election polls.

» Always pay attention to the polls' margin of error.

» Poll results can affect public opinion.

» Sampling errors, response bias, and other potential flaws inevitably confer a measure of uncertainty on any survey.

Public Opinion in a Democracy

If the public is to have any meaningful role in governing, political leaders must listen to them. But here's the uncomfortable question: Do the people know enough to influence government? Is the public rational and capable of self-government? Or are we, as political scientist David Sears suggested in a recent essay, "an ignorant and easily duped electorate?"[24] Let's look at two different views.

Ignorant Masses

"The masses are asses!" insisted Walter Lippmann in his path-breaking book, *Public Opinion* (published in 1922). Lippmann, a well-known political journalist and cultural critic, believed the typical American was distracted by celebrities and minor scandals, rarely followed policy issues closely enough to understand the details, and yet readily offered up personal views on any topic. Paying attention to uninformed masses was no way to run a country. Lippmann, along with many others, believed that governing involved technical decisions that were best left to well-trained experts.[25]

In 1960, four University of Michigan professors published a book that hit America like a thunderclap. *The American Voter* used careful data analysis and came to the same conclusion as Lippmann had: Americans are politically ignorant; they do not even offer logically consistent answers during a survey. One of the authors, Philip Converse, later coined the term ***nonattitudes*** to describe the response of many Americans to polls. When people were asked the same questions at different times, they tended to change their answers—sometimes radically. Moreover, changes in their responses were random: People did not switch their positions in response to new information or in changing contexts, but rather offered up different and even diametrically opposed views for no apparent reason.[26]

Recent research echoes this view suggesting that most people do not function as "rational actors" who seek and analyze information, weigh evidence, and choose candidates (or support policies) that advance their preferred views. Rather, people rationalize preconceived biases and react to unconscious cues. They may not even be aware of why they are making the choices they make.[27]

Nonattitudes: The lack of a stable perspective in response to opinion surveys.

The Rational Public

The alternative view was captured in a book-length response to *The American Voter* called *The Rational Public*. The authors, Benjamin Page and Robert Shapiro, agreed that yes, most voters were inattentive to policy issues and uninformed about political details. However, measured across large groups, public opinion moves in coherent, stable ways that signal shared views about policy issues.[28]

Page and Shapiro argued that most of us use **information shortcuts** to arrive at reasonable judgments about politics and government. These shortcuts are often derived from our direct personal experience. Homeowners grasp the importance of interest-rate changes, and shoppers feel inflation's effect on rising prices. They develop an intuitive sense of the performance of the economy. Likewise, citizens notice impacts of other policy outcomes on their daily lives, as they notice that trains or buses are running on time or mail is arriving late. Through a steady and often unwitting process of making everyday evaluations, voters arrive at reasonably well-established positions on candidates or policy issues.

Journalist James Surowiecki summarized this perspective in the title of his book: *The Wisdom of Crowds*. Even if any individual does not have clear views, argued Surowiecki, a large crowd, taken together, adds up to a rational

Information shortcuts: Cues about candidates and policies drawn from everyday life.

public. In fact, a random collection of people, he continued, is actually wiser than a group of experts when it comes to devising the best solution to a policy dilemma.

Overall if the group is of sufficient size—at least a few dozen—and members feel free to speak their minds, they will zero in on a good collective decision. Often these are innovative, outside-the-box solutions. Experts, on the other hand, are typically trained in similar ways and are subject to **groupthink**: They tend to reinforce one another's existing prejudices.

Surowiecki illustrated his point by going back to an old English county fair. A prize was offered to whoever could guess the correct weight of a giant ox on display. Cattle experts weighed in with their own well-founded opinions, but all were considerably off the mark. More than eight hundred locals offered up guesses as well. Although no one hit the correct weight (1,198 pounds), averaging the crowd's collective estimate came out at 1,197—just one pound below the correct total, and much closer than that offered by any agricultural or farming expert.[29]

Governing By the People

The optimistic view about the wisdom of the crowd restores traditional hopes about self-rule. However, if public opinion is to guide government, three conditions must be met.

1. The people know what they want and guide government decisions.
2. The public can clearly communicate its desires to political leaders.
3. Political leaders pay attention to public views and respond.

Groupthink: The tendency among a small group of decision makers to converge on a shared set of views. It can limit creative thinking or solutions to policy problems.

James Surowiecki discusses the power—and danger—of crowds, including online "mobs."

What Do YOU Think? | **How Closely Should Elected Officials Follow Public Opinion?**

Should the government approve a pipeline delivering gas from Canadian tar sands to Texas refineries? When the debate began, the public supported the project but, in 2015, the Obama administration refused to issue a permit to build the pipeline, aligning itself with a Democratic Party concerned about global climate change and the environment.

The Trump administration reversed the decision in response to Republican desires for energy independence—and despite the fact that public support has dropped and polls show that the public disapproved of the pipeline, 51 percent to 42 percent. Is it okay for presidents to override public opinion?

Elected officials must lead. We elect leaders and expect them to fulfill their campaign promises. Both presidents responded to the people who voted them into office. Furthermore, presidents can be privy to more information about an issue than the general public. In these cases, they must override the opinion of the majority.

Public opinion should dominate. Even though individuals may not know all the details of a policy issue, a large group of people tends to provide reliable information and make good choices that are reflected in polls. Furthermore, polls measure and communicate the values and views of the people. Elected officials should look to these polls to inform their decisions.

Do the People Know What They Want? Although the opinion polls suggest that the public has distinct preferences, public views often fail to provide a guide for policymakers. For example, after the economic collapse between 2008 and 2010, polls showed a majority of Americans were angry at Wall Street banks. But when Congress and the Obama administration tried to translate this public discontent into concrete legislative solutions, popular consensus evaporated. Should we regulate derivatives as we do stocks and bonds so that their trading is transparent? Half the public said yes, half said no. Limit CEOs' pay or the multimillion-dollar bonuses the financial wizards receive each year? Maybe, or maybe not, Americans told surveyors. Does the public know what it wants? In a general way, it probably does. But political leaders have to supply the policy specifics.

How Do the People Communicate Their Desires? It is difficult for the people—even a clear majority—to convey their views to policymakers. As we have seen, **survey research** can offer a snapshot of public opinion but is hard to translate into specific polices.

Of course, democracies also rely on elections. Candidates who win often claim they have a **mandate**: The people have spoken. But it is often difficult to translate an election into support for any single policy. In 2016, republicans won the presidency and both chambers of Congress. But even with that mandate, they were not able to eliminate Obamacare, build a border wall, or rewrite the immigration laws. As previous administrations also learned, even a clean sweep of elective branches does not automatically translate into policy success.

Do Leaders Respond to Public Opinion? On the surface, the answer seems clear: yes! Politicians are hooked on polls. President Trump routinely tweets out any uptick in his **approval rating**, while Democratic critics are quick to report downturns. Candidates running for office spend, collectively, more than a billion dollars on opinion surveys. President Bill Clinton was said to poll on everything—including where to go on vacation.[30]

Polls matter most in setting the **policy agenda**. Public opinion helps shape which topics governing officials pay attention to in the first place. If the public thinks something is important, political leaders will usually respond.

Big changes in public opinion have an especially significant effect on Congress. Members are often reluctant to legislate in the face of strong popular opposition. Americans may ignore many topics, but when large numbers of us pay attention to

Survey research: Systematic study of a defined population, analyzing a representative sample's views to draw inferences about the larger public's views. Also termed *opinion poll*.

Mandate: Political authority claimed by an election winner as reflecting the approval of the people.

Approval rating: A measure of public support for a political figure or institution.

Policy agenda: The issues that the media covers, the public considers important, and politicians address. Setting the agenda is the first step in political action.

● *Public opinion alerted politicians to the anger at big banks—but did not provide an answer for what to do about it.*

something, politicians generally respond. That is exactly what we saw at the start of this chapter with marijuana and same-sex marriage.

Although collective public opinion holds some sway, the opinions of some groups matter more than others. As we have seen, pollsters target the opinions of likely voters—individuals they expect to participate in elections. Social movements, interest groups, and political parties work to collect and transmit their views and can have a more direct influence on public policies. By participating in the political system, your voice is more likely to be heard.

The Bottom Line

» Some Americans have viewed public opinion as an unreliable, even dangerous, guide to government policymaking, based in part on voter ignorance.

» Others argue that, in practice, a "rational public" is the best source of democratic decision making.

» One way to combine these clashing views is to focus not on what individuals know about politics but on how the many different popular views add up to a "wisdom of crowds."

» If public opinion is to guide politics, three conditions must be met: The public must know what it wants; its views must be effectively communicated; and leaders must pay attention.

» Even strong public opinion may not be specific enough to offer policy guidance.

» All government officials constantly have to weigh doing what they think is best against doing what the public desires. Popular views can help set governing agendas.

Getting Involved: Political Participation

In some ways, Americans are highly engaged in politics; in other ways Americans are downright apathetic. In this section, we explore the many pathways to participation in the political system. Some stretch back over two hundred years; others are just emerging on the political scene today. Altogether, they break into three broad categories: traditional participation, civic volunteerism, and direct action.

Traditional Participation

The 2020 election campaign has already begun to fire up millions of people. Will Donald Trump run for—and win—a second term? Can former Vice President Joe Biden or Senator Elizabeth Warren capture the Democratic

TABLE 6.3 **Rates of Traditional Political Participation**

22% of Americans have attended a political meeting on local, town, or school affairs.
13% have been an active member of a group that tries to influence the public or government.
10% have attended a political rally or speech.
7% have worked or volunteered for a political party or candidate.
7% have called into a live radio or TV show to express an opinion about a political or social issue.
1.7% have donated to political campaigns.
0.03% have donated $200 or more to political campaigns.
Source: Pew Research Center

nomination, or will a member of the rising generation take the helm? Many of these candidates' supporters engage in traditional politics. **Traditional participation** means getting involved in politics through formal government channels—organized by federal and state constitutions and developed over time. Voting, working for a candidate, signing petitions, or writing letters to the newspaper are all ways of becoming active (see Table 6.3).

Traditional participation: Engaging in politics through the formal channels of government and society.

Voting. Voting is the most important aspect of political participation in the United States. Yet over 120 million eligible Americans did not vote in 2018. Recall from Chapter 2 that the Constitution leaves most election details up to the states. There are many subtle ways that a state can encourage (or discourage) voters by making it easier (or harder) to vote. If you have voted, you know the basic drill.

First, register to vote. Seventeen states and the District of Columbia make the process much easier by permitting registration and voting on the same day. Oregon was the first state to automatically register voters.

Second, cast your vote. Only a few years ago, this meant arriving on Election Day at your assigned polling place. But today, thirty-seven states permit early voting—again to make voting more convenient—and more than a third of the ballots are cast before Election Day. Washington, Colorado, and Oregon conduct elections by mail.

If you do vote on Election Day, bear in mind that some states limit voting facilities—creating long lines, which will discourage some voters. In November 2018, voters waited over three hours in Reno, Nevada, so that all voters in line had a chance to cast their ballots. Record turnout—the highest for a midterm election since 1966—meant late poll closings in Texas and Georgia, and some Maryland polling stations ran out of ballots.

Once you get to the head of the line, you will encounter polling workers. They are usually unpaid volunteers—another form of political participation. They will direct you to a voting booth, often adorned with distinctive blue curtains.

● *Why is voting turnout lower in the United States than in many other countries? Perhaps it's because some governments make it difficult. Pictured here are the long voting lines in Atlanta, Georgia.*

Inside, you find one of many different voting mechanisms. Some jurisdictions use touch screens; some states use voting machines with levers; and in others you mark paper ballots. In 2016, an allegedly Russian-sponsored hacking of Democratic Party servers led to congressional hearings and federal investigations about electronic voting machines being tampered with, and even calls for a return to paper balloting. Others suggest new technologies, like blockchain voting—an online method that is far more difficult to hack.

If many different offices are listed on the ballot, perhaps along with an issue referendum or two (which we discuss in Chapter 8), it might take you several minutes to work your way down the ballot and make all your choices.

Electoral Activities. Beyond voting, Americans engage in other electoral activities. They volunteer to get out the vote for favorite candidates. They go to meetings and rallies. They post signs on their lawns and bumper stickers on their cars. They donate money.

Voice. If Americans vote less, they are quick to express their opinion. One in five contacts a government official—about everything from potholes to immigration policy. To the surprise of many people, legislators—and especially members of Congress—devote considerable time to constituent inquiries.

Civic Voluntarism

Civic voluntarism: Citizen participation in public life without government incentives or coercion, such as getting together to build a playground.

Not all participation runs through politics. Many Americans volunteer for causes or donate money for local charities. These are forms of **civic voluntarism**, working together to address problems through society.

When the French visitor Alexis de Tocqueville, whom we met earlier in this book, traveled through the United States in 1831–1832, he was struck by Americans' eagerness to get involved. In *Democracy in America*, Tocqueville repeatedly remarked on the way Americans joined together to build roads, schools, and hospitals; in France, he noted, such projects would require elaborate layers of government approval—and in England, would need the patronage of a lord.[31]

The United States is at or near the top of the international charts on volunteering.[32] And the millennial generation—adults between 18 and 34 years—is the most active in modern U.S. history when it comes to devoting time for worthy causes. Over the past decade, the proportion of teenagers who volunteer has more than doubled. Résumé padding for career advancement? Recent studies say no. Figure 6.7 shows the major reasons why younger millennials get involved.

Voluntary engagement comes in many forms. People serve in a food bank, teach English as a second language, join a volunteer fire department, or help raise money for high school basketball uniforms. Many Americans respond to crowd-funding requests on sites such as Kickstarter, GoFundMe, and others.

Volunteers may not see their work as political, and indeed getting involved is often related to a hobby or enthusiasm, rather than public service. Whatever the motivation, however, voluntary activity tends to draw people into the common sphere. And once there, the payoff is clear. If you volunteer, you are more likely to vote, pay attention to political affairs, and otherwise engage in public life. As we saw in Chapter 1, successful democracies require a vibrant civic spirit.

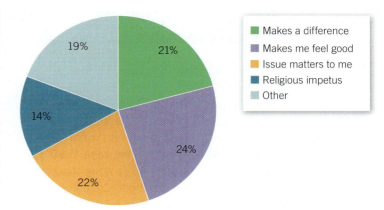

- Makes a difference
- Makes me feel good
- Issue matters to me
- Religious impetus
- Other

● **Figure 6.7** *Americans aged 15 to 25: Reasons for volunteering. (Brookings Institution)*

Direct Action

When people feel that the traditional forms of participation are not working, they sometimes seek change outside of normal channels and take **direct action**. This is the world of demonstrations, marches, armed standoffs, and riots.

Protest politics can invoke the highest American aspirations. Or they can reflect nativism, prejudice, and unbridled anger. The goal is generally to call attention to a cause and to foster a movement around it. Of course, direct action can blur into electoral politics. Protests can spark political movements that then penetrate political institutions. The #MeToo movement against sexism and gender inequity arose in part from the women's marches against the insensitivity of those in power. A record number of women candidates and victors in the 2018 midterm elections represents an institutional change growing out of protest.[33] The Tea Party also began as a protest movement and, before long, candidates for public office began aligning themselves with the movement. Occasionally, direct action goes further and violates the law—sometimes through proud acts of **civil disobedience**. Protesting slavery in 1849, Henry David Thoreau urged his countrymen: "if [the law] requires you to be the agent of injustice to another, then, I say break the law. Let your life be a counter friction to stop the machine." Martin Luther King, Jr.

Direct action: Participating outside of normal political and social channels through civil disobedience, demonstrations, and even riots.

Civil disobedience: Protesting laws one considers unjust by refusing to obey them—and accepting the punishment.

● *Civic volunteerism: Americans work together to solve social problems.*

What Do YOU Think?

Would You Have Protested?

Go back to the Civil Rights protests pictured on pages 153–154—young people at a sit-in are humiliated, those on a Freedom Bus beaten and almost burned alive. College students carried out the sit-ins and Freedom Rides. A question for you—one we often ask ourselves: **If you were in college between 1960 and 1962, would you have joined in?** It would have taken conviction, courage, and (for most students) a willingness to ignore parents horrified by the risks.

What would you have done? Explain why. Now consider the protests taking place on campuses today. How are they similar? How are they different? Have you considered taking part yourself? Explain why.

Political voice: Exercising one's public rights, often through speaking out in protest or in favor of some policy change.

picked up this theme in his eloquent Letter from Birmingham Jail, where he wrote to white liberals about why black Americans would break unjust laws rather than wait quietly for reform.

Great American rallies mark high points in our political history. After millions of Americans gathered to promote cleaner air and water at the first Earth Day in April 1970, Congress passed major clean-air legislation within a month, and a Clean Water Act followed soon after that. A series of "Rally for Life" marches in the 1980s–1990s helped advance the anti-abortion cause in Congress and many state legislatures. That type of **political voice** is the lifeblood of American democracy.

Direct action is not always part of the proud democratic legacy. Violent protests in Seattle cost an estimated $20 million—and also put antiglobalization on the political agenda. White Nationionalist activists in Charlottesville claimed they were defending southern heritage but shocked most Americans with their anti-Semitic and harsh racial attitudes. Were they taking political action? Recklessly destroying property? Violating hard won American norms? Or all of the above?

Finally, direct action also includes a dark legacy of violence and injustice. Recall how the entire system of Jim Crow was kept in place by a tradition of lynching—a form of American terrorism.

The Participation Puzzle

This chapter confronts us with a puzzle: American voting rates are very low compared to those in other nations. Under 60 percent of the voting age population turns out in presidential elections and 40 percent in midterms. Yet some Americans are quick to get involved in direct action.

Perhaps the level of citizen participation reflects the rules that govern the electoral system. Low voter turnout may partially reflect the barriers to voting that have been erected over the years: registration requirements, voting on

Compare voter participation by country and group.

a working day, and so on. Historic barriers restricting the African American vote in the South and the immigrant vote in the North may also contribute to low turnout today. In contrast, some democracies go so far as to *require* voting.

At the same time that voting is low, strong First Amendment rights have fostered a tradition of taking to the streets to demonstrate strongly held views. Here's the fundamental question: Is the American system a miracle of mass participation? Or one designed to limit citizen access? Or, in the spirit of American federalism, is it a state-by-state patchwork of both?[34]

The Bottom Line

» Traditional participation involves engaging politics through formal government channels. Voting is the most familiar form of traditional political participation.

» Americans participate in politics year-round. One in five contacts a public official in the course of a year.

» Civic voluntarism is a form of engagement with public life that operates outside of government—but enhances democracy.

» Direct action seeks change by going outside the formal channels of government. It has a long legacy in the United States that goes back to the nation's founding and includes some of the nation's great reform movements.

Why Do People Get Involved?

Whether they are voting, volunteering, or expressing their political voice, some Americans feel more inspired to participate than others. What makes Americans more likely to engage in political activity? Let's look at five major factors: background, friends, community, mobilization, and—surprisingly—government benefits.

Background: Age, Wealth, Education, and Race

Age. Older people vote more often. Figure 6.8 displays voting rates for different American generations. Note that *young* adults vote less, in election after election. In fact, given their distinctive opinions, if young people voted as regularly as older people, they would profoundly change American politics. Instead, younger voters are more likely to try and influence politics through direct action and are far more likely to participate online.

Wealth. High earners tend to be much more involved in public life than those farther down the income ladder—and the higher the income, the more likely individuals are to get involved in politics.[35]

▷

Learn about the role of the younger Americans in the 2012 election.

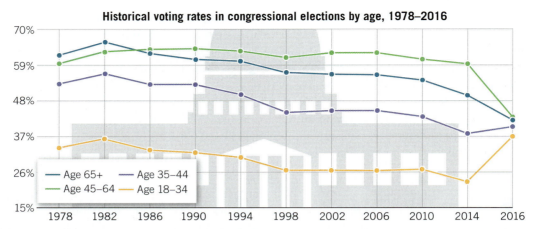

Historical voting rates in congressional elections by age, 1978–2016

Legend:
- Age 65+
- Age 45–64
- Age 35–44
- Age 18–34

● **Figure 6.8** *Voter turnout in congressional elections, by age. (U.S. Census Bureau)*

Education. Education also predicts political involvement. It is no surprise that education closely tracks income. Figure 6.9 shows that the more education, the higher the voting levels. Less than 30 percent of the people who did not finish high school normally vote in presidential elections; citizens with a college degree are more than twice as likely to vote. People with a college degree are far more likely to be politically involved in other ways than those who did not finish high school. Voters with less education, however, played a critical role in 2016 due to their strong support of Donald Trump.

Race. If we were writing this book fifteen years ago, we would have had to add another major category: race. Traditionally, African Americans voted in lower numbers than white Americans. Gradually, however, the gap began to close and for the first time in American history, black Americans voted at a slightly higher rate than white Americans when Barack Obama ran for president. Hispanic turnout jumped from about 8 percent in 2016 to between 11 and 12 percent in 2018, perhaps signaling a new trend.[36] As their numbers grow, they are becoming an increasingly important political force.[37]

Friends and Family. Another way to predict whether someone will vote or volunteer is to find out whether their parents and closest friends do. On average, someone whose family or peers vote regularly is likely to do so as well.

An even more powerful inspiration is being *asked* to get involved by people close to you. Political science studies find that face-to-face encouragement is the most reliable route to political activity. Direct personal contact—even with strangers—gets results. This finding appears to hold for many forms of participation—and in many nations. Protesters are often part of personal networks.[38]

Community. The type of community you live in also makes a difference. In some places, neighbors are more trusting and people are more likely to get

Social capital: Relations between people that build closer ties of trust and civic engagement, yielding productive benefits for the larger society.

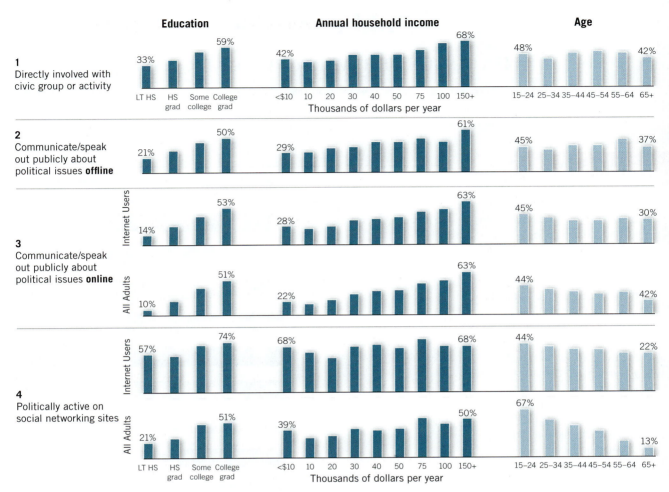

● **Figure 6.9** *Percentage involvement in civic activities by education, income, and age (Pew Research Center). Note: "LT HS" means "less than high school; failed to graduate."*

involved—in local activities such as block watches, school fundraisers, or community gardens. Those types of communities also see higher voting rates. We call this spirit of being high on volunteerism and public participation—**social capital**. Communities that score high on social capital tend to house happier, healthier residents. One related worry about millennials: They exhibit lower levels of trust, generally speaking, than previous groups of young Americans. This makes social capital harder to generate in the rising generation.[39]

Political Mobilization. Political parties are powerful sources of **political mobilization**—urging millions of people to get involved, especially at election time (see Chapter 11). When it comes to **issue advocacy**, however, interest groups have become our mobilizers-in-chief. At times, issue advocacy campaigns and social movements threaten to take over a party—as happened with the Tea Party Movement and the Republican Party after 2009.[40]

Political mobilization:
Efforts to encourage people to engage in the public sphere: to vote for a particular candidate (and donate money, work on the campaign, etc.) or to get involved in specific issues.

Issue advocacy: Organized effort to advance (or block) a proposed public policy change.

Public Rallies

WHAT ISSUES DRAW PEOPLE TO PROTEST?

Americans participate in politics for many different reasons. Participation in public rallies has climbed in recent years. Which issues draw people into the streets? Here are the top twelve issues in 2018. They include both liberal causes (women's and LGBTQ rights, environment/energy, minimum wage) and conservative ones (abortion, gun rights, the removal of Confederate monuments). Today, more protesters come from the left.

THINK ABOUT IT

Look back at issue polls from the year you were born, or even just five years ago (both Pew and Gallup websites list these year by year). Which topics seemed of highest interest then? What has changed in the United States to explain the shift to this set of issues?

Are there any issue(s) that you would add to this list, as likely sources of mass protest in coming months? Is there Anything you'd *like* to see on the list that isn't— something that arouses your passion enough to join a march or rally?

Source: Washington Post *and Kaiser Family Foundation.*

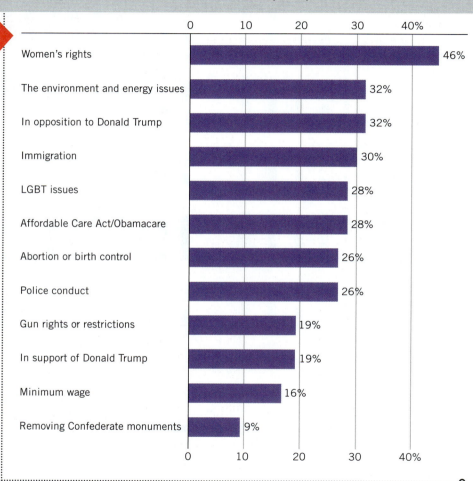

Issue	Percentage
Women's rights	46%
The environment and energy issues	32%
In opposition to Donald Trump	32%
Immigration	30%
LGBT issues	28%
Affordable Care Act/Obamacare	28%
Abortion or birth control	26%
Police conduct	26%
Gun rights or restrictions	19%
In support of Donald Trump	19%
Minimum wage	16%
Removing Confederate monuments	9%

In the eyes of professional political mobilizers—advocacy groups, campaign strategists, and other members of the enormous "political industry" based in Washington, DC—each of us is a potential resource. They spend a great deal of money and energy trying to inspire us: to sign a petition, write our congressional representatives, send them a check, and get out and vote.

Government Beneficiaries. A fifth factor encouraging participation in public life may strike you as odd at first glance: receiving some types of government benefits. If you receive a federally guaranteed student loan, or are covered by your parents' health insurance past age twenty-one, you are a beneficiary. Researchers have shown that when the government rewards service—as when returning soldiers receive free or discounted college tuition through the GI Bill—recipients are considerably more likely to get involved as volunteers and to exercise their public voice.[41]

These spurs to participation all focus on individual factors. Being asked, imitating your parents and friends, living in an active community, responding to incentives, or receiving government benefits influences your own inclination to engage in the public sphere. But there is also a larger backdrop to participation as well.

Historical Context

Major shifts in the economy and in politics affect both the intensity and the types of participation. In the rural South during the early to mid-twentieth century, for example, an infestation of boll weevils (tiny insects that feed on cotton plants) devastated the cotton crop. Many African American subsistence farm workers, whose livelihood was gone, moved to cities (in both the south and the north). Suddenly surrounded by new kinds of communities, many plunged into civil rights movements—and changed American politics.

Context deeply influences opportunities for political engagement.[42] During some historical periods, Americans have been more likely to engage in public life than at other times. For example, workers (in the 1930s) and students (in the 1960s) flocked into direct action politics in massive numbers. Today—with Americans organizing across the political spectrum on many college campuses—we appear to be in another high participation moment.

Talking POLITICS

HOW MOBILIZERS SEE US

Political strategists have a language of their own. Below are some of the terms you'll hear if you work in politics long enough.

Grassroots: A movement for political reform that is sparked at the local level, "from the ground up"—figuratively, from the grassroots.

Astroturf: A movement for reform that *appears* to be from the grassroots but is actually mobilized by political professionals.

Dog whistling: Using insider, "coded" language to rouse constituents or interest-group members who care strongly about an issue—such as making religious references that nonbelievers won't get. (The rather rude analogy is from training dogs, which hear high-frequency whistles that other animals—including humans—cannot.)

The Bottom Line

» People participate in politics at very different rates.

» Five factors influence their decision to get involved: background characteristics such as income and education; family and friends; the community they live in; political mobilization efforts; and receipt of government benefits from programs that treat beneficiaries with respect (e.g., Social Security).

» Political mobilization also is influenced by the larger social and historical context.

Talking POLITICS

HOW MOBILIZERS SEE US

(Continued)

Actorvist: A professional actor involved in political issue campaigns, increasingly valuable in winning attention for one's cause. George Clooney and Oprah Winfrey, both of whom speak out in favor of gun control, Chuck Norris, who actively supports a strong military, and Demi Lovato, on mental health, are among the many "actorvists." Also sometimes heard is "raptivist," rappers who get involved in political causes: Chance the Rapper, for example.

Voter turnout: A measure of what proportion of eligible voters or voting age voters cast a ballot in a given election.

Paradox of voting: For most individuals, the cost of voting (acquiring necessary information, traveling to polling site, and waiting in line) outweighs the apparent benefits. Economic theory would predict very low voter turnout, given this analysis.

What Discourages Political Participation?

Back to the American paradox: Although Americans more actively engage in politics than citizens of other nations, **voter turnout** in the United States is low. Why? Political scientists list many reasons:

- Elections are held on Tuesdays—when many people work. Many other nations vote on weekends.
- The United States holds frequent elections—national, state, and local.
- The United States also holds primary elections, which are staggered throughout the year in different states.
- Finally, registering to vote can be burdensome and complicated. To put it bluntly, some states try to discourage some voters.

Economist Anthony Downs famously asked why anyone should vote. His theory, the **paradox of voting**, suggests that it makes little sense for an individual to expend the time and resources necessary to vote. One person is not going to change an election. The paradox: Apparently rational people show up by the millions to vote each year. Downs could have said the same thing about joining a protest march or posting online. Yet, here again, Americans take to the streets, and post petitions on Facebook. Why?

Well, as we saw in the previous section, people get many benefits from participating: a sense of involvement, of duty performed, of belonging to a community. So some political scientists flip the question: Instead of asking "why do people vote," they ask the opposite: "Why don't more people vote in the United States—as they do in other nations?" There are four broad reasons to explain why people of all ages, income levels, and educational backgrounds do not participate in political life: alienation, barriers to participation, complacency, and shifting mobilization patterns.[43]

Alienation

Alienation from public life may be described as a feeling of powerlessness or inability to control one's own political fate. Most alienated people ignore politics. When they get involved, it is usually not through traditional channels but through direct action, especially protests. A sense of alienation is reported more often in the United States among members of historically excluded groups, especially African Americans.[44] Alienation is also higher among younger people and recent immigrants. Recently, alienation levels have soared among white men who failed to finish high school.

These findings raise a question: Do some groups feel alienated because they lack a history of participation? Remember, one predictor of whether a person will get involved in politics is whether his or her peer group or parents are actively engaged.

The sheer number of elected offices and the high frequency of U.S. elections can result in public weariness and disengagement, especially when campaigns feature seemingly endless negative advertisements. Sharp partisan differences also play a role. Rising polarization and angry debates lead many Americans to "hate politics and politicians." The millennial generation appears to be particularly uncomfortable with the high levels of conflict between the parties.[45]

Finally, alienated citizens charge the political establishment with focusing on matters that avoid real problems. Government officials, they contend, seem more interested in winning elections. They do not address the deeper issues that many people care about—growing inequality, a

● *A negative ad in a 2018 Pennsylvania campaign for the U.S. House. Attack ads mobilize partisans and discourage moderates from participating.*

sense of being left behind, fears about the erosion of the nation's moral fabric. The 2016 presidential election featured two candidates, Donald Trump and Bernie Sanders, who embodied this alienation—and stunned political observers with their unexpected success. However, the 2018 midterm elections, with the highest turnout in a half-century, suggest that alienation can be overcome.[46]

Consider how this negative ad influences you.

Institutional Barriers

When Will Walker, a young black farmer, arrived to cast his vote in Tuscaloosa, Alabama, in 1964, he was first required by state law to pass a literacy test, supposedly designed to prove that he was capable of exercising political judgment. None of the white voters streaming past Will to the voting booths had to take such a test. Will shrugged and turned to the paper before him, brandished by an unfriendly poll worker. He had brushed up on his basic U.S. government facts, and he knew plenty about the various candidates running for election. Yet no amount of studying could have prepared Will for questions such as these:

- The electoral vote for president is counted in the presence of two governmental bodies. Name them: _____ and _____.
- The president is forbidden to exercise his or her authority of pardon in cases of _____.
- If the president does not wish to sign a bill, how many days is he or she allowed in which to return it to Congress for reconsideration? _____ days.
- At what time of day on January 2 each four years does the term of the president of the United States end? _____.

Will filled out as many of the twenty questions as he could and he did better than most political science majors might today. But he was turned away from the polls. Alabama allowed only black voters with a perfect score to vote.

Why do some countries have higher voter turnout than others?

As a result, many counties across the Jim Crow South featured voting registration rates among African Americans that approached zero.

Most of these overtly racist obstacles to participation were eliminated during the 1960s, although some critics continue to point out structural barriers to participation in American public life—such as the disenfranchisement of individuals convicted of a crime, even after they have served their sentence.

The incentives and barriers to voting can be subtle: How difficult is it to register? How long does voting take place? How long are the lines in the different precincts?

Democrats have generally tried to simplify voting rules. They have sponsored such changes as the National Voter Registration Act of 1993, usually referred to as the "motor voter law," which permits citizens to register to vote when they receive their driver's license. On the other side, Republicans in many states have tightened restrictions on voting. They argue that more careful monitoring reduces fraud and that voting should be treated as a privilege that takes time and energy. Accordingly, many states have introduced new voting regulations: tougher identification requirements, limits on same-day registration, reductions in the voting periods, purging Americans who have not voted for six years from the list of registered voters at the polls, and so on. Opponents call this "voter suppression" and charge that it is an effort to limit young people, minorities, the disabled, and people with lower incomes from voting. In 2018, the Supreme Court took a "hands-off" approach to state government voting actions.

Complacency

Some people do not participate because they are satisfied. If there are no urgent problems to be solved, why bother? Interest groups attract more new members and raise more money when the group's core issues are threatened. The election of President Trump boosted membership in the American Civil Liberties Union (ACLU) and mass shootings generally increase membership applications to the National Rifle Association, as gun supporters fear government restrictions.

John Kenneth Galbraith described another type of complacency as the "culture of contentment": Wealthy people will use their resources—time, money, contacts—to sustain their "contented" way of life. Those less well-off are increasingly discouraged from political participation.[47]

Donald Trump, after winning the election in 2016, thanks in part to mobilizing new voters, continued to hold campaign-style rallies as president—here, in Michigan in 2018.

Is there still a culture of contentment in pockets of American life? What do you think? Do you see evidence of complacency around you?

Shifting Mobilization Patterns

Before the 1960s, when political parties were Americans' main source of political mobilization, wealthy and poor people were organized to participate in roughly similar proportions. A surge in advocacy-group organizing since the 1960s has boosted the public's collective voice in politics. Movements on behalf of consumer rights, the environment, and many other causes represent a major gain in public leverage. These gains, however, have primarily benefited the relatively well-off, who can devote resources of time and money to public involvement.[48]

 **The Bottom Line**

» Participation in civic life tends to vary by age, income level, and education.

» Several other factors have fueled a decline in Americans' political participation in recent years. These include alienation, barriers to voting, complacency, and shifting mobilization patterns.

New Avenues for Participation: The Internet, Social Media, and Millennial Participation

The millennial generation is the most wired group in history. New technologies have engendered new forms of participation—liking a candidate's Instagram feed, commenting on an online opinion piece, or retweeting a politician's statements—and embarrassments. Today, political participation has expanded to include online activities and social media. Like many new styles of politics, **clicktivism** (or #politics) has triggered a hot debate.

Is clicktivism a powerful new form of participation that can change the way we do politics for the better? Or is it a threat to popular government? Or, less dramatically, does "participating" on a smartphone screen negatively affect the experience of civic involvement? Once again, there are multiple sides to the story. Some observers predict a vibrant new era of citizen participation. Others take a much less sunny view and warn about fragmented communities, central government control of emerging outlets, and viral malice.[49]

Clicktivism: Democratic engagement in an online age: point your mouse, click, and you have donated funds, "liked" a candidate, or (in some states) even cast your vote.

Scenario 1: Rebooting Democracy

First, optimists begin by pointing out how *active* Internet users are (see Figure 6.10). People seek out news, follow links, and access a world of information.

Second, people can easily respond. The Internet offers multiple opportunities for talking back: Check the "Like" icon, fire off an irate email, add a

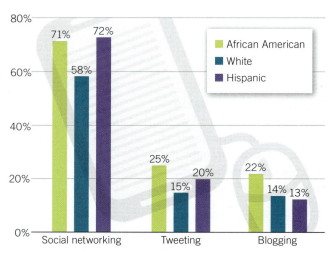

● **Figure 6.10** *Who is socially active online? A view by race and ethnicity (Pew Research Center).*

Use social media to spur political participation.

comment, or tweet a network of like-minded people. Democracies, when they are working well, *hear* their people. New technologies give individuals many opportunities to exercise their political voice.

Third and related, the Internet vastly expands the range of commentary. Traditionally, political pundits were limited to a small circle of well-known personalities and authors. Today if you have something to say you can launch a blog, tweet dozens or hundreds (or millions) of followers, or post news and opinions for your Facebook friends. YouTube videos and Instagram stories go viral all the time. People post petitions on change.org. Crowdfunding platforms such as Kickstarter raise significant funds for civic and political causes.

Fourth, the new media democratizes news production. Rather than wait for a news van and reporters, bystanders capture important events and upload them. Suddenly, everyone sees a shooting or an angry candidate flinging a racial slur.

Fifth, the Internet offers new ways for politicians and parties to reach out. Donald Trump continues to treat his Twitter followers—now more than 50 million—to a daily stream of pungent observations and stinging insults.

In sum, optimists argue that social media and other Internet-based sources promote active users; link people to one another; permit citizens to bypass the talking heads and make their own comments; and offer politicians a powerful tool to mobilize, connect, and collect. None of these factors ensure that the new media will help refresh American democracy. But they suggest a great deal of promise.

Scenario 2: More Hype and Danger than Democratic Renaissance

All this potential, however, might be squandered. Technological change might harm democracy rather than enhance it. Critics level three main charges against the Internet and social media as vehicles for political participation.[50]

First is the sustained power of *central control*, by governments or corporations, over the Internet and its users. "Facebook has more power in determining who can speak and who can be heard around the globe than any Supreme Court justice, any king, or any president," noted law professor Jeffrey Rosen. Social media companies determine what speech violates their community standards, when to cooperate with security agencies, and how to monetize information about your shopping habits.[51] Competing with public officials and tech companies for control are cybercriminals, as hackers constantly seek to steal sensitive political information (the Pentagon, for example, is attacked by hackers millions of times *each day*).[52]

Second, with more than 1.8 billion websites on the Internet, the sheer volume and variety of available information are mind boggling. The resulting chaos—known as the **din**—can overwhelm participation. Researching a

Din: Shorthand for the sheer volume of information and noise generated by online sources. It can be a disincentive to participate politically.

specific topic involves wading through a forest of hearsay, contradiction, malice, and deliberate misinformation.

Try to do an Internet search for this chapter's topic, "political participation." As of 2018, we found more than 30 million relevant Internet sources. Which ones provide valuable or even usable details about participation in the public sphere? Merely to scan each site for one minute would take sixteen years.

Third, the Internet incubates lies, malice, and falsehoods. Rumors start and spread. Racism, anti-Semitism, misogyny, and character assassination all flourish in the hyper-connected, often anonymous new media. No, Hillary Clinton was not running a child-sex ring out of a Washington, DC, pizza parlor—though a man who saw that "news" online traveled from North Carolina and fired three rifle shots to "save the children." Like so many others, this dangerous falsehood metastasized on the Internet. The democratic promise of the Internet comes with a dark side.[53]

In sum, critics worry that the Internet and social media will have a corrosive effect on American democratic participation. They point out that the government monitors Internet behavior; meanwhile, corporations gather information from every click and swipe. Yes, people can post and blog, but not many develop an audience. Finally, the Internet generates malice and trolling as easily as communication and community.

Does Social Media Increase Political Participation?

Whatever its downside, the new social media has become a fact of political life. It opens more and more opportunities for broad participation and policy innovation (see Table 6.4). For example, Mobile, Alabama, engages Instagram to fight urban blight. Fairfax County, Virginia, uses social media to boost pet

TABLE 6.4 **Social Network Site (SNS) Users' Participation Rates**

	% OF SNS USERS WHO HAVE DONE THIS	% OF ALL ADULTS WHO HAVE DONE THIS
"Like" or promote material related to political/social issues that others have posted	38	23
Encourage other people to vote	35	21
Post your own thoughts/comments on political or social issues	34	20
Encourage others to take action on political/social issues that are important to you	31	19
Belong to a group that is involved in political/social issues or working to advance a cause	21	12
Follow elected officials, candidates for office, or other elected officials	20	12
Source: Pew Research Center		

adoption rates. Government "hackathons" invite people to pitch their civic-improvement ideas. And everywhere, citizens use smartphones to show one another what their public officials are doing. Also social media users are more likely to participate in politics than the general public.

What explains this correlation between social media and participation? Perhaps individuals who are inclined to become involved in politics are more likely to be social media users. Or do people become engaged by what they see and hear online—and then act? Or is there a bandwagon effect?

The bandwagon effect has been successfully employed in the past to encourage voter turnout and other types of political participation. But skeptics point out that although the bandwagon effect within social media may galvanize participants in the short term, it is unclear whether it sustains traditional political engagement. Although the critics offer valuable caveats, participation via new social media is here to stay. It will continue to morph and change—and with it, the ways we participate in government.

How the Millennial Generation Participates

Millennials (eighteen to thirty-four year olds) vote less than other age groups, both in the United States and in many other nations. They are less likely to get involved in political campaigns. They do not identify strongly with either political party—as of 2018, 45 percent of millennials called themselves independents. That is far more than any other generation—no other age cohort reaches 40 percent independent. Millennials are also more likely to identify as liberals more than any previous generation did when they were the same age.[54]

Millennials participate in their own distinctive way: From working in hospitals to helping out in programs for at-risk kids, young adults today volunteer at unusually high rates. And they are willing to endorse government more than any other generation. Should we have a bigger government doing more things like guaranteeing healthcare for all? Only the millennials say yes, at a 57 percent rate. In contrast, 64 percent of the silent generation, enjoying the two largest government programs—Social Security and Medicare—say "no" (see Table 6.5). Why?

TABLE 6.5 **Support for Bigger Government Highest Among Younger Generations**

WOULD YOU RATHER HAVE . . .			
GENERATION	SMALLER GOVERNMENT, FEWER SERVICES	BIGGER GOVERNMENT, MORE SERVICES	DEPENDS
Millennial	38	53	9
Gen X	51	40	9
Boomer	59	32	8
Silent	64	22	14
Source: Pew Research Center			

Younger generations display a high level of trust in public officials, but relatively low levels of trust in their fellow citizens.[55] How does a generation that is skeptical of their fellow citizens but not of government participate? You probably know the answer to that: through social media and the Internet. This generation of "digital natives" comments on politics, captures (and uploads) the world around them, and networks online. For millennials and the generations that follow, the future of political participation lies in the question: How will clicktivism affect our democracy?

Political scientists have one concern about this generation. Young America is diverse, eager to build social capital by volunteering, and feels strongly about many political issues. But it has not translated that energy into traditional modes of political action—at least not yet.

The Bottom Line

» The Internet, and especially social media, has launched a revolution that is changing the way Americans participate politically.

» An online and social media revolution is changing the way Americans participate in politics.

» It may refresh American Democracy. Or diminish it.

» Millennials participate in these new methods, but are less likely to vote, belong to a party, or get involved in traditional politics.

Conclusion: Government by the People

Americans founded their nation on an inspiring idea: the consent of the governed. Lincoln put it beautifully, in his Gettysburg Address, when he prayed that "government . . . by the people shall not perish from the earth." But just how do we maintain those democratic dreams? They demand that public opinion guides—or at least influences—the government and that the people get involved in government affairs.

Public opinion surveys are the most widely used effort to understand the popular mind. Scientific techniques have refined polling to a point of remarkable accuracy—especially when elections draw near.

Yet, a great debate swirls around public opinion itself. Many have called it whimsical or uninformed. Others are more optimistic: Collective decisions—the wisdom of crowds—are often wiser than those made by well-trained experts. Public officials have a major effect on setting the agenda, framing issues, and signaling popular views. They can take the lead in encouraging us to be better stewards of democracy. However, a politically active and informed public is a crucial check on those officials.

Today, enormous political energy sparks across the political spectrum—from the effervescence of the Trump loyalists on the right to the call for social justice on the left. The key to the future lies in finding a way to channel that energy into everyday politics. Today, young Americans are more likely to volunteer and engage through social media. The question for political scientists focused on the future is whether they will get involved in traditional politics. Finding a way to make traditional politics vital and relevant is the key to living up to Ben Franklin's challenge and "keeping the republic."

CHAPTER SUMMARY

Check your understanding of Chapter 6.

🟢 Scientific surveys have come a long way since the *Literary Digest* in 1936. Professionals now design well-specified polls that capture popular views with a high degree of accuracy. However, be cautious when reading polls, such as those without a well-defined sample (e.g., online surveys). Always pay attention to the margin of error when interpreting results.

🟢 Political socialization is the study of the forces that shape public opinion. The most important are demographics such as race, gender, religion, and economic interests; family and friends; community; party affiliation; and defining events such as war.

Need to review key ideas in greater depth? Click here.

🟢 In a democracy, public opinion should guide the government. But are the people capable of self-rule? From the Constitutional Convention to contemporary social scientists, many experts consider public opinion uninformed and unreliable.

🟢 Others respond that the public, taken as a whole, is a rational, reliable source of government decision-making. Even if individuals do not know much, there is wisdom in crowds.

🟢 Public officials generally balance public opinion with their own beliefs about the best decisions.

🟢 Popular views can be especially important in setting the agenda: If something seems important to the public (and the media), politicians respond. Congress, in particular, pays attention to spikes in public opinion. Presidents find it easier to get their policies passed when public opinion is strongly in favor of those policies.

🟢 Participation in civic and political life is a longstanding American tradition. Today, Americans still exhibit higher levels of voluntarism than citizens of other countries. However, our rates of participation in politics and government have fallen to disturbing levels.

🟢 People participate in public life in three broad ways: First, by participating through traditional mechanisms: voting, going to rallies, contributing to campaigns, and contacting public officials.

🟢 Second, by contributing to civil society through volunteering and getting involved in the community.

● Third, Americans have been quick to get involved in direct action when traditional mechanisms seem unresponsive. This is the politics of demonstrations, protest movements, and even armed confrontations.

● An online and social revolution is changing the way Americans participate in politics. It may refresh American Democracy. Or diminish it.

● Mass engagement in politics and other civic activities is the lifeblood of American democracy, helping to explain why analysts are so anxious to expand participation.

KEY TERMS

Flashcard review.

Approval rating, p. 197
Bandwagon effect, p. 193
Boomerang effect, p. 194
Civic voluntarism, p. 200
Civil disobedience, p. 201
Clicktivism, p. 211
Demographic group, p. 191
Din, p. 212
Direct action, p. 201
Electoral activities, p. 200
Framing effects, p. 192

Groupthink, p. 196
Information shortcuts, p. 195
Issue advocacy, p. 205
Likely voters, p. 191
Mandate, p. 197
Margin of sampling error, p. 192
Nonattitudes, p. 195
Paradox of voting, p. 208
Policy agenda, p. 197
Political elites, p. 189

Political mobilization, p. 205
Political socialization, p. 186
Political voice, p. 202
Push poll, p. 192
Response bias, p. 193
Sampling frame, p. 191
Social capital, p. 205
Survey research, p. 197
Traditional participation, p. 199
Voter turnout, p. 208

STUDY QUESTIONS

1. "The masses are asses," wrote one observer. He was summarizing a perspective that public opinion is not a reliable guide to government. Why, exactly, is public opinion unreliable?

2. "Public officials must always balance public opinion with their own beliefs."

a) Explain why.

b) What problems face political leaders who *always* follow the polls in deciding what to do?

c) What problems face political leaders who *never* follow the polls in deciding what to do?

d) How can polls help leaders who already know what they want to do?

3. Define the following terms: A push poll. A sampling frame. The margin of error. The Bradley effect.

4. What does it mean to "frame an issue"? Illustrate using the issue of obesity.

5. What are the different categories of involvement in civic or political life? Which appeals to you most? Least? Why?

6. Which distinguishes the millennial generation when it comes to participation in civic and political activities?

7. Does "clictivism" enhance democracy? Or diminish it? Describe the arguments on both sides. Which is more persuasive to you and why?

 Go to **www.oup.com/us/Morone** to find quizzes, flash cards, simulations, tutorials, videos, and other study tools.

IN 1961, THE AMERICAN MEDICAL Association

enlisted actor Ronald Reagan to help fight President John F. Kennedy's healthcare plan. Reagan cut a vinyl record that the medical association mailed to every physician's home. "If this program passes," warned the future president, "we will . . . spend our sunset years telling our children and our children's children what it was like in America when men were free." Doctors' wives invited their friends for coffee, played Reagan's message, and then wrote letters to Congress opposing national health insurance. Congress voted down the program, although another version passed four years later—now known as Medicare.

In 1993, the Health Insurance Association of America aired television ads opposing President Clinton's health plan. The ads featured "Harry and Louise," a middle-aged couple concerned that national health insurance would create a bureaucratic monster and wreck their healthcare. "They [Washington bureaucrats] choose," intones the ad. "You lose." Congress soon buried Clinton's health proposal. It took nearly two decades until President Obama succeeded in getting a comprehensive healthcare plan passed.

In 2016, Republican presidential nominee Donald Trump took to Twitter and vowed to end that health law, known as the Affordable Care Act (ACA) or "Obamacare." In 140-character bursts, Trump channeled outrage at this Big Government intrusion—and kept going once he took office. President Trump's Twitter attacks on the ACA were retweeted and "liked" by tens of thousands of followers—encouraging Republican officeholders to repeal it.

Each snapshot captures the media technology of a different era, and the politics they channeled. In 1961, a recording reached an elite audience, which responded by mailing letters to Congress. In 1993, a TV ad ran in select markets and then spread farther via pundits—and helped bring down a presidential initiative. A quarter-century later, a posting instantly

● *Media photographers swarm Facebook CEO Mark Zuckerberg during his appearance before a joint hearing of the Senate Judiciary and Commerce committees.*

In this chapter, you will:

- ● Learn how media coverage of politics is changing.

- ● Consider the democratic promises and pitfalls of mainstream and social media.

- ● Explore how the media is (and is not) biased.

- ● Understand the rules that channel the media into its current forms.

- ● Discover how U.S. media is distinctive.

- ● Assess how media coverage influences politics, campaigns, and elections.

Donald J. Trump
October 31, 2017 · 🌐

It's time to repeal and replace Obamacare once and for all. I will FIX it, but the Washington Democrats must END the obstruction. Americans WILL get the top quality healthcare they deserve!

👍❤️😆 50K   7.5K Comments 6.2K Shares 921K Views

🟢 *From LP record albums to tweets and Facebook posts: Evolving media technologies have changed American politics—and journalism.*

reached millions of social-media followers, generating reaction in new media formats (Instagram, Twitter, Facebook) and traditional ones (newspapers, radio, TV). Three major changes mark the evolution of issue campaigns across sixty years:

- First, *information is cascading faster and faster.* As media outlets multiply, consumers rush to keep up with the never-ending flood of news.

- Second, *today's media includes many more voices and formats.* Proliferating media options contribute to a more polarized public, as people follow sources that align with their worldview.

- Third, *the new media permits the public to be much more active.* You can comment on an Instagram or Facebook posting far more easily than you could respond to a record in 1961 or a TV commercial in 1993. The public also can act as media watchdogs and information providers by posting smartphone videos—supplying coverage formerly controlled by large media organizations.

What is the media?[1] It is all the ways people obtain information about politics and the world: Instagram, television, Facebook, podcasts, newspapers, Snapchat posts, Reddit threads, blogs, Twitter feeds, and more. Media outlets are the major information bridge between citizens and government.

The successive rise of radio, television, and the Internet each had a profound impact on American political culture. Fifty years ago, everyone heard the same

Hear Reagan's "Operation Coffee Cup" recording.

See the Harry and Louise ad.

BY THE NUMBERS
The Media

Number of daily newspapers in print in the United States in 1850	254^2
Number in 1900	$2,226^3$
Expected number in 2020	700^4
Percentage of Americans who get news from social-media sites, 2018	68
Percentage of Internet-using Americans who trust information from social media sites	33
Percentage of Americans who trust information from traditional news sources	72^5
Percentage of Republicans and Democrats (respectively) approving of how news media performs its "watchdog" role, 2011	58, 58
Percentages in 2018	$38, 82^6$
Number of journalists for broad-interest websites (such as Slate.com) accredited to cover the U.S. Senate, 2009	2
Number accredited in 2019	more than 90
Percentage of news-media advertising revenue earned by digital sites, 2011	20.4
Percentage in 2017	43.6^7

Is anything important lost about news reporting and publishing in the transition from analog (newspapers) to digital? Do you trust mainstream news sources or web-based ones more? Why?

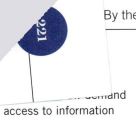

...demand access to information through digital devices that feature interactive participation with content.

newscast and debated the same issues. Today, each person tunes into their own news source and links to their personal network. *What do you think* about the **new media**: Does the vast expansion in outlets enhance democracy? Diminish it? Or some of both?

Who are we? The United States is an immense, ongoing argument over political ideas. The media brings the people into political debates; it is the link between leaders and citizens. The national media reflects America itself: raucous, fast-changing, multicultural, forceful, loud, and lucrative. It sparks intense policy debates at home. It broadcasts America to the world.

Media and American Democracy

Media outlets perform three essential functions in a democratic system: providing information, acting as a public watchdog, and helping shape the policy agenda. Let us take a closer look at all three.

Providing Information

First, media coverage *informs the public*. Without media bridging the gap, the public would be ignorant of most political events: Most of us cannot attend sessions of Congress, the Supreme Court, or our city or town council—much less track the literally thousands of public matters that government addresses each year. When the media does its job well, we are more informed voters and more engaged citizens.

Are there limits to this information-providing role? Imagine that you are a Republican with many Democratic friends. You send them a news article that crushes one of their cherished beliefs. But rather than changing their minds, the story reaffirms what they already "know." Research shows that new information rarely influences people who have strongly held opinions.

However, new information *can* have an impact on less politically aware people. About a third of the public has few strong political views and rarely follows news. This group *is* open to media influence. Here is a paradox: The news media is most likely to influence those who pay the least attention to it. Because this group does not follow politics and government very closely, only news stories with a **loud signal** are likely to reach them.

Fact-check the media.

Loud signal: Widely reported media stories with an unambiguous message.

Public watchdog: Media coverage that alerts the public when a problem arises in politics or society.

Watching Officials

Second, the media serves a **public watchdog** function, scrutinizing government for corrupt or illegal acts, misleading statements by leaders, failed consumer protections, and other flawed decisions or government processes. *Washington*

Post reporters brought down the Nixon presidency by doggedly covering the Watergate scandal. In every election, candidates' public statements (on social media, during debates, or in campaign appearances) are scoured by media outlets for accuracy and consistency. Is a candidate misleading the American public? Reporters keep careful score.

Politicians often complain about media coverage. President Trump fights back directly, denouncing journalists who criticize his views or who ask questions he considers unfair. More than half a million people "liked" Trump's July 2017 post of himself appearing to beat up a man with the CNN logo as its head.[8] Serving as a watchdog for democracy has never been easy.

> **Donald J. Trump** ✔
> @realDonaldTrump
> Follow ⌄
>
> Bob Iger of ABC called Valerie Jarrett to let her know that "ABC does not tolerate comments like those" made by Roseanne Barr. Gee, he never called President Donald J. Trump to apologize for the HORRIBLE statements made and said about me on ABC. Maybe I just didn't get the call?
>
> 8:31 AM - 30 May 2018

> **Donald J. Trump** ✔
> @realDonaldTrump
> Follow ⌄
>
> The Failing and Corrupt @nytimes estimated the crowd last night at "1000 people," when in fact it was many times that number - and the arena was rockin'. This is the way they demean and disparage. They are very dishonest people who don't "get" me, and never did!
>
> 7:35 AM - 30 May 2018

● *Reporters serving as "watchdogs" can become targets of sharp coverage themselves.*

Shaping the Policy Agenda

Editors and reporters have enormous influence on what Americans think *about*. Media executives listen to the political din and pluck out stories to headline. Those become the topics that politicians address, Congress investigates, talk shows debate, and you discuss and retweet. When an issue commands widespread attention, we say it is on the **policy agenda**. The first step toward action is to get your issue—homelessness, immorality, animal cruelty, whatever—onto the policy agenda, which often requires an attentive journalist.

Setting the agenda is one of the news media's most important influences. Politicians, think tanks, interest groups, citizens, and experts all try to influence the agenda, but issues can arise seemingly out of nowhere. During the 2016 NFL preseason, San Francisco 49ers quarterback Colin Kaepernick—incensed by what he called inequitable treatment of African Americans—remained seated and later knelt while the national anthem was played. As media coverage mounted, other athletes—professional, college, and high school—joined Kaepernick, fueling news coverage. Many Americans, including President Trump, felt that the athletes were disrespecting the U.S. flag and those who died defending it. Media attention kept these issues on the national agenda well into 2018–2019.

Does the public attend to an issue because the media covers it? Or does media coverage arise because the public is interested? Political scientists found that the issues that people absorb from media sources became more important to them.[9] When the media focuses on an issue, its importance—or salience—generally rises in public perception.

Policy agenda: The issues that the media covers, the public considers important, and politicians address. Setting the agenda is a key step in political action.

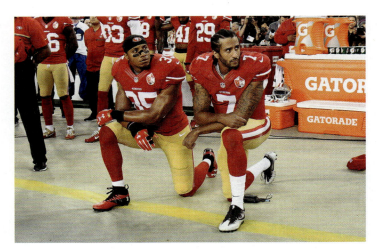

● *Media coverage of Colin Kaepernick's protest spotlighted the treatment of African Americans—and, on the other side, respect for the flag and what it stands for.*

Priming: Affecting public perceptions of politicians or issues by reporting on topics in ways that either enhance or diminish support.

Framing: The way an issue is defined; every issue has many possible frames, each with a different tilt in describing the problem and highlighting solutions.

The media's focus on some stories and not others affects public perceptions of politicians and policy issues. This influence is known as **priming**. For example, because the Republican Party generally supports smaller government, stories about government incompetence *prime* the public to sympathize with Republican views. Stories about the plight of the elderly or hard-working poor people prime voters to share Democrats' outlook.

When a media outlet emphasizes a particular slant in a story, it is **framing** an issue. Consider the decision in 2018 by Republicans in Congress and the Trump administration to scrap the "Volcker Rule," passed in the wake of the 2008–2009 financial meltdown to prohibit banks from making risky investments with customer deposits. Business-friendly outlets, such as *Fortune*, framed the story as relief from overzealous regulators: "It's Time to Just Kill the Volcker Rule," blared a typical headline. On the left, articles complained that "Republicans Are Sowing the Seeds of the Next Financial Crisis."[10] Mainstream media organizations tend to seek a balance, often describing for their audience two or more competing frames. The *New York Times* take on the Volcker Rule, for example, was headlined "Bankers Hate the Volcker Rule. Now It Could be Watered Down."[11]

Often, media framing is invisible to the public because it reflects dominant social values of the time. The issue of equality was once framed as a problem concerning white men: Could they achieve the American dream in an industrial system devoted to profits? Later, mass social movements reframed the issue as one that spoke directly to race, ethnicity, and gender.

In short, framing defines the nature of a problem, organizes potential solutions, and diminishes alternative policies. A lesson all political leaders learn quickly: If you are not actively shaping the terms of debate, your opponents will. As one academic wrote: "Frame or Get Framed."[12] Media coverage plays a crucial role—often, *the* crucial role—in issue framing.

The Bottom Line

» A vast change is under way in media formats, driven by rapid technological advancement.

» Media outlets continue to perform essential democratic functions: providing information, acting as public "watchdogs," shaping what news is reported (agenda setting), setting the context for a topic (priming), and describing it in specific ways (framing).

U.S. Media Today: Traditional Formats Are Declining

Fifty years ago, three national TV networks and the daily paper all delivered essentially the same news to an audience with few options for responding to reporters' coverage. Most households subscribed to one newspaper. Your grandparents' choice: tune in or not. Today, new technologies—and the Internet companies that invent and manage them—are shaking up both media and government.

As Figure 7.1 shows, digital sources are replacing traditional media, especially television. Back in 2002, TV was the chief source of news for 82 percent of the public; by 2017 that figure had fallen to 50 percent—down seven percentage points in just one year. Americans under the age of 55 have switched decisively to digital sources. Newspapers and magazines continue a long slide from their one-time dominance. In contrast, radio hangs on—almost everyone listens, in the car or to podcasts.

Social media sites such as Facebook or Instagram generally do not perform their own reporting: They rely on a combination of links to traditional news sources, partisan sites, and public comments. New media formats include podcasts, crowd-funded reporting, and multimedia platforms that tell stories through digital media, like the hugely popular *Serial* podcasts that include short videos, letters, maps, and other clues online. Major stories are funded each year through Kickstarter and similar crowd-funding sources; this removes traditional gatekeepers such as producers and editors from agenda setting, or deciding which issues receive priority coverage.

What are the implications of this fast-changing landscape? We can learn more by focusing on developments in each of the major media.

Newspapers and Magazines: Rise and Decline

Newspapers have always been midwives to American democracy. The *Federalist Papers* first appeared as articles in the *New York Independent Journal*. George Washington subscribed to ten newspapers. His most famous communication, the Farewell Address, was a letter addressed to his "fellow citizens" and printed in the papers.

In the 1830s, newspapers became the first **mass media**—just when the vote expanded to include all white men. Papers cost one penny and reflected the highly partisan and often corrupt politics of the era. The *New York Herald* gave the readers what they

Mass media: Information and entertainment for broad popular audiences including newspapers, magazines, radio, and television.

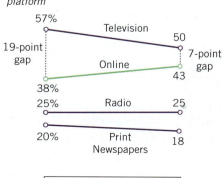

% of U.S. adults who *often* get news on each platform

57% Television 50
19-point gap
Online
7-point gap
38% 43
25% Radio 25
20% Print Newspapers 18

2016 2017

● **Figure 7.1** *Sources of political news. (Pew Research Center)*

wanted—murder, fire, suicide, and crime. That profit-driven journalism disgusted the old elites but made the *Herald* the most widely read newspaper in the world.

Newspaper influence grew steadily. The 1898 Spanish-American War arose because banner headlines blamed Spain for sinking an American battleship in Havana Harbor and helped bully the McKinley administration into the conflict. By the turn of the twentieth century, there were some 2,200 newspapers in the United States.[13] Even after the rise of radio and television, newspapers remained the major source for political information. Now, after more than two centuries atop the media, newspapers are waning, with magazine circulation falling as well. Advertisers who once guaranteed profits have migrated to the Internet, and so have readers. Occasionally an "angel investor" comes along—Jeff Bezos, Amazon's founder and CEO, spent $250 million to buy the *Washington Post* and its affiliated papers—but such investments are rare.

Radio Holds Steady

The first commercial radio stations began airing in the 1920s. President Franklin Roosevelt, during the Great Depression of the 1930s, delivered informal weekly radio addresses known as "fireside chats." Hearing Roosevelt's voice personalized the relationship between Americans and their president. Indeed, political scientists link this development to the rise of the **personal presidency**.

Radio's golden era lasted just thirty years. By the mid-1950s, television had become king. However, radio still has a role in national politics. Conservative talk radio arose in the late 1980s; after Rush Limbaugh syndicated his daily talk show, fellow conservatives followed him onto the airwaves. Limbaugh pioneered the argument that became an article of conservative faith: The mainstream media is biased, so dial in here. Liberals tried to counter with their own talk shows, but their efforts foundered, in part because fewer liberals view the media as biased.

Compared to television, public radio has a large presence in the United States: National Public Radio (NPR)'s audience is over thirty-eight million listeners a week. Roughly 15 percent of NPR's funds come from the federal government, prompting ferocious criticism from conservatives, who argue that taxpayers should not be supporting "liberal" radio shows. (The independent

Personal presidency: The idea that the president has a personal link to the public. Made initially possible by the new twentieth-century technology of radio.

● *Franklin Roosevelt used the new medium—radio—to speak directly to citizens in their homes. The result: the rise of the personal presidency. Changing media helped introduce a change in our politics.*

organization AllSides rates NPR news programs as centrist, though found their editorial commentary to be inching left in late
2017–2018.)[14]

Podcasts also enable radio to thrive as
a news provider. The fastest-growing media format today, podcasts attract millennial listeners alongside older radio news
consumers, and launch investigative stories
of their own. Online media companies such
as Slate, as well as traditional organizations like the *Washington Post*, host multiple podcasts on their sites.

Television: From News to Infotainment

Television burst onto the American scene
in the 1950s, revolutionizing both entertainment and politics. President Kennedy
sensed TV's power and gave the first live

● *Kennedy pioneered the televised news conference—and his approval rating soared to 70 percent. Presidents now had to be telegenic in live performance. Once again, the media shifted the expectations and role of the presidency.*

press conference in February 1961. Sixty-five million people—one in three
Americans—tuned in. The young, charismatic president was a natural television performer: Again a new media technology intensified the link between the
people and their president.

The Rise of Cable.   Two networks, CBS and NBC, monopolized the television
news business during the 1960s and 1970s. Interested Americans all watched
the same version of the day's events

Technology broke the monopoly. Cable stations began airing in the 1970s;
they lingered on the fringe of the media until 1991, when an upstart named
Cable News Network (CNN) showed a live video of American rockets explod-
ing into Baghdad at the start of the Gulf War. CNN introduced a new model:
It reported news all day long. No more waiting for the evening network news.
A new format was born: the twenty-four-hour news cycle. Thirty years ago,
White House staff, and the reporters who covered them, all relaxed around
5 p.m. Today, the cycle never ends.

In 1996, Rupert Murdoch launched Fox News, a network with a conservative slant. As Republican viewers headed for Fox, other cable networks—most
notably MSNBC—moved to the left and developed shows with a liberal spin.
Eventually, cable channels filled every political niche—Fox offerings such as
Hannity on the right, shows like *Hardball with Chris Matthews* in the center,
and the *Rachel Maddow Show* on the left (Figure 7.2). As households switched
to cable, political leaders' communications tended mainly to reach members of
their own party.[15]

News sources believed to be objective

	All Americans %	Republican %	Independent %	Democrat %
FOX	24	60	16	3
CNN	13	4	11	21
NPR	10	1	12	15
Local News	5	4	5	5
BBC	5	3	7	9
MSNBC	4	0	4	7

● **Figure 7.2** *Political polarization fuels Americans' belief that the media (especially that favored by the other side) is biased. Here, trust levels vary by political outlook. (Gallup/Knight Foundation)*

President Trump chats with *Fox & Friends* hosts.

Infotainment: The blurred line between news and entertainment.

Infotainment. As cable channels proliferated, the line between news and entertainment began to evaporate. Late-night talk show hosts gleefully lacerated the political losers of the day. Politicians responded by lining up as on-air guests. A threshold was crossed when Senator John McCain, the Republican nominee for president in 2008, announced his candidacy on *David Letterman*—with bandleader Paul Shaffer blasting out "Hail to the Chief." Donald Trump has elevated blurred lines to an art form, appearing repeatedly on the *Fox & Friends* morning show and reportedly speaking frequently with the popular anchor Sean Hannity.[16]

This blend of news and entertainment is known as **infotainment**. One worry raised by scholars and media executives alike: As infotainment spreads, Americans already inattentive to politics will be less likely to vote or otherwise participate politically.[17]

Amid this colorful scene, network and cable news gained viewers during the 2016 campaign and its aftermath, after several years of decline. This partly reflects the irresistible spectacle of Donald Trump, who told the *New York Times*, "newspapers, television, all forms of media will tank if I'm not [president] because without me, their ratings are going down the tubes."[18]

Overall, the TV picture reflects the entire media. A broadly shared view of the world, as interpreted by the nightly network news, has shattered. Instead, Americans consume infotainment in separate ideological and cultural enclaves.

New Media Rising

The trend toward personalized news and information accelerated to hyper-speed after the arrival of digital media formats. You can click a Facebook link, read content from, say, *The Wall Street Journal*, post a comment on Instagram, debate classmates in an online chat room, and surf over to YouTube for a clip posted by an eyewitness. Digital media permits readers to respond immediately, to share, and to learn more—often through multiformat platforms.

Media analysts raise three concerns about the new media. First, web-based outlets aggregate news and sometimes provide background context and multiple links, but most stories are developed by traditional reporters. If newspapers and TV networks cannot generate revenue, they will not survive. As these sources cut their own costs, news coverage gets thinner and less reliable. Will the reporting function migrate to another media institution? This is already happening in some cases, with online reporters for sites such as *Vox* or *Slate*; digital media outlets doubled their reporting staffs between 2008–2017, but are still dwarfed by traditional organizations.

Second, important stories may get lost. Newspapers and local TV news always covered the "hot" topics (war, murder, high school sports) along with less exciting civic issues (such as school board meetings and wetland controversies). Because everything was bundled together into one package, the popular stories paid for the civics lessons. As mainstream media, especially local newspapers, downsize staff, there may be no way to subsidize coverage on limited-interest (but very important) issues such as local education. Traditional media must generate ever more dramatic headlines to keep up with alluring "clickbait" fare online, dulling audiences' attention to vital but complicated policy stories. Media scholars report that this effect is particularly strong among millennials: "When the goal is to attract young viewers, sensational and novel [stories] often drown out news of more significance that lacks excitement."[19]

Third, traditional media tends to include a variety of viewpoints. Conservative and liberal columnists appear side-by-side on the Op-Ed page; pundits from Left and Right serve on the same Sunday morning news show. Facebook and Instagram deploy algorithms to filter stories based on viewer preferences, emphasizing items that fit a user's worldview.[20] The result: Each of us inhabits a shrinking "echo chamber," encountering media reports that fuel our views and prejudices.

As exposure to diverse viewpoints shrinks in the new-media age, **fake news**—stories that are made up, or twisted to promote a particular viewpoint—appears to be expanding.[21] A natural tendency, fueled by a president who criticizes mainstream media as fake-news purveyors, is to characterize as "fake" news anything with which you disagree. But empirical evidence suggests that deliberately misleading views, or ideology masquerading as fact, is increasingly common among digital-media sites—particularly on scientific

Learn about the first Pulitzer Prize awarded to an online-only news site.

Fake news: The deliberate spread of falsehood or misinformation—often a charge made by politicians facing unfavorable stories.

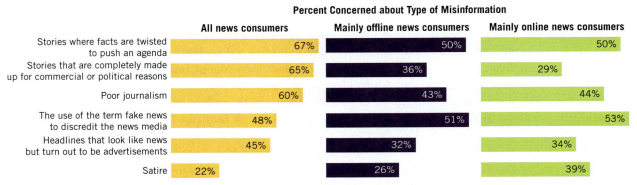

Percent Concerned about Type of Misinformation

	All news consumers	Mainly offline news consumers	Mainly online news consumers
Stories where facts are twisted to push an agenda	67%	50%	50%
Stories that are completely made up for commercial or political reasons	65%	36%	29%
Poor journalism	60%	43%	44%
The use of the term fake news to discredit the news media	48%	51%	53%
Headlines that look like news but turn out to be advertisements	45%	32%	34%
Satire	22%	26%	39%

● **Figure 7.3** *Proportion of those who are very or extremely concerned about each type of misinformation, by main source of news. (Reuters Institute/Oxford University Press)*

subjects such as climate change or environmental harms.[22] Americans express concern about misinformation both online and offline (Figure 7.3).

Other observers predict the new media will usher in a golden era of citizen participation. The Internet and social media sites turn us all into potential news providers. Traditional news awaited the arrival of a camera team and print reporters. Now anyone can record an event on her smartphone, post it to YouTube, Instagram, or Twitter, and watch it go viral. Private citizens posting videos of young black men killed by police helped inspire the Black Lives Matter movement, for example.

Likewise, new technologies allow for greater transparency. In 2018, the *New York Times* obtained a cache of emails and other documents from the political analysis firm Cambridge Analytica, showing that the firm used data illegally obtained from Facebook to target individual voters. The evidence caused Cambridge Analytica to cease operations, and landed Facebook in a political crisis.

The Bottom Line

» Thirty years ago, TV networks, magazines, and newspapers delivered roughly the same news. Today, media outlets cater to every perspective—left, right, and center. Americans no longer share a single news source.

» Previous waves of rising "new" media—newspapers, radio, and television—changed the nature of news reporting, affecting political institutions.

» Today these now-traditional institutions are in serious decline. All are losing ground as the place Americans go for news. Digital sources such as Facebook and Instagram are taking over—especially among young people.

> » The new media raises major concerns, including: Do the benefits—everyone's ability to contribute to "news" and increased transparency—outweigh losing traditional reporting sources and rising incidence of "fake news"? Will these more democratic formats find large audiences, or are we fragmented into individual niches? And can new media invent revenue sources that will enable them to cover vital but sometimes obscured stories, especially about local issues?

Is the Media Biased?

Charges of media bias are finding wider public agreement. In 1984, a substantial majority of Americans (58 to 42 percent) agreed that media sources are careful to separate fact from opinion. Today just 32 percent affirm this statement of media objectivity, while 66 percent view media as *not* separating fact and opinion. Nearly half of Americans cannot name a single "objective" news source.[23]

On the right, traditional news organizations are decried as hostile to conservatives, their reporters overwhelmingly liberal: "97 percent of donations from mainstream media [reporters] go to the Democrat[ic] party," complained a GOP congressman.[24] Liberals see media as biased toward corporate power. Bernie Sanders and his supporters charged during his 2016 presidential campaign that "the corporate-owned media is inherently biased against the slate of issues his 'revolution' is built upon due to their business interests."[25]

Widespread charges of bias are worth taking seriously. When the public mistrusts media organizations, U.S. government suffers—given the importance of a free press to American democracy. Republicans and independents continue to view the media with high degrees of suspicion (Figure 7.4), even as Democratic support rose after President Trump's victory.

Learn about organizations that monitor the media.

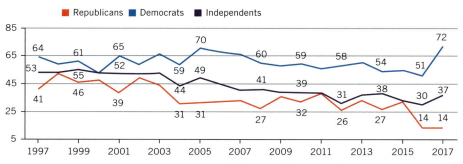

● **Figure 7.4** *Trust in U.S. Media*
Source: (Gallup)

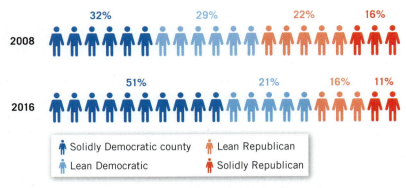

● Figure 7.5 *Jobs in media are increasingly clustered in counties that lean Democratic.*
Source: (Politico)

Are Reporters Politically Biased?

Conservatives are correct that mainstream media reporters are much less likely to identify as Republican (7 percent, in a 2014 study) than does the national population (around 25 percent). Most journalists call themselves independent, especially local reporters, where the number runs well above 60 percent.[26] This partly reflects geography: As Figure 7.5 displays, a large proportion of mainstream and online journalists now live among other coastal elites—in cities and counties that vote overwhelmingly Democratic.[27] Just as you are more likely to share political opinions with those living around you, so might reporters.

Though a few studies have found favoritism, dozens of studies fail to show a systematic bias among mainstream media reporters in favor of Democratic candidates or liberal policy positions. Scholars have searched for bias in campaign coverage and in what policy issues receive coverage. Perhaps reporters' views creep into their *framing* of which issues matter. Researchers find no evidence to suggest that policy frames in mainstream media systematically favor liberal views.[28]

What about the Left's claim that corporate ownership encourages journalists to favor the status quo and avoid hard-hitting stories on poverty, marginalized people, or radical social movements? Political scientists found that news organizations that stood to benefit financially from legislation (the 1996 Telecommunications Act) covered the Act more favorably than outlets realizing no financial gain. Other research demonstrates that newspapers tend to run content favoring their advertisers, but extensive study has found no pervasive inclination to ignore less well-off Americans in favor of the wealthy and powerful.[29]

There *is* hard evidence of a much deeper bias in the news media—the need to attract an audience. Media organizations' principal bias arises in their core purpose: attracting coverage and making money. Media outlets present stories that will draw viewers.

Profits Drive the News Industry

What does the media actually sell? The answer is not news about government actors or elections. Media sells its audience to advertisers. Thus the core goal is to expand the audience. When ratings rise, business prospers; when they fall,

Explore the role of the media in agenda setting.

networks replace anchors and newspapers cut staff. As Sam Zell, former CEO of the media giant Tribune Company, bluntly told his reporters: "You need to help me by being a journalist who focuses on what readers want and therefore generates more revenue."[30]

These financial realities give news reporters a strong incentive to align their politics with their audience. For large outlets—TV networks, national newspapers—that means the political center, where most Americans are comfortable. Hence people on both the Left and Right complain about bias; the center—where most stories are pitched—*is* to the left of conservatives and to the right of liberals.

At the same time, each publication and network seeks its own audience. Conservative communities usually tune in to more conservative sources, and vice versa. In short, the market forces each news source toward the politics of its audience. That pressure is just the start of audiences' influence on the media. Other market biases include the search for drama, conflict, and scandal.

Drama Delivers Audiences

Journalists find it difficult to generate audience excitement about a school board meeting or a healthcare proposal. Miners trapped below the earth–Now *that* pulls people to their televisions and Twitter feeds. A good drama has a narrative arc with a beginning, middle, and end. It features a protagonist (the miners), pathos (anxious spouses), a villain (the coal company or government regulators), drama (will they be rescued before air runs out?), an ending (tired but jubilant miners hugging their families), and a take-home message (worry about mine safety).

Do not be fooled by the political moral at episode's end. Real mine safety raises complicated—and potentially boring—policy issues that attract few viewers. Be assured that when the state legislature debates mine safety, the cameras and reporters will be off chasing the next drama.

Local news gets much of its drama from crime. A classic rule of thumb guides local TV news: "If it bleeds, it leads." Many good things may have happened that day, but the lead story will feature the most grisly event. The images are familiar to the point of cliché—a breathless reporter live on the scene, yellow tape blocking the area, grim-faced cops or firefighters in the background, weeping relatives in a daze, and perhaps a blank-faced perpetrator blinking into the camera.

● *Media outlets, driven by a bottom-line concern for expanding audiences, tend to emphasize sensational stories—especially about violent crimes such as carjacking. This image led the news in West Palm Beach, Florida, although car thefts had fallen by 66 percent over the previous two decades.*

The need for drama also transforms election coverage. Election reporting rarely focuses on the issues—an audience turnoff. Instead, the dramatic spotlight is on the protagonists, their families, their strategies, their dirty tricks, and their blunders. Elections have a built-in narrative arc as well: a *beginning* (candidates throw their hats into the ring), a *middle* (who had the best week?), a *conclusion* (someone wins), and a *take-home message* (the loser had a fatal flaw that other candidates should avoid). In 2016, media outlets debated whether Americans' thirst for drama-filled coverage led reporters and editors to provide Donald Trump with more free publicity than other candidates.[31]

Political debates—whether about the environment, education, or taxes—reflect the same pressure to build a narrative. Regardless of the issue, media coverage focuses on drama and conflict, heroes and villains, winners and losers. This tendency exacerbates media bias. For example, despite a dramatic drop in U.S. crime rates over the past twenty years, most Americans believe that crime is actually rising.[32] The constant coverage, especially on local news, misleads viewers to imagine criminals running rampant everywhere.

Click on your favorite news website. What dramatic narrative frames the lead story? Pundits criticize media stories for lacking substance. However, as a student of political science, you have learned to examine the *institution* and its incentives. The media, seeking a large audience for advertisers, covers whatever attracts the most attention. Simply calling for serious coverage will not change the incentives built into the media market.

Investigative "Bias"

Other media biases stem from journalistic norms. Two are especially powerful: skepticism and fairness. Back in the early 1960s, Washington reporters were a small, white, male club with a code that winked at White House extramarital affairs or falling-down drunks in Congress. Then the moral intensity of the civil rights movement, administration efforts to manipulate media during the Vietnam War, and the **Watergate scandal** all made the old accommodations seem irresponsible. How could reporters go easy on segregationists or liars?

Watergate was especially significant in fostering skepticism. Reporters investigated a burglary of Democratic Party headquarters that led directly to the White House. President Nixon had secretly taped conversations in the Oval Office; while addressing the botched burglary, the Supreme Court forced the release of the tapes. Their content stunned Americans,

Watergate scandal: A failed effort in 1972 by Republican operatives to break into Democratic Party headquarters in the Watergate office complex in Washington, DC. President Nixon tried to cover up the event—eventually causing him to resign from the presidency.

● Conflict sells. Following Hurricane Harvey's devastation of Houston, news outlets ran stories about widespread looting and other crimes. In response, Houston Mayor Sylvester Turner declared "looting will not be tolerated" and ordered a city-wide curfew. The initial stories proved to be greatly exaggerated; Houston saw fewer property crimes (and no shootings, despite initial reports) in Harvey's aftermath than during ordinary times.

What Do YOU Think?   Is the Media Objective?

After Congress repealed the Fairness Doctrine that forced media to provide opposing viewpoints, some outlets began to cater to partisan audiences. Today, 46 percent of Americans cannot name an objective news source, and many feel that the media is doing a poor job serving our democracy.[33] Do you agree?

Not enough objectivity. Media organizations should serve as a platform for the expression of opposing views—vital to the democratic process. They should also clearly distinguish facts from opinions to restore public trust in media—and other governing institutions.

Enough objectivity. Even though some media sources are partisan, the public has access to a range of sources—from Fox to CNN to MSNBC—providing a wide range of viewpoints. I can gather a fuller picture of critical issues and arrive at a better interpretation of events by following multiple sources.

Too much objectivity. Media reports bend over backward to give all sides a fair hearing. Journalists are very knowledgeable about politics; I want to hear their views, not just "unbiased" recitations of facts and politicians' opinions.

who could hear their president order aides to "stonewall" the Watergate investigations. Even more shocking, the presidential tapes bristled with ethnic slurs and foul language.

In response, reporters redefined their roles. Rather than acting as chummy insiders, they became skeptics, aiming to pierce official propaganda and finding the hidden truth. Media emphasizing their "watchdog" function led relations between the press and politicians to turn more adversarial. Each time journalists felt misled by an administration, their skepticism grew. For example, George W. Bush insisted that Iraq owned dangerous weapons that threatened the United States. (It did not.) Barack Obama promised Americans, "If you like your health plan, you can keep it." (Not all could.) Reporters' mission became uncovering lies and bad behavior.

The Fairness Bias

The effort to be fair introduces an unexpected bias. Reporters energetically try to present both sides of every topic. However, when issues do not have two equal sides, the effort creates the impression of a debate that does not exist. Companies that market tobacco, unhealthy foods, or toxic products, for example, have learned that they do not need to win the debate. They simply sponsor research and announce that there are two sides to the issue. The fairness bias then leads the media to report the two sides as equivalent—even if one of the sides was manufactured by an interested party.

The Bottom Line

» Both conservatives and liberals complain of media bias. However, the media generally reflects the politics of its audience—to the left of conservatives and to the right of liberals.

» The media's deepest bias comes from its need to appeal to advertisers. That puts an emphasis on drama, scandal, and conflict—exacerbating partisan political divisions.

» Media efforts to be objective and balanced can introduce new biases such as "fairness."

 How Governments Shape the Media

We have seen how technology constantly changes the media. The media, in turn, changes politics. In this section, we examine how political rules shape the development of the media.

Democratic nations organize their media in three different ways: First, *governments fund* media outlets. This **public ownership** model is familiar in many nations—but generally not the United States. Second, governments can *regulate* media to ensure protection of the public interest. Third, governments can stand aside and let the *market* guide media; the assumption of the market model is that private companies will give the people (and advertisers) what they want.

Public ownership: A situation in which media outlets are run by the government and paid for by tax dollars.

The First Amendment Protects Print Media from Regulation

You have already encountered the primary political rule governing print media—the First Amendment: "Congress shall make no law . . . abridging the freedom of speech or of the press." Given strict Supreme Court decisions prohibiting government interference with the press, it is very difficult to censor news (a practice known as prior restraint), to convict someone of slander or libel (spoken or written lies), to restrict pornography, or to forbid hate speech. Reporters also fiercely protect their sources. A *New York Times* reporter, Judith Miller, went to jail for three months rather than reveal her source for a story about a CIA agent named Valerie Plame.

Market forces and audience feedback impose the limits that do exist. American newspapers, paid for by local advertisers, generally reflect local mores. They are tame compared with, for example, English tabloids. Web-based news outlets likewise reflect the outlook of their parent companies and of their audience. New-media consumers can respond swiftly to coverage they see as biased or inappropriate, through "comments" sections and organized Twitter and Facebook campaigns. When the gossipy site Gawker printed an article outing a gay Condé Nast executive, readers tweeted a torrent of objections, calling the story an unwarranted example of "gay shaming." Gawker soon removed the article.

Regulating Broadcasters

Radio and television fall into a separate category. They have been subject to government regulations from the start. As radio stations spread in the 1930s, their signals began interfering with one another. In 1934, Franklin Roosevelt's administration created the Federal Communications Commission (FCC) to referee the industry. The agency was founded on a basic political philosophy: The airwaves belong to the public. The FCC would license stations on a given frequency—preventing signals from overlapping—but in exchange, stations were required to be "socially responsible." When a station secured or renewed its license, it had to prove it operated in the public's interest. When television emerged, the FCC expanded its jurisdiction to include it.

In 1949, the FCC issued the **fairness doctrine**, requiring radio and TV stations to give equal time to each side of a public issue. The rule reflected the era's expectations: sober, nonpartisan coverage of news and politics. Even absent strict enforcement, the fairness doctrine led stations to shy away from political controversies altogether, to avoid the bother of achieving balance.

In the 1980s, the Reagan administration challenged the idea of public responsibility enforced by regulatory agencies. Instead it viewed media as a private commodity, not a public good: End government regulations and let consumers use the market to enforce what they value. The FCC repealed the fairness doctrine in 1983, with huge consequences. Under the fairness doctrine, each talk show with a point of view had to be balanced by another talk show from the opposite perspective. A station that broadcast conservatives such as Rush Limbaugh would be required to air an equal amount of liberal programming. Repealing the rule opened the door to today's media landscape: a rich, raucous menu of news and politics that reaches across the political spectrum.

Government regulation of new media is evolving as technology changes. In 2015, following a vigorous debate pitting new-media companies such as Netflix and large

Fairness doctrine:
Regulation that required media outlets to devote equal time to opposite perspectives.

● *Fierce political support for net neutrality did not change FCC commissioners' minds in 2018.*

Internet service providers such as Comcast against consumer rights advocates, the FCC established "net neutrality" rules. These prohibited Internet providers from charging more for certain content or from giving preferential treatment to certain websites ("pay to play"). Three years later, net neutrality was killed by a party-line vote of FCC commissioners. Some states, including California and Washington, wrote their own net neutrality laws—and were sued for interfering with interstate commerce. Will high-paying customers have access to faster Net service? Can customers be charged a premium for using popular social-media sites such as Instagram? Without guaranteed net neutrality, no one knows for certain.

Protecting Competition

Consolidation: The process whereby a media company acquires other companies and threatens to dominate the market.

The market model is based on competition. If one corporation captures too much market share, might it diminish consumer choice? This question arose when corporations moved to control companies across different media markets—print, radio, and television. Some observers warned that a few dominant companies could stifle the marketplace of ideas. By 2010, the top two radio companies, Clear Channel and CBS, controlled so many stations that they broadcast to a larger audience (263 million) than all twenty-four of the remaining radio networks combined. **Consolidation**, from this perspective, threatens free speech and fair debate.

Telecommunications Act of 1996: A major overhaul of communications law that allowed companies to own outlets in multiple media markets such as radio, television, and magazines, and removed limits on how many outlets one company can own.

Those favoring deregulation respond that today's media takes so many different forms, from radio stations to online news, blogs, and tweets, that stiff competition for consumer attention is inevitable. The **Telecommunications Act of 1996** permitted many forms of cross-ownership. Two decades later, consolidation leaves a few media companies controlling vast swaths of American airwaves.

 **The Bottom Line**

» Democratic nations organize their media in three ways: government ownership, regulation, and markets. The United States relies on the latter two models, regulation and markets.

» The First Amendment protects print media from most government regulation.

» Broadcast media in the United States was originally regulated by agencies such as the FCC, which imposed the fairness doctrine—a reflection of a less partisan era. Today's FCC further reduced its own power by ending "net neutrality."

» Deregulation, new technologies, and the rise of multiple media have created the spectrum of perspectives that mark American media today. At the same time, a handful of giant media companies now controls much of the content we see and hear. This contributes to our partisan and conflicted politics.

Media Consolidation

WHO PRODUCES, DISTRIBUTES, AND OWNS THE MEDIA?

Our fast-changing media landscape reflects sweeping consolidation. Three decades ago, media content—
what Americans read, watch, and hear—was spread across more than 50 companies.

CIRCLES SIZED BY MARKET CAPITALIZATION

Distribution   Content

AT&T
$211B market cap
24M video subs
16M broadband subs

TO BUY

Otter Media $1B

DirecTV

TO BUY

Turner (CNN, TNT, TBS)

Time Warner $75B

Warner Bros, studios

HBO

Oath (Yahoo/AOL)

Verizon
$206B
5M video
7M broadband

Go 90

Dish $15B
13M video
(including Sling)

Charter $67B
17M video
24M broadband

Cox $34B**
~4M video
~5M broadband

CBS

CBS $20B

CBS Interactive/CNET

Showtime

Paramount

TO BUY

Viacom $12B

Viacom Media (MTV, Comedy Central, BET)

Discovery, Food Network, HGTV

Discovery Scripps ~$25B

Sony Pictures $31B*

Columbia pictures

Sony Pictures TV

i24NEWS

Altice USA $13B
3M video
4M broadband

News 12 Networks

Lionsgate/Starz $4.9B

Lionsgate TV

Starz

Lionsgate Films

IFC Films

AMC, IFC, BBC America

AMC $3.6B

Fox cable (Fox News, FS1, Nat Geo)

20th Century Fox Studios

21st Century Fox $74B

Fox broadcast

TO BUY

ESPN

ABC

Marvel Studios

Disney $155B

Lucasfilm

Sky $31B
23M video/broadband

39% STAKE

CONTESTED BID

NBC

Dreamworks

Comcast $148B
22M video
26M broadband

E!, Bravo, CNBC

Universal Studios

> ### THINK ABOUT IT
>
> How many major companies control the creation of media content? How many control the distribution of this content?
>
> Today, media giants provide more than 90 percent of content. Is this problematic? Why or why not?
>
> *Source: Rani Molla and Peter Kafka, "Here's who owns everything in Big Media today," Recode, June 18, 2018*

Media Around the World

The American media is different from that of other nations. The "watchdog" tradition, combined with near-absolute freedom of the press to say what they wish, is stronger in the United States than most other countries. Most nations also began with government-operated broadcast media—an option the United States has little pursued, apart from public television (PBS) and radio (NPR). However, differences may be eroding. American media has gone global, and in some countries, leaders even complain about the "Americanization" of their media—moving from public to private ownership.[34]

Government-Owned Stations

When radio developed in the 1920s, democratic leaders worried about the new medium's potential power. What if demagogues seized the airwaves? Rather than leave radio and, later, television programming to private entrepreneurs, many countries introduced public stations that were owned by the government and funded through taxes. To this day, the publicly owned BBC is the largest network in Britain, attracting 32 percent of the TV market.[35] Most other democracies also have popular public stations. One exception is Italy, where for 50 years the Berlusconi family has controlled the nation's three largest TV channels. Silvio Berlusconi parlayed that control into four terms as prime minister. Now consider the United States, where public television draws barely 2 percent of TV watchers. Are you concerned about private control of America's airwaves? Or is this a fine example of the market at work? In many democratic countries, rising commercial media has cultural leaders concerned that the U.S. mix of infotainment and polarized news outlets will soon follow.[36]

Censorship

A different media model dominates authoritarian nations: The government directly controls the media and censors every story. This was long common practice around the world. Government censorship, limiting open information and political debate, has always been the tool of tyrants. Democracies can only operate with the free flow of ideas and information.[37]

New media challenges authoritarian regimes' ability to control information. When the Internet is blocked, innovative networks can spring up to spread the news while new technologies permit people to receive content outside official channels. A key future question is whether (and how) citizens in authoritarian countries will successfully seize the democratic potential of new media forms. In China, for example, Facebook, Google, YouTube, and Twitter are officially blocked, and current rules require all images and words from even partly foreign-owned companies to be approved by government agencies before being broadcast in China. Whatever the answer, the crucial link between media and popular government extends far beyond the United States to every nation.

American Media in the World

American media industries have enormous reach. In one typical week in June 2018, *Jurassic World: Fallen Kingdom* was the highest grossing film in fourteen of twenty-five countries tracking box-office receipts, from Italy to South Africa to Tunisia; *Ocean's Eight* was on top in three others, including Australia and Colombia; and *Avengers: Infinity War* led in China. American television has a similarly wide influence, both in entertainment and news; CNN is shown in virtually every corner of the world. The U.S. media model, emphasizing markets and consumer choice, has a major impact in both democracies and authoritarian nations.

Every nation has its own media style. Governments remain a major content provider (and regulator) in most industrial nations. Looking abroad illustrates how distinctive the U.S. model remains. Few other nations feature a system of private entrepreneurs operating within a framework of very light regulatory oversight.

 **The Bottom Line**

» Rapidly changing media outlets link citizens to their politics around the world. An open media is a vital key to making democracy work.

» The American model of media as private enterprise is spreading. However, most other democracies retain more government regulation than the United States.

» Authoritarian nations censor their news reporters. New media forms challenge government control of the news, but the censors are keeping pace.

Media in Context: War, Terrorism, and U.S. Elections

Every aspect of media influence on politics is on display during two dominant American events: military conflicts, including responses to terrorism, and election campaigns. Framing issues, emphasizing drama and "infotainment," and the fragmenting of story lines in our new-media age all come to the fore.

Covering Wars and Terrorism

When America engages in military conflicts, reporters embed with the troops. Mathew Brady's portraits of Civil War carnage helped establish photography's mass appeal. Wars and terrorist attacks fuel media's inclination to cover striking conflicts. Questions arise in every war about whether media is "sensationalizing" the conflict by providing particularly gruesome images.

● *Vietnam War coverage: Images such as this—a South Vietnamese general shooting a handcuffed Vietcong prisoner in the head—were debated as too violent for American viewers in the 1960s.*

Others warn that wartime media coverage must not give "aid and comfort to America's enemies," as a U.S. general charged during the Vietnam conflict. During the Iraq War, reporters covered alleged American military misdeeds, such as waterboarding torture. Did the coverage portray U.S. soldiers unfairly, diminishing support for the war back home? What responsibility do journalists have for balanced reporting, including of atrocities by our wartime enemies? And how able are traditional media outlets, with reduced budgets for foreign correspondents, to provide big-picture coverage of complex conflicts in Afghanistan and Iraq?

Media coverage of terrorist attacks also raises questions about journalistic ethics. Should the media faithfully report any government claim about foiled terrorist plots, for example? Some experts worry that extensive media coverage of terrorism may heighten the chance of a subsequent attack, as misguided actors seek journalistic fame through terrible crimes. Should the Islamic State, for example, be given the media's "oxygen of publicity" for beheadings and other horrific acts?

Political science research suggests that reporting may spur further terrorist acts. One recent study concluded that a *New York Times* article about a terrorist attack in any specific country increased the number of ensuing attacks in that country by as much as 15 percent.[38]

The Campaign as Drama

American reporters cover electoral campaigns like horse races—obsessed with who will cross the finish line first. With the advent of digital media, the pace of information accelerates; one result is that coverage of presidential campaigns now devotes much less time to the candidate's actual views. In 1968, the average **sound bite** of a candidate speaking on the news ran for over forty seconds. Today, that clip lasts under eight seconds.

Sound bite: A short audio clip; often refers to a brief excerpt from a politician's speech.

See the controversial "Daisy" ad from the 1964 Johnson campaign.

Throughout the campaign, reporters' antennae are always up for hints of scandal. When one appears, the entire media rushes to cover it. Every speech and debate is carefully combed over for blunders; sites such as "FactCheck.org" review candidates' claims during stump speeches and debates. Does this media whirlwind matter to election outcomes? The short answer: rarely. Effective campaigns develop rapid-response teams that deal with whatever crisis gusts through the media on that day.

Without the charge of a presidential race, midterm campaigns such as 2018 can seem relatively dull. However, scandals, endlessly reported by journalists desperate for material beyond the candidates' daily stump speeches, can knock a candidate out of a race or out of office, as ex-Governor Eric Greitens of

Missouri discovered in 2018—after steamy revelations of an affair with his hair-dresser. And any attention at all, in (say) a U.S. House open seat or state lieutenant-governor roundup of candidates, is welcome; so-called "free media" can amplify a message—and validate it ("*The Wall Street Journal* wrote about my candidacy!") with voters.

Candidate Profiles

Campaign coverage typically features a media profile of each candidate—simplistic, exaggerated, and very hard to escape. Once the portrait develops, it reverberates through the world of infotainment. Behavior that "fits" immediately gets airtime, reinforcing the narrative.

● *Media coverage of terrorist attacks: a New York City trail of mayhem in a rented truck. Might 24/7 reporting raise the chances of further attacks?*

In Bernie Sanders's 2016 presidential race, media portrayed Sanders as an insurgent, whose critiques of U.S. financial institutions attracted progressive Americans, especially young voters. Hillary Clinton became an Establishment figure, with reporters noting her long history in Washington institutions such as the State Department, the Senate, and the White House as First Lady. Sanders's surprising staying power was in part thanks to the framing of his candidacy by journalists.

Campaigns respond to shrinking sound bites by creating visual images that will speak louder than the inevitable punditry. Waving flags, cheering crowds, or bales of hay down on the farm all convey images—regardless of media voiceovers.

Candidates spend extraordinary sums on advertising. Some ads have become classics, usually because of their wicked stings; they seep into news coverage and become part of the campaign narrative. That can amplify the signal enough to reach the voters in the middle who are not paying much attention. In 1964, perhaps the most famous ad ever was run by President Johnson's campaign, to fuel fears of GOP presidential candidate Barry Goldwater as dangerously unsuited to supervise American nuclear weapons. A girl plucked petals off a daisy, counting "10...9...8..." Then an ominous male narrator took over, counting down to 1, when the screen filled with a nuclear mushroom cloud. The "Daisy Ad" was only shown once, but achieved huge currency when networks aired it again and again.

New media raises the prospect of transformed campaigning. Social media outlets such as Facebook and Twitter enable candidates to circumvent the mass media and speak directly to supporters: Donald Trump, a master of online campaigning, continued his high-volume tweeting in the White House. Digital messaging offers a dynamic way to mobilize supporters behind a cause.

Ironically, the mainstream media eagerly reports on successful new media campaigns—amplifying that success by publicizing it.

The Bottom Line

» Reporting on war and terrorism has long attracted more viewers than almost any other political story. Ethical questions about media coverage continue to reshape editors' approach to these dramatic stories.

» Media coverage of campaigns reflects patterns of the contemporary media. It emphasizes drama, conflict, and the horse race narrative.

» Campaigns attempt either to influence the media or to bypass it and speak directly to supporters. These efforts in turn become subjects of media coverage.

Conclusion: At the Crossroads of the Media World

The media reflects the United States—and broadcasts it to the world. American media has many critics. Conservatives blast the mainstream media's "liberal bias"; progressives lament the stifling influence of corporate media ownership. Another line of concern: Millennials, engaging media through smartphones, find it hard to filter the endless stream of news and information arriving from every social-media corner. Remember what makes American broadcast media unusual: It has always been a commercial enterprise. Whatever draws an audience generally flourishes.

America's media reflects the American people. The fifth-largest network in the United States is the Spanish-language Univision. And the multilingual media does not stop at Spanish: The Dish satellite menu includes a hundred foreign-language stations. Sixty million Americans have at least one parent born abroad, and the media reflects that reality.

Here is another important indicator: The ten largest religious networks have more than 350 affiliates. The largest, INSP (formerly the Inspiration Network), reaches an estimated 85 million households—roughly on par with ESPN.

As we have seen, television in every demographic is being squeezed by the Internet and the new media. Netflix now has more than 125 million subscribers, and may be the largest U.S. "TV network" within the next few years. In this booming new category, it is America's young people who are driving the change—pioneering new technologies and picking winners and losers among sites and applications. A onetime "digital divide" is now shrinking, as African American and Latino youth catch up to white youth. In forums such as Twitter, they have nudged their way to the top among the young.

Who are we? A multinational and multicultural society, bustling with changes and beaming images to the world—through television, films, blogs, Instagram posts, streaming Netflix shows, and tweets.

Pessimists lament the collapse of our national community. Every political side now has its own news shows. Americans do not just disagree about values—they rarely hear or see the same reality. Mainstream newspapers and networks are losing money, affecting their capacity to collect the news. As details about national and international events get sketchier, the void is filled by loud, ill-informed opinions. The entire news apparatus dashes after drama, conflict, and scandal. Important issues such as education, the environment, and healthcare are downplayed in this chase for an audience. To pessimists, today's media—fragmented, declining, sensationalist—exacerbates the conflicts in American politics.

In contrast, optimists see a thriving democracy in which people are active and engaged. Polarized debates in Washington merely reflect an energetic nation undergoing enormous change. As media outlets expand and go digital, people's choices grow richer. Today, the United States has a broad lineup of news, information, and analysis. Mainstream journalists try to present objective reports. Cable channels and radio stations fire up partisans. And new media—Internet-based outlets such as Instagram and Facebook—permit people, especially young people, to engage in political dialogue as never before. The media stirs up the best features of American politics: broad participation and strong opinions that leaders cannot help but hear.

CHAPTER SUMMARY

🟢 The media helps *set the policy agenda*, *prime* the electorate, and *frame* issues.

🟢 Media stories affect public opinion—especially among people who do not have strong political views.

🟢 Media platforms have expanded from traditional television, radio, and newspapers to include online news sites, podcasts, Facebook, Twitter, and more.

🟢 Media technology changes rapidly, and each change reshapes the connection between citizens and their leaders—a crucial criterion for democracy. Does today's media strengthen or weaken American democracy?

🟢 Newspapers, magazines, television, and radio face shifting business models, and rush to adopt new formats such as on-demand streaming and podcasts. Online news is now the main source for people under thirty. The enormous number of news sources spans the political spectrum and blurs the line between entertainment and news.

● The media is biased—though mainstream reporters do not seem to tilt coverage. The deepest bias arises because the media is a business requiring an audience to generate revenue. Therefore the news emphasizes drama, conflict, and scandal.

● In most other democracies, the government plays a central role in the media world. In authoritarian countries, the new social media poses a threat to the old model of information control and censorship.

● The new social media is changing the nature of news and information. On the upside, active users can choose, respond, report, comment, critique, create, and share. Candidates and parties have new ways to connect. On the downside, the ready availability of news on the Internet has challenged the pay models of traditional print outlets, leading to a new media environment that facilitates the spread of rumors and even lies. Americans less and less often share the same news.

● Media's influence gives it considerable power over American politics. Whether that power is used for the public benefit is a much-debated question—perhaps most sharply when it comes to covering urgent topics such as war, terrorism, and election campaigns.

● In many ways, the media reflects America. What we watch and hear tells us who we are.

KEY TERMS

Consolidation, p. 238
Fairness doctrine, p. 237
Fake news, p. 229
Framing, p. 224
Infotainment, p. 228
Loud signal, p. 222

Mass media, p. 225
New media, p. 222
Personal presidency, p. 226
Policy agenda, p. 223
Priming, p. 224
Public ownership, p. 236

Public watchdog, p. 222
Sound bite, p. 242
Telecommunications Act
of 1996, p. 238
Watergate scandal, p. 234

STUDY QUESTIONS

1. Where do most Americans get their news—local television, network television, newspapers, or the Internet?
2. Which sources do millennial Americans rely on most for their news?
3. Name two problems most analysts see in the decline of the newspaper. Do you agree that these are problems? Why or why not?

4. How is the American media biased? Describe three of its biases.
5. Name three ways in which the American media is different from that of other nations. Be sure to consider the questions of ownership, objectivity, and investigation.
6. Choose a news source and look at today's headlines. Can you find a "media narrative"

in these stories? Do you see a narrative arc, drama, conflict, good guys, and bad guys? Can you come up with a more objective way to present the story?

7. Research a presidential candidate for the 2020 election. What does she or he stand for? Now design a campaign commercial for that candidate. Put him or her in the best possible light using visuals and voiceovers. Post your creation on YouTube.

8. Pick a story. Read its coverage in the *New York Times*. Now compare this coverage with that of two other sources: the BBC and Al Jazeera. Identify at least one difference in the way the other two outlets covered the story.

Go to **www.oup.com/us/Morone** to find quizzes, flash cards, simulations, tutorials, videos, and other study tools.

8 Campaigns and Elections

THE RULES FOR WINNING THE PRESIDENCY

were clear. Raise a lot of money, build a sophisticated team, and win over the party leaders.[1] The 2016 presidential campaign seemed perfectly predictable. Team Jeb Bush raised a whopping $116 million. On the Democratic side, Hillary Clinton was not far behind. Then Donald Trump broke all the rules: He seemed indifferent to fundraising, he did not build a serious campaign organization, he did not run any commercials, and he was crude and insulting—to Latinos, African Americans, U.S. prisoners of war, women, immigrants, newscasters, donors, and even Republican elder statesmen.[2] Trump mocked many of the sixteen other Republican candidates who could not get airtime—as the media obsessed over the latest Trump outrage. By the end of the campaign, estimates suggested that Trump had swung $2 billion worth of free media coverage—much of it negative. Yet he won primary after primary. Despite the cold shoulder from almost every past Republican presidential candidate and most officeholders ("trickle-down racism," charged former presidential candidate, Mitt Romney), Trump won the nomination. On the Democratic side, Senator Bernie Sanders—a rumpled, little known, 74-year-old democratic socialist with a Brooklyn accent representing Vermont—also broke the rules: He lashed the rich, lambasted party leaders for ignoring everyday people, and won 23 contests and 43 percent of the votes in the Democratic primary.

When political scientists published their models before the general election, the median (or middle one) predicted correctly that Democratic presidential candidate Hillary Clinton would receive 51 percent of the popular vote. A surge of white (mostly male) voters from economically distressed communities, however, gave Trump the Electoral College and powered one of the biggest upsets in American campaign history. It was a very close call. If 78,000 votes in Wisconsin, Michigan, and Pennsylvania (out of a total of 12 million) had gone the other way, Hillary Clinton would have won.

● *Republicans and Democrats confront one another during a raucous campaign event. The question for political scientists and citizens: How much do campaigns matter?*

In this chapter, you will:

● **Learn what is unique (and what is not) about American elections.**

● **Reflect on how democratic American elections are today.**

● **Examine the influence of money in elections.**

● **Explore presidential and congressional campaigns.**

● **Identify the keys to a successful campaign for Congress.**

● **Consider election reforms.**

● *Alexandria Ocasio-Cortez, a former Bernie Sanders organizer, jolted the political establishment by upsetting powerful Democrat Joseph Crowley in a New York City primary.*

There's always another election coming up. Two years later, the 2018 midterm shook up American politics. Republicans gained ground in the Senate, but Democrats won control of the House of Representatives and made inroads with suburban voters. What's next? Another election, of course. All eyes turn on the next great prize: the election of 2020.

Sometimes, political scientists suggest, campaigns barely matter. More fundamental factors—such as the economy and the president's approval rating—determine who wins the election. Not the hyped-up, media-saturated, roller-coaster campaign. Do campaigns matter?

In fact, campaigns are essential to electoral outcomes. This chapter will show you how and why.[3] We will not just focus on the White House. Thousands of candidates run for positions from U.S. senators to judges to municipal drain inspectors. *Who are we*? A nation of elections. Americans vote more often and for more officers—on every level of government—than the people of most other nations. Through elections, Americans choose leaders, philosophies, policies, and an attitude toward the rest of the world.

Both Donald Trump and Bernie Sanders pose an overarching question for campaigns and elections in the United States: Do the rules governing our voting reflect the people? Should it better reflect public views? Or perhaps, as some of the founders thought, American electoral machinery should be *less* sensitive to the whims of public opinion.[4]

How Democratic Are U.S. Elections?

Time, place, and manner clause: The constitutional clause that delegates control of elections to the state governments.

The Constitution sidestepped a crucial matter: Who votes and how. It left the election details—the **"time, place, and manner"**—up to the states. Every state builds its own electoral process—and our federalist conflicts have always filtered right into the voting rules. For example, felons can vote from jail in Maine, only after they have passed through parole and probation in Texas, and almost never in Florida. We can evaluate how well elections enhance popular rule by focusing on four dimensions: frequency, breadth, voting barriers, and the role of money.

BY THE NUMBERS
Campaigns and Elections

Years in which American women first voted (in New Jersey)	**1797–1807**
Year in which women in all states could vote	**1920**
Number of people filing to run for president in 2016	**1,812**
Number filing who were "serious" Republican candidates	**17**
Number of candidates named Prince of Darkness, Satan Lord of the Underworld H. Majesty	**1**
Sequential rank of Iowa and New Hampshire in presidential primary season	**1, 2**
Percentage of U.S. population that is non-Hispanic white, 2017	**61.3**
Percentage of Iowa's and New Hampshire's population, respectively, that is white	**86, 91**
Number of Americans who voted in the 2016 presidential race	**128.7 million**
Number of Americans who did NOT vote in the 2016 presidential race	**100 million**
Percentage of Americans who support limits on money spent in political campaigns (2018)	**77[5]**
Percentage of voting-age population who turned out, 1916 and 2016	**61.6, 54.8**
Number (and percentage) of House or Senate incumbents who lost in 2016	**4 House (0.9%), 2 Senate (2%)**

Who participates in campaigns and elections and how does that influence our democratic process?

Frequent and Fixed Elections

One way to hold public officials accountable is to require them to face the public frequently. The United States schedules elections for national office more often than most other democratic countries. House members are chosen every two years, presidents every four, and Senators every six. Add in state and local elections and there is never a year in the United States without major elections.

In parliamentary democracies, the prime minister generally decides when to hold an election as long as there is at least one within a set period, usually five years. In contrast, American national elections are on a fixed date (chosen back in 1845)—politicians do not have the luxury of deciding when to stand before the people. On the first Tuesday after the first Monday in November of every even-numbered year, Americans elect all House members and a third of the Senate; every fourth year, we elect a president. Special elections are held if an officeholder dies or resigns, and each state sets the date of the primary elections that determine which candidates represent a political party for each office. The timing and frequency tilts U.S. elections in a more democratic direction.

Do you see any drawbacks to frequent elections? All that campaigning consumes a great deal of time, money, and energy. House members are always running for reelection. As a Canadian prime minister once remarked: "In your system, you guys campaign for 24 hours a day, every day for two years. You know, politics is one thing, but we have to run a government."[6]

Over 520,000 Elected Officials

Not only are U.S. elections unusually frequent compared to most countries, but an enormous *number* of positions are elected—from presidents to municipal drain inspectors. Today, even judges are elected (in 39 states covering 87 percent of all state judges). No other country elects judges, since they are supposed to be above politics. Critics charge that fundraising and campaign promises compromise the impartiality of state judges. But elections remain the American way.

To get a feel for the numbers see Table 8.1, which lists elected officials representing the residents of Iowa City, Iowa. Count them up: There are 58 elected officials for Iowa City alone. That's one measure of democracy in action. Is this a good way to give the people influence over government? Or does it make informed judgment impossible by overwhelming them with too many choices? What do you think?

Barriers to Voting

There are plenty of barriers to voting. Registration requirements were introduced in the nineteenth century to limit voting; today eight states strictly require a photo ID and many others make registration burdensome; thirty-three states restrict voting by felons after they have done their time. Other states purge voting lists (which makes it harder to register), offer fewer voting stations in some neighborhoods (check out the long lines featured on all the news feeds on Election Day), and the list goes on. On the other hand, some states make it easy: Seventeen states permit same day registration (including the six with the highest turnout in 2016) and sixteen states saw more than half the population vote

| TABLE 8.1 | **Who Do You Vote for in Iowa City?** |

NATIONAL OFFICIALS	
1 U.S. president	
2 U.S. senators from Iowa	
1 U.S. representative from Iowa's Second District	
STATE OFFICIALS	
1 governor	
1 lieutenant governor	1 secretary of state
1 attorney general	1 state treasurer
1 agriculture secretary	1 state auditor
1 state senator	1 state representative
COUNTY OFFICIALS	
1 supervisor	1 sheriff
1 treasurer	1 attorney
1 auditor	1 recorder
TOWNSHIP/CITY OFFICIALS (IOWA CITY IS BOTH A CITY AND A "TOWNSHIP")	
1 clerk	
3 trustees	
7 school board members	
4 education agency directors	
7 city council members (who elect one member as Iowa City mayor)	
9 agricultural extension members	
1 soil and water conservation commissioner	

Elected versus Appointed Positions?

There are too many elective positions.
The public is asked to vote too often. Few voters can learn about so many races. The United States should appoint more experts who could handle the technical aspects of government.

No, we need to encourage people to vote more often.
Reducing the number of elected officials would be unhealthy for our democracy. Voting permits the people to hold their public officials directly to account. It's the best check on government officials.

by mail or vote early. The point: It's all up to the states. Some encourage voting, others raise barriers. Why? Usually, the majority party protects itself by adjusting the voting rules—a tendency that goes all the way back to the first elections.[7]

Financing Campaigns: The New Inequality?

Enormous sums flow through U.S. elections, triggering another set of fears. Does money tilt the process?

Too Much Money? The price tag for the 2016 presidential and congressional races combined: $6.5 billion (Figure 8.1). Those billions raise a perennial question: Is there too much money in American political campaigns?

Many critics say yes. Public officials on every level devote enormous amounts of time and energy raising money. As a result, some people fear that wealthy people may be able to bury candidates and (more important) political issues that they do not like. Polls consistently show overwhelming majorities want to reduce the role of money in U.S. elections. In 2002, Congress responded with the Bipartisan Campaign Reform Act (known as McCain–Feingold), which limited the amounts individuals, corporations, and organizations could give.

Bipartisan critics pushed back. Both Mitch McConnell (R-KY), the Republican Senate leader, and the American Civil Liberties Union argued that supporting campaigns is a form of free speech. The Supreme Court has largely accepted this perspective. In *Citizens United v. The Federal Elections Commission*, the court ruled (5–4) that the free speech clause of the first amendment protects corporations, unions, and other groups who wish to support candidates or causes. In *McCutcheon v. Federal Elections Commission*, the court struck down limits on the total donations an individual can make (again 5–4). The law still limits how much you can give an individual candidate running for office, but not how much you spend overall by donating to parties, to multiple candidates, and on issue ads.[8]

Americans oppose the rising tide of campaign cash, but for most, the issue is not a high priority. After all, think about those campaign numbers in context: The $6.5 billion spent on all national races in 2016 was less than two-thirds of what Americans spent at Taco Bell and less than a third of the estimated amount spent on pornography during the same year. What do you think: Is contributing to campaigns a citizen's right? Or is it turning our democracy over to the wealthy?

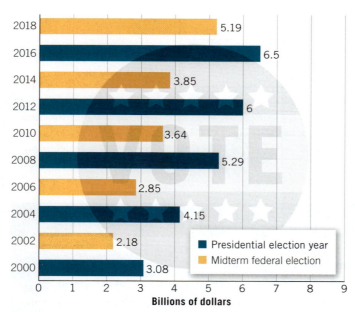

● **Figure 8.1** *The cost of national elections (inflation-adjusted dollars). (Open Secrets)*

Democracy for the Rich? Do the wealthy dominate elections—maybe even squeezing out the people's influence? There are three major concerns.

First, does one party get an advantage? Some groups do contribute mainly to one party. For example, labor unions financially back Democrats (by a ten-to-one margin, in recent elections), and some industries—such as oil and gas companies—largely support Republican candidates. But most business sectors traditionally split their donations about evenly between the two major parties. In 2016, for example, Comcast gave $1.9 million to Democrats, $2.1 million to Republicans; Northrup-Grumman, the fourth largest defense contractor, contributed $1.8 million to Democrats and $2.5 million to Republicans. Most corporate sectors wanted a seat at the table in both parties. Are the Republicans now pulling ahead, as many Democrats fear? If so, it has not begun to show in total spending. In the 2018 midterms, Democrats outraised Republicans by more than by more than $300 million in the House and $140 million in the Senate. The entire price tag for the midterm: 5.2 billion.[9]

Second, parties may not get an advantage but incumbents certainly do. They generally overwhelm their challengers. In 2018, sitting Senators amassed $14.6 million on average. Their opponents scraped together just 1.9 million on average. Perhaps that is one reason the reelection rates in 2018 were 93% (House) and 88% (Senate). This lopsided funding has a big impact, not in the headline presidential contest and high profile Senate races, but down the ballot in the low profile Congressional races.[10]

Third, critics worry that the need to raise funds—always more and more money—makes officeholders especially sensitive to their funders. Big donors confidently chuckle that they are "buying a seat at the table"—they can always get in the door to talk to elected officials. Mick Mulvaney, head of the Consumer Financial Bureau put it bluntly: When he was a congressman, he said, "If you're a lobbyist who never gave us money, I didn't talk to you."[11] Still, research has not yet found a systematic link between contributions and political influence.[12]

Major Donors: Easier to Give. OK, you have made your fortune and you want to contribute to your favorite candidate. What are your options? First, many corporations and advocacy groups organize **political action committees** (**PACs**) to donate to candidates. PACs, which must include 50 or more contributors, may legally contribute $10,000 to any one candidate—$5,000 for the primary campaign, $5,000 more for the general election.

Want to contribute more? The **super PAC** was born in 2010 after the Supreme Court struck down laws limiting "independent" political spending by corporations and unions (in *Citizens United v. FEC*). Super PACs, formally known as "independent expenditure-only committees," may raise unlimited sums from virtually any source—business firms, unions, or individuals—and spend as much as they like to openly support or oppose political candidates. Unlike traditional PACs, they are not supposed to directly contribute to or coordinate with the candidate's political campaigns. But that rule is difficult

Political action committee (PAC): An organization of at least 50 people, affiliated with an interest group, that is permitted to make contributions to candidates for federal office.

Super PACs: Organizations that raise and spend unlimited amounts of money to promote a candidate or publicize a cause. However, they may not directly contribute to a candidate or coordinate with a campaign.

Money in Elections

THE NEW RULES

Since 2010, the Supreme Court rulings in *Citizens United v. FEC,* and *McCutcheon v. FEC,* have weakened the limits on campaign contributions and enabled super PACs to emerge. Although per candidate and per PAC limits still exist, the caps on the number of candidates or PACs a donor can contribute to have been lifted.

THINK ABOUT IT

How has the amount of money a single donor can contribute to candidates, party committees, PACs, and super PACs changed?

How does the lifting of caps affect wealthy donors who hedge their bets by contributing to multiple candidates? How will this affect elections and democratic representation?

Sources: Washington Post *Information Graphics; Open Secrets*

		2010	2018
Candidates	Limit for each candidate	House and Senate candidates $5,200 each	House and Senate candidates $5,400 each
	Limit for all candidates in an election cycle?	**YES** Total possible contribution: $48,600	**NO LIMIT** By giving each candidate the maximum amount. one donor could contribute $2,527,200
Party committees	Limits	$74,600	$1,197,400
PACs	Limit for each PAC	$5,000 each	$5,000 each
	Limit for all PACs	**YES** Total possible contribution: $74,600	**NO LIMIT** By giving each PAC the maximum amount. one donor could contribute **$Millions**
Number of super PACs		0	Over 2,300

to enforce as close associates generally run the super PACs lined up behind a candidate.[13]

Despite all this money flowing into campaign coffers, Shaun McCutcheon, a conservative Alabama businessman, was frustrated by the campaign finance laws that capped his overall donations. In *McCutcheon v. FEC*, the Supreme Court agreed (5–4). The law still limits how much you can give an individual candidate, but not how much you spend overall by donating to parties and issues ads. The top seven contributors in 2018 gave just under $300 billion, evenly split between the parties.

What is left after the Court's ruling is a patchwork of regulations. No one may contribute more than $2,700 to any individual candidate or $5,000 to an old-fashioned PAC (not to be confused with Super PACs, which have no limits). One way around that limit is through **bundling**: convincing colleagues and friends to donate at or near the maximum amount, then delivering all the checks together.

Another source of campaign-related funds: **527 groups**, named for the section of the U.S. tax code that regulates them. Although 527 groups are forbidden from advocating directly on behalf of any candidate's election, they can accept and spend unlimited amounts for "issue advocacy." They may not explicitly support or oppose a candidate, but the ads they run can be indirectly supportive—or scathing. "Senator Jones is a tree killer who hates the environment" is an acceptable message for a 527 group; "Vote against Senator Jones" is not.

PACs, super PACS, bundlers, 527s: In the 2016 presidential contest, these outside groups spent an estimated $1.04 billion—beyond the roughly $2 billion raised by the presidential campaigns. Each innovation raises a fresh round of questions about democracy and campaign spending. Does this help or hurt democracy? Does contributing funds to a legislator buy anything valuable for donors? Should the system be changed to reduce the influence of monetary contributions? Or is spending money on campaigns a vital form of free speech? We will come back to these questions at the end of this chapter.

Bundling: A form of fundraising in which an individual persuades others to donate large amounts that are then delivered together to a candidate or campaign.

527 groups: Organizations that raise and spend unlimited amounts for "issue advocacy" but are forbidden to coordinate their efforts with any candidate or campaign.

 **The Bottom Line**

» Are American elections truly democratic? Americans vote more often than the citizens of most democracies.

» Americans vote for more offices—from state judges to school board members—than the people in other democracies. Some critics suggest we vote on too many offices.

» The most familiar question about American democracy today fixates on the role of money in campaigns. PACs, super PACs, and 527s have become fixtures in national elections. Recent court decisions have significantly expanded the ability of wealthy donors and outside groups to spend large sums in support of their preferred candidates, party, and causes.

🔵 Presidential Campaigns and Elections

The presidency is the greatest electoral prize but winning is brutal. Running is expensive, exhausting, and often humiliating. Yet, in every presidential race, dozens take up the challenge.

Who Runs for President?

Onetime candidate Morris "Mo" Udall, who ran in 1976, said afterward, "You have to be a little crazy to run for president." The U.S. Constitution, however, only requires that candidates be American citizens, aged 35 years or older who have resided in the country for 14 years or more.

Serious presidential candidates generally have experience as elected officials—and, in the past half-century, both parties have nominated candidates with one of three offices on their résumé—vice president, governor, or senator. The last president to come directly out of the House of Representatives? James Garfield in 1880. Businesspeople with no experience in public office? None ever won the presidency—until Donald Trump in 2016 (Table 8.2). In all American history, Donald Trump is the first newcomer to navigate the political process. How did he do it? Read on.

The Three Phases of Presidential Elections

Presidential campaigns involve three distinct stages: the *nomination process*, the *party convention*, and the *general election*. Each stage requires very different political strategies, played out amid the white-hot lights of global media coverage.

● *Presidential Candidate Vermin Supreme placed fourth in the 2016 New Hampshire Democratic primary on a platform of time travel research, zombie alert preparation, and ponies for all.*

| TABLE 8.2 | **The President's Résumé** | | | |

The President's Résumé

YEAR	WINNER	PREVIOUS POSITION	LOSER	PREVIOUS POSITION
1960	John Kennedy	Senator	Richard Nixon	Vice president (1953–1961)
1964	Lyndon Johnson	Vice president (1961–1963)	Barry Goldwater	Senator
1968	Richard Nixon	Vice president (1953–1961)	Hubert Humphrey	Vice president (1965–1969)
1972	Richard Nixon	Incumbent	George McGovern	Senator
1976	Jimmy Carter	Governor	Gerald Ford	Vice president/Incumbent
1980	Ronald Reagan	Governor	Jimmy Carter	Incumbent
1984	Ronald Reagan	Incumbent	Walter Mondale	Vice president (1977–1981)
1988	George H. W. Bush	Vice president (1981–1989)	Michael Dukakis	Governor
1992	Bill Clinton	Governor	George H. W. Bush	Incumbent
1996	Bill Clinton	Incumbent	Bob Dole	Senator
2000	George W. Bush	Governor	Al Gore	Vice president (1993–2001)
2004	George W. Bush	Incumbent	John Kerry	Senator
2008	Barack Obama	Senator	John McCain	Senator
2012	Barack Obama	Incumbent	Mitt Romney	Governor
2016	Donald Trump	Real Estate Developer, Reality TV Star	Hillary Clinton	Secretary of State, Senator, First Lady

Winning the Nomination

The grueling process begins with the invisible primary (also known as the money primary). Candidates toss their hat in the ring and then build an organization, compete in televised debates, and scramble for media attention. Before the first vote was cast in the 2016 race, five Republican candidates had already dropped out—doomed by low polls, anemic fund raising, and weak debate performances.

Next, the candidates run the gauntlet of state contests. Iowa begins with a **caucus** where activists in each precinct meet to select delegates who will vote for a candidate. Here's an opportunity to break out of the pack—or suffer an unexpected setback. In 2016, Texas Senator Ted Cruz won 27.6 percent of the vote, followed by Donald Trump (24%) and Florida Senator Marco Rubio (21%). After only 186,000 voters had spoken, Republicans had their front-runners. On the Democratic side, the presumed nominee, Hillary Clinton, barely held off Vermont Senator Bernie Sanders, 48.8 percent to 49.6 percent—Sanders showed he was a serious contender.

Next, on to New Hampshire's **primary**. In a **closed primary**, only party members go to the polls and vote for a nominee. In an **open primary**,

Caucus: A local meeting of voters to select candidates to represent a political party in a general election or to choose delegates who select candidates at a convention.

Closed primary: A vote cast by party members to select candidates to represent the party in the general election

Open primary: A vote cast by any eligible voter to select candidates to represent the party in the general election

voters can participate in either party's elections. New Hampshire's primary is semi-closed because independents may vote in either party's primary. New Hampshire produced a political earthquake: Donald Trump won easily, making him the Republican front-runner with Ohio Governor John Kasich a distant second. And Bernie Sanders smashed to victory with over 60 percent of the vote.

After that, candidates negotiate a wide range of contests with different rules and norms. Candidates hopscotch the country trying to amass delegates (while raising money)—until **Super Tuesday** when both parties schedule multiple elections on a single date. Party leaders generally hope to have a winner by Super Tuesday so that the nomination process does not drag on too long and damage the eventual nominee. In 2016, Hillary Clinton won 511 delegates on Super Tuesday but Bernie Sanders hung on with 348 of his own and the contest continued. On the Republican side, Cruz, with 232 delegates, continued to challenge Trump who by then had 332.

Both parties require that a winning candidate attract a majority of the convention delegates. In 2020, the magic number is 1,237 for Republicans and 2,382 for Democrats. The parties assign each state a number of delegates based on state population and party loyalty in the last election.

In the past, Republicans used a **winner-take-all** system, under which the winning candidate receives all the delegates for that state. Democrats, in contrast, have generally employed a system of **proportional representation**, allocating delegates based on the proportion of the vote a candidate wins. In 2016, the GOP primaries required proportional representation until mid-March, when states could choose to allocate all their delegates to the outright winner (seven states did so). Why all this rigmarole? Republican Party activists wanted a process that did not get decided too soon—before their candidate had been fully tested (as happened with John McCain in 2008)—but they did not want the contest to drag out so long as to damage the winner (Mitt Romney in 2012).

The traditional rules are clear: Primary season candidates must make strong first impressions, compete well in state after state, avoid errors or outrageous statements in a dozen or more debates, and manage a campaign team that, as the contests continue, can swell to thousands of people. They also may have to carefully calibrate their issue positions.

In 2016, Donald Trump broke all the rules: He made outrageous statements and did not bother with a professional campaign team. So, why did he win the primaries?

First, day after day, he dominated the news feeds. Trump had already attracted the public attention as a businessman and celebrity—from his bestselling book, *The Art of the Deal*, to his own reality television show, *The Apprentice*. To many people, Trump was a symbol of economic success.[15] Trump's outrageous statements kept him in the limelight. *The Art of the Deal* explained: "Good publicity is preferable to bad, but . . . bad publicity is sometimes better than no publicity at all. Controversy, in short, sells."[16]

Super Tuesday: The date on the presidential primary calendar when multiple states hold primaries and caucuses.

Winner-take-all: The candidate winning a simple majority (or, among multiple candidates, a plurality) receives all electoral votes or primary delegates. Sometimes called "first-past-the-post."

Proportional representation: The allocation of votes or delegates on the basis of the percentage of the vote received; contrasts with the winner-take-all system.

Why Iowa and New Hampshire?

Two years before each presidential election, politicians, campaign advisors, and the media descend on two small states. By tradition, Iowa's caucuses and New Hampshire's primary are the first two presidential contests—giving them an outsized influence in the process. Should they continue to have such an important say in choosing the president?

Yes. Small states such as these test the candidates' abilities through one-on-one meetings with small groups—a very different challenge than the media campaigns reliant on heavy fundraising that follow in the large states. These small states reveal the men and women behind the slick media presentations.

No. Iowa ranks thirtieth in population and is 86 percent white; New Hampshire forty-second in population and 91 percent white. Two highly unrepresentative states eliminate many candidates before any large state has even had a chance to vote.

Second, Trump emphasized American economic decline even as the Obama administration touted a solid growth rate. Trump understood that many individuals felt left out of the economic recovery—and he targeted his pitch directly to them. These individuals formed a vital component of his early base of supporters.[17]

Third, questions of identity have grown increasingly intense and prominent in American politics. What appeared to be mistakes—bashing immigrants, racially insensitive language, and so on—spoke to a segment of voters that resented cosmopolitan, urban, coastal, multicultural elites. Recent work in political science suggests that the Trump campaign managed to mobilize the issue of white identity, especially among white voters with low education—some of whom had voted for President Obama.[18]

Finally, both Trump's success and Bernie Sanders's strong showing can be attributed—in part—to the nature of voter turnout in primary elections. Far fewer Americans vote in primary elections than in general elections; those who do vote tend to be more ideological than the more centrist fall electorate. Conventional political wisdom holds that candidates must run more to the extreme—farther left for Democrats, farther right for Republicans—to capture the nomination and then move back to the middle for the general election. Both Trump and Sanders energized their base supporters—ardent conservatives and progressives, respectively. Each, in a very different way, conveyed an authenticity to an electorate deeply cynical about politics and politicians. And, as the contest moved on to the next stage, Trump broke yet another convention: He doubled down on his own base instead of tacking to the center.

Organizing the Convention

Political party conventions showcase the party's presidential nominee on a national stage. They also gather party insiders from across the United States for several days of meetings and celebration. Advocacy groups and corporate

Electoral bounce: The spike in the polls that follows an event such as a party's national convention.

See excerpts from the 1960 Nixon–Kennedy debate.

interests flock to the conventions as well: Everyone jockeys to be noticed by a potential future president and his or her closest advisers.

When it works well, the convention can provide the nominee an **electoral bounce**, a temporary boost in the polls. A star-studded Democratic convention gave Hillary Clinton a bounce, despite furious opposition from Sanders supporters. That boost vaulted her into a lead she never relinquished in the polls—until Donald Trump won the election.

The General Election

After the convention, the campaigns shift into overdrive. With just three months between the convention and Election Day, every hour matters. Campaigns scramble to stage media events, blast the opposing candidate, tweet, post, and meet with donors.

General elections usually feature three debates between the nominees, as well as one vice presidential debate. Pundits scrutinize the performances, search for gaffes, and report the overnight polls. The truth, however, is that most viewers have already made up their minds and debates normally have only a slight impact on the race.

Winning Presidential Elections

The CIA, the FBI, and the National Security Agency jointly reported that Russian President Vladimir Putin had run a sophisticated operation to tilt the election to Donald Trump. The Russians spread disinformation through Internet trolls, hacked the computer systems of both major parties, and leaked the emails of Democratic leaders online ahead of the Democratic National Convention.[19] Most analysts, however, are skeptical that Russian cyberactivities influenced the results of the elections.[20] What factors did—and do—win presidential races? Along with the candidates themselves—their speeches, gaffes, debate performances, and responses to the unexpected— a variety of factors help determine the winner.

● *Chicago 1968 Democratic National Convention: Angry protests both in and outside the hall created an image of disarray and crisis. This convention symbolized the collapse of the old Democratic coalition. Republicans would take the White House in five of the next six elections.*

Economic Outlook. Bill Clinton's headquarters in 1992 featured a famous whiteboard reminding campaign staffers: "It's the Economy, Stupid." If the economy is performing poorly, the party holding the presidency is likely to suffer.

Even with a fairly strong economy in 2016, the growing difference between the haves and the have-nots proved to be a major issue. In the Democratic primaries, Bernie Sanders spoke to frustrations over America's growing inequality. Donald Trump painted a dark picture of the state of the nation that seemed baffling to prosperous elites but resonated in the towns and small cities of middle America.[21]

Demographics. Once upon a time, each party worked to build a winning coalition, relying on its base of likely supporters and reaching out to undecided groups in the middle. After the 2012 election, the Republican Party did an "autopsy" to explain why it had lost the presidency and slipped (minus two seats) in the Senate. Major conclusion: The party failed to appeal to growing ranks of millennials and minorities, especially Hispanics. In 2016, Republican primary voters spurned that advice and turned to a candidate who shouted out the perils of immigration, disparaged immigrants, and was unpopular with a majority of young voters.

His harsh words propelled Trump to victory in the primaries and then, rather than pivot for the general election, Trump doubled down on anti-immigrant rhetoric. He spoke directly to the party demographics: older, whiter, more male. White voters had not given a Democratic nominee more than 43 percent of the vote in 35 years. Democrat Hillary Clinton overwhelmingly won the black vote (an estimated 88%), Latino (65%), Asian (65%), and people under 30 (55%). But she only managed 37 percent of all whites voting.[22]

War and Foreign Policy. Most Americans pay far more attention to domestic issues—especially those that touch their pocketbooks. Occasionally, however, foreign-policy issues become pivotal, especially when the nation is at war. For example, the 9/11 attacks helped George Bush win reelection three years later in 2004. In 2016, Republicans sharply criticized Hillary Clinton for a terrorist attack in Benghazi, Libya, that killed four American embassy officials during the time she served as secretary of state. During the campaign, however, she took far more hawkish (or aggressive) views than Donald Trump.[23]

Still, 2016 was a normal year: Few voters named foreign policy as a major influence on their choice of candidate. Even so, Trump questioned support for traditional U.S. allies and alliances (like NATO, the alliance that won the Cold War) and expressed admiration for Russian leader Vladimir Putin.[24] Most Washington insiders were aghast at Trump's foreign-policy statements.

● *Over 70 million Americans tuned into the Kennedy and Nixon debate in 1960—launching the age of televised campaigning. The more charismatic Kennedy won the White House by the slimmest of margins—.001 percent.*

Explore domestic
issues and party
platforms.

Domestic Issues. Every presidential candidate has a list of favorite programs and strategies. Bill Clinton discussed education, energy, Medicare, and Medicaid so often that his staff started calling his campaign E2M2. Donald Trump promised job creation, infrastructure, a hard line on immigration, and a strong nationalist trade policy—the United States would not be pushed around anymore, he said. The candidates' issue preferences are important, not because they will decide the election (highly unlikely), but because they set the agenda for the presidency. True to form, President Trump moved immediately to limit immigration, challenged alliances like NATO, and challenged other countries—from China to Rwanda—with trade restrictions.[25]

The Campaign Organization. One truism that every would-be president knows: It is essential to assemble a team of talented, loyal advisers capable of charting a plan for victory. This is an immensely difficult task. Building a large, multistate organization—often from scratch—tests every candidate's executive skill.[26]

Political scientist Samuel Popkin argued that a strong campaign chief of staff could be a decisive factor in whether campaigns thrive or founder.[27] Again, Donald Trump was unusual. He relied on his own instincts and the advice of a small circle—despite Republican pleas that he defer to seasoned political managers. Instead he kept shaking up his team, bringing on Steve Bannon, whom the BBC described as a "bare knuckled populist," to direct the final months of the campaign.[28]

Parties Matter. Many analysts expected moderates to abandon Donald Trump and go over to Clinton in droves. He was too toxic, too divisive, too racist, too sexist, and too unpredictable. What analysts overlooked was the force of party attachment in a partisan era (see Chapter 11). Even a candidate that blasted many of the party's traditional policy positions still commanded the loyalty of the vast majority of Republicans. In the end, 92 percent of Republican men and 91 percent of the women came home to vote for the party's nominee—just a hair below Governor Romney's 93 percent party loyalty.[29]

Trump supporters
chant "Build
the wall" on the
Mexican border.

The Electoral College and Swing States. The Electoral College vote in almost all states is winner take all, so the outcome of most presidential elections hinges on a few states. Democrats know they will win in New York and California. Republicans know they will sweep the Deep South. Both parties compete to win swing states—states that might go either way in a race—to amass 270 Electoral College votes. Swing states keep changing. In 2016, the battle was in some ten to twelve states including Colorado, Florida, Iowa, Nevada, New Hampshire, North Carolina, Ohio, Pennsylvania, Virginia, and Wisconsin.[30]

Hillary Clinton won the popular vote by 2.9 million votes—48.2 percent, compared to Trump's 46.1 percent. So how did Trump win the Electoral College? Razor thin margins in three states the Democrats had held for 24 years—Michigan (10,700 votes out of 4.7 million cast), Wisconsin

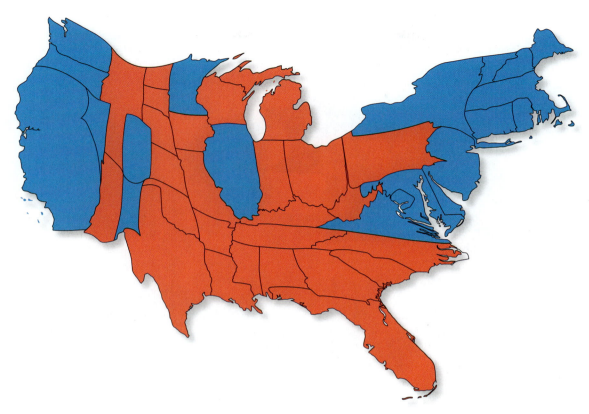

● **Figure 8.2** *The electoral map in 2016 with state size morphed to show size of Electoral College vote. Blue is Democrat, Red Republican. Note how Trump's victories in Pennsylvania and Ohio loom large. (Mark Newman)*

(22,000 votes out of 4 million), and Pennsylvania (44,000 out of 6 million)—gave the Trump campaign all 46 Electoral College votes in those three states and the election. In addition, Democrats tend to concentrate in urban areas. In California and New Jersey, where approximately 95 percent of the population lives in urban centers, Clinton won 61.7 percent and 57.3 percent of the popular vote, respectively.[31] Republicans are more efficiently (at least for maximizing Electoral College votes) spread out over rural and suburban America (Figure 8.2).

But here's a crucial historical point: The states are always evolving. Forty years ago, California was reliably Republican, Texas Democratic. American politics is always changing.

Finally, the biggest number in the 2016 election was 100 million. That's the number of people who did NOT vote—and it is almost as many as voted for the two major candidates *combined* (128.7 million). All of those non-voters could be a blockbuster source of change—if a party or a candidate could find a way to get them to vote (Figure 8.3).[32]

That Elusive Winning Recipe. There is no sure recipe for winning a presidential election. They occur so rarely—the 2016 contest was only the eighteenth since

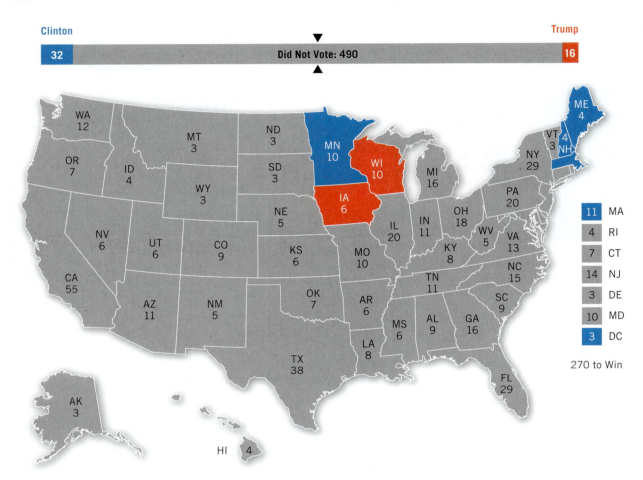

Clinton

| 32 | Did Not Vote: 490 | Trump | 16 |

11	MA
4	RI
7	CT
14	NJ
3	DE
10	MD
3	DC

270 to Win

● **Figure 8.3** *If "not voting" had been a candidate for the 2016 presidential race, "not voting" would have won the Electoral College in almost every state. (270 to Win)*

World War II—and involve such an immense array of influences that journalists, historians, and political scientists spend years trying to draw lessons from each campaign.

In 2016, demographics mattered (Figure 8.4). White working-class people (especially men) had long tilted Republican (Figure 8.4). Now that tilt grew. White people with a two-year college degree or less strongly favored Trump. Suburban and rural America went Republican, too. Trump spoke to the economic anxieties of those left behind in an era of jarring inequality. He channeled the grievance some people felt toward cosmopolitan urban elites; rural middle America believed that urban and coastal areas did not share their values and received an unfair portion of government benefits—a point one political scientist emphasized in charting the changes to Wisconsin politics —even before the 2016 election.[33] That resentment may be exacerbated by uneasiness with immigration, racial changes, and the prospect of a majority–minority nation.[34]

Still, a great question hangs over the Republican future: Will they find a way to reach minority and millennial voters as those populations grow? In 2016, the white vote, which typically breaks Republican, fell from 72 to 70 percent of eligible voters—still a majority but a slowly, steadily diminishing one. Meanwhile, voter turnout from groups that lean Democratic, Hispanics and African Americans, grew. The first indicators from the 2018 midterm suggested the trend continues. As in the recent past, African Americans voted in high numbers, comprising approximately 12 percent of all voters. Hispanic turnout, however, jumped: Hispanics made up 8 percent of all midterm voters in 2014, but 12 percent in the 2018—a 50 percent increase. These voters pose a major challenge for both political parties: Will Democrats continue to win them over on issues such as undocumented immigration? Or can Republicans make inroads by stressing moral values and the American dream? However the votes trend, the future of electoral politics may lie in these rising demographic groups.[34a]

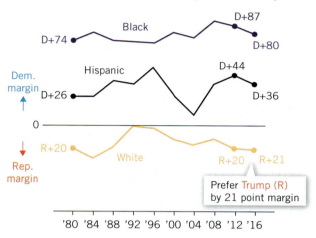

In 2016, Trump won whites by virtually the same margin as Romney in 2012

Presidential candidate preference, by race or ethnicity

● **Figure 8.4** *Whites supported the Republican candidate in 2016 by roughly the same margin as in 2012, but the education gap widened. (Pew Research Center)*

Predicting Presidential Elections

Predicting presidential outcomes is a national pastime. Social scientists have developed sophisticated models to predict long before the election. Some even believe that all the campaign excitement is irrelevant: Mathematical models will pick the winning party even before the campaigns get into the field.

What goes into a model? Each has a slightly different recipe but most political scientists emphasize the economy, presidential approval, and fatigue with the party in power—with just one exception, no party has controlled the White House for more than two consecutive terms in the last 72 years.

How did the political science models do? Table 8.3 shows the results: The models were amazing—and still wrong. Eight of the eleven models, all run months before the voting, came within 1 percent of the results: Clinton wins 51 percent of the two-party vote. Yet the models face limits. They could not deal with the jagged permutations of the Electoral College.

The Bottom Line

» Nearly all of the serious candidates are experienced politicians. No candidate without public sector experience had ever won the presidency—until Donald Trump.

» The three phases of the campaign—nominating process, party conventions, and general election—require different political strategies.

» Election outcomes are influenced by many factors: economic performance, wars, organization, party loyalty, demographics, and the Electoral College.

TABLE 8.3 Political Science Models Predict the Elections

FORECASTER	PERCENTAGE OF TWO-PARTY VOTE CLINTON WILL WIN	PERCENTAGE POINTS BY WHICH THE MODEL MISSED (0 = PERFECT)
Michael Lewis-Beck and Charles Tien, *Political Economy*	51.0	0.0
James Campbell, *Convention Bump and Economy*	51.2	–0.2
James Campbell, *Trial Heat and Economy*	50.7	0.3
Brad Lockerbie, *Economic Expectations and Political Punishment*	50.4	0.6
Bruno Jerôme and Veronique Jerôme-Speziari, *State-by-State Political Economy*	50.1	0.9
Christopher Wlezien and Robert Erikson, *LEI and Polls; Post Conventions*	52.0	–1.0
Thomas Holbrook, *National Conditions and Trial Heat*	52.5	–1.5
Andreas Graefe, J. Scott Armstrong, Randall Jones, and Alfred Cuzan, *Pollyvote*	52.7	–1.7
Alan Abramowitz, *Time for a Change*	48.6	2.4
Helmut Norpoth, *The Primary Model*	47.5	3.5
Source: Oxford University Press (OUPblog)		

🔵 Congressional Elections

Congressional elections feature a colorful kaleidoscope of races across the country. Every two years, all 435 House districts hold an election, with an additional 33 or 34 Senate seats in play as well. It's a political junkie's dream.

Candidates: Who Runs for Congress?

Almost anyone can run. Convicted felons, rodeo clowns, and little-known college professors have won unexpected victories. As Table 8.4 shows, there are few limits on candidacy.

But winning is not easy. The average race costs over $1.7 million; to make it to the Senate, you will need on average $10.5 million (depending on where you are running, of course.)[35] Most candidates spend hours on the phone raising money. The personality traits that inspire candidates to run for Congress—self-confidence, leadership ability, interest in politics—rise as people move up the political ladder.

The median net worth of House and Senate members in 2018 was $511,000 (meaning half are above, half below). More than a third are millionaires.[36]

TABLE 8.4	**Requirements for Running for Congress**
Age	Successful House candidates must be at least 25 years old to take office; senators must be at least 30.
Citizenship	House candidates must have been a U.S. citizen for at least seven years—nine for the Senate.
Residence	Candidates must live in the state, although not necessarily the House district, where they are seeking election.

However, congressional races attract relatively few top American business and cultural celebrities—there are not many Mark Zuckerbergs, Warren Buffetts, or Oprahs in Congress. And when the famous or wealthy mount a run, they often lose. Maryland businessman David Trone spent $13 million of his own money unsuccessfully seeking the Democratic nomination for an open House seat in 2016. World Wrestling Entertainment CEO Linda McMahon spent $100 million on her two failed Senate races in 2010 and 2012—although the publicity helped make her President Trump's head of the Small Business Administration.[37]

Each time one party targets a Senate candidate, the other party matches it. The price tag for Texas's Senate race in 2018 approached $120 million, close to the record set in Pennsylvania's 2016 contest. Even little New Hampshire's 2016 Senate race cost more than $100 million. The results reflected what political scientists have long found: Money alone rarely swings congressional elections. But with 468 races, the big money makes it hard to challenge most incumbents.[38]

If neither money nor celebrity guarantees a seat, here is a more promising shortcut to Congress: be related to a member. One in eight members of Congress

● Left: Frederick Frelinghuysen, New Jersey delegate to the Continental Congress (1779) and later U.S. senator (1793–1796). Right: Frederick's great-great-great nephew Rodney Frelinghuysen served in the U.S. House from 1995 to 2018. He was the sixth Frelinghuysen to represent New Jersey in Congress.

● *A new generation: 2018 saw the largest number of women run for and win election elected to Congress. Here, California Republican Young Kim stops on the campaign trail, poised to become the first Korean-American women in Congress.*

has relatives who already served (including twenty members who hold their parent's seat). Since 1947, there has usually been a Kennedy in office in Washington—today, Congressman Joe Kennedy (D-MA). Other families—Bush, Adams, Roosevelt, Clinton—have built dynasties over the years.[39]

Still, political amateurs dominate each crop of new candidates challenging sitting House members. About one in six of these challengers is an elected official, usually from the state legislature; another 10 percent or so serve in nonelected government positions—often as former congressional staff. The remaining candidates—generally around three-quarters of the total are new to government service. Senate candidates, because they run statewide, tend to be more experienced. Most are political veterans.

Women are just as likely as men to win elections to Congress, but the parties have been slower to recruit them as candidates, women were less eager to run, and when they ran they were more likely to draw primary challenges than men.[40] In 2018, however, an astonishing 3,379 women were running for political office. When the votes were counted, there were over 100 in the House of Representatives and over 125 in both chambers breaking the previous record—101 in the previous Congress. By party, women representatives break over five to one toward the Democrats.

Members of large minority groups (African Americans, Latinos, and Asian Americans) tend to run much less often than Caucasians. As we saw in Chapter 5, their ranks are slowly growing, especially in the House Democratic Caucus.

Talent and experience are vital in congressional races. Party leaders know that recruiting skilled candidates—more political background, better education—gives them a leg up in the contest between Democrats and Republicans for power in Congress. A candidate's background also has an impact on the quality of representation in Washington. How well Congress carries out its work depends on the political ability of its members.

The Power of Incumbency

If you talk to sitting members of Congress about reelection, you will see the worry wash over their faces. House and Senate officeholders face an increasingly volatile electorate: Voters are less predictable and harder to reach through traditional advertising. Now that virtually every utterance is digitally preserved, candidates have to be more careful about what they say. The popular Virginia Senator (R) George Allen was caught on videotape at a campaign rally calling an Indian American "macaca," a slang racial insult. The clip went viral. Allen tried to deny it, to laugh it off, and eventually apologized, but he could not shake the media storm and wound up narrowly losing. Allen, who was being touted as a presidential contender, never recovered. Many candidates have been caught saying embarrassing things that come back to haunt them.

Despite this treacherous electoral environment, most incumbent House and Senate members win. Even in 2010, when Republicans won the largest Republican landslide since 1890, more than nine of every ten incumbents survived. In 2018, 93% of House members and almost 88% of Senators won reelection. The power of incumbency held again. But there is one caveat: Twenty six mainly moderate Republicans retired in this election cycle—perhaps fearing a backlash against the party in power.

At first glance, this **incumbency advantage** is a mystery. As we explore in Chapter 10, Americans give Congress a resounding thumbs down. In 2018, approval ratings for Congress hovered between 13 percent and 20 percent—not the lowest on record, but close. What did the voters do? They voted the rascals right back in. Incumbents won more than 90 percent of the races (see Figure 8.5).

What explains these consistently high incumbent success rates? For one thing, members have become skilled at running *against* Congress. They position themselves as reasonable individuals fighting against a dysfunctional institution—a position known as Fenno's paradox (named after a much loved political scientist). The way Congress operates—stalemate on the big issues, lots of little favors to constituents—makes the stance an easier sell. "I'm for expanding aid to needy children," say liberal members, "but I can't get it past the Republicans on Capitol Hill. Oh, and how about that new aquarium I funded?" GOP members tell a similar story.[41]

Go online to hear Senator George Allen's "macaca moment."

Incumbency advantage: The tendency for members of Congress to win reelection in overwhelming numbers.

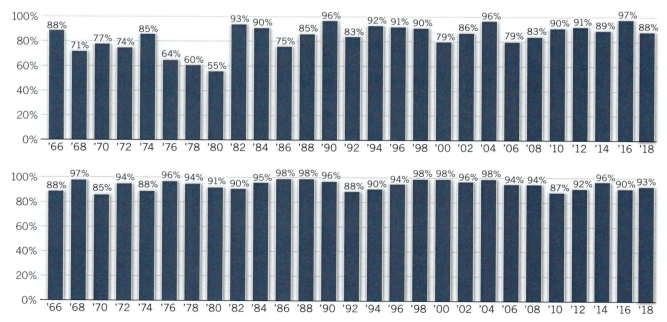

● **Figure 8.5** *Senate (top) and House (bottom) reelection rates, 1964–2016. (Open Secrets)*

Finally, money (again). Most congressional races feature very well-funded incumbents running against underfunded challengers. In short, members are attentive to constituents, raise money, and already have staff and name recognition. Most win reelection. Here is the paradox: People despise Congress but reelect their representatives.[42]

Patterns in Congressional Elections

Here's another familiar pattern: In most **midterm elections**, the president's party loses congressional seats—termed **midterm loss**. In the last forty midterm elections (going back to 1938), the president's party picked up seats in either chamber of Congress only five times—and only a handful each time. In contrast, the president's party lost double-digit House seats eight of twelve times. In 2018, the pattern held in the House: The Democrats picked up over 30 seats and won control of the chamber. But Republicans gained at least 3 Senate seats—the best showing by an incumbent party in more than 50 years (see table 10.5).

Another intriguing pattern: America at war. Although we might expect voters to support the president's party, the opposition usually wins seats in the congressional election following a war's outbreak.

Midterm elections: National elections held between presidential elections, involving all seats in the House, one-third of the Senate, thirty-six governors, and more.

Midterm loss: When the party of the president loses seats in Congress during the midterm elections. This has occurred in almost all midterm elections.

TABLE 8.5 Midterm Congressional Election Results, 1970–2018

ELECTION YEAR	PRESIDENT	SEAT GAIN	
		HOUSE	SENATE
2018	Trump (R)	**D+32***	**R+3***
2014	Obama (D)	R+13	R+9
2010	Obama (D)	R+63	R+6
2006	G. W. Bush (R)	D+30	D+6
2002	G. W. Bush (R)	**R+8**	**R+2**
1998	Clinton (D)	**D+5**	(No change)
1994	Clinton (D)	R+54	R+8
1990	G. H. W. Bush (R)	D+8	D+1
1986	Reagan (R)	D+5	D+8
1982	Reagan (R)	D+26	(No change)
1978	Carter (D)	R+15	R+3
1974	Ford (R)	D+48	D+3
1970	Nixon (R)	D+12	**R+1**

The president's party has won seats in a midterm election only four times (indicated in **bold**) in the past 42 years.
*Results as of Novermber 16, with some races still too close to call.

Redrawing the Lines: The Art of Gerrymandering

Membership of the House of Representatives is fixed at 435 and the population keeps shifting. Every ten years, the census measures population changes and **reapportions** House seats. In 2010, Texas—with its growing population—gained four seats, Florida gained two, and New York and Ohio each lost two. Following reapportionment, states redraw the boundaries of the election districts, a process called redistricting.

Many state legislatures seize the opportunity and redraw district that boost the majority party—known as a **gerrymander**. In a **gerrymander**, the party in control of the state legislature draws the lines to help itself. See Figure 8.6 for a hypothetical example. Imagine a state called PoliSciLand that has two districts that are 100 percent Republican (A and B) and one district that is 100 percent Democratic (C): PoliSciLand sends two Republicans and one Democrat to Congress. Then an enterprising Republican on the redistricting committee says, "Hey, we're the majority in this PoliSciLand legislature. Let's redraw the congressional districts our way."

Check out the result: By drawing the district lines horizontally instead of vertically, Republicans take the Democratic district and split its voters into three different congressional districts. Instead of one district with 100 percent Democratic voters and two that are 100 percent Republican, PoliSciLand now has three districts, each 33 percent Democratic and 66 percent Republican.

Reapportionment: Reorganization of the boundaries of House districts following the U.S. census, constitutionally required every ten years. The lines are redrawn to ensure that each House member represents roughly the same number of constituents.

Gerrymander: Redrawing an election district in a way that gives the advantage to one party.

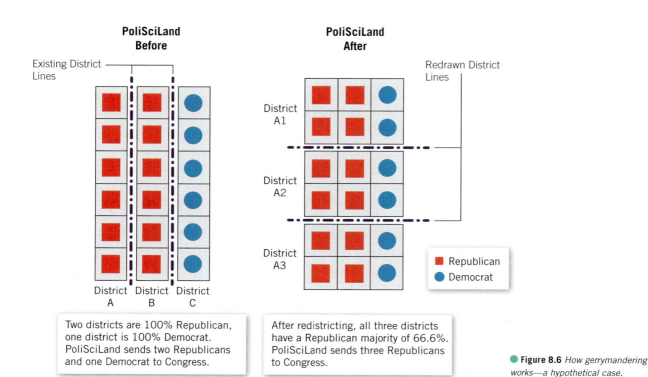

PoliSciLand Before

Existing District Lines

District A | District B | District C

Two districts are 100% Republican, one district is 100% Democrat. PoliSciLand sends two Republicans and one Democrat to Congress.

PoliSciLand After

Redrawn District Lines

District A1

District A2

District A3

■ Republican
● Democrat

After redistricting, all three districts have a Republican majority of 66.6%. PoliSciLand sends three Republicans to Congress.

● **Figure 8.6** *How gerrymandering works—a hypothetical case.*

● *The original gerrymander: Massachusetts, 1812.*

Safe district: A district consisting of voters who have historically voted for one party over the other by a large majority.

How does gerrymandering work?

Assess current debates on redistricting.

Today information technology permits carefully crafted boundaries designed to help one party. The two main techniques are packing (placing all the like-minded voters into one district) and cracking (spreading them out so that they form a minority in many districts). Our imaginary PoliSciLand cracked the Democratic district.

Redistricting processes in most states are messy and politically charged. Many results look at least as bizarre as the original gerrymander. Together, the political parties have perfected the practice—although Republicans dominated the 2010 state level elections and became masters of the art: In 2016, Republicans won the total popular vote for the House by less than 1 percent but reaped a big advantage in number of seats held: 241 to 194. The gerrymander has led to the famous political quip: Before the people choose their representatives, the representatives pick their people.

Gerrymandered districts also tend to be **safe districts**—where voters are likely to vote for one party over another by a large ("safe") majority. But here's an unexpected twist: Legislators are safe from the other party, but not from activists in low turnout primaries who charge that the legislators have betrayed the party's values. In this way, gerrymanders also push both Democrats and Republicans away from compromising with the other party—for fears of being "primaried."

Nonpartisan Districting and Minority Representation

Does all this seem unfair to you? Some reformers call for nonpartisan commissions that would divide states into natural communities and not tilt to any political side. California passed a law to establish just such a nonpartisan commission after the 2010 census—other states have followed. The results are often compact, contiguous districts faithful to existing geographic communities—and legislators at the state and U.S. House level scrambling to win their new district lines. (We will return to this reform at the end of the chapter.)

In the past, some states used gerrymanders to create majority–minority districts—packed with African American voters. For black Democrats, it was an anguishing call because it split two sides of their political identity: It delivered more black representatives, but fewer Democrats. In 1995, the Supreme

Court stopped the practice.[43] Despite dire predictions, the black congressional caucus continued to grow, jumping from 29 House members in 1995 to over fifty after the 2018 election.

In 2018, the Court unanimously permitted highly partisan districts in North Carolina, Wisconsin, and Maryland, then bitterly divided (5–4) in a ruling on a Texas case. The majority held that courts should "presume" that states are acting in "good faith" and not aiming to suppress minority votes. Four liberal justices dissented and two declared there was "undeniable proof of intentional discrimination."[44]

Gerrymandering
Texachusetts

The Bottom Line

» Every two years, all 435 House seats and a third of the Senate seats are up for election.

» Few restrictions govern who may run.

» House and Senate incumbents have powerful built-in advantages when running for reelection.

» The president's party generally loses House and Senate seats during the midterm election.

» Decennial redistricting of House seats can result in some strangely shaped—and politically motivated—districts, known as gerrymanders.

How to Run for Congress

Are you ready to run your own race for Congress? It won't be easy, but following our advice will increase your chances. Here are our four keys to winning a congressional election:—*money, organization, strategy,* and *message.* Even if you are not planning to run, remember these as you watch congressional races.

Key 1: Money

First and foremost, you will need funds to mount a legitimate challenge—up to $2 million in many House districts, and five or six times that if you are running for the Senate. Where does all the money go? TV advertising, direct mailing, radio spots, voter data, consultants, offices, phone banks, computers, and lawn signs. Unless you are wealthy you will "dial for dollars." Your staff prepares **call lists** and you spend your days desperately filling your war chest.

Call list: A long list of potential donors who candidates must phone.

Open seat: A seat in Congress without an incumbent running for reelection.

Candidate-centered elections: A system in which individual candidates decide to run, raise their own money, and design their own strategy—as opposed to party systems, in which political parties play these roles.

CAMPAIGN LINGO

Want to know what your advisers are talking about? Here are a few insider terms from the campaign trail.

Robocall: Automated phone call used to contact thousands of voters simultaneously; may feature a recorded message by the candidate or a popular personality—or an attack on the opponent.

Advance team: Campaign staffers who arrive at the site of major events (e.g., a speech) ahead of time to organize the site and build crowds.

Field/GOTV: The staff and volunteers who engage one-on-one with the public on behalf of the candidate.

To boost your chances of winning, wait for an **open seat**—one with no incumbent running. Taking on sitting members is difficult and expensive.

Key 2: Organization

You also will need a well-constructed team to run for Congress. Somebody has to recruit and train your speechwriters, fundraisers, social media coordinators, and supportive community leaders. Once, the local Republican or Democratic organization did all that work. Over the past four decades, Americans have shifted to **candidate-centered elections**. Candidates themselves decide to run, raise money, grab airtime, and organize their own campaigns. You will usually have to build your own organization from scratch.

There is a side benefit to assembling a talented team. Political insiders see hiring established pollsters, media experts, and so forth as the sign of a competitive campaign. Funders, seeing a possible winner, will start directing more money your way. Most rookie congressional candidates decry the "professionalization" of campaign politics—then hire experienced insiders to help them win.

Key 3: Strategy

A fat bankroll and seasoned organization cannot compensate for a common candidate mistake—a weak campaign strategy. Uncertainty is a central fact in every election. Political winds shift, opponents do the unexpected, unpredictable events demand a response. Incumbent members tend to stick to the strategy that got them there last time. Challenges must invent a strategy that plays well to their political values and personal strengths.

Two elements of successful congressional campaign strategies are vital: building a coalition of supporters and connecting with voters. Every state or district includes local business leaders, political activists, religious leaders, and identity group spokespersons. Attracting some of them—and, presumably, their followers—is essential. A coalition-building strategy also targets broader groups likely to vote for a party's candidate.

During the 1980s and 1990s, House Republican candidates forged coalitions of conservative, middle-aged, white, Protestant, relatively affluent voters. By 2006, this reliable lineup had fragmented in many places, and Democrats won 47 of 48 contested House seats to retake control of the chamber. By 2010, a new Republican coalition, now fueled by Tea Party activists and featuring a larger proportion of lower-income, disaffected white voters, regained control of the House. Notice how fast the winds shift in contemporary electoral politics. In 2018, the Democratic Party was able to take back control of the House of Representatives.

Candidates primarily reach voters through the media. Candidate strategies need to include plenty of high-profile events—speeches, press conferences, nursing home visits—that attract media coverage. The coverage may be more positive if you offer fresh ideas helping the district or state. If you cannot build crowds because of your low **name recognition**, you may resort to more creative approaches—bring in a local celebrity. Anything for airtime!

You also will need a smart social media strategy. Instagram, tweets, Google banner ads—anything to grab eyeballs for your campaign. But do not forget old-fashioned politicking. Knocking on someone's door and meeting face-to-face is still, by far, the best way to win votes.

Sadly, there is another effective strategy: **negative campaigning**. This seeds doubt in voters' minds about your opponent. Much as you may find this strategy repugnant, conventional wisdom suggests "going negative" works. However, there is good news: Recent work in political science suggests that negative ads may not change many minds and may not actually win elections.[45] The jury is still out, however, so you can expect that the other side's opposition researchers will portray you in the least flattering light possible. The point is not to change people's minds but to discourage the weaker supporters on the other side—with the hope that going negative will keep them home on Election Day.

Key 4: Message

Finally, you have to give people a good reason to vote for you. Candidates with a clear, powerful message sometimes topple better-financed and more elaborately organized opponents. In 2014, an unknown economics professor with a shoestring budget ($200,000) named David Brat upset House Majority Leader Eric Cantor. In 2018, a 28-year-old progressive activist Alexandria Ocasio-Cortez upset Joe Crowley, the fourth most powerful Democrat in the House, with just one-tenth his budget. Both longshot candidates had the same message: Their opponents had become Washington insiders and lost touch with the district and its values.

In the relatively rare case that a first-time challenge like yours is victorious, what can you expect as a freshman member of Congress? (Yes, *freshman*: The term is the same as in high school or college, and the learning curve is just as steep!) What comes next?

A *new campaign*, starting immediately. For House members, the next election looms just two years away. Senators have a more relaxing six years—but must run statewide, which in high-population or sprawling states is very time consuming. Winning an election to become a congressional "sophomore" can be especially difficult. The legendary House Speaker Sam Rayburn told each incoming House freshman class, that "a member of Congress can be elected by accident, but seldom reelected by accident." Voters back home will watch a first-term member especially closely, as will his or her colleagues on Capitol Hill.

As a sitting representative or senator, you may join your colleagues in denouncing Washington as corrupt and in need of reform. Is the American electoral system in need of reform? And if so, how?

Conclusion: Reforming American Elections

Does the U.S. electoral system work? In this chapter, we highlighted many concerns. Is it a problem that we keep sending the same representatives back to an unpopular Congress? That big spenders often win? That gerrymanders impact elections? Here we introduce three popular reforms.

Gerrymanders: We could limit partisan districts by asking neutral panels to draw the lines—eight states do so for congressional districts, fourteen for state legislators. The goal: rational, compact, community-based districts that do not tilt to either party. The proposals always face a challenge: Can we really trust the experts to find truly neutral districts? Indeed, is there any such thing? Iowa has tried to address the objection by giving the job to a nonpartisan panel and then forwarding their plans to the state legislature for an up or down vote. In some states, such as Arizona, statewide votes have forced the reform on reluctant legislators. Legislators sued but the Supreme Court narrowly sided with the voters, 5–4.[46]

Money: Doesn't money skew our politics, obsess legislators (and their challengers), and stack the deck to incumbents? A relatively small amount on the state level can sink an incumbent, threaten a judge, or even flip a legislature.

One simple reform, proposed by Democrats in 2016: forbid anonymous donations (known as "dark money"). Let the public know exactly who is funding that oppo (negative research) shop. More ambitious reformers call for publicly financed elections, in which (as in most other advanced democracies) the government provides equal funding to each candidate and allows relatively small donations from the public. This would create a more even playing field between incumbents and challengers. Several states have tried, but courts have struck down efforts to limit private contributions.

There is a deeper question: Does money buy influence? The connection may seem obvious to you, but political scientists, examining the data from every angle, have had a hard time proving that contributing to a campaign leads to policy payoffs after the election. Big donors enjoy personal access to their representatives, but efforts to trace favors back to contributions have so far come up empty. However, subtle forms of influence, especially over small issues (like items in the tax code) are difficult to measure.

Campaign finance reform polls well, but it also has strong critics—including a narrow Supreme Court majority which has repeatedly blocked efforts in the name of free speech. If a candidate excites you, why shouldn't you send money to him or her? Those who disagree point to a more fundamental question: Why give large organizations—corporations, labor unions—the same right to free speech as citizens? The debate remains intense but the institutional barriers to finance reform (mainly courts) are steep.

Term Limits: The president is limited to two terms. So are governors in thirty-six states. Why not limit members of Congress to, say, twelve years of service? Here many political scientists are skeptical. The problem is that good legislating takes skill. Term limits clear out legislators just when they have learned how to become effective.

For all the problems we have described, campaigns and elections offer a vital way to participate. Repeated electoral waves leap over all the barriers and sweep new people, new voices, and new ideas into office. Each generation of Americans decides whether to shake up the system of campaigns and elections or to leave things in place. In 2016, the totally unexpected won out; 2018 saw a surge of victories for women, people of color, and a rare increase for the incumbent Republicans in the Senate.

We are especially proud of our many students who have run (and won!) seats in state legislatures and Congress. We hope that you get engaged too. If you have read this chapter carefully, you understand the many challenges. But leaping into elections—as voters, volunteers and, even candidates—remains the only way to ensure government by the people.

CHAPTER SUMMARY

🟢 Elections define democracies.

🟢 A key question in this chapter: Are American elections democratic enough?

🟢 American electoral systems are unique because:

- We vote on a huge number of offices—over 520,000.

- We vote often compared to other nations.

- Federal elections for the House of Representatives take place every even-numbered year.

- In some places, there are elections every year.

🟢 The Constitution puts the states in charge of running elections, instructing them to manage

Check your understanding of Chapter 8.

"the time, place, and manner." But it is silent on crucial matters—such as who has the right to vote.

🟢 In the last 60 years, all presidents have had one of just three jobs on their résumés: vice president, governor, or senator. Donald Trump became the first president in American history with no public sector experience.

🟢 The road to the White House passes through three stages: primaries, the party convention, and the general election.

🟢 The most familiar question about American democracy today involves the role of money in election campaigns. PACs, super PACs, and 527s have become fixtures in national elections.

🟢 The only constitutional limits to running for Congress are age, citizenship, and residency in the state.

🟢 Winning a race for Congress takes money, organization, strategy, and message.

🟢 Every ten years, the state legislatures redraw their congressional districts to keep up with changes in the population. The *gerrymander* is a district that is redrawn to help one party.

🟢 Across time, striking patterns have emerged in congressional elections: The president's party loses seats in the midterm elections, results have grown more volatile (with the party in power shifting often), and war spells trouble for the president's majority.

Need to review key ideas in greater depth? Click here.

KEY TERMS

Flashcard review.

527 groups, p. 257
Bundling, p. 257
Call list, p. 275
Candidate-centered elections, p. 276
Caucus, p. 259
Closed primary, p. 259
Electoral bounce, p. 262
Gerrymander, p. 273

Incumbency advantage, p. 271
Midterm elections, p. 272
Midterm loss, p. 272
Name recognition, p. 277
Negative campaigning, p. 277
Open primary, p. 259
Open seat, p. 276
Political action committee (PAC), p. 255

Proportional representation, p. 260
Reapportionment, p. 273
Safe districts, p. 274
Super PACs, p. 255
Super Tuesday, p. 260
Time, place, and manner clause, p. 250
Winner-take-all, p. 260

STUDY QUESTIONS

1. What one federal office could the people originally vote for directly?

2. What does the Constitution say about who can vote? What is the importance of the "time, place, and manner" clause.

3. For further study: Is the American system of elections democratic enough for the twenty-first century? Defend your position by pointing to features that make it more (or less) democratic.

4. Describe the American system of campaign finance. What are PACs? How about super PACs? What influence on the system did the 2014 *McCutcheon v. FEC* Supreme Court decision have?

5. For further study: What is campaign finance reform? Make an argument for or against campaign finance reform. If possible, explain how recent research supports your argument.

6. Describe the three stages of the presidential campaign.

7. You have decided to run for Congress. What four things will your campaign need to be successful?

8. What is negative campaigning? Why do candidates rely on it?

9. For further study: If you were running for Congress, would you use negative campaign ads on your opponent? Why or why not?

10. Describe three reforms that have been suggested for campaigns and elections in the United States. Now, pick one and argue for or against it. Be sure to defend your position.

 Go to **www.oup.com/us/Morone** to find quizzes, flash cards, simulations, tutorials, videos, and other study tools.

9 Interest Groups and Political Parties

YOU HAVE BEEN HIRED as a new congressional staffer—and today is your first day at work on Capitol Hill. (Congratulations!) You arrive during the crazy busy legislative season. The office is bustling, and nobody has time to get you oriented. In fact, you barely know where you are assigned to sit . . . and now the legislative director has asked you to prepare a detailed analysis of "papa," or at least that's what you heard her say. A sympathetic colleague explains that she meant "PAHPA," which Google tells you is the Pandemic and All-Hazards Preparedness Act. Your diligent Internet search shows only that the act is due to be reauthorized next year; the bill hasn't yet been introduced. And your analysis is due by tomorrow morning.

Where to begin?

Quick, call the Congressional Research Service, the research arm of Congress. They're glad to help you out, they say—but it will take a few weeks. *Weeks*? You have only hours. Depending on your party affiliation, you try the Democratic or Republican Study Group, which summarizes legislation for their party's Congress members and staff, but they haven't analyzed this topic yet.

You feel like slinking out of the office before anyone notices and disappearing into a completely different career. Then salvation arrives, in the form of an elegantly bound, meticulously researched report on PAHPA reauthorization. All the details you need on chemical and biological threats, as well as potential flu pandemics—which House and Senate members are pushing which views, the party politics involved, even the technical details—are laid out clearly. You're not sure whether to cry or laugh with relief. Who *wrote* this? You look around to thank your angel of an officemate. Not here, your colleagues smile: over on **K Street**. An interest-group lobbyist sent it directly to you. As this chapter shows, that report that saved your job is at the heart of what interest groups do in Washington.

● *Dana Loesch, spokesperson for the National Rifle Association (NRA), among the most politically powerful interest groups in America.*

In this chapter, you will:

● Learn what interest groups and parties do in the U.S. government—and how they do it.

● Investigate why people identify with one party (or why they don't).

● Analyze a paradox: Americans like their parties and don't like partisanship.

● Reflect on whether the United States has grown too partisan—and whether interest groups and lobbyists wield too much power.

K Street: A street in downtown Washington, DC, that is home to the headquarters for many lobbying firms and advocacy groups—and thus synonymous with lobbying.

Interest groups have become central to American government. At the same time, lobbyists and the interest groups they represent consistently receive among the lowest approval ratings of any professionals, inside or outside of politics. Political parties are also vital in the U.S. political system. And also rank low in public esteem. In a typical poll, 42 percent of independent voters (not registered with either party) had an unfavorable view of *both* parties; only 8 percent were favorable.[1]

In this chapter, we will explore the origins and current practices of both interest groups and parties in American government. Are interest groups and parties a good thing for American democracy—and for you?

Pause and consider: How many interest groups work on *your* behalf? None, you say? In fact, like most Americans, you are represented by dozens of groups—advocates who push for clean air, safe food, religious freedom, affordable student loans, and virtually every other cause or issue. Your college or university probably has representatives who lobby to promote the school's concerns—at the state capitol and in Congress—and your student fees or tuition probably help pay for their work. Even your favorite subject, political science, has a national association that is based in Washington, DC—and a lobbyist devoted to its interests. You are a participant in what one expert terms our "interest-group society."[2]

You also live in a nation that has long been organized by political parties; a party is a *group that shares political principles and is organized to win elections and hold power.* As voting rights spread in early America, parties stepped in to organize the major questions of the day: Big government or small? Slavery or abolition? Should immigrants get to vote? By the mid-1800s, parties were the largest, most influential political organizations in the nation. Today, national elections, congressional votes, policy decisions, judicial rulings, state government, and our own political opinions are all stamped by party influence.

Who are we? A deeply partisan people who helped invent the contemporary political party—and also the political home of modern interest-group lobbying. Among Americans' top complaints about our political system today: We are a nation of too many lobbyists and special interests, and we are too bitterly divided by party.

More than two centuries ago, James Madison warned against interest groups—he called them "factions" and in *Federalist* no. 10 described them as the "mortal disease" that always killed off popular government. His solution? *Increase* the number of interest groups. That way, none would become too powerful and they would have to work together to accomplish anything. Increase the number of groups? That is one piece of advice the United States has certainly taken.

A decade after Madison wrote, George Washington—on departing the presidency he had done so much to establish—described parties in similarly harsh terms. "Let me warn you," he intoned, "in the most solemn manner against the baneful effects of the spirit of party."[3]

Concerns about **special interests** and about excessive party influence have both surged periodically since these two famous warnings. Populists in the Great Plains in the 1890s, 1960s student radicals, Bernie Sanders and Donald Trump supporters today: Reformers across U.S. history charge that the political system may be tilted toward some people—particularly the rich and powerful—and that party leaders and lobbyists are paving the way. But do not let the outcry obscure a basic truth: Interest groups and parties are not just "them"—they're us.

The United States is an interest-group society. It is also home to the first mass political parties. These two institutions, interest groups and parties, each convey popular views to public officials. Here is this chapter's big question: Do parties and interest groups enhance democracy? Or does one or the other (or both) pose a threat to government by the people in the twenty-first century? We consider the two institutions separately, starting with interest groups and then turning to parties.

Special interest: A pejorative term, often used to designate an interest group whose aims or issue preferences one does not share.

The Many Roles Interest Groups Play

A woman approached longtime Texas Congressman Kent Hance and promised to vote for him under one condition: "Promise me you'll never talk to any of those lobbyists in Austin" (the state capital).

"Ma'am" responded Hance, "I sure wish I could promise you that, but I simply can't."

"Why not," she asked.

Safely assuming the woman was a Baptist, Hance replied. "Why ma'am, if a religious issue came up for a vote, I wouldn't dream of taking a position until I had talked to the lobbyist for the Southern Baptist Convention."

"You mean that our church has a lobbyist?" asked the astonished woman.

"It sure does," said Hance with a smile, "and a very fine Christian gentleman he is."[4]

Most people do not think of Baptists as special interests with lobbyists. But they are. What is an interest group? Dozens of lobbyists, pushing private agendas on Capitol Hill and working their inside political connections? It's much simpler: **Interest groups** are *organizations whose goal is to influence government.*

Notice two important elements in that definition. First, *organization*: A collection of wheat farmers begins to resemble an interest group only when they meet regularly to discuss and manage their concerns. The second is *influence government*: Plenty of organized groups have no contact with public officials. When those wheat growers join the American Farm Bureau Federation and press

Interest group: An organization whose goal is to influence government.

BY THE NUMBERS

Total number of U.S. House and Senate members who are not Republican or Democratic (out of 541)	**2**
Total number of national parties fielding a presidential nominee, 2016	**9**
Total number of parties (other than Republican or Democratic) getting at least one electoral vote in the last 45 years	**0**
Estimated number of interest groups engaged in U.S. politics	**More than 200,000**
Number of members claimed by National Rifle Association	**nearly 5 million[5]**
Estimated number of professionals lobbying the U.S. government	**90,000[6]**
Total spending reported by healthcare interest groups, 2017	**$561,231,163[7]**
Total spending on lobbying by the city of Houston, Texas, 2018	**$260,000**
Percentage of Americans who identified as Democrats, Republicans, and independents, respectively, September 2018 Gallup poll	**29, 26, 43**
Percentage of Americans who identified as Democrats, Republicans, and independents, respectively, November 2005 Gallup poll	**34, 33, 30**
Total amount spent on lobbying by the Chamber of Commerce, 1998–2018	**$1.5 billion**
Appropriation to fund all U.S. House and Senate salaries/operations, 2019	**$2.2 billion[8]**
Reported expenditures on lobbying, U.S. corporations, 2018	**$2.7 billion[9]**
Median pay CEO for top 50 largest Washington nonprofit trade associations, 2018	**$1.3 million[10]**

Do parties and interest groups have too much power in our democratic system?

Congress for subsidies to keep crop prices stable, then they are an interest group.

At least two hundred thousand interest groups are active in American politics today. How do they carry out their work of trying to influence government? Along three main paths: informing, communicating, and mobilizing.

Informing Members

The U.S. government is sprawling—House members represent more than 700,000 constituents, Senators represent millions. Students, small business owners, rocket scientists, and Baptists do not have the time (or the knowledge) to follow the many government policies affecting them. That's where lobbyists step in. *Interest groups inform their members* about what's go-

● *Lobbyists representing Amazon, Google, Facebook, and other tech industry giants prepare for a congressional hearing on net neutrality.*

ing on in politics. The political science lobbyist, for example, gives presentations to faculty members on how Congress feels about funding your professors' research.

Communicating Members' Views

Second, interest groups *communicate members' views to government officials.* How? Often by hiring a **lobbyist** who already knows her way around Washington or the state capital. Put simply, a lobbyist contacts government officials on behalf of a particular cause or issue. Plenty of people try to influence government—like college students, who fan out across their state capital each year, asking legislators to oppose higher student fees or appropriate more funding for science labs. Though some reject the label, they are "lobbyists," by this expansive definition. *Professional lobbyists* are paid by clients to influence lawmakers. They are often experts (remember that PAHPA report) and generally enjoy access to the halls of power.

For example, the AARP hires lobbyists to communicate members' views to government on a wide range of issues affecting seniors, from Social Security benefits to disability insurance.[11] In 2006, when President Bush tried to add a new prescription drug benefit to Medicare, Democrats thought they had the votes to block the legislation on Capitol Hill. Then the AARP threw its weight behind the bill—and it passed.

Lobbyist: A person who contacts government officials on behalf of a particular cause or issue.

Mobilizing the Public

Third, interest groups *mobilize the public:* They encourage groups of people to get involved. Their lobbyists develop Facebook and Instagram alerts, TV ads, direct-mail postcards, and tweets, all meant to provoke action.

● *Vaping advocates seek to appeal to both public and lawmakers.*

Many Americans care about abortion, for example, and want to do more than simply vote for candidates who share their position. Pro-life and pro-choice groups offer members many opportunities to *do something*. Interest groups mobilize on many issues, from gun rights to climate change. They help people get involved: contact Congress, join a rally, or meet policy makers. And they make a difference: Members of Congress are extremely aware of the messages coming in. One killer response to any lobbyist pushing an issue: "I haven't heard from a single constituent on that one."

Groups often duel with their rivals in political arenas. The tobacco industry and its lobbyists promote vaping as a healthier alternative to smoking. Anti-vaping activists push back, pointing out that fruit or candy flavor e-cigarettes attract teens who are then more likely to start smoking real cigarettes.[12] Tobacco and vaping-company lobbyists mount "education" campaigns to promote the benefits of vaping compared to smoking; public-health groups respond.

How well do interest groups represent your concerns? If you care about something already on the government agenda, groups are very likely promoting your view in Washington. More obscure topics, and less powerful interests, have a harder time getting heard. However, if you have strong opinions about a policy that seems to be overlooked, do not despair. American political history is full of "crackpots" who believed in outlandish things—ending segregation, cleaning up polluted rivers, putting airbags in every car, slashing personal income-tax rates—ideas that eventually won out.

Through their work informing members, communicating views to political officials, and mobilizing the public, interest groups play an important role in democratic societies. They are inevitably controversial because they are in the thick of every political debate.

What Interest Groups Do for Democracy

Whether our interest-group system represents all (or most) people triggers heated debates, both among political scientists and across the public. Some hold that as long as the American political process is open to a wide range of different groups, then governmental policies should roughly correspond to public desires—a view known as **pluralism**. No single set of interests dominates our system, pluralists insist, and all the different groups pushing and tugging allow the collective good to shine through. This is a latter-day rendering of James Madison's argument in *Federalist* no. 10: The answer to the problem of interest groups is—more interest groups.

Pluralism: An open, participatory style of government in which many different interests are represented.

● *"Bring cancer to its knees through lobbying": Citizen-lobbyist Amanda Rubeck joins fellow "Cancer Action Network" volunteers at the Indiana State House for Lobby Day 2018. Pluralist theorists point to examples such as Rubeck and conclude that democracy works.*

● *Power elite theorists, in contrast, see interest groups as part of a cozy, interlocking network that perpetuates themselves in power.*

Two pessimistic theories respond to the pluralists. Many Americans fear that the proliferation of interests and groups is bogging the entire system down in stalemate: Political scientists call this **hyperpluralism**. Any time a group promotes a policy—paying teachers more, constructing a highway, building a border wall, fighting climate change—there is always another group to oppose it because they do not want to pay the taxes or fear harm to the environment or think the policy unfair. Policy "gridlock" is often the result of the immense buildup of lobbyists in Washington and state capitals—and the growth of what one scholarly article recently described as "vicious, street-fighting hyperpluralism."[13]

Others worry that the playing field is tipped too far toward the richest and most powerful people. This **power elite theory** portrays a group of wealthy, influential Americans—mostly from the corporate sector—who mingle with one another regularly, promote their shared (class) interests, and hire lobbyists to do the daily work of influencing government on their behalf.

Power elite analysts look at the makeup of President Trump's cabinet—nearly all leaders of high-powered American companies before joining the administration—and conclude that the theory of intersecting influences is alive and well.[14] Or they note that every current U.S. Supreme Court justice attended Harvard or Yale Law School.

Political scientists supply numbers that back the elitist perspective. Lobbying, these researchers note, is dominated by business: 53 percent of the lobbying organizations and 72 percent of the expenditures represent business interests. In contrast, public interest lobbying weighs in at about 5 percent of lobbying efforts. And groups supporting less privileged people employ just 2 percent of the lobbyists in Washington. The results, say power elite theorists, reflect the conclusion of a famous political scientist back in 1960: The chorus of political groups "sings with a decidedly upper class accent."[15]

Hyperpluralism: The collective effect of the vast number of interest groups slowing and stalemating American policymaking.

Power elite theory: The view that a small handful of wealthy, influential Americans exercise extensive control over government decisions.

Which view—pluralist, hyperpluralist, or power elite—is correct? Political scientists cannot say for sure. It is difficult to tell whether big business or other powerful groups regularly win their policy aims. For every example that affirms the power of elites in the American system, another story suggests the opposite—that small business or retired people or environmental advocates prevail. Hyperpluralists note that *neither* group is getting all that much from Washington, as big bills are bottled up for years. Perhaps each theory captures part of the truth.

We return later in this chapter to the question of how well Americans are represented in general. By now you understand the central issue: the extent of interest groups' influence in American politics and policymaking.

Types of Interest Groups

Political scientists divide the teeming world of interest groups into three main categories: *economic* groups, which primarily serve members' financial interests; *citizen* groups, which are organized to advance the public interest (as they define it) or a particular cause or viewpoint; and *intergovernmental* groups, featuring one level or branch of government trying to influence another.

Economic Groups. Economic groups lobby for financial benefits for their members—whether a business (like Google or Disney), a labor union (the Teamsters), or a *trade association* representing professionals in a specific sector—architects, nurses, or even sex workers (who have organized in some states[16]). Economic groups often pursue the narrow interests of their members. For example, the American Petroleum Institute (API) is a trade association representing oil and gas companies. The API lobbies for tax benefits, favorable trade deals, and reducing environmental regulations.

● *Citizen action groups engage the public in lobbying efforts across the United States; here, a New York State chapter fights proposed cuts in government services.*

Citizen or Public Interest Groups. What about the rest of us? Hundreds of thousands of *citizen groups*, also called *public interest groups*, exist in American politics. They cover the political spectrum, and represent every conceivable issue and group of people, even those at society's margins: The National Alliance to End Homelessness, for example, is a well-respected Washington interest group. Single-issue organizations, such as People for the Ethical Treatment of Animals (PETA), fit into this category, as do those established to promote a political viewpoint, such as the American Conservative Union.

Professional associations have a built-in constituency (after all, most lawyers join the American Bar Association). In contrast, citizen groups have to work hard to recruit and retain members. Many get a boost when an issue seems to be losing ground. For example, when the Trump administration pulled out of the Paris Agreement to fight climate change, hundreds of citizen groups joined U.S. mayors, governors, business leaders, and university members to lobby under the #WeAreStillIn banner.[17]

Public interest organizations face a problem: *free riders*. Why join a citizen group, pay dues, and even spend time in meetings when you could stay home and let others do the hard work. Some people do the work, but everyone benefits. How do these groups attract members?[18]

Log on to the website of a public interest group—Greenpeace or the National Rifle Association (NRA), and you will see major swag available. Tote bags, curated trips to Yosemite, gun-safety videos, travel mugs—all free or discounted for joining. In political science terms, these *material benefits* help attract new members. Others join because of *expressive benefits*: The group expresses values that its members share, such as social justice or individual freedom. Still other people may join an interest group for solidarity. Think of your own experience as a Girl Scout or sorority member: It can feel very powerful to be part of the group. Interest-based organizations tap into that feeling and engage members based on shared social fellowship.

Intergovernmental and Reverse Lobbying. America's fragmented federalism creates a curious form of interest-group lobbying: Public officials (often from one level of government) form organizations to influence other public officials (from another level of government). The National Governors' Association (NGA), for example, includes all fifty states' governors—conservative and liberal alike. Because states share a strong interest in federal funding for social programs (Medicare, Social Security, Medicaid), infrastructure projects (highways, bridges, and schools), and much else, the NGA lobbies the White House, Congress, and federal bureaucrats.

Government officials even lobby interest groups—termed **reverse lobbying**. Officials convene behind closed doors with key interest groups before moving forward on a proposal. The Obama administration quietly met with lobbyists representing the insurance industry, pharmaceutical companies, physicians, and other healthcare stakeholders before releasing its health plan. Republican officials huddle with oil and coal executives before issuing new energy rules. Although scornfully criticized by opponents, reverse lobbying occurs on every level of government. When a public official proposes something new, she often makes the round of sympathetic lobbyists to drum up support for her proposal.[19]

Explore PETA and other interest groups in depth.

Reverse lobbying: Attempts by government officials to influence interest groups on behalf of their preferred policies.

Michael B. Hancock ✔
@MayorHancock

[Follow]

Mayors are the ones implementing legal marijuana. We know what works & what doesn't. Teaming up w/ @MarkFarrellSF, @MayorJenny, @LibbySchaaf, @tedwheeler & @mayorheidi in a first-of-its-kind coalition to help cities, states & Congress prepare for legalization #MayorsMJCoalition

The Government for Responsible U.S. Cannabis Policy Coalition will push for Congress and the Administration to take action.

#MayorsMJCoalition

● *Intergovernmental lobbying in action. In summer 2018, U.S. city leaders announce the Government for Responsible U.S. Cannabis Policy Coalition formed to lobby Congress and the White House to respect state laws on marijuana policy.*

 **The Bottom Line**

» Interest groups, or organizations that seek to influence government, employ lobbyists to pursue benefits for their clients or membership.

» Groups serve their members by communicating political information to them, analyzing and relating members' views to policymakers, and mobilizing people to act politically.

» A long debate continues among pluralist, hyperpluralist, and power elite theorists about whether the collective public is well represented by interest groups.

» Interest groups come in several types: economic groups such as businesses or labor unions; citizens or public interest groups; and intergovernmental organizations that lobby other branches of government—or even private interest groups.

Interest Groups and the Federal Government

Lobbyists are everywhere in the American political system. Let's take an inside look at how they work.

The Multiple Roles of Lobbyists

Another Monday morning in Washington, DC; all over the capital, lobbyists are starting their workweek. Some head straight to Capitol Hill to catch up with any staffer (or, ideally, Senate or House member) they might bump into. Others gather in boardrooms for breakfast with lobbyists sharing similar interests—protecting the environment or promoting family values—to review the week's urgent legislation.

Lobbyists wear many different hats. Some interest groups are large enough to hire specialists—staff members dedicated to researching policy issues or developing media advocacy campaigns. Lobbying firms also hire outside scientists, consultants, and other experts to assist them. But most Washington representatives juggle several roles. It's all part of the job.

Researchers. The typical interest-group representative spends significant time every day studying political trends, monitoring government programs, and analyzing policies. This was the work that saved you with that PAHPA report in the chapter opening.

Witnesses. Congressional committee hearings feature testimony from interest groups. Executive agencies convene expert lobbyists for advice on how to implement a law. Professional lobbyists attend congressional hearings, following every utterance. Experienced Washington eyes read the signs—a questioning look to a senator's aid here, a note passed to a witness there—to help inform their clients of what is likely to happen.

Position Takers. Washington groups issue statements declaring their organization's positions. Every January, for example, the powerful U.S. Chamber of Commerce—which represents more than two million U.S. businesses—holds a press conference to announce the group's goals for the coming legislative season. The AFL-CIO, representing more than 60 labor unions, weekly posts a "Working People List" of leading issues in Washington and the states.

● Lobbyists work at all levels of government. Here, they pack a hearing in Lansing, Michigan, on the state's electricity laws.

Coalition Builders. Affiliated groups often band together in coalitions, allowing them to share information and split the job of contacting lawmakers. More than 25 groups joined a coalition in 2016–2017 to advocate for government-subsidized Internet connections for low-income Americans.

Social Butterflies. There is a social side to the job that many interest-group representatives relish. One lobbyist we know starts his mornings in one of the House cafeterias. Strategically located at a table by the cash register, he exchanges gossip and tidbits with a steady stream of staffers and an occasional House member. It's just his way of staying in the loop.

Iron Triangles

Do interest groups wield power? The traditional answer was yes. The model of Washington power used to be the **iron triangle**—tight, closed links among three powers: interest groups, congressional committee chairs (and their staff), and administration officials. The iron triangles dominated each narrow area of politics and policy.

> **Iron triangle:** The cozy relationship in one issue area between interest-group lobbyists, congressional staffers, and executive branch agencies.

Consider one example: *farm subsidies.* For decades, many American farmers—growing crops from corn to tobacco—have received "price supports," or subsidies worth millions of dollars, from the U.S. government. Critics charge that this practice is a huge giveaway of taxpayer dollars. Agricultural experts explain that weather and other uncertainties endemic to farming make a system of crop insurance and production management necessary. During the 2018 farm bill reauthorization, farm subsidies were targeted for cuts. Legislators in both parties pointed to the need to rein in spending, but when the smoke cleared, the price supports remained. However, the the bill remained stalled over work requirements for food stamp recipients.[20]

In some accounts, a classic iron triangle explains the staying power of farm subsidies. Congressional staffers on the agriculture committees (in Figure 9.1)

Lobby Congress on a specific issue.

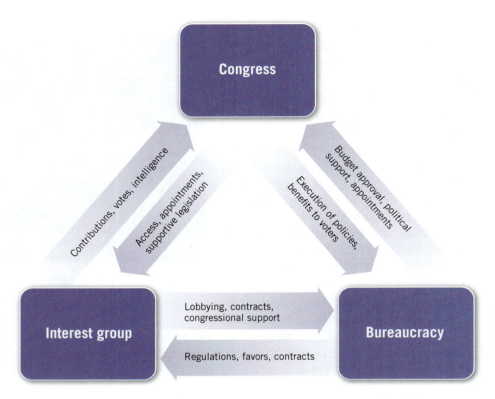

● **Figure 9.1** *Iron triangle: The classic image of interest-group power features a close relationship between Congress, lobbying groups, and federal government bureaucracy.*

Revolving door: The tendency of Washington's most seasoned lobbyists to move from government work (e.g., as a presidential advisor) to lobbying and back again.

Issue network: Shifting alliances of public and private interest groups, lawmakers, and other stakeholders all focused on the same policy area.

have close relationships with lobbyists for various farm groups, who encourage them to appropriate funds managed by bureaucrats in the Agriculture Department. If the bureaucracy balked at implementing subsidies, it might find its congressional appropriation cut the following year—so it keeps the programs humming along. The combination of executive branch, legislative branch, and lobbyists—the iron triangle—seems unstoppable.

To make the triangle still stronger, the Washington players frequently move from one point of the triangle to another. Congressional staffers, for example, take jobs as lobbyists. The changes are known as the **revolving door**.

In reality, however, farm policy may be the last vestige of the old system. Iron triangles flourished into the 1960s, thanks to a closed (old boy) system. Then, an "advocacy explosion" brought a flood of new interest groups and broke open the old triangles.

Rise of the Issue Network

Over the past 30 years, iron triangles have largely given way to a very different image of looser, more open **issue networks**. More and more positions demand to be heard; more experts join the scene; and the growth of congressional

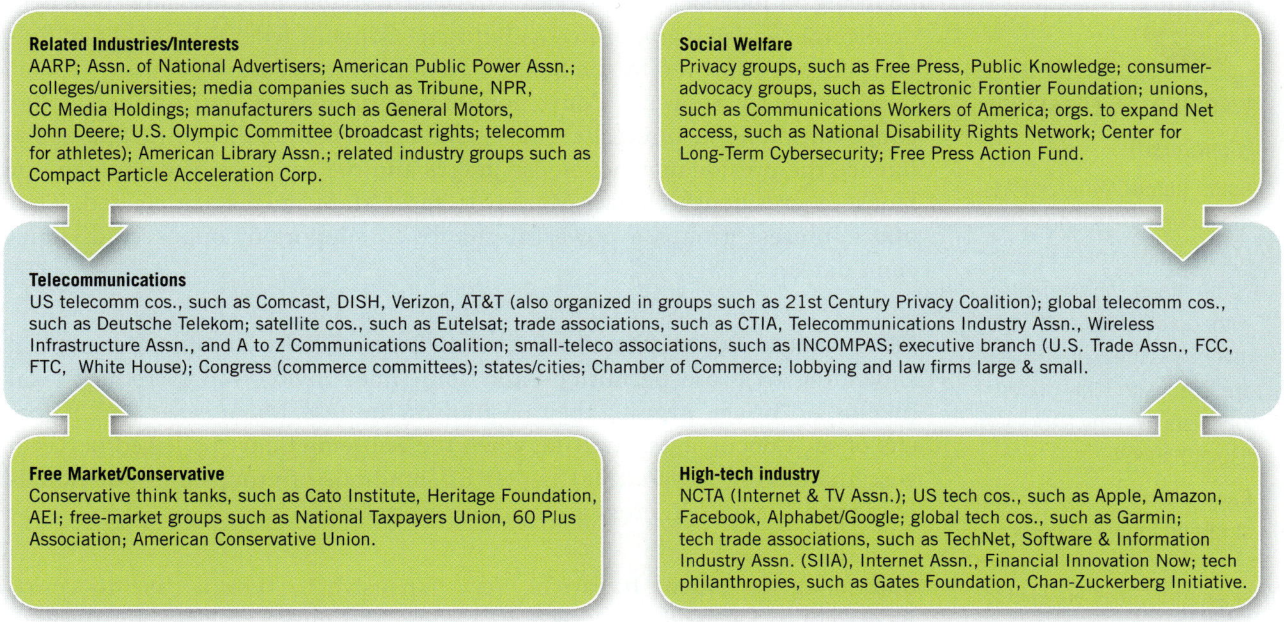

Related Industries/Interests
AARP; Assn. of National Advertisers; American Public Power Assn.; colleges/universities; media companies such as Tribune, NPR, CC Media Holdings; manufacturers such as General Motors, John Deere; U.S. Olympic Committee (broadcast rights; telecomm for athletes); American Library Assn.; related industry groups such as Compact Particle Acceleration Corp.

Social Welfare
Privacy groups, such as Free Press, Public Knowledge; consumer-advocacy groups, such as Electronic Frontier Foundation; unions, such as Communications Workers of America; orgs. to expand Net access, such as National Disability Rights Network; Center for Long-Term Cybersecurity; Free Press Action Fund.

Telecommunications
US telecomm cos., such as Comcast, DISH, Verizon, AT&T (also organized in groups such as 21st Century Privacy Coalition); global telecomm cos., such as Deutsche Telekom; satellite cos., such as Eutelsat; trade associations, such as CTIA, Telecommunications Industry Assn., Wireless Infrastructure Assn., and A to Z Communications Coalition; small-teleco associations, such as INCOMPAS; executive branch (U.S. Trade Assn., FCC, FTC, White House); Congress (commerce committees); states/cities; Chamber of Commerce; lobbying and law firms large & small.

Free Market/Conservative
Conservative think tanks, such as Cato Institute, Heritage Foundation, AEI; free-market groups such as National Taxpayers Union, 60 Plus Association; American Conservative Union.

High-tech industry
NCTA (Internet & TV Assn.); US tech cos., such as Apple, Amazon, Facebook, Alphabet/Google; global tech cos., such as Garmin; tech trade associations, such as TechNet, Software & Information Industry Assn. (SIIA), Internet Assn., Financial Innovation Now; tech philanthropies, such as Gates Foundation, Chan-Zuckerberg Initiative.

● **Figure 9.2** *Today, scholars generally see a more extensive network of actors influencing policy than that pictured by the classic iron triangle. Here, the issue network that influences telecommunications policy. (Authors' compilation based on Berry and Wilcox)*

staffs all broke apart the cozy triangles. Now the lobbyists representing farmers confront colleagues representing environmental groups, taxpayer associations, or farm representatives from African nations. In short, as political scientist Mark Peterson put it, the iron triangles have largely dissolved into "looser, less stable, less predictable, and more diverse patterns of interaction and decision."[21]

Figure 9.2 illustrates an issue network focused on telecommunications policy. Notice how much more complicated than a simple triangle it is. Welcome to the life of a Washington lobbyist today! To negotiate these networks—to faithfully represent members and attract new clients—modern interest-group representatives cannot count on a few reliable contacts with the chair of a congressional committee and a few bureaucrats. Instead, they must cultivate connections across Capitol Hill and in multiple executive departments and agencies. They also may have to master the byzantine ways of the judicial branch.

Interest Groups and the Courts

Iron triangles and issue networks portray interest groups engaging with the two elective branches, Congress and the presidency. What about the courts, which play a major role in policymaking (described in Chapter 13)? Interest groups have almost no access to Supreme Court justices and very little connection to other federal (or senior state) judges. But interest groups still manage to weigh in on judicial decision making. They do so in three main ways.[22]

Talking POLITICS

WASHINGTON LOBBYING

Drop: Set of brochures and position papers left behind by a lobbyist after visiting a legislator's office.

Fly-in: A series of Washington meetings, usually on Capitol Hill, organized by lobbyists for their out-of-town clients.

Bird-dogging: Posing tough questions to an elected official, often at a public event. Advocacy groups often engage in this tactic to advance their cause and win attention.

WASHINGTON LOBBYING

(*Continued*)

Gucci Gulch: Areas outside the House Ways and Means and Senate Finance committees, which deal with lucrative tax and revenue issues; the hallways are lined with high-priced lobbyists wearing expensive (Gucci) shoes.

Rainmakers: Lobbyists adept at raising funds for politicians or causes; when they collect large sums, they are said to be "making it rain."

Third House: In Washington, as well as many state capitals, lobbyists are viewed (not necessarily positively) as a co-equal "third branch" of government, given their expertise and access.

Lobbying on Judicial Confirmations. One way to shape court decisions is to help determine who gets *appointed* as Supreme Court or federal judge. Each federal judge is approved by the Senate. That process used to be routine. Today, however, every Supreme Court nomination prompts a multimillion-dollar confirmation fight. Interest groups spend heavily on public campaigns to influence the presidents who choose judges and the senators who confirm—or block—a president's choice. Moreover, most state judges are elected. That offers interest groups a powerful chance to support or oppose individual candidates.

Filing Amicus Curiae (literally, Friend of Court) Briefs. Groups interested in a pending case are permitted—and sometimes invited—to introduce legal memos, or "briefs," arguing their position on the case. Major cases attract dozens of such documents: In 2018, when the Supreme Court reviewed partisan gerrymandering (covered in Chapter 8), hundreds of groups and individuals filed more than 50 different amicus curiae briefs.

Sponsoring Litigation. It can be very expensive to take a case to court. Researching the issues, paying the lawyers, and pursuing litigation through multiple appeals can cost millions of dollars. Interest groups often take up a legal cause, contributing both money and expertise. When the Supreme Court agreed to review establishment clause rules about what counts as state sponsorship of religion—for example, whether government funds can go to Catholic schools or whether a state courthouse can post the Ten Commandments—the American Civil Liberties Union (liberal) and the Federalist Society (conservative) provided substantial expertise and financing. In fact, interest groups often choose the topic, recruit the plaintiffs, and fund the legal action—all to advance their cause.

The Bottom Line

» Lobbyists perform a wide range of roles, from researchers to social butterflies.

» Lobbyists working in some traditional areas still form "iron triangles" with congressional staff and executive branch officials.

» More fluid "issue networks" featuring lobbyists as central players increasingly characterize today's complex policymaking environment.

» Successful lobbyists master information, do in-depth analysis (which allies can use), engage in political campaigns, and form close ties with one of the two major parties.

» Interest groups also lobby the judicial branch by funding confirmation battles, filing amicus curiae briefs, and financing litigation.

Interest Groups and Power

Should Americans worry that interest groups are intimately involved in the details of policymaking—writing bills, organizing litigation, and shaping outcomes? It's difficult to find hard evidence about interest groups' power—did this bill pass because lobbyists pushed for it? Maybe it passed despite them? Without a smoking gun, we fall back on the usual suspects: *numbers* and *money*.

Lobbyists in Washington

How many lobbyists are there in Washington? Around 11,500 professionals registered as congressional lobbyists in 2018, but that number represents a small fraction of the total. Lobbyists can avoid registering if they spend less than 20 percent of their work time on "lobbying activities," a loosely defined term. Although legal penalties apply to those failing to disclose lobbying work, not a single criminal case has been filed under this law. Add up all the grassroots advocates, political consultants, trade association representatives, and others who can claim to be under the 20 percent threshold and the number of people peddling influence in Washington is closer to 100,000.[23]

Tens of thousands of lobbyists all chase members of Congress, congressional and White House staff, and executive bureaucrats. Many commentators see these numbers as decisive evidence of interest-group influence. Lobbying is increasing in state and local government as well. Companies that used to focus on Washington are diversifying: Google had lobbyists in just two states in 2006; by 2015, it had expanded to thirty states, and through lobbying coalitions like the Internet Association it now has lobbying boots on the ground in all 50 states.[24]

Do big (and rising) numbers suggest an ability to win? Not necessarily. Recent research suggests that, as lobbying networks become denser, it becomes easier for interest groups to block undesirable legislation, and harder for them to advance new aims.[25] That veto power echoes the hyperpluralist view described earlier. Still, are lobbyists really writing most bills and pushing their passage through Congress and state legislatures? For now we can say: No research substantiates that claim.

Interest Groups' Spending

Interest groups from Wall Street financial interests to California almond growers spend an estimated eight billion dollars each year attempting to influence Washington policymaking. This does not include spending on political campaigns, discussed later in this chapter. Or the money spent on state and local government decisions.

How do interest groups invest in campaigns?

This $8 billion figure is inexact. Official Senate and House records indicate that *registered* lobbyists reported spending nearly $3.37 billion on lobbying activities in 2017 (see Figure 9.3). Because many of those seeking to influence Congress never bother to register, analysts estimate that total spending is about 2.5 times the reported amount.[26]

Amazon's Lobbying Interests

HOW DO INTEREST EXPAND AS COMPANIES GROW?

Many companies, such as Amazon and other technology/e-commerce, claim they wish to stay out of politics. But like most of its fellow tech companies, Amazon lobbies on an increasing number of issues, as shown in the graph.

How did the number and types of issues change as Amazon grew from a five-year-old company in 2000 to an IT giant in 2017?

Based on what you have learned about business interest groups and lobbying in this chapter, why might a Seattle-based company spend so much time and money in Washington, DC?

Source: Senate Office of Public Record

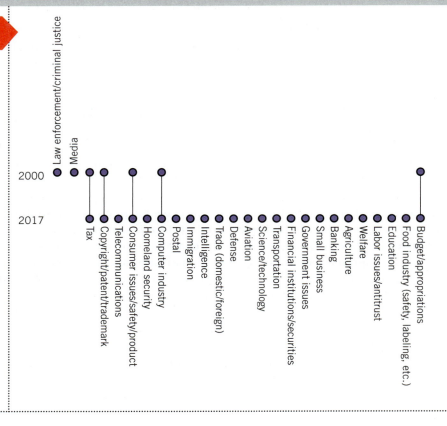

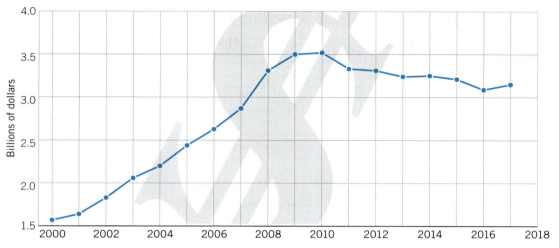

● **Figure 9.3** *Trends in spending by registered lobbyists, 2000–2017, in billions of dollars. (Center for Responsive Politics)*

Clients of private groups and members of public groups together provide those billions of dollars, which are spent on lobbyists' salaries, research costs (remember that neatly bound report!), the expense of running a Washington office, travel, and so forth. Table 9.1 lists the top-spending interest-group clients for 2017. Of the various sectors represented (healthcare, oil/gas, telecommunications, military contractors, real estate, and seniors), most of these big spenders are corporate interests. Does that fuel the power elite view? Or is it merely a waste of money, given that business loses plenty of policy battles?

When an issue of great importance to a group or industry comes up in Washington, affected groups boost their spending. Amazon was already devoting millions to its lobbying efforts when, in 2017-18, the Trump administration took up tax rates for online retail and US Postal Service shipment costs. In response, Amazon doubled its in-house lobbying team (to 28) in one year and quadrupled lobbying spending, compared to three years earlier. Other "e-tail" firms also boosted their lobbying activities.

Some analysts look at these hikes in spending and conclude that they prove interest groups' extensive political influence. But the truth is more complicated. We might ask, for example, what Amazon and other e-commerce companies got for all their spending. An internet-sales tax that they strenuously opposed was, at the last minute, pulled out of the 2018 spending bill over President Trump's objections.[27] Then the Supreme Court reversed its precedent and permitted the states to tax online sales.[28] The battle continues and, along with it, the lobbying swirl.

Our conclusion about all that money: It probably did not influence many votes. On a high-profile issue such as Internet taxation, most members of Congress have very strong views. Seasoned politicos can predict most of the votes before the debate begins. What are the lobbyists spending funds on, then? They are supporting the members that agree with them or trying to soften up the few members who may be persuadable on this topic.[29]

Watch President Trump criticize Amazon in 2018—spurring it to double its lobbying force.

TABLE 9.1	Biggest-Spending Lobbying Clients, 2017

LOBBYING CLIENT	TOTAL AMOUNT SPENT
US Chamber of Commerce	$82,190,000
National Assn of Realtors	$54,530,861
Business Roundtable	$27,380,000
Pharmaceutical Research & Manufacturers of America	$25,847,500
Blue Cross/Blue Shield	$24,330,306
American Hospital Assn	$22,094,214
American Medical Assn	$21,535,000
Alphabet Inc	$18,150,000
AT&T Inc	$16,780,000
Boeing Co	$16,740,000
Open Society Policy Center	$16,110,000
DowDuPont	$15,877,520
National Assn of Broadcasters	$15,460,000
Comcast Corp	$15,310,000
Lockheed Martin	$14,464,290
Amazon.com	$13,000,000
Southern Co	$12,970,000
National Retail Federation	$12,890,000
NCTA The Internet & Television Assn	$12,790,000
Oracle Corp	$12,385,000
Source: Center for Responsive Politics	

A clearer sign of lobbying heft may be an adjustment in a bill or a policy. Energy companies, for example, successfully pushed to include an "offset program" in climate change legislation that allowed them to more easily meet reduced emissions targets. This technical policy change underlines an important truth: The more obscure the provision, the better the chances interest groups and their lobbyists have of winning. The less the public is aware of a topic, the more room Congress has to deliver favors.

We turn now to an extended look at political parties in the U.S. system. We will return in a concluding section to possible reforms of both interest groups and parties.

The Bottom Line

» Because of the difficulty of directly measuring interest-group influence in government, researchers turn to familiar metrics such as the number of lobbyists and the monies they spend on lobbying.

» Beginning in the mid-1960s, an advocacy explosion saw lobbyist numbers climb dramatically. Resources devoted to lobbying also rose sharply beginning in this period. And lobbying spread to state and even local governments.

» Despite their extensive presence and spending, lobbyists are not likely to change congressional minds on high-profile votes; their role is more akin to supporting the members already on their side. Votes on more obscure or highly technical topics are easier for lobbyists to sway.

Political Parties and U.S. Government

Just as Americans express concern about excessive lobbying influence in government, the rise in partisanship has received plenty of criticism. A wide divide has opened between the parties on almost every issue—and separates Americans into two hostile camps. Seventy percent of politically engaged Democrats say Republicans make them "afraid," "angry," and "frustrated"— and most active Republicans feel the same way about the Democrats.[30] In summer 2017, partisan antipathy reached a new height when a former volunteer for Democrat Bernie Sanders's presidential campaign opened fire on the Republican team practicing for a congressional baseball game, critically injuring one legislator and wounding several others. The gunman lived in his van and belonged to a Facebook group called "Terminate the Republican Party."[31]

All this might tempt you to echo George Washington: Do we really need parties? The answer is yes. Let us see why.

What Political Parties Do

Love them or hate them, parties are an essential part of American government. They have five major roles: championing ideas, selecting candidates, mobilizing voters, organizing government action, and integrating new voters.

Parties Champion Ideas. U.S. politics reverberates with ideas, and every candidate takes a position on scores of them. How do voters keep it all straight? Parties create a brand that enables people to identify others who roughly share their views. If you strongly support environmental activism, citizenship

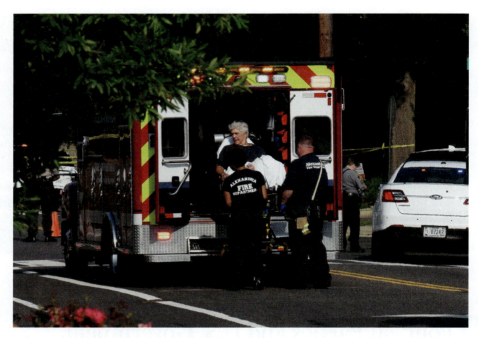

● *Representative Roger Williams (R-TX) is placed in an ambulance after a gunman opened fire on congressional Republicans practicing for an annual charity game.*

for undocumented immigrants, robust social programs, a woman's right to choose, and high-speed rail, you are probably a Democrat. If, on the other hand, you care more about lowering taxes, reducing the size of government, getting tough on undocumented immigrants, supporting traditional families, and outlawing abortion, you are probably a Republican. Prefer to mix and match from the lists? You're likely an independent who belongs to neither party—though political scientists know that most independents usually vote for one party.[32]

Parties are always evolving. Candidate Donald Trump challenged many traditional Republican views–he mocked free trade deals and staunchly defended Russia—but once in office he won support from a sky-high 90% of Republicans. Many reversed their positions to endorse his.

Parties Select Candidates. Parties choose the candidates who will run for election. Republicans began with seventeen contenders running for president in 2016 and voted, state by state, until they had selected Donald Trump. The two major parties select candidates to run for office at every level of government—except local government, which often relies on **nonpartisan elections**.

Parties Mobilize the Voters. Party leaders work to attract votes for their candidates. The parties raise money, hire consultants, craft advertisements, take

Nonpartisan election:
An election in which candidates run as individuals, without any party affiliation. Featured in many towns and cities.

● Parties socialize new groups into politics. When evangelical Christians started getting involved in politics in the 1970s and 1980s, Republican leaders were there to show them the ropes. Here, President Ronald Reagan speaks to evangelical leaders.

● Barack Obama supporters celebrate his presidential reelection. For the first time in history, African Americans voted at a higher rate than white voters when Obama ran for president.

polls, and organize phone banks. They have also become adept at suppressing the other side's votes through negative advertising.

Parties Organize Governing Activity After the Election. Once the election is over, parties work to enact programs that deliver on their party platform. Leaders set agendas, line up votes, and organize their teams in Congress, in presidential administrations, and in the state governments.

Parties Help Integrate New Groups into the Political Process. Parties transmit basic lessons about politics and government (details may differ, depending on the party). Party messages have attracted immigrants, young voters, evangelical Christians, high-tech entrepreneurs, and many more into the American polity. Savvy party leaders seek overlooked groups they can rally. Barack Obama galvanized black Americans who, in 2012, and perhaps 2008 (counts differ), turned out at higher rates than whites for the first time in American history.[33] Four years later, Republican nominee Donald Trump attracted votes from white males without a college degree who felt abandoned by both Democrats and Republicans.

Political parties carry out these five functions in the United States—and in other countries with democratic governments. But there's something more distinctive about the American **party system**: The United States has always relied on just two major parties.

Two-Party America

In January 2019, all 435 members of the House of Representatives, 98 of 100 senators, and all 50 governors were either Democrats or Republicans. Why is the United States so resolutely devoted to the number two when it comes to party politics?

Party system: The broad organization of U.S. politics, comprising the two main parties, the coalition of supporters backing each, the positions they take on major issues, and each party's electoral achievements.

One reason for this two-party tradition rests on ideas (Chapter 1). Democrats and Republicans often take different sides in the great American debate over ideas. For example, Republicans see liberty as freedom from government coercion while most Democrats emphasize "freedom from want" and support government programs that will ensure everyone has the basics.

As you know by now, institutions reinforce ideas. In this case, the winner-take-all electoral rules keep third parties out. The Libertarian or Green Party may win 20 percent of the national vote, but if it fails to win a majority in any state or congressional district, it is shut out from both Congress and the Electoral College. In contrast, most other democracies operate multiparty systems. Their proportional representation systems award a party that won 20 percent of the vote roughly 20 percent of the seats in the legislature. A French sociologist, Maurice Durverger, drew the conclusion: American-style elections (often described with a horse racing metaphor, "first past the post") yield two parties; proportional representation produces many parties.

The U.S. rules push every group to join one of the two major parties. When candidates try to break out of the two-party system, they are accused of being "spoilers"—throwing the election to the opposing party. This is precisely what happened in the 2000 presidential election. In Florida, Republican George W. Bush won 48.847 percent of the vote; Democrat Al Gore won 48.846 percent of the vote; and Green Party candidate Ralph Nader won 1.635 percent of the vote. Bush's 0.001 percent margin gave him all 25 electoral votes in Florida and made him president. Disappointed Democrats blasted Ralph Nader for drawing just enough liberals to throw the election to the Republicans. The Florida experience reinforced for many Democrats a key institutional lesson: Work within the two parties.

Other institutional forces reinforce the two-party system. State laws determine who gets on the ballot, and they often make it very difficult for a minor-party candidate to be listed. In Florida, for example, after reforms in 2011 that *eased* restrictions, a third party still needs to collect more than 112,000 notarized signatures simply to list its candidate on a presidential-primary ballot—a high bar for a small party.

The advantage of America's two-party system: It is predictable and stable. In nations with many parties, each election is followed by negotiations among the parties trying to form a majority coalition that sometimes collapses before the next scheduled elections.

There are also disadvantages to two-party dominance in the United States.[34] For starters, it is less representative. In 2018, approximately one-third of the voters in Massachusetts voted for Republican congressional candidates. Is it fair to end up with nine Massachusetts Democrats—and no Republicans—in Congress? Voters in proportional representation systems like Germany's or Japan's generally have more choices for national or local office; people passionate about a cause—environment, religion, free markets—often can find a party devoted to that cause. Perhaps you are wondering if the United States has ever made significant room for additional parties? That's easy to answer: No!

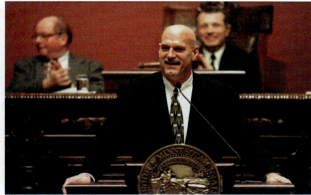

● *Wrestler-turned-governor Jesse Ventura, a member of the Reform Party.*

Third Parties in American Politics

Theodore "Teddy" Roosevelt is one of the most colorful figures in U.S. political history: a military hero who suffered from asthma, a big-game hunter who adopted an orphaned bear cub (giving rise to the familiar "teddy bear"). When Roosevelt came out of retirement to run as a Progressive Party candidate, he became the only third-party presidential candidate to come in second—but he still got clobbered by Woodrow Wilson, who won 435 electoral votes to Roosevelt's 88.

Table 9.2 lists all third-party presidential contestants who gained more than 5 percent of the popular vote or more than ten electoral votes since 1840. It is a short list, without a single candidate who came close to winning. And most third parties lasted just one term (or four years) at the national level. Roosevelt's Progressive Party, for example, elected some fifteen members to Congress and spearheaded important reforms—but dissolved within four years. The "Tea Party," which has attracted considerable attention in American politics in recent years, is not an organized national party, but a label that Republican candidates adopt to signal their conservative views.

On the state level, third parties have done only slightly better. In 2018, 169 libertarians and 143 Green Party members held office (remember, that's out of 520,000 elected officials).[35]

Minnesota was the only state to elect a third-party candidate governor. Jesse Ventura, a former professional wrestler (known as "The Body"), rode his blend of outsized personality and blunt common sense to the governor's mansion as a Reform Party candidate in 1998. In the last quarter-century, four other states have elected governors outside the major parties: Alaska (1990), Connecticut (1990), Rhode Island (2010), and Maine (1994, 1998). All four winners were independents rather than representatives of third parties.

Despite their history of electoral failure, minor parties matter. They provide a vehicle for people to express alternative views. Third-party movements have injected strong and controversial views into American politics. They have

Reforming The
Two-Party System
in Iowa

TABLE 9.2 **The Road to Nowhere: The Most Successful Third-Party Presidential Contenders, 1840–2019**

ELECTION	THIRD-PARTY CANDIDATE(S), PARTY	PERCENTAGE OF POPULAR VOTE (NO. OF ELECTORAL VOTES)
1856	Millard Fillmore, American (Know-Nothing) Party	22% (8)
1860	John Bell, Constitutional Union Party	12.6% (39)
1892	James Weaver, People's Party	8.5% (22)
1912	Theodore Roosevelt, Progressive Party	27.4% (88)
	Eugene Debs, Socialist Party	6% (0)
1924	Robert La Follette, Progressive Party	16.6% (13)
1948	Strom Thurmond, States' Rights (Dixiecrat) Party	2.4% (39)
1968	George Wallace, American Independent Party	13.5% (45)
1980	John Anderson, National Unity Party	6.6% (0)
1992	Ross Perot, United We Stand Party	18.9% (0)
1996	Ross Perot, Reform Party	8.4% (0)

fought for the abolition of slavery, the direct election of senators, gender equality, eliminating child labor, the prohibition of drinking, the income tax, limits on immigration, and smaller government.[36] When a third-party cause becomes popular, one of the major parties tends to adopt it—as they did with every issue in the previous sentence.

America's Party Systems: Origins and Change

Political parties are always evolving—in response to a third party or to new issues, or new ways of winning elections. Every few decades the entire U.S. party system changes. We can identify at least six distinctive "party systems" stretching across American history.

Beginnings: First Party System (1789–1828). Early Americans thought political parties ruined good government. The immensely popular George Washington (a strong Federalist) twice won the presidency without campaigning and his vice president, John Adams, won the third presidential election. But, throughout the 1790s, leaders disagreed on a crucial issue: How strong should the central government be? Politicians who supported strong national government established the Federalist Party; those who wanted to leave power with the states formed the Democratic-Republican Party. Thus, the political parties emerged. In 1800, party competition finally broke into the open as Thomas Jefferson (Democratic-Republican) defeated Adams—the first party change in the presidency. The Democratic-Republicans won the next six presidential elections and controlled Congress for 24 years (see Table 9.2).

The fading Federalists charged Jefferson with winning "on the shoulders of slaves."[37] With a base in the south, his Electoral College count was inflated by adding three-fifths of a vote for each slave (discussed in Chapter 2). In fact, slaveholders held the presidency for most of the next forty years, thanks in part to the three-fifths rule.

The first party system set a durable pattern: two main parties contesting elections and building coalitions. One party dominated until new issues or changing rules swept in a new constellation of parties, ideas, and interests—in short, a new party system.

Rise: Second Party System (ca. 1828–1860). When Andrew Jackson won the presidency in 1828, some twenty thousand Democrats (many of them angling for government jobs) swarmed into Washington for his inauguration. Supreme Court Justice Joseph Story spoke for the old-style gentry: "The reign of King Mob seemed triumphant."[38] What he really saw: the birth of modern party politics.

In just three decades, political parties had evolved into a form that we would recognize today. Party competition grew fierce; voting rights expanded to most white males; enthusiastic party members threw themselves into politics.

The birth of modern politics came with serious downsides: fewer rights for the small population of free blacks. Elected officials dispensed jobs to their followers as the "spoils of office"—a corrupt patronage system of government (discussed in Chapter 12).[39]

The parties themselves changed. The Federalists vanished. Andrew Jackson's supporters rebranded Jefferson's party as Democrats; his opponents called themselves "Whigs"—named after a British party that opposed royal tyranny.

The Democrats favored small farmers, embraced immigrants (and stuffed ballots in their hands almost as soon as they landed), pursued genocidal Indian Removal, defended slavery, and plunged into war with Mexico. Whigs favored business, stronger government, and infrastructure projects; meanwhile, they struggled to limit the influence of immigrants and included most abolitionists in their ranks.

Neither party could duck the issue of slavery. As the United States spread west, every new territory and state raised the same urgent question: Should slavery be permitted? Democrats answered, leave it to the states and territories. Whigs from the North and the South could not agree with

● *The new Irish and German immigrants, identified by the type of liquor they prefer, steal American democracy in this nativist critique of urban (Democratic) voters during the second party period.*

one another and the issue destroyed the party. A new party system arose—and clarified the future of slavery in the United States.[40]

War and Reconstruction: Third Party System (1860–1896). Abraham Lincoln helped form a new party—the Republican Party. The Republicans strongly supported free labor (which today we call capitalism) and opposed the expansion of slavery. When Lincoln won the presidential election of 1860, southern "fire-eaters" persuaded the region's leaders that slavery was in peril. They split from the union, the Lincoln administration fought to stop them, and the nation entered its bloody Civil War (1861-1865).[41]

After the war, Republicans drew on their party to help rebuild the nation. Republicans promoted black rights; in all, 16 black Americans served in Congress and more than 600 won seats in state legislatures. Democrats limited former slaves' freedom to travel, vote, or seek employment—often resorting to violence—and eventually restored white dominance.[42]

By the 1870s, each party had a strong regional identity. Democrats controlled the former Confederate states, which became known as "the Solid South." Republicans dominated the Northeast and the Midwest. After 1872, elections became very close, the presidency changed hands with each election, and two (of five) winners lost the popular vote but won in the Electoral College—something that did not happen again until 2000 and 2016.

Beginning in the 1870s, European and Asian immigrants streamed into the cities. Powerful political organizations—**party machines**—dominated urban government. Managed by **party bosses**, the machines provided immigrants with food, shelter, jobs, and a sense of belonging. In exchange, the party could count on a large block of votes. The machines grew notorious for bribery and corruption.

Reformers eventually cleaned up city politics (although the hardiest machines lasted well into the twentieth century) through a series of institutional reforms that included banishing the parties themselves. Today, parties remain crucial on the national and state level, but many cities have nonpartisan elections. In fact, you can measure how strong the urban reformers were in any city by checking whether the parties are still involved in local elections.

Business and Reform: Fourth Party System (1896–1932). In 1892, a radical Populist party swept out of the west and won over a million votes. Even so, the Democrats won the presidency and both houses of Congress. Then a terrible economic depression hit the country. In the 1894 midterm, the Democrats lost 116 seats—the biggest drop ever. In the 1896 presidential election, Populists joined the Democrats to challenge the status quo but were defeated by Republicans termed the "millionaires' party." After President William McKinley was assassinated in 1901, his vice president, Theodore Roosevelt, stepped into the White House, challenged the "millionaires' club," and began to sponsor reforms.

The central debates of the fourth party system featured support for business on one side, and pressures for equality (championed by the Progressive movement) on the other. Should women be granted the vote? Should the government

Party boss: The senior figure in a party machine.

Party machine: A hierarchical arrangement of party workers, often organized in an urban area to dominate power politics; they helped integrate immigrants into the political system—but at the price of bias and corruption. Most active from the mid-nineteenth to the early twentieth centuries.

THE BOSS STILL HAS THE REINS

● *Cartoonist Thomas Nast mocks one corrupt politician, Boss Tweed, at the reins of New York's Democratic Party*

● *One policy both parties agreed on for most of the fourth party system: prohibiting the sale of alcohol. The 1920s became a boom time, marked by rising new industries such as advertising, automobiles, and electricity. Then the economy collapsed in 1929–1930, taking down Prohibition and the entire fourth party system.*

regulate emerging corporate giants, such as Standard Oil or the Central Pacific Railroad? Should state government regulate child labor? And limit the workday for men and women? To Progressive reformers, led by Roosevelt, the answer was yes, yes, yes.

The 1920s were a boom time, marked by the dominance of business and rising new industries such as advertising, automobiles, and electricity. Then the economy collapsed in 1929–1932, taking the fourth party system down with it.

Depression and New Deal: Fifth Party System (1933–1968). Another President Roosevelt, Teddy's distant cousin Franklin, helped define the fifth party system. The Great Depression (1929-1941) unhinged party politics, crippling a Republican Party associated with economic incompetence.

After three years of economic misery, Franklin Delano Roosevelt (FDR) brought a new Democratic coalition into power—firmly blaming the "unscrupulous money changers" (the old "millionaires' club") for the nation's "dark days."[43] Roosevelt's **New Deal** focused on jobs, infrastructure, government aid to the elderly (Social Security), temporary assistance for the needy, and new federal agencies to manage them all.

The Democratic Party coalition included an unusual mix: the Solid South, big-city machines with their ethnic supporters, labor unions, farmers hurt by rising agricultural prices, and African Americans. Many black men and women had migrated north, where they were recruited into local Democratic parties. That created tension within a party that now included both African Americans and southern segregationists. Democrats kept the coalition together—and hung on to their southern majority—for another thirty years, but as they became

New Deal: Broad series of economic programs and reforms introduced between 1933 and 1936 and associated with the Franklin Roosevelt administration.

known as the party of civil rights, white southern voters shifted to the "**Grand Old Party**" (**GOP**).

Grand Old Party (GOP):
Longstanding nickname for the Republican Party; ironically, bestowed early in the party's history, in the 1870s.

The Sixth Party System: The Parties at Equal Strength (1972–Present). Republican presidents Richard Nixon (1969–1973) and Ronald Reagan (1981–1989) developed a "southern strategy" to win middle-class white votes. By 1981, Reagan launched a direct assault on the fifth party system with a conservative mantra: Government is not the solution to our problems. Instead, he said, government is the source of many problems. Eventually, even Democrats began to echo Reagan. Democratic president Bill Clinton announced that "the era of big government is over."[44]

Republicans dominated the fourth party period and Democrats the fifth. The sixth party era eventually introduced something new: neither party in control. Instead, very close elections swing party control back and forth. And with very close elections comes growing partisanship.[45]

The sixth party period is already one of the longest-lived. Political historians watch carefully to see if one party or the other finally establishes dominance—and inaugurates a new party era.

Why does party period matter? Why should we care what party system we are in? Because a new party system means new politics. Shifting coalitions, ideas, and leaders determine how America is governed.

The Bottom Line

» Political parties perform five major functions: They champion ideas, select candidates, mobilize voters, organize government action, and integrate new groups into the political process.

» America's two-party style has endured for more than two hundred years. Since 1866, Democrats face off against Republicans. Election rules help explain this dominance. Third parties challenge but none has ever managed to break through.

» We count six party systems since the founding of the United States. The latest, which began in 1972, is marked by very close elections.

 # Who Joins? Party Identification

Party identification: Strong attachment to one political party, often established at an early age.

The strong attachment many Americans feel to their party is called **party identification**, and it deeply affects how individuals see politics. Where do party identities and differences come from? And who is attached to each party?

Building Party Identification

Party loyalty often starts with family and includes demography—race, gender, age, and so on. The Democratic Party is younger. Men break Republican, women Democratic (see Figure 9.4).[46] The Republican Party is mostly white;

Strong groups for Democratic and Republican parties

% of each group that identifies as . . .

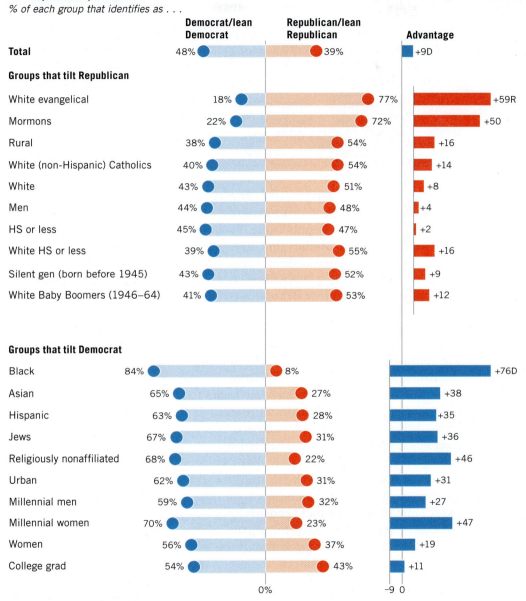

	Democrat/lean Democrat	Republican/lean Republican	Advantage
Total	48%	39%	+9D
Groups that tilt Republican			
White evangelical	18%	77%	+59R
Mormons	22%	72%	+50
Rural	38%	54%	+16
White (non-Hispanic) Catholics	40%	54%	+14
White	43%	51%	+8
Men	44%	48%	+4
HS or less	45%	47%	+2
White HS or less	39%	55%	+16
Silent gen (born before 1945)	43%	52%	+9
White Baby Boomers (1946–64)	41%	53%	+12
Groups that tilt Democrat			
Black	84%	8%	+76D
Asian	65%	27%	+38
Hispanic	63%	28%	+35
Jews	67%	31%	+36
Religiously nonaffiliated	68%	22%	+46
Urban	62%	31%	+31
Millennial men	59%	32%	+27
Millennial women	70%	23%	+47
Women	56%	37%	+19
College grad	54%	43%	+11

0% –9 0

● **Figure 9.4** *Party demographics. White, male, older evangelical voters are more likely to vote Republican while Black, Asian, female, young and urban voters are more likely to vote Democrat. (Pew Research Center)*

the Democratic Party is increasingly diverse. Political scientists John Sides, Michael Tesler, and Lynn Vavreck argue that underlying contemporary partisanship is a fierce identity politics—with white identity on the right and multicultural identity on the left. These identities shape views on immigration, social welfare policies, and the government itself.[47]

What Do YOU Think? **Personality and Party**

Consider your own personality and party preference. Does recent political science research help predict your view— and the views of the people around you?	**Yes.** I believe that Democrats are more likely to seek new experiences and Republicans are more likely to emphasize duty and discipline.	**No.** I think there are different traits that explain party identification. (Please specify which traits you think matter most.)	**Interests, not personality.** I don't believe personality predicts politics. We are rational creatures pursuing our own self-interest regardless of personality.

Other traits also matter. Urban dwellers are Democrats, suburbanites lean Republican, and rural voters are strongly Republican. White evangelicals and Mormons are reliably Republicans, secular people Democrats. Even personality seems relevant. Studies find that people who exhibit more "openness" (eagerness to explore new experiences) are more likely to be Democrats. Those who measure high in "conscientiousness" (strong sense of duty, discipline, impulse control) tend to be Republicans.[48]

Another influence on party affinity comes down to the moment when voters form attachments. Certain times seem to carry magic for a political party— John Kennedy's 1960 election drew millions toward the Democratic Party, as Ronald Reagan's 1980 election did for the Republican Party.

No mass shift in party identification has shown up for the last twenty-five years. Current poll numbers show that around 27 percent of the electorate identifies as Democratic and about 25 percent as Republican. Recently, we have seen a surge in independents who are weary of both parties. At 44 percent, their numbers are now larger than either party.[49] Why? The intense conviction among the party members may make others less willing to identify themselves. Still, most independents vote faithfully for one party or the other and feel just as strongly about the shortcomings of the other party. Only about 12 percent of the population are true independents.[50]

One factor may be slowly shifting the balance toward the Democratic Party: When Ronald Reagan whipped Jimmy Carter in the 1980 presidential election (489-49 in the Electoral College), the electorate was almost 90 percent white. By 2020, the white electorate is estimated to be down to around 68 percent—and falling. Of course, groups can and do shift parties. Still, the demographic trend suggests an urgent message for the Republican future: Diversify the base.[51]

The Power of Party Attachment

Party identification shapes three key aspects of public involvement: participating, "filtering," and ideology.

Voting/Participation. Party identity is a very strong predictor of your voting habits. In 2016, for example, 89 percent of Democrats voted for Clinton while

Explore party values and factions.

91 percent of Republicans voted for Trump. Analysts measuring the strength of party attachment find that strong partisans tend to be very loyal **straight-ticket voters**, sticking with their party's candidates right down the ballot. Their opposite? **Split-ticket voters**, who make their choices candidate by candidate.

Voting rates are higher among those with strong party identification. Only 60 million (27 percent of eligible voters) cast a ballot in the 2016 presidential primaries. The key to every election is turning out the party's **base voters**—those who deeply identify with the party—while winning over some independents.[52]

Filtering. Party identification also plays a *filtering* role. Filters influence what signals in the media environment people accept or reject. As one political scientist wrote, "people tend to project favorable characteristics and acceptable issue positions onto the candidates of the party they favor."[53] In a set of experiments, social scientists asked respondents to rate a generic series of political candidates based on photos and detailed biographies. Each was sometimes described as a Democrat, sometimes as a Republican, and sometimes as an independent. The study found that self-identified Democrats preferred the candidates described as "Democrats," the Republicans preferred Republicans. The candidate's policy positions, appearance, and family background were all less important than the party label.

Ideology. The parties diverge sharply on many issues. Should we provide government support to people who cannot take care of themselves? Democrats say yes (71 percent); Republicans say no (only 24 percent agree). Should we make every effort to improve the position of minorities, even if it means preferential treatment? Most Democrats (52%) but few Republicans (12 percent) agree. Do you believe in God as described in the Bible? Republicans are more likely to say yes (70 percent) than Democrats (45 percent). On all these indicators, differences between the parties have more than doubled in the past fifteen years.[54]

Of course, even with the growing intensity of party ideology, no party is a monolith. Each includes multiple factions with different—sometimes very different—ideas. Let us take a look at the factions within the parties today.

Republican Factions

Republicans are often lumped together as conservatives, but significant differences exist. Consider six different Republican factions.

Populists or Trumpists. These men and women are skeptical of elites in both parties, believing that they have turned their back on conservative values—and more generally, on America. They are strong nationalists, vehemently oppose immigration, and are skeptical of international trade agreements. President Trump leads this wing of the party. Referring to this faction of the party, Senator Bob Corker (R-TN) commented, "People no longer care about issues. They [only] want to know if you're with Trump."[55]

Religious Traditionalists. Some conservatives support a return to what they consider America's Christian origins. They oppose abortion, affirmative action,

Straight-ticket voter: Votes for the same party for all offices on a ballot.

Split-ticket voter: Votes for at least one candidate from each party, dividing his or her ballot between the two (or more) parties.

Base voters: Party members who tend to vote loyally for their party's candidates in most elections.

Every party has fringe groups. Strong language about immigration brought white nationalists back into the national spotlight when some endorsed Donald Trump.

Watch Donald Trump's populist supporters during the campaign.

and same-sex marriage and support school prayer, gun rights, and restrictions on immigration.

Fiscal Conservatives. This faction supports tax cuts, opposes government spending, and wishes to reduce the size of government. They voted for the sweeping Trump administration tax cut, but wish to see its costs balanced with cuts in the large entitlement programs—Social Security and Medicare (see Chapter 14).

Libertarians. Libertarians are passionate defenders of individual liberty and free markets. They oppose government involvement in education, environmental regulation, health care (which sounds conservative), as well as abortion, marijuana, or same sex marriage. This faction tends to be wary of the Trump administration.[56]

Neoconservatives. Neoconservatives support strong U.S. intervention to spread democracy and free markets around the world and believe that the United States should exercise its military muscle to improve the world.[57]

Moderates. Moderates, a once-proud Republican faction, tend to be fiscally conservative but will consider tax increases along with spending cuts and are willing to compromise with Democrats to get things done. A quarter of self-identified Republicans describe themselves as moderates, but they face scorn from populist Republicans who dismiss moderates as RINOs: Republicans in Name Only.

Democratic Factions

Democrats also encompass very different groups. Today, 13 percent label themselves conservative, 50 percent liberal.[58]

Progressives. Progressives occupy the Democratic left wing. They are strong environmentalists, embrace universal healthcare, support immigrant rights, advocate a woman's right to reproductive freedom, and are especially concerned about economic inequality. Many backed Senator Bernie Sanders in the 2016 primaries and responded to Trump's election by helping launch the #MeToo movement.

The Civil Rights Caucus. Many Democratic Party members trace their political commitment to the spirit of the civil rights movement. They advocate for groups that have historically faced discrimination, especially racial minorities, recent immigrants, LGBTQ people, and women. They build "rainbow" coalitions, fight against discrimination, support social programs, and join in declaring sanctuary cities.

Organized Labor. Unions have been a major source of campaign contributions, votes, and workers for the Democratic Party. Unions strongly support jobs programs, infrastructure projects, and workers' rights. Labor traditionally opposes globalization, free trade agreements, and environmental regulations. Republicans have made major inroads, especially among white working men.[59]

Centrists. In the 1990s, some centrist Democrats embraced a "Third Way" between the farther-left progressives in the party and Republican conservatives. For example, they balanced environmental protection with "smart growth." The third-

● *Every party has fringe groups. Left-wing antifa protesters smash windows and set fires amidst reports that conservative activist Milo Yiannopoulos would come to the University of California, Berkeley campus.*

way theme was especially important during the Bill Clinton years. Centrists are fiscal conservatives who urge the progressive caucus to tack to the center. But in a highly polarized era, this is becoming an increasingly hard sell.

Why so many factions—ten across the two parties? Because the parties themselves are changing. Partisanship and electoral dynamics (like safe districts where the only real threat to an officeholder is in the primary) have moved national officials in both parties away from the middle. Populists (among Republicans) and progressives (among Democrats) are feeling especially emboldened. Still, both parties include multiple perspectives. Add variations across states and regions, and the perspectives multiply. The crucial point: Parties are always boisterous combinations of views. Are you unmoved by every one of these perspectives? Then you are a genuine independent!

The Bottom Line

» Most Americans identify strongly with Republicans or Democrats, though the number of independents has been rising.

» Strong party identification is a result of many factors, including parental influence, political context, and even personality type.

» Party identification shapes our ideas and the way we filter information and vote.

» Each party features multiple factions.

🧍 Party Organization

With so many factions, running a party is a complicated job. The work falls on three different groups: the party organization, the party in government, and the party in the electorate—each with national, state, and local dimensions. By now you will recognize the classic feature of American political institutions: a very complicated organizational chart.

The Party Bureaucracy

The central organization for both parties is a national committee—the Republican National Committee (RNC) and the Democratic National Committee (DNC). These committees raise funds for the party, coordinate election strategies, decide which local races to fund, organize a national convention every four years, and prepare the **party platform**—the party's statement of purpose and its position on issues.

The committees also issue and enforce the party's rules for primary elections, from the presidential level downward. Important members of the DNC and RNC include the state party chairs and vice chairs, who typically are the most faithful activists in each party.

Traditionally, the leaders of the **party organization** are anonymous insiders who oversee the primary process. During the 2016 primaries, Bernie Sanders charged that the Democratic National Committee (DNC) was openly siding against him. A blockbuster email trove, published by WikiLeaks (the result of a Russian intelligence hack), seemed to prove him right, as high-level staffers wrote things such as "he's never going to be president." With their behind-the-scenes activity exposed, DNC Chair Debbie Wasserman Schultz and other staffers resigned in disgrace.

Party in Government

The **party in government** gets the recognition. These are the government officials in each party, and include elected leaders, appointed officers, individuals running for political office, and their staffs. The party in government tries to enact the policies they support—and to stop their rivals from enacting theirs.

There is a constant struggle for influence within each party in government. Presidents usually command their own party—as Donald Trump now does the Republicans. The party that does not control the presidency often sees a contest as

Party platform: The written statement of a party's core convictions and issue priorities. Generally revised every four years, in time for the national party convention.

Party organization: The portion of a political party that includes activists, state/local leaders, and affiliated professionals such as fundraisers and public relations experts.

Party in government: The portion of a political party's organization that comprises elected officials and candidates for office.

● Sanders supporters at the Democratic convention protested bias of the Democratic National Committee (DNC). The role of the conventions is to bring the different factions together.

congressional leaders, governors, and presidential candidates all vie to put their own stamp on the party.

Party in the Electorate

What is left after the party organization and office holders? We are! Each party's followers make up the **party in the electorate**.

The Big Tent

The media generally focuses on the best-known party leaders. Political parties thrive, however, when all their elements—organization, office holders, and public supporters—work together. That means voicing the same message, getting enthused about shared principles, and embracing the party symbols—right down to the bumper stickers.

American federalism makes unanimity difficult. Local officials run the party in each state. Democrats in a conservative state such as Alabama often have more in common with many Republicans in their own state than they do with liberal Democrats in San Francisco or New York. The opposite is true for more liberal Republicans in New York or Massachusetts.

Party organizations always make tactical calculations: Do they put their resources in a few swing states that they have a good chance of winning in the next election cycle? Or should they spread their resources across many states—even supporting candidates who are long shots—with the aim of slowly building up their party in places where it does not often win?

Federalism pushes each of the two major parties to adopt a "big tent" approach: spread themselves wide, embrace divergent views, and hope any resultant ideological muddle does not turn off too many party members. However, many party members reject the big tent approach and insist on sticking to their political principles—which can make for tumultuous politics within each party.

> **Party in the electorate:** The largest (and least organized) component of a political party, drawn from the public at large: registered members and regular supporters.

Distinguish between the groups that make up a party.

The Bottom Line

» Parties include three groups: the party organization, the party in government, and the party in electorate.

» Both major parties in the U.S. adopt a "big tent" approach, relaxing ideological purity in order to attract a broad range of supporters.

Party Competition . . . and Partisanship

Parties began to lose their influence over politics in the 1960s. Interest groups muscled in on their territory, mobilized voters, and shaped issue positions. Americans began to identify with movements and organizations—civil rights, environmentalism, the right to life, libertarianism. The parties floundered. By the 1970s and 1980s, books featured titles like *The Party's Over* and *The Decline of American Political Parties*.[60]

Parties Rise Again

Even as political scientists declared the death of parties, their revival began. Money led the way. Campaign finance rules limited contributions to candidates—so the PACs and Super PACS began to pour their money into the DNC, the RNC, and congressional campaign organizations. Now the parties could fund candidates, who became more dependent on the parties as a result.

Partisanship Intensifies

The two parties regularly used to work together to craft legislation. The Senate passed the 1964 Civil Rights Act thanks to Northern Republicans and Democrats; Congress passed the Clean Air Act, a blockbuster environmental bill, almost unanimously (there was only one negative vote) and it was signed into law by Republican President Richard Nixon; and in 1997, the Republican majority worked with Democratic President Bill Clinton to extend health insurance to seven million children. Cross-party majorities were not unusual because there was as much difference *within* each party as there was between the parties. Democrats were so bitterly divided over civil rights that they could barely hold a **party caucus** during the 1950s–1960s.

Today strong differences within the parties have diminished. Factions remain, as we saw, but party members are far less diverse in their views. The strongest divisions are now between the two parties. By 2010, every single Republican in the U.S. Senate had a voting record to the right of even the most conservative Democrat. Ideological conflict in both the House and the Senate now breaks down almost completely along party lines. This partisan divide makes the political contest—over ideas, programs, and even the meaning of America—louder and angrier than it has been in more than a century. Across government, **partisanship** is rising. It is also increasing among the public.[61] Here's how partisan Americans have become: Half of all Republicans (and 30 percent of Democrats) report they would be "displeased" if their child married someone from the opposite party.[62]

With two intense parties thriving, elections have grown very close. Since 2000, the Senate has changed hands four times, the presidency three times, and the House three times—a turnover rate last seen in the nineteenth century (see Table 9.3).

Who influences whom? Are partisan officials fanning the flames of party difference among the public? Or do activists within each party push their leaders to take stronger positions against the opposition? Or perhaps media outlets such as Fox News and MSNBC, catering to conservatives and liberals, respectively, have driven the people into their party corners? The answer is probably yes to all three questions.

Party caucus: A meeting of all House or Senate members of one or the other main party, usually to discuss political and policy strategies.

Partisanship: Taking the side of a party, or espousing a viewpoint that reflects a political party's principles or position on an issue. Cheered by political scientists (for giving people real choice) but decried by political reformers who wish the parties would work together.

TABLE 9.3 Party Control of U.S. National Institutions Since 2000

ELECTION YEAR	CONTROL OF PRESIDENCY	PARTY IN CONGRESSIONAL MAJORITY (SIZE OF MAJORITY)	
		SENATE	HOUSE
2000	**R (Bush)**	**50–50 (later +1 D)***	R (9 seats)
2002	R (Bush)	**R (2 seats)****	R (24 seats)
2004	R (Bush)	R (10 seats)	R (29 seats)
2006	R (Bush)	**D (2 seats)**	**D (37 seats)**
2008	**D (Obama)**	D (19/20 seats)	D (79 seats)
2010	D (Obama)	D (6 seats)	**R (49 seats)**
2012	D (Obama)	D (10 seats)	R (34 seats)
2014	D (Obama)	**R (8 seats)**	R (59 seats)
2016	**R (Trump)**	R (4 seats)	R (45 seats)
2018	R (Trump)	R (3 seats)***	**D (32 seats)***

Ten changes of control in ten elections is a remarkable level of turnover.

*After May 2001, when Senator Jim Jeffords switched parties, Democrats controlled the Senate.
**Bold denotes party control switched after that year's election.
***As of November 12 with some races undecided

Should we worry about the rise in partisan division? Public opinion surveys repeatedly report dismay at partisan rancor. What exactly are Americans worried about when they express their displeasure?

First, Americans feel that party divisions lead to gridlock—a slowdown in government's ability to get things done. Second, bitter partisanship, as one commentary put it, "breeds bad public policy."[63] Third, a toxic partisan climate is said to drive more public officials away from government service. And fourth, it leads to disenchantment, worrying divisiveness, and the erosion of civil discourse among the public.

Is partisanship really generating these types of bad government outcomes? Some political scientists break with popular wisdom and argue that the fears of partisan breakdown are exaggerated: American government—replete with checks, balances, and federalism—was designed to move incrementally. Delay is part of the normal process. **Divided government** (when at least one house of Congress is controlled by a party different from that occupying the White House) has long been loud, divisive—and unexpectedly productive.[64]

Divided government: Periods during which at least one house of Congress is controlled by a party different from the one occupying the White House.

What Do YOU Think?   Should We Try to Diminish Partisanship?

When Supreme Court Justice Anthony Kennedy resigned, a political war erupted. Conservatives urged President Trump to nominate a real conservative who would tip the balance of the court to the right. Liberals vowed a fierce battle to push for someone more moderate—like Justice Kennedy. What do you think of the partisanship that's fueling this and other debates?

Yes, partisanship is harmful.
It leads to paralysis and extremism. It tempts public office holders—like justices and presidents—to dangerously expand their powers. Worse, it is turning people off from politics, and that will create problems for us in the long run.

No, partisanship is healthy.
President Trump won the election promising to appoint conservative judges. The problems of partisanship originate from strong ideas and close elections. These arguments are useful and part of the democratic process. We should encourage intense views and strong arguments— that's what introduces bold new ideas. People who oppose can have an impact where it counts—at the ballot box!

Maybe.
Some partisanship is useful, but today the parties are taking disagreement too far. Every branch of government must be a mix of strong ideas and compromise.

Today, however most political scientists are drawing a more pessimistic conclusion. The parties clash over almost everything and, increasingly, on every level of government. Divided government increasingly yields political paralysis. And the dangerous result may be that gridlock in Congress drives ever more power to the executive branch.

Which side is right? For now, be aware that there are two sides to the argument about whether rising partisanship is harming American government. However, as the debates go on, social scientists—like the general public—tilt increasingly toward the pessimistic perspective.[65]

The Bottom Line

» The political parties are thriving—and highly competitive. Recent national elections have featured narrow margins of victory in presidential races and frequent shifts in party control.

» This competition has helped fuel a rise in partisan differences, evident among both national policymakers and the U.S. public.

» Most Americans—and many social scientists—believe that partisanship is affecting the quality of American government. The intensity of the conflict, they believe, will weaken our institutions.

ℹ Conclusion: A Political System Ripe for Reform?

Calls for reforming the U.S. political system are as old as the system itself. Today, many people call for new laws that regulate interest groups and reduce partisanship. Here are some popular proposals. Can you think of some others?

1. Regulate Interest Groups

Should we impose tighter regulations on lobbyists? Today, they are governed by restrictions imposed in 1995. The House banned virtually all gifts; the Senate permitted inexpensive trinkets such as T-shirts—up to a value of fifty dollars per year for any senator from a given lobbyist. This **gift ban** law was designed to make it more difficult to "buy" favors from a member of Congress.

Loopholes in the 1995 law swiftly appeared. The House prohibition on lobbyists buying meals for congressional members or their staff was clarified to cover only meals consumed while sitting down, presumably at a restaurant. "Finger food," such as hors d'oeuvres eaten standing up at cocktail parties, slipped through as a legitimate expense—enabling lobbyists to continue sponsoring fundraisers for congressional members and their staffs (who famously love the free food). Lobbyists could also pay for a meal with lawmakers as

Gift ban: A regulation that eliminates (or sharply reduces the dollar amount of) gifts from interest groups to lawmakers.

● Do interest groups representing large corporations have greater access—and therefore power— than other groups? This protester certainly thinks so.

long as the member or staffer was a "personal friend." Imagine how many new friendships were born after that ruling!

Stories like the "finger food exception" inspired Congress to tighten the gift ban and bar former senators from lobbying their old colleagues for two years after leaving the Senate. Yet today, interest groups continue to offer benefits to members of Congress and state legislatures—including overseas junkets.

Maybe the best counter to the influence of lobbyists in Washington is the public going to the polls. Elected representatives are responsible for the policies they make. If they've been influenced to make bad ones, reformers can call them out in a primary or in a general election.

2. Proportional Representation

America's winner-take-all system simply selects the highest vote recipient in each of 435 single-member House districts—and that reduces the number of House or Senate members who are not from one of the two major parties to almost zero. A proportional representation system provides minor parties with representation equivalent to their electoral support. America would soon have representatives of the environmental party, the pro-immigration party, the anti-immigration party, and the libertarians. Would this be a desirable change?

Supporters believe that moving to proportional representation would give voters more choices, possibly increasing voter turnout. It would enhance policymaking by ensuring that a wider spectrum of options is considered, better reflecting the nation's ideological and civic diversity. Many advocates predict that more women and minority-group representatives could be elected. Any state could experiment with this change.[66]

3. Reduce Partisanship in Government

Reformers promoting this approach sometimes call for a "postpartisan" American politics. Ideas include limiting negative campaigning, reducing the role of outside advocacy groups in campaigns (attempts to do so have been struck down by the Supreme Court), and adopting public financing (implemented in a few places, but without notable reduction in partisan polarization).

So far, attempts at unity have been swamped by disagreements. Neither governors nor governed have shown much inclination to change their practice of decrying partisanship while fiercely embracing their party and its ideas. Nor are interest groups likely to diminish in importance or number.

Here is a different way to think about partisanship and interest-group lobbying. Consider first the rich history of party politics in America, extending across six party systems. Those years have often seen a spirit that the Greeks called *agonistic*—a willingness to disagree with your adversaries while acknowledging their views as legitimate. In a democracy, successful political ideas must not just be rationally sound. We must also contest them, and we do this through party competition. Perhaps *stronger* parties, providing clear alternatives and articulating "core commitments" in a forthright way, is an antidote to our current gridlock and hyperpolarization.[67]

Multiplying interest groups, covering most sides of most policy issues, similarly can be a positive force in U.S. government. The expanded number of groups translates into better representation of a wide range of interests. Not *all* interests, to be sure: People seeking assistance from government typically must possess some combination of resources, organization, and a favorable political context.[68] Even so, advocates' ability to negotiate the system—and connect directly to lawmakers and party leaders—means that many Americans and their interests are well represented today.

Ultimately, the United States has always been a nation based on ideas— and intense disagreements about what they mean. Citizens leaping into the fray are essential to democracy. The greatest dangers come not from strongly held views, but from political apathy. If parties and interest groups mobilize Americans and get us involved, that is a significant plus. But if our hyperpartisan and lobbyist-drenched times instead turn people away from government and politics, that represents a real risk. It may take a millennial generation that instinctively seeks *balance*—between work and life, and toward healthy disagreement—to restore what is best in the long American tradition of party and interest-group politics.

CHAPTER SUMMARY

● Interest-group lobbying has long been a vital feature of U.S. government and politics. Interest groups are deeply engaged in all parts of our policymaking system, and groups have sprung up to represent virtually every imaginable professional, personal, and identity-based interest, providing their members with information about federal policies and conveying those members' concerns to Washington.

● Public anxiety centers on interest groups' reputed power to affect policymaking. Groups spend billions of dollars each year to advance their views, and they swarm over Washington (and, increasingly, state capitals) in large numbers. Interest groups are active in all three branches of government; in each, they both seek and provide information—the currency of politics. They also work on (and help finance) political campaigns and are closely intertwined with leadership of both Republican and Democratic parties.

● The United States' two-party style has endured for over two hundred years, with Democrats and Republicans its main standard-bearers since 1856.

● The foundational American ideas and the organization of our elections help explain the

Check your understanding of Chapter 9.

dominance of the two parties. Third parties arise periodically, but none has ever managed to break through and seriously challenge two-party rule.

Need to review key ideas in greater depth? Click here.

● The system of two parties—and the contest between them—regularly shifts as new party systems arise. Each change in party system creates new coalitions of voters and new ideas to inspire the voters.

● A substantial majority of voting-age citizens identifies strongly with one of the two major parties, though a growing number declare themselves independents. The powerful sense of party identification is a result of many factors, including parental influence, political context, and even personality type.

● Party identification in turn helps shape our voting patterns, the way we filter political information, and our bedrock ideas about politics and government.

● Each major party works to unite their key figures and followers under one "big tent." These include the *party in government* (elected politicians, their staffs, and affiliated political professionals); the *party organization* (party chairs, the national committees, and the state party leaders); and the *party in the electorate* (the millions of people who identify with the party).

● Most U.S. citizens—and many social scientists—believe that partisanship and interest-group proliferation are both affecting the quality of the U.S. government. The intensity of the conflict, they warn, will weaken our institutions.

KEY TERMS

Flashcard review.

Base voters, p. 313
Divided government, p. 320
Gift ban, p. 321
Grand Old Party (GOP), p. 310
Hyperpluralism. p. 289
Interest group, p. 285
Iron triangle, p. 293
Issue network, p. 294
K Street, p. 283
Lobbyist, p. 287

New Deal, p. 309
Nonpartisan election, p. 302
Partisanship, p. 318
Party boss, p. 308
Party caucus, p. 318
Party identification, p. 310
Party in government, p. 316
Party in the electorate, p. 317
Party machine, p. 308
Party organization, p. 316

Party platform, p. 316
Party system, p. 303
Pluralism, p. 288
Power elite theory, p. 289
Reverse lobbying, p. 291
Revolving door, p. 294
Special interest, p. 285
Split-ticket voter, p. 313
Straight-ticket voter, p. 313

STUDY QUESTIONS

1. Name the three main theories about the effects of interest groups (pluralism, for example, is one). Describe each. Which strikes you as most persuasive?

2. Describe the traditional *iron triangle*. Explain the *issue network* that has now in large part replaced it.

3. Describe three ways that interest groups try to affect Supreme Court decisions.

4. One of the most important elements of lobbying success is gathering information. Explain how and why.

5. What are the two main reasons U.S. politics is usually limited to two political parties?

6. What is proportional representation? In your opinion, should we adopt it in the United States?

7. What is party identification? Name three factors that influence party identification.

8. Describe the factions in each party. Which is the most powerful today? Can you think of any others?

9. Make a strong argument in favor of partisanship. Now summarize the argument against it. Finally, tell us which you agree with and why (and as always, feel free to defend your views).

 Go to **www.oup.com/us/Morone** to find quizzes, flash cards, simulations, tutorials, videos, and other study tools.

10 Congress

HIGH DRAMA ON THE U.S. SENATE FLOOR:

July 28, 2017. After a raucous all-night debate, John McCain—military hero, Republican presidential nominee, and recently diagnosed with the brain cancer that would claim his life a year later—strode into the chamber. His was the decisive vote on a bill to repeal the Affordable Care Act, a President Trump campaign promise and GOP priority. Two Republicans had already voted "no" on repeal, joining all 48 Democratic senators. McCain paused as the chamber held its breath; instead of speaking his vote, he extended his arm . . . and turned his thumb down, signifying a "nay" vote.

The bill had failed. The ACA would continue to provide affordable health insurance to more than 20 million Americans. And the U.S. Senate again proved to be an institution where deliberation and compromise sometimes balance partisan loyalty.

The ACA story began a decade earlier, in the House of Representatives. Over four months, three different House committees produced two different bills: Then House Speaker Nancy Pelosi (D-CA)—the first female Speaker in American history—combined elements of both bills into a single act. Pelosi and her top lieutenants met with House coalitions: conservative Blue Dogs, the liberal Progressive Caucus, the Congressional Black Caucus, the Hispanic Caucus, abortion opponents, and others. Each wanted to change the bill. After bargaining for seven feverish months, Pelosi brought the legislation to the House floor; after a fierce all-day debate, the legislation squeaked through by a vote of 220 to 215 as the clock neared midnight.

In the Senate (with 100 members), two more committees produced two *more* bills—making five different versions, each one topping a thousand pages. The Senate majority leader, Harry Reid (D-NV), then hammered out a compromise Senate-style: Reid met not with separate groups but one by one with individual senators, searching for the magic 60 votes. After eight months of negotiating, an exhausted Senate voted yes early on

● *U.S. Senate Majority Leader Mitch McConnell (R-KY), flanked by fellow Senate leaders, speaks to reporters. Bitter party polarization in recent years, which resulted in legislative inaction, has led scholars to term the modern Congress a "broken branch" of government.*

December 24, 2009. Now, the House and Senate had to negotiate the differences between their bills, requiring three more months of horse trading.

Throughout the entire process, only one Republican voted for the legislation – though party pressure forced him to change his mind before the final tally. When the ACA finally passed, Republicans immediately introduced a bill to repeal the new law and scheduled dozens more repeal votes over the next several years.[1]

Many analysts now dub Congress the "broken branch" of American government. They criticize the House and the Senate for their archaic rules and dysfunctional gridlock. "The Senate has literally forgotten how to function," sighed Senator Angus King (Independent-ME), in 2018. "We're like a high school team that hasn't won a game in five years."[2]

As the McCain drama testifies, even after the 2016 election—with Republicans controlling both chambers of Congress and the presidency—the Capitol Hill stalemate on most major issues continued. Congress did pass more than 200 bills and resolutions in both 2017 and 2018, including a sweeping tax cut. But commentators on left and right alike emphasized what *was not* accomplished across President Trump's first two years, from ACA repeal to major infrastructure improvements to the president's wall along the U.S./Mexican border.

Who are we? A vibrant people who are suspicious of government. Congress builds that suspicion into its governing process. Is Congress indeed "the broken branch of government"? Or does it reflect the American spirit by slowing down policymaking and ensuring that deliberation and stability reign?

Assess current debates on healthcare.

Introducing Congress

The Constitution places Congress at the center of American government. The document's first and longest article provides a detailed accounting of legislative organization and authority (Table 10.1).

This is a formidable set of powers. For most of American history, Congress ruled. After the Civil War, President Andrew Johnson brooded in the White House while Congress passed bills redefining the nation, including the postwar constitutional amendments ending slavery and guaranteeing voting rights to black Americans. A half-century later, when Senator Warren Harding won the presidential election of 1920, one of his old Senate buddies told him to "sign whatever bills the Senate sends you . . . and don't send bills for the Senate to pass."[3]

By the middle of the twentieth century, however, Congress had become increasingly deferential to the White House, especially in foreign affairs. Today, the nation looks first to the president to manage the economy, deploy troops,

BY THE NUMBERS

Congress

Percentage of Americans who approved of Congress, fall 2018 polls	19[4]
Percentage who approved of Congress, fall 1998	55
Percentage of House members reelected in 2018	93
Percentage of Senators reelected in 2018	88
Number of bills considered by 115th Congress, 2017–2018 (as of November 12, 2018)	10,689
Number considered by 95th Congress, 1977–1978	18,045[5]
Number of African Americans in the Senate, 1950	0
Number of African Americans in the Senate, 2019	3
Number of women in the House of Representatives, 1949	7
Percentage of those women who were Republicans, 1949	57
Number of women in the House of Representatives, 2019 (as of November 12, 2018)	102
Percentage of those women who were Republicans, 2019 (as of November 12, 2018)	16
Annual salary for member of Congress	$174,000
The House Speaker's annual salary	$223,500

Members of Congress collectively look more like the nation they represent, churn out thousands of bills each year, and are paid far less than leaders in other fields (business, nonprofits, academia). Yet public approval ratings for Congress are at rock bottom. How do you explain Americans' disdain for Congress?

TABLE 10.1 **Constitutional Powers of Congress**

From Article 1, Section 8 (unless otherwise noted).*
Financial. Raise revenue through taxes and borrowing, pay national debts, "provide for the common defense and general welfare," and regulate trade and commerce among the American states and with other countries.
Legal. Establish U.S. citizenship laws, regulate bankruptcy laws, issue U.S. money, punish counterfeiters, establish a patent system, fix national weights/measures standards, and enact laws subject to presidential approval. Impeach presidents and federal judges.
Institutional. Organize the judicial and executive branches, establish a postal system (Article 2, Sec. 2), set up and control the national capital (Washington, DC, since 1797), admit new states, and exercise control over U.S. territories (Article 3, Sec. 3). Alter or amend the time, place, and manner of states' election laws related to congressional elections (Article I, Sec. 4).
National defense. Declare war, regulate rules for prisoners of war, and raise and fund the U.S. Army, Navy, and other defense forces.
Additional congressional powers are provided by constitutional amendment. For example, the Thirteenth (1865), Fourteenth (1868), and Fifteenth (1870) Amendments authorize Congress to enforce African Americans' civil rights, as you read in Chapter 5.

address crises, and pursue policy objectives. We call the Affordable Care Act "Obamacare," and credit President Trump for the 2017–18 tax cut, even though Congress worked out most of the details on each.

Still, Congress remains near the center of American government. Presidents may command more public attention, but they need cooperation from the House and Senate to advance their policies. We judge presidents in part on whether their programs win approval from Congress, as explained in Chapter 11. Moreover, Congress's importance extends far beyond the vital responsibility of lawmaking. As much as any other institution in U.S. government, it is Congress that answers the question, *Who are we?*

Two Chambers, Different Styles

Congress reflects two faces of the American people in its basic makeup. Like most other national legislatures, Congress is bicameral, comprising two "houses" or chambers. The larger *House of Representatives* includes 435 members, divided among the states based on population size, along with six nonvoting delegates from Washington, DC, Puerto Rico, Guam, and other U.S. territories. All House members serve two-year terms, and each represents a district of approximately 730,000 people.

The House is organized around a relatively clear set of rules and procedures. The majority party wields centralized control through a powerful leadership team. In the **116th Congress** (2019–2020), Democrats won the majority; this positioned Democratic leader Nancy Pelosi to become Speaker of the House and to control which issues reach the **floor**, and frequently to get them passed.

116th Congress: The Congress elected in November 2018, meeting in 2019–2020. The first Congress met in 1789–1790. Each Congress is elected for two years and numbered consecutively.

Floor: The full chamber, either in the House or the Senate. A bill "goes to the floor" for the final debate and vote, usually after approval by one or more committees.

The Senate is made up of 100 members, two from each U.S. state, each elected for a six-year term. The Democrats lost the Senate in 2014; Republicans retained a majority after 2018. An old truism (attributed to Mark Twain) declared "every senator a little king."[6] To this day, each Senator possesses a remarkable degree of autonomy. Any senator—even the most junior—is able to halt the entire body's consideration of a bill merely by placing a **legislative hold** on it.

For example, the Senate must vote to approve every U.S. ambassador nominated by the president. Normally, this is a routine formality. Cassandra Butts, an experienced government worker, was proposed in 2014 as new ambassador to the Bahamas. She excitedly awaited confirmation. Months, then years passed: First one senator put a hold on all State Department nominations, then Senator Tom Cotton (R-Arkansas) put holds on Butts as well as two other proposed ambassadors. What troubled Senator Cotton? A complaint about a Secret Service leak of private information, unrelated to Butts or the Bahamas. Cotton wanted the administration's attention, so he did what any senator may: halted the body with a one-man veto.[7]

Films, such as *Mr. Smith Goes to Washington*, feature a noble **filibuster**— "democracy's finest show"—a lone senator standing up bravely for justice. But much of the time filibusters or holds involve narrowly focused issues, such as Senator Cotton's. Actual public filibusters—taking the floor and speaking for hours—have largely disappeared from the Senate. Instead, senators quietly issue a legislative hold by informing the leadership that they object to a particular bill.

The two congressional chambers present a familiar contrast. Americans, as we saw in Chapter 1, embrace direct democracy—and the centralized House can move swiftly on national legislative priorities. Americans also fear government power and seek stability: Enter the independent senators, slowing legislation down with filibusters and holds. Legend has it that Thomas Jefferson, who had been in Paris during the Constitutional Convention, asked George Washington why the Constitution established two chambers in Congress. "Why," responded Washington, "do you pour your tea into the saucer?" "To cool it," replied Jefferson. "Just so," returned Washington, "we pour House legislation into the senatorial saucer to cool it." Whether the exchange actually took place, it captures the traditional contrast between House and Senate.[8]

Is today's Senate too good at the task of cooling legislation? Cooperation between the two parties, essential for getting around the filibuster or hold, has diminished—the tone in the once courtly Senate increasingly

Legislative hold: An informal way for a senator to object to a bill or other measure. The action effectively halts Senate proceedings on that issue, sometimes for weeks or longer.

Filibuster: Rule unique to the U.S. Senate that allows any senator to hold the floor indefinitely and thereby delay a vote on a bill. Ended only when 60 senators vote for cloture.

● *Swearing in a new Congress.*

See two filibuster versions: Senator Smith's noble moment, in the movie *Mr. Smith Goes to Washington* and a real-life example from then-Senator Rand Paul. latter: https://www.youtube.com/watch?v=E1_9nSzG_hk

resembles the partisan House. Across the United States, schoolteachers, police officers, and everyone else dependent on federal funding had to wait for agonizing months in 2017 while the Senate and House bickered over a federal budget while missing deadline after deadline. Imagine trying to plan a statewide vaccination program or organize a Mars launch with no idea what your budget will be. Do we need a more nimble, responsive government in the twenty-first century? Or is the senatorial function of slowing things down more important than ever?[9]

The House and Senate Each Have Unique Roles

The Constitution also grants each branch a measure of unique authority. All budget measures must originate in the House. The House holds the power to impeach public officials—including the president—for "high crimes and misdemeanors." After the House impeaches (or indicts) an office holder, the Senate holds a trial and decides whether to remove them. The Senate also has exclusive authority over two important matters. The president negotiates treaties with other countries, but the Senate must approve them by a two-thirds majority. Sixty-seven votes is a very high bar in today's politics, and presidents have found creative ways around it.

The Senate also has sole power to review presidential appointments—the Constitution calls it "advice and consent." Each nominee for the Supreme Court, for example, must win Senate confirmation. Here is another place where some political scientists see a broken branch: Although in the minority, Democrats delayed or blocked more than 100 of President Trump's nominees for judiciary and executive-branch positions in 2017 and 2018—just as Senate Republicans had blocked 73 Obama judicial nominees in 2016. Again the question: A broken branch? Or healthy limits on presidential power?

What Do YOU Think?   Senate Filibusters and Legislative Holds

	Yes.	**No.**	**Not sure.**
President Donald Trump is the latest in a long line of critics to demand the Senate end its distinctive filibuster rule.[10] Should senators be allowed to hold up legislative initiatives until their opposition can round up 60 votes to stop their stalling action? What do you think?	Filibusters and holds ensure independence and protect minority rights. They are also a time-honored tradition. They force the two parties to work together.	The 60-vote rule makes a mockery of majority rule and causes gridlock, slowing policymaking to a crawl. Today, the minority often refuses to work with the majority regardless of the issue. It is time to rewrite Senate rules and end the filibuster and legislative hold.	Ponder this question as you read the rest of the chapter.

» Congressional powers, as granted under the Constitution, are extensive and clearly defined.

» America's Congress is bicameral: The House has 435 members (plus six nonvoting members), elected every two years. The 100 senators serve six-year terms.

» House and Senate work together in many areas, most notably passing legislation; each chamber has distinctive powers, such as the Senate's sole authority to approve presidential appointments and treaties.

» The two chambers of Congress reflect different national priorities. Populists appreciate the responsive House; advocates of stability embrace the more deliberate Senate, where rules such as the filibuster and hold make it more difficult to pass legislation.

» Less legislation and more partisanship have Congress watchers debating: Is this a broken branch of government?

Congressional Representation

Members of Congress represent their constituents in multiple ways. They must live in the same state or district—which is known as *geographic* representation. They may share views about political issues—or *substantive* representation. Some also resemble the people they represent in terms of race, ethnicity, gender, age, national origin, and so on, termed *descriptive* representation.[11]

Access an interactive map of African Americans in the House and Senate throughout U.S. history.

Does Congress Reflect America?

A half-century ago, every senator was white. Only two African American members sat in the House of Representatives. Today, Congress more closely resembles the country it represents—in some respects.

As Figure 10.1 shows, the Congressional Black Caucus (one of several **congressional caucus** groups) has grown to over fifty members (including nonvoting representatives from Washington, DC, and the Virgin Islands). Latinos entered Congress more slowly, but their recent rise in numbers is also striking. Forty members are Hispanic. More than a dozen members are Asian and four are Native American. Despite the growth, Congress has a long way to go before it reflects America. Overall, only 22 percent of the House and just 9 percent of the Senate are members of racial minorities—compared to 36.7 percent of the population.

Among historically underrepresented groups, the number of women in Congress has risen most rapidly. In 1980, there were 17 women in the House; in 2019, the number was over 100—more than 23 percent of all members. In the Senate in 2019, there were a record twenty-four women—nearly a quarter of the chamber. These numbers are rising—but still a far cry from parity.

Congressional caucus: A group of House or Senate members who convene regularly to discuss common interests; they may share political outlook, race, gender, or geography.

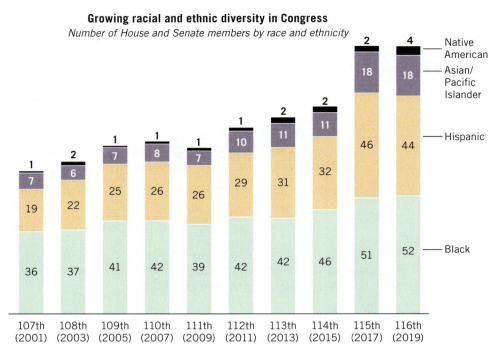

Growing racial and ethnic diversity in Congress
Number of House and Senate members by race and ethnicity

Native American
Asian/ Pacific Islander
Hispanic
Black

107th (2001) 108th (2003) 109th (2005) 110th (2007) 111th (2009) 112th (2011) 113th (2013) 114th (2015) 115th (2017) 116th (2019)

● **Figure 10.1** *Growing racial and ethnic diversity in Congress.* (Pew Research Center; authors' compilation)

The United States ranks below the top 90 among legislatures around the globe on the percentage of women in the larger national chamber. Yet some marvel at how things are changing.

The religious makeup of Congress has changed dramatically over the last half-century. Until recently, it was overwhelmingly Protestant. Today, Catholics make up nearly a third of Congress (reflecting their proportion of the population); Jews make up 5 percent of the House and 8 percent of the Senate (more than twice the percentage in the population); there are 17 Mormons, four Muslims, two Buddhists, one Hindu, and one atheist in Congress today.

How important is descriptive representation? If you are a conservative, evangelical woman who deeply believes in the right to life, you may be dismayed that Nancy Pelosi (a liberal who strongly supports abortion rights) is the most powerful woman in the House. She represents you descriptively (you are both women) but not substantively (you share few ideas or policy preferences). You might say that Speaker Pelosi does not represent your interests at all.

Trustees and Delegates

Each member of Congress faces the same conundrum: Do what you think is right? Or do what your constituents want?

Do the Right Thing. One view holds that representatives owe us their expertise and judgment. They possess considerably more information than their constituents. Just like your doctor or your lawyer, your House and Senate members' job is to pursue what is best for you. And if you disagree with the result, you can vote for their opponent in the next election. This perspective, as we saw in Chapter 2, is known as the *trustee* view of representation.

Do What the People Want. Another view holds that true representation involves House or Senate members faithfully following popular preferences. A lot of congressional choices involve basic values. You do not need more information to know how you feel about the right to own guns, or whether healthcare is a universal human right. A legislator, according to this view, should take voting instructions directly from his or her constituents. This is the *delegate* view of representation.

Political scientists recognize that the rules help tilt individuals one way or another (the institutional perspective again).[12] When the constitutional framers required House members to run every two years, they favored the delegate view: Pay close attention to the people, or lose your job. Each senator has six years between elections; the rules enable them to think more like trustees, to act as they think best.

What makes for good representation? The theoretical answer is simple: *Representatives effectively pursue their constituents' substantive interests.* The trick comes in figuring out those interests and promoting them through the complicated legislative process. At election time, the people judge whether their members of Congress effectively pursued their interests. To political scientists, this is how a well-operating representative system works.

This theorizing barely registers with most members of the House and Senate. They come to Congress with a clear perspective that informs their important votes. They rarely spend time pondering what stance to take on gun rights or on national health insurance. The answers are part of their basic philosophy, forged years before they arrived in Congress. Most politicians do not pander—at least not on large, visible issues. They know what they believe, and they rarely say merely what they think their audience wants to hear.[13] However, a great outcry from the constituency can moderate even strongly held views. Members pay close attention when they receive a loud signal from their constituents.

The Bottom Line

» Members of the House and Senate represent Americans in geographic, descriptive, and substantive ways.

» Along with these different styles of representation, members can act as delegates or trustees. Representatives can faithfully follow what the people want or do as their political experience, instincts, and core principles dictate.

Getting to Congress—And Staying There

How do members of Congress spend their days? From occasional glimpses of C-SPAN you may imagine Congress as a sustained feast of debates, but members of the House and the Senate spend relatively little time on the floor. Table 10.2 displays the typical workweek of a member of the House. Not a lot of time left for quietly contemplating the major issues of the day, is there?

The Permanent Campaign

Congressional members spend extensive time on the campaign trail. House members face the voters every two years—more frequently than many other national legislatures. Even senators, with a more comfortable six years between races, must keep their campaign operation humming along. Notice, in Table 10.2, that members spend as much time raising money as they do on committee meetings or floor action. Does this constant pressure to attract donations and votes discourage members of Congress, or potential candidates, from running? Most representatives stay in office a long time. And when a seat in either chamber opens because of retirement or death, a lengthy list of office seekers from both parties is usually ready to run.

Recall the Constitutional Convention compromise: House members were elected directly, while senators were to be insulated from the whims of public opinion and chosen by state legislatures. Not until 1913 did the public vote for senators, when the Seventeenth Amendment was ratified. Did the state legislatures pick more elevated senators than the people did? Not necessarily.

TABLE 10.2 **Average Division of Time of a U.S. House Member**

Meeting with staff (mostly in Washington)	19%
Meeting with constituents (mostly in district)	19%
Ceremonial events (in district; some in Washington)	13%
Fundraising calls/meetings	11%
Committee meetings (hearings, member meetings)	8%
Floor action (votes, debates, morning business)	7%
Office work (email, reading, legislative drafting)	6%
Informal talks (with colleagues, lobbyists, media)	6%
Caucus meetings (all-party or subgroup gatherings)	5%
Other (miscellaneous)	5%
Source: Congressional Management Foundation	

In the very first congressional elections, Virginia's legislature passed over James Madison for the Senate; the people of his district had better sense and elected him to the House, where he immediately pushed through the Bill of Rights.

Another important influence on House elections is **reapportionment**. Every ten years the U.S. census determines which states have gained or lost population, and because each district must be the same size, House seats are reapportioned accordingly. In 2010, Texas gained four new seats, Florida gained two, and New York and Ohio each lost two. The new districts are drawn by the state legislature, and fierce political battles surround the way the lines are drawn (as we saw in Chapter 8).

Home Style: Back in the District

Members of Congress spend a lot of time back in their district or state. Often they are literally returning home to families who have decided to stay in Seattle or St. Louis or Scranton, rather than move to Washington. Today, more than 100 House members, most of them conservative Republicans, proudly refuse to settle into a Washington residence and sleep on a cot in their office. Most members leave Capitol Hill on Thursday evenings and only return on Monday evening or even Tuesday morning.

Back home, members are kept hopping. District staff line up events for members to meet with constituents, give talks about Washington issues, cut ribbons on new office buildings or schools, visit with local party leaders and elected officials, and raise funds for their next election. Senators and House members, while in Washington, often hold Facebook or Skype meetups with constituents—reflecting the importance of staying in touch.

A Government of Strangers

Through the twentieth century, members of Congress lived in Washington. Senators or representatives worked together during the day and socialized during evenings and weekends. In fact, a bar for members, called the Hole in the Wall, was located between the House and Senate chambers.

Today, most legislators are not in Washington long enough to get to know one another. They dash in, spend three days packed with congressional business, and dash home. This schedule makes it more difficult for Congress to get things done, because it is now a collection of strangers. The tortured legislative process—described at this chapter's start—is further complicated by diminished personal ties.

Why do members rush home each week? Because it helps them win reelection—an ever-present concern. When political scientists explain and predict congressional behavior, they often assume that reelection is a member's primary or even only goal.[14] Although many members genuinely pursue their political ideals, the pressure for reelection significantly shapes congressional behavior.

Reapportionment: Reorganization of the boundaries of House districts, a process that follows the results of the U.S. census, taken every ten years. District lines are redrawn to ensure rough equality in the number of constituents represented by each House member.

The Bottom Line

» Members of Congress are always running for office. Fundraising takes up a huge amount of time and attention.

» Members pay special attention to their home style: Most go back to their constituency every week—compressing normal congressional business into the period from Tuesday through Thursday.

» Congress has become an institution of strangers. Most members focus intensely much of the time on reelection.

Congress at Work

When members of the House and Senate do gather in Washington, they have a staggering to-do list: managing the nation's legislative business, investigating executive branch activities, staging public hearings about everything from auto safety to U.S. aid to Zimbabwe. And raising money for reelection. How—and where—do they accomplish all that work?

The City on the Hill

The huge Capitol building is perched on an actual hill; its majestic marble dome dominates the Washington skyline. Traditionally, no building in the District of Columbia except the Washington Monument may be taller. The Capitol building is also the heart of a small city within a city. Six grand office buildings house the members and their staff. Three ornate structures house the Library of Congress, which has mushroomed from Thomas Jefferson's personal book collection into the world's largest library.

This City on the Hill includes a dozen restaurants, two gyms, a chapel, a bank, a post office, and a warren of "hideaways": small unmarked offices for senior members. Add another half-dozen staff buildings, several elegant townhouses rented most nights for fundraising events, a small high school for congressional pages—young men and women who run errands on the House and Senate floor—and even a subway, to shuttle members back and forth between their office buildings and the congressional chambers.

Inhabitants of this "city" include the 541 members of Congress, along with more than 22,000 staff members, who range from well-paid senior policy experts to summer interns; the 250-member Capitol police force; and the U.S. poet laureate, appointed by Congress. And do not forget the thousands of lobbyists. It all adds up to a very busy place.

How much are members paid? As of 2019, the rate is $174,000 for House and Senate members, a figure frozen since 2009.[15] Leaders earn a slightly higher salary; The House Speaker is the highest paid at $223,500. Constituents

TABLE 10.3 Annual Average Salaries by Profession

CEO, top 500 company	$13.9 million
NBA player	$7.1 million
NFL player	$2.7 million
U.S. president	$400,000
Surgeon	$251,890
Senior U.S. executive branch official (capped since 2010)	$199,700
Member of Congress	**$174,000**
Lawyer	$147,950
Personal financial advisor	$124,140
Pharmacist	$121,710
Aerospace engineer	$115,300
Political scientist	$98,620
Web developer	$74,110
Elementary school teacher	$60,830
Plumber	$57,070
Child/family social worker	$48,430

Sources: Sporting Intelligence; Bureau of Labor Statistics (March 2018 report); U.S. Office of Personnel Management

frequently complain that congressional salaries are too high. But comparable leaders in other areas—from business managers to academic deans—are paid much more (see Table 10.3). If your professional aim is to make money, running for Congress is not your best bet.

Congressional staff members are a major presence in this company town. As Congress became more professional after World War II, it saw a steady increase in assistants, researchers, committee experts, legal counsel, and the like. By the 1990s, House and Senate staff leveled off at around 27,000; the number is about 22,000 today. Many college graduates take entry-level positions, because there are many opportunities to move up quickly. We have both worked on Capitol Hill—it is an exciting job for the men and women, many right out of college, who dominate staff positions.

New Hill staffers soon hear the question: *"Who are you with?"* Working for a congressional leader, a committee chair, or a nationally known figure can catapult even new staffers up the Washington pecking order.

Capitol Hill life runs on a unique rhythm. Congress usually remains in session, apart from holidays, from the beginning of January through early August;

Talking POLITICS

CAPITOL HILL BUZZWORDS

Christmas tree: A bill packed with "riders," or benefits for constituents: a dam in one district, a new government building in another, and a science lab at a state university.

Must-pass: A bill considered so vital that Congress *has* to enact it, such as legislation funding the annual operations of the U.S. government. Because of this necessity, must-pass items are loaded up with "rider" items (see "Christmas tree," above).

Senate Swamp: Area across from the Capitol's Senate steps where one or more Senators gather for media appearances on hot topics; often issue-based rallies are held in the "Swamp" as well.

● *Congressional staff at work. With C-SPAN on TV in the foreground, staffers discuss a key upcoming vote in 2018.*

members return after Labor Day and rush to finish for the year in early October during election (even-numbered) years. In non-election years, the session lasts longer—Obamacare passed the Senate on December 24, 2009. When in session, the Hill buzzes with action, especially when members are in residence Tuesday through Thursday.

Members of Congress know that they stand in the vortex of history. Every move—such as the deep bow made by clerks carrying House bills to the Senate and vice versa—reflects a legacy that may stretch as far back as the Virginia House of Burgesses, which first convened in 1619.

Minnows and Whales: Congressional Leadership

When Lyndon Johnson (D-TX) served as Senate majority leader in the 1950s, he divided colleagues into two camps: "whales," who could enact landmark legislation, and "minnows," who dutifully followed. Most whales are chairs of important committees or part of the formal leadership structure.

The House and Senate feature very different leadership styles. The smaller, more collegial Senate—where any member, again, can bring the entire body to a halt—usually requires patient, consensus-minded leadership. Majority leaders do not so much lead as manage Senate procedures, cajoling proud senators to move legislation along. Recently, the traditionally consensual Senate has begun to behave more like the partisan House, making it still harder to forge agreements. The larger House, run on majoritarian principles, permits much tighter central control from the Speaker and other top leaders.

House Leadership

Democrats and Republicans each choose a party leader from their ranks. When a new Congress opens after an election (in January of odd-numbered years), the majority party votes its leader to the top post in Congress, the **Speaker of the House**. The Speaker serves as the public face of the House. He or she is simultaneously an administrative officer, a political spokesman, and a party leader.

As chief administrative officer of the House, the Speaker presides over the chamber on special occasions (e.g., when a president delivers the State of the Union address to Congress). The Speaker rules on procedural issues, chooses members for committees, assigns legislation to committees, and "maintains order and civility"—although civility is increasingly difficult to sustain.

The Speaker sets the House's agenda and determines which bills are considered and when. Speakers negotiate with the Senate and the executive branch.

Speaker of the House:
The chief administrative officer in the House of Representatives.

And they help manage the Rules Committee, which sets the terms of the debate for every piece of legislation that reaches the House floor. The Speaker sometimes works with Rules to hold the majority together or to derail opposition on important votes.

As leader of the majority party, the Speaker also spins issues in their party's favor and serves as the party's public face. That leads the opposition to portray them as ruthless partisans. It takes a nimble politician to juggle the different roles the Speaker must play. Speaker John Boehner tried to build consensus in the party, but was toppled after five years in 2015 by ultra-conservative young Republicans impatient for change.[16]

● *Departing House Speaker Paul Ryan (R-WI) announces his retirement in 2018. The 2018 midterm elections positioned Democratic House leader Nancy Pelosi to take over.*

The House majority leader, as second in command, acts as the majority party's floor manager, negotiator, and spokesperson. The majority leader also serves as the Speaker's eyes and ears, tracking party members' actions and preferences. Steny Hoyer (D-MD) currently holds this position. Aiding the Speaker and majority leader is the majority whip, responsible for party discipline, who utilizes a loyal team to determine party members' position on issues and ensures that they vote as the leadership directs. The majority whip leads a team of nine deputy whips, each responsible for members from a different region.

The minority has the same leadership structure, with one big difference: no Speaker. The top Republican in the 116th Congress, minority leader Kevin McCarthy (R-CA), is joined by the minority whip in trying to thwart the Democratic majority. All leaders must do a lot of arm-twisting and deal-cutting to persuade colleagues to vote the party line.

Senate Leadership

To lead the Senate, take all the difficulties involved in managing the House—and quadruple them. Senate rules, such as the filibuster and the hold, give each individual senator a great deal of autonomy. The Senate leadership must turn to personal skills, especially expert negotiation, to advance their party's goals.

The senators elect a majority leader—currently Mitch McConnell (R-KY)—who does not even formally preside over the chamber. The Constitution gives that job to the vice president. In practice, vice presidents rarely show up in the Senate, appearing for very important votes (to break a possible tie) and on ceremonial occasions. Likewise, the **president pro tempore**—currently Charles Grassley (R-IA)—has presiding authority at certain formal occasions. Otherwise, every senator presides in turn over the body, serving rotating half-hour stints. A staff member stands by the presiding member's side, helping him

President pro tempore:
Majority party senator with the longest Senate service.

or her to negotiate the complex rules (with a pedal that shuts off the microphone if the presiding Senator gets confused).

Senate whips from both the majority and minority parties serve the same functions as in the House—though they command much less power to demand party discipline, owing to the Senate's individualistic ways. This difficulty extends to the majority leader. It is hard to set the Senate's agenda or command floor action in a context of unlimited debate and amendments, with the constant threat of a hold or filibuster. Majority leaders and their team mostly influence which policies will be considered on the Senate floor, and in what order, usually in consultation with the minority leader.

Committees: Workhorses of Congress

Learn about your representatives and the committees they serve on.

The regular duties of congressional lawmaking play out mainly in committees. Committees draft legislation, sponsor hearings, oversee the executive branch, and draft the federal budget. Every year, the administration sends its priorities to Congress. Leadership duly assigns issues to committees, where many die a quiet death.

The Enduring Power of Committees

Table 10.4 lists the types of congressional committees. The basic committee structures and operation have been remarkably resilient, despite decades of pressure for reform. How have they managed to duck calls for change?

Two reasons: First, inertia—it is hard to remake Congress, given the layers of tradition and complex rules. Second, in their own way, committees work. The committee system permits busy members to each become an expert on a narrow range of topics (especially in the House, where members typically serve on one primary committee). Committees enable Congress to devise fairly sophisticated legislative solutions to the many issues competing for attention.

The committee system is yet another way American government separates powers. It means that Congress winds up with multiple centers of authority, making the legislative process slower and harder for the public to follow. But

TABLE 10.4 Congressional Committee Types

Standing committees: Permanent bodies, with fixed jurisdiction (Table 10.5 lists them all). House and Senate standing committees vary widely in prestige: The oldest are traditionally the most influential, though some newer ones (such as Intelligence, created after 9/11 in both chambers) deal with significant topics. Standing committees are further divided into multiple *subcommittees*, organized around areas of expertise.
Select committees: Created for a defined time to investigate a particular issue; also called *special committees*.
Joint committees: Made up of both House and Senate members to address topics of continuing importance. These committees can remain in place for decades; the Joint Committee on Taxation has existed since 1971, for example. *Conference committees*, introduced later in this chapter, are temporary joint committees, created to consider a specific piece of legislation.

the division of labor allows an institution—with distracted, busy members—to accomplish more. The 115th Congress was able to dispatch more than 10,500 bills, although that number was nearly twice as high forty years ago.

The standing committees (see Table 10.5) provide a main avenue to send favored services, or "pork," home to a representative's district. Members of the Appropriations Committee—which decides how U.S. funds are spent—are informally called "cardinals," like the ruling cadre in the Vatican. Other members

TABLE 10.5 **House and Senate Permanent Standing Committees, 116th Congress (2019–20)**

U.S. HOUSE COMMITTEES	U.S. SENATE COMMITTEES
Agriculture	Aging (Special)
Appropriations	Agriculture, Nutrition, and Forestry
Armed Services	Appropriations
Budget	Armed Services
Education and the Workforce	Banking, Housing, and Urban Affairs
Energy and Commerce	Budget
Ethics	Commerce, Science, and Transportation
Financial Services	Energy and Natural Resources
Foreign Affairs	Environment and Public Works
Homeland Security	Ethics (Select)
House Administration	Finance
Intelligence (Permanent Select)	Foreign Relations
Judiciary	Health, Education, Labor, and Pensions
Natural Resources	Homeland Security and Governmental Affairs
Oversight and Government Reform	Indian Affairs
Rules	Intelligence (Permanent Select)
Science, Space, and Technology	Judiciary
Small Business	Rules and Administration
Transportation and Infrastructure	Small Business and Entrepreneurship
Veterans' Affairs	Veterans' Affairs
Ways and Means	

Earmark: A legislative item usually included in spending ("appropriations") bills that directs Congress to fund a particular item in a district or state.

approach them to request **earmarks** in the form of items in appropriations bills: a dam in one district, funds for highway construction in another. Appropriations members saw their power diminished in 2012, after Congress's decision to outlaw earmarks; within a year, however, Congress found creative ways to fund the practice.

The committee system makes Congress far more efficient. But there is also a harsher reality. Committees fragment Congress into small fiefdoms, hide action from public view, and make it easier to do favors for well-placed constituents (a tax break or a phone call to get a pesky regulator to back off). The fragmentation also makes it more difficult to pass major legislation or to address large national problems. Only about 6 percent of the bills and proposals assigned to committees ever make it to the floor.

The organization of Congress again raises the dilemmas of American democracy: Is the system biased toward the powerful? Does the bias against action frustrate the popular will or simply reflect Americans' wariness of government (or both)?

Leadership and Assignments

After the 2018 Congressional election, many House members found excuses to check in with the new Speaker: They were jockeying for committee assignments. The Speaker is a key player in assigning members (and chairs) to each committee—a vital decision, given the power committees wield. Each party votes on members' committee assignments, and seniority remains a vital factor in determining chairs, but decisions require the Speaker's blessing. Over in the Senate, assignments involve more give-and-take but ultimately rest in the majority leader's hands. Minority party assignments are recommended by minority leaders in both chambers.

Members compete fiercely to join the most influential committees. Once they are on a committee, representatives and senators often stay for many years—gaining power and influence, and aspiring to become chair. Traditionally (but not always), the chair is the longest serving committee member. Members generally seek to join committees that reflect the concerns of their district. When political scientist David Price (D-NC) won a seat in Congress in 1993, he requested a seat on the House Banking (now Financial Services) Committee. Why? Because his district had a strong banking and financial services sector.[17]

Committees can bury a bill, completely rewrite it, report out an unrealistic version, or boost the chances of success with a strong bill. Skilled committee chairs broaden the jurisdiction of their committee by claiming pieces of bills. As we saw in the chapter opening, five different committees shaped Obamacare. Each committee has its own process and political slant.

Jurisdictional squabbles can erupt into battles for influence between committees when their responsibilities overlap. The House and the Senate each have different committees for Homeland Security, Intelligence, and Foreign Affairs. Sometimes they all hold hearings on the same issue, and because legislation is assigned to every committee that has jurisdiction over the topic, overlapping authority means multiple committees wrestling to shape the same bill.

The Bottom Line

» Congress resembles a small city. Its residents include the 541 members of Congress, 22,000 staff members, and an army of lobbyists. The city includes its own amenities, traditions, and slang.

» House leadership includes a Speaker, majority and minority leaders, and ten whips. Successful leaders in the House impose discipline on their party members. The Senate allows far more individual action. Party leaders and whips have fewer ways to impose discipline.

» Congressional committees are the efficient, adaptable workhorses of Congress. However, the committee system also fragments Congress, hides action from public view, accommodates constituents seeking individual favors, and makes it difficult to pass major legislation.

Legislative Policymaking

As the Affordable Care Act's convoluted passage testifies, congressional law-making can be boiled down to five words: *Complex process. Difficult to win.* The last decade saw thousands of bills submitted each year (see Figure 10.2). Less than 3 percent made it through the process to become law.

Americans complain about politicians' inability to ban abortion, regulate assault rifles, or reduce the federal budget deficit. Pundits explain these failures by invoking "American culture" or "powerful lobbyists." Here is a more accurate explanation: Congressional rules make it very hard to do any of these things—even when a majority of legislators (and the nation) are in support. Let's find out why by taking a close look at the procedure.

Drafting a Bill

Anyone can petition Congress to consider a bill, but only members of the House and Senate have the right to introduce one. Every piece of legislation

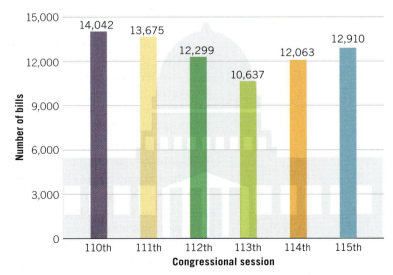

● **Figure 10.2** *Bills and other resolutions introduced in Congress: 115th, as of November 12, 2018. (GovTrack)*

TABLE 10.6	Examples of Creative Legislative Titles
Clarifying Lawful Overseas Use of Data (CLOUD) Act (2018): Allows U.S. law enforcement (with a judge's subpoena) to obtain American citizens' private data from servers anywhere in the world.
EGO (Eliminating Government-Funded Oil-Painting) Act (2013): Ban federal funding of official portraits of government officials.
Personal Responsibility in Consumption Act (2006): Immunize fast-food companies against lawsuits by obese consumers.
What Really Happened Act (2002): Require instant TV replay in all major sports.
Note: Only the first of these bills passed.

needs at least one primary sponsor, whose name is inscribed on the first page. Major bills are often referred to by the sponsors' names, with some creative exceptions (see Table 10.6).

Bills can feature any number of co-sponsors, or members who agree to have their names listed as supporters. The main sponsors usually try to sign on many members, especially powerful ones such as committee chairs, as co-sponsors.

Anything can be introduced as legislation—no matter how peculiar. Congressman Ron Paul (R-TX) once introduced a bill mandating that the Treasury buy a one-inch-wide strip of land stretching down the middle of the United States from Canada to Mexico. All goods or people crossing that line would be charged a toll, eliminating the need for other taxes or government fees. The bill did not make it out of committee.

Bills' sponsors rarely write the legislation themselves. Some bills include language taken from state legislation, or even other countries' parliaments. Senior members adapt junior colleagues' bills for their own use. Many bills go to Congressional Research Service experts for drafting help. Bill drafters also consult outside sources, including executive branch officials, lobbyists, and academics. And members copy themselves; as each new session begins, congressional offices dust off and reintroduce bills that failed last time.

There is a great art to bill drafting, involving major political choices. How much money should we ask for in spending bills? How much can we change current laws? Do we dare test existing constitutional limits? Many bills include bargaining chips—provisions the sponsors are willing to negotiate away to win over skeptics. Legislation to reduce elementary school class sizes may also promise healthier lunches in all public schools. When the serious bargaining starts, nutritious lunches may be dropped to satisfy budget hawks. Drafters are also aware that if the law passes, it may well end up involved in litigation, which puts a premium on clarity and precision.

Once the bill is drafted and the co-sponsors have signed on, it is ready for the next step: submission.

View an example of a congressional bill, its description, supporters, and status.

Submitting the Bill

The Senate typically introduces bills as the legislative day opens, around noon on Tuesdays, Wednesdays, and Thursdays. Let's peek inside the chamber.

The presiding officer taps his or her gavel, bringing the stir of conversation to a halt. Members pause as the Senate chaplain recites a prayer. A bustle breaks out as the chaplain concludes. Routine administrative motions (such as approving records of the previous day's proceedings) are followed by morning-hour statements—short speeches that celebrate home state achievements. A constituent is turning 100 years old, or a softball team won the state title.

Watch closely: A senator snaps her fingers. A page dashes down the aisle, takes the senator's document, and places it in a wooden tray beside the bill clerk. The clerk writes a number on the first page (bills are numbered serially, starting each session with S.1), notes the senator's suggestion for committee referral, and places it in a tray. That night it is printed. A bill has been born!

The House is less ritualized, in keeping with its democratic spirit, but bill introduction continues an old-fashioned practice. Representatives carry proposed bills down to the rostrum. They hand their legislation to the clerk or drop it in a mahogany box, called the "hopper." From there, bills are delivered to the Speaker's office, where they are assigned a number—starting each session with H.R. 1—and referred to committee.

Committee Action

The House leadership normally assigns each bill to committees with jurisdiction over the topic. Once they are assigned a bill, committees perform four major tasks.

1. Committees Hold Hearings on Policy Topics. Witnesses submit written testimony for staff members and reporters; unless they are senior government officials or celebrities, they are limited to a five-minute presentation at the **committee hearing**. When they begin, a little green light goes on; at the four-minute mark, a yellow light goes on. At five minutes, a red light blinks. Nervous rookies stop mid-sentence; veterans ignore the lights and talk serenely on—until the chair bangs the gavel.

The staff assembles a list of who is testifying. Witnesses generally include White House officials and cabinet heads—whose testimony has to be cleared with the Office of Management and Budget (OMB; introduced in Chapter 11).

Celebrities are popular witnesses, attracting media attention. Angelina Jolie

Committee hearing: A way for committees to gather information and gauge members' support for legislation. Hearings usually feature witnesses who submit testimony, make an oral presentation, and answer questions from members of Congress.

● *Celebrity congressional witnesses include . . . Elmo! Elmo "testifies," with the help of music industry executive Joe Lamond, before the House Education Appropriations subcommittee in support of funding for school music programs. When he finished, Elmo tried to eat the microphone.*

has appeared before Congress five times on international aid issues; Kourtney Kardashian spoke to the Senate about safety measures in the cosmetics industry. More often, witnesses include interest-group lobbyists, think tank experts, academics, and pollsters reporting public opinion on the issues.

Hearings also can get tough. When the CEOs of three big U.S. automakers went to Congress for a bailout, Representative Brad Sherman (D-CA) needled them about flying to Washington on corporate jets.

Rep. SHERMAN:	I'm going to ask the three executives here to raise their hand if they flew here commercial.
Mr. MULALLY [Ford CEO],	**(No response.)**
Mr. WAGONER [GM],	
Mr. NARDELLI [Chrysler]:	
Rep. SHERMAN:	Second, I'm going ask you to raise your hand if you're planning to sell your [private] jet . . . and fly back commercial.
Messrs. MULALLY,	**(No response.)**
WAGONER,	
NARDELLI:	
Rep. SHERMAN:	Let the record show no hands went up.
Rep. ACKERMAN:	It's almost like seeing a guy show up at the soup kitchen in [a] tuxedo. . . . I mean, couldn't you all have downgraded to first class or jet-pooled or something to get here?

Other members asked the CEOs if they would give up their hefty compensation packages and work for one dollar a year. Nardelli, the Chrysler chairman, declined with a muttered, "I'm good." The CEOs learned their lesson: When they next testified before Congress, they rode to Washington in cars manufactured by their company.

2. Committees Prepare Legislation for Floor Consideration. Committees are the primary source of policy development in Congress. Members and committee staff, drawing on their collective knowledge, assess and revise each bill that comes before them.

Major rewrites of bills occur in **committee markup sessions**, when the committee gathers to work through the legislation's language, line by line. The result, called a "chairman's mark," is hot property among lobbyists and

Committee markup session: A gathering of a full committee to draft the final version of a bill before the committee votes on it.

reporters; it contains many of the details that will become law if the legislation wins approval.

Following markup, the committee holds a vote on whether to report a bill to the full House or Senate. When the Senate Finance Committee took up a $1.5 trillion tax-reform bill in November 2017, it considered 355 amendments over four days—incorporating nearly 100 before voting to approve by a party-line vote of 14 to 12. All that work in just one Senate committee—and usually at least one other committee is negotiating another version—in this case, the Senate Budget, which plowed through several dozen more amendments before voting 12 to 11 to send an amended tax bill to the Senate floor.

Committee votes are pivotal moments in a bill's career. If a bill is voted down in committee—not reported, in Congress-speak—it is usually dead. Those voted through by a narrow margin face tough sledding on the floor, and the Speaker may decide never to bring the closely divided measure up for a vote.

3. Committees Also Kill Legislation. Of the more than 4,000 bills referred to the 40 House and Senate standing committees each year, only about one in eight sees any action. Items judged less important or not politically viable may be quietly tabled. Some bills are proposed just to win approval back home or otherwise score political points; committees usually bury them swiftly. In the past, bills died in committee without public acknowledgment of how members voted. A key reform of the 1970s required all committees to keep full records of important votes.

4. Committees Exercise Oversight. Congress's work is not done when legislation passes. House and Senate standing committees monitor the executive branch, making sure cabinet departments and agencies perform their roles properly. This supervision can be high-stakes: Oversight hearings investigate scandals; review major issues such as protection against terrorism; and evaluate presidential appointees. Committees also continue to monitor the programs that they have passed: Is the agency spending its budget properly? Are people benefitting from the program?

Floor Action

After a successful bill makes it through all relevant committees, its next stop is the House or Senate floor. Now its chance of becoming law increases dramatically. Of bills that make it to the floor, more than half are enacted. But legislation may take a long time to achieve floor consideration—leaders rarely call up a bill until they think they have the votes to win.

Getting to the Floor. House and Senate floor procedures are very different. After a Senate committee approves a bill, it is placed on the "business calendar," from which it is called up for consideration on a schedule worked out by the majority and minority leaders. Only bills that receive **unanimous consent**—agreement

The House Armed Services Committee holds a 15-hour markup session!

Unanimous consent: A Senate requirement, applied to most of that body's business, that all senators agree before an action can proceed.

● *Senator Susan Collins (R-ME), among a handful of pivotal votes on the 115th Congress's signal legislative achievement, a $1.5 trillion tax bill, surrounded by reporters. The bill was delayed reaching the floor for days while Collins and two other holdout Republican senators pondered how to vote.*

by all senators—can be brought to the floor. One objection and the bill is put on hold.

In the House, majority party leaders exert more control over what makes it to the floor. They may start by rewriting a bill—sometimes because multiple committees cannot come to agreement among themselves. Other times, the majority leadership rewrites legislation to get the measure through.

Once it confirms a bill's language, the House Rules Committee issues a directive governing the floor process: for example, which type of amendments may be proposed. The membership of the Rules Committee is tilted to favor the majority party, and the committee chair works closely with the Speaker to ensure that floor action will follow the leadership's wishes. The Senate, in contrast, allows virtually unlimited consideration on the floor; amendments of all kinds just keep on coming.

In both chambers, once bills make it to the calendar, they can get stuck there—sometimes for an entire session. A logjam of legislation or failure to achieve unanimous consent may be the reason. Or it might be the result of coordination issues between House and Senate, given the requirement that legislation has to move through both chambers. Achieving 100 percent agreement to allow a bill to come up for a vote often involves elaborate negotiations.

On the Floor. Eventually a bill's moment arrives. Supporters hope their measure will be taken up in the House and Senate around the same time, knowing that legislation may only pass one chamber during a session—another form of death sentence. In the 115th Congress, bills to prohibit taxpayer funding for abortion require all states to honor "concealed carry" gun laws, and repeal the Affordable Care Act all sailed through the House—and died when the Senate failed to act on them.

In both chambers, floor action on legislation follows the same procedures. First, a bill is assigned a floor manager—usually the legislation's main sponsor, but on big issues the chair of the committee or subcommittee that reported the bill takes up this role. The manager handles amendments and controls the time for debate. Majority and minority party members each have a specific number of hours and minutes to discuss the legislation, determined in the Senate by agreement between party leaders and in the House by the Rules Committee.

Then the political maneuvers really start. In both the House and Senate, floor action involves amendments, procedural moves, and eventually a final vote—all accompanied by a lot of talk. Members rarely change any votes with

Sponsor a bill on immigration reform and see if you can get it passed.

their eloquence. But floor speeches are not empty oratory. Congress watchers know that who chooses to speak, and what they say, matters. Whips listen closely and adapt their floor strategies to secure a majority in support of party-approved amendments and the vote for passage.

Members of the minority party often express frustration at the leadership's hardball tactics. In 2016, the Senate considered six gun-control measures in the wake of a terrorist mass murder at an Orlando gay dance club. House Republican leaders refused even to hold committee hearings on the issue—leading furious Democratic members to stage a rare sit-in on the House floor.

House rules permit leaders to introduce creative strategies to get their legislation through. They can extend the time allocated for debate (while a few more arms are twisted). They sometimes permit members to vote "yes" on multiple contradictory motions knowing only one (the last vote or the one with the most votes) will really count; this procedural antic permits members to tell angry constituents, "Don't blame me, I voted for that bill!"

Senate leaders, far from inventing new rules, are more likely to breathe a sigh of relief after steering a bill to the floor. There, a further obstacle lurks: the filibuster or legislative hold. A senator may halt all activity in the chamber by refusing to yield the floor or issuing a hold; the only way to stop him or her is through a **cloture vote**, which requires the approval of three-fifths of the Senate—192 votes.

Filibusters used to be rare events. Between 1927 and 1960, there were only 18 efforts to break a filibuster (or cloture filings). Not a single one succeeded in *invoking cloture,* or stopping the filibuster and permitting a vote on the issue. As you can see in Figure 10.3, the Senate invoked more clotures in the 1970s; they became even more common in the 1990s and 2000s, when the

Cloture vote: The Senate's only approved method for halting a filibuster or lifting a legislative hold. If 60 senators—three-fifths of the body, changed in 1975 from the original two-thirds—vote for cloture, the measure can proceed to a vote.

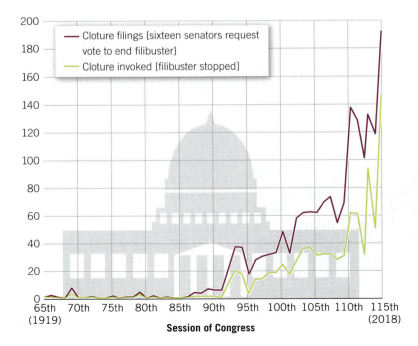

● **Figure 10.3** *Cloture votes are called to end a filibuster or hold. When they are successful, cloture is invoked and the blockage ends. Notice how they used to be rare events. The 113th Congress (2013–2014) set the record for cloture votes until the 115th Congress (2017–2018) when the numbers spiked again. (U.S. Senate)*

legislative hold became a regularly used tactic. The new Republican minority (2007–2015) broke all records and averaged 161 cloture filings a session. Not to be outdone, Democrats pushed for more than 180 filings in the 115th Congress (not all cloture requests are caused by the minority party, but most are). Sixty votes has effectively become the new Senate threshold for passing legislation.

The Vote

Once amendments are voted down or adopted, the time for speeches has expired, and the leadership reckons it has a winning majority; it is time for a final floor vote. On uncontroversial matters, a **voice vote** of all members is sufficient. But several dozen votes each session are judged important enough to require a **roll-call vote**. In the Senate, a clerk still calls the roll, alphabetically scrolling through senators by last name, with each responding "yea" or "nay" (or "present," to abstain). Because the much larger House would take hours to vote in this way, roll calls are done electronically. Representatives use a voting device about the size of a credit card that they plug into kiosks located around the House chamber.

Roll-call votes on major bills are among the most important public acts a member of Congress performs. These votes attract a great deal of attention from constituents, lobbyists, the media, and potential campaign opponents—who might use an unpopular vote to attack an incumbent.[18]

Conference Committee

Legislation must pass the Senate and House in identical form to proceed to presidential action. If different versions of a bill pass—and technically a single comma in a 500-page bill counts as a "difference"—a conference committee must reconcile them. These special sessions, made up of lawmakers from both chambers, provide a golden opportunity for disgruntled members or attentive lobbyists to revisit a bill. Interested parties who failed to get a favorite item included during committee or floor action now have another chance. "An apple and an orange could go into conference committee," lamented President Ronald Reagan, "and come out a pear."[19] No joke: The conference can write a significantly new bill, though sections that were identical in House and Senate versions cannot be altered in conference. Conference committees are rarer in Congress in recent years, but still are held on high profile bills.

House–Senate conferences, if successful, yield a single version of a bill. Each chamber then has an "up-or-down" floor vote—no further amendments permitted. Opponents in the Senate may launch another filibuster, hoping to win supporters who object to the compromises made with the House. In recent years, however, the two chambers have increasingly negotiated with one another prior to passage in

Voice vote: A congressional vote in which the presiding officer asks those for and against to say "yea" or "nay," respectively, and announces the result. No record is kept of House or Senate members voting on each side.

Roll-call vote: A congressional vote in which each member's vote is recorded, either by roll call (Senate) or electronically (House).

To track your House and Senate members' votes, enter their names at Congress.gov.

● *C-SPAN televised live the December 2017 House–Senate conference committee to resolve differences in their respective versions of a tax reform bill.*

a process known as "ping pong." That yields bills that match. The number of conferences has declined from more than fifty a session in the 1990s to under ten today.[20]

Presidential Action: Separated Powers Revisited

Even after all that, the legislation still faces another hurdle. No bill becomes law until the president takes action, usually by signing it (bills also become law within ten days of passage, if Congress remains in session). On important issues, a signing ceremony often takes place in the White House Rose Garden. Presidents sign multiple copies of the bill, handing out pens to the original sponsors and other high-ranking congressional members in attendance.

Presidents can also **veto** legislation. If the president says no, Congress has one more shot at passing the legislation. It is a high bar, though. To deny or override a veto, both chambers need a two-thirds majority: at least 67 senators and 291 members of the House have to say "no" to the president. Only in this way can a bill become law without presidential approval. Figure 10.4 summarizes how a bill becomes law.

We cover more details about veto practices in Chapter 11 on the presidency. Fortunately for most legislative advocates, presidential opposition is rare: George W. Bush and Barack Obama vetoed 12 bills each. President Trump did not exercise the veto power during his first two years in office.

Veto: The constitutional procedure by which a president can prevent enactment of legislation passed by Congress.

The Bottom Line

» The power of an officially sanctioned law inspires the introduction of thousands of bills in Congress each year. Most proposed legislation (97 percent) never becomes law.

» Congressional committees are the central actors in legislative policymaking, holding hearings and marking up (or deleting) bills to prepare them for floor action.

» Floor procedures are another intricate part of the process. Once passed by both House and Senate, legislation may still face a conference committee, a presidential veto, or both.

Why Is Congress So Unpopular?

Congress, the "people's branch," may be expected to win the most public support among our national political institutions. But it is by far the least popular. Since the 1970s, Congress has come in last among government institutions in virtually every survey, often by a great margin. Today, Congress is less popular than at any other time in modern history and less popular than, well, almost anything—including the Internal Revenue Service (see Figure 10.5).[21] And yet, as we saw in Chapter 8, Americans re-elect well over 90 percent of their representatives, year after year. Why?

Explore why incumbents are reelected despite Congress' unpopularity.

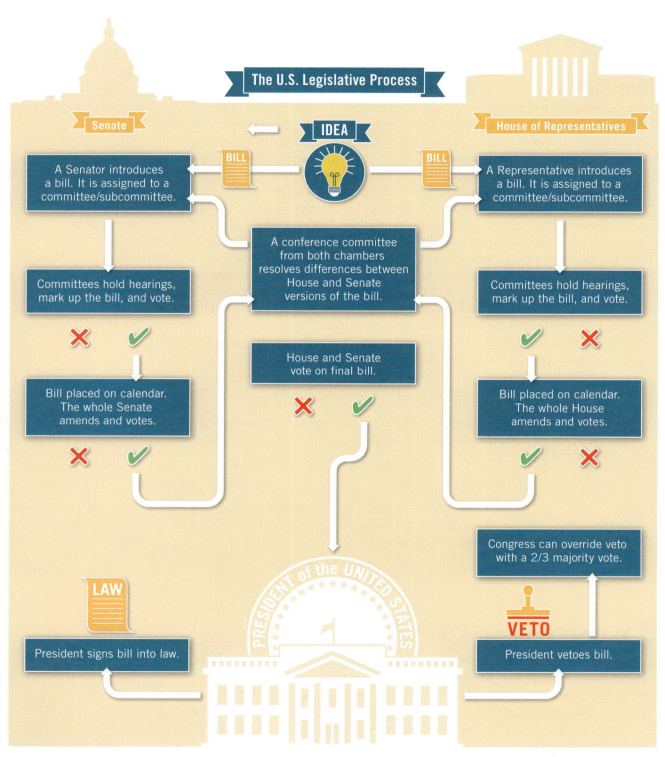

The U.S. Legislative Process

Senate

IDEA

House of Representatives

BILL — A Senator introduces a bill. It is assigned to a committee/subcommittee.

A Representative introduces a bill. It is assigned to a committee/subcommittee. — **BILL**

Committees hold hearings, mark up the bill, and vote.

A conference committee from both chambers resolves differences between House and Senate versions of the bill.

Committees hold hearings, mark up the bill, and vote.

Bill placed on calendar. The whole Senate amends and votes.

House and Senate vote on final bill.

Bill placed on calendar. The whole House amends and votes.

Congress can override veto with a 2/3 majority vote.

LAW

President signs bill into law.

PRESIDENT of the UNITED STATES

VETO

President vetoes bill.

● **Figure 10.4** *How a bill becomes a law.*

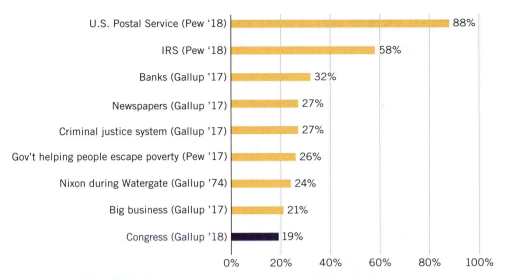

● **Figure 10.5** *Public approval of Congress, compared to other institutions. Across 2018, Congress's approval rating remained between 15 to 19 percent; it fell as low as 7 percent in 2014 (Gallup).*

Constituents tend to like their own representatives and senators, who receive far higher approval numbers than Congress as a whole. And individual members have become adept at running against the Congress they serve in. But what makes the institution itself so unpopular? The public dislikes both partisan fighting and gridlock.

Partisan Polarization in Congress

Congress has exhibited partisan differences since its origins. Strong party disputes, fueled by regional and racial divisions, led nineteenth-century members to carry swords, pistols, or Bowie knives into chambers. One historian entitled her description of Congress before the Civil War, *The Field of Blood*.[22] In one especially famous act of violence, a southern House member, Preston Brooks, slipped onto the Senate floor after a rousing anti-slavery speech by Charles Sumner of Massachusetts in 1856 and beat Sumner unconscious with a cane. Sumner, trapped at his desk which was bolted to the floor, absorbed so many blows that he was unable to resume his Senate duties for nearly three years.

Subsequent combat in the House or Senate was mostly, but not entirely, limited to words. During the 1950s and 1960s, large Democratic majorities in both chambers masked differences—mostly between southern conservatives and liberals from other regions of the country—within the Democratic caucus. Cross-party conflict rose during the 1980s, as Republicans gained congressional seats. When the GOP won control of the Senate in the 1980s and challenged Democrats for control of the House after 1990, the fault lines between the parties cracked open.[23] The proportion of House votes in which a majority of Democrats voted against a majority of Republicans increased by more than 50 percent during the 1990s and early 2000s.[24] In a similar telling measure,

Partisan Polarization

HOW HAS IT CHANGED OVER TIME?

For more than 100 years, congressional parties displayed considerable ideological overlap, represented by the narrow gap between median Democratic and Republican voters on the upper left (1994) display.

THINK ABOUT IT

How has that gap changed since 1994?

While this growing gap between the parties is usually criticized, are there any *advantages* to such a wide ideological divide?

Think about yourself and your politically engaged friends and relatives. Do you prefer highly partisan candidates? What impact might your choices have on the work of Congress?

Source: Pew Research Center

Democrats and Republicans more ideologically divided than in the past

Distribution of Democrats and Republicans on a 10-item scale of political values

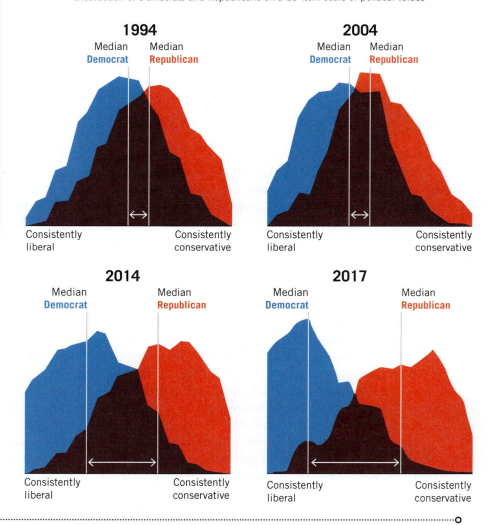

What Do YOU Think? Is a Partisan Congress a Good Thing?

Should Congress seek more cross-party agreement? Today's "partisan" Congress features a significant ideological divide between conservative Republicans and progressive Democrats. Partisanship helps guide how members pursue the goals they believe in and try to persuade the public. What do you think?

Yes, a partisan Congress is a good thing.	**No, Congress is too partisan.**
It permits the public to choose between very different political philosophies. Take undocumented immigration: For decades, both parties in Congress had largely indistinguishable positions. Now, Republicans introduce bills to increase deportation and build a wall, while Democrats denounce the GOP for separating migrant children from parents and call for an extension of the "Dreamers" program.	The parties may disagree, but they do not reflect public views. Most Americans are moderates willing to listen to the other side. Rising partisanship also hampers cooperation necessary for Congress to pass important legislation. Congress should seek compromises in the national interest.

party cohesion—the proportion of each party's House or Senate members who vote with the party majority—remained at or above 90 percent each year after 1990, after historically varying from the mid-60s to the low 80s. In other words, the parties in Congress were digging in against each other, with ever-fewer members willing to look for middle ground.

Titles of recent books about Congress underscore the point. These include: *Fight Club Politics: How Partisanship Is Poisoning the House of Representatives*; *The Broken Branch: How Congress Is Failing America and How to Get It Back on Track*; and, by a sitting House member, *Drain the Swamp: How Washington Corruption Is Worse Than You Think*.[25]

There are two perspectives on polarization. Most political scientists believe the parties are now, for the first time in modern U.S. history, sorted by ideology. Republicans have moved steadily to the right over the past quarter-century, and Democrats more recently are swinging leftward; this encourages both to be more partisan. Others see "asymmetrical polarization": The Republicans, inspired by a fiery conservative movement, are the ones who have pressed the partisan fight in the name of their ideals. Democrats have, at least till very recently, remained more or less in the same place according to this perspective.[26]

Divided Government

How to explain the rise in partisan "gridlock" in our era? Divided government, say some.[27] Divided government occurs when each party holds at least one of the three national elective institutions: the presidency, House, or Senate. One or both houses of Congress led by a party opposed to the president, the argument goes, will result in a legislative standoff—as well as more aggressive congressional investigations of the White House and a slowed-down policymaking process. Although prominent political scientists have questioned this conventional wisdom, [28] in recent years the highly polarized Congress and frequent clashes with the White House bear out the idea that divided government leads to policy stalemate. One result: a "virtual disappearance of regular order in Congress"—that is, bipartisan lawmaking according to long-established norms.[29] Another is continuing declines in Congress's approval rating among the American public.

The Bottom Line

» Congress has grown more partisan. Today, the parties themselves are more ideologically consistent. This makes for sharper conflict, but it also gives people clearer choices.

» Does divided government lead to more gridlock? Political scientists argued in the past that it does not. Today, the growing ideological purity of the parties and the regular use of legislative holds suggest that divided government hampers Congress's ability to solve America's problems.

Some Popular Reforms—And Their Limits

Should we care that Americans do not like Congress? Many observers—and thoughtful members—worry that continued public disapproval will erode the institution's effectiveness. Others fret that potential young political talent is discouraged by public disapproval from considering a congressional career (as either staffers or members). Still another danger: A deadlocked Congress permits the executive branch to make policy on its own. We explore that worry in Chapter 11.

Each year, reformers propose various fixes to improve Congress. We have already discussed one such reform: imposing term limits (see Chapter 8). Here we discuss two other popular reforms: limits on lobbyists and public education about what Congress really does.

Limit Lobbyists

Americans have called for years for reductions in lobbyists' influence in Congress. Chapter 9 chronicled extensive lobbying reforms, including bans on gifts and meals. Both reform packages were greeted with yawns from the public: Congressional approval ratings dropped after each was implemented.

As we discussed in Chapter 9, one person's special interest is another's cherished protector of a vital program. Lobbyists represent virtually everyone. And they link together our vast public and the complicated structures of national governance.

Even so, congressional organization—with its arcane processes and multiple committees and subcommittees—creates many opportunities for special interests to win favors and block initiatives. The problem is not their power over the big issues, on which members have strong views, but in the obscure items to which few pay attention, even though millions of dollars (or other benefits) can be gained or lost with a few strokes of a legislator's pen.

How to limit such deals? Perhaps James Madison had the answer in *Federalist* 10. When energy companies seek special benefits, environmental groups blow the whistle (and vice versa); when public hospitals push higher pay for CEOs, taxpayer groups challenge their arguments. Perhaps the solution to the problem of interests really is more interests. That would mean reforming the way Congress does business—to make sure that a wider array of interests are heard on every issue—rather than eradicating lobbying.

Educate the Public

Most reform proposals include an earnest plea for better education about Congress. Many Americans do not know their House member's name and cannot begin to explain how bills become law. Perhaps with more knowledge, the public would be more sympathetic.

● *Public disapproval of Congress.*

Political scientists John Hibbing and Elizabeth Theiss-Morse instead argued that Americans' problem with Congress was not lack of knowledge. Rather, Americans dislike logrolling and bargaining; we dislike committees and bureaucracy; we dislike political partisanship (and parties); we despise interest groups. Americans disdain the slow pace of congressional lawmaking, which inevitably involves hashing things out, bickering, and back-scratching. In sum, concluded Hibbing and Theiss-Morse, although Americans love democracy in the abstract and demand transparency in politics, many Americans disapprove of core features of democracy in practice.[30]

The Real World of Democracy

This chapter has tried to describe the complex and often muddled congressional process. Our goal is to increase your appreciation for the messiness of democracy, as carried out in the people's branch. Another way to view all the bargaining, partial solutions, noisy debates, and compromising is as faithfully representing a diverse, divided American public. Congress is the most open, transparent institution in our system of government. It is also full of flaws and limits—just like the humans it serves.

The Bottom Line

» Some popular reforms propose limiting the influence of lobbying groups in Congress.

» Others emphasize the importance of educating the public about the workings of Congress. We would recommend education about the "messy" nature of legislating in a diverse democratic nation.

🔵 Conclusion: Congress and the Challenge of Governing

Congress does some important things very well—representatives and senators are remarkably responsive to individuals seeking help. Direct constituent service, at home in the district and state, is often superb. That is one reason why re-election rates are so high.

But as our individual needs have become better supported, Congress has grown less capable of solving big societal problems—such as immigration, healthcare, crime, inequality, wage stagnation, or global warming. The over-arching question throughout this chapter is whether the U.S. Congress has lost its ability to achieve big collective aims, or whether it still muddles through precisely as the constitutional framers intended.

Congress has certainly proven capable of broad achievements. Medicare and Social Security, to take two giant congressional programs, have cut the rate of poverty among elderly Americans by more than half and provided seniors with generous health benefits.

Genuine democratic, popular government can be chaotic and sometimes unseemly. But it is essential. The people's branch will have to find a way to govern effectively—and to win back popular approval—if American democracy is to flourish.

CHAPTER SUMMARY

Check your understanding of Chapter 10.

🟢 Congress operates under complicated rules that make action difficult. Americans debate whether Congress still works the way it is intended—blunting too much government action. Or whether it has become "the broken branch."

🟢 America's Congress is bicameral: The House of Representatives contains 441 members (435 voting; six represent territories like Guam and Puerto Rico) elected every two years; in the Senate, 100 senators serve six-year terms.

🟢 The two chambers of Congress reflect different national priorities. Populists appreciate the responsive House; advocates of stability embrace the more deliberate Senate.

🟢 Members of the House and Senate represent Americans in multiple ways. These include:

- *Geographic representation*: Constitutional election rules say members must live in the state or district they represent.
- *Descriptive representation*: Does the assembly look like the people?
- *Substantive representation*: Do members of Congress effectively pursue constituent interests?

🟢 Members of Congress are always running for office, raising funds and returning most weeks to their constituency. Normal congressional business occurs from Tuesday through Thursday.

● Congress is increasingly an institution of strangers who do not know one another well.

● Congressional leadership in the House includes a Speaker, majority and minority leaders, and ten whips. Successful House leaders impose discipline on their party members. In the Senate, party leaders and whips have fewer institutional tools with which to keep members in line.

● Congressional committees have proved efficient and adaptable over the years, preparing legislation and conducting oversight of the executive branch. However, the committee system also fragments Congress, hides action from public view, and makes it difficult to pass major legislation.

● Floor procedures are another intricate part of the legislative process. Once passed by both House and Senate, legislation may still face a conference committee, a presidential veto, or both.

● Congress has grown more partisan. More ideologically consistent parties make for sharper conflict, but it also gives people clearer choices.

● The difficult path to legislation raises a key question about Congress: Should we cheer the slow-moving process as a way to limit government? Or should we worry that the institution is not up to addressing America's vital problems?

Need to review key ideas in greater depth? Click here.

KEY TERMS

116th Congress, p. 330
Cloture vote, p. 351
Committee hearing, p. 347
Committee markup session,
  p. 348
Congressional caucus, p. 333

Earmark, p. 344
Filibuster, p. 331
Floor, p. 330
Legislative hold, p. 331
President pro tempore, p. 341
Reapportionment, p. 337

Roll-call vote, p. 352
Speaker of the House, p. 340
Unanimous consent, p. 349
Veto, p. 353
Voice vote, p. 352

Flashcard review.

STUDY QUESTIONS

1. Discuss the following reforms:
   a) Public financing for all congressional elections, even if that means raising taxes.
   b) Abolishing the Senate filibuster and legislative hold.
   c) Limiting lobbyists' access and/or influence.
2. How did Congress lose so much power to the president? Should power be more balanced between the two branches?

3. Why is Congress so partisan today? Can you think of ways to reduce partisanship? Are there any advantages to drawing strong lines between Republicans and Democrats?
4. Should it be easier to pass laws through Congress? What, if any, benefits do all the checks and balances provide?
5. Why is Congress so unpopular with the American people? In your view, does Congress deserve its low approval ratings?

 Go to **www.oup.com/us/Morone** to find quizzes, flash cards, simulations, tutorials, videos, and other study tools.

11 The Presidency

GEORGE WASHINGTON, the first president of the United States, faced a problem. He had to persuade 13 independent-minded states to think of themselves as one unified nation. Washington decided to foster unity by touring the new country. He set out with assistants, slaves, horses, and dogs. As the party approached each town, the president mounted a great white steed and cantered handsomely into the cheering throngs, his favorite greyhound trotting at his side. Washington named the dog Cornwallis, after the British general who surrendered to end the Revolutionary War. Poor Cornwallis the greyhound died while touring the southern states, but his name reminded the people that they were part of a proud and independent nation. Everywhere Washington went the people greeted their president with ringing bells, cheers, songs, speeches, parades, and flags. The crowds felt, at least for a day, like Americans.[1]

Who are we? Each president offers a different answer. Washington may be our greatest president, not because of his domestic programs or foreign policies—at the time, critics were scathing about both. Instead, Washington embodied the new nation. He championed American ideals, spoke to national aspirations, introduced new ideas, and personified the nation's sense of identity—both to Americans and to the world. All presidents do the same—some more successfully than others.

The president's role is difficult partly because Americans rarely agree about who we are. The United States are often the *Un*-United States. Washington took slaves on his unity tour. Didn't slavery violate the new nation's ideals? Many Americans knew that it did.

Almost 230 years after Washington's tour, newly inaugurated President Donald Trump signed an executive order barring citizens from seven Muslim-majority nations from entering the United States—without consulting administrators or legal experts. The results: Chaos at the borders; civil rights attorneys dashed to the airports to defend visitors abruptly pulled out of lines; multiple federal courts put the ban on hold. The president pressed on. His administration rewrote the travel ban in light of court

● *President Trump signs a travel ban during his first week in office.*

In this chapter, you will:

● See how the Constitution defines the presidency.

● Focus on presidential power.

● Learn what presidents do.

● Reflect on presidential popularity—and greatness.

● Consider the personal side of the office.

● Tour the Executive Office of the President and meet the team around a president.

rulings, and eventually, a bitterly divided Supreme Court (5–4) upheld it. The Court majority was clear: The law gave the president authority over the nation's borders. Six months later, the president signed another controversial order barring most transgender individuals from serving in the U.S. military. It reversed an executive order signed by his predecessor, Barack Obama. Again, the president's order set off a scramble in his own agency, this time the military; a debate in Congress; and more litigation.

Many constitutional experts read these executive orders as emblematic of swelling presidential power.[2] President Obama had seized presidential authority to protect immigrants and transgender individuals; President Trump expanded that authority still further to keep people from some countries out of the United States and some Americans out of the military. Many Americans despaired as neither Congress nor the Court, both dominated by conservatives, was willing to question his authority.[3]

But there is another way to see it. The case illustrates how the president is enmeshed in a complex institutional web. The president clearly took his policy to the people during the election, then had to adjust it to address the Court's constitutional concerns, work with the bureaucracy to organize an orderly process, maintain support in Congress (which can override the bans), and work out the legal arguments with the Justice Department.

Today, the presidency raises precisely the same question the delegates debated at the Constitutional Convention: How much authority should the president wield? From Washington's tour to Trump's bans, the presidency reflects the same three themes:

> *The president personifies America.* More than any other individual, presidents tell us who we are—and what we are becoming. As Americans grow more partisan, this traditional role becomes more challenging. Most Republicans believed (incorrectly) that Barack Obama was born in Kenya—and was therefore not eligible to be president.[4] Fast forward to the present, when Democrats return the favor and chant "not my president" during protests against Donald Trump.
>
> *The president injects new ideas and themes into American politics.* Our discussion of Congress emphasized the institutional rules of the game; the presidency places more focus on individuals and ideas. President Trump promised a new approach to border security—and that quickly rose to the top of the nation's political agenda.

BY THE NUMBERS
The Presidency

Number of presidents in the last 85 years	**14**
Split between Republican/Democratic presidents in the 85 years	**7 from each party**
Length, in months, of the shortest presidency (William Henry Harrison)	**1**
Length, in months, of the longest presidency (Franklin D. Roosevelt)	**145**
Number of presidents younger than Barack Obama when they were elected	**2**
Number of presidents older than Donald Trump when elected	**0**
Election year of last president without a college education (Harry S Truman)	**1945**
Birth year of first president to be born in a hospital (Jimmy Carter)	**1924**
Year in which first woman (Victoria Woodhull) ran for president	**1872**
Number of presidents who were sons, nephews, or cousins of prior presidents (John Quincy Adams, Benjamin Harrison, Franklin D. Roosevelt, George W. Bush)	**4**
Estimated proportion of presidents who have had extramarital affairs	**1 in 3**
Number of presidents to hold a patent (Abraham Lincoln, for an invention to free boats trapped on a sandbar)	**1**

Who do Americans elect to the highest office—and how representative are they?

The president has enormous powers—at least on paper. That authority, and how presidents use it, returns us to the fundamental question: Is the presidency too powerful for a democratic republic? Or is the office too weak to do what Americans demand of it? Perhaps the same president can be both too strong and too weak. Keep this question of authority in mind as you read the chapter.

Defining the Presidency

Time travelers from the nineteenth century would easily recognize today's Senate or Supreme Court. However, the modern White House would stun them. The presidency is the branch of the federal government that has changed the most.

Up till 80 years ago, Americans could walk right in the front door of the White House and greet the president. In 1829, during President Andrew Jackson's inauguration, supporters mobbed the mansion and forced the president to climb out a window for his own safety; aides placed tubs of whiskey and orange juice on the lawn to lure the crowds outside. When William Henry Harrison won the presidency in 1840, so many men milled about the White House hoping to get a government job that the president-elect could not find an empty room to meet with his cabinet.

Today there are no more mobs in the White House. Presidents have redefined their roles and renegotiated their powers. The presidency is a different institution. Partly all the changes arise because each president has the opportunity to reshape the office. One reason the presidency is so fluid lies in the job description. By now, you know where to look for that: the Constitution.

Defined by Controversy

The Constitutional Convention faced three tough questions when it defined the presidency. First, *should the United States even have a president?* Traditional republics feared executive power. The founders of the United States feared the English king as too powerful; but they worried that the state governments did not have enough executive power and were too feeble to govern effectively.

Their job was to find a happy medium. In the end, they selected a single president and established simple qualifications for the post: a natural-born citizen at least 35 years old who had lived in the United States for at least 14 years.

● *Different eras: After Andrew Jackson's inauguration, Americans crushed into the executive mansion—aides used whiskey punch to draw the crowds outside.*

Second, *how long should the president serve?* The delegates at the Constitutional Convention considered terms of four, six, seven, eight, eleven, and 15 years. Alexander Hamilton passionately argued for a lifelong term—an elected king. The Convention finally settled on four years, with no limit to the number of terms. In 1945, the Twenty-Second Amendment limited presidents to two terms.

Third, *how should the United States choose its president?* Delegates to the convention feared that the public did not know enough, the state legislatures were too self-interested, and Congress would become too powerful if given the task of appointing the executive. They finally settled on a roundabout method, the Electoral College. The states each get electoral votes equal to their congressional delegation. Who would elect the electors? The convention simply left the matter to the states (see Chapter 2).

Political scientists still debate the Electoral College because it distorts the popular vote. It has put the popular vote loser in the White House in two of the last three presidencies. Major population centers—New York, Los Angeles, Houston—are all ignored during presidential elections because they are in states that safely give their majority (and all their electoral votes) to one party or the other.[5]

The President's Powers

Article 2 of the Constitution, which defines the presidency, seems puzzling at first glance. Article 1 meticulously defines everything Congress is empowered to do: The instructions run for 52 paragraphs. In contrast, Article 2 says very little about who the president is and what the president does. Thirteen short paragraphs define the office. This vague constitutional mandate is one reason why the office keeps evolving.

The Constitution is especially terse when it gets to the heart of the presidency: the powers and duties of the chief executive. It grants the president a limited number of **expressed powers**, or explicit grants of authority. Most are carefully balanced by corresponding congressional powers. Table 11.1 summarizes this balance.[6]

Learn about executive privilege and other presidential powers.

Expressed powers: Powers the Constitution explicitly grants to the president.

TABLE 11.1 The President's Expressed Powers

The president is commander in chief of the army, navy, and state militias. But Congress has the power to declare war, set the military budget, and make the rules governing the military.
The president can grant pardons and reprieves for offenses against the United States.
The president can make treaties (with the approval of two-thirds of the Senate), appoint ambassadors (with the advice and consent of the Senate), and select Supreme Court justices and other officers (again, with Senate approval).
The Constitution also authorizes presidents to solicit the opinions of his officers (the cabinet members) and requires presidents to report on the state of the Union.

Delegated powers: Powers that Congress passes on to the president.

Inherent powers of the presidency: Powers assumed by presidents, often during crisis, on the basis of the constitutional phrase "The executive power shall be vested in the president."

Executive agreements: An international agreement made by the president that does not require the approval of the Senate.

Executive privilege: Power claimed by the president to resist requests for authority by Congress, the courts, or the public. Not mentioned in the Constitution but based on the separation of powers.

The president draws real authority from a simple phrase at the end of the section: "take care that the laws be faithfully executed." Congress votes on legislation and then sends it to the executive branch to put into effect. In other words, Congress grants **delegated powers** to the president. For example, Congress passes legislation that aims to improve hospital care. It delegates power to the executive branch, which issues a detailed rule saying that hospitals will receive lower federal payments if patients develop infections after surgery.

Presidents claim a third source of authority: **inherent powers**. These are not specified in the Constitution or delegated by legislation, but are implicit in the vague Article 2 phrase "The executive power shall be vested in a president." During crises, presidents have often seized new "inherent" powers. During the Civil War, for example, President Lincoln took a series of unprecedented military actions with no clear legal basis. He imposed censorship, ordered a naval blockade, and issued orders while Congress was not in session. President Obama exercised inherent powers to launch an air campaign against ISIS, a radical Islamist organization in Iran and Syria. Did he need congressional approval? The administration said no. The president's claim of inherent powers is not the last word on the matter. Congress may pass legislation in response and the Supreme Court often weighs whether the president has overstepped executive authority.

Modern presidents have expanded presidential power in informal ways. As we shall see later in this chapter, presidents regularly issue executive orders, negotiate **executive agreements** with other nations, and claim **executive privilege**—all ways of bypassing Congress. Throughout this chapter we will encounter subtle ways the presidents have used their office to expand their power.

The result is a fluid definition of presidential power. Presidents regularly renegotiate the limits of the office through their actions at home and abroad. More than any other institution, the presidency is a constant work in progress. The arc of presidential history begins with a modest constitutional grant of power that has grown through the years.

This discussion brings us back to the question we posed at the start of the chapter: Has the president become too powerful? We turn to that question in the next section.

 **The Bottom Line**

» Presidents serve a four-year term and can run for re-election once.

» They are elected indirectly, via the Electoral College.

» The president has three types of powers: expressed in the Constitution, delegated by Congress, and inherent in the role of chief executive.

» In theory, Congress passes laws and the president executes them. In reality, presidents constantly negotiate the limits of their power—which often expands during crises.

🔵 Is the Presidency Too Powerful?

The constitutional framers wrestled with the same issue we debate today: *power*. How much authority do presidents need to protect the nation and get things done? When does the office's reach violate the idea of limited government?

An Imperial Presidency?

During George Washington's national tour, a few Americans fretted about his nine stallions, gold-trimmed saddles, personal attendants, and all that adulation. Washington, they whispered, was acting more like a king than the president of a homespun republic. They were articulating a constant American theme: The president has grown too mighty. Flash forward two centuries.

When President Trump landed in London, the English press reported that 1,000 staff members came along with him. The presidential parties included lawyers, secretaries, speechwriters, military aides, physicians, and personal chefs. For the English visit, they required 750 hotel rooms. U.S. fighter jets flew in shifts, providing continual air cover. Today, American presidents travel like emperors.[7]

How about weaker individuals? George Washington's successor, John Adams, did not have to worry about cheering crowds. Critics mocked the chubby second president as "His Rotundity." Adams attracted so little attention that he regularly swam naked in the Potomac River (until a woman reporter allegedly spied him, sat on his clothes, and demanded an interview). Even Adams, however, aroused widespread fears about executive power when he signed the Alien and Sedition Acts, which gave the executive broad powers to deport "dangerous aliens" and punish "false, scandalous, and malicious" speech. The president seemed to be trampling the First Amendment by silencing criticism.

Some defend the expansion of executive power. The **unitary executive theory** contends that the Constitution puts the president in charge of executing the laws, and therefore no one—not Congress, not the judiciary, not even the people—may limit presidential power when it comes to executive matters. Many executive decisions demand swift, decisive, and sometimes secretive action. Only an empowered president, the argument goes, can make those instantaneous calls.[8]

The unitary executive is controversial. Arthur Schlesinger Jr., a celebrated historian, warned of an **imperial presidency**. Very powerful presidents, he feared, become like emperors: They run roughshod

Unitary executive theory: The idea that the Constitution puts the president in charge of executing the laws and that therefore no other branch may limit presidential discretion over executive matters.

Imperial presidency: A characterization of the American presidency that suggests it is demonstrating imperial traits and that the republic is morphing into an empire.

🟢 *President Obama arrives in Los Angeles aboard Marine One—surrounded by support aircraft.*

over Congress, issue secret decisions, unilaterally deploy force around the world, and burst past the checks and balances that limit presidential power. Critics worry that imperial features have become part of the presidency itself. Republicans bitterly argued that the Obama administration's overreach had created another imperial presidency.[9] Now Democrats say the same about the Trump administration. Many contemporary scholars echo the fears: With Congress deadlocked, suggests political scientist Francis Fukuyama, supporters cheer when presidents act decisively—even if it pushes the boundaries of presidential power. Power appears to be flowing to the president.[10]

At issue are two vital principles: We need a president who is strong enough to lead the country and face our problems. But if presidents become too strong, we lose our republican form of government. This is a deep paradox in American politics: *We need powerful leaders; we fear powerful leaders.*

A Weak Office?

At the same time, the presidency also can seem very weak. Every modern president has complained about his inability to get basic goals accomplished. Congress, courts, the opposing political party, the media, interest groups, and bad luck can all humble a president. Since 1960, only four (of eleven) presidents have completed two full terms. What type of "imperial" presidency is that?

Presidents often appear weakest when they wrestle with domestic issues. Even under the best of circumstances it is difficult to get major legislation through Congress. The president nominally runs the executive branch, but the bureaucracy is immense and often difficult to control—and cabinets are staffed by officials the Senate must approve. Introducing changes through the American political process is extremely difficult, even for the savviest presidents.

For a case study of weak presidency, take Jimmy Carter. Congressional relations turned frosty early in his term, after Carter unexpectedly vetoed a spending bill. Then the economy soured; interest rates spiraled toward 20 percent and unemployment reached 10 percent. Gas prices soared, forcing customers in some regions to wait in long lines at gas stations.

Carter did not seem to have an answer to all the woes besetting the nation. A mischievous editor at the *Boston Globe* captured one reaction to Carter's speech when he designed a mock headline, "More Mush from the Wimp." By mistake, the headline ran in the first edition.[11] A few months later, militant Iranian students took 53 Americans hostage at the U.S. embassy in Tehran and held them for 444 days. A weak president seemed to be completely overwhelmed by events.

Even President Trump, who made progress on many of his goals (rolling back regulations, cutting taxes, restricting immigration from Muslim countries, winning conservative Supreme Court appointments) struggled to get much of his agenda through Congress in his first two years: He failed to repeal Obamacare (by a single vote in the Senate), to build a border wall, to change the immigration laws, or to slash federal spending.

Back and forth goes the debate. Is the president getting too powerful and breaking free from popular control? Or is the president not up to the job of governing a superpower? To answer this question, let us take a closer look at just what presidents do.

The Bottom Line

» Americans want a powerful president; Americans fear a powerful president.

» The executive branch has grown far stronger over time, especially when it comes to foreign policy.

» Presidential power is limited, especially when it comes to domestic matters.

What Presidents Do

Over time, presidents have taken on many jobs. Some are described in the Constitution. Presidents seize other powers as they respond to crisis or jockey for political advantage. By now, the president has accumulated an extraordinary number of hats (and helmets).

Commander in Chief

The Constitution lays it out simply: "The president shall be the Commander-in-Chief of the Army and Navy of the United States and the militia of the several states, when called into the actual service of the United States." Congress declares war and presidents manage it.

For many years, the United States had a small standing army and called men and women to service in wartime. After each war, the army quickly demobilized. This approach reflected classical theory. In great republics such as Athens and Rome, citizens took up arms when enemies loomed and then returned home when the crisis had passed—just as George Washington had done during the American Revolution. Peacetime armies were, according to the traditional perspective, a recipe for empire or monarchy.

After World War II, however, the United States faced off against the Soviet Union in the Cold War. An army of around 250,000 (in 1935) grew into a force of more than two million and spread across the globe. Back in 1835, Tocqueville mused that the Constitution gave the president "almost royal prerogatives which he has no occasion to use." Now the occasion had arrived, and the president's power grew.[12]

Today, America's active-duty force numbers over 1.3 million, with another 808,000 in reserve (see Figure 11.1). In 2018, military spending topped $681 billion. And that does not include the Department of Veterans Affairs, Homeland Security, intelligence agencies, and other related efforts. The military operates approximately 750 installations around the globe. In short, the

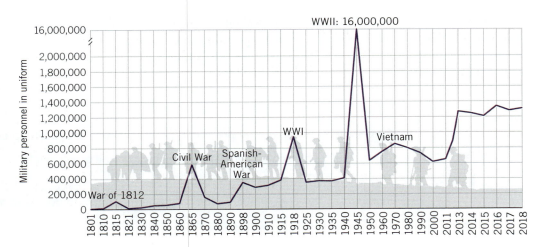

● **Figure 11.1** *The military and how it grew, 1800 to 2018: Traditionally, the United States called soldiers to war and then demobilized afterwards. The United States began to play a global role after the Spanish–American War (Historical Statistics/ Statistical Abstracts and the US Department of Defense).*

commander in chief oversees the world's largest fighting force. That role, by itself, makes the president one of the most powerful individuals in the world.

Meanwhile, checks on the commander in chief have faded. The Constitution authorizes Congress to declare wars, but since the nuclear age dawned in 1945, presidents rarely have waited for Congress to act. Facing the doomsday threat of nuclear missiles, military response time is measured in minutes—too fast for congressional deliberation.

In an effort to regain some of its authority, Congress passed the War Powers Act (1973), which permitted the president to send forces into combat "in case of a national emergency created by an attack on the United States ... or its armed forces." When presidents deploy troops they must notify Congress within 48 hours and win its approval within 60 days. In practice, presidents have unilaterally deployed troops and shown contempt for the War Powers Act. Even when they sometimes do turn to Congress, it is very difficult to vote no when Americans are in combat.[13]

Three developments have further increased the president's authority: America's powerful military machine, always poised for deployment; new technologies, such as drones, that permit presidents to target enemies around the globe; and perceptions of perpetual threat—first from the Soviet Union, now from terrorists.

Presidents are deeply engaged with their military role. They traditionally start each day with a security briefing that reviews all the dangers stirring around the world; they have a large national security staff; and—the great symbol of our nuclear age—they are never more than a few feet away from "the football."

If you see the president in person, or a wide-angle shot on television, you can glimpse a military officer standing about 20 feet away and clutching a medium-size black briefcase, known as "the football." What is in the bag? The answer is classified, but over the years the public has learned that it is a mobile communications center locked into the American nuclear arsenal. Every minute of every day the American president is steps away from a kit that would enable him or her to launch an attack that could obliterate any nation from the face of the Earth.

Top Diplomat

The Constitution gives presidents the lead role in foreign affairs. Presidents and their international advisors set a framework for the U.S. role in the world. Foreign policy crises differ vastly from everyday domestic politics. Passing laws is a long, complicated process full of compromise and constraint. During international crises—hostage situations, terrorist attacks, the outbreak of war, or simply international negotiations—all eyes turn toward the president and his team. Often presidents must make fast decisions with immediate consequences. John F. Kennedy captured the intensity, a few weeks after taking office, in a late-night phone call to former vice president Richard Nixon during his first international crisis. "It really is true that foreign affairs is the only important issue for a president to handle, isn't it?" queried Kennedy. "I mean who gives a shit if the minimum wage is $1.15 or $1.25 compared to something like this?"[14]

● *A uniformed officer with "the football"—a briefcase that contains launch codes for the nuclear arsenal. The football is never more than a few feet away from the president.*

Foreign diplomacy is not just about trouble spots. The State Department manages 305 embassies, consulates, and diplomatic missions around the world. Presidents must hash out American relations with nearly 200 nations that range from "special friends" to distant allies to avowed enemies. Intricate questions arise about how to approach each country: Should the president shake hands with our nation's enemies? Every smile or snub sends a diplomatic message. A president sets the tone and the policy for all these relationships.

President Trump has stunned allies by disparaging their leaders and their policies—attacking the prime minister of Canada as "very dishonest and weak" and calling Great Britain's Brexit plan "very unfortunate."[15] Although President Trump's comments have violated the polite language of diplomacy, he has pursued a larger goal: to fundamentally reorient American foreign policy. After World War II, American leaders from both parties built a web of alliances to promote Western—and sometimes—global interests: military alliances such as NATO, economic agreements to lower tariffs and facilitate

● *Body language and diplomacy: President Trump confronts the G-7 leaders including German Chancellor Angela Merkel (center) and Japanese Prime Minister Shinzo Abe (with folded arms).*

free trade and special accords on issues such as climate change (the Paris Climate Accords). Promoting his America First policy, President Trump has bluntly questioned whether many of these institutions serve U.S. interests.[16]

The president charged that NATO members were not paying their fair share for the alliance and insisted that they speed up their agreement to increase their military budgets to 2 percent of GDP by 2024—and then, in a meeting with the allies, upped that goal to 4 percent of GDP.[17] In an effort to push wealthy European countries to pay for their own defense, he ordered the Pentagon to study the impact of withdrawing troops from Germany (a key NATO member and ally). Congress responded with a bipartisan, nonbinding resolution supporting NATO. The exchange illustrated how the president now dominates the power over diplomacy. But it also shows how Congress could reassert its own powers over U.S. global engagement.[18]

The First Legislator

The Constitution authorizes presidents to *recommend measures* for Congress's "consideration," report to Congress *information on the state of the Union*, and *veto legislation* they oppose.

Assess current debates on climate change.

Recommending Measures.   Until modern times, presidents generally avoided legislative affairs. Dwight Eisenhower (1953–1961) was the last president to try to leave legislation to Congress. His cabinet officers complained, and before long Eisenhower was recommending measures—and blasting Congress when they failed to approve them.

Today, presidential candidates define the legislative agenda. President Donald Trump campaigned on repealing Obamacare, restricting immigration reform, cutting taxes, and renegotiating trade agreements—precisely what the 115th (2017–2018) Congress undertook. Congressional leaders have their own lists. Top White House advisors lobby for favorite programs. And unexpected issues constantly spring up and require presidential attention.

State of the Union.   The Constitution invites the chief executive to report on the state of the Union "from time to time." Today the "SOTU," as insiders term it, is an annual event, delivered with great fanfare before Congress, Supreme Court justices cabinet members, and a national television audience. The speech announces the president's legislative program for the year.

Following the SOTU address, each issue undergoes a second round of debates within the administration: Does it really fit our budget? Can we make it work smoothly? Did Congress cheer or yawn when the boss rolled it out? What was the public reaction? Most policies have friends and enemies in the administration—and if you get your favorite program funded, I may not get mine. The process is a bureaucratic version of a knife fight. Proposals that survive go up to Capitol Hill, where they face the long, complicated congressional process we described in Chapter 10.

● Across the ideological divide: President Ronald Reagan (a Republican) and Speaker of the House Tip O'Neill (D-MA) negotiate the budget. "Maybe Tip and I told too many Irish stories," wrote Reagan in his journal after one long night of tall tales.

Presidential "Batting Average." Only members of Congress can formally propose a law, so presidents rely on supporters in each chamber to submit their bills. Then they rely on a crucial team that the public rarely sees. The White House congressional liaison prods, bargains, negotiates, and sometimes even bullies Congress over legislation. Frustration inevitably sets in. To the executive branch, legislators seem overly parochial as they focus on their states and districts. Still, most presidents quickly learn the same lesson: Work closely with Congress. Managing relations with House and Senate members is one of the most important presidential skills.

One measure of a president's success is their "batting average"—how many of their bills get through (see Table 11.2). There are many different ways to keep score: all the bills the president endorses, the most important bills, or bills that the other party opposes. You can see that when the same party controls the White House and Congress, known as unified government, the batting average is much higher—usually around .800. When the opposition party controls Congress (divided government), the average usually falls below .500. Some political scientists have argued that divided government makes for a more effective legislative process. But notice how divided governments (the orange lines) have been yielding less agreement in recent years. President Obama enjoyed the highest batting average in the past 75 years when both houses of Congress were Democratic, and the second lowest average when he faced a divided Congress.

Of the presidents since World War II, President John Kennedy signed the most legislation in his first year (684). Who signed the least number? President Trump with 96 bills.[19]

Veto. When Congress passes a law, presidents have the authority to sign or **veto** (*veto* means "I forbid," in Latin). A veto blocks the legislation unless two-thirds of both chambers vote to **override** it, a very high bar. Presidents have ten days to return the legislation to Congress with a message explaining why they

Veto power: The presidential power to block an act of Congress by refusing to sign—and returning it to Congress with objections.

Override: The process by which Congress can overcome a presidential veto with a two-thirds vote in both chambers.

TABLE 11.2	Presidential Batting Average:

Measuring the proportion of congressional bills on which the president took a position that passed

PRESIDENT	PARTY	YEARS IN OFFICE	CONGRESSIONAL CONTROL	PERCENTAGE VOTES SUPPORTING PRESIDENT'S POSITION OF CONGRESSIONAL
Ronald Reagan	R	1981–1986	Mixed control (R Senate, D House)	67.4
Ronald Reagan	R	1987–1989	Democrats control Congress	45.4
George H. W. Bush	R	1989–1993	Democrats control Congress	51.8
Bill Clinton	D	1993–1994	Democrats control Congress	86.3
Bill Clinton	D	1995–2000	Republicans control Congress	48.1
George W. Bush	R	2001–2006	Republicans control Congress	80.9
George W. Bush	R	2007–2008	Democrats control Congress	43.0
Barack Obama	D	2009–2010	Democrats control Congress	92.0
Barack Obama	D	2011–2013	Mixed control (D Senate, R House)	52.8
Barack Obama	D	2015	Republicans control Congress	35.7
Donald Trump	R	2017–2018	Republicans control Congress	90.4 (Through 11/12/18)

- ■ *President's party controls Congress*
- ■ *Opposition party controls Congress*
- ■ *Congress split*

have rejected it. If the president does nothing, the bill becomes law in ten days, a move known as a "pocket veto."

The veto is a formidable weapon. In the past 80 years presidents have rejected more than 1,400 bills. Congress managed to override just 60 times: a congressional "batting average" of 4 percent. Recently the veto has become a more partisan weapon, as conflict between the parties has escalated. Franklin D. Roosevelt, Harry Truman, and Jimmy Carter all flourished the veto pen against a Congress controlled by their own party; in their first two years the

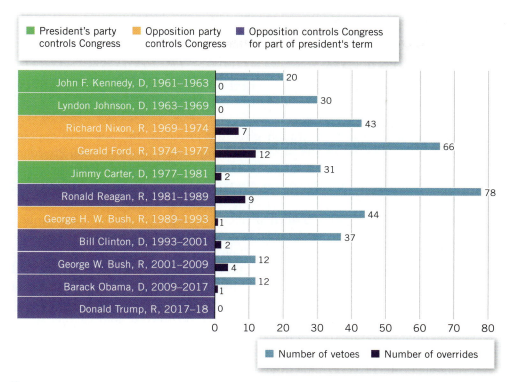

● **Figure 11.2** *Presidential vetoes and overrides. Note that vetoes were far more common 50 years ago, even when the same party controlled Congress and the White House. Congress rarely manages to override a presidential veto. (U.S. Senate)*

three presidents struck down 73, 74, and 19 bills, respectively. In contrast, the most recent presidents—Clinton, Bush, Obama, and Trump—have been far more sparing in their use of their veto power (see Figure 11.2).

A president's veto rarely comes as a surprise. As Congress works on a law, the president's congressional liaisons are ever-present. Administration officials may threaten a veto to shape the legislation in ways they prefer. When negotiations get especially intense, the president also can go public and challenge individual members or Congress as a whole.

Congress.   Congressional leaders in turn can threaten to bury another bill the president wants or openly defy a president to veto popular bills. After all the back-and-forth, presidents have developed yet another strategy: They can voice their displeasure while signing bills into law.

Signing Statements.   Bill signing has become a great Washington ritual, especially for popular legislation. Congressional sponsors flank the president, who has a big pile of pens to hand out to the program's key supporters while cameras capture the smiling moment.

In recent decades, presidents have increasingly issued **signing statements** as they sign a bill into law. These statements may offer their

Signing statements: Written presidential declarations commenting on the bill that is being signed into law— often including criticism of one or more provisions.

administration's interpretation of the law—one sometimes at odds with Congress's expressed ideas.

Chief Bureaucrat

As chief bureaucrat, the president has the powers to make appointments and issue executive orders.

Appointments.   The Constitution gives the president the power to appoint the executive branch leaders, subject to confirmation by the Senate. President Washington took the top officers of the major departments and organized them into a cabinet to advise him. By 1800, the executive branch numbered 200 office holders.[20]

Today, the executive branch includes 15 departments and 2.6 million employees—a number that has leveled off in recent years. Add the military, and the executive branch tops four million. Presidents appoint some four thousand **political appointees** who direct the executive agencies; the rest are **civil servants** who stay on from one administration to the next (all discussed in Chapter 12).

The Trump administration has shattered one record: four cabinet secretaries fired in the first year—and five in a year and half. No earlier president dismissed more than one. Supporters cheer the full throttle, take-no-prisoners approach; others worry that large organizations such as the cabinet agencies suffer when there is rapid turnover at the top.

Executive Orders.   As chief executive, presidents wield powers that do not need to go through Congress. They can sign **executive orders**, with the force of law, setting guidelines for federal agencies. Some are simply instructions for operating the executive branch: organizing a new advisory board, for example. Others involve controversial decisions. They can be issued with fanfare or executed secretly. Recent executive orders include: regulatory rollbacks, bans on entry from selected countries (described at the start of this chapter), enhanced border security, restrictions on lobbying, and an effort to strip funds from sanctuary cities.

Some presidential scholars insist that executive orders are unconstitutional— the Constitution never mentions them. However, courts generally permit the orders as part of the "inherent powers" of the presidency.[21] The Supreme Court has only struck down eight executive orders—five of Franklin Roosevelt's, two of Bill Clinton's, and one of Barack Obama's—out of more than 13,850 going back to the Washington administration.

Some observers worry that, yet again, authority is leaking away from Congress as presidents—from both parties—use a traditional form of executive power to expand the scope of their office. More and more, worry the critics, presidents use executive orders to make policy unilaterally, from the White House. Congress, mired in partisan stalemate, has been slow to respond.[22] There is, however, an inherent weakness in governing by executive order: The

Political appointees: Top officials in the executive agencies appointed by the president.

Civil servants: Members of the permanent executive branch bureaucracy who are employed on the basis of competitive exams and keep their positions regardless of the presidential administration.

Executive order: A presidential declaration, with the force of law, that issues instructions to the executive branch without any requirement for congressional action or approval.

next administration can repeal it with an executive order of its own—far easier than persuading Congress to roll back a policy.

Economist in Chief

Economic authority is one power the Constitution definitely does *not* grant the president. It places the power of the purse—taxing, spending, borrowing, and regulating commerce—firmly in congressional hands. However, during the Great Depression of the 1930s, the Roosevelt administration seized responsibility for putting the nation back to work, launching one recovery program after another. "Take a method and try it," insisted Roosevelt. "If that fails, try another. . . . Above all try something."[23]

The idea took root: The president became responsible for a smooth-running economy. When Roosevelt died, Congress legislated the Council of Economic Advisers to help presidents oversee the economy. Today, the president and a host of advisors monitor economic conditions. White House economists vet every plan and proposal for its impact on American prosperity; they help formulate policy on almost every issue—taxing, spending, trade deals, and the projected costs of a new federal holiday. Presidential popularity and the party's chances of holding onto the office in the next election are heavily influenced by economic conditions.

During the Trump administration's first two years, the economy boomed—and, as always, credit went to the administration in power. The president himself played a very active role: placing tariffs on aluminum and steel; launching a trade war with China and renegotiating trade deals such as NAFTA (with Mexico and Canada). Despite the deep discomfort of most economists with tariffs and trade wars, the economy continued to prosper right through most of 2018, although growth slowed across the second half of the year. What will be the long-term consequences? Stay tuned!

The Head of State

Most nations have a ceremonial head of state who stands above partisan politics and represents the nation. The queen of England, the emperor of Japan, and the president of Israel all play this nonpolitical role while their prime ministers make the policies that govern their countries. Citizens of the British Isles do not need to check their political affiliation when they

● *The president as head of state: President Bill Clinton and First Lady Hillary Clinton wear traditional kente cloth. They are waving to thousands of cheering Ghanaians. With them is then-president of Ghana, Jerry Rawlings.*

Executive Orders Issued, Per Day

WHICH PRESIDENTS RELIED MOST ON THIS POWER?

Presidents exercise many forms of power. Although the Constitution separates power among the branches, all presidents have issued executive orders that have the force of law but do not require congressional approval.

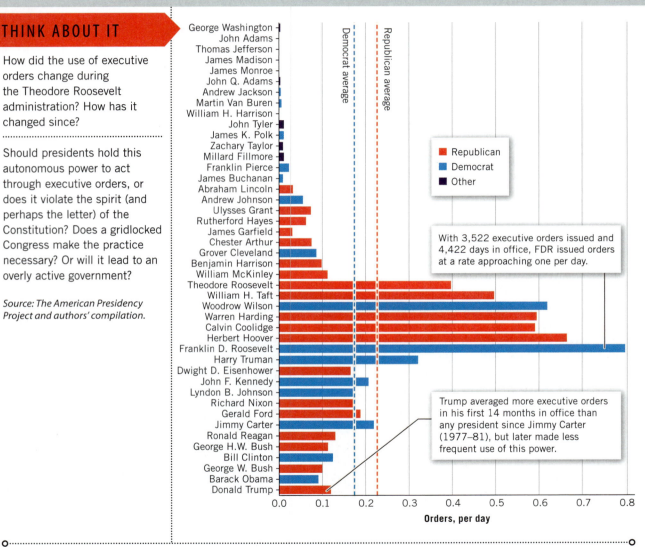

With 3,522 executive orders issued and 4,422 days in office, FDR issued orders at a rate approaching one per day.

Trump averaged more executive orders in his first 14 months in office than any president since Jimmy Carter (1977–81), but later made less frequent use of this power.

Legend: Republican, Democrat, Other

Orders, per day

sing "God Save the Queen." In contrast, the presidents of the United States play both roles. They stand for the nation even while they fight for their party. Balancing these roles can be difficult.

Presidents spend a lot of time in their ceremonial role. They throw out the first pitch during the World Series, spare a turkey every Thanksgiving, light the White House Christmas tree and menorah, and smash a bottle of champagne across the bow of a new aircraft carrier. When presidents travel abroad they represent all Americans, not just their party or their supporters.

Party Leader

George Washington repeatedly warned the country against political parties and the strife they would bring. However, by his second term, rival parties sprang up and thrust yet another role onto the president: party leader. This role sharpens the tension we described in the last section. There is a very fine line between leading the nation (and standing for everyone) and leading the Republicans (which means defeating Democrats).

Can anything tamp down the partisan conflict? Yes: The secret ingredient is fear. When a president grows very popular, opponents will often go along out of fear that the voters might punish them if they do not. Presidents, who get more votes in a district than a House member, or more votes in the state than a senator, can be very persuasive—as long as their poll numbers remain high.

The Bully Pulpit: Introducing Ideas

President Theodore Roosevelt was bursting with ideas, opinions, exhortations, and warnings. He called the presidency itself a "bully pulpit" (today we might say "awesome brand multiplier"). Roosevelt knew that an active president has the country's ear, an opening to introduce and promote new ideas.

Most presidencies are marked by a few big ideas. In his inaugural address, John F. Kennedy called the nation to public service. "Ask not what your country can do for you," said Kennedy. "Ask what you can do for your country." Ronald Reagan championed a very different idea when he called government the source of our national problems; individuals pursuing the American dream and trying to get rich were, he declared, the real source of national vitality. Successful presidents arrive in office with powerful ideas—and persuade the public to embrace new visions of our political life. A sign of a fading party is a cupboard bare of fresh ideas.

"The power of the presidency," as political scientist Richard Neustadt famously put it, "is the power to persuade."[24] Persuasion includes the ability to take an unfamiliar notion and get the whole nation to talk about it. Throughout this book, we have focused on the power and importance of ideas in American politics. The presidency is the institution best geared to inject new ideas into our great national conversation.

Theodore Roosevelt takes full advantage of his bully pulpit.

The Impossible Job

How can anyone juggle so many different presidential roles? The honest answer is that no one can. Even great presidents cannot handle all their jobs well all of the time. Still, this is what we demand of our chief executive.

Each presidential role requires different strengths and skills. No person will have them all. However, the bully pulpit can help: Bold ideas bring together the many threads of this huge task. They make a presidency coherent. Without that, presidents may seem overwhelmed, skittering from one task to another without a broader vision.

Finally, note one theme that runs through every role: Presidential authority has grown in every aspect of the office. The president's many roles are one more way to measure the swelling power and importance of the office. That brings us back again to the central paradox of the executive: The presidency grows ever more powerful, yet the role has grown so large that no one person can perform every aspect of it well.

The Bottom Line

» The president wears many hats and helmets. Some are specified in the Constitution. Others have developed over time.

» Presidential roles include commander in chief, top diplomat, first legislator, head bureaucrat, economist in chief, head of state, and party leader. Presidents also are uniquely situated to introduce new ideas—tying together these many different roles.

» The president's authority has grown in every one of these roles. It is difficult to do so many things well.

Presidential Leadership: Success and Failure in the Oval Office

Presidents try to manage perceptions of their performance. They address the public, use (and bypass) the media, schedule eye-catching events, and rely on polls to hone their message. How do we know if they have succeeded? We will examine three different measures: polls, historical rankings, and the great cycles of political time.

Managing the Public

As the only nationally elected official (excepting the vice president, who is elected as a package with the president), presidents develop a relationship with the people, which they cultivate by **going public**—directly addressing citizens to win support. Each new form of media—radio, television, Twitter, Snapchat—shifts the way presidents go public.

John F. Kennedy demonstrated the full power of the media when he held the first live, televised press conference in February 1961. It was a smash hit, with 65 million viewers; Kennedy's approval ratings climbed to 75 percent and stayed high for 16 months. Kennedy had shifted how presidents connect to the public: People saw him, heard him, and related directly to him. Few people gave Donald Trump much chance in the 2016 Republican primary, much less the general election. What did they overlook? His savvy in going public.

Today, presidents continue to look for ways to connect with Americans. They give campaign speeches before roaring crowds—even when the next election is years away. They speak directly to the camera from the Oval Office. They travel across the nation. They tweet. Each is designed to win the public over—sometimes for a specific policy, sometimes for a broad presidential agenda.

Presidents constantly balance going public with playing "the inside game"—quietly working with Congress and the bureaucracy to get things done. Which is more effective? That depends on the time and circumstance. But every president—going public or playing the inside game—strives to shape public perceptions.[25]

Images are often more important than words. Presidents hug disaster victims, play basketball with the troops, or wave to cheering throngs. The image can turn negative in an instant. President Johnson playfully lifted his beagle by the ears in front of the press (cruel!). President Ford slipped and fell in public (clumsy!). President George H. W. Bush threw up at a state dinner in Japan (you can imagine!). In a complicated world, a single picture can distil popular perception. Images have an impact—positive or negative—when they seem to reveal the president's true strengths or weakness. The key point is simple: *Presidents constantly try to manage their image in the public eye.*[26]

Our 24/7 media era complicates the effort to touch the public. The sheer volume of information flowing through the media means that only the most important events will command attention for long. The president's message now requires constant repetition, amplification, and—to grip viewers—a touch of novelty and drama. Going public is a rapidly changing art form.

The White House runs a sophisticated polling operation that guides its outreach efforts. The president's daily schedule frequently includes briefings from the administration's pollster. The president's team scrutinizes the findings, not to develop new policies but to recalibrate the ways it presents its message. President Trump has proven especially adept at bending the news cycle with his tweets—to the delight of some and the chagrin of others.[27]

Going public: Directly addressing the public to win support for oneself or one's ideas.

What Do YOU Think? Go Public or Play the Inside Game?

Pick an issue you care about: immigration or climate change or something else. Now, what would you advise the president to emphasize?	**Go Public.** In the era of Obama and Trump, presidencies are almost like social movements—keep your supporters mobilized.	**The Inside Game.** To really make progress, you have to work quietly with individual members of Congress and the bureaucracy.	Of course, every president does both, but on every issue has to stress one or the other.

Some political scientists caution that it is very difficult to move public opinion. The bully pulpit is most powerful, suggest political scientist George Edwards, when presidents recognize and exploit changes that are already in the political air.[28]

Approval Ratings

Every week, another raft of poll reports charts the president's performance. These have become a rough barometer of the administration's success. Any one poll can be misleading (as we saw in Chapter 6), but if you eliminate the outliers—the polls that are much higher and lower than the others—and scan the rest, you will have a snapshot of the administration's ratings that are reverberating through the media, and around the country.

Presidents riding high in the polls find governing easier. The press corps and Washington insiders are slightly more deferential. Members of Congress watch the president's popularity in their own states and districts, and think twice about opposing him or her. As the president's approval rating sinks, criticism rises. Congressional allies back away. Press coverage turns sour. The late night talk shows serve up mockery.

All administrations run through polling cycles; no president stays above 50 percent approval for an entire term. Average out differences across administrations and roughly the same pattern generally emerges: High approval scores at the start, usually above 60 percent; a slow decline that bottoms out midway through the second year; a gradual ascent and peak toward the end of the fourth year (see Figure 11.3). With luck, it rises above 50 percent in time for re-election. A dip

● Lyndon Johnson lifting his beagle by the ears. The president was trying for a lighthearted moment but quickly felt the backlash from outraged pet lovers.

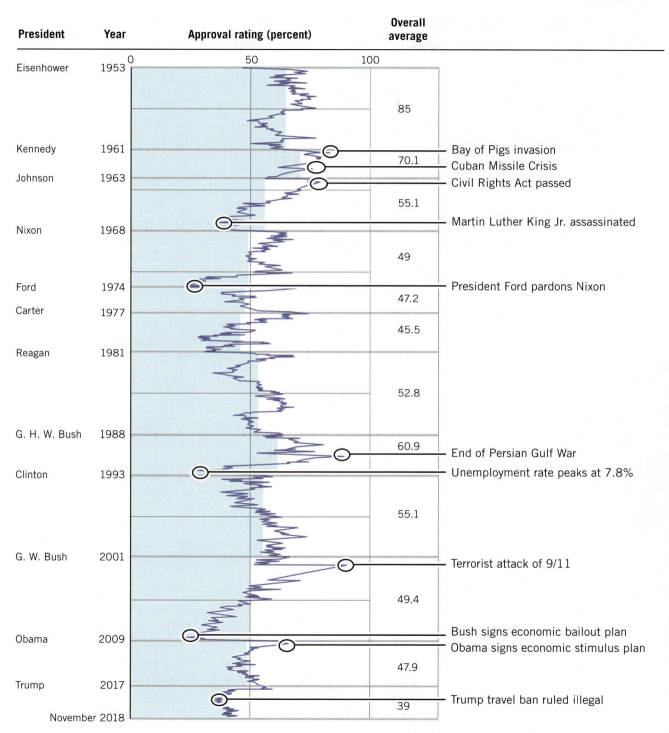

President	Year	Approval rating (percent)	Overall average	
Eisenhower	1953		85	
Kennedy	1961			Bay of Pigs invasion
			70.1	Cuban Missile Crisis
Johnson	1963			Civil Rights Act passed
			55.1	
Nixon	1968			Martin Luther King Jr. assassinated
			49	
Ford	1974			President Ford pardons Nixon
			47.2	
Carter	1977		45.5	
Reagan	1981			
			52.8	
G. H. W. Bush	1988		60.9	
Clinton	1993			End of Persian Gulf War
				Unemployment rate peaks at 7.8%
			55.1	
G. W. Bush	2001			Terrorist attack of 9/11
			49.4	
Obama	2009			Bush signs economic bailout plan
				Obama signs economic stimulus plan
			47.9	
Trump	2017			Trump travel ban ruled illegal
	November 2018		39	

● **Figure 11.3** *Presidential job approval. Every administration goes through polling cycles—rising and falling in public esteem. Note how approval ratings are affected by important events and political decisions. (Gallup)*

George W. Bush visits the scene of the 9/11 terrorist attack. The dramatic days following the attack drove President Bush's approval ratings to one of the highest levels ever recorded by Gallup.

See President George W. Bush's dramatic bullhorn speech at Ground Zero.

after re-election and a rise at the end. Of course, every administration offers its own variation.[29]

Dramatic events create spikes in approval (or disapproval). The two highest ratings on record boosted George H. W. Bush after a quick, dramatic victory in the first Gulf War, as well as his son George W. Bush after he responded to terrorist attacks on the World Trade Center in September 2001 by standing defiantly on the rubble with a bullhorn, surrounded by cheering firefighters. Each Bush peaked at 89 percent approval rating in Gallup polls. Such spikes in popularity are usually temporary. A year after his military triumph, George H. W. Bush's approval rating had fallen below 40 percent and he lost his re-election campaign. The younger Bush narrowly won re-election but ended his time in office tied for the lowest ratings after a full term.

Polls offer immediate public feedback, but they do not reflect an administration's historical importance or long-term success. For that we can turn to a different type of poll.

Presidential Greatness

Back in 1948, historian Arthur Schlesinger Sr. asked a panel of historians to rank the presidents. Their choice for the top three: Abraham Lincoln, George Washington, and Franklin D. Roosevelt.

Poll after poll followed—we list four different versions in Table 11.3. In each, a different panel of historians and political scientists ranks the presidents in order from great to failed.

Liberals and conservatives rarely disagree about how the presidents rank. Ronald Reagan is an exception, though his ratings from left-leaning scholars have climbed in recent polls. Such agreement returns us to the question: What makes a great president?

There are plenty of answers. President Harry Truman said that all the great presidents were decisive. Political scientists Marc Landy and Sidney Milkis suggested that great presidents redefine the presidency. Our view is that great presidents redefine America; they reshape the way the nation sees itself.[30] Or, to put it slightly differently, *great presidents tell us who we are*. Their definitions of America resonate with the public and endure over time.[31]

Greatness in Context: The Rise and Fall of Political Orders

Presidents are not masters of their destiny. The times make the presidents as much as they make the times. Individual presidents fit into national cycles of politics and power. Presidential scholar Stephen Skowronek described each

TABLE 11.3	**Rating the Presidents**

Here are the results of four independent polls by historians and political scientists (you can find dozens of them). Historian Arthur Schlesinger polled historians in 1948; his son Arthur Schlesinger Jr. repeated the exercise with historians and political scientists in 1996; the United Kingdom Center for the United States Presidency (USPC) provided rankings from a foreign scholarly perspective; and the American Political Science Association (APSA) conducted a survey in 2015.

	POLITICAL PARTY	SCHLESINGER (1948)	SCHLESINGER, JR. (1996)	USPC 2011	APSA 2015
George Washington	None	2	2	3	2
John Adams	Federalist	9	11	12	15
Thomas Jefferson	Dem–Repub.	5	4	4	5
James Madison	Dem–Repub.	14	17	14	13
James Monroe	Dem–Repub.	12	15	13	16
John Q. Adams	Dem–Repub.	11	18	20	22
Andrew Jackson	Democratic	6	5	9	9
Martin Van Buren	Democratic	15	21	27	25
William H. Harrison	Whig	—	—	—	39
John Tyler	Whig	22	32	37	36
James K. Polk	Democratic	10	9	16	19
Zachary Taylor	Whig	25	29	33	33
Millard Fillmore	Whig	24	31	35	37
Franklin Pierce	Democratic	27	33	39	40
James Buchanan	Democratic	26	38	40	43
Abraham Lincoln	Republican	1	1	2	1
Andrew Johnson	Democratic	19	37	36	41
Ulysses Grant	Republican	28	24	29	28
Rutherford Hayes	Republican	13	23	30	30
James Garfield	Republican	—	—	—	31
Chester Arthur	Republican	17	26	32	32
Grover Cleveland	Democratic	8	13	21	23
Benjamin Harrison	Republican	21	19	34	29
William McKinley	Republican	18	16	17	21
Theodore Roosevelt	Republican	7	6	5	4

(continued)

TABLE 11.3 (continued)

	POLITICAL PARTY	SCHLESINGER (1948)	SCHLESINGER, JR. (1996)	USPC 2011	APSA 2015
William H. Taft	Republican	16	22	25	20
Woodrow Wilson	Democratic	4	7	6	10
Warren Harding	Republican	29	39	38	42
Calvin Coolidge	Republican	23	30	28	27
Herbert Hoover	Republican	20	35	26	38
Franklin D. Roosevelt	Democratic	3	3	1	3
Harry Truman	Democratic	—	8	7	6
Dwight D. Eisenhower	Republican	—	10	10	7
John F. Kennedy	Democratic	—	12	15	14
Lyndon B. Johnson	Democratic	—	14	11	12
Richard Nixon	Republican	—	36	23	34
Gerald Ford	Republican	—	28	24	24
Jimmy Carter	Democratic	—	27	18	26
Ronald Reagan	Republican	—	25	8	11
George H.W. Bush	Republican	—	24	22	17
Bill Clinton	Democratic	—	20	19	8
George W. Bush	Republican	—	—	31	35
Barack Obama	Democratic	—	—	—	18

Political order: The set of institutions, interests, and ideas that shape a political era. Great presidents reconstruct the framework, launching a new order.

presidency as part of a great historical pageant: the rise and fall of **political orders**. A political order is a set of ideas, institutions, and coalitions that dominate an era.[32] In Skowronek's telling, orders rise and fall in three steps. Every president fits somewhere in the cycle.

Step 1: A New Order Rises. Outstanding leaders take over the presidency and shake up the political system. An Abraham Lincoln, Franklin D. Roosevelt, or Ronald Reagan introduces a fresh philosophy of government. Each leads a political party with new allies and new ideas into power. The public responds enthusiastically to this bold break with old political ways.

Step 2: The Order Refreshed. Every governing coalition eventually grows tired. The great president who boldly articulated its themes is gone. Many of the original goals are won. New problems arise that have nothing to do with the philosophy that fired up the party in the first place. The ideas begin to look out of date; the great coalition begins to unravel. In fortunate times, a new leader will come along and infuse the party with a fresh variation of the old philosophy, renewing the aging order.

Step 3: The Old Order Crumbles. No order lasts forever. Over time, the party finds its ideas increasingly irrelevant. The old order feels outdated, a political dinosaur.

Every president comes to Washington with fresh hope and promise. Political historians look back and see that they operate within a cycle. Some (Lincoln, Roosevelt, Reagan) take office as the head of a new coalition with fresh ideas. Others come to Washington at the end of an era (Herbert Hoover, Jimmy Carter). They face a far more difficult governing challenge. To some extent, the rankings in Table 11.3 reflect each president's place in political time.

The Burden of Office

Talk of greatness should not obscure the inescapable fact about the presidency: It is an exhausting job that takes a visible toll on the incumbents. The Oval Office houses a vulnerable human being. Presidents get sick, take dubious drugs, get drunk, overeat, have affairs, contemplate suicide, fret about ailing parents, and burn with insecurities. None can escape the human condition.

Learn about presidential achievements.

Presidents are usually very talented—or they would not have gotten to the White House. As with all people, however, they have strengths and weaknesses, vast skills and blind spots.[33]

These inevitable human limits return us to our central question: Has the presidency developed too much power for any one person to handle?

The Bottom Line

» Presidents try to manage public perceptions of the job they are doing. They get immediate feedback from polling.

» Great presidents change the way Americans see themselves. They change what government does. They forge a new answer to the question, Who are we?

» Individual presidents don't completely control their own destiny. They operate in the historical cycle of political orders.

The President's Team: A Tour of the White House

When Herbert Hoover moved into the Oval Office in 1929, he presided over a presidential staff of four administrative assistants plus 36 typists, clerks, and messengers. That was it. No speechwriter, no press secretary, no congressional liaison; no chief of staff, no drug czar, no budget director. Today, the presidency is more than a person or an idea or a party. It is a bureaucracy staffed by thousands of people.

The Political Solar System: Presidential Appointments

Every time a new president is elected, thousands of people hope for a job. University professors who have always dreamed of government service, students who worked on the campaign, business executives looking for a plum on their résumé, and supporters who believe the president-elect will make America a better place: All want to work for the new administration.

To get a job in a presidential administration, do not start by being modest. You must campaign: One executive angling to be a senior Treasury Department official a few years back tasked four subordinates to do nothing but promote his name to the administration's transition team in charge of selecting top appointees (yes, he got the big job).

Let's take a tour of the offices near the presidency. A crucial opening point: Power is always measured by proximity to the president. The executive branch is like the solar system, with the president as the sun and everyone else rotating around him. The ultimate name drop in any Washington, DC, conversation is "When I was talking to the president. . . ." Most people who work for the president are in an orbit somewhere past Pluto: They never get any face time. Let us look at who does.

The Vice President

Traditionally, the vice president's primary job was to stand in the wings in case the president died. That awful transition has happened eight times in American history, four times by murder. There were at least four more close calls: Assassins fired point-blank at Andrew Jackson (the gun jammed), Franklin D. Roosevelt (the shooter missed the president and killed the mayor of Chicago), Gerald Ford (a bystander grabbed the gunwoman's arm, diverting the shot), and Ronald Reagan (the bullet lodged less than an inch from his heart).

In addition to standing by in case of catastrophe, vice presidents preside over the Senate and cast a vote in case of a tie. There is not much power in presiding, and the vice president only appears in the Senate chambers on special occasions.

Otherwise, a vice president's responsibilities are entirely up to the president. For a long time, the role was meager. Senator Daniel Webster rejected the

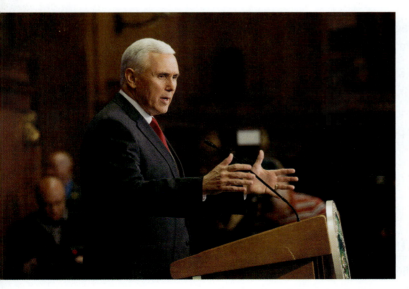

● *Vice President Mike Pence served six terms in the House before being elected Governor of Indiana.*

vice-presidential nomination in 1848 with an acid comment: "I do not choose to be buried until I am really dead." Bad move: Webster would have become the thirteenth president when Zachary Taylor died in the White House. Franklin Roosevelt's vice president, John Nance Garner, offered the most famous assessment of the post when he said the job was "not worth a pitcher of warm piss."[34]

The weak vice presidency continued well into the twentieth century. Harry Truman had barely met with President Roosevelt when FDR's death in 1945 catapulted him into the Oval Office. "Boys," he said when he met the press the next day, "if you ever pray, pray for me now." In 1960, reporters asked President Eisenhower what ideas Vice President Nixon had contributed. "If you give me a week," quipped the president nastily, "I might think of one."

The vice presidency became important during the Carter administration (1977–1981). From Carter through Trump, six of the past eight presidents were Washington outsiders who had never held a federal job; every newcomer chose a vice president with federal government experience—Vice President Mike Pence, for example, served six terms in Congress. Slowly but surely, vice presidents gathered the emblems of power: a seat at cabinet meetings (1950s), an office in the White House (1970s), a vice-presidential jet (Air Force 2, in the 1970s), a growing staff, and—perhaps most important in status-obsessed Washington—regular meetings with the president.[35]

The Cabinet

Members of the cabinet have two primary roles: They run executive branch departments, and they meet to discuss policy with the president in cabinet meetings. Once the cabinet served as a president's governing team. Today the cabinet has grown to 15 members; add the vice president and other important officers on the president's staff and meetings are too large to serve as a real decision-making body. We discuss the cabinet, and the hundreds of thousands of federal bureaucrats who work under cabinet secretaries in the executive agencies, in Chapter 12.

In most administrations, a handful of cabinet officers rise above the rest and shape administration policy. Political scientists call them the "inner cabinet": the secretaries of State, Defense, Treasury, and Justice— precisely the quartet in Washington's original cabinet. Most other cabinet secretaries operate far from the centers of power. Departments such as Transportation and

● *President Nixon worked closely with National Security Advisor and later Secretary of State Henry Kissinger.*

Energy have vital roles to play. But, unless they have personal connections or unusual responsibilities, they are rarely part of a president's inner circle.

Cabinet secretaries often come to see issues from the perspective of their own bureaucracy rather than the administration or the party. After all, they are surrounded by tens of thousands of employees who do a lot of work with limited resources and look to the secretary to champion their causes. Richard Nixon's close adviser John Ehrlichman groused that the administration chose solid, budget-cutting conservatives to run the cabinet departments—and then watched their appointees run off and "marry the natives."[36]

Presidents must manage the tension between senior cabinet officials and White House advisors. At one cabinet meeting during the Carter years, the secretary of Housing and Urban Development summed up her frustration by blurting out: "We can move government forward by putting phones in the White House staff offices and then using them." Translation: No one in the White House even returns my phone calls. Why all the frustration? The president's inner circle (and the real center of power) had shifted from the cabinet to the White House staff.[37]

The Executive Office of the President

Executive Office of the President (EOP): The agencies that help the president manage daily activities.

Influence over government policy has steadily leaked into the **Executive Office of the President** (**EOP**), made up of agencies that help a president manage his daily activities. These roughly 1,800 administrators and advisors surround the chief executive. Many are experts who stay on from one administration to the next. Conservatives, frustrated with cabinet agencies that failed to pursue their values, have most eagerly expanded the EOP. Richard Nixon created or revamped four EOP offices, Ronald Reagan added three more. Today every president—left, right, or center—relies on them.

Table 11.4 illustrates the offices in the Executive Office of the President. The list reflects the hats and helmets that the president wears. Organizing a new EOP office or an office within the White House Office (discussed below) is one way for administrations to signal the things they consider most important. Richard Nixon added the Council on Environmental Quality, George W. Bush an office for his faith-based initiatives, Barack Obama created an Office of Digital Strategy, and Donald Trump, the first businessman in the White House, created an Office of American Innovation.

In the EOP, a familiar clash gets especially intense. On the one hand, most EOP employees are experts on specific issues—drug policy, healthcare, or the budget. On the other, they have to serve each president's political philosophy (not to mention re-election prospects). Slowly the balance between these goals has tipped toward politics.[38] Let's visit the most important offices in the EOP.

Central clearance: The OMB's authority to review and "clear" (or okay) anything a member of the administration says or does in public.

The Office of Management and Budget (OMB). This is the most powerful agency in the executive branch—known (not very fondly) as "the agency that says no." The OMB uses its authority over the federal budget to manage the entire executive branch. During the Reagan administration, the agency acquired its most powerful weapon—**central clearance**: the power to review and "clear"

TABLE 11.4	**Offices in the Executive Office of the President, 2019**		
OFFICE	EMPLOYEES	YEAR ORGANIZED	ORGANIZED BY
White House Office	450	1939	F. D. Roosevelt
Council of Economic Advisers	27	1946	Truman
National Security Staff	58	1947	Truman
Office of the U.S. Trade Representative	240	1963	Kennedy
Council on Environmental Quality	24	1969	Nixon
Office of Management and Budget	487	1921/1971	Harding/Nixon
Office of the Vice President	25	1972	Nixon
Office of Science and Technology Policy	32	1976	Ford
Office of Administration	234	1977	Carter
Domestic Policy Council	25	1985	Reagan
Office of National Drug Control Policy	84	1988	Reagan
Homeland Security Council	18	2001	G. W. Bush
Executive Residence	96 (full-time)	—	—

(or OK) anything a member of the administration says or does in public. All members, from the secretary of defense to an analyst in the Small Business Bureau, must submit every speech they make, opinion piece they write, congressional testimony they deliver, or policy they propose to OMB for its approval. Until they get OMB's nod, they may not say or publish a word.

The OMB vets every administration proposal. When Congress passes a bill, OMB coordinates every administration member's recommendations about whether to sign or veto. Imagine how frustrating it is for energetic new secretaries to take charge of departments, only to learn they must clear every formal statement with OMB.

Before the Nixon administration organized the OMB in 1971, fiscal control was much looser. President Lyndon Johnson famously low-balled his economic estimates. One day, instructing a young senator from Massachusetts named Ted Kennedy, Johnson warned him not to let economic projections slow up his favorite bills and illustrated the point with Medicare. "The fools [at the Bureau of the Budget] had to go projecting [Medicare] down the road five or six years, and when you project it the first year it runs $900 million."[39] Those anticipated costs, complained LBJ, cost him votes in Congress; he advised the new senator to stop economists from interfering with important proposals. The era of simply suppressing cost estimates is long past. Today, OMB requires cost-benefit analyses for every policy—the institutional rules of governing empower an economic perspective. Still, the future is never certain and the savvy political operator knows plenty of ways to massage the numbers.

The Council of Economic Advisers. Meet another clutch of economists. The council and its chair keep an eye on the whole economy, private as well as public. This office does economic analysis for the president: unemployment predictions, productivity measurements, economic forecasts, and all the rest.

Settle a military crisis from the White House.

The National Security Council (NSC). The NSC brings together powerful officers involved in national security: secretaries of state, defense, energy, and treasury (economists again); the chair of the Joint Chiefs of Staff; and others who the president choses. The national security advisor directs the council and must work for consensus across all the different perspectives and formidable personalities. In some administrations, the national security advisor is as influential as the secretaries of state or defense—although the Trump administration saw an unprecedented three NSC advisors in its first 14 months.

The Heart of Power: The White House Office (WHO)

Our tour ends at the heart of power. The White House Office is part of the Executive Office of the President, but it also stands apart. This group of 400 or so advisors, aides, and associates work directly for the president, most of them in the West Wing. At the center sits the **Chief of Staff**, the president's gatekeeper, traffic cop, and coordinator. Other important offices include speechwriters, White House counsel (the president's official lawyer), and the legislative affairs team.

Chief of Staff: The individual responsible for managing the president's office.

Until President Obama, the two parties organized their White House Offices very differently from one another. Franklin D. Roosevelt set a mixed example for Democrats: creative chaos. Roosevelt surrounded himself with gifted intellectuals, gave them overlapping tasks, and let them freelance from issue to issue. In theory, bold ideas would flow. Many Democratic administrations tried to mimic Roosevelt. John Kennedy valued broad-minded intellectuals and encouraged them to weigh in on any subject. So did Bill Clinton; early in his administration, staffers would jump in and out of meetings and conversations regardless of their assigned tasks. The bull sessions went on deep into the night.

In contrast, Republicans like clearly defined organization and tasks. Republican executives usually model their organization on the military or traditional business: Crisp lines of authority go from the president to the Chief of Staff. Everyone has a clearly defined role.

Now, that's changed. The Obama White House was tightly organized— almost Republican in style. President Trump seems to thrive on creative chaos—encouraging aides and confidantes to drop by the Oval Office, hiring and firing White House officials at an unprecedented clip, and assigning tasks to people he trusts regardless of their background.

No matter the style, the Chief of Staff makes the White House run. He or she directs traffic through the president's office, oversees the schedule, sums up the decisions that are made, and follows up to see that those decisions are understood and implemented. The office requires a strong, talented, smooth, competent administrator familiar with the levers of power.

The White House staff is like a little village, full of folkways that reflect the presidents' values. For example, Ronald Reagan put special emphasis on his speechwriting team; they spent hours watching his past speeches to learn his rhythms and his way of thinking. The president reworked their draft speeches with great care. Reagan's successor, George H. W. Bush, thought the president should speak more plainly and rejected all the attention on crafting speeches. He demonstrated the new order by stripping the speechwriting team of its White House Mess (dining hall) privileges. The village recognized a major demotion.

When a new president comes to town, attention focuses on his cabinet selections. The wise observer knows to track more subtle appointments to the White House Office. After all, no matter how brilliant the secretary of labor or how experienced the secretary of HHS, they will have to rely on unseen advisors in the White House to convey their ideas, programs, and problems to the president. The route to influence—the path to "yes" on any program—runs through the White House Office staff.

Unlike the high-ranking members of the cabinet agencies, most EOP staffers are not subject to Senate confirmation. They are elected by no one, overseen only by the Chief of Staff, and often have regular access to the president's ear.

Talking POLITICS

SPEAK LIKE A WEST WING INSIDER

Want to learn to talk like a member of the White House staff? Start practicing now. Casually toss off something like: "I'm given to understand that WHO is the real force in the EOP." Those are two indecipherable acronyms (the more the better) and, of course, the passive voice: You don't want to risk revealing your sources!

What Do YOU Think?   Do Presidents Need Such a Large Staff?

The Executive Office of the President (EOP) now houses more than 1,800 staff members, from economic and foreign-policy advisers to communications specialists. All answer directly to the president and his top aides; most do not even require Senate confirmation. By comparison, President Lincoln had four personal assistants, and when Franklin D. Roosevelt took office 82 years ago, he had a staff of 36. Does the modern presidency require such a large staff?

Yes, absolutely. Given the immense range of responsibilities on their shoulders, presidents need reliable, trustworthy experts and assistants to analyze intelligence and economic data, to assess overseas threats, and to help manage public perceptions of the president. In fact, it's surprising there isn't more support (Congress, after all, has more than 20,000 staffers).

No—start staff cuts immediately. Modern technology could make the presidency far more efficient. CEOs run major companies with far fewer staff reporting to their office. Other sectors are able to function with far fewer personnel; so could the White House.

Not sure. The huge array of presidential staff reportedly work incredibly hard, and the White House certainly has a plateful of duties. But perhaps the large staff reflects too much power in the executive? If Congress reasserted its traditional powers, we could cut back this EOP army.

Should the president's advisors, rather than the experienced cabinet secretaries confirmed by the Senate, dominate the executive branch? Again, we confront the fundamental question: power and control versus democracy and enhanced accountability. Perhaps granting authority to White House staff makes the whole federal leviathan more responsive to the will of the people. Most democracies are, ultimately, ruled by experts. American government is run in part by men and women with a sharp eye on winning the next election.

One final feature of the White House staff strikes most newcomers: Its members are young—much younger than the staff running other governments, large corporations, universities, or major nonprofit organizations. Cabinet secretaries with years of experience often complain that their access to the president is governed by young people in their twenties and thirties.

The First Spouse

One team in the White House Office does not fit any traditional political category: the office of the president's spouse. Traditionally, the "First Lady" role was simply that of hostess. Eleanor Roosevelt broke the mold and pioneered a new role, the First Lady as activist. Eleanor was a powerful liberal, a popular symbol of the New Deal, and a forceful advocate for Franklin and his policies. In effect, she became a one-woman campaign for social and labor reform. A *New Yorker* cartoon captures the First Lady's tireless campaign. Deep underground, two sooty coal miners stop their labors as one remarks with surprise: "For gosh sakes, here comes Mrs. Roosevelt!"

What did Melania Trump mean?

Few First Spouses were as active or committed as Eleanor Roosevelt, but she set a pattern of policy engagement that her successors have followed. Lady Bird Johnson chose "beautification" of American cities and highways. Nancy Reagan became a spokesperson for the war on drugs. Mrs. Reagan was the first to achieve that mark of status, an office in the West Wing. Bill Clinton assigned his wife, Hillary, the signature policy initiative of his presidency, national healthcare reform. In fall 1993, Hillary Clinton's performance in a series of congressional hearings drew praise from both parties; it did not save the healthcare reform but signaled the start of her own political career—and established a new ceiling for First Ladies' contributions to presidential action.

Melania Trump has focused on children. Her "be best" program addresses child well-being, cyberbullying, and opioid

● The first spouse in the media storm: Melania Trump, wearing a jacket that read, "I really don't care, do u?" set off much commentary when she traveled to an immigrant center on the U.S.-Mexico border to visit children who had been separated from their parents. Was she criticizing the media for its critical treatment of the president's border policy? Or the president's policy itself?

abuse. Political scientists—especially those interested in gender and power—have begun to pay particular attention to the role of the First Spouse.[40]

The Bottom Line

» Each president directs a massive organization—the executive branch of the federal government.

» Cabinet secretaries manage the great bureaucracies of the executive branch of government.

» Over time, executive branch policymaking has migrated from the cabinet to the Executive Office of the Presidency—the network of offices that help the president manage the government.

» The president's innermost circle is the White House Office. These close advisors—often relatively young—include the Chief of Staff, speechwriters, legislative liaison, and the office of the First Spouse.

🔵 Conclusion: The Most Powerful Office on Earth?

In 2017, a new president arrived, bursting with ideas and campaign promises—and raising, once again, fundamental questions about the presidency. President Trump seemed to make policy on the fly: threatening leaders of other countries, holding high profile summits, announcing the rollback of regulations, renegotiating treaties and trade deals, pushing Congress to cut taxes, naming conservative justices to the courts. At the same time, the president fumed over Congress's refusal to change immigration law, to allocate money for a border wall, or to cut spending.

The presidency is a far more powerful office than it was a century ago. Has it grown too powerful for a republic? Or is it too hobbled to carry out the mandate of the public? Perhaps it is most accurate to say that the same president can be both too powerful and too weak, depending on the issue, the circumstances, and the incumbent. As you watch the Trump administration, ask yourself whether the president is too powerful—or not powerful enough.

The Trump presidency also raises another concern among political scientists: Does Donald Trump violate the norms—a basic civility toward political opponents, respect for judges and courts, deference to the rules—that protect democratic governance?[41] Strong democracies rely, not just on formal laws, as Alexis de Tocqueville stated, but also the "reason and mores" that limit power and guide behavior. Once they are broken, they may be hard to re-establish.[42]

Who are we? The president offers us an answer—actually, several different answers. Americans seek a powerful, confident figure at their government's center. At the same time, we fear strong executives and hem them in with a labyrinth of checks and balances. We want our collective democratic voice ringing in the ears of our national leaders but also want our security protected in ways that may require secrecy and fast, decisive choices. We are a people who demand small government—yet complain when every need is not speedily met by the executive branch. We are a complicated, diverse, paradoxical people—like the presidency that reflects and serves us.

CHAPTER SUMMARY

Check your understanding of Chapter 11.

● *The president personifies America.* More than any individual, the president tells us who we are—and what we are becoming.

● *The president injects new ideas into American politics.* Our discussion of Congress emphasized the institution, the rules of the game; the presidency puts more focus on individuals and ideas.

● The president has three types of powers: those expressed in the Constitution, those delegated by Congress, and those inherent in the role of chief executive.

● The executive branch has grown far more powerful over time, especially when it comes to foreign policy.

● The office of the president constantly raises the same fundamental question: *Is the president too powerful for a democratic republic? Or, on the other hand, is the office too weak to do what Americans demand of it?* Or, perhaps, the president is both too strong and too weak at the same time.

● The president wears many hats and helmets. Presidential roles include commander in chief, top diplomat, first legislator, head bureaucrat, economist in chief, head of state, and party leader. The president's authority has grown in every one of these many roles. At the same time, it is difficult to do so many different things effectively.

● Presidents try to manage public perceptions of the job they are doing by going public and getting feedback from polls. Individual presidents do not completely control their own destiny. They operate in the historical cycle of *political orders.*

● Over time, executive branch policy has flowed from the cabinet secretaries to the Executive Office of the President—the network of offices that help the president manage the government.

● The president's innermost circle is the White House Office. These close advisors—often relatively young—include the Chief of Staff, speechwriters, legislative liaison, and the office of the First Spouse.

Need to review key ideas in greater depth? Click here.

KEY TERMS

Flashcard review.

Central clearance, p. 392	Executive order, p. 378	Override, p. 375
Chief of Staff, p. 394	Executive privilege, p. 368	Political appointees, p. 378
Civil servants, p. 378	Expressed powers, p. 367	Political order, p. 388
Delegated powers, p. 368	Going public, p. 383	Signing statements, p. 377
Executive agreements, p. 368	Imperial presidency, p. 369	Unitary executive theory,
Executive Office of the	Inherent powers of the	p. 369
President (EOP), p. 392	presidency, p. 368	Veto power, p. 375

STUDY QUESTIONS

1. Some people have suggested changing the president's term to one seven-year term without the possibility of re-election. What do you think? How would that shift the incentives that currently face a first-term president?

2. Why is the Constitution more vague about presidential than congressional powers? What problems—and benefits—does that ambiguity create?

3. What do you think: Is the president too strong? Or too weak? Defend your opinion.

4. Name seven different roles the president plays. Which do you consider the most important right now? How well do you think the president is carrying out this role today?

5. How well do you think President Trump goes public—appealing to the American public to support his policies? Do *you* respond positively to his speeches and legislative requests?

6. Should presidents care about their approval ratings from the American public? Why or why not?

7. Explain the role of the OMB. What does this agency do? What perspective was it designed to bring to the policy debates?

8. Describe the role of a First Spouse. Despite getting involved in policies, she is often more popular than the president. Why do you think that is so?

 Go to **www.oup.com/us/Morone** to find quizzes, flash cards, simulations, tutorials, videos, and other study tools.

12 Bureaucracy

THE MISSOURI BOOTHEEL is a rural region in the south-west corner of the state – and, yes, on the map, it does look like a boot's heel. Back in 2010, the region faced a public health crisis. There were not enough hospitals, clinics, or other health providers to serve this Mississippi Delta area of farmland, small towns, and rolling hills. Obesity and diabetes rates were rising sharply, and newer scourges like opioid addiction stretched resources even more.[1]

The Bootheel was not unusual. Healthcare providers are often scarce in rural America. In the Bootheel, health care advocates did something that may surprise you: They called for help from bureaucrats. The Health Resources & Services Administration, a part of the Department of Health and Human Services, responded with a solution: A digital network connecting six far-flung health centers across the region; the network coordinated care and advised residents in each neighborhood when a service provider or mobile clinic was coming to their area.[2]

Health outcomes in the Bootheel improved after the network went into place.[3] Note the unexpected heroes who improved health care: Bureaucrats in Washington, DC, working with bureaucrats in Missouri and local health professionals, as well as private advocacy groups (such as The Bootheel Network for Health Improvement).

Bureaucrats helping? That's not a story most people expect to hear. Most Americans hold a very low opinion of the federal bureaucracy. Sixty percent, in a 2018 poll, agreed that "unelected or appointed officials in the federal government have too much influence in determining federal policy."[4] Politicians campaign for office against faceless bureaucrats in Washington, portraying them as "armies of regulators descending like locusts," in the words of Senator Ted Cruz (R-TX). President Obama promised to shrink government programs "that do not work."[5] The Trump administration pushed an elaborate reorganization plan that would merge and cut entire agencies.

This chapter tells a different story about the federal bureaucracy. Yes, we'll look at the standard critiques – and the important points they

● *A rural physician working long hours. Rural regions such as Missouri's "Bootheel" have fewer physicians, clinics, and hospitals and are underserved by health professionals. That's where government bureaucrats are able to help.*

- Learn how the bureaucracy developed, how it is meant to work, and why programs and processes sometimes fail.

- See how federal agencies do their job.

- Examine the different types of agencies that comprise the public service.

- Consider who—if anyone—controls the bureaucracy.

- Review possible reforms—and affirm what works well in our massive, sprawling federal bureaucracy.

make. But we also present the other side reflected in the Bootheel story: health policy bureaucrats partnered with local leaders to improve lives in rural Missouri. Bureaucrats, despite their terrible reputation, perform valuable, even life-saving services. The bureaucracy makes government run.

The criticism of generic bureaucrats melts away when pollsters ask about specific agencies. For example, two-thirds of Americans give high marks to the U.S. Postal Service, the Centers for Disease Control, and NASA.[6] Bureaucrats look a lot better when we focus on what they actually do.

Who are we? In many ways, a country of bureaucrats: U.S. national departments and agencies employ 2.6 million civilians (and nearly 4 million including active-duty military). Nineteen million Americans work for state and local governments. That totals 23 million people on government payrolls—more than one in every ten working-age adults. What's more, the federal bureaucracy resembles the population it serves more than any other branch of government (Figure 12.1). Remember that Congress is overwhelmingly white, male, and middle-aged; all presidents have been male and, except for Barack Obama, they have all been white. The U.S. civilian bureaucracy is far more diverse, although Trump administration appointees to federal agencies and departments have reversed a decades-long trend toward increased diversity.

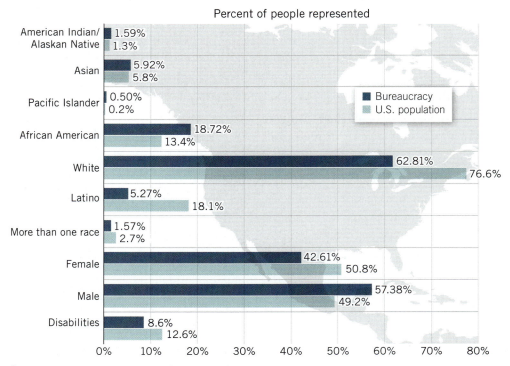

Percent of people represented

- American Indian/Alaskan Native: 1.59% / 1.3%
- Asian: 5.92% / 5.8%
- Pacific Islander: 0.50% / 0.2%
- African American: 18.72% / 13.4%
- White: 62.81% / 76.6%
- Latino: 5.27% / 18.1%
- More than one race: 1.57% / 2.7%
- Female: 42.61% / 50.8%
- Male: 57.38% / 49.2%
- Disabilities: 8.6% / 12.6%

■ Bureaucracy　■ U.S. population

● **Figure 12.1** *U.S. civilian bureaucracy demographic characteristics. (U.S. Census)*

The Bureaucracy

Number of cabinet departments, U.S. executive branch, 2019	**15**
Number of independent agencies/commissions, such as the CIA or Postal Service	**67**[7]
Number of departments during the George Washington administration (1789)	**4**
Number of departments during the Theodore Roosevelt administration (1905)	**7**
Number of ministries (e.g., cabinet departments), Japanese government, 2001	**20**
Number of Japanese ministries in 2019, following extensive restructuring in recent years	**12**
Total federal bureaucracy workforce	**3.9 million**
Percentage of that total who are active-duty military	**34**[8]
"Hidden workforce" of federal contractors and grantees	**5.3 million**[9]
Number of women, in U.S. history, who have headed cabinet-level departments	**36**
Number of those named since 1975	**34**
Miles of hallways in the largest U.S. federal building, the Pentagon	**17.5**
Maximum annual salary earned by a civil servant (GS-15, top of scale), 2019	**$136,659**
Average layers of upper management in large U.S. cabinet departments	**64**

The federal bureaucracy was modernized in the 1890s. How has it changed since?

Does its diversity make the bureaucracy more representative? Not necessarily. One of the great challenges every national bureaucracy faces is how to synchronize its work with the people's will. How can a bureaucracy of 2.6 million unelected federal workers govern democratically? An efficient and effective federal bureaucracy is essential to good government. How does it fit with democratic governance?

The Trump administration illustrates the tension. It came to Washington claiming a mandate to shake up American government and immediately ran into a bureaucratic wall: rules, rules, rules. The president soon discovered that announcing (or tweeting) a policy change had to be followed by a very careful and rigorously defined process. How does that process work? Read on!

How the Bureaucracy Grew

Predicting storms near Miami, keeping tabs on elections in Brazil, Nigeria, and India, and tracking suspected terrorists worldwide all require large, well-coordinated bureaucracies—as the National Oceanic and Atmospheric Administration (NOAA), the State Department, and the Central Intelligence Agency (CIA) are intended to be. This section examines where the U.S. bureaucracy came from, how bureaucracies are organized, and some of the problems that hamper their success.

Birth of the Bureaucracy

Spoils system: A system in which government jobs are given out as political favors.

Universalistic politics: A government that is run according to transparent rules, impartially applied.

In the nineteenth century, U.S. government jobs were political prizes. Men got their posts—as officers in the army, postmasters in rural towns, or tax collectors in ports—because they helped politicians win elections. When George Washington Plunkitt, a colorful New Yorker, decided to enter politics, he went to the local party boss with a marketable commodity: votes. He won his position by delivering the votes of all his friends and neighbors.[10]

This system was inefficient, unfair, and corrupt. Senator William Marcy, another New Yorker, gave the system its name when he declared, "To the victor belong the spoils." Giving jobs to political friends became known as the **spoils system**.

Reformers fought for years to break this corruption. Jobs, they insisted, should be distributed on the basis of merit, not political connections. These good-government advocates championed what we now call **universalistic politics**: a government of impartial rules that apply equally to everyone. That ideal was the basis for bureaucratic government in the United States.[11]

Battles erupted between reformers and defenders of the spoils system. In 1881, a crazed office seeker assassinated President James Garfield. Suddenly, the reformers had a martyr for their cause. The spoils system, they said, had caused the president's assassination. Popular outcry pushed a reluctant

James Garfield is assassinated in the Baltimore train station by a frustrated job seeker. Reformers blamed the spoils system and used the tragedy to introduce the civil service.

Congress to pass the **Pendleton Civil Service Act** (1883), which required the federal government to hire well-qualified individuals who took demanding exams to win their posts. It was the first step toward the civil service—another name for the bureaucracy—that runs the government today.

Reformers fighting for efficient government had a big advantage: There were jobs that needed doing. As American society and economy grew more complex, the spoils system (which too often attracted the lazy and the incompetent) failed to answer the nation's needs. Five key forces pushed the United States toward a modern bureaucracy.

War. Each time the United States mobilized for war, the bureaucracy grew. Matters of life and death could not depend on political hacks; military efforts spurred a search for competent administrators and well-organized offices. After each war, government maintained some of the new jobs. The number of civilian employees doubled during World War I and tripled during World War II. The second war, more than anything else, led to the large national bureaucracy we have today.[12]

"Your Honor, this woman gave birth to a naked child!"

● *Late nineteenth-century moral reformer Anthony Comstock and his quest to stamp out any signs of smut. His effort helped build a sophisticated postal bureaucracy.*

Morality. American government actively regulated morality right from the start. Enforcing moral rules required the creation of increasingly sophisticated agencies. For example, the effort to outlaw all liquor (under Prohibition, which lasted from 1920 to 1933) created a powerful new enforcement agency in the Department of the Treasury.[13]

Economics. Over time, the federal government assumed responsibility for economic performance. This created many new government offices—commissions designed to regulate business (starting in 1887 with efforts to manage the giant railroads); the Federal Reserve, intended to stabilize banking (created in 1913 after a series of financial panics); and a host of offices and agencies in response to the Great Depression (in the 1930s).

Geography. The United States spread rapidly across the continent. Keeping the far-flung nation together required a more sophisticated postal service (including the famous Pony Express), new forms of transportation, the distribution of public lands to homesteaders, and repeated military actions against Native Americans.

Race/Ethnicity. Slavery and civil rights concerns constantly engaged the federal government—leading, to the Civil War and the subsequent occupation of southern lands by the federal army. Likewise, shifting immigration policies,

Pendleton Civil Service Act: The law that shifted American government toward a merit-based public service.

often based on ethnicity (the Chinese Exclusion Act of the 1880s, for example), required a huge network of federal officials deciding who was permitted to settle in the United States.[14]

Each of these forces—war, morality, economics, geography, and race/ethnicity questions—pushed the United States toward more professional bureaus and agencies. The Pendleton Act of 1883 laid the cornerstone for the civil service that developed into a national bureaucracy by 1900 (after the Spanish-American War). By 1946 (after World War II), the country had developed many of the agencies that govern America to this day.

The Bureaucratic Model

What is a bureaucracy supposed to look like? The German social scientist Max Weber (1864–1920) reduced it to five characteristics that, in theory, mark all modern bureaucracies—including the American civil service. As we consider each, remember that this is how the bureaucracy is *supposed* to operate, not how it always does.[15]

Hierarchy. All bureaucracies have a clear chain of command. Each individual reports to the person above him or her all the way up to the president—or the queen, or the pope, or the university chancellor. Every individual along the chain has well-defined superiors and subordinates. Weber noted that the desire to move up the ladder makes most individuals sensitive to their superior's orders. In this way, the efforts of thousands of people can be coordinated.

Figure 12.2 shows the hierarchy of the U.S. Department of Energy (DOE), starting with the cabinet secretary and moving through elaborate subsets of assistants, deputies, and associate administrators. This chart lists the top 57 positions; some 15,000 men and women work in the agency (and another 40 thousand work under contracts with the DOE). The principle of hierarchy allows leaders to coordinate their subordinates' work.

Division of Labor. Bureaucracies divide up complex programs and assign each piece to an individual or a group, who are experts at their specialized tasks. The hierarchy coordinates all the specialists into a smoothly working operation. For example, the division of labor permits the State Department to staff each region of the globe, each language, and most countries.

Fixed Routines. Rather than making things up as they go along, bureaucrats are expected to follow well-specified codes of conduct called standard operating procedures (SOPs). Have you ever been stopped for speeding? The highway patrol's routine, from requesting your license and registration to checking for outstanding warrants, is fixed routine. Each step in the SOP has a purpose.

Equal Rules for All. The ideal is always the same in a bureaucracy: The rules apply equally to everyone. The spoils system was all about whom you knew. In contrast, the bureaucratic official is not supposed to care whose daughter you are or what special story you have to tell.

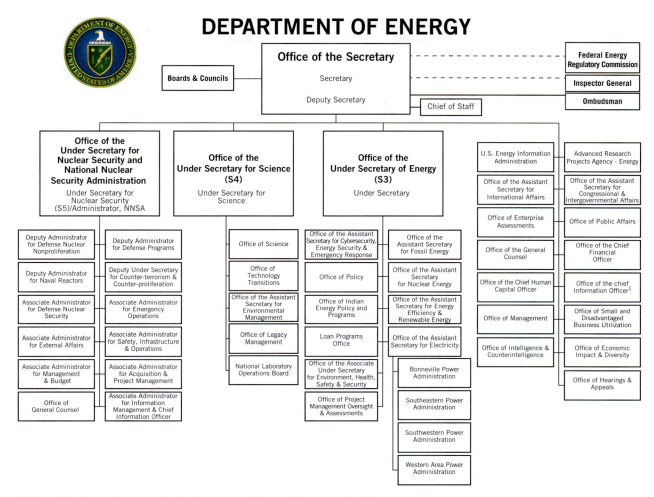

● **Figure 12.2** *Organizational chart for the Department of Energy. (US Department of Energy)*

Technical Qualifications. Because bureaucracies value expertise, people are hired based on their qualifications. For example, consider Figure 12.2. On the right of the organizational chart, note an Advanced Research Projects Agency (ARPA, which supports research into the origins of the universe). George Washington Plunkitt got his job by rounding up votes for New York's Democratic Party; in contrast, the ARPA staff are hired thanks to their scientific expertise.

Bureaucratic Pathologies

These five characteristics look good on paper. However, bureaucracies often work very differently in practice.

Almost everyone has an annoying or alarming bureaucrat story. You may have experienced one in dealing with your university: for example, "You cannot take this course until you take that one"—even though you took it at another school. People who deal with the federal government regularly experience this kind of bureaucratic error.

Hear about bureaucratic pathologies and processes.

Here's a great example. Starting in 2010, eight-year-old Mikey Hicks, an ordinary American boy with no ties to terrorism, was stopped and interrogated every time he and his family boarded a plane. The Transportation Security Authority (TSA) explained that his name was on the agency's no-fly list (a real suspect had a similar name). It took the TSA months to remove Mikey from the list. And while the TSA agents were grilling Mikey, a *real* terrorist, Umar Farouk Abdulmutallab, boarded a Northwest Airlines flight and unsuccessfully tried to blow it up. No one asked him any questions, even though two months earlier, his father, a prominent businessperson, had reported that his son was training at an Al Qaeda camp for terrorists in Yemen.

Why do these errors happen? Because every feature of the ideal bureaucracy has its potential downside, known as **bureaucratic pathologies**.

Bureaucratic pathologies:
The problems that tend to develop in bureaucratic systems.

- **Rote.** Some bureaucrats slavishly follow familiar standardized routines despite new developments. The failure to adjust can lead to problems, even tragedies. When members of an organization strictly follow SOPs, they avoid responsibility—and potential blame—by hiding behind assigned routines.

- **Imperialism.** Bureaucracies compete just like private companies. They want bigger budgets and better staffs. This status seeking can lead them to grow immense and waste time in turf wars.

- **Turf war.** Agencies often do overlapping jobs. This replication leads to tensions about who is responsible for what. For example, there are approximately 19 intelligence agencies in the federal government. Agencies such as the FBI and CIA that view each other as competitors often fail to share vital information.

- **Lack of coordination.** Even well-run agencies may lack mechanisms for cooperating with other agencies. This is because their routines are internal to the agency and do not apply to other organizations. If the agencies are imperialistic or fighting a turf war, the problem can become acute.

- **Clientelism.** Agency routines may favor some constituents over others. If the Department of Agriculture sends out complicated forms to qualify for loans, they favor agricultural corporations (which have bookkeepers and secretaries) over small family farms with little time to complete 50-page forms. The bias may not

● *A threat to national security? Mikey Hicks was subjected to intense questioning every time he flew—thanks to a glitch in the no-fly list. Bureaucratic pathologies include an inability to break routines.*

be explicit, but is built into the SOPs. And because the favored clients—big farms—do not complain, the routine continues.

What was the problem for Mikey? Primarily, the problem of rote. Once his name was on the watch list, the agency kept running through its routine and questioning him. Because the agency faced serious trouble if it crossed a real terrorist off the list, the routine for removing names requires more checkpoints and approvals than does adding a name. Why did the real terrorist slip through? Here, the problem was a *lack of coordination*, compounded by a *turf war*: different security agencies failed to communicate. Umar Farouk Abdulmutallab's father contacted one agency, which neglected to pass the information to another.

● *Farmers rally in West Fargo, North Dakota, in 2018. Close ties between "Big Ag"—giant agribusiness operations—and the U.S. government arouse complaints: an example of the bureaucratic pathology termed* clientelism.

The story of bureaucratic pathology often eclipses every other aspect of the subject. This is a mistake. We could not run the military, deliver the mail, operate an airport, or predict the weather without bureaucratic agencies. The key question for all governments is this: How do we produce the benefits of bureaucracy while minimizing the pathologies?

The Bottom Line

» Government jobs were originally distributed as spoils, or political rewards. Reformers challenged this system and eventually built a national bureaucracy.

» The ideal bureaucracy has five characteristics: hierarchy, division of labor, fixed routines, equal rules for all, and technical expertise.

» Bureaucracies are prone to pathologies, such as hewing too closely to a routine, fighting over turf, favoring some clients over others, and refusing to coordinate. These are all exaggerations of the very features that make bureaucracies efficient.

What Bureaucracies Do

After Congress passes a law or the president issues an executive order, the bureaucracy puts it into effect. Sometimes this work involves routine administrative action: Congress appropriates funds for Social Security, and bureaucrats at the Social Security Administration issue the checks. Just as often, implementing laws and executive orders requires complicated

Push a program through the bureaucracy.

judgments. Sometimes Congress sidesteps difficult questions to avoid a conflict or an unpopular decision, sometimes the laws or executive orders are vague, and sometimes legislation requires technical details that Congress leaves to the bureaucratic experts. In each of these cases, the bureaucracy follows a two-step process of putting a law into practice: rule-making and implementation.

The process is extremely important. When officials in the Trump administration tried to introduce changes, they discovered that they could not simply issue a new policy overnight. Instead, each change had to follow a well-organized procedure. Opponents could (and did) go to the courts and block any change that missed a step.[16]

Proposed rule: A draft of administrative regulations published in the *Federal Register* for the purpose of gathering comments from interested parties.

Rule-making

Rule-making showcases classic bureaucratic principles in action: a fixed process with multiple steps, always carried out the same way (Figure 12.3). First, the agency studies the law and proposes a "rule" that spells out how the new program will operate. For example, in 2018, the Department of Health and Human Services (HHS)—responding to an executive order by President Trump—proposed reducing prices of pharmaceutical drugs, which are often two to three times higher than the cost of the same drug in other countries.

Sounds simple enough, right? Not at all, once rule-makers at HHS dug into the details. Would the massive purchasing power of Medicare—which provides care for 57 million Americans aged 65 and over—be leveraged by allowing program administrators to negotiate prices with drug companies. No! Why? This practice has long been forbidden by Congress, thanks to effective lobbying by pharmaceutical companies. Should more generic drugs be brought more quickly to market? Not so easy, owing to elaborate safety rules—not to mention effective lobbying by large pharmaceutical companies. And so on: The bureaucracy's job is to spell out these types of details.

After the agency has drafted the language, it sends the **proposed rule** to the Office of Management and Budget (OMB) for approval. After the OMB gives its okay, the agency publishes the proposed rule in the *Federal Register*, the daily journal of the federal government.

Who reads the *Federal Register*? In theory, any citizen can read it online or at a library, and comment on proposed rules if they wish. In practice, most people are unaware it exists,

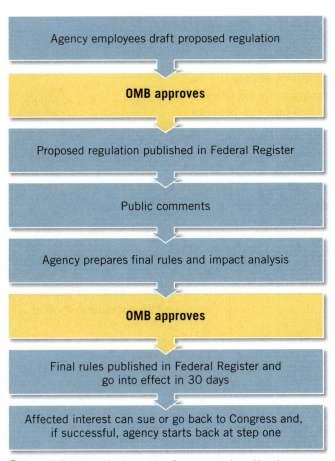

● **Figure 12.3** *Rule-making in practice. Government rule-making showcases classic bureaucratic principles in action: a fixed process with multiple steps always carried out in the same way. (Office of Management and Budget)*

while lobbyists and lawyers pore over it like the latest hot novel. The day we wrote this chapter, the *Federal Register* included proposed rules on air quality (from the Environmental Protection Agency), and a final rule regulating coastal shark harvest limits off the Atlantic coast of the United States (from NOAA).[17] You can be sure that lawyers and lobbyists for manufacturing companies with high pollution emission rates and fishing fleets bombarded the agencies with comments (also published in the *Federal Register*, along with a response to the comments from the officials who drafted the rule). Environmental and consumer groups also join the conversation.

President Trump, with Department of Health and Human Services Secretary Alex Azar, announces a plan to lower pharmaceutical prices. Many months of HHS rule-making later, the plan's details remained the subject of much debate.

The agency reviews all comments and makes changes—a process which can take months or even years—and proposes a **final rule**, along with an analysis of the likely impact of the new rule. Back it goes to the OMB, which has 30 days to review the final rule. Then the final rule is published in the *Federal Register*. Thirty days later, the regulation goes into effect. The final rule is not necessarily the end of the process, however. An individual citizen, group, or corporate firm objecting to the result can sue the agency for misinterpreting Congress's intent. Or it can appeal to its allies in Congress to criticize the rule and push the agency to restart the process.

Final rule: The rule that specifies how a program will actually operate.

In practice, lobbyists for affected industries and concerned consumer groups negotiate with the agency as proposed and final rules are written. They offer advice or may threaten to sue. Once in a while, when a rule taps into a broader controversy, this debate spills over into public view. During 2017–2018, the EPA proposed repeal of a "Clean Power" rule directing states to curb carbon pollution from power plants. Coal producers and power-plant operators originally fought the rule as a direct attack on their livelihood; the proposal to repeal drew fire from environmental groups—and the battle is likely to drag on in the courts for years.[18]

View a video about the history and operation of the *Federal Register*.

Apart from occasional flash points (e.g., the EPA and carbon emissions), rule-making involves a narrow slice of American life (e.g., shark harvesting) that takes place far from the public eye. Congress gets plenty of media coverage when it considers legislation. But negotiations over rules take place in the shadows, where only the most informed experts understand what is going on. This hidden debate shapes every law, executive order, and public policy. It may be technical, but it involves all of us. Today's proposed rules are about countering climate change and ensuring a steady food supply; tomorrow's could affect student loans and affordable housing. How can the public possibly control these battles that occur deep in the bureaucratic leviathan? Read on.

Regulating Health Systems

DO WE HAVE TOO MANY REGULATIONS?

Health systems must comply with hundreds of regulatory requirements issued by state and federal bureaucratic agencies.
These regulations are designed to ensure patient safety and compliance with a wide expanse of policies.
The judiciary and Congress also affect the regulation, providing oversight.

THINK ABOUT IT

Identify three institutions that create regulations for health systems and note what types of regulations they issue.
Are you surprised that any of the agencies are involved in healthcare regulation?

Some argue that our health system is too heavily regulated—restricting medical innovation and driving up costs. Do you agree or disagree? Are there areas that should be more or less strictly regulated?

Source: American Hospital Association

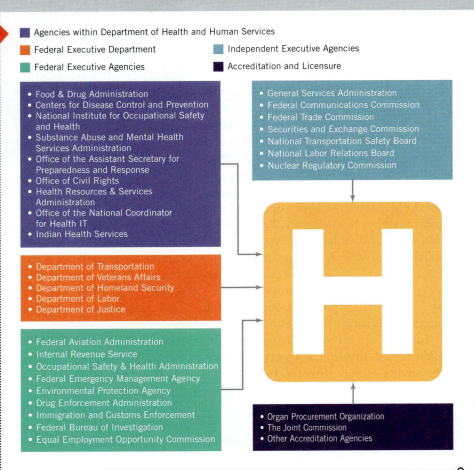

Legend:
- Agencies within Department of Health and Human Services
- Federal Executive Department
- Independent Executive Agencies
- Federal Executive Agencies
- Accreditation and Licensure

Agencies within Department of Health and Human Services
- Food & Drug Administration
- Centers for Disease Control and Prevention
- National Institute for Occupational Safety and Health
- Substance Abuse and Mental Health Services Administration
- Office of the Assistant Secretary for Preparedness and Response
- Office of Civil Rights
- Health Resources & Services Administration
- Office of the National Coordinator for Health IT
- Indian Health Services

Independent Executive Agencies
- General Services Administration
- Federal Communications Commission
- Federal Trade Commission
- Securities and Exchange Commission
- National Transportation Safety Board
- National Labor Relations Board
- Nuclear Regulatory Commission

Federal Executive Department
- Department of Transportation
- Department of Veterans Affairs
- Department of Homeland Security
- Department of Labor
- Department of Justice

Federal Executive Agencies
- Federal Aviation Administration
- Internal Revenue Service
- Occupational Safety & Health Administration
- Federal Emergency Management Agency
- Environmental Protection Agency
- Drug Enforcement Administration
- Immigration and Customs Enforcement
- Federal Bureau of Investigation
- Equal Employment Opportunity Commission

Accreditation and Licensure
- Organ Procurement Organization
- The Joint Commission
- Other Accreditation Agencies

Implementation

After the rules are in place, bureaucracies implement the new policies. The shark fishing fleets have to be inspected, power-plant emissions regulated, and government services such as GI Bill benefits or Veterans Administration medical care delivered to recipients. Who does this work? Mostly **"street-level bureaucrats"**: those who interact directly with the public—welfare officers, police, teachers, poultry-plant inspectors, and so on. They implement government policies by running programs and carrying out oversight.

Implementation is the last step in a long process. The president and/or members of Congress proposed the law; the House and Senate passed it; the courts upheld it; and the bureaucratic agency proposed draft rules, gathered comments, and published final rules in the *Federal Register*. Bureaucrats are active at every stage in the process. For example, they sometimes shape proposed programs by suggesting legislative language to allies in Congress and testifying before congressional committees that are considering the law.

Executive bureaucrats often develop close alliances with members of Congress as well as with interest-group lobbyists. A specialist in the EPA might spend years working with "green" members of Congress, along with the environmental groups and industries most affected by the regulations. As another example, the Bureau of Alcohol, Tobacco, Firearms, and Explosives connects frequently with gun makers and members of Congress who care about guns. Some criticize these arrangements as too cozy (recall the iron triangles discussed in Chapter 9). In any case, recognize that the bureaucracy is not walled off from other actors in government. It is part of the process all along the way.

● *A street-level bureaucrat in action. A local official in the Modesto, California, Health Department measures the growth of a young client as part of the Women, Infants, and Children program.*

Street-level bureaucrats:
Public officials who deal directly with the public.

The Bottom Line

» Once a law is passed or an executive order is signed, the executive bureaucracy takes the lead on implementation.

» Bureaucrats propose rules, publish them in the *Federal Register*, gather comments, rewrite the rules, and publish the final version. The law or executive order is now in effect.

» Implementation activity is not carried out by bureaucratic officials alone; Congress, interest groups, cabinet officials and sometimes even presidents all weigh in. Because the work is technical, it mostly takes place far from the political limelight.

» Bureaucratic officials take part in every step of the political process—from proposing legislation to putting it into effect.

Civil servants: Members of the permanent bureaucracy who are employed on the basis of competitive exams and keep their positions regardless of the presidential administration.

BUREAUCRACY BUZZWORDS

Bureaucrat: You need to be more proactive.

Meaning: You should have protected me from myself.

Bureaucrat: We want you to be the executive champion of this project.

Meaning: I want to be able to blame you for my mistakes.

Bureaucrat: We need to syndicate this decision.

Meaning: We need to spread the blame if it backfires.

Bureaucrat: I see you involved your peers in developing your proposal.

Meaning: One person couldn't possibly come up with something this stupid.

Bureaucrat: Our agency is going through a paradigm shift.

Meaning: We have no idea what we've been doing, but in the future we shall do something completely different.

(Source: H. George Frederickson, *Up the Bureaucracy*).

How the Bureaucracy Is Organized

Each presidential administration names the heads of the government bureaucracy—about four thousand people known as political appointees. The Senate approves the highest-ranking twelve hundred or so, who include cabinet secretaries, their assistants and deputies, the ambassadors to countries around the world, and other top figures. Their role: steer their agencies in the direction charted by the president.

Under these four thousand appointees toil some 2.6 million **civil servants** who work at their jobs regardless of which party occupies the White House. Imagine the tensions when a new political appointee (often a campaign official) arrives touting the new president's philosophy to an office of career officials. Those long-serving bureaucrats usually have far more expertise than the political appointee who has just been named their boss. The civil servants know that before long (on average, three years), the eager new appointee will move on, to be replaced by another. The civil servants are acutely aware of the rules, regulations, and SOPs that guide their agency. They literally tell their new bosses what they can do and how they should do it.

Civil servants have developed a vocabulary of their own, often caricatured as "bureaucratese"—the cautious, cover-your-backside language of experts with lifetime positions who are tasked with providing three trillion dollars' worth of federal services every year (see Talking Politics). Master these lines, and you will be ready for an internship in the executive branch!

The federal government's organizational chart includes four types of agencies: cabinet departments, autonomous bureaus, independent regulatory agencies, and the bureaucracy's service organizations. Let us take a closer look at each.

The Cabinet Departments

President George Washington's cabinet had just four departments: State, Treasury, War (now called Defense), and the Office of the Attorney General (now the Justice Department). Over time, presidents added new departments until the cabinet reached its current size of fifteen. Table 12.1 lists each department, the year it was founded, and total employees.

Because State and Treasury are the two oldest departments, the secretaries of state and the treasury sit next to the president in cabinet meetings. The younger the agency, the farther away from the president the secretary sits. A similar protocol exists for any formal event—the leaders of the oldest departments enter first, with the secretary of the newest department (currently Homeland Security) bringing up the rear. In the event of a catastrophe, the secretary of state is fourth in line to take over the presidency, followed by each cabinet secretary—again in the order the agencies were founded.

The Challenge of Governing. Nominating cabinet secretaries and other bureaucratic leaders is part of the fanfare of a new administration. The president sings the nominee's praises and the media speculates about fresh policy directions. Imagine that you are in the secretary's shoes: Here are the hurdles you will face.

TABLE 12.1 U.S. Executive Bureaucracies

DEPARTMENT (WITH YEAR OF FOUNDING)	CURRENT EMPLOYEES (AS OF 2018)
State 1789	73,624*
Treasury 1789	78,734
Defense 1789	749,060 civilians; 1.3 million uniformed military
Justice 1789	111,778
Interior 1849	69,761
Agriculture 1862	73,231
Commerce 1903	35,757
Labor 1913	14,424
Health and Human Services (originally 1953 "Health, Education, and Welfare")	65,866
Housing and Urban Development 1965	7,697
Transportation 1966	53,568
Energy 1977	14,249
Education 1979	3,842
Veterans Affairs 1989	372,127
Homeland Security 2002	193,326
ADDITIONAL FEDERAL AGENCIES	
Social Security Administration	59,680
Environmental Protection Agency	14,172
National Aeronautics and Space Administration	17,581
General Services Administration	11,757
Other independent agencies	55,486
U.S. Postal Service (a semi-independent federal agency since 1971)	503,000
Executive Office of the President (detailed in Chapter 11)	1,869
Total Civilian Federal Service	**2,580,589** (excluding active-duty military**)**
Estimated number of federal contractors and grantees	**5.3 million**

Source: U.S. Office of Personnel Management.
*49,737 foreign service staff overseas, 10,191 U.S. civil servants, and 13,696 foreign service officers

First, you must win Senate confirmation. In the increasingly partisan Washington environment, any past indiscretion may force you to withdraw. If all goes well, you take office when the president does, in late January.

Next, you select your team – they are not yet in place when you take office. You pick names for your deputies, assistants, and leaders in your agency. Next, you'll send them all to the White House for a thumbs up. The White House staffers may have their own favorites, so you'll have to negotiate over some of their choices. The FBI examines every nominee's background, which can sometimes take many months. After that, each nominee goes to the Senate for confirmation.

● *Trump meets with his cabinet. Notice the size of the group—too large for serious policy debates.*

If a proposed political appointee gets caught in a bottleneck—at the White House, the FBI, or (most likely) in Congress—it can be a year or more before team members are in place. In September 2001, President George W. Bush did not yet have most of his security team in office when the terrorists attacked September 11, eight months after Inauguration Day. After 500 days in office, the Trump administration still had not filled 204 of the top 605 posts in the executive branch.[19] As Washington has grown more partisan, the confirmation process has become more difficult.

New secretaries also must manage a large bureaucracy that they know very little about. Cabinet secretaries usually do not have any experience with the many facets of their department. President Trump's first secretary of the Department of Homeland Security (DHS), John Kelly,[20] was previously a Marine Corps general. Although he was familiar with homeland security issues, Kelly did not know much about immigration, the Coast Guard, or the Animal and Plant Health Inspection Service—all bureaus now under his direction.

Compare Parliamentary Systems. Governments with parliaments—such as England, Japan, or Israel—are different from the U.S. when it comes to bureaucratic leadership. In all these nations, senior members of the legislature become ministers, the equivalent of cabinet secretaries in the United States. No one sends in a résumé to become a department head: You have to win an election to parliament and work your way up the party hierarchy. There is no long confirmation process, no hostile congressional oversight, no checks and balances between executive and legislative branches.

By comparison, the U.S. Constitution bars members of Congress from taking "any civil office"—to join the bureaucracy or the judiciary, they must resign their House or Senate seat. (Congressman Mike Pompeo, a Kansas Republican, had to resign his House seat to become CIA Director under President Trump;

he subsequently was named Secretary of State.) The founders, as always, insisted on checks and balances.

Cabinet Meetings. Fifteen department heads gather around a White House conference room table with the president, vice president, and as many as ten additional senior leaders, including the White House Chief of Staff and the CIA Director.

Explore major agencies within the bureaucracy.

Does the whole group—department secretaries plus additional cabinet-level officials—serve as a president's central advisory team? No. There are too many of them. With twenty-five or more people around the table, plus dozens of staff lining the walls behind them, it is hard to have a serious discussion. That's why cabinets meet less often in recent years: Donald Trump convened his full cabinet only nine times during his first year in office.

The Rotating Bureaucracy. The turnover at the top rung of the U.S. bureaucracy is unique. No other democracy works in this way—nor does any other major institution. No private company, nonprofit organization, or university routinely asks thousands of outsiders to take over for three or so years, then step aside and make way for a new crop of leaders.

Management consultants would run screaming from the room if you suggested setting up a business in this way. We cannot look to the Constitution for justification, because it does not mention cabinet departments. Many political scientists, however, think the bureaucracy does work. The civil service does its job, often quite well. And the political leadership comes to the job with a definite philosophy, based on a president's central ideas.

Scholars of public policy generally agree that stability is desirable among political appointees during a presidency.[21] President Trump raised concerns when he replaced five cabinet-level officials in his first hundred days—far more than any other administration in history; the six presidents prior to Trump all together replaced only *one* cabinet official during their first hundred days in office.

Pairing a suitable philosophy with skilled political leadership can make a real difference in an agency's management. An example is the Federal Emergency Management Agency (FEMA), which responds to natural disasters. When the George W. Bush administration came to office, they installed an inexperienced (but politically connected) campaign donor, Michael Brown, as FEMA director.

FEMA responded feebly to Hurricane Katrina, a massive storm that flooded New Orleans in 2005. The media depicted widespread desperation: more than 1,800 people lost their lives in the storms and subsequent flooding—with scant federal response. Director Brown lost his job, and President Bush's popularity ratings tumbled.

President Obama, learning from his predecessors, appointed an experienced FEMA director, W. Craig Fugate, who had directed emergency services under Governor Jeb Bush in Florida. The agency received high marks when another devastating storm, Hurricane Sandy, hit the East Coast in 2012. The FEMA example illustrates another important point about the federal bureaucracy. Calling for smaller government sounds promising on the campaign trail.

● *FEMA's response to disasters (Hurricane Katrina on left; Maria on right) remains a White House flashpoint. The agency's response to Hurricane Maria's September 2017 devastation in Puerto Rico was widely criticized, recalling the aftermath of Hurricane Katrina in New Orleans a dozen years before.*

However, each corner of the sprawling government establishment has a job to do; almost all deliver services that people rely on. That responsibility makes cutting government agencies difficult in practice.

The Cabinet and Diversity. Like the bureaucracy they lead, the secretaries and cabinet-level officials increasingly reflect the American public. Until the mid-1960s, just two women had served in the cabinet in all of American history—and not a single African American, Latino, or Asian. Since the 1980s, every president appointed a diverse set of secretaries that reflects the nation. President Trump has slowed that trend, appointing the most heavily white and male group since George H. W. Bush came to office in 1989.

Other Agencies

Nearly three-quarters of the federal bureaucracy—about 1.9 million civilians—works in the cabinet departments. Two other categories of federal workers each offer a different twist on the bureaucracy.

Executive Agencies. Independent executive agencies have more specific assignments than do the cabinet departments. The Environmental Protection Agency, for example, is entirely focused on the difficult job of overseeing the environment. In contrast, the Department of the Interior has responsibilities that include—among many other things—supervising Indian affairs, national parks, geological surveys, oceans and energy, and surface mining.

The more than thirty independent executive agencies perform a wide range of jobs: They land astronauts on the moon (NASA), send Americans on service projects around the world (Peace Corps), manage the banking system (Federal Reserve), monitor elections (Federal Election Commission), and investigate violations of civil rights in the workplace (Equal Employment Opportunity Commission).

Independent Regulatory Commissions. Another type of bureau originally emerged to regulate business. In the 1880s, farmers and small business complained bitterly about the railroads' arbitrary freight rates and pleaded for government controls. However, powerful railroad owners dominated the state legislatures and Congress. How could consumers be protected against these wealthy "robber barons"? Reformers organized a regulatory agency, the Interstate Commerce Commission (ICC), that would operate separately from Congress and the White House and regulate industry—free from corrupting lobbyists and politics.

Independent regulatory commissions (IRCs)—designed to be independent from political influence—perform many different jobs: The Federal Election Commission, established in 1975, oversees U.S. electoral practices; the Securities and Exchange Commission oversees financial markets (see Figure 12.4). The sixteen IRCs each have the authority to issue regulations, enforce laws, and settle disputes—essentially combining legislative, executive, and judicial powers in one agency. A commissioner, nominated by the president and confirmed by the Senate, runs each agency for a fixed term that does not overlap with the president's term—another way to minimize political influence.

To understand an industry well enough to monitor its activities, regulators need relevant expertise. Commissioners are frequently drawn from the ranks of the regulated industry. Ironically, the effort to keep the regulatory commissions independent of Congress and the White House leaves them more susceptible to industry influence. Critics charge that the independent regulatory agencies are "captured" or "acquired" by the industry and simply do its bidding.

There is no escaping the politics that pervade the independent regulatory agencies. Still, the "**regulatory capture**" argument is often overstated. Consumer groups also lobby, provide information to, and sue the agencies. Moreover, agency civil servants often work hard to achieve their institution's goals—and express pride in its independent stance.

Regulatory capture: The theory that industries dominate the agencies that regulate them.

In the past forty years, reformers have promoted *deregulation*—abolishing the agencies and letting free-market competition protect consumers. The original ICC was dismantled in 1995. The Civil Aeronautics Board, a regulatory commission that protected the airline industry by limiting competition, was abolished in 1985, with good and bad consequences—frequent-flier programs, fewer airlines, and huge fluctuations in fares. Today, business-friendly Republicans target the Consumer Financial Protection Bureau, created to aid consumers in the wake of the 'Great Recession' of 2008-09, for elimination.[22]

Deregulation brings us full circle. Once, farmers and small business pleaded for relief from predatory markets. Now, a new generation of reformers offers a solution to creaky regulatory agencies: Return to the markets.

An Army of Their Own. A small support army maintains and services the massive office buildings housing the executive branch, most notably the Office of Personnel Management (OPM) and the General Services Administration (GSA).Do you want to work for the U.S. government as a civil servant? OPM manages the giant "USAJobs" website, listing hundreds of thousands of federal bureaucracy job openings each year. Once you apply for your position, your application will be read and screened by OPM staff. Whatever your job in the

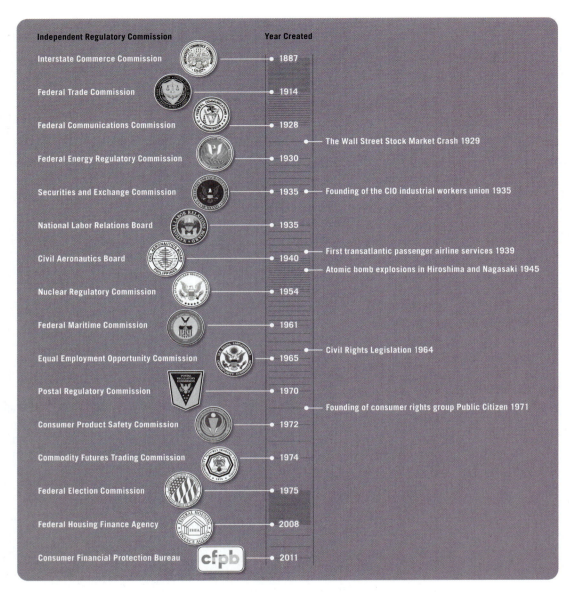

Independent Regulatory Commission

Independent Regulatory Commission	Year Created	
Interstate Commerce Commission	1887	
Federal Trade Commission	1914	
Federal Communications Commission	1928	
Federal Energy Regulatory Commission	1930	The Wall Street Stock Market Crash 1929
Securities and Exchange Commission	1935	Founding of the CIO industrial workers union 1935
National Labor Relations Board	1935	
Civil Aeronautics Board	1940	First transatlantic passenger airline services 1939
Nuclear Regulatory Commission	1954	Atomic bomb explosions in Hiroshima and Nagasaki 1945
Federal Maritime Commission	1961	
Equal Employment Opportunity Commission	1965	Civil Rights Legislation 1964
Postal Regulatory Commission	1970	
Consumer Product Safety Commission	1972	Founding of consumer rights group Public Citizen 1971
Commodity Futures Trading Commission	1974	
Federal Election Commission	1975	
Federal Housing Finance Agency	2008	
Consumer Financial Protection Bureau	2011	

Figure 12.4 *Congress creates independent regulatory commissions in response to stock market failures, the rise of new technologies, or other emerging social needs.*

government, GSA manages all the details of maintenance and supply. Your building just got painted? GSA did the work—or hired and supervised the company who did it under contract. Do you need a shipment of forest fire–fighting helicopters (for the National Park Service) or a more sophisticated smartphone (at the OMB)? GSA is your one-stop shopping spot.

Private contractors: Private companies that contract to provide goods and services for the government.

Private Contractors. Another category of employees does not work directly for the government. They come from private companies that provide goods and services under contract to the government. An estimated 5.3 million **private contractors**

now perform many jobs once handled directly by government employees.[23] For example, the military increasingly relies on private firms to provide meals, transportation, security services, and even commando teams. Besides war-related efforts, private companies provide a full range of government services, spreading to homeland security, international diplomacy, prison management, and garbage collection.

Why contract out government services? First, private companies, foundations, and nongovernmental organizations often have special skills and resources they can bring to a job. Second, private companies can sometimes do a better and cheaper job. Do the benefits of "privatizing" government services outweigh the costs? We will explore at chapter's end.

● *Private contractors continue to provide security in war zones, including Iraq; here, private guards protect a U.S.–Iraqi diplomatic meeting.*

Executive branch agencies and commissions face the same leadership challenges as those we described in the cabinet departments. The appointment process is cumbersome. Partisan politics slow it down further. New appointees scramble to learn the bureaucratic ropes, even as the to-do list piles ever higher—and meanwhile the administrative team takes months or even years to get into place. Then, after about three years, the leadership moves on and the selection process begins again.

The Bottom Line

» The federal bureaucracy includes fifteen cabinet departments, as well as other types of bureaucracies. Executive agencies focus on one type of issue, such as environmental quality; independent regulatory commissions oversee specific industries; and service agencies keep all the people and materials moving along. An additional 5.3 million private contractors are licensed to provide goods and services for the government.

» The president appoints a few thousand executive-branch leaders, another 2.6 million bureaucrats are members of the permanent civil service. The cabinet and civil service have grown far more diverse in the past thirty years.

» The cabinet and other appointed executives provide political direction; civil servants provide expertise and continuity.

» Among the many challenges to a smoothly functioning system is the time—often more than a year—that it takes a new administration to get its leadership team in place.

Who Controls the Federal Bureaucracy?

Managing four million civilian bureaucrats and military personnel, and more than five million private contractors is a daunting leadership responsibility—and a giant management headache. It is also crucial for democracy. Self-rule requires mastering the bureaucracy. But who is in charge?

The People

In a democracy, the federal government must ultimately respond to the people. But actual popular control faces a core problem: Much of what the bureaucracy does is too technical for direct public engagement.

How does the Internal Revenue Service (IRS) compute tax penalties for S corporations that wrongly elect to amortize anticipated losses with write-downs? What is the maximum engineering pendular sway ratio on truss-style bridges? When the chemical compound bisphenol-A, widely used in plastics, leaches into bottled drinking water, how dangerous is it to public health? Few Americans can develop informed opinions about such matters. We need someone to act on our behalf.

The President

In theory, the president controls the bureaucracy. The Constitution is clear: "The executive Power shall be vested in a President." The president is the bureaucrat in chief, a form of control that is known as **overhead democracy**: The people elect presidents who, through their appointees, control the bureaucracy from the top.

In practice, most presidents are frustrated in their efforts to manage the millions of men and women under their command. Harry Truman famously commented on his successor, General Dwight D. Eisenhower: "He'll sit here and he'll say 'Do this!' and 'Do that!' *And nothing will happen.* Poor Ike, it won't be a bit like the army. He'll find it very frustrating."[24]

Presidents quickly discover that the bureaucracy has its own preferences, processes, and routines. When President Richard Nixon, a Republican, came to office, Democrats had run the government for twenty-eight of the previous thirty-six years, and Nixon believed that many career civil servants were Democrats waiting for the next liberal administration. "If we don't get rid of these people," Nixon wrote bluntly, "they will sit back on their well-paid asses and wait for the next election to bring back their old [Democratic] bosses."[25] During the Trump administration, some White

Overhead democracy:
A system by which the people elect the president, who, through political appointees, controls the bureaucracy from the top.

● *Does the public control our federal bureaucracy? This cartoonist suggests otherwise.*

Every president complains that "the bureaucracy" is unresponsive to their goals. Career civil servants— hired long before a new administration is elected— owe their loyalty to their department or agency, not to the president or the appointed head of their bureau. Is this tension a problem?

Yes: "Deep State" Equals Gridlock. Career bureaucrats can hinder innovation, which our government needs desperately to keep up with a 21st century economy and global political crises. When bureaucrats block an elected president's goals, they are also acting against the popular will. I would vastly increase the proportion of politically appointed civil servants and simplify the process of putting them in place.

No: Leave Experts in Charge. The complex demands of governing our $8 trillion federal bureaucracy require technical expertise and seasoned experience. Career bureaucrats have been a central feature of the executive branch for well over a century, and are responsive to bosses who are approved by the Senate and appointed by the president—hence subject to democratic norms. Stability is a key feature of the American government's ability to succeed—and adapt as necessary, not as an impatient new administration insists.

House officials voiced a similar concern that a "deep state" of career bureaucrats (and some disloyal political appointees) were thwarting the president's policy goals.

Congress

Although bureaucrats "belong" to the executive branch, the legislative branch wields authority as well. Congress shapes the bureaucracy through four powers.

- *Funding.* Congress funds nearly all executive branch programs since it determines the federal budget. If Congress rejects a bureaucratic proposal, or an agency head crosses a powerful subcommittee, that program or department may find its budget slashed by congressional appropriators.

- *Oversight.* Congress has formal power to supervise the executive branch, including both White House and federal bureaucratic operations. Policing department and agency actions is normally a routine operation—making sure that funds are properly expended or that programs achieve their stated goals. But Congress can extend its oversight authority into investigations of executive branch actions. The mere mention of oversight hearings is a major threat to the bureaucracy.

- *Authorization.* Congress often has to reauthorize laws after a specified number of years. For example, Congress first passed a farm bill in 1933 and it has to be reauthorized every five years. The legislation covers farmers, conservation, nutrition, forestry, energy and more. The politics grows intense as Congress can change programs or even deny their reauthorization.

- *Reorganization.* Finally, Congress can change the structure of executive branch organizations. Currently, Congress is considering a White House proposal to merge the Department of Labor and the Department of Education.[26]

These four sources of power add up to extensive congressional influence. Agency heads and cabinet secretaries are often more responsive to Congress—with its power of the purse and oversight authority—than to the president. Bureaucratic leaders regularly lobby Congress for additional funding or authority. They also frequently complain, however, about congressional "micromanagement."

Principal-agent theory: Details how policymakers (principals) control the actors who work for them (agents)—but the agents may have far more information.

Political scientists view the relationship between Congress and the bureaucracy through **principal-agent theory**. This approach analyzes how a principal (in this case, Congress) hires an agent (the bureaucracy) to do a job. Problems arise when the agent has much more information than the principal. How do you control a bureaucracy when there is "information asymmetry," that is, when "they" (bureaucrats) know a lot more than "you" (busy House and Senate members) do? The answer: Make sure their interests are the same as yours. And the fear of being hauled before a congressional panel and threatened with loss of funding is enough to make most bureaucrats worry about congressional desires.

Interest Groups

Interest groups closely engage bureaucrats as they administer the laws. Lobbying groups comment extensively on proposed rules. As bureaucrats finalize rules and implement programs, they routinely engage interest-group representatives from industry and consumer organizations, whose cooperation may be necessary to make the program work smoothly. Over time, close relations may develop, making lobbyists influential in regular operations of executive agencies. Interest groups also publicly complain about or even sue overzealous regulators. The result: another set of influences on bureaucrats in action.

Bureaucratic Autonomy

Partly because they have so many would-be masters, bureaucrats wind up with considerable autonomy in their work. Many civil servants have strong views about their field, whether that is exploring space, ensuring fair elections, or keeping the homeland safe. They also have an interest in increasing their own autonomy—applying their best judgment to the problems they face.

Whistleblower: A federal worker who reports corruption or fraud.

Some federal bureaucrats, termed **whistleblowers**, call attention to abuses within their department or agency. In many cases, permanent civil servants blow the whistle on fraudulent or misbehaving political appointees higher up in the department or agency. In 2017-18, for example, several whistleblowers detailed abuses of office by EPA Administrator Scott Pruitt, including extravagant travel and security spending and falsifying his official calendar. Pruitt resigned under fire in summer 2018.[27]

This search for autonomy is especially true for government officials who deal directly with the public—the street-level bureaucrats who implement public policy. General policies are formulated in the higher administration, but it is street-level bureaucrats who actually run the programs, constantly using their own judgment. For example, a police officer may write you a speeding ticket—or let you off with a warning.[28]

Or take a more complicated case. A mother missed the application deadline for WIC, a program providing vouchers for meals to low-income families with children. Do you give her the benefit card anyway? On the one hand, the rule says no; on the other hand, her children may go hungry if you don't. In case after case, street-level bureaucrats decide what to do—giving them enormous influence over how to apply the rules. Program beneficiaries quickly learn about the power of the bureaucrats they see repeatedly.

Moreover, at the street level, every program has its own tone. Some programs (for example, Social Security) generally treat their beneficiaries with respect; others (like Temporary Assistance for Needy Families) take a more disciplinary stance.[29]

Democracy Revisited

Many agents—the president, Congress, courts, and interest groups—exert some control over the bureaucracy. Bureaucrats try to maximize their own discretion to do what they think is best. Do all these clashing forces add up to democratic control?

The answer is yes and no. At times, these different forms of democratic control offer a rough form of popular oversight. Administrations that focus on delivering services can have considerable success; presidents who seek to change the direction of federal policy can sometimes succeed; congressional oversight often improves responsiveness. But all the levers for democratic control are blunt instruments. Effectively using them takes constant attention. In the next section, we examine three reform proposals to improve popular control.

 **The Bottom Line**

» In a democracy, the public must control the government bureaucracy. The question is how.

» Different actors exert influence over the bureaucracy: the president (who names the leaders), Congress (through funding and oversight), and interest groups.

» Bureaucrats still operate with considerable autonomy, especially those at the "street level."

🔵 Reforming the Bureaucracy

Americans ask a great deal of the bureaucracy, but—as reported at the start of the chapter—we do not like it much. Let us look at the usual criticisms and then explore some solutions.

Critiques

Three major sources of disapproval focus on cost, inertia, and public mistrust.

Cost. Critics complain about the high cost of the bureaucracy and its programs. As a proportion of America's gross domestic product (GDP), however, the cost of the bureaucracy—as well as the number of federal bureaucrats—has remained steady over the past forty years (see Figure 12.5). And although every politician criticizes waste and fraud, the agencies of the bureaucracy meet real needs—which is one reason elected officials find them difficult to cut. The only president who significantly reduced nonmilitary civil servants since World War II is Bill Clinton, who slashed the civil service by 400,000 bureaucrats. Donald Trump has cut the size of individual departments, such as Treasury, but increased others like Interior and Veterans Affairs; the net effect has been little change.

Inertia. In our restless, innovative nation, the slow, rule-bound, hierarchical bureaucracy never seems to keep up. Why do NASA flights, such as the space shuttle, always take off from Florida, despite uncertain weather and a growing population potentially endangered by crashes? Because an obscure 1950s rule prohibited the flight of test aircraft west of the Mississippi River. Remember: once bureaucratic routines are set, they are hard to change.

Inertia also comes from clashing political desires. For example, the government is prohibited—again by bureaucratic regulations—from purchasing

● **Figure 12.5** *Cost of the federal bureaucracy as a proportion of GDP; federal programs cost slightly less than 30 years ago. The bottom line shows the percentage of the GDP that is discretionary spending (programs that Congress, presidents, and department heads can control); the top line shows the percentage of the GDP that is spent on all federal programs, including those required by law: Social Security, Medicare, and Medicaid are the largest. (Congressional Budget Office)*

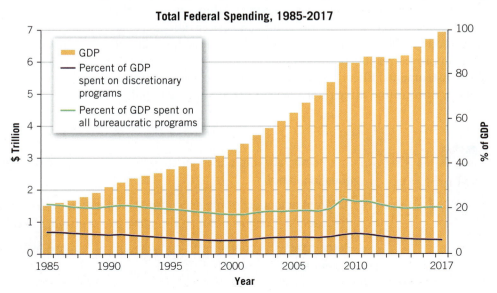

knives, forks, and spoons from abroad. Employees on State Department business are prohibited from flying aboard non-American airlines. It is often less expensive to buy foreign goods or to fly on international carriers. Why don't bureaucratic rules shift to accommodate this reality? Because multiple political constituencies demand different things. Congress, reflecting many voices, insists on both efficient purchasing policies *and* "buying American."

Clashing rules reflect different goals and values: We want to spread government contracts around the country, ensure social equity, stimulate innovative programs, and support American producers. These desires can clash with one another—and with lower costs or faster services. Which priority deserves the most weight? The effort to choose among them is what democracy is all about. It is a debate that never ends.

More troubling is the increasing difficulty of recruiting the "best and the brightest" to government service. Individuals tapped for senior positions face a long process—and, often, hardball politics. Then appointees arrive on the job and discover that civil service pay scales have only inched up since 2010.

Public Mistrust. Politicians from both parties bash the bureaucracy. Republican Ronald Reagan announced that "government is not the solution to our problem" and declared, "It is time to make [bureaucrats] stand by our side, not ride on our back." Democrat Bill Clinton declared, "The era of big government is over."

Fueling public mistrust of bureaucrats are scandals and mistakes, many covered in detail by a 24/7 media mix of headlines, blogs, and tweets. In an institution as large as the federal bureaucracy, examples of error, corruption, and fraud are inevitable. Government officials are human, prone to personal flaws and errors like anyone else. But in an environment of constant bureaucracy bashing, the bad news is far more prominently reported than are bureaucratic achievements, which only reinforces the general image of a corrupt, lazy bureaucracy riding "on our backs."

Proposed Reforms

The bureaucracy's reputation for being expensive, slow-moving, and scandal-ridden has attracted a long history of reform efforts–including these three popular proposals.

Open Up the System. The public's faith in government tumbled after the late 1960s with an unpopular war in Vietnam, civil rights unrest, and the Watergate scandal. One response was a concerted attempt to make the executive bureaucracy more transparent. Sunshine laws,

● *Businesswoman turned bureaucrat. Lillian Salerno, who ran a successful healthcare business, joined the Department of Agriculture in 2009 to manage a rural-development program providing some $30 billion annually in grants and low-interest loans to farmers in rural America.*

Freedom of Information Act (FOIA): A 1966 law that facilitates full or partial disclosure of government information and documents.

which require public hearings and citizen input, open bureaucratic debates to public view. The **Freedom of Information Act** (**FOIA**) extends citizen access to agency and department deliberations. Any individual or news organization may file a FOIA request to see an unreleased government document. Today, every federal agency has its own website that tries to explain its priorities and processes.

Bureaucratic officials sometimes resist these efforts. Some worry about the potentially chilling effect on communication by politically motivated FOIA requests: as one headline asked, "Is the Freedom of Information Act Stifling Intellectual Freedom?"[30] Advocates of openness continue to push for more access.

Reinventing Government. During the Clinton administration, Vice President Al Gore ran a sweeping "Reinventing Government" project designed to cut bureaucratic delays, reduce costs, decentralize management, and empower employees to make decisions. President Trump in summer 2018 announced a major bureaucracy overhaul that he promised would save billions of dollars.[31]

A call for efficiency works only up to a point. Most businesses have a clear and simple goal: maximize returns for investors. In contrast, bureaucratic agencies have many constituencies with multiple goals. For example, if the Department of Agriculture focuses on farmers and helps to maintain price levels, complaints will arise from consumers (high prices), environmentalists (disappearing topsoil), and even foreign governments (protections may violate free trade). Efficiency *sounds* good. However, government officials are called on to juggle many different goals: They have to be fair, responsive, objective, focus on the national interest, and attend to international trade rules. Being efficient at one goal often clashes with being efficient at another.

● *An employee of the Immigration and Customs Enforcement's Stewart Detention Center in Lumpkin, Georgia, waits for the front gate to be opened. The detention center is operated on contract by the Nashville-based Corrections Corporation of America.*

Privatization. If the bureaucracy seems slow and inefficient, perhaps private companies can do the job better. As we explored earlier in this chapter, one powerful trend in government has been outsourcing public services to private firms. For-profit companies collect garbage, manage prisons, protect the homeland, cook for the troops, and launch commando raids abroad.

The movement for privatizing federal (and many state) programs took flight in the 1970s and received a boost from President Reagan in the 1980s. His administration turned some forty thousand government jobs over to private contractors, for reported savings of more than six hundred million dollars. That number grew steadily through the 1990s, with another sharp increase after the 9/11 terrorist attacks and ensuing wars in Afghanistan and Iraq.[32] Today, over five million private contractors serve federal, state, and local governments.

Private firms often can do a job at lower cost. But the savings are at least partly offset by the need for government supervision. What happens when private managers—worrying about the bottom line—cut corners or violate rules? More and more often, public–private partnerships that combine bureaucratic supervision and protections with private-sector expertise are the preferred approach.[33] That's how health care improved for Missouri's Bootheel residents, in our chapter-opening story: Private providers worked with local, state, and national government officials as well as public-health groups.

The Bottom Line

» Critics of the bureaucracy focus on cost, inertia, and public mistrust.

» Solutions include sunshine reforms, reinventing government to make it more constituent friendly, and privatizing some of its functions.

Conclusion: The Real Solution Lies with You

President Kennedy came to office amid a burst of idealism and declared, "Ask not what your country can do for you—ask what you can do for your country." Inspired by the young president, the early civil rights movement, and the general optimism of the era, many college graduates streamed into public service. Today, fewer Americans are attracted to government service: Just 6.1 percent of U.S. federal employees are under thirty, compared to more than 9 percent in 2010.[34] Can this trend change? What would draw *you* into working for the government?

Politicians from both parties take shots at the bureaucracy. They freeze pay and downsize

● *Wanted: a few good bureaucrats!*

departments. Many Americans applaud these moves, given our opposition to "Big Government" that extends right back to the nation's founding. Yet the bureaucracy performs many jobs we need and value, from managing our national finances to predicting the weather to defending the United States. Ultimately, our democratic government is only as good as the bureaucracy that puts public policy into effect. And this brings us back to your generation's commitment to public service, and what public officials can do to foster it.

CHAPTER SUMMARY

Check your understanding of Chapter 12.

🟢 The U.S. federal bureaucracy does a vast amount of work in governing the country—and more closely resembles the nation's population than other branches. However, Americans express deep ambivalence about our bureaucracy, rating it very low in opinion polls.

🟢 The American bureaucracy was established in reaction to the spoils system, dominant between 1828 and 1901. A merit-based hiring system has been in place for more than a century.

🟢 In theory, all bureaucracies share five characteristics: hierarchy, division of labor, fixed routines, equal rules for all, and technical qualifications.

🟢 Bureaucrats in the United States, as in other countries, perform a wide range of functions—from managing the nation's defense and national economy to providing food stamps and tax cuts. The bureaucracy is specifically charged with implementing the laws passed by Congress and signed by the president. This typically involves an administrative rule-making process, as well as delivery of services and carrying out of programs.

🟢 Since the 1930s, the federal bureaucracy has grown to nearly four million employees—two-thirds civilians and one-third active-duty military. This growth has occurred despite anti-"big government" sentiment among Americans; helping to overcome this opposition have been the twin forces of war and enforcing morality.

🟢 Organizing such a sprawling set of cabinet departments and agencies, populated by civil servants and political appointees, is an immense job.

🟢 It is not readily apparent who is in charge of managing the bureaucracy. Many players have a role, including the public, the president, Congress, and interest groups. The result of all those masters: Bureaucrats have considerable discretion in how they work.

🟢 This freedom can lead to serious tensions between Americans' democratic ideal of representative accountability and an unelected, often-*un*accountable workforce of civil servants.

🟢 Public disapproval of the bureaucracy arises from different complaints. Our executive bureaucracy costs too much, say some critics; others argue that bureaucratic inertia makes it difficult to respond to policy crises. Well-reported scandals influence Americans' perceptions of our bureaucracy, driving up mistrust.

● Reform efforts include enhancing the transparency of bureaucratic practices, reinventing government to improve responsiveness and reduce layers of management, and privatizing government services.

Need to review key ideas in greater depth? Click here.

KEY TERMS

Flashcard review.

Bureaucratic pathologies, p. 408

Civil servants, p. 414

Final rule, p. 411

Freedom of Information Act (FOIA), p. 428

Overhead democracy, p. 422

Pendleton Civil Service Act, p. 405

Principal-agent theory, p. 424

Private contractors, p. 420

Proposed rule, p. 410

Regulatory capture, p. 419

Spoils system, p. 404

Street-level bureaucrats, p. 413

Universalistic politics, p. 404

Whistleblower, p. 424

STUDY QUESTIONS

1. Is the U.S. federal bureaucracy too large? Do we need four million people working for the government—in addition to several million more hired under federal contracts? If you would like to see a smaller bureaucracy, where would you start cutting workers?

2. Who *should* run the bureaucracy? Do bureaucrats have too much discretion in how they perform their duties? What are the respective merits of a "street-level" or "top-down" management style? And should presidents (or Congress, or interest groups) have more authority to exert their will on the bureaucracy?

3. You have just learned about some unsavory doings in your bureaucratic agency or department. Do you blow the whistle? Or do you keep quiet, knowing your job could be in danger? What factors would affect your decision?

4. Should we mount a major push for reforming the bureaucracy? What type(s) of reforms would be most useful? Or are the various agencies and processes, such as rulemaking, working pretty well already?

5. Given your expanded knowledge of the bureaucracy, are you more or less likely to be interested in working in an executive office like the Treasury Department or EPA? Does this seem like a promising way to exercise your civic spirit? Why or why not?

Go to www.oup.com/us/Morone to find quizzes, flash cards, simulations, tutorials, videos, and other study tools.

13 The Judicial Branch

JUNE IS a good time to visit the Supreme Court's iconic marble steps. Most decisions are announced then as the Court ends its annual term. During two days in June 2018, the Court issued three major decisions with sweeping implications for American politics and society—each by a 5–4 vote. In *Trump v. Hawaii*, the Court ruled that the president's authority to secure the country's borders enabled his controversial ban on travelers from eight mostly majority-Muslim nations. In *National Institute of Family and Life Advocates v. Becerra*, the Court blocked a California law that required religious "crisis pregnancy centers" to inform women about abortions. And, in *Janus v. American Federation of State, County and Municipal Employees*, the Court ruled that workers who do not join unions may not be forced to pay for collective bargaining—a decision that struck down a 40 year precedent and dealt a serious blow to labor unions.[1]

All three cases reflected the powerful role the judiciary plays in American politics. During the battle to ratify the Constitution, Alexander Hamilton predicted that the judiciary "will always be the least dangerous" and "the weakest" branch of government, for, he reasoned, it has "no influence" over "the sword" (the president controls the army) or "the purse" (Congress is in charge of the budget).[2] Yet since 1789, the U.S. judiciary has accumulated sweeping authority. It strikes down laws, rules, and regulations that violate the Constitution—as the courts interpret it.

We have seen the great reach and power of the Supreme Court throughout this book. For example, it struck down hard-won congressional compromises and protected slavery (in *Dred Scott*, 1857); it first permitted segregation (*Plessy v. Ferguson* in 1896) and then rejected it (*Brown v. Board of Education*, 1954); it swept away a network of state laws prohibiting abortion (*Roe v. Wade*, 1973). More recently, the Supreme Court rejected bipartisan efforts to limit money flowing into American elections; struck down sections of the Voting Rights Act that empowered the federal government to monitor election laws in places with a history of racial discrimination;

● *Union activists protest the Supreme Court ruling in* Janus v. AFSCME, *which held that public employee unions cannot require nonmembers to pay fees to the union.*

In this chapter, you will:

● **Consider how the law reflects the American people—and our national culture.**

● **Learn how the judicial system operates.**

● **Examine the courts' role in American politics.**

● **Explore the inner workings of the Supreme Court.**

● **Reflect on how judges decide cases.**

● **Review landmark judicial cases.**

overturned a law that permitted the government to deport immigrants who had committed felonies; and permitted Ohio to purge voter lists of people who had not recently voted.[3] These cases were all the more controversial because each was decided by a single vote: 5–4.

The previous two chapters, on the presidency and on the bureaucracy, asked whether each still fit into a democratic framework. The question becomes even more pointed for the federal courts. Unelected officials with lifetime appointments wield the power to overrule the long, hard, democratic process of forging legislation in both Washington, DC, and the states. The founders believed that the more political branches of government—the president and Congress—needed the courts to check them. Has that check now grown too powerful? And too politicized?

Who are we? A nation founded on the world's oldest constitution, which directly or indirectly governs almost every aspect of our collective life. The courts apply the Constitution to the problems we face. Small wonder that the United States has been a nation of courts, lawyers, and people ready to sue.

We begin with the basics. What does the court system look like? How does it make decisions? How did it amass so much power over American politics, government, and daily lives? Throughout we will ask the same fundamental question: Does the American political system effectively balance the authority of elected officials and lifetime judges? The answer starts with the basic character of the American people: *Who we are.*

Who Are We? A Nation of Laws . . . and Lawyers

The United States relies on courts to resolve more matters than most nations. The result is a deeply legalistic political culture.

Embracing the Law—and Lawsuits

Litigation: The conduct of a lawsuit.

Lawsuits, or **litigation**, are a near-constant feature of American public life. The annual U.S. criminal caseload includes 35 to 40 million cases filed in state courts. Traffic violations add another 55 million cases to the total. Federal courts open approximately 400,000 new cases a year (notice that federal cases equal about 1 percent of the number in state courts). Another three quarters of a million cases enter the bankruptcy courts. Add all of these up and the United States approaches 100 million legal actions a year. And that is before we get to all the cases heard in specialized federal courts.

BY THE NUMBERS
The U.S. Judiciary

Original number of Supreme Court justices	5
Year in which the number of Supreme Court Justices was set at 9	1869
Number of Supreme Court justices appointed, 1882–1910	18
Number of Supreme Court justices appointed, 1982–2010	9
Average number of years a Supreme Court justice served before retiring from 1790–1954	16.5
Average number of years a Supreme Court justice served before retiring from 1970–2018	26
Number of Acts of Congress ruled unconstitutional per year from 1800–1900	0.2 (or 22 in all)
Number of Acts of Congress ruled unconstitutional per year 1900–1999	1.3
Number of Acts of Congress ruled unconstitutional per year 2000–2018	2.0[4]
Number of chief justices in American history	17
Number since 1953	4
Total number of cases heard by Supreme Court, 1987–1988 term	155
Total number of cases heard by Supreme Court, 2017–2018 term	79
Vacancies on the Supreme Court filled in Obama's eight years	2
Vacancies on the Supreme Court filled in the first two years of the Trump presidency	2
Estimated number of Americans who served on federal juries in 2016	44,000
Estimated number who served on juries in state or local courts	1.4 million

How has the character and role of our judicial system changed over time?

Courts are the primary sites for settling disputes. Advocacy groups, private citizens, and corporations go to court as a "first-strike" option. Litigation is an essential part of the rule-making process (discussed in Chapter 12). Business competition spills into the courts. Most other industrial nations rely more on **mediation** in noncriminal cases; citizens also are more likely to defer to civil servants. In contrast, Americans sue. Only a few other nations—most notably, Great Britain and Denmark—have as many suits per capita as the United States does.

Mediation: A way of resolving disputes without going to court, in which a third party (the mediator) helps two or more sides negotiate a settlement.

Trust in Courts

The law was once prestigious. Tocqueville described early nineteenth-century lawyers as democracy's natural aristocrats and noted that the American people trusted them.[5] Not anymore.

Today, law, lawyers, and the legal system all face shrinking reputations. In 2018, only 37 percent of Americans reported "a great deal" of confidence in the Supreme Court (see Figure 13.1).

In 2016, Justice Scalia died and the Republican-controlled Senate refused to hold hearings on President Obama's nominee, Merrick Garland. A year later, the Senate swiftly confirmed Donald Trump's nominee, Neil Gorsuch. Approval rose 15 percent among Republicans and fell 10 percent among Democrats.[6] Smart politics? Or the growing politicization of an institution that should be above politics?

Even when the judiciary's prestige ebbs, it still ranks roughly the same as that of the president (37%) and towers over Congress (just 11% in June 2018).

Courts in American Culture

Images of law and lawyers run through American culture, with the image alternating between heroism and cynicism. In *To Kill a Mockingbird*, Gregory Peck's Atticus Finch wins the African American community's respect when he passionately defends a black man unjustly accused of rape: "In our courts all men are created equal," he proclaims at the film's climax. "That's no ideal to me. That is a living, working reality." The book and movie's racial idealism reflected

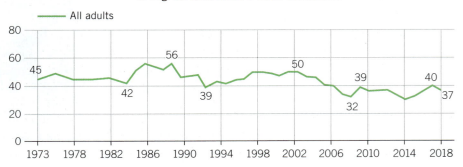

Americans' Confidence in the U.S. Supreme Court
% A great deal/Quite a lot of confidence

● **Figure 13.1** *The Supreme Court gradually declines in public esteem (Gallup, 2018).*

the optimism of the early 1960s. Julia Roberts played another legal heroine, the real-life Erin Brockovich, a clerk without any legal training whose indefatigable work led to a major environmental suit against Pacific Gas and Electric for contaminating the water supply of Hinkley, California. Images of law as a type of crusade—for racial justice, environmental protection, or national security—reflect and reinforce cultural images of political idealism.

● *Images of law in popular culture. Here, the cast of Suits.*

The Bottom Line

» The United States relies on courts and litigation more than most other nations.

» Trust in the Supreme Court has declined in recent years.

» Law continues to play an important role in American popular culture—portrayed in both idealistic and cynical terms.

Organizing the Judicial Branch

The Constitution offers detailed instruction for Congress (Article 1) and vague rules for the executive branch (Article 2). The judiciary gets the least attention of all. The Constitution vests judicial power in the Supreme Court, without specifying the number of justices, and empowers Congress to design the rest of the federal court system. As usual, Americans run this branch of government in a distinctive way.

Divided We Rule

By now you know the story: When Americans see government power, they divide it. Two chambers of Congress, with layers of committees and subcommittees; an executive branch split into departments, agencies, commissions, and White House offices; a federalist system of national, state, and city officials all cooperating, competing, and overlapping. Court powers also are divided.

Most other nations feature a single, unitary system of courts. In contrast, the United States exhibits *judicial federalism*. Both federal and state court systems are further divided into layers. The federal system has three layers, as do most states (see Figure 13.2): Lower courts conduct trials, appellate courts hear appeals, and a supreme court in both state and federal systems renders a final verdict. The national Supreme Court is the ultimate arbiter for all cases involving the Constitution or federal law. Millions of cases are filed each year;

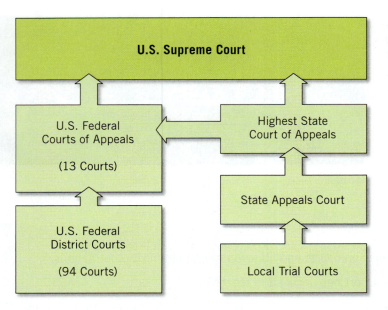

U.S. Supreme Court

U.S. Federal
Courts of Appeals

(13 Courts)

U.S. Federal
District Courts

(94 Courts)

Highest State
Court of Appeals

State Appeals Court

Local Trial Courts

● **Figure 13.2** *Organization of the U.S. federal courts system.*

around ten thousand appeals reach the Supreme Court, which only accepts about 80. That leaves a great deal of authority in the lower ranks of the judiciary.

State and Local Courts

Local trial and state appeals courts are the workhorses of the judiciary. State courts are responsible for all cases that arise under state law; they rule on everything from antitrust disputes to murder cases and from medical malpractice to marijuana possession. Each state organizes its judicial system in its own way—so there is considerable variation around the nation.

The first stop in most cases is a state trial court. Appeals are handled in state appellate courts and then a supreme court for final appeals (Texas and Oklahoma have two top courts). Appeals from state courts may be heard by the U.S. Supreme Court. Many landmark cases originate—and are sometimes settled—in state courts. *Roe v. Wade* (which struck down a Texas law banning abortion) and *Bush v. Gore* (halting the recount of disputed presidential ballots in Florida) began in state courts. However, very few of the millions of state cases ever reach a federal judge, as these cases did.

Judicial Selection

Do you think you might like to become a state judge? There are surprisingly few formal requirements. You may not even need a law degree. Twenty-two states and the federal courts require no formal training before judges start hearing cases. Most judges first make their name as lawyers, although many come from government or academia. And do not bother lobbying the governor unless you are from one of the sixteen states where governors select the judges. Two others leave selection to the state legislature. Most elect judges and others subject them to re-election after a term (thirty-eight states hold elections). Terms last between two and fourteen years.[7]

The idea of electing judges is controversial. After all, the courts are meant to be above partisan politics, protecting rights and weighing evidence without political pressures. Elections, say the critics, undermine the courts' ability to stand up for the rights of unpopular minorities. Moreover, campaign contributions and promises could lead to bias and even corruption on the state benches. Former Supreme Court justice Sandra Day O'Connor has been an especially vocal critic of electing judges; she calls the campaigns "tawdry and embarrassing."[8] Still, the United States is the land of five hundred thousand elected officials.

What Do YOU Think? **How Should States Select Their Judges?**

| Which of these three approaches to judicial selection in the states seems best to you? | **Let the people vote.** The people are the best guardians of their own welfare. Let them decide who should be their justices. No matter how courts are organized, it is naive to think that politics can be kept out of the equation. Today, 70 percent of the public thinks that justices sometimes let their own political views influence their rulings. Because politics is inevitable, the public should have a direct voice in judicial selection.[9] | **Appointment by a governor.** The state's governor (with the advice and consent of the state senate) will have valuable information about the candidates and can keep better track of which justice is doing a good job. It also avoids the problems introduced by elections: campaigning, fund-raising, potential corruption, and the temptation to win votes by making promises that could later compromise the court. | **Merit committees.** Courts must be above politics. They must defend the rights of minorities and unpopular views. The only way to ensure such fairness is to let impartial merit commissions make the selection. The commission's nominees can then be voted up or down by the legislature. | **Unsure.** You will probably develop a stronger opinion by the end of the chapter. |

Federal Courts

Federal courts hear three types of cases. First, they handle crimes that violate federal laws, issues that involve federal treaties, or cases touching on the Constitution. Examples range from the dramatic to the mundane: terrorism, immigration, organized crime, civil rights, patents, or flag burning. Second, they decide disputes that spill across state lines—for example, interstate drug trafficking or conflicts between parties in different states (with at least $75,000 in dispute). Finally, after state courts have ruled on a case, the parties can appeal to federal courts—if a federal issue is involved.

Most federal cases begin in one of the ninety-four **district courts**, which together house just under 700 judges. Every state has at least one district court, and the larger states (e.g., California and Texas) have as many as four. District courts determine the facts of the case (did John Smith try to blow up a federal building?), they build a record detailing the evidence, and they then apply the law to reach a ruling. Cases at this level are heard by a single judge.

District court judges, like all federal judges, are appointed by the president, subject to "advice and consent" review by the Senate, and hold their office for life. Until recently, the Senate routinely approved nearly all judicial appointments, sometimes with very little scrutiny. In today's hyperpartisan Congress,

District courts: The first level of federal courts, which hear the evidence and make initial rulings.

● *Judicial elections: emblem of democracy—or path to corruption?*

Circuit courts: The second stage of federal courts, which review the trial record of cases decided in district court to ensure they were settled properly.

however, the opposition party generally challenges judicial nominations—slowing them down in the hopes that their party will take the presidency and fill the empty seats.

When the Republicans gained the Senate in 2014, they applied the brakes to the Obama administration's judicial appointments. By 2016, the administration's last year, almost 300 positions were vacant. With the Trump administration in power, Democrats return the favor and try to slow down the appointments. By summer 2018, there were 152 vacancies on the federal bench and 88 nominees awaiting confirmation.[10]

Above the ninety-four district courts are thirteen federal appellate courts, known as **circuit courts**. A party that loses in district court can appeal to this next level. Three circuit court judges hear each case, usually to determine whether the district court made the correct ruling. They rule on the basis of the record established on the lower level: There is no jury and no cross-examination. Some 180 judges serve these circuit courts, collectively ruling on nearly seventy thousand cases in a typical year. As with the district courts, the circuit courts are organized geographically and referred to by their number: Figure 13.3 displays the current organization. Appeals from Ohio, for example, go to the Sixth Circuit Court of Appeals in Cincinnati. Some types of cases (like those involving patents or international trade) go directly to a court known as the U.S. Court of Appeals for the Federal Circuit. As with district court judges, those on the circuit courts are nominated by the White House and are subject to Senate confirmation.

Sometimes multiple versions of a case reach different district and circuit courts. Rulings on the Trump administration travel ban were handed down in five districts from Hawaii to Massachusetts. At the next level, two circuit courts eventually accepted appeals. The Supreme Court eventually overturned the Ninth Circuit when it ruled in favor of the ban.

Specialized Courts

The federal judiciary also includes a set of specialized courts, each covering a specific subject such as military justice, tax disputes, terrorism, and bankruptcy The caseloads rise and fall as society changes: Bankruptcy claims, for example, have dropped from more than 1.5 million (during the Great Recession) to about 796,000 in 2017. After 9/11, the FISA court, which rules on federal requests to conduct electronic intelligence saw its caseload (and its prominence) soar.

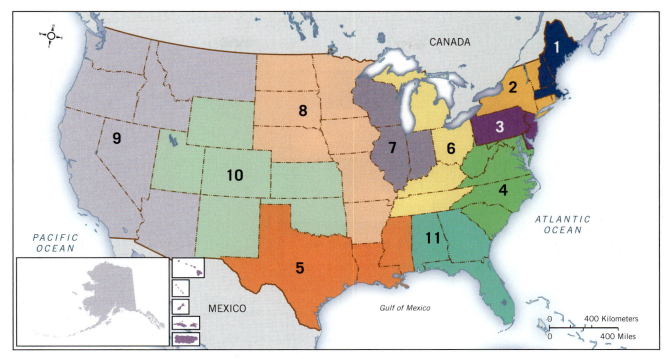

● **Figure 13.3** *The federal circuit courts. In addition there are two courts, one for Washington, DC, and one for specialized cases, which are not shown here (Federal Judicial Center.)*

The president appoints (and the Senate confirms) judges to all these courts. Unlike other federal judges, however, they do not serve for life. Bankruptcy judges, for example, serve renewable 14-year terms.

The U.S. military runs its own separate court system, addressing breaches of justice by members of the armed forces. These courts have been a source of controversy since President George W. Bush called for military tribunals to try defendants charged with terrorism against the United States, many of whom were held as enemy combatants in Guantánamo Bay, Abu Ghraib, and other detention centers around the globe. The Obama administration first suspended the military trials, but after Congress resisted moving the trials to civilian courts, the administration reinstated the tribunals with some changes in their rules. In rare cases, tribunals are permitted under the Constitution. The last large-scale use of military tribunals occurred after World War II, to try Nazi war criminals.[11]

Together, these specialized courts, ranging from bankruptcy to military, constitute something of a "third judiciary" alongside state and federal courts. Periodically, critics advance proposals for a new type of special court, usually to deal with some technical area of law they believe regular citizen juries cannot handle adequately. The latest proposals focus on medical malpractice, where multimillion-dollar damage suits turn on ambiguous "medical errors."

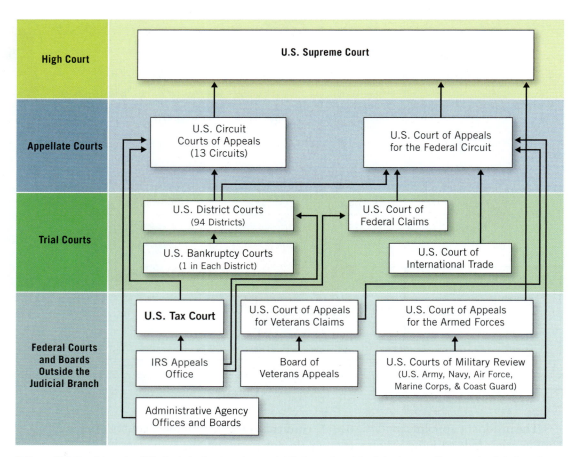

● **Figure 13.4** *Special courts within the federal system. A more detailed snapshot of the federal system illustrates that it is, in reality, far more complicated than the simple tripartite system of district, circuit, and supreme courts.*

Specialized courts offer another example of the fragmented and complicated judicial branch—as Figure 13.4 vividly demonstrates.

Diversity in the Federal Judiciary

Do federal judges reflect America's population? No. Just below one-third of judges are women, and nearly three-quarters are white. Twelve-and-a-half percent of federal judges are African American (compared to 12.2% of the population), 9.7 percent are Hispanic (compared to 16.3%), 2.9 percent are Asian American (compared to 4.7%), and only one federal judge is Native American. The past six presidents, going back to 1977, each left the federal bench more diverse though the Trump administration, in its first 17 months in office, reversed the trend (Table 13.1); 90 percent of its nominees were white and 72 percent male (Figure 16.5).[12]

Does it matter if the judge presiding over a case is female or Latino? Supreme Court Justice Sonia Sotomayor suggested that it did, ten years before

| TABLE 13.1 | How Presidents Compare on Racial and Ethnic Diversity of Appointed Judges | | | | | | |

PRESIDENT	JUDGES	WHITE	BLACK	HISPANIC	ASIAN	OTHER	% NONWHITE
Trump	67	60	1	1	5	0	10*
Obama	324	208	58	31	18	0	36
G. W. Bush	324	266	24	30	4	0	18
Clinton	372	282	61	23	5	1	24
Bush	188	169	11	8	0	0	10

Source: Pew Research Center
*As of September 30, 2018

she was appointed to the Court. "I would hope that a wise Latina woman," Sotomayor said, "with the richness of her experience would more often than not reach a better conclusion than a white male who hasn't lived that life." In other words, personal experience will inform judicial decisions. The comment provided cause for reflection—and also raised controversy. Former House Speaker Newt Gingrich claimed that a white male judge making a similar claim on behalf of white men would be forced to resign.[13] The remarks sparked controversy—but was it correct?

Research suggests that black judges are more likely to vote in favor of affirmative action,[14] more likely to find violations of the Voting Rights Acts,[15] more likely to side with lesbian, gay, bisexual, or transgender claimants, and more likely to accept black defendants' claims of police misconduct.[16] Likewise, women on the bench rule somewhat differently from male judges in gender-related cases: Women are roughly 10 percent more likely to find discrimination—as are male judges if they are serving on a panel with a female judge.[17]

What Do YOU Think?   Identity on the Bench

Do you agree with Justice Sotomayor's comment that a person's life experience can deeply inform his or her judgment about politics, culture, and other matters?

Agree. Every person inevitably brings his or her life experience to important decisions and justices are no different. That's why diversity on the bench is so important.

Disagree. Judges should rule on the basis of law. Their background is irrelevant and should not cloud sound legal judgment based on the laws and the facts of the case.

The Bottom Line

» State courts handle the vast majority of cases. Nearly all states divide their judiciary into three levels: trial courts, appeals courts, and a state supreme court. A majority of U.S. states elect their judges.

» Federal courts rule on cases involving constitutional questions, federal laws, and federal treaties. They are divided into ninety-four district courts, eleven appeals courts, and the Supreme Court.

» Federal justices are selected by the president and confirmed by the Senate, and they hold their position for life. Party polarization in Congress has created a serious problem of unfilled judgeships.

» Numerous additional federal courts handle everything from bankruptcy to military matters.

The Court's Role

Alexander Hamilton's assurance that the judiciary would play a minor role in American government did not last long. John Marshall, the longest-serving chief justice in U.S. history—held the office from January 1801 to July 1835—helped establish the U.S. courts as unusually powerful. How did Marshall do it?

Judicial Review

The breakthrough came in the landmark case *Marbury v. Madison*. Marshall asserted that the Supreme Court has the authority to overrule any act of Congress that violates the Constitution.

The case arose after John Adams lost the 1800 election and, during his final hours as president, made "midnight appointments" that installed his supporters in judicial positions. The new president, Thomas Jefferson, came to office with very different political views and vehemently opposed the last-minute appointments. Jefferson directed his secretary of state, James Madison, to destroy the appointment letters—including one naming William Marbury as justice of the peace for the District of Columbia. The Judiciary Act of 1789, which established the position, referred some cases (involving writs of mandamus, or direct orders to government officials) directly to the Supreme Court. Marbury duly petitioned the Court to order Madison to deliver his commission. This action constituted a high-stakes early test of the Court's authority.

Marshall and his fellow justices faced a trap. If the Court ruled in favor of Marbury, the recently elected President Jefferson would ignore the Court—and diminish its importance in the new federal government. Marshall found an ingenious way around Jefferson's defiance and vastly expanded the Court's role in American governance.

How do judges interpret the Constitution?

Led by Marshall, a unanimous Court ruled that Congress, in drafting the Judiciary Act of 1789, had erred in granting the Supreme Court the direct authority (or "original jurisdiction") to decide the question. The Constitution implied that the Supreme Court should rule on such cases only on appeal from the lower courts. However, the Constitution was silent on what would happen if Congress passed a law that clashed with the Constitution. Marshall filled in the blank with a dramatic move: "It is emphatically the province and duty" of the Court, wrote Marshall, to judge "if a law be in opposition to the Constitution." With that, Marshall established the court system's mighty power of **judicial review**—although that authority is never mentioned in the Constitution itself.

● *John Marshall denied Marbury's suit and, in the process, asserted the power of the Supreme Court to strike down acts of Congress when they violated the Constitution.*

Judicial review: The Court's authority to determine whether legislative, executive, and state actions violate the Constitution and overrule those that do.

The Court decided the case by striking down Section 13 of the Judiciary Act of 1789—the section that referred writs of mandamus directly to the Supreme Court. Because Section 13 was the basis of Marbury's petition, the Court ruled that it had no constitutional authority to force the administration to deliver the petition. President Jefferson opposed Marshall's clever move, denouncing the "despotism" and "oligarchy" by which unelected officials "usurp[ed]" control of the Constitution from elected ones. But what could Jefferson do? In asserting the Court's power, Marshall had sided with the president and denied Marbury his petition. Jefferson had no way to defy a Court case that he had won. By apparently relinquishing power, Marshall permanently strengthened the federal judiciary.[18]

Marshall deftly addressed a basic issue in American government, with profound implications that reverberate in the present day. When there is doubt about what the Constitution holds or implies, the Supreme Court continues to claim that it is the one that makes the call.[19]

Activism Versus Restraint

The Supreme Court was slow to wield the power it had asserted. It did not overrule another act of Congress for 54 years, until the *Dred Scott* decision struck down the Missouri Compromise and declared that black people were "so far inferior that they had no rights which the white man was bound to respect."[20] That decision brought the issue of slavery to a boil in 1857 and established a pattern: Many of the most intense disputes in American politics wind up decided in court.

The judiciary has stepped up the pace with which it overrules Congress. In the 150 years following *Marbury*, it struck down just 22 federal laws; in the 25 years between 1990 and 2018, it struck down 59, including laws

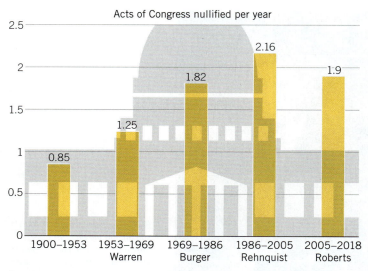

Acts of Congress nullified per year

- 1900–1953: 0.85
- 1953–1969 Warren: 1.25
- 1969–1986 Burger: 1.82
- 1986–2005 Rehnquist: 2.16
- 2005–2018 Roberts: 1.9

● **Figure 13.5** *Acts of Congress nullified by the Supreme Court* (Journal of Legal Metrics).

designed to limit flag burning, guns near schoolyards, child pornography, violence against women, barriers to voting, limits on gambling, and same-sex marriage (see Figure 13.5).

Today, the Supreme Court is embroiled in many intense debates. We began the chapter with three examples. Other hot questions include: May Congress limit campaign contributions? Can the White House regulate emissions from power plants to combat global warming? Is the right to bear arms limited? Does the right to privacy forbid states from banning or curtailing abortions? Each of these questions was removed from the court of public opinion, or the jurisdiction of elected officials, and settled by the Supreme Court—generally by a 5–4 vote.

The Supreme Court also reviews state and local statutes. This Court did not have to maneuver to win this power. The Constitution's "supremacy clause" declares that "this Constitution and the laws of the United States . . . shall be the supreme Law of the Land" (Article 6). The Judiciary Act of 1789, which established the federal court system (yes, the same act that created William Marbury's position), granted the Court authority to enforce the supremacy clause and to strike down state laws that clash with the Constitution or with federal statutes. The judiciary has been more active on this level; striking down state actions at about six times the rate it overturns federal laws. Over time, federal courts have declared almost 1,100 state and local laws unconstitutional and ruled that more than another 200 state and local laws were preempted—or superseded—by federal law. Landmark cases overruled state laws that established segregation, forbade child labor, outlawed abortion, established school prayer, limited private property rights, or prohibited same-sex marriage.

The growing number of rulings that strike down legislation raises an enduring question: How energetic should courts be in reviewing cases? **Judicial activism** takes a vigorous approach to reviewing the other branches of government and believes that courts must be vigilant in protecting rights. Between the 1950s and the 1970s, liberal activists were in the Supreme Court majority. During this period, the Court struck down segregation, forbade school prayer, and found a right to privacy in the penumbra (or shadow) of the Constitution.

Judicial restraint holds, on the contrary, that the courts should overturn the elected branches of government reluctantly and as a last resort. The terms—*activism* and *restraint*—are easily politicized. Conservatives bitterly

Judicial activism: A vigorous or active approach to reviewing the other branches of government.

Judicial restraint: Reluctance to interfere with elected branches, only doing so as a last resort.

attacked liberal judicial activism during the civil rights era of the 1950s to early 1970s; as the courts turned conservative, however, liberals began to criticize activist judges for being eager to overrule the will of the people's representatives.

The idea of activism recalls our discussion in Chapter 2 about how to read the Constitution. Is it a living and evolving document, as the pragmatists believe? Or should we insist on faithfully reconstructing the original meaning, as originalists think we should do? The difference between these positions is less stark than it might appear. The Constitution can be ambiguous; it often requires a nimble analysis to apply it to any contemporary case.

The Judicial Process

The judiciary's role goes far beyond weighing constitutionality. Legal cases constantly raise the question of how a law should be applied in a specific dispute. The court's job is to determine legislative intent. We saw this in the bureaucratic rule-making process in Chapter 12). If lobbyists do not like the new regulations for inspecting poultry slaughterhouses, they can go to court and claim that the regulatory agency has mistaken what Congress intended when it authorized those inspections. Ultimately, the court has to rule on what Congress meant to do—perhaps in the distant past. Because lawsuits are a regular feature of policymaking, federal courts stay very busy interpreting the intent of the other branches.

Often there is no legislative record or executive action to settle a case. The American colonists introduced an English system known as **common law**. Common law (also known as *case law*) is a system of law developed by judges in deciding cases over the centuries. Because legal judgments should be consistent from case to case, each time a court settles a case it sets a **precedent** that will guide similar cases in the future. Over the years, the common law offers a rich legal heritage to guide judges in settling disputes. In countries without a common law tradition, such as France, judges may not rule unless there is a statute or regulation to guide them.

American courts handle two different types of cases. **Civil law** handles cases between two parties. William Marbury sues James Madison for his commission; a young man sues his Catholic diocese because a priest molested him; a major corporation sues a local pizza chain for borrowing its corporate logo. **Criminal law** involves cases where someone is charged with doing something prohibited by the government such as stealing your car.

The party who complains—Marbury, the man who was molested, or the government coming down on an alleged criminal—is called the **plaintiff**; the party that is sued is the **defendant**. In court cases, the plaintiff is listed first and the defendant second; thus, the case is called *Marbury* (the plaintiff) *v. Madison* (the secretary of state who did not deliver the commission). When a party loses in a lower court, it becomes the plaintiff on appeal; that is why you see case titles such as *Trump v. Hawaii* (the travel ban case).

Discover how to pursue a case through the court system.

Common law: A system of law developed by judges in deciding cases over the centuries.

Precedent: Judicial decisions that offer a guide to similar cases in the future.

Civil law: Cases that involve disputes between two parties.

Criminal law: Cases in which someone is charged with breaking the law.

Plaintiff: The party that brings the action in a lawsuit.

Defendant: The party that is sued in a court case.

Too Much Power?

Should nine unelected, lifetime appointees wield this much power in a twenty-first-century democracy? Add to that the circuit and district court federal judges, all appointed to their post for life: How can we say "the people" rule over the judicial branch?

Both our litigious society and the range of judicial authority—from judicial review to common law—give the courts the power to shape American policy. American courts profoundly affect American politics. Are they the guarantors of American constitutional rights? Or an outmoded throwback to an earlier, more elitist age? You can get a better sense when we look behind the scenes at the inner workings of the Supreme Court later in the chapter.

Or Still the "Least Dangerous" Branch?

Although the courts are undeniably powerful, every institution faces limits. The courts operate with four different types of restraints.

First, the federal courts have *no electoral base*. Their prestige and mystique are balanced by a lack of democratic authority. This has made some past courts careful about confronting elected officials. For example, the Supreme Court delayed the ruling in *Brown v. Board of Education* (striking down segregated schools) for almost two years while the justices struggled to reach unanimity. Chief Justice Earl Warren felt that such an important case—challenging segregation laws across many states—should have the backing of all nine members, because a major decision that went against popular opinion could harm the Court's authority and prestige.

Second, courts have relatively *limited resources* compared to other units of government. Senators generally have more than 50 staff members and can call on the Congressional Research Service and Government Accountability Office houses, which have hundreds of experts reporting in detail on any question a member may raise. In contrast, most federal judges have only two or three clerks—young staffers, usually fresh from law school with little judicial experience—who serve them for less than a year. Supreme Court justices, whose decisions can shape the course of government for generations, have at most four clerks, who serve for a year or two.

The courts also command small budgets. The Supreme Court operates on an annual budget of around 90 million dollars a year. The entire federal judiciary—13 circuit courts, 94 district courts, and the Supreme Court—receives less than $7 billion. That is about the same budget as that of NOAA, the federal weather service.

Third, courts are by definition *reactive decision makers*. Executive branch agencies or legislators can tackle problems and devise solutions. Courts await disputes; cases must come to them. True, most major issues eventually do wind up before the courts—but, unlike the other branches they do not define the problem or shape the question that is being disputed.

Finally, the courts must rely on other branches for *enforcement*. The Court rules. Other actors—in and out of government—implement the decisions.

The Supreme Court could strike down school desegregation; it could not, however, enforce the decision by sending troops to Little Rock or cutting the budgets of schools that refused to comply. In fact, the *Brown* decision was blocked for years by intransigent state and local officials (until the civil rights protests finally moved Congress to pass the Civil Rights Act). President Andrew Jackson made the point dramatically. When the Supreme Court struck down a Georgia law, because the state had no "dominion" over the Cherokees, he reputedly said, of the chief justice: "John Marshall has made his decision, now let him enforce it."[21]

The Bottom Line

» Chief Justice John Marshall asserted the Court's authority to review acts of Congress for their fit with the Constitution in *Marbury v. Madison*. The Judiciary Act of 1789 authorized the Court to review state laws.

» At first the Court rarely struck down acts of Congress, but it began to do so at a quicker pace after the 1970s.

» There are two general approaches toward defining the courts' role in government: *activists* believe in a vigorous judiciary scrutinizing the other branches; judicial *restraint* holds that courts should intervene rarely and reluctantly.

» The vital overarching question remains the same one that Chief Justice Marshall and President Jefferson crossed swords over more than two centuries ago: Is the Court acting in ways that are indispensable for democracy? Or in ways that threaten it?

The Supreme Court and How It Operates

Tucked away at the top of the majestic marble Supreme Court building on East Capitol Street, among all the justices' offices and conference rooms and libraries lined with leather law books, is . . . a small basketball court. Known as the "highest court in the land," the court is used exclusively by Supreme Court insiders: the justices' clerks, both current and former; a few staff members; and occasionally even one of the justices. We can imagine the basketball court as symbolic of the Supreme Court itself: exclusive, little known, and open to a tiny membership for a lifetime.

Hearing Cases

The Supreme Court is in session for nine months each year, traditionally opening on the first Monday in October. The justices generally stay out of public view, except when the Court meets to hear *oral arguments*—the presentation of a case that the Court has agreed to review. The Court is open to the public, first

● The Court hears a case in 2018. The chief justice sits at the center and the seats closest to his are occupied by those justices with the most seniority. From left, Kagan, Alito, Ginsburg, Kennedy (since replaced by Kavanaugh), Roberts, Thomas, Breyer, Sotomayor, and Gorsuch. Only sketches such as this one are permitted in the Supreme Court; no photographs or TV coverage.

come first served. If you are in Washington, we recommend you go.

Supreme Court oral arguments do not resemble the courtroom scenes on TV. The justices are the sole audience. Any case that the Supreme Court agrees to hear has usually already been thoroughly aired by at least one lower court. Normally, cases are heard in one hour, and each side's lawyer—called "counsel" in Court-speak (whether it is one lawyer or many)—is granted 30 minutes to make his or her best argument. When the Court took up the Obamacare case, *National Federation of Independent Business v. Sebelius*, it signaled the importance of the case by scheduling six hours over three days of oral argument.

The justices usually interrupt the presenting lawyer with questions—some supportive, others combative. They may also deliver mini-speeches of their own; lawyers never dare interrupt a Supreme Court justice, even if their 30 minutes are slipping away.

Before the hearing, both sides submit written briefs spelling out their argument. Other interested parties may submit their own briefs, endorsing one side. The outside contributions are known as **amicus curiae** (Latin for "friend of the court") briefs. A creative, well-written amicus curiae brief, sometimes wind ups being included in a justice's written opinion on the case.[22]

Are oral arguments important? Perhaps not. Justice Clarence Thomas told one interviewer that they influence his colleagues "in five or ten percent of the cases, maybe." Chief Justice John Roberts once added, "The judges are debating among themselves and just using the lawyers as a blackboard."[23] What matters far more are the written briefs that the counsels submit.

Amicus curiae: A brief submitted by a person or group that is not a direct party to the case.

Selecting Cases: Formal Requirements

How do the justices decide which cases to hear? Losing parties in lower courts may file a petition with the Supreme Court—stating the facts of the case and setting out detailed arguments as to why the Court should hear it. The petitions are split up among the justices and their clerks; on selected Fridays, the justices meet to choose the cases they will hear. At least four judges have to vote to hear a case for it to make it to the Supreme Court; that requirement is known as the **rule of four**.

When the justices agree to hear a case, the Supreme Court issues a *writ of certiorari* (legal-speak for "to be informed") demanding the official record from the lower court that heard the case. Roughly ten thousand petitions are filed with the Supreme Court each year, and some 70 or 80 are accepted—less than 1 percent. How do cases make it into that tiny group? That remains one of the great mysteries of American government. The Court never gives any

Rule of four: The requirement that at least four Supreme Court judges must agree to hear a case before it comes before the Court.

formal explanation for why it decided to grant certiorari to this case and not another.

Formally, a case must meet three conditions before it is even eligible for the Supreme Court—or any other court; these requirements apply at all judicial levels. The case must involve a *legitimate controversy*, that is, an actual dispute between two parties. Supreme Court justices do not deal with hypothetical matters; no federal court offers "advisory opinions" about something that might someday happen.

Second, the parties bringing a case must have *standing*: They must prove an actual harm (or imminent harm) to receive a hearing. Merely being distressed about a distant environmental disaster is not enough to provide standing; you must prove that this oil spill directly affects your livelihood (or your health or your property).

Finally, if the Court's proceedings will no longer affect the issue at hand, it is considered *moot*—irrelevant—and the case is thrown out. A famous example occurred in *Roe v. Wade*, where a federal district court dismissed the case as moot because the plaintiff, "Jane Roe" (real name: Norma McCorvey), had already delivered her child. The Supreme Court rejected this view, noting that the typical length of legal appeals processes meant that pregnancies would usually conclude too soon for a court decision to be reached.

Listen to oral arguments on the *Fisher v. University of Texas at Austin* affirmative action case.

Listen to oral arguments on the *United States v. Texas* immigration case.

Selecting Cases: Informal Factors

Thousands of cases each year meet the standards—controversy, standing, and mootness. Informally, we can identify four additional factors that help predict whether a case is more or less likely to be accepted by the Court.

First, the Supreme Court is more inclined to hear a case when two lower courts decide the legal question differently (usually two federal courts, but sometimes federal and state). Different rulings in similar cases require some resolution, hence the Court considered during its 2016–2017 term whether the North Carolina Supreme Court or federal district court was right about allegedly racially biased redistricting practices in the state.

Second, justices are inclined to grant certiorari to cases in which a lower-court decision conflicts with an existing Supreme Court ruling. In 1989, the Court ruled in *Penry v. Lynaugh* that a death sentence was sometimes permissible for criminals under the age of 18. More than a decade later, the Missouri Supreme Court declared that the death penalty for nonadults was "cruel and unusual punishment," citing a recent Supreme Court ruling that struck down capital punishment for mentally disabled people. The Supreme Court agreed and, in *Roper v. Simmons*, reversed its 1989 decision.

Third, the Supreme Court is more likely to hear cases that have significance beyond the two parties involved.

Fourth, the Supreme Court is especially likely to hear a case when the U.S. government is a party. The solicitor general—the attorney who represents the Department of Justice—is involved in almost half the Court's cases. Historically, the solicitor general had a "home court advantage" and won most cases for its client, the United States Government. Not anymore. President Obama's legal

● *Supreme Court Justice Ruth Bader Ginsburg as meme—the notorious R.B.G.— a play on rapper Biggie Smalls, aka the notorious B.I.G.*

team won just 44 percent of the time (the worst record in at least a century) and, in the Trump administration's first year, the administration record was, likewise, 43 percent.[24]

The Court hears cases from early October through late April. It usually issues its rulings on Monday mornings in May and June. Those Mondays are very exciting—and, for those involved in a case's outcome, very anxious occasions. No one knows when the Court will hand down a decision in a given case.

Conference Sessions and Written Decisions

What do the justices do when they are not on the bench, hearing oral arguments? Justices keep busy writing opinions (usually with substantial assistance from their clerks, who prepare drafts and discuss details with their boss); deciding which cases to hear in the future; and reading briefs for upcoming oral arguments. And, most intriguing of all, the justices meet in conference.

Supreme Court conferences, which usually take place on Thursday and Friday afternoon, are closed to everyone except the justices. They sit around a conference table; by tradition, the most junior justice sits nearest the door, opening it only to allow a staff member to wheel in carts piled with materials for the next case under consideration. The Supreme Court's collective decisions take place in conference.

Majority opinion: The official statement of the Court.

Concurrent opinion: A statement that agrees with the majority opinion.

Dissent: A statement on behalf of the justices who voted in the minority.

Justices discuss the cases they have heard, indicate their votes, and the chief justice, if he is in the majority, assigns the job of writing the **majority opinion**. Otherwise, the senior member of the majority assigns the job. The majority opinion is the official statement of the Court. Any justice who wishes to can issue a **concurrent opinion** explaining why he or she voted in favor of the majority outcome—different justices come to the same conclusion for different reasons. Justices who disagree about the outcome write a **dissent** indicating why they voted against the majority. Some dissents become celebrated or form the basis for a future judicial shift in thinking.

Supreme Court Clerks

Supreme Court clerks, usually recent law school graduates, exercise a remarkable amount of influence. They help the justices write opinions and reach decisions. The clerks also perform initial screening of the thousands of certiorari petitions that reach the Court each year.

Although the process is kept strictly private, the clerks reject many of the petitions, choosing a smaller set of a few hundred potential cases for the justices' consideration. Just think about this: A small group of unelected people in their twenties influence whether a case will reach the Court—and possibly shape American government.

Are you interested in serving as a Supreme Court clerk? It is a tough position to get; more than 1,000 apply each year and only three dozen or so land the job. After completing your law degree (JD), you generally serve one year in a lower-court clerkship—for a district court judge or in a state supreme court. During that year, you apply to a specific Supreme Court justice's chambers. (Some aspirants apply to all nine to maximize their chances of being selected.) If you make it to the interview stage, get ready for the toughest grilling of your life. Justice Antonin Scalia's famous interviews covered, as one veteran put it, "the law—all of it."[25]

Supreme Court clerks who elect to stay in public service often go on to important posts or become professors at top law schools. If you decide instead to go into private practice, you will be a hot commodity, and "court clerk bonuses" for signing with a law firm have been as high as $250,000.

Confirmation Battles

In June 2018, Justice Anthony Kennedy announced his retirement. Kennedy had leaned to the right but was, generally, the justice in the middle, between four strong conservatives and four strong liberals. Kennedy wrote a blockbuster opinion in *Obergefell v. Hodges*, which guaranteed the right to same-sex marriage (5–4) and was cheered by the Left, but also authored *Citizens United v. FEC*, which opened the door to campaign spending by corporations, 5–4 (see Chapter 8) and was cheered by the Right.

The succession battle began immediately. President Trump selected Brett Kavanaugh, a U.S. circuit-court judge who had been a staff member in the George W. Bush White House. Ratings of his prior opinions pegged him as a stalwart conservative. Many court watchers expected the Kavanaugh appointment to tilt the Court significantly to the right—ensuring a five to four majority, at least until the next retirement. Liberal groups mobilized against the Kavanaugh nomination, but Republicans had the votes and, after four days of hearings, confirmation seemed assured—until an unexpected bombshell.

A psychology professor, Christine Blaney Ford, publicly stated that Kavanaugh had sexually assaulted her at a high-school party 36 years before. Ford's charges resulted in an additional Senate Judiciary hearing—with Ford and Kavanaugh as the sole witnesses. Kavanaugh, alternately furious and tearful, denied Ford's allegations. After a supplemental FBI investigation, the Senate approved Kavanaugh's confirmation by a 50-48 vote.

● *Supreme Court nominee Robert Bork testifying at his confirmation hearing. His nomination was a watershed in the politicization of the Court. Before Judge Bork, the major focus was competence; now, the focus is on political perspectives.*

Given the lifetime tenure and the immense influence often wielded by the Supreme Court justices, one of the most significant moments on the American political calendar is the appointment of a new justice. Confirmation hearings have become partisan debates engaging a wide range of interest groups and national campaigns, all designed to influence the Senate Judiciary Committee, which holds hearings on a nominee and issues a recommendation to the Senate.

Until recent decades, confirmations were usually uncontroversial. Justice Anthony Kennedy was confirmed unanimously (see Table 13.2). Nomination politics changed dramatically in 1987, when President Ronald Reagan nominated Robert Bork to the Court. Bork certainly seemed qualified: He was a national authority on antitrust law; and he had been acting attorney general and a circuit court judge.

Bork, however, was also a no-apologies conservative who would replace Justice Lewis Powell, a moderate "swing vote." Liberal groups mobilized to oppose the nomination. Democratic senators, led by Ted Kennedy, criticized what they called "Robert Bork's America." After 12 days of hearings, the Senate defeated the nomination, 58 to 42. What surprised observers was the swift rise of organized opposition based not on the candidate's qualification, but on his judicial philosophy. Conservatives coined a new word to describe the phenomenon: *Borking*. They have returned the favor. Every judicial appointment, like Kavanaugh's, now faces a partisan nomination fight: packed hearings, demonstrations (pro and con), intense media coverage, polls serving up regular updates on how the nominee fares in the public view, and millions of dollars of advertisements running back in the states to influence key Senate votes.

The battles simply reflect the stakes that have developed in a highly partisan era when the two parties each stand for very different policies and principles. A single vote makes the difference on a host of issues: the right to privacy and abortion, gun control, the rights of criminals, campaign finance, immigration, healthcare reform, the rights of terrorism suspects—and the list goes on. Small wonder that the debates over each new justice get so heated, especially when

● The Senate Judiciary Committee grills Brett Kavanaugh before a packed hearing room—and a national audience.

● Bork: to turn down a competent nominee for political reasons.

TABLE 13.2 **Supreme Court Nominations and Confirmations**

Nomination votes have gotten closer over the years. Before the Bork appointment, qualified justices were easily confirmed. Notice that Kennedy, like many justices before him, won confirmation unanimously. As partisanship rose, the court grew politicized, unanimous votes disappeared and the hearings became more contentious. Debates become especially heated when a swing vote—such as Justice Kennedy—is up for replacement. It is much easier to replace a liberal with a liberal or a conservative with a conservative.

JUDGE	AGE AT TIME OF APPOINTMENT	APPOINTED BY (PRESIDENT)	SELECTED FROM	YEAR	SENATE VOTE		PUBLIC OPINION	
					YES	NO	YES	NO
Brett Kavanaugh	53	Trump	United States Court of Appeals	2018	50	48	46	45
Neil Gorsuch	49	Trump	United States Court of Appeals	2017	54	45	48	35
Elena Kagan	50	Obama	U.S. Solicitor General	2010	63	37	44	34
Sonia Sotomayor	55	Obama	U.S. Court of Appeals	2009	68	31	56	36
Samuel Alito	55	G. W. Bush	U.S. Court of Appeals	2006	58	42	54	30
John Roberts	50	G. W. Bush	U.S. Court of Appeals	2005	78	22	60	26
Stephen Breyer	55	Clinton	U.S. Court of Appeals	1994	87	9	—	—
Ruth Bader Ginsburg	60	Clinton	U.S. Court of Appeals	1993	96	3	53	14
Clarence Thomas	43	G. H. W. Bush	U.S. Court of Appeals	1991	52	48	58	30
Anthony Kennedy	51	Reagan	U.S. Court of Appeals	1988	97	0	—	—
Robert Bork	43	Reagan	U.S. Court of Appeals	1987	42	58	38	35

a nominee's political philosophy differs from his or her predecessor. Donald Trump's surprise presidential victory owed in part to his promise to nominate a conservative to the Court. "The least dangerous branch" was not designed to be in the eye of the political hurricane.

The Bottom Line

» The Supreme Court generally hears cases on the basis of petitions requesting a review of lower-court decisions. Four justices must vote to hear a case before it becomes part of the 1 percent that comes before the Court.

» To be heard in federal court, a case must meet criteria involving controversy, standing, and mootness. Other factors that make it more likely that the case will be heard include the scope of the question, a clash between lower courts or between a lower court and previous Supreme Court decision, and requests from the solicitor general.

» Cases involve oral arguments, written briefs, and conferences with only the justices present. The chief justice assigns a majority opinion; others write concurring or dissenting opinions for the record.

» Confirmation to the federal bench—and especially to the Supreme Court—was once a polite affair that largely involved questions of competence. Today, confirmations are some of the most politically charged dates on the political calendar. This discord raises an important question: How does the charged politics that surrounds the Court affect its own workings—and its standing with the public?

Judicial Decision Making and Reform

How do judges reach their decisions in a case? Social scientists emphasize four different perspectives.

The Role of Law

In theory, justices decide cases on the basis of the legal facts as laid out in the documents submitted. They read the law, consider the intent of its framers, and place it in the context of the Constitution.

Stare decisis: Deciding cases on the basis of previous rulings or precedents.

According to long-established principle, justices generally abide by previously decided cases. This is known as **stare decisis** (literally, "stand by the things decided"). Occasionally, the Supreme Court concludes that the precedents were wrongly decided and overrules a past decision. It has reversed itself 236 times—more than it has struck down acts of Congress. Still, legal theory suggests that the Supreme Court rules on the facts, guided by precedent. As Chief Justice John Roberts stated at his confirmation hearing, "Judges are like umpires. Umpires don't make the rules; they apply them. . . . My job is to call balls and strikes."[26]

The umpire metaphor is appealing. However, legal cases are often ambiguous. Applying the Constitution, more than two centuries after it was written is rarely simple or straightforward. Political scientists who study Supreme Court decisions have found another perspective with a good deal of analytic power.

Ideology and Partisanship

Ideology provides another guide to the judicial mind. Political scientists have generally found that the justices' beliefs are the most powerful predictor of how they will vote, especially on difficult cases. Some studies look at the party identification of the justices, others at their ideology prior to confirmation, and still others at the views of the presidents who appointed them. No matter how ideology is measured, one study after another suggests a strong relationship between the justices' beliefs and their votes (see Figure 13.6). In brief, we can predict the justices' votes, over time, with considerable accuracy, based on their political orientation.[27]

Ideology lines up with the judicial philosophy we discussed earlier. *Pragmatists* (who see a living, changing Constitution) will approach cases differently from *originalists* (who believe we must interpret the document's text literally). Likewise, activists may be quicker to strike down acts of Congress, state laws, and court precedents. Conservatives charged liberal justices with being overly activist during the Warren Court (1953–1969); today, liberals repeat the complaint about conservative justices. Ultimately, simple political perspective—liberal versus conservative—is one of the most effective ways of explaining how justices rule.

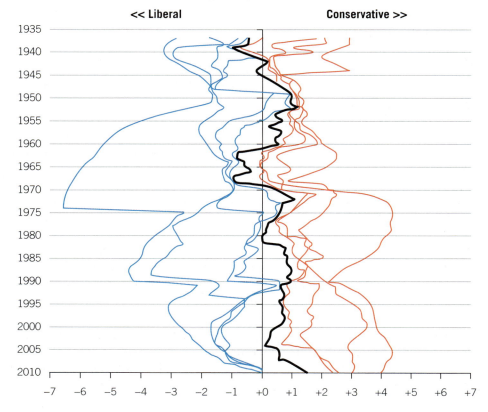

Ideology of Supreme Court Justices

● **Figure 13.6** *Ideology and voting on the Supreme Court. (Nate Silver, FiveThirtyEight)*

How Americans View the Supreme Court

LIBERAL OR CONSERVATIVE?

Americans are divided over their view of the Supreme Court as too liberal, too conservative, or just right. These views are influenced not only by Court decisions but also by new appointments.

How has the public view of the Court shifted over time? How have Court decisions impacted this view? How have views changed since the appointment of Justice Gorsuch in 2017?

Does the conviction that judges rule on the basis of ideology require us to rethink the way we appoint the justices or how the Court operates? Or is it desirable in our party-polarized age that justices exhibit strong viewpoints as so many politicians and ordinary citizens do today, thereby better representing the public?

Source: Gallup

Major shift in views of Court's ideology
% saying the current Supreme Court is . . .

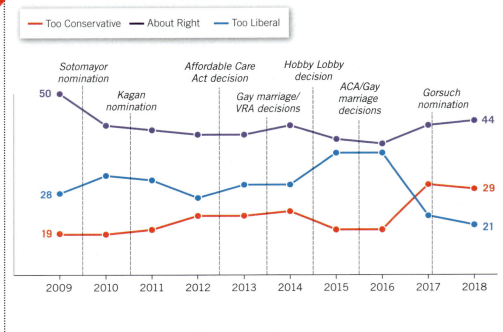

Too Conservative — About Right — Too Liberal

Sotomayor nomination
Kagan nomination
Affordable Care Act decision
Gay marriage/ VRA decisions
Hobby Lobby decision
ACA/Gay marriage decisions
Gorsuch nomination

50 · 44
28 · 29
19 · 21

2009 2010 2011 2012 2013 2014 2015 2016 2017 2018

The public has come to share the scholarly view about how justices decide. In recent polls, a full 70 percent of the public say that Supreme Court justices "are often influenced by their own political views." Just 24 percent think the justices "generally put their political views aside."[28]

The Court has long broken along the partisan divide: Four members were conservative—and, according to one study, rank among the seven most consistently conservative voters in the past 50 years: Chief Justice Roberts and associate justices Thomas, Alito, and Gorsuch all vote conservative more than 70 percent of the time. Justice Anthony Kennedy tended to vote conservative but provided a swing vote for liberals about one-third of the time. And Associate Justices Ginsburg, Breyer, Sotomayor, and Kagan vote liberal between 60 and 70 percent of the time. In recent years, the justices have begun to read their dissenting opinions aloud, a striking step designed to attract public attention to their dissatisfaction, which they often express in strong terms. Keep an eye on Justice Kavanaugh, as many court watchers expect him to provide a fifth strong conservative vote.[29]

Investigate the background of the justices.

The ideological model has its limits and by no means explains all votes. In 2017–2018, 39 percent of the cases were decided unanimously—much lower than the previous year (59% unanimous) or 2013–2014 (a record 65%). Ideology does not play a role in many technical cases.

Even so, the idea that the Court often rules on the basis of politics poses a dilemma for our democratic system. The Court is designed to stand above politics, to interpret and explain the rules without partisan consideration. That is the reason justices are selected for life. When they rule on the basis of political ideology—and are widely seen as doing so—they raise a problem for the legitimacy of this powerful institution.

Collegiality and Peer Pressure

A third factor shaping Court decisions is *collegiality*, or to put it more bluntly, *peer pressure*. Persuasion is a regular feature of Court discussions; justices appear to change positions in some cases based on legal arguments and personal appeals of colleagues. They also may change their votes for strategic reasons—trading votes in different cases.[30] Past generations appeared to engage in more give-and-take—in the 1950s and 1960s, at least one justice would switch his vote in about half of all cases.[31] Today, justices appear to be more settled in their convictions.

Another angle on the idea of "peer pressure" arises from the larger legal community. A few hundred people—law professors, law students, legal bloggers, congressional members, committee staff on the House and Senate Judiciary Committees, interest-group activists—carefully watch every judicial decision. The audience's judgment about a specific judicial opinion can be laudatory or scathing. Once classic analysis concluded that "judicial reputation" played an important role in explaining why justices moved left or right during their service on the Court.[32]

Institutional Concerns

Finally, justices sometimes appear to think about the interests of the Court as an institution. They spend many years on the bench and worry about the standing of the Court—before public opinion, a hostile Congress, or a skeptical executive. As we saw earlier, Justice Marshall carefully considered the role and standing of his institution as he crafted his complicated opinion in *Marbury v. Madison*. Some recent studies underscore the importance of this perspective.[33]

During much of 2016, with the Court down to eight justices, four members—two liberals and two conservatives—came together and tried to forge a consensus in as many cases as possible. They argued that constant deadlock would diminish the reputation of the Court. Four others (two liberals and two conservatives) responded that it would not help the cause of justice by compromising their judicial philosophies. Which side would you agree with?

The Bottom Line

» Four different perspectives help explain how justices make their decisions.

» First, we should pay attention to their own explanation: They follow precedent and the facts of the case.

» Political scientists are more likely to find that ideology is the best predictor in the long run. Recently, the public also has taken this view. It poses a dilemma for American governance: An institution designed to be above politics is increasingly seen as essentially political. That perception has helped turn confirmation hearings volatile.

» Two final factors also play a role: collegiality and institutional protection.

Nineteen Cases You Should Know

The history of American court cases includes a long list of famous—and occasionally infamous—decisions. Here we list 19 cases that every student of American government should be familiar with, organized chronologically.

1. *Marbury v. Madison* (1803)

Without Marshall's momentous decision, we may not have judicial review—or courts so deeply engaged in U.S. government and policymaking. You read about this one earlier in this chapter.

2. *McCulloch v. Maryland* (1819)

James William McCulloch was a clerk at the Baltimore branch of the National Bank of the United States. The state of Maryland levied an annual tax on all banks "not chartered by the state" of Maryland; at the time the National Bank

● Chief Justice Roger Taney, who served on the Court from 1836 to 1864, authored the Dred Scott decision—often described as the worst decision in Court history.

● Dred Scott, a slave, sued for his own freedom and that of his two daughters, arguing that he had been taken to Illinois and the Wisconsin Territory, both free areas. The Court rejected his bid for freedom, 7–2.

was the only one. On behalf of the bank, McCulloch refused to pay the Maryland tax and sued. The Maryland Supreme Court ruled against McCulloch, arguing that the Constitution said nothing about establishing a bank—the national bank was unconstitutional in the first place.

Taking a loose interpretation of the Constitution (rather than a strict construction that would have limited Congress to doing only what was explicitly allowed), Chief Justice Marshall upheld the constitutionality of the bank. Marshall argued that Congress had every right to establish a national bank under the Constitution's necessary and proper clause (which authorizes Congress to do anything that is "necessary and proper" for "carrying into execution" the powers it was granted).

Furthermore, declared the Court, Maryland was forbidden to tax the national bank. "The power to tax," declared Marshall for the unanimous majority, "involves the power to destroy."[34] The states had no such power over federal institutions because the collective American citizenry had established a national government with the Constitution's ratification. The Court's action affirmed the federal government's superiority to state governments in all specific instances named by the Constitution; this decision marked a significant advance toward American nationhood.

3. *Dred Scott v. Sandford* (1857)

As tensions mounted over the spread of slavery into the West, Chief Justice Roger Taney inserted the Supreme Court squarely into the middle of the debate. Writing for a 7–2 Court majority, Taney ruled that Dred Scott, a Missouri slave who was taken to a free state and later back to Missouri, was still a slave. He might have stopped there.

The Court, however, went on to rule that Congress did not have the power to prohibit slavery in the territories. Taney continued, in passages that are shocking to read today: Blacks, he insisted, were "beings of an inferior order and altogether unfit to associate with the white race." They were not and could never become U.S. citizens. The bottom line: Slavery could not be restricted in any western territory.[35] Many constitutional historians choose *Dred Scott* as the worst Supreme Court decision in American history (for more details, see Chapter 5).

4. *Santa Clara Co. v. Southern Pacific Railroad* (1886)

Santa Clara Co. v. Southern Pacific Railroad was a complicated tax case, decided unanimously without much notice, but it reverberates through our politics today. California forbade corporations from deducting their debts from their taxable property. The Court ruled that California had acted improperly because corporations should be treated as persons and afforded the Fourteenth Amendment right of equal protection. The case established a precedent—later expanded—that enhanced the power of corporations. By 1938 Justice Hugo Black would complain that the Fourteenth Amendment had been written "to protect weak and helpless human beings," not to "remove corporations in any fashion from the control of state governments." A decade later, Justice William O. Douglas added: "The *Santa Clara* case becomes one of the most momentous of all our decisions. . . . Corporations were now armed with constitutional prerogatives." The bottom line: *Santa Clara* set a precedent that, with time, gave corporations all the legal benefits of individual citizens. The legal theory in *Santa Clara* helped inform the Court when it struck down campaign finance laws (in *Citizens United* and other recent cases).[36]

5. *Plessy v. Ferguson* (1896)

In 1890, a Louisiana statute required that railroads maintain separate cars for black and white ticket holders—it was part of a network of laws pushing African Americans into second class citizenship. Homer Plessy deliberately challenged the law by refusing to move to the "colored car" on an East Louisiana Railroad train. The case eventually reached the Supreme Court, where Plessy's lawyers argued that the segregation violated his Fourteenth Amendment rights. (Remember that the Fourteenth Amendment, passed after the Civil War, guaranteed to all Americans "equal protection under the law.") The Court rejected Plessy's argument and upheld Louisiana's law, cementing the infamous doctrine of "separate but equal" for nearly 60 years (until *Brown v. Board of Education*). The decision permitted racial segregation, and in the next ten years the Jim Crow system went firmly into place with the Supreme Court's blessing.

The sole dissenting justice, John Marshall Harlan (note his first and middle names), wrote a blistering critique of the decision, predicting accurately

● *Keith Plessy and Phoebe Ferguson, descendants of the two men named in the famous case, have become friends and formed a foundation to promote innovative ways of studying civil rights. The battle for civil rights is passed on from generation to generation. Now it is in your hands.*

that *Plessy* "will prove as infamous" as the *Dred Scott* case and insisting that the Constitution must be "color blind."

Go online to see a discussion of the Plessy case.

6. *Lochner v. New York* (1905)

The rise of mass industry and manufacturing in the late nineteenth century bred strong demands for worker protection. Several states passed laws limiting working hours and banning child labor. New York State's worker protections, passed in 1897, included a "Bakeshop Act" that prohibited anyone from working more than ten hours a day, or 60 hours a week, in a bakery.

Joseph Lochner, a bakery owner in Utica, was fined for requiring employees to exceed the 60-hour weekly limit. He took his case to court, insisting that the Fourteenth Amendment protected his right to establish free contracts with his workers, independent of state influence.

Two New York courts denied Lochner's appeals. In a 7–2 ruling, the Supreme Court reversed the New York decisions, holding that the Bakeshop Act was an invalid exercise of the state's power. The decision ushered in a 30-year **Lochner era**, during which courts repeatedly struck down state economic and labor regulations, including minimum wage laws, in the name of individual economic liberty. Governments could not interfere with the private right to contract by introducing worker protections.

Lochner era: A period from 1905 to 1937, during which the Supreme Court struck down laws (e.g., worker protection, minimum wage laws) that were thought to infringe on the right to contract.

7. *Muller v. Oregon* (1908)

Oregon limited the number of hours women could work. Whereas Lochner ruled that the state could not regulate men's hours, the court chose to treat women differently. The Court ruled that "the difference between the sexes does . . . justify a different rule respecting a restriction of the hours of labor." The concern about "healthy mothers" justified the state intervention.

Louis Brandeis defended the law with an innovative strategy. He disposed of the legal arguments in two pages and then compiled page after page of data—health statistics, medical evidence, the experience of other nations. From that time forward, this kind of statistical brief, brimming with data, would be known as a "Brandeis brief."

The case is particularly important for gender readings of the law. Yes, women won labor protections, but note how: The decision rested on the idea that a woman was different from a man and, more to the point, that her role as child bearer and mother was more important than her role as worker.

8. *Schenck v. United States* (1919)

Charles Schenck, the secretary of the U.S. Socialist Party, printed and distributed leaflets expressing opposition to a U.S. military draft in World War I. Schenck was convicted under the Espionage Act of aiding the enemy during wartime. Insisting that he was exercising his First Amendment free speech rights, Schenck took his appeal to the Supreme Court.

Oliver Wendell Holmes Jr. wrote the decision for a 9–0 majority that upheld Schenck's conviction. For the first time, the Court formally marked out

● Lawyer Louis Brandeis, later a Supreme Court justice, relied on social science data to win Muller v. Oregon. *To this day, we call an argument that emphasizes social science research rather than legal argument a "Brandeis brief."*

Clear and present danger: Court doctrine that permits restrictions of free speech if officials believe that the speech will lead to prohibited action such as violence or terrorism.

boundaries around protected speech: Words presenting a "clear and present danger" were legitimate subjects of legislative prohibitions. The **clear and present danger** test guided the court for 50 years—it was rewritten in 1969. Recall that a "test" is a general principle designed to guide future court decisions on a topic (for more detail, see Chapter 4).

9. *National Labor Relations Board v. Jones and Laughlin Steel Corporation* (1937)

Jones and Laughlin was the nation's fourth-largest manufacturer of steel—an industry that had aggressively opposed unions. The company fired ten workers who tried to launch a union and was sued by the labor board for violating the Wagner Act (of 1935), which protected the right to unionize. The company responded that the Wagner Act violated the Constitution. The lower courts both agreed that precedent was on the company's side.

In a 5–4 decision, Chief Justice Charles Evans Hughes reversed the lower-court decisions and held that Congress had the power, under interstate commerce, to regulate the company's treatment of its workers. This decision broadly expanded congressional power to regulate economic matters. It meant that the Court—by a one-vote margin—would accept New Deal legislation. We can understand the enormous scope of this new ruling when, three decades later, Congress used its authority over interstate commerce to outlaw segregation in hotels and restaurants (with the Civil Rights Act of 1964, discussed in Chapter 5).

Along with another case, *West Coast Hotel Company v. Parrish* (also decided 5–4 in 1937), the courts now permitted legislatures to regulate relations between business and workers. The cases meant the end of the "Lochner era." Today, conservative judicial activists are eager to roll back congressional use of the interstate commerce power. Some even call for a return of the Lochner era.

● *Fred Korematsu refused to enter a Japanese internment camp. Today, his lifelong fight on behalf of civil liberties is commemorated by the "Fred Korematsu Day of Civil Liberties and the Constitution."*

10. *Korematsu v. United States* (1944)

During World War II, President Roosevelt's executive order forced Japanese Americans out of their homes and into hastily constructed internment camps. Fred Korematsu, a California native, was arrested for defying the order. The Court ruled 6–3 that the need to defend against espionage during wartime justified the order—and its violation of equal protection. The case was one of the first to use the **strict scrutiny** of government actions: The Court is primed to strike down any law that singles out a race or ethnicity unless there is a very strong reason for doing so (see Chapter 5 for discussion). In this case, the Court ruled, the government's action met the standards of strict scrutiny.

The case was infamous for its mistreatment of Japanese Americans. In 1983, a federal district court in California used the new information to vacate (or void) Korematsu's conviction. The Court formally reversed the precedent of Korematsu in 2018—in *Trump v. Hawaii*.

Strict scrutiny: A form of judicial review that requires the government to have a "compelling government interest for any law that singles out race or ethnicity."

11. *Brown v. Board of Education* (1954)

This landmark decision, decided unanimously, declared that segregating schools for black and white children violated the equal protection clause of the Fourteenth Amendment. As Supreme Court Justice Earl Warren put it, "separate schools are inherently unequal." The decision boosted the civil rights movement and led the way for an end to legal segregation. It overturned *Plessy v. Ferguson*, described earlier (for more details, see Chapter 5).

13. *Mapp v. Ohio* (1961)

Cleveland police received a tip in 1959 that local resident Dollree Mapp was harboring a suspected bombing fugitive, and they swarmed her house without a search warrant. The police found no fugitive—but they did find obscene material, at the time legally forbidden in Ohio. Mapp was arrested and convicted. The Supreme Court reversed her conviction and, drawing on the Fourth Amendment (prohibiting unreasonable searches and seizures), devised the "exclusionary rule," stating that illegally obtained evidence cannot be admitted in a criminal trial. The Court extended this federal rule to cover state cases (incorporating part of the Fourth Amendment) and ruled that, because the evidence against Mapp was obtained without a search warrant, she could go free. The conservative majority on the Roberts Court recently rolled back the exclusionary rule, and there is some speculation that it may be abolished altogether (for more details, see Chapter 4).

13. *Gideon v. Wainwright* (1963)

Clarence Gideon was accused of a minor theft from a Florida pool hall. Lacking funds to hire a defense attorney, Gideon represented himself at his trial—a relatively common practice into the early 1960s. He was swiftly convicted, but he appealed his sentence based on the state's failure to provide a competent defense lawyer.

The Supreme Court held that Gideon was wrongly convicted and ordered a new trial. The *Gideon* legacy: Anyone charged with a serious criminal offense has the right to an attorney. Moreover, the state must provide a lawyer to any defendant unable to afford legal counsel. *Gideon* was the first in a series of landmark judicial decisions upholding the rights of defendants in criminal proceedings, including the so-called *Miranda rights* to counsel during police questioning. Recently, the Court has strengthened the right to counsel, holding that it applies to plea bargain cases where a defendant is offered a deal: plead guilty, avoid a trial, and receive a lighter sentence (for more details, see Chapter 4).

14. *Lemon v. Kurtzman* (1971)

Religion is another constitutionally guaranteed freedom attracting frequent judicial attention: Recall from Chapter 4 that the First Amendment both guarantees the *free exercise* of religion to every person and forbids the *establishment* of religion. It erects what Thomas Jefferson termed a "wall of separation" between church and state.

In *Lemon v. Kurtzman*, the Court created a three-prong test for judging whether government action violated the first amendment by "establishing" a religion. The law could not create "excessive government entanglement" in religious affairs; it must not inhibit religious practice; and the law must have a secular purpose. Any law that violates any of these tests is unconstitutional.

The Court has been growing more permissive about allowing religious practices. For example, in *Town of Greece v. Galloway* (2014) the Court ruled (5–4) that the town's practice of starting its monthly meetings with a prayer did not violate the establishment clause. Despite the new, more permissive orientation, the Court has repeatedly refused to strike down the Lemon test (for more detail, see Chapter 4).

15. Roe v. Wade (1973)

The *Roe v. Wade* decision, written by Justice Harry Blackmun, struck down a Texas statute outlawing abortion—and expanded the personal right to privacy under the Constitution (for more detail, see Chapter 4).

16. United States v. Nixon (1974)

This case revolved around the Watergate break-in and the historic political debate that ensued. President Nixon refused to turn over audiotapes of White House conversations, along with other requested materials, to the special prosecutor investigating Watergate, on the ground of "executive privilege," a sweeping claim of presidential immunity. Chief Justice Warren Burger (appointed by Nixon five years before) upheld the doctrine of executive privilege but concluded that presidents could not invoke it in criminal cases to withhold evidence. Nixon acquiesced—and resigned as president a month later as a result of what the nation heard on the tapes.

The politics of abortion inflame passions, mobilize demonstrations, and shape American politics. For over forty years, the judiciary has been the central arena for this conflict.

17. Bush v. Gore (2000)

High drama surrounded a recount of some of Florida's disputed ballots in the 2000 presidential election, stretching well past the November 7 election date. On December 8, Florida's Supreme Court ordered a manual recount of ballots; George W. Bush's lawyers, fearing this would result in an advantage for Vice President Gore, appealed the decision to the U.S. Supreme Court. The Court, acting with unusual speed because of the urgency of the issue—a presidential election hung in the balance—halted the recount the very next day. Three days later, Chief Justice Rehnquist handed down a 5–4 ruling that no constitutionally valid recount could be completed by Florida's December 12 deadline. As a result, George Bush won Florida's 25 electoral votes and, with them, the presidential election.

Listen to the Supreme Court oral argument for Bush v. Gore (2000).

18. *National Federation of Independent Business v. Sebelius* (2012)

This blockbuster decision took on two controversial features of the Obama administration health reform law. Can the federal government require individuals to carry health insurance? Proponents said yes: Congress has the power to regulate interstate commerce (see case number 9, *NLRB v. Jones and Laughlin*). Chief Justice Roberts and the four conservative justices ruled that Congress does *not* have the power under interstate commerce to require that people buy health insurance. Then, very dramatically, the chief justice broke with the conservatives and ruled that Congress does have the power to tax—and this is a tax. The Obama reform was upheld. However, Roberts got Supreme Court watchers buzzing. Remember, conservatives have long wanted to curtail the congressional use of interstate commerce. Was Roberts handing conservative jurisprudence a victory, perhaps a return to the Lochner era that conservatives have been calling for, even while upholding the Obama healthcare law? Time will tell.

In the other part of the case, the Court ruled 7–2 that Congress could not change the rules of the Medicaid program and require states to expand their Medicaid program to cover everyone under the poverty line (the federal government paid 90% of the costs). It could only encourage the states to participate. Was this, wondered analysts, a new rollback of the federal government's power over federalism? Again, time will tell. The true scope of a case like this often takes years to reveal itself.

19. *Obergefell v Hodges* (2015)

When John Arthur was dying of ALS, his husband, Jim Obergefell, wanted the death certificate to list him as the surviving spouse. However, Ohio law refused to recognize same-sex marriage. In *Obergefell*, the Court ruled (5–4) that denying marriage licenses to same-sex couples violated the due process and the equal protection clauses of the Fourteenth Amendment. The ruling, authored by Justice Kennedy, required every state to accord same-sex marriages all the rights and conditions that accompany opposite-sex marriages. Again, Justice Kennedy's retirement raises the question of how future decisions might affect this ruling.

What Do YOU Think? Name Another Landmark Case

Why didn't we take our list to a nice round number? To leave room for your choice. Think about the many cases we have already discussed in this book (especially in Chapters 4 and 5). Then pick one that you think should be added to the list: What would it be?

Hint: Some cases that are frequently seen as landmarks include *Loving v. Virginia* (which struck down bans on interracial marriage); the *Trump* (immigration) and *Janus* (union dues) cases that opened this chapter; *Citizens United* (striking down campaign finance legislation, discussed in Chapter 8); *Miranda* (the right to remain silent; see Chapter 4); *Tinker* (student free speech; see Chapter 4); or *Bakke* (affirmative action; see Chapter 5);

The Nineteen Cases—and the Power of the Court

This list illustrates the wide range of questions addressed in U.S. federal courts. These cases also illustrate the formidable reach of the judiciary over American politics and government.

Many of these cases were very controversial when decided—and some remain disputed today. Such controversy repeatedly raises the question we have asked throughout the chapter: Does the Supreme Court (and do courts in general) overstep democratic boundaries when ruling on such momentous political matters? How deferential should they be to the people's representatives? Each case introduces a different kind of judgment call—not just on the substance of the case but also on the scope of the Court's authority.

The Bottom Line

» A few judicial decisions become landmark decisions, significantly reshaping American politics and society.

🔵 Reforming the Courts

We go to court more frequently than citizens of most nations. But we are dubious about the legal system in general. Some suggest providing more resources to the court (which operates with tiny staff and small budgets). Perhaps that would attract talented judges and reduce the caseload burden. Let's consider two other reforms.

Term Limits

Judicial term limits (often proposed as 18 years) would help address the fear of "unelected judges" overruling the elected branches, for justices would cycle off the Supreme Court with each election.[37] Justices could move to the appellate bench—satisfying the constitutional requirement of lifetime appointment. Judicial term limits would still keep the Court insulated from political tumult—18 years is a long time—while providing for a regular circulation of new judges with fresh perspectives.

Share Authority with Congress

Some scholars believe Congress should have the authority to modify Court precedents—essentially sharing the power to interpret the Constitution. Of course, the Court decides the case between the two parties in a suit. But Congress might revise the Court's general policies. In *Federalist 81*, Alexander Hamilton suggested that Congress "may prescribe a new rule for future cases" even if it violates Court precedent. As we have seen, the Court asserted the power to interpret the Constitution. Perhaps that power should be shared with Congress. What do you think?[38]

The Bottom Line

» Two reform proposals for the courts: Term limits and shared responsibility with Congress.

Conclusion: Democracy and the Courts

Courts wield an unusual amount of influence in the United States—far more than courts in most other nations. The court's powerful role will always be vexing for a simple reason: The courts are designed to serve as a check, ultimately, on the democratic majority. The courts, when they are acting properly, stop the people and their representatives from violating the Constitution or from harming minority rights. However, as the steady parade of 5–4 decisions discussed in this chapter indicates, what exactly the Constitution means is often a highly controversial matter. Further, with the benefit of hindsight, we see that the Court has interpreted the Constitution in ways that reduce rights in cases such as *Dred Scott*, *Plessy*, *Korematsu*, and many others while they protect them in others. A powerful Court always faces a very delicate balance: Protect the Constitution and minority rights while deferring to the democracy, to the people, and their representatives.

CHAPTER SUMMARY

Check your understanding of Chapter 13.

● The judiciary has a central place in U.S. government and politics—as well as in our legalistic national culture.

● Americans express uneasiness about their judicial system, despite their faith in the rule of law.

● Compared to other advanced democratic nations, U.S. courts possess a great deal of influence over our politics and government. This is primarily because of the power of judicial review, asserted long ago by Chief Justice John Marshall. Once again, Americans found a way to separate and fragment power—continuing the work begun in the Constitution.

Need to review key ideas in greater depth? Click here.

● Alongside their uncommon influence, courts are hemmed in by restrictions such as limited resources, stare decisis requirements, and their lack of an electoral base (at the federal level).

● The judiciary has affected a vast range of areas through its Constitution-interpreting authority, from religion and race to economic regulations and even presidential election outcomes. This impact is evident through a set of landmark cases—each of which typically arouses great controversy, leading to renewed calls for limits on judicial activism. Originalist and pragmatist schools have very different views of what constitutes such "activism."

● The Supreme Court marks the pinnacle of judicial—and constitutional—authority in the United States. Its operations, often carried out behind closed doors, are the subject of fascinated speculation: How do nine justices decide? The leading theories: They follow the rule of law; they are guided by their ideology; they are moved by peer pressure; and they are concerned about the institution of the courts.

KEY TERMS

Flashcard review.

Amicus curiae, p. 450
Circuit courts, p. 440
Civil law, p. 447
Clear and present danger, p. 464
Common law, p. 447
Concurrent opinion, p. 452
Criminal law, p. 447

Defendant, p. 447
Dissent, p. 452
District courts, p. 439
Judicial activism, p. 446
Judicial restraint, p. 446
Judicial review, p. 445
Litigation, p. 434
Lochner era, p. 463

Majority opinion, p. 452
Mediation, p. 436
Plaintiff, p. 447
Precedent, p. 447
Rule of four, p. 450
Stare decisis, p. 456
Strict scrutiny, p. 464

STUDY QUESTIONS

1. Should the judiciary have less power in American government and politics? If so, how would you propose to restrain judicial authority in practice?

2. The Supreme Court, prior to Justice Scalia's death, for several years had been 33 percent women, around the same proportion as in other federal courts (district and circuit). Does that seem unjustly low to you, given that women make up nearly 52 percent of the U.S. population? What about the fact that none of the eight justices is Protestant in a country that is

around 51 percent Protestant? Should we care about the religious preferences of Supreme Court justices?

3. Do Supreme Court clerks—and other federal judges' clerks—have too much influence, given their relatively young ages? Should they serve for longer than one year, given the importance of the work they do?

4. Should we mandate more transparency for judicial operations? Televise Supreme Court oral arguments, for example? Require that

Court conferences be transcribed and publicized? Are there any benefits to the secrecy that characterizes the federal judiciary?

5. Should the federal judiciary be the last line of defense in protecting Americans' constitutional rights and liberties? Why or why not? And if not, what other institution or group of people should have this responsibility? Be specific: How would another actor or group protect rights and liberties better than federal judges, and ultimately the Supreme Court, do today?

 Go to **www.oup.com/us/Morone** to find quizzes, flash cards, simulations, tutorials, videos, and other study tools.

14 Domestic and Foreign Policy

"DRILL, BABY, DRILL!" The call echoed out across GOP rallies in 2008, as vice-presidential nominee Sarah Palin stirred campaign crowds with promises of American energy independence and lower gas prices. Palin and fellow Republicans promoted drilling in U.S. coastal areas with extensive oil and natural gas deposits. Russia and Middle Eastern countries controlled 80 percent of world oil supply and 70 percent of the gas supply, while the United States claimed only 7 percent of each.[1] Alaskans and others also embraced off-shore drilling because of the number of jobs it would create. Democrats countered that offshore drilling would leach toxic chemicals into pristine waters, decimate marine life, and harm humans as well as other species including the endangered polar bear. Once in office, Democratic President Barack Obama banned all new offshore drilling. Then, in 2018, the Trump administration reversed the ban and opened up oil and natural-gas drilling in nearly all United States coastal waters.[2]

Environmental activists denounced the administration's move and sued to block the new policy. Members of Congress were split, though not necessarily along party lines: House and Senate members from both parties who represented coastal states and districts raised strong objections, in many cases joined by their states' governors. Florida Governor Rick Scott, a close Republican ally of Trump's, received an exception allowing the state's coastal drilling ban to remain, protecting the tourism industry that thrives on the state's inviting shores.

During 2018, thousands of Hondurans, fleeing violent gangs and searching for a way to make a living, wove their way through Central America toward the United States. A group called *Pueblo Sin Fronteras* (people without borders), which advocates for open borders, organized the caravan. President Trump turned images of the caravan into an effective midterm campaign issue, promising to bar undocumented immigrants and refugees alike from crossing into the United States, in order to uphold

● *Oil rigs in the wilderness? The Obama administration banned new offshore drilling. President Trump revoked the policy. Congress, governors, and the courts all leapt in to the dispute: Many actors have a hand in making American policy.*

the rule of law and protect American jobs and security. Democrats slammed the president for stirring up prejudices and driving away those people in greatest need of humanitarian assistance.[3]

Officials in the White House, Congress, and courts were not just debating environmental and immigration rules, but what government should do. In other words, they were making public policy. Exchanges such as these about both domestic and foreign policy decisions have far-reaching implications, affecting tens of millions of Americans and many more millions around the world. Policy debates also return to this book's familiar chapter-opening question: *Who are we?*

Perhaps Americans are best described in terms of the policies we enact—and those that we reject or abandon. Why do we provide hefty government subsidies to farmers growing corn, dairy, and beef but virtually none to growers of fruits and vegetables? Why do we ban diplomatic relations with Cuba but embrace Bahrain as an ally, despite both countries' terrible human-rights records?[4] Why do we closely regulate sex but not violence in movies? Why are thousands of U.S. troops still fighting in Afghanistan? These and thousands of other policy decisions contribute to the kaleidoscopic portrait of who we are.

All the actors introduced in this book—interest groups, Congress, the media, executive branch officials, the courts, the public, and more—come together to create public policy. Here we will look at both domestic and foreign policymaking, treating the two in turn.

Public Policymaking in Five (Not-So-Easy) Stages

Policies often take the form of laws, but they can also be regulations, presidential executive orders, funding formulas (determining who gets how much), military actions, established norms, or action plans. Think of an issue you care about: clean drinking water, infant mortality, or protection from terrorism. Policy issues play out through public policymaking—whether in controlling waterborne pollutants, encouraging prenatal care and mandating safe infant delivery rooms, or devising effective antiterrorism efforts at home and overseas.

Making policy is an elaborate process, involving five stages. Figure 14.1 displays these stages graphically. We organize our trip through the public policy system by exploring each of these in turn.

1. Agenda Setting

Policymaking does not begin in earnest until public officials recognize a problem as worthy of government attention. President Obama, arriving in office in 2009, identified nuclear power as a renewable, "clean" alternative to coal

BY THE NUMBERS
U.S. Public Policy

Number of laws passed, 115th Congress (2017–2018), *as of Nov. 15, 2018	**277**
Number of laws passed, 80th Congress (1947–1948), labeled the "Do-Nothing Congress" by President Truman	**906**
Average number of new federal regulations introduced each year, George W. Bush Administration	**3,985**
Average number during Barack Obama Administration	**3,640**
Number during first year of Donald Trump Administration	**3,281**
Number of new international treaties the United States entered into, January to July 2018	**31**[5]
Total U.S. economic activity, 2018	**Over $20 trillion**[6]
2019 U.S. federal budget deficit (estimated)	**Over $1 trillion**[7]
U.S. military spending as a percentage of all global military spending, 2017	**35%**
Rank in the world of the U.S. economy's size, 2018	**1**
Rank of the Chinese, Japanese, and German economies, respectively	**2, 3, 4**

Who makes public policy in the United States? What impact do these policies have domestically and internationally?

and oil—two finite energy sources that give off air pollution when burned. Nuclear power developers planned new construction across the United States, encouraged by tax incentives and relaxed regulatory restrictions. Then, in 2011, a **focusing event** changed Americans' minds about nuclear power. A massive tidal wave hit a nuclear plant in Fukushima, Japan. Safety mechanisms failed,

Focusing event: A major happening, often of crisis or disaster proportions, that attracts widespread media attention to an issue.

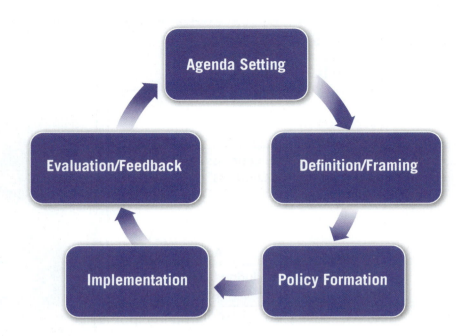

● **Figure 14.1** *The five stages of policymaking.*

part of the plant melted down, and a radioactive leak affected water, land, and air for miles around. The disaster quickly made nuclear plant safety a high-level agenda item for American policymakers. Government support for new nuclear construction disappeared, and regulators' scrutiny sharpened, halting expansion plans.

Focusing events such as the Fukushima nuclear meltdown are critical to shaping **policy agendas**. Those agendas, as we saw in Chapter 7, are typically the source of fierce competition, because the policy system can emphasize only a few priorities at any time.

Once an issue hits the agenda, debates erupt about how to describe the topic—moving us to the next stage.

Policy agenda: The issues that the media covers, the public considers important, and politicians address. Setting the agenda is the first step in political action.

2. Framing

Translating agenda items into proposed policy solutions requires answering a series of questions: What are the root causes of the problem? How bad a problem *is* this? How should public officials respond, if at all? Most agenda issues involve framing questions like these; the answers can differ greatly depending on who is making the argument.

Consider an example from education policy. Every three years, a world-wide sample of 15-year-olds takes exams in reading, math, and science. When the latest results were released, in 2017, American secondary school students finished well behind their counterparts from many other advanced countries. Parents, teachers, and businesses anxious to hire well-trained employees in a globally competitive market all agreed: Scores had to improve.

That consensus merely placed the issue on the agenda. Then disputes about defining, or framing, the problem began. Was it that many U.S. classrooms were overcrowded, with too few teachers to provide personalized instruction? Were officials in the Department of Education better positioned to address mediocre test scores, or should solutions come from the local level?

These different ways of "framing" issues, also called *problem definition*, help determine which policy responses the government considers. Federal government officials had no formal say in education policy until the mid-1960s, when Congress established an extensive program of national funding through the Elementary and

● *Focusing event: A nuclear plant in Fukushima, Japan, burns after a partial meltdown following a giant tsunami. The tragedy caused U.S. public approval for nuclear power to plummet, affecting plans to expand American nuclear energy production.*

Secondary Education Act. The U.S. Department of Education was created later still, in 1979. Champions of local control of education have fought to limit federal activity ever since. As issues are framed and reframed, policy actors translate their preferred solutions into proposed laws, propelling policymaking to a third stage.

3. Policy Formation

After a problem reaches the policy agenda and the debate settles into one or two primary frames, a wide-ranging process of policy formation is underway. Members of Congress (and often state and local legislators) draft bills, hold hearings, and hammer out compromises in committee meetings and floor debates. Executive branch experts weigh in. Advocacy groups and industry lobbyists swarm around lawmakers; judicial rulings reshape the policy debate; and media experts opine on multiple platforms.

Analyzing Policy, Ex Ante.   Technical studies are also vital to policy success. Policy analysis involves constructing scientific measures of a proposal's costs and benefits ex ante—before it passes and goes into effect. Such assessment efforts are central to policymaking in the United States and other advanced industrial nations.

One evaluative approach involves **cost-benefit analysis**. In 2018, with gas prices at historic lows, President Trump recommended a 25-cent per gallon hike in the federal gasoline tax, to pay for a massive infrastructure improvement

Cost-benefit analysis:
A typically complex study of the projected costs and benefits associated with a proposed policy.

● *Should federal officials manage education policy, or leave it to local school districts? Education Secretary Betsy DeVos, with President Trump's backing, seeks to shift federal funding toward "school choice," including support for charter schools and religious instruction.*

plan (including improved highway maintenance). For a quarter-century, the national gas tax has remained at 18.4 cents per gallon, after slowly rising over the preceding 60 years from a penny per gallon. To estimate an ideal tax increase, experts from government, lobbying firms, and academia performed a cost-benefit analysis.

The first step in a cost-benefit analysis is to list all the expected costs of a policy proposal, as well as all the expected benefits. For the gas tax, researchers identified two primary categories of cost and five main areas of benefit. The results are summarized in Table 14.1.

Researchers then "monetize" (assign dollar values to) these costs and benefits, using elaborate formulas. In the gas tax example, the estimated *costs* of a higher tax are around 78 cents per gallon: 54 cents for the increased price of services (such as higher costs of goods transported by truck) and 24 cents in direct costs to drivers paying the increased tax. That is a steep cost for each gallon of gas, but the predicted *benefits* were considerably higher, as measured in the value of enhanced public health and transportation infrastructure. Adding together the estimated savings yielded a $1.81 benefit per gallon, as Table 14.2 shows—so the national gas taxes could be raised by just over a dollar per gallon: $1.81 in benefits, minus the 78-cent cost.

TABLE 14.1   Gas Tax Costs/Benefits

GAS TAX COSTS
Direct cost of the tax to drivers (those in rural areas, and with lower incomes, would be hardest hit).
Higher price of services dependent on transportation, such as shipping goods by truck.
GAS TAX BENEFITS
Reduced urban air pollution (thereby improving public health).
Reduced CO_2 emissions (slowing the pace of climate change).
Reduced U.S. dependence on imported oil.
Diminished traffic congestion (saving drivers time).
Reduced traffic accidents (because people drive less or switch to mass transit).

TABLE 14.2 **Cost-Benefit Valuation of a Proposed Gas Tax**

COSTS OF GAS TAX	VALUE*	BENEFITS OF GAS TAX	VALUE*
Direct cost to drivers	$0.24	Public health (reduced air pollution)	$0.43
Transportation services	$0.54	Climate (reduced CO_2 emissions)	$0.13
		Reduced oil imports	$0.11
		Time saved (less traffic)	$0.58
		Reduced accidents	$0.56
TOTAL	**$0.78**		**$1.81**

*Values are estimated per gallon of gas.
Source: Authors' calculation, combining several existing models.

From Cost-Benefit Analysis to Politics.   Cost-benefit and other ex ante evaluations are widely used in policymaking, with significant impacts on both legislative votes and judicial decisions. These analyses alone, however, do not determine policy.

President Trump's 2018 proposal to more than double the gas tax, to a total of some 43 cents/gallon, was greeted with headlines such as "Trump's Gas Tax Goes Nowhere in Congress."[8] With gas prices rising as the midterm elections approached, the plan was quietly abandoned. Political considerations can overcome even a positive policy analysis.

If legislative and executive branch preferences align just right, and the cost-benefit analysis comes out positive, a figurative **policy window** opens.[9] Might a new policy be launched? There is no guarantee of success, especially at the national level. Policy windows rarely stay open for long. But organized, determined advocates who master the rules of the policy game can successfully navigate this formation stage.

Policy window: A figurative description of the opportunity—often brief, measured in days or weeks rather than years—to pass a bill in Congress or a state legislature.

4. Policy Implementation

When a new law is passed, policymaking moves to the implementation stage. As you read in Chapter 12, this bureaucracy-dominated process happens out of public view and is not widely understood. Does this shift mean that the work of policy implementation is less politicized? Many American political thinkers and actors have thought so; back in 1887, future president and political scientist, Woodrow Wilson described bureaucratic activity as "a technical science." Wilson insisted that "administrative questions are not political questions."[10]

As Wilson learned 30 years later as president, implementing public policy is a highly political event. Implementation involves two main steps: working out a law's specifics, primarily through the rulemaking process introduced in Chapter 12, and then delivering government services or enforcing new regulations. Both these steps attract intense political interest—and fighting—among communities affected by the policy change.

Rulemaking Revisited.

Recall from Chapter 12 that each aspect of a new law requires a separate rule, each spelled out in painstaking detail. For example, one part of the Affordable Care Act (ACA) mandates that dependents up to age 26 remain eligible for health insurance through their parents; the previous cutoff age was 18 (21, for students enrolled in college). In the ACA, this requirement was spelled out in only a couple of sentences. However, the Department of Health and Human Services rule specifying details—who was eligible, under what circumstances, penalties for violation, and so forth—ran to more than 25 single-spaced pages in the *Federal Register*.[11]

With such room for maneuvering, complaints abound about bureaucratic overreach. President Trump, soon after arriving in office, announced a "2 for 1" requirement—every new regulatory action by an executive agency or department had to be accompanied by the *elimination* of two existing rules.[12] But thousands of career civil servants and a thicket of existing rules and regulations make significant changes difficult. In fact, rulemaking has proceeded under Trump at a pace similar to previous presidencies.

Thumb through the *Federal Register* online.

Top-Down Delivery.

Once the final rule setting out a policy's details has been issued, it is time to provide the benefits or regulations that the law was designed to produce. As the American national government stepped up its level of domestic policy activity following World War II, delivery of public services was established as a "top-down" process. Cabinet secretaries and agency heads were firmly in charge of the process. Lower-level bureaucrats and "policy clients" (the people government was serving) were mainly concerned with *compliance*, or doing what they were told to do.

Many policy planners still promote this top-down model of delivering government benefits and services. It works best when a policy is relatively simple, with clear, well-specified goals. Imagine a national ban on sales of a food product tainted by potentially fatal bacteria, for example. A high-ranking figure, such as the secretary of agriculture or the head of the Food and Drug Administration, issues a public warning. Government inspectors ensure that the dangerous product is removed from grocery shelves, law enforcement officials investigate the cause of the outbreak, and prosecutions may follow. The public's role is simple: avoid the tainted product. The policy aim is clear, as are the lines of authority.

● *Tainted food—and top-down policy response. When the FDA receives reports about possible dangerous food products—such as these Goldfish-brand crackers in 2018—the agency, along with the Department of Agriculture, supervises a national top-down recall.*

As you know well by now, most issues involve many interested actors, leading to struggles over jurisdiction. Authorities are frequently stymied in their attempts to police pot growers, for example, given all the conflicting local, state, and federal regulations governing medicinal marijuana—especially with several states and Washington, DC, now permitting limited legal marijuana sales (see Figure 14.2).[13]

Bottom-Up Delivery.   For complicated policies, "bottom-up" provisions of public services or regulations can be more effective than top-down efforts to command and control outcomes. Bottom-up service delivery starts with street-level bureaucrats, introduced in Chapter 12. Examples include the social worker who calls on needy families to make sure their food stamps have arrived, the IRS agent who checks to confirm that your charitable claims are all legitimate donations, and the air-traffic controller who brings your flight safely in for landing.

All these policy providers and regulators work directly with the public, and they can exercise discretion in making decisions. Certainly a hierarchy is still in place, with cabinet secretaries and agency heads at the top. But when street-level officials are allowed a measure of autonomy, or input into decision making, government services are often delivered more efficiently and regulations are put in place with less disruption. These street-level actors may even ignore superiors' orders and do what they consider best, based on their experience. Is this democracy in action—or bureaucracy run amok?

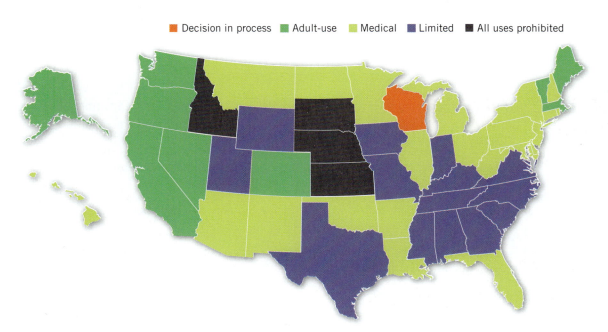

● **Figure 14.2** *Marijuana policy in the states, as of fall 2018. A series of conflicting federal (including Congress, executive agencies, and courts) and state policy decisions has left this area a patchwork—illustrating the complexity of policy implementation. (National Cannabis Industry Association)*

5. Policy Evaluation and Feedback

A solution has been formulated, passed into law, and implemented: The new service is being delivered or new regulation put in place. Has our policymaking story now ended? Not at all. We still have to assess whether the new program actually works.

This is the stage of policy evaluation. Policy evaluators analyze how well a policy is meeting its stated goals. Does a school-lunch program need tweaking because its benefits are not reaching many kids? Should we abandon an ineffective government effort to reduce tax fraud and try something else? Significant policies are usually subjected to ex post evaluations—based on actual results. These tend to follow a prescribed sequence. An evaluator compares a policy program to the original goals that Congress and executive branch rule-makers affirmed. The evaluator could be a government agency, an academic or think tank analyst, an interest group, a court-appointed independent authority—or all of these, as prominent programs often attract multiple evaluations. The evaluator collects and assesses relevant information and data; makes a judgment about program effectiveness; and issues recommendations.[14]

When a law is introduced, advocates fight hard to frame the policy change positively, advance it through Congress, and win the president's signature. Many monitor rulemaking as well. Now imagine an ex post evaluation that suggests the policy is not working well. These supporters will probably not agree; instead they may criticize the "flawed" evaluation and commission a competing review. Likewise, after a positive evaluation, the opposition—which fought the new policy all the way from framing to rulemaking—rarely gives up and admits that its criticisms were wrong.

 **The Bottom Line**

» U.S. policymaking involves five stages. Policies do not proceed neatly from one to the next, but the "stages" idea is a useful way of distinguishing among different actions carried out by policy officials.

» The first of these stages is agenda setting. Widespread attention turns a concern into a policy issue.

» Stage two: problem definition and framing features debates about how to describe an issue and which solutions are most viable.

» Stage three: policy formation. Legislative and executive action develop the policy idea into concrete terms.

» Stage four: policy implementation. Rulemaking and service delivery put the policy into action.

» Stage five: Evaluation and policy feedback. Now, policy makers determine whether a policy works—and that often start debates all over again.

U.S. Social Policy

Public policy comes in many forms. *Fiscal policy* has to do with matters of finance, such as monetary supply and budgeting; *foreign policy* covers topics including wars, defense, diplomacy, and trade agreements. We take each up as this chapter proceeds. Most other issues are grouped together as *social policy*, involving individual or group well-being. Health, housing, education, employment, criminal justice, child welfare, and old age security: all these areas make up social policy. Also under this heading are controversial topics such as abortion, same-sex marriage, and recreational drug use.

● *During the Great Depression new federal social policies were created at a rapid clip. Traditional policies, such as "poor relief," were expanded as well in response to social need.*

From colonial days onward, "poor relief" offered support for needy Americans. Benefits were limited, however—and came with a price. People on relief sometimes faced the loss of their personal property and the right to vote. The able-bodied unemployed were often forced to work or were jailed, although laws varied from state to state. Even with all these limits, poor relief was the largest single budget item in most early American towns and cities.[15] The term was still used well into the twentieth century, especially during the Great Depression.

That terrible economic downturn, starting in 1929, helped lead to more extensive federal social policies, many arising from Franklin Roosevelt's New Deal. Among the numerous social programs run or financed by the U.S. government today, three deserve attention here.

Old-Age Insurance: Social Security

Since 1935, Social Security has provided Americans aged 65 and older—provided they have lived in the United States at least five years—with a monthly living stipend. Though Americans can receive a reduced stipend if they retire at 62, the eligibility age for the full stipend was recently raised to 66, with Congress still debating whether to raise it another year or two. Social Security payments vary with income: A worker who retires making $65,000 a year would currently receive around $1,813 per month. The original act also created an unemployment insurance program, paid benefits to disabled workers and their families, and offered financial assistance to low-income families with children. One constant over the years: Social Security's financing comes from a payroll tax on all eligible workers.

In 2018, Social Security paid some $984 billion to more than 61 million workers, supported by payroll taxes from more than 142 million employees. At nearly 5 percent of the nation's **gross domestic product (GDP)**, Social Security is the largest single federal government program.

Assess current debates on Social Security.

Gross domestic product (GDP): The value of all the goods and services produced in a nation over a year. For 2019, the U.S. GDP is an estimated $21.4 trillion.

Social Security and Medicare are perhaps the two most fiercely defended U.S. government programs. Some analysts suggest that their continued rapid growth (together, these programs cost more than $1.75 *trillion* in 2019) is outpacing U.S. taxpayers' ability to support them. Concerned policymakers float ideas like raising the eligibility age to 68 or even 70. Such a change would save tens of billions of dollars—but also delay older Americans' ability to begin drawing these vital benefits.[16] Any hint of a cut in either and senior citizens respond vehemently, as do the House and Senate members who represent them. Are you willing to tackle cutting Social Security and Medicare (and, while you are at it, Medicaid)?

Yes, reform the Social Security and Medicare programs. The budget savings of even minor adjustments—such as raising the eligibility age—would be immense.	**No, leave Social Security and Medicare intact.** We must balance the American budget in other areas, not on the backs of our grandparents. Reforms also could have devastating political consequences because the opposing party would sound the alarm immediately.

The old-age benefits provided by Social Security have helped lift many seniors out of poverty, yet urgent alarms have been sounded for decades about the financial burden of supporting the program. Those concerns grow more urgent today, as Social Security moves inexorably toward a one trillion dollar annual cost—as the huge "baby boomer" generation increasingly receives benefits. A major debate turns on the gravity of the problem. Many moderates and conservatives argue that Social Security poses a dangerous economic risk as it moves inexorably toward a one trillion dollar annual cost. Many liberals argue that the program is necessary and relatively small adjustments (increasing the retirement age, raising taxes, limiting benefits) will fix its cost problem. Once again: a debate over problem definition.

Unemployment Benefits

As the Great Depression stretched into the 1930s, some 34 million Americans (more than a quarter of the 122 million population) lived in households with no full-time wage earner. Across the United States, unemployment rates reached shocking levels, topping out at 80 percent of able-bodied adults in Toledo, Ohio. In 1935, the Social Security Act included a provision for joint federal–state unemployment benefits, funded like old-age insurance through a payroll tax on employees. States administer the program, with federal oversight and funding assistance.

During the recession of 2008-9, unemployment levels rose from less than 4 percent in 2008 to above 10 percent in 2009. Unemployment was below 4 percent by 2018 for the first time since 2000.

Health and Disability: Medicare/Medicaid

In the early 1960s, America ranked as the wealthiest nation in the world, but barely half of the nation's seniors had health insurance. Even with Social Security, an estimated third of those over 65 lived in poverty, in significant part because of the cost of healthcare.

After a Democratic landslide in 1964, Congress passed Medicare (in 1965) as an amendment to the Social Security Act. As with old-age and unemployment benefits, Medicare was financed through a payroll tax on employees. And as with Social Security, the program grew rapidly after it was implemented in 1966. Today, some 55 million Americans receive Medicare benefits; by the late 2020s, the program is expected to serve nearly 80 million people, as the last of the baby boomer generation (born between 1945 and 1964) retire. The program costs $750 billion today, and is projected to grow to more than $1.5 trillion annually.

As the battle over Medicare raged in 1965, a companion measure to provide health insurance to disabled and low-income people, dubbed "Medicaid," was passed. Each state was encouraged (but not required) to establish a Medicaid program of its own; Arizona was the last to sign on, in 1982. Over time, a variety of additional benefits were added to Medicaid, including dental and nursing home coverage. Today Medicaid serves over 72.5 million Americans. Obama Care extended Medicaid to everyone below 138% of the **poverty line**, although the Supreme Court ruled that states could decide for themselves whether to expand the program (so far, 36 have said yes).

Figure 14.3 displays costs for the three biggest entitlement programs (Social Security, Medicaid, and Medicare), plus interest on the U.S. federal debt, measured as a percentage of the expected U.S. GDP. Together, these

Explore Medicare/ Medicaid policies in depth.

Federal Poverty Line: The level of income (calculated each year for both individuals and families) below which people are considered to live in poverty, become eligible for some federal benefits. The Federal poverty line in 2018 was set at $12,100 for a single individual.

Where the Money Goes
Federal spending as a percentage of GDP, 1947–2047

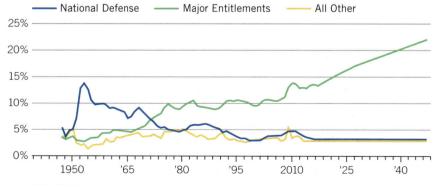

Note: 2018–2047 projections

● **Figure 14.3** *Spending on the largest entitlement programs plus interest on the U.S. national debt totals 14 percent of U.S. GDP. That total (green line) is projected to sharply increase in coming years; defense (blue line) and other spending (gold line) remain flat relative to GDP.* (Wall Street Journal)

entitlement programs will require very tough choices about spending on other programs and about increasing tax rates to fund them.

The Bottom Line

» Social policymaking in the United States is typically more controversial, and features less expansive coverage, than social policymaking in other advanced industrial nations.

» Wars, along with severe economic downturns, have been major sources of expansions in American social policies across U.S. history.

» Three large social programs—Social Security, unemployment insurance, and Medicare/Medicaid—are especially significant in U.S. government.

Entitlement program:
A government benefit program whose recipients are *entitled* by law to receive payments. Social Security, Medicare, and Medicaid are the three largest.

Fiscal policy: Taxing and spending policies carried out by government, generally in an effort to affect national economic development.

Monetary policy: Actions of central banks such as the U.S. Federal Reserve, designed primarily to maximize employment and moderate inflation.

Economic Policymaking: Fiscal and Monetary Policy

People judge their governments foremost on economic performance. Bill Clinton's presidency is widely considered a success because the economy roared ahead during his time in office. Compare Clinton's predecessor, George H. W. Bush, who after the Gulf War (1990–1991) enjoyed the highest popularity rating among modern presidents. Barely a year later, an economic downturn battered Bush's public opinion ratings and left him a one-term president.

Economic policy is carried out in two primary ways. Government decisions about taxing and spending is termed **fiscal policy**. Managing the economy through central banks' control of the money supply, directly affecting unemployment and inflation rates, is known as **monetary policy**.

Fiscal Policy

Well into the twentieth century, the U.S. government's fiscal policy can best be described as "laissez-faire," a French term meaning "leave it alone." Most presidents and Congressional leaders sought to balance the (relatively small) federal budget, with limited tax or spending authority. That changed during wartime, when military needs drove tax collections and spending (mostly for defense) temporarily much higher.

During the Great Depression, national economic devastation led Franklin Roosevelt and his policy advisors to more actively manage the levers of fiscal policy. Large New Deal programs were funded through government spending at an unprecedented scale. The resulting budget deficits—federal funds flowing out much faster than tax revenues coming in—reflected a Keynesian approach to national economic policy, named for an influential early twentieth-century British economist, John Maynard Keynes. Keynes recommended pump-priming during economic downturns: pouring government funds into a faltering economy and cutting taxes; that would give consumers and businesses more money (as well as confidence in the economy) and induce them to start spending and hiring again.

Post-World War II American policymakers, brimming with confidence about their ability to manage the economy, adopted taxing and spending policies as a routine national practice. Since then, through conservative and liberal presidents and across Democratic and Republican control of Congress, active fiscal policy has continued.

The parties differ on which fiscal levers to pull. During economic downturns, Democrats are likelier to favor expanded spending—the Obama administration passed a large stimulus package designed to rescue the national economy from the brink of disaster. Republicans generally prefer tax cuts, claiming that the economy benefits as consumers spend more of the windfall.[17] Hence party leaders, led by President Trump, praised the 2017 tax cut as fueling economic growth.[18]

Though fiscal policymaking may sound straightforward, few policy areas are more controversial in practice. In summer 2018, for the second consecutive year a government shutdown loomed, as Congress and the White House debated budget details. "Our budget process is totally broken," lamented Republican Senator Bob Corker (R-Tenn.).[19]

Monetary Policy

Following the collapse of the venerable Lehman Brothers investment bank in fall 2008, with other giant financial institutions tottering, the U.S. government leapt into action. The main actors were not presidents or congressional leaders, but more obscure figures: the Federal Reserve chairman, the treasury secretary, and the chair of the Federal Reserve Bank of New York. And the economic tools they applied had nothing to do with taxes or spending: Instead, the conversation was about liquidity and the national money supply.[20]

These experts deployed monetary policy in response to the gravest financial crisis in 75 years. By manipulating the national money supply and interest rates, they aimed to increase employment while holding inflation (the rate at which the price of goods and services rises) in check. Although the White House and Congress are the chief architects of fiscal policy, monetary shifts are carried out by central bankers. In the United States, the main actor is the Federal

● *Though rarely recognized in public, Federal Reserve chair Jerome Powell is a key figure in managing the nation's money supply—a central feature of U.S. economic policy.*

Explore the concepts of monetary and fiscal policy.

Reserve System, comprising a headquarters in Washington, DC, along with 12 bank branches around the country. The current Federal Reserve (or "Fed," in Washington-speak) director is Jerome Powell.

The Federal Reserve deploys several tools, such as buying Treasury securities (issued to pay for the national debt) and setting dollar reserve levels that banks are required to hold; these actions allow them to influence interest rates. The Fed reduces interest rates to stimulate economic growth, making it easier for businesses to borrow money to expand production, increase hiring, or invest in research and development; similarly, individuals can borrow at lower interest rates to buy new homes or consumer goods. If economic demand is growing too fast, the Fed raises interest rates to reduce inflationary pressures that raise prices and result in an economic slowdown.

The Bottom Line

» The U.S. government employs both fiscal policy and monetary policy to affect the economy.

» Taxes and spending are the chief levers of fiscal policy. During economic downturns, Republicans prefer to enact tax cuts; Democrats favor spending programs.

» The Federal Reserve is the main architect of monetary policy. By adjusting interest rates and the national supply of money, the Fed works to affect inflation and unemployment.

Economic Policymaking: The Federal Budget Process

Federal budget deficit: The gap between revenues received by the national government (primarily through individual income and corporate taxes) and spending on all public programs.

"It's a good policy idea, but we don't have the budget to pursue it." That phrase has been repeated countless times in Washington in recent years, as policy-making has become more oriented around the budget. This bottom-line focus owes primarily to the U.S. **federal budget deficit**—the gap between how much our national government spends and how much we take in through taxes and fees. The deficit for fiscal year 2019, which began October 1, 2018, is projected as slightly over $1 trillion dollars, around 4.7 percent of GDP; at the end of in 2016, that figure was 2.5 percent (still far short of 2009's record high deficit of $1.3 trillion, or 9.8 percent of GDP).[21]

Can the historic deficits projected for coming years be reversed, and is such an effort even desirable? To tackle budget reform, we have to first grasp the basics of how national government budgeting works. Much of American domestic policymaking is organized around our budget process.

Budget politics involves three primary stages, beginning with the White House (see Figure 14.4).

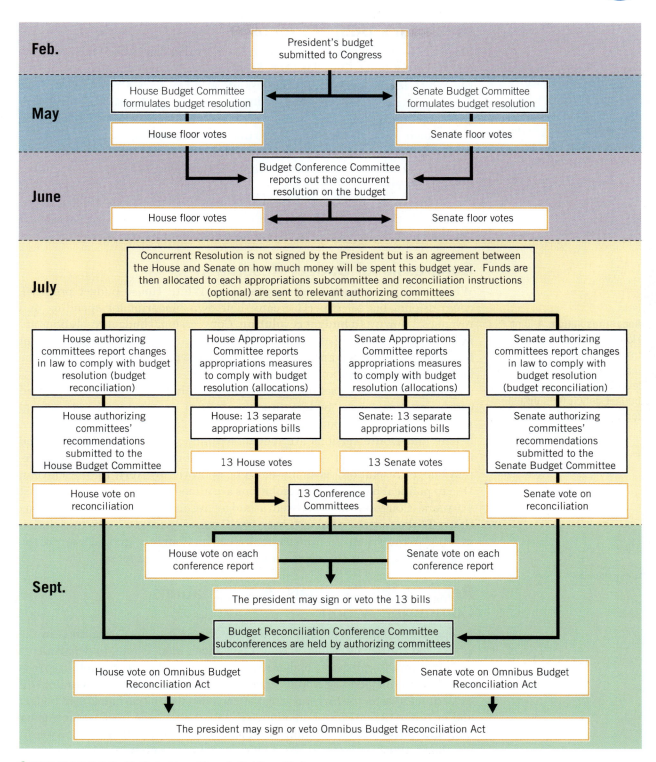

Feb.
President's budget submitted to Congress

May
House Budget Committee formulates budget resolution
Senate Budget Committee formulates budget resolution

House floor votes
Senate floor votes

June
Budget Conference Committee reports out the concurrent resolution on the budget

House floor votes
Senate floor votes

July
Concurrent Resolution is not signed by the President but is an agreement between the House and Senate on how much money will be spent this budget year. Funds are then allocated to each appropriations subcommittee and reconciliation instructions (optional) are sent to relevant authorizing committees

House authorizing committees report changes in law to comply with budget resolution (budget reconciliation)

House Appropriations Committee reports appropriations measures to comply with budget resolution (allocations)

Senate Appropriations Committee reports appropriations measures to comply with budget resolution (allocations)

Senate authorizing committees report changes in law to comply with budget resolution (budget reconciliation)

House authorizing committees' recommendations submitted to the House Budget Committee

House: 13 separate appropriations bills

Senate: 13 separate appropriations bills

Senate authorizing committees' recommendations submitted to the Senate Budget Committee

House vote on reconciliation

13 House votes

13 Senate votes

Senate vote on reconciliation

13 Conference Committees

Sept.
House vote on each conference report
Senate vote on each conference report

The president may sign or veto the 13 bills

Budget Reconciliation Conference Committee subconferences are held by authorizing committees

House vote on Omnibus Budget Reconciliation Act
Senate vote on Omnibus Budget Reconciliation Act

The president may sign or veto Omnibus Budget Reconciliation Act

Figure 14.4 *U.S. federal budget process (House Budget Committee).*

President's Budget Proposal

Since the 1921 Budget and Accounting Act, presidents have been the first movers in federal budgeting. For each **fiscal year** (**FY**), which starts October 1, the White House submits to Congress in early February a proposed budget. This document details projected federal spending for thousands of different government programs. Its assembly begins many months earlier in the executive branch, with each cabinet department and federal agency compiling its expected spending totals. The Office of Management and Budget has the massive task of coordinating all these estimates; the Treasury Department chimes in with expected revenue figures.

Unlike most other countries, the president's budget proposal is just that—a proposal. Congress is free to ignore it. That is what it did with President Obama's budget proposal in 2016 and President Trump's two years later.

Congressional Budget Resolution

While executive branch analysts shape the White House budget proposal, congressional budget experts create their own blueprint for spending and revenues, known as a **budget resolution**. Congressional budget resolutions are not binding laws. Instead, they provide a general "sense of Congress" about budgetary expectations and guide the committees responsible for finishing the budget during summer and fall.

Budget resolutions set out overarching spending expectations in 19 broad categories, known as "budget functions." Each committee spends several months assembling a budget resolution, which must pass the full chamber. Senate and House versions are inevitably different, and must be reconciled in a conference committee. The joint outcome, formally known as a "concurrent budget resolution," is supposed to be approved by April 15 of each year. Due to political battles, these resolutions are almost always late. Over the past 40 years, Congress has approved a budget resolution on schedule only six times. To the surprise of many observers, Congress passed a budget resolution in 2018. To the Trump administration's chagrin, Congress ignored many of the proposed budget cuts in order to smooth passage of the proposal.

Reign of the Cardinals: Appropriations Committee Action

A separate step in this process involves the Appropriations Committees in the House and the Senate, which specifies how much money flows to departments and programs. Recall from Chapter 10 that, because of their central role in spending decisions, members of Appropriations are informally known on Capitol Hill as "cardinals," after the high-ranking Vatican officials. The cardinals split budget authority into 13 separate jurisdictions (see Table 14.3). Some areas are far smaller than others: the District of Columbia appropriation is around $645 million yearly, less than 1/100th of the $700-plus billion for national defense.

Each of these 13 areas is assigned to a separate Appropriations subcommittee in the House and Senate, which handles budget planning for all policy areas

Fiscal year (FY): In budget calculations, the "new year" beginning October 1 and ending the following September 30. Organized many decades ago for accounting purposes.

Budget resolution: A joint House–Senate creation that outlines targets for federal spending, revenue levels, and the resultant budget deficit (or surplus) for the coming fiscal year.

Discover how to balance the budget.

| TABLE 14.3 | **Appropriations Subcommittees: Areas of Jurisdiction** |

Agriculture; Food and Drug Administration
Departments of Commerce, Justice, and State
Department of Defense
District of Columbia
Energy and Water Development
Foreign Operations
Department of Interior
Departments of Labor, Health and Human Services, and Education
Legislative Branch
Military Construction
Department of Transportation
Department of Treasury; U.S. Postal Service
Department of Housing and Urban Development; Veterans Administration

under its jurisdiction. Some, such as Labor, Health and Human Services, and Education (known informally on the Hill as "Labor-H"), supervise thousands of individual programs.

Because they only deal with **discretionary programs**, which require legislative action to explicitly authorize spending, the 13 appropriations bills cover about a third of all U.S. government spending. Social Security, Medicare, and Medicaid are considered *mandatory spending* because they are funded annually, based on a formula, without requiring Congress's reauthorization each year. Thus, a giant chunk of the U.S. federal budget, nearly two trillion dollars, flows automatically and is essentially untouchable.

Discretionary programs: Non-entitlement program spending, subject to the decision ("discretion") of Congress each year.

Appropriations bills are supposed to be signed by September 1. With the start of the fiscal year looming on October 1, federal agencies and departments have a month to finalize their plans for spending funds and delivering services. As with other deadlines in the budget process, this September 1 marker is far more often missed than hit: 1995 was the last time that all 13 appropriations bills were passed before the new fiscal year.

If one or more bills are not approved, Congress may combine all the outstanding appropriations measures into a single giant "omnibus" spending bill. This legislation is typically cobbled together with only days to spare before the September 30 end to the fiscal year.

Continuing resolution (CR): A congressionally approved act required when no national budget has been passed before the start of a new fiscal year. This extends spending at current levels for a prescribed period of time.

More often than not, Congress fails even to pass an omnibus bill, leaving some areas unfunded as the new fiscal year opens. In that case, the president asks Congress to pass a **continuing resolution (CR)**, which keeps the dollars flowing—usually at the just-ended fiscal year's rate—for a specified period, usually two weeks or a month. In some years, Congress is forced to pass CR after CR. Otherwise, the government runs out of spending authority for discretionary programs and shuts down—as almost happened in 2017. President Trump, in his first budget cycle, warned that he would not again tolerate a giant omnibus bill followed by continuing resolutions. Congress clearly got the message, as appropriations bills during 2018 proceeded close to the published schedule.

Ultimately, budgeting involves the fundamental choices that help define how we Americans see ourselves. Foreign-policy decisions are also governed by budget considerations, although presidents tend to have more spending and operational leeway to act in this realm. We will now turn to policymaking in the international arena.

The Bottom Line

» The U.S. budget process, when on schedule, runs from early February through October 1 and encompasses a presidential proposal, a concurrent budget resolution, and appropriations bills.

» In practice, the process rarely runs on time, and various "fixes" such as omnibus bills and continuing resolutions keep the budget system functioning.

» Although the details can be obscure, budget battles in Washington are among the most dramatic features of U.S. policymaking because of the high stakes involved.

Foreign-Policy Goal No. 1: Security

Foreign policy defines American relations with external nations, groups, and problems. It involves countless decisions, large and small: trade rules with Japan, China, and Uruguay; whether to intervene in genocide; and when to deploy military force. American foreign policies change the world. They also boomerang back home and change the United States.

Three goals guide foreign policy: National security, prosperity, and spreading American values. Sometimes these goals clash with one another. As we describe each, think about which seems most important to you.

First, the United States must defend itself. *Security means protecting the nation and its values from external threats.* But what constitutes a threat? Should policymakers focus on terrorists? North Korea's rising military power? Economic competitors like China? Or perhaps the greatest danger comes from global warming, or limits on natural resources. Different dangers require different strategies.

Military Primacy

Every administration, whether Democratic or Republican, seeks security through a powerful military. The United States spends as much on its armed forces as the other top six nations combined. The Department of Homeland Security, intelligence agencies, and the Veterans Administration add more than $200 billion to the total.

Why spend so much more on defense than other nations? Because U.S. military strategy is based on the theory of **primacy**: Maintain an unrivaled military force that can overwhelm any enemy. Is this expensive doctrine necessary? That depends on how we see the world.

● *Realists see a world bristling with threats. Here, North Korean troops celebrate their nation's 70th birthday.*

Basis for Primacy: Realism

Two main views of the U.S. role in the world have colored American foreign-policy debates since the 1950s. **Realism** sees the world as dangerous, full of tough rivals competing for advantage. The best way to protect the nation is to maximize military and economic power. Realists see the international system as an anarchy—individual states struggle for dominance in a lawless international arena. The only hope for peace and stability: Powerful states assume leadership and establish order.

As a result, realists emphasize international security threats around the world—terrorists, rivals, and rogue states. In an unstable world, say the realists, the United States must build a powerful military to use as a deterrent—and if necessary deploy it against threats to American interests.

Realists debate what type of international order is most stable: unipolar (led by one nation), bipolar (led by two) or multipolar (with multiple powers). During the cold war, the international order was bipolar (with the United States and the Soviet Union competing for dominance). Today Americans ask: What type of international order is emerging? Will it prove stable?

Realism offers a strong perspective that underpins the doctrine of primacy. Yes, it is expensive to maintain such a large army. But today, no other military has the same reach, and none can move as swiftly to respond to trouble around the globe. Realists insist that it is the price of security.

A Different View: Liberalism

A very different perspective suggests that the best way for nations to secure peace and prosperity is to work together. **Liberalism** focuses on identifying common goals, building international organizations such as the United

Primacy: The doctrine asserting that the United States should maintain an unrivaled military.

Realism. A doctrine holding that nation–states seek to amass power to ensure their self-preservation.

Liberalism: A doctrine that views nation–states as benefiting most from mutual cooperation, aided by international organizations.

Nations, and exchanging cultural ambassadors—from rock stars to football teams. Together nations can create a world that moves beyond self-interest.

Liberal critics of the realist strain in U.S. foreign policy raise an alarming question: Could building such a large military make the United States *less* secure? Liberals identify three potential problems with military primacy.

Security trap: The idea that using military force creates multiple, often unforeseen, problems.

First, they warn of a **security trap**: Using military force often produces a backlash. It humiliates other nations and leaves them more susceptible to anti-American sentiments.[22] When the United States deploys its military, civilians are inevitably killed—some one hundred thousand civilians died during the invasion and occupation of Iraq from 2003 to 2011.[23] Civilian casualties are not America's responsibility alone—but they are sobering and they create resentment.

Second, military primacy costs more than 700 billion dollars annually. This economic burden shifts spending from other priorities. Liberal thinkers argue that mutual engagement with other nations is more likely to foster increased trade, enhancing everyone's economic well-being.

Finally, liberal thinkers are joined by conservatives in warning that too much emphasis on military power undermines liberty. As we saw in Chapter 1, Americans long feared that a large army would turn a republic into an empire. That critique evaporated during the Cold War. Facing communists armed with atomic bombs, America could not afford to worry about the problems posed by a standing army. Once communism fell, however, critics argued that it was time to downsize the military.

Soft power: The influence a nation exerts through culture and commerce; a contrast to attempted influence through force.

Those promoting cuts in military spending face the same problem we have seen in almost every chapter: entrenched institutions. Many local economies depend on military bases, military contractors, or military suppliers. It is always hard to cut any budget.

Soft Power

Packed stadiums around the world shout out the words at Beyoncé or Florida Georgia Line concerts. To foreign policy analysts, they are another source of American influence. Political scientist Joseph Nye calls it "**soft power**": Use culture and economics to persuade rather than coerce (hard power). Soft power is an important part of liberal foreign policy. The United States is the world's second leading tourist destination (just behind France) with 75.6 million visitors in 2017. American music, movies, and television are everywhere. People line up outside Apple stores (not to mention Starbucks or McDonalds) from Rome to Shanghai. Sharing these cultural experiences forms bonds among people, which create a different type of security.[24]

● *Soft power: American lattes are welcome where the army is not. Here, Starbucks in the heart of the Forbidden City, the imperial palace in Beijing, China.*

Foreign Aid and National Security

The United States is the largest foreign aid donor in the world. Many Americans believe we spend far too much—and from the realist perspective, it is a drain on our economic resources. in fact, the United States devotes less than half a percent (about 0.54%) of gross national income—half as much as China or France. Too much—or too little?[25]

Those with a liberal view of America's role in the world believe that assisting other nations is an important path to security. It builds goodwill and helps lift nations out of the poverty that breeds extremism. Others counter that financial assistance only makes other nations reliant. Moreover, foreign aid often flies straight into the pockets of the rich and the powerful. Whatever side you take, remember that foreign aid forms a tiny part of U.S. spending.

 **The Bottom Line**

» Two leading foreign-policy views, realism and liberalism, differ sharply on how best to ensure security for Americans and allied countries.

» To pursue the first goal of American foreign policy, security, realists urge the United States deploys a large military and maintains a policy of primacy.

» Liberal thinkers prefer diplomacy and other forms of multinational cooperation, soft (or cultural) power, and foreign aid.

American Foreign-Policy Goal No. 2: Prosperity

The United States is a superpower because of its economy. In the long run, national power always rests not on armies but on economic engines. The second goal of foreign policy: keep that economic engine strong.

Back in 1960 the United States accounted for 40 percent of the world's economic output, a figure that today has dropped by half. That still ranks the U.S. as the world's largest economy, but some analysts believe the international order is turning multipolar. Growing centers of economic power in Asia and Europe may challenge U.S. supremacy in the years ahead. The Trump administration's trade war (more on that below) is a direct response to the fear of decline.

Economic Superpower or Nation in Decline?

At first glance, the United States certainly does not look like a declining power. The American economy is 45 percent larger than China's, almost four times larger than Japan's, and larger than 163 other nations *combined* (see Figure 14.5). The American dollar is the international reserve currency—used in foreign trade and investment. And English has become the language of international affairs.

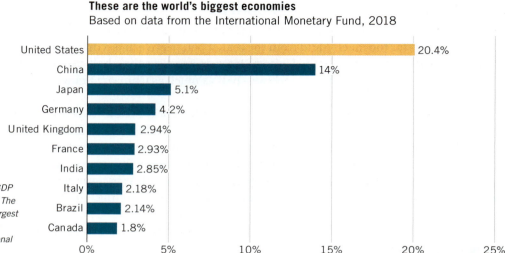

These are the world's biggest economies
Based on data from the International Monetary Fund, 2018

- United States — 20.4%
- China — 14%
- Japan — 5.1%
- Germany — 4.2%
- United Kingdom — 2.94%
- France — 2.93%
- India — 2.85%
- Italy — 2.18%
- Brazil — 2.14%
- Canada — 1.8%

● **Figure 14.5** *The nation's GDP as percentage of world total. The United States remains the largest economy—though China has been catching up. (International Monetary Fund)*

Although the U.S. economy remains by far the world's largest, China appears to be rapidly catching up. Its economy has been growing twice as fast. If current economic trends continue (a very big if), the Chinese economy will surpass America's in the decades ahead. Two other growing areas could also be potential rivals: the European Union and India.[26]

Another possible risk: The United States buys more from other nations than it sells to them. This imbalance, known as a **trade deficit**, has existed every year since 1975. Is it a problem? Economists differ. Many believe that the United States cannot continue running high deficits without eventual economic consequences.

Trade deficit: The deficit arising when a nation imports (or buys) more goods from foreign nations than it exports (or sells) to them.

Some critics also worry that the United States is failing to invest in its *infrastructure*—its roads, train tracks, air terminals, and public transportation. Travelers to Asia marvel at the sleek airports and railroads. Does the Chinese growth of the past decade mean that authoritarian governments are more efficient at organizing the economy than America's democracy is? Here is an issue where President Trump and the Democrats agree—though their different approaches have, so far, blocked efforts to rebuild American infrastructure.

How do these concerns add up? Pessimists worry that other nations, especially China, will overtake the United States economically. Optimists disagree. America has run both trade and budget deficits for almost 50 years, and the financial sky has not fallen. Yes, politicians bicker, but they do not diminish the energy of American inventors. Entrepreneurial genius has powered the information age through Microsoft, Apple, Google, Facebook, Amazon, and the Internet itself. The United States remains an economic powerhouse.[27]

A nation in decline? Or an entrepreneurial dynamo setting the pace for the world? You can keep your own score in the years ahead by tracking just one measure of world power: the size of the American economy relative to the rest of the world.

Free Trade

In 2018, President Trump shocked most Americans—including leaders of his own party—by launching an all-out trade war on China. Why were so many so concerned? For the past 50 years U.S administrations championed **free trade**—*the idea that goods and services should move across international boundaries without government interference.* Until World War II, most governments tried to protect their own industries by slapping tariffs on foreign goods—special taxes that made foreign competitors more expensive than local products. This type of favoritism is called **protectionism** because it is designed to protect local industries, such as steel and aluminum, from foreign competition.

In theory, free trade helps businesses and consumers in every country, because it offers more choices and lower prices. If Detroit can make better cars at a lower price, consumers from Kansas to Kazakhstan should be able to buy them. And because a quarter of all American economic activity involves foreign trade, there is a lot of money on the table.

American policy makers pushed for both bilateral trade agreements with individual countries and, more important, multilateral treaties with many nations—the most important resulted in the **World Trade Organization** (**WTO**), which oversees international trade rules. Democratic President Bill Clinton used enormous political capital to push another multilateral agreement, the North American Free Trade Agreement (NAFTA), through Congress in 1994. NAFTA phased out taxes on imports and exports between Canada, Mexico, and the United States. Economists generally agree: NAFTA boosted economic growth in all three countries.

However, NAFTA's costs and benefits are not evenly spread out. Many U.S. companies shifted operations to Mexico, leaving hundreds of thousands of workers at least temporarily without jobs. Opposition to free trade deals grew. In the last 30 years, presidents have pressed free trade deals; in Congress Democrats generally opposed and Republicans supported them.

Then Donald Trump led the Republicans into a sharp U-turn. He insisted that trade deals like NAFTA must be renegotiated—and then followed through by targeting first Mexico and then Canada. He forcefully articulated a backlash against the international trade regime. Why? We will see in the next section.

Challenges to Free Trade

Almost every policy textbook repeats the same thing: Free trade makes everyone better off. However, many Americans strongly disagree. Free trade faces four main challenges.

First, critics of free trade charge that it is cheaper to produce goods in nations that pollute, outlaw unions, reject safety standards, and keep wages low. If global agreements are not carefully negotiated, jobs will flow to those nations—leaving American workers and their communities high and dry. Some critics suggest an alternative to free trade: **fair trade**—emphasizing worker protections and environmental standards. Fair trade can be built into trade

Free trade: Goods and services moving across international boundaries without government interference.

Protectionism: Efforts to protect local business from foreign competition.

World Trade Organization (WTO): An international organization that oversees efforts to open markets and promote free trade.

Examine the concepts of free trade and protectionism.

Fair trade: Trade that emphasizes the inclusion of environmental and labor protections in agreements so that nations do not receive unfair advantages by exploiting workers or harming the environment.

Projections for Economic Growth

WHICH ECONOMIES ARE GROWING THE FASTEST?

The United States has the largest economy but this chart shows what international economists predict for the immediate future.

THINK ABOUT IT

Which countries are expected to grow most rapidly? Which nations are lagging?

Looking purely at these economic projections, what would you advise the president to do? Find a way to slow China's growth? How? Or, alternatively, build an alliance of like-minded nations? If so, which nations would you pick to make deals with?

Finally, which nations seem least important in economic terms?

Source: IMF

% of est. global growth (2017–2019) in real GDP

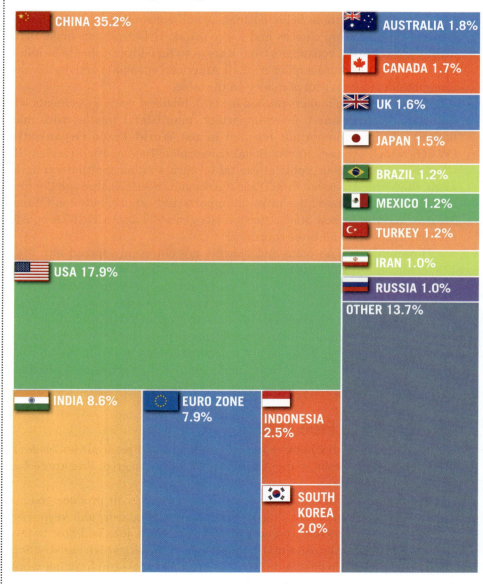

CHINA 35.2%

USA 17.9%

INDIA 8.6%

EURO ZONE 7.9%

INDONESIA 2.5%

SOUTH KOREA 2.0%

AUSTRALIA 1.8%

CANADA 1.7%

UK 1.6%

JAPAN 1.5%

BRAZIL 1.2%

MEXICO 1.2%

TURKEY 1.2%

IRAN 1.0%

RUSSIA 1.0%

OTHER 13.7%

deals that reduce trade barriers. That way, say proponents, companies in different nations compete under the same rules.

Second, free markets cause social displacement, at least in the short run. What happens to software engineers in Austin, Texas, who find their jobs migrating to Bangalore, India? Most nations have not put policies in place to help workers who are displaced by international competition. Even if everyone is better off in the long run, as free trade advocates argue, politics reflects troubles in the short run.

Third, as international markets have expanded to facilitate the huge sums involved in free trade, they have grown volatile. The Greek debt crisis, a Chinese stock market crash, and Turkey's financial troubles all reverberated through the global economy. Liberal economists such as Paul Krugman warn that free markets create a wild ride full of booms, bubbles, and busts.[28]

Fourth, long before President Trump came to office, American leaders promoted free trade only until they ran into powerful interests. When government helps American farmers, it violates the rules of free trade that the government itself is championing. Because few politicians are willing to take on the farm lobby or the rural states, American farm subsidies stay in place despite different administrations' commitment to free trade.

Today, President Trump has openly embraced protectionism. His administration placed tariffs on aluminum, steel, washing machines, and solar panels to force other nations to fully open those markets to American goods. Trading partners fired back, imposing tariffs on American products. From farmers exporting soy to Harley Davidson selling choppers to distillers making bourbon, American exporters faced retaliation; they expressed worries about losing market share and upsetting trade agreements negotiated over decades. But the administration pressed firmly on—adamant about forcing China, Europe, Turkey, and even Rwanda to fully open their markets. With the same determination, President Trump renegotiated North American Trade Agreement between Mexico, Canada, and the United States in order to deliver on his campaign promise to "get a better deal" for U.S. workers.[29]

Political reaction was mixed. For starters, trade wars run counter to bedrock traditional Republican doctrine. Most experts believe that tariffs hurt the nation that imposes them by reducing competition, choking innovation, and raising prices; some feared an international economic crisis if the tariffs stayed in place. On the other side, some liberal Democrats cheered. Senator Sherrod Brown, running for reelection in Ohio, embraced the tariffs. The AFL-CIO, a leading union, also praised the policy. They believe that free trade hurts workers in high income nations. Notice the peculiar lineup: Populists on both the left and the right against moderates in the center.

Energy

Foreign policymakers keep a close eye on energy supplies. The United States consumes almost 20 million barrels of oil a day, a fifth of the world total. In the last 30 years, America has fought three major wars in the Middle East—which has an estimated 60 percent of the world's oil reserves.

Watch 2016 presidential candidates Bernie Sanders and Donald Trump criticize a free trade agreement, the TPP.

Assess current debates on free trade.

Today, the energy story is changing rapidly. Natural gas and renewable energy supply 40 percent of American needs. Together, the United States and Canada now produce almost 80 percent of the nation's annual consumption. The United States is approaching energy independence.[30]

Economic Weapons

American officials use economic relations as carrots to reward other nations or as sticks to punish them—for attacking another country, trying to build nuclear weapons, or hacking American elections. Economic sanctions include the following:

- A *boycott*, or refusing to buy goods or services from a country.
- An *economic embargo*, or restricting the flow of trade into a country. Sometimes the Navy or the Air Force enforces the embargo.
- *Divestment*, or refusing to invest in another country. Local governments and private actors can also use this strategy.
- *Freezing assets*, or seizing bank accounts and other financial assets that foreign nationals have invested here. This strategy targets elites by stripping them of their foreign bank accounts.
- *Withholding foreign aid*—if the country is receiving any.

Applying these economic sanctions requires building an international coalition. If other countries refuse, the United States may lose a market for its own goods without applying any real pressure. Being the world's largest economy makes a difference; when the Trump Administration renewed economic sanctions on Iran, European firms discovered that the United States would punish them for violating the sanctions. Few valued their Iran business over trade with the United States.

 **The Bottom Line**

» A second goal of foreign policy is to protect prosperity. Economic strength is the ultimate source of power on the world stage.

» Today, the U.S. economy is the largest in the world, but many Americans and allies around the globe wonder: Will the United States maintain its economic strength relative to other nations?

» American economic policy has been guided by pursuit of free trade—the dropping of barriers to international commerce. Resistance has grown to free trade, among President Trump and allies as well as congressional Democrats. Many support *fair* trade.

Foreign-Policy Goal No. 3: Spreading American Ideals

Investigate the economy, military, and politics of other nations.

Realists—and many liberals—believe that every nation's foreign-policy goal can be simply described: blunt self-interest. However, explaining American action only in terms of power or prosperity misses something important.

American leaders often justify foreign-policy action as promoting values such as liberty and democracy. George Washington, in his first inaugural address, declared that the new nation existed to spread "the sacred fire of liberty and . . . the republican model of government." The United States entered World War I, said President Woodrow Wilson, because "the world must be made safe for democracy." A century later, Secretary of State Hillary Clinton described American foreign policy as "upholding universal values and human rights," warning "If we . . . let our policies diverge too far from our ideals, our influence will wane."[31]

The belief that the United States plays a special role in world affairs is known as **American exceptionalism**. America's deepest interest, according to this view, lies in promoting the peace, freedom, and democracy that will benefit all people.[32]

American exceptionalism: The view that the United States is unique, marked by a distinct set of ideas such as equality, self-rule, and limited government.

Some observers warn that American exceptionalism is a dangerous myth. It can lead Americans to reduce complicated reality into a simple clash between good and evil. And it can blind American policy makers to other perspectives and interests.[33]

A faith in America's special destiny, whether truth or myth, makes foreign policy more controversial. Political science research suggests that advancing democratic values and economic growth in underdeveloped countries helps everyone. According to the **theory of democratic peace**, nations with legitimate democratic governments do not go to war with each other.[34] While Republicans have traditionally emphasized a faith in American exceptionalism, President Trump is deeply skeptical of the idea: As a foreign policy realist, he emphasizes national self-interest.

Theory of democratic peace: Theory that strongly democratic nations are less likely to engage in wars with one another.

The Bottom Line

» The United States tries to spread its own values of democracy and freedom—a third foreign-policy goal.

Who Makes Foreign Policy?

What is misleading about the following newspaper headlines?

- "The United States Warns Syria About Attacks on Protesters"
- "South Korea Seeks to Balance Relations with China, United States"
- "Iran Threatens Saudi Arabia"

They all describe nations as if they were *unitary actors*, or individuals with minds of their own. Every chapter in this book has told a different story. The United States constructs politics out of many perspectives, interests, institutions, and arguments. So does every other nation. Foreign policy emerges out of negotiation. Several major players have a seat at the table when American foreign policy is made.

Congress

The Constitution balances responsibility for foreign policy between Congress and the president. Congress has the power to declare war, to set the military's budget, and to ratify treaties. Over time, defense—and, more generally, foreign policy—shifted away from Congress to the White House. Congress has not declared war since 1941 despite major wars in Korea (where 36 thousand Americans died), Vietnam (another 58 thousand), the Persian Gulf, the Balkans, Afghanistan, and Iraq. Congress is divided, slow to act, focused on domestic issues, and always running for reelection. For all these reasons, it has let foreign policymaking slip to the executive branch.

In 1973 Congress tried to reassert some control by passing the **War Powers Act**, which requires presidents to get congressional permission for military action after troops are in the field for no more than 60 days. Presidents often ask Congress for support before they commit troops (see Chapter 10 for details). And when wars drag on and grow unpopular, Congress asserts itself: It holds hearings, rallies opposition, and squeezes the budget.

The Constitution requires the Senate to ratify international treaties with a two-thirds vote—a very high bar in our partisan era. To get around the requirement, presidents sign *executive agreements* with other nations; these have the same legal effect as formal treaties but do not require the two-thirds vote. The Constitution also makes Congress responsible for confirming top foreign-policy appointments. Again, partisan politics has slowed this process in recent years.

In short, Congress has evolved from a partner to a type of check on the executive. The executive branch crafts international policies. It then must win over Congress for funding, legislation, confirmations, and cooperation. In effect, Congress pushes back when presidential policies become unpopular.

War Powers Act: Legislation passed in 1973 to increase congressional involvement in undeclared wars. It requires Congress to approve military action undertaken by the president in no more than 60 days.

NADIA MURAD

● *Activists also play a role in American foreign policy. Here, Nadia Murad tells a rapt Senate hearing on the Islamic State: "I was raped and sold and was abused [by ISIS] but I was lucky." Her mother and six brothers were all killed in one day.*

The President

The president commands the military, negotiates treaties, rallies Americans during crises, and oversees relations with allies and foes alike. Presidents and their team decide whether, when, and how to intervene around the globe. They balance foreign policy with domestic priorities and political calculations.

Recent administrations have demonstrated the enormous power inherent in the president's foreign-policy role. Ironically, modern presidents have more authority and less experience. Early presidents all had a rich foreign-policy background. Most recent presidents have arrived in the White House with no experience in international affairs. Trump's victory came, in part, from a great wave of distrust toward Washington insiders—such as candidate Hillary Clinton, former Secretary of State.

Although presidents take the lead, they have many partners in conducting international affairs. One key to presidential success is wisely managing the enormous foreign-policy bureaucracy. Each office in the pyramid does a different job and sees the world in its own way.

The State Department

The State Department, the first cabinet agency established under the Constitution, manages diplomatic relations with more than 200 nations. State is responsible for negotiating treaties, distributing foreign assistance, and managing daily contact with other nations.

Discover how to
negotiate agreements
with foreign entities.

State Department officers are interested in understanding other nations and cultures. They learn foreign languages, live abroad, and favor diplomatic solutions—usually multilateral. The department is sometimes accused of being out of step with majority American opinion, which can favor skeptical disengagement.

The critiques lead to a serious problem: The State Department is chronically underfunded. Its offices around the world lack key personnel. . From this perspective, the United States is ceding the crucial area of diplomacy to rivals like China—which are taking full advantage of American indifference. The Trump Administration, with its tough realist world view, has proven especially skeptical of the diplomats' role. After twenty months in office, the administration still has no ambassador in 78 nations—and has not even nominated ambassadors to 34 countries including Australia, Sweden, Mexico, Ireland, or Chile.[35]

The Department of Defense

The Department of Defense (DOD) manages the military. It is the largest organization in government and the biggest employer in the United States. The DOD is responsible for over two million military personnel, seven hundred thousand civilian employees, and troops deployed in 177 nations from Turkey to Djibouti. They are all led by the secretary of defense, who is always a civilian. The department is housed in a huge five-sided office building known as the Pentagon.

Defense Department officials see the world very differently than the State Department. The DOD makes military calculations, toting up risks and threats, assets, and strategy. A familiar Washington lament concerns the frequent failure of these two important cabinet departments to coordinate with one another. At the same time, Defense is internally divided by rivalry between the services. The Army, Navy, Air Force, and Marine Corps all strive to deploy their own tactical assets during military operations. These tensions can create such confusion that, in one notorious case, a Marine involved in the invasion of Grenada had to use a pay phone to report details back to Washington. The Chairman of the Joint Chiefs of Staff, America's top military figure, is charged on behalf of the president and secretary of defense with coordinating the branches—a tall order, given rivalries among them.

Intelligence

The United States has a large and complicated intelligence community. More than 15 different agencies and offices gather information from around the world. The best known is the Central Intelligence Agency, which is responsible for foreign intelligence. The Departments of State, Defense, Energy, and the Treasury all have their own foreign intelligence operations, as do the military branches. The Federal Bureau of Investigation is responsible for domestic intelligence, which often has to be coordinated with information from abroad.

In theory, each intelligence office and agency monitors a different spectrum of threats. In reality, they have overlapping jurisdictions and act as rivals (a familiar theme in the foreign-policy bureaucracy). They are slow to share information or communicate. There is a standard answer to turf wars such as the one in the spy community: Create a new agency and charge it with coordinating all the others. In 2004, after hearings into the 9/11 terrorist attacks exposed the chaos, Congress created a director of national intelligence charged with bringing order to American intelligence. Did this mandate impose coordination or simply inject one more voice into the contest? Answer: Both.

The National Security Council

The National Security Council (NSC), part of the Executive Office of the President, brings the most important foreign-policy officers together to advise the president. The NSC includes the president and the vice president, along with the secretaries of state, defense, and homeland security. It also includes the director of national intelligence, the head of the Joint Chiefs of Staff, and others who the president may name. Very different perspectives and personalities come together in this high-powered group to shape foreign-policy decisions.

Other Executive Agencies

Many other bureaus and agencies engage in foreign policy. The president's economic team plays an important role. The Office of the U.S. Trade Representative negotiates trade deals. The Labor Department leads business groups abroad. The Department of Homeland Security brings together a host of agencies ranging from the Coast Guard to the Immigration Service. Each agency and office pushes to define foreign-policy problems. Each seeks to put its own spin on America's approach to the world.

Interest Groups and the Public

Organized groups play an active role in foreign policymaking—far more than in most other nations. On high-profile issues such as trade agreements, every side mobilizes and lobbies. Some groups focus support for specific countries, while others lobby for specific causes: Human rights groups and Christian organizations concerned about religious persecution in other nations are among the most familiar interest groups on Capitol Hill.

Public opinion and the media can also have a powerful impact. The public generally pays little attention to foreign policy. When a foreign-policy issue does move to the forefront of American politics, the media plays it up and the public leaps in with its opinions. Wars are the most common major events, and they often follow a cycle. At first, the American majority rallies around the flag and throws its support to the president and the troops. Inevitable anti-war demonstrations get scant media attention. Over time, especially if the war bogs down or its purpose grows murky, as in Vietnam or Iraq, the public turns against the action.

Fragmentation or Success?

The policies produced by these many agencies, offices, legislators, and groups—all pulling and hauling and scrambling for influence—are typical of American government. It is chaotic, messy, unpredictable, open—and often democratic. Yet there is always the foreign-policy difference: At the end of the process, the president can make a decision and break the stalemate—deploy the Navy, issue a warning, embrace one foreign leader and challenge another, sign an executive agreement with one nation, cut off an agreement with another. Strong presidents have considerable leverage. Despite the messy process, U.S. foreign policy has been relatively successful through much of the nation's history.

The Bottom Line

» Many different individuals and institutions shape foreign policy.

» Congress and the White House were originally foreign-policy partners. During the Cold War, checks and balances diminished. Today, the president takes the lead and Congress offers a check.

» The most important executive agencies in foreign policymaking are the State Department, the Defense Department, and the National Security Council.

» Other important foreign-policy influences include intelligence agencies such as the CIA, economic bureaus, interest groups, corporations, foreign governments, the media, and the public.

» Is the messy, fragmented system swirling around the president an effective way to generate new ideas? Or is it too chaotic for the twenty-first century? Or both?

🔵 Grand Strategies in U.S. History

American leaders create an overall framework to meet the challenges of the time. Their **grand strategy** includes everything from a military doctrine to ways of seeing and interpreting the world. The United States has adopted and then moved away from four different grand strategies over the past century. Once a strategy is in place it can be very difficult to change—until a dramatic event breaks up the old order. Today, many different interests and forces struggle to shape a new grand strategy for our time.

Grand strategy: An overarching vision that defines and guides a nation's foreign policy.

Standing Alone (1918 to 1939)

Although the United States was rarely **isolationist**, through most of its history it acted alone. President Washington broke the alliance with France that had helped win the Revolutionary War, and America did not enter another peacetime alliance for 150 years. This perspective is known as **unilateralism**—American foreign policy should be independent and self-sufficient.

Isolationism: The view that America should remain free from wars and most other international engagements.

Unilateralism: A doctrine holding that the United States should act independently of other nations. It should decide its own interests—not in coordination with partners and allies.

World War I was horrific. The fighting bogged down in trenches in eastern France, and hundreds of thousands of men died moving the battle line back and forth a few miles. After three years, the United States entered the war and quickly tipped the balance. U.S. President Woodrow Wilson championed a new international order after the war. The United States would spread democracy to every nation and join with other countries in a collective security organization called the League of Nations.

Wilson's highly moral and multilateral vision met with furious opposition. Many Americans were scornful of the European leaders who had blundered into the terrible war. Some became isolationists; most remained unilateralists. In the years following World War I, the American grand strategy was simple: The United States would intervene, unilaterally, only when its own interests were threatened. The United States sent ships and troops around the world—to Russia (during and after the Bolshevik Revolution), Mexico, Panama, Turkey, China, and many other places. It almost always acted independently and minded its own interests.

The Cold War (1945 to 1989)

When World War II began in 1939, many Americans wanted nothing to do with another foreign war. "America first," they said. On December 7, 1941, Japan attacked the naval base at Pearl Harbor, sank 11 ships, and killed 2,400 men. On that day, the era of standing alone ended.

Following World War II, American policy changed. Facing a hostile Soviet Union armed with nuclear weapons and as the newly emerged leader of the Western world, American leaders argued that the United States could no longer afford to go it alone. **Multilateralism** means acting together with other nations to pursue common goals.

Multilateralism: A doctrine that emphasizes operating together with other nations to pursue common goals.

When the war ended in September 1945, the only rival to the United States was the Soviet Union, whose armies occupied the nations of Central Europe.

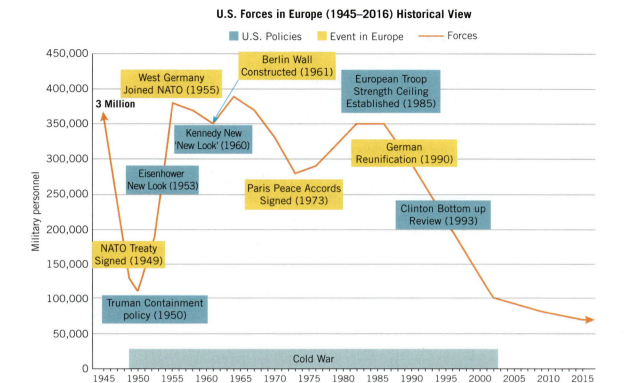

U.S. Forces in Europe (1945–2016) Historical View

● **Figure 14.6** *U.S. Troop Strength in Europe during the Cold War. For 50 years, the United States, operating with its allies (through the North Atlantic Treaty Organization, or NATO), focused on containing the Soviet Union in its sphere by stationing troops in Europe and elsewhere (U.S. European Command).*

Many observers warned that the Soviets were poised to extend their control. The Truman administration decided to accept the Soviets' current sphere of influence but to oppose every effort to expand it, a policy known as **containment** (see Figure 14.6). The crucial test came in 1947. The Democratic administration asked a Republican Congress to pour funds into Greece and Turkey to stop them from turning to communism.

Although the United States retained economic and military primacy, it joined with other nations in **multilateral organizations** dedicated to opposing communism and spreading democracy and capitalism. It broke with its own past to help establish multiple organizations: the United Nations (formed in 1945), the Organization of American States (OAS, 1948), and the North Atlantic Treaty Organization (NATO, 1949). Senator Vandenberg gave the era its famous slogan when he quipped that American party politics "stopped at the water's edge." In other words, Democrats and Republicans would no longer disagree (at least, not too loudly) about international affairs.[36]

All the same, the era posed new and difficult questions for American leaders. Should the United States support brutal dictators if they joined us in fighting communists? Should it resist popular democratic movements if they seemed to

Containment: American Cold War strategy designed to stop the spread of communism.

Multilateral organization: An international organization of three or more nations organized around a common goal.

John F Kennedy's
Speech in
Berlin—"I am a
Berliner"

Ronald Reagan's
Speech in Berlin:
"Tear down this wall"

See footage of the
joyous destruction
of the Berlin Wall
in 1989.

tilt toward communism? The debate grew heated. However, with thousands of American and Soviet missiles still threatening a nuclear holocaust, the Cold War framework remained in place—until Soviet communism suddenly collapsed.

The New World Order (1989 to 2001)

Around the world, people gaped at the incredible television footage in November 1989. Germans were clambering onto the Berlin Wall and ripping it apart. For almost 30 years, the wall—running through Berlin and separating communist Germany from democratic Germany—had been the symbol of the Cold War. President John Kennedy had looked out at the wall and declared, "All free [people], wherever they may live, are citizens of Berlin." Ronald Reagan had stood on the same spot and challenged the Soviet leader, "Mr. Gorbachev, tear down this wall." Now the East German guards stood awkwardly by, uncertain what to do, as the delirious mob did just that. Within two years, the entire Soviet empire collapsed. The framework that had guided American foreign policy for more than 50 years was suddenly irrelevant. What next?

President George H. W. Bush proclaimed "a new world order," with an active, multilateral march toward free markets and democracy. The United States should use its unchallenged military strength to make the world more peaceful, democratic, and secure.

The War on Terror (2001 to 2009)

The 9/11 attacks killed almost three thousand people. The attacks shut down American institutions from coast to coast—financial markets in New York, Disney World in Florida, the great arch in St. Louis, and air travel across American skies (for five days). In the stunned aftermath, the George W. Bush administration constructed a formidable new foreign-policy framework. To define the attacks as a crime would have brought in the American justice system. Instead, the administration declared them an act of war and responded with a "war on terror." That choice changed America's role in the world.

During the Cold War, the United States operated on the theory of *deterrence*: build a military so overpowering—including nuclear weapons—that other nations will be afraid to attack. Deterrence is aimed at other governments, not terrorist or insurgents.

What can be done against such amorphous foes? President George W. Bush

● *One of history's turning points: Jubilant Berliners climb the Berlin Wall as communism collapses. Suddenly, American foreign policymakers needed an entirely new grand strategy.*

adopted a strategy of **preemptive war**: attack them before they can strike at us. Responding to terrorist threats, the United States launched long and costly wars in Afghanistan and Iraq; it launched air strikes or sent special forces into Libya, Syria, Yemen, Cameroon, and many other hot spots. But in combating terrorism, conventional means of warfare—such as invading another country—proved less effective than policing measures such as gathering intelligence and punishing criminal behavior.

In the aftermath of 9/11, an act of Congress created the Department of Homeland Security. Related legislation, the USA Patriot Act, gave police and security personnel far more latitude to monitor, search, and detain suspects both abroad and at home. Many Americans feared these policies would weaken the United States by undermining its bedrock values—liberty and the rule of law.

The War on Terror, the Obama administration's troop withdrawal from Iraq, and popular uprisings called the "Arab Spring" destabilized the Mideast. Dozens of terrorist organizations arose, most prominently the Islamic State of Iraq and Syria (ISIS). Although the Obama administration stopped using the term "War on Terror," both the United States and its NATO allies continued fighting terrorists with intelligence, drone strikes, and special forces. The goal remains important but no longer defines the U.S. role in the world.

The Next Grand Strategy

Today, American grand strategy is up for grabs. The Obama administration developed a modest foreign policy with four interlocking components: maintain American military and economic primacy; reduce American military commitments (as the president put it, "don't do stupid shit"); operate through international organizations ("lead from behind," said the president); and pivot toward Asia.[37]

President Trump came to office with an "America First" policy: realist, deeply impatient with international organizations, and ready to reset relations with undemocratic nations. Trump's tough positions have caused American approval, which had been high during the Obama years, to plummet internationally.[38]

The new unilateralism draws a sharp response from multilateralists who believe that we cannot solve modern problems by ourselves: Only international cooperation can defeat terrorism, reverse climate change, secure prosperity, end starvation, stop ethnic killing, resist global pandemics, reduce the international traffic in drugs and sex, and end violence against women.

One pressing issue that cannot be solved through an unilateral, isolationist approach is the spread of nuclear weapons. Five nations openly possess them (the United States, England, France, Russia, and China). Four others have likely developed them (India, Pakistan, North Korea, and Israel). A few foreign-policy experts argue that the spread of these weapons makes wars less likely, because either side can annihilate the other.[39] Most observers believe the

Preemptive war: The effort to attack hostile powers before they launch attacks. Highly controversial because it sanctions striking first.

● *Diplomatic breakthrough? Or same old pretense? In 2008, North Korea blew up a cooling tower at the Yongbyon nuclear complex to emphasize its commitment to abandoning its nuclear program. Eight years later, having successfully exploded a hydrogen bomb and tested intercontinental missiles that could reach the U.S. mainland, North Korea blew up tunnels at its Punggye-ri nuclear site as show of good faith following President Trump's meeting with North Korean leader Kim Jong Un.*

opposite: As nuclear weapons spread to less stable nations, they are more likely to be used or to fall into the hands of extremist groups.

President Trump warned North Korea "of fire and fury like the world has never seen" if it continued to threaten others and develop nuclear weapons. He then made an unprecedented move: meeting North Korean leader Kim Jong-Un in a summit focused on containing the dangers of a nuclear nightmare. Might the summit lead to a breakthrough peace in Korea? Time will tell.

Today, another threat looms: cyberweapons. Russia, China, and North Korea have turned online viruses and other cyberweapons (developed in the United States) on western nations, threatening power grids, governments, banks, and more. Vulnerable Western nations may find it more effective to cooperate rather than go it alone.[40]

Interested in grand strategies in foreign policy, and what might be next for the United States? Watch closely in coming years: Time will tell how a new strategy develops, how successful it might be, and how deep its roots will sink.

The Bottom Line

» The United States forged four grand strategies in the twentieth century: It stood alone and acted unilaterally (1918–1939), it led the democratic nations in multilateral coalitions during the Cold War (1945–1991), it debated a new world order after the Cold War (1991–2001), and it launched a war on terror (2001–2009).

Conclusion: Policy Matters

As you go about your day today, recognize all the different ways you encounter the policy system. Notice the "USDA Organic" label on your breakfast cereal or yogurt container. Hopping in your car or on your bike? The cost of any gas you buy, the condition of the roads you travel on, the street signs you navigate by: All are the result of often hard-fought policy decisions. Federal agencies license and manage the electromagnetic spectrum that you use to communicate by smartphone or watch TV (devices that were likely assembled abroad, under treaties negotiated by foreign-policy experts), regulate the safety of the gym where you work out, and inspect the food you buy. Headed to class? Policy decisions determined the subsidy supporting you and the rates you pay on any student loans you hold—and if you attend a public university, they may have some say over the curriculum you study.

These are just a few of the ways in which public policy helps shape your daily experience. As a member of this vast but often surprisingly accessible democracy, you have the ability (and now, we hope the enhanced knowledge) to shape those policy decisions in turn. May you find a fulfilling role in the great continuing American experiment: government by the people.

CHAPTER SUMMARY

● Public policymaking involves choices: Should we launch a manned mission to Mars? Open formerly protected lands to oil and gas drilling? Pull out of the NAFTA treaty? Understanding those choices is the essence of politics and government in America.

● Five stages, from *agenda setting* through *evaluation*, mark the process of domestic policymaking. These are not a blueprint for action, but most policy achievements pass through all five.

● The largest U.S. programs are social policies such as Social Security, Medicare, Medicaid, and unemployment insurance. Longtime American resistance to big government helps to explain their slow growth.

● Heightened attention to fiscal and monetary policy, combined with harder economic times, has elevated the importance of budgeting in American politics. The federal budget process is a complicated machine that rarely meets its key deadlines—largely because the financial stakes are so high.

● Foreign policy explores how the United States engages the world. Is the United States the richest and most powerful country, still the global leader, or is it a declining superpower?

● The three goals of American foreign policy are security, prosperity, and spreading American values. These three goals sometimes conflict.

Check your understanding of Chapter 14.

● The United States spends as much on its military as do other leading powers combined. Primacy suggests that it should act with unparalleled power. The security trap suggests that an effort to maintain primacy builds resentments and resistance. Soft power leads instead through culture and values.

● American policymakers must make two basic choices: isolationism versus active engagement with the world; unilateralism (going it alone) and multilateralism (working with other nations in organizations and associations).

Need to review key ideas in greater depth? Click here.

● The United States is responsible for a fifth of the world economy, nearly 50 percent more than its nearest rival, China. However, China's economic growth rate in recent years has been much higher than that of the United States.

● U.S. economic policy long revolved around free trade—reducing barriers to trade between nations. Today, free trade meets resistance.

● Prime responsibility for foreign policy has shifted from Congress to the executive. However, foreign policy is the outcome of many agencies and groups pushing for their own interests and advantage.

● Twentieth-century grand strategies included isolationism (1918–1939), multilateral engagement during WWII and the Cold War (1942–1989), the search for a new world order (1991–2001), and the war on terror (since 2001).

KEY TERMS

Flashcard review.

American exceptionalism, p. 501
Budget resolution, p. 490
Containment, p. 507
Continuing resolution (CR), p. 491
Cost-benefit analysis, p. 477
Discretionary programs, p. 491
Entitlement program, p. 486
Fair trade, p. 497
Federal budget deficit, p. 488
Federal poverty line, p. 485
Fiscal policy, p. 486

Fiscal year (FY), p. 490
Focusing event, p. 475
Free trade, p. 497
Grand strategy, p. 506
Gross domestic product (GDP), p. 483
Isolationism, p. 506
Liberalism, p. 493
Monetary policy, p. 486
Multilateralism, p. 506
Multilateral organization, p. 507
Policy agenda, p. 476
Policy window, p. 479

Preemptive war, p. 509
Primacy, p. 493
Protectionism, p. 497
Realism, p. 493
Security trap, p. 494
Soft power, p. 494
Theory of democratic peace, p. 501
Trade deficit, p. 496
Unilateralism, p. 506
War Powers Act, p. 502
World Trade Organization (WTO), p. 497

STUDY QUESTIONS

1. Think of a policy issue you care about. How is it currently *framed* in national or local discussions? Would you frame it differently?

2. What is the difference between an ex ante and ex post policy evaluation? How are both useful in helping shape a government program?

3. Why are our largest entitlement programs—Social Security, Medicare, and Medicaid—so expensive?

4. How important, in your view, is balancing the U.S. budget?

5. Which qualities characterize successful policy entrepreneurs?

6. Name the three foreign-policy goals that the United States pursues. Discuss the relative importance of each goal. If you had to stress one, which would it be?

7. Describe "American exceptionalism." Do you consider it a truth, a myth, or something in between? Defend your answer.

8. If you could adopt a major reform to the American policymaking process, what would it be? (Choose from among options in the last section of this chapter, or propose your own.)

 Go to **www.oup.com/us/Morone** to find quizzes, flash cards, simulations, tutorials, videos, and other study tools.

APPENDIX I

THE DECLARATION OF INDEPENDENCE

When in the course of human events, it becomes necessary for one people to dissolve the political bands which have connected them with another, and to assume, among the powers of the earth, the separate and equal station to which the Laws of Nature and of Nature's God entitle them, a decent respect to the opinions of mankind requires that they should declare the causes which impel them to the separation.

We hold these truths to be self-evident, that all men are created equal, that they are endowed by their Creator with certain unalienable Rights, that among these are life, liberty and the pursuit of happiness. That to secure these rights, governments are instituted among men, deriving their just powers from the consent of the governed; that whenever any form of government becomes destructive of these ends, it is the right of the people to alter or to abolish it, and to institute new Government, laying its foundation on such principles and organizing its powers in such form, as to them shall seem most likely to effect their safety and happiness. Prudence, indeed, will dictate that Governments long established should not be changed for light and transient causes; and, accordingly, all experience hath shown, that mankind are more disposed to suffer, while evils are sufferable, than to right themselves by abolishing the forms to which they are accustomed. But when a long train of abuses and usurpations, pursuing invariably the same object evinces a design to reduce them under absolute despotism, it is their right, it is their duty, to throw off such government, and to provide new guards for their future security. Such has been the patient sufferance of these colonies; and such is now the necessity which constrains them to alter their former systems of government. The history of the present King of Great Britain is a history of repeated injuries and usurpations, all having in direct object the establishment of an absolute tyranny over these States. To prove this, let facts be submitted to a candid world:

He has refused his assent to laws, the most wholesome and necessary for the public good.

He has forbidden his governors to pass laws of immediate and pressing importance, unless suspended in their operation till his assent should be obtained; and, when so suspended, he has utterly neglected to attend to them.

He has refused to pass other laws for the accommodation of large districts of people, unless those people would relinquish the right of representation in the legislature, a right inestimable to them and formidable to tyrants only.

He has called together legislative bodies at places unusual, uncomfortable, and distant from the depository of their public records, for the sole purpose of fatiguing them into compliance with his measures.

He has dissolved representative houses repeatedly, for opposing with manly firmness his invasions on the rights of the people.

He has refused for a long time, after such dissolutions, to cause others to be elected; whereby the legislative powers, incapable of annihilation, have returned to the People at large for their exercise; the State remaining in the mean time exposed to all the dangers of invasion from without, and convulsions within.

He has endeavored to prevent the population of these States; for that purpose obstructing the laws for naturalization of foreigners; refusing to pass others to encourage their migrations hither, and raising the conditions of new appropriations of lands.

He has obstructed the administration of justice, by refusing his assent to laws for establishing judiciary powers.

He has made judges dependent on his will alone, for the tenure of their offices, and the amount and payment of their salaries.

He has erected a multitude of new offices, and sent hither swarms of officers to harass our people, and eat out their substance.

He has kept among us, in times of peace, standing armies without the consent of our legislatures.

He has affected to render the Military independent of, and superior to, the civil power.

He has combined with others to subject us to a jurisdiction foreign to our constitution and unacknowledged by our laws; giving his assent to their acts of pretended legislation:

For quartering large bodies of armed troops among us;

For protecting them, by a mock trial, from punishment for any murders which they should commit on the inhabitants of these States;

For cutting off our trade with all parts of the world;

For imposing taxes on us without our Consent;

For depriving us, in many cases, of the benefits of Trial by Jury;

For transporting us beyond Seas to be tried for pretended offences;

For abolishing the free System of English Laws in a neighbouring Province, establishing therein an Arbitrary government, and enlarging its Boundaries so as to render it at once an example and fit instrument for introducing the same absolute rule into these colonies;

For taking away our charters, abolishing our most valuable laws, and altering fundamentally the forms of our governments;

For suspending our own legislatures, and declaring themselves invested with power to legislate for us in all cases whatsoever.

He has abdicated government here, by declaring us out of his protection and waging war against us.

He has plundered our seas, ravaged our coasts, burnt our towns, and destroyed the lives of our people.

He is at this time transporting large armies of foreign mercenaries to complete the works of death, desolation and tyranny, already begun with circumstances of cruelty and perfidy scarcely paralleled in the most barbarous ages, and totally unworthy the head of a civilized nation.

He has constrained our fellow citizens taken captive on the high seas to bear arms against their country, to become the executioners of their friends and brethren, or to fall themselves by their hands.

He has excited domestic insurrections amongst us, and has endeavored to bring on the inhabitants of our frontiers, the merciless Indian savages, whose known rule of warfare, is an undistinguished destruction of all ages, sexes and conditions.

In every stage of these oppressions we have petitioned for redress in the most humble terms; our repeated petitions have been answered only by repeated injury. A prince whose character is thus marked by every act which may define a tyrant, is unfit to be the ruler of a free people.

Nor have we been wanting in attentions to our British brethren. We have warned them from time to time of attempts by their legislature to extend an unwarrantable jurisdiction over us. We have reminded them of the circumstances of our emigration and settlement here. We have appealed to their native justice and magnanimity, and we have conjured them by the ties of our common kindred to disavow these usurpations, which, would inevitably interrupt our connections and correspondence. They, too, have been deaf to the voice of justice and of consanguinity. We must, therefore, acquiesce in the necessity, which denounces our separation, and hold them, as we hold the rest of mankind, enemies in war, in peace friends.

We, therefore, the representatives of the United States of America, in general Congress, assembled, appealing to the Supreme Judge of the world for the rectitude of our intentions, do, in the name, and by the authority of the good people of these colonies, solemnly publish and declare, that these united colonies are, and of right ought to be free and independent states; that they are absolved from all allegiance to the British Crown, and that all political connection between them and the state of Great Britain, is and ought to be totally dissolved; and that, as free and independent states, they have full power to levy war, conclude peace, contract alliances, establish commerce, and to do all other acts and things which independent states may of right do. And for the support of this declaration, with a firm reliance on the protection of Divine Providence, we mutually pledge to each other our lives, our fortunes and our sacred honor.

THE CONSTITUTION OF THE UNITED STATES OF AMERICA

We the People of the United States, in Order to form a more perfect Union, establish Justice, insure domestic Tranquility, provide for the common defence, promote the general Welfare, and secure the Blessings of Liberty to ourselves and our Posterity, do ordain and establish this Constitution for the United States of America.

Article I

Section 1

All legislative Powers herein granted shall be vested in a Congress of the United States, which shall consist of a Senate and House of Representatives.

Section 2

The House of Representatives shall be composed of Members chosen every second Year by the People of the several States, and the Electors in each State shall have the Qualifications requisite for Electors of the most numerous Branch of the State Legislature.

No Person shall be a Representative who shall not have attained to the Age of twenty five Years, and been seven Years a Citizen of the United States, and who shall not, when elected, be an Inhabitant of that State in which he shall be chosen.

Representatives [and direct Taxes]* shall be apportioned among the several States [which may be included within this Union, according to their respective Numbers, which shall be determined by adding to the whole Number of free Persons, including those bound to Service for a Term of Years, and excluding Indians not taxed, three fifths of all other Persons].** The actual Enumeration shall be made within three Years—after the first Meeting of the Congress of the United States, and within every subsequent Term of ten Years, in such Manner as they shall by Law direct. The Number of Representatives shall not exceed one for every thirty Thousand, but each State shall have at Least one Representative; and until such enumeration shall be made, the State of New Hampshire shall be entitled to choose three, Massachusetts eight, Rhode-Island and Providence Plantations one, Connecticut five, New York six, New Jersey four, Pennsylvania eight, Delaware one, Maryland six, Virginia ten, North Carolina five, South Carolina five, and Georgia three.

---

*Modified by the Sixteenth Amendment.
**Negated by the Fourteenth Amendment.

When vacancies happen in the Representation from any State, the Executive Authority thereof shall issue Writs of Election to fill such Vacancies.

The House of Representatives shall choose their Speaker and other Officers; and shall have the sole Power of Impeachment.

Section 3

The Senate of the United States shall be composed of two Senators from each State, chosen [by the Legislature thereof]* for six Years; and each Senator shall have one Vote.

Immediately after they shall be assembled in Consequence of the first Election, they shall be divided as equally as may be into three Classes. The Seats of the Senators of the first Class shall be vacated at the Expiration of the second Year, of the second Class at the Expiration of the fourth Year, and of the third Class at the Expiration of the sixth Year, so that one third may be chosen every second Year, [and if Vacancies happen by Resignation, or otherwise, during the Recess of the Legislature of any State, the Executive thereof may make temporary Appointments until the next Meeting of the Legislature, which shall then fill such Vacancies].**

No Person shall be a Senator who shall not have attained to the Age of thirty Years, and been nine Years a Citizen of the United States, and who shall not, when elected, be an Inhabitant of that State for which he shall be chosen.

The Vice President of the United States shall be President of the Senate, but shall have no Vote, unless they be equally divided.

The Senate shall choose their other Officers, and also a President pro tempore, in the Absence of the Vice President, or when he shall exercise the Office of President of the United States.

The Senate shall have the sole Power to try all Impeachments. When sitting for that Purpose, they shall be on Oath or Affirmation. When the President of the United States is tried, the Chief Justice shall preside: And no Person shall be convicted without the Concurrence of two thirds of the Members present.

Judgment in Cases of Impeachment shall not extend further than to removal from Office, and disqualification to hold and enjoy any Office of honor, Trust or Profit under the United States: but the Party convicted shall nevertheless be liable and subject to Indictment, Trial, Judgment and Punishment, according to Law.

Section 4

The Times, Places and Manner of holding Elections for Senators and Representatives, shall be prescribed in each State by the Legislature thereof;

*Changed by the Seventeenth Amendment.
** Modified by the Seventeenth Amendment.

but the Congress may at any time by Law make or alter such Regulations, except as to the Places of chusing Senators.

[The Congress shall assemble at least once in every Year, and such Meeting shall be on the first Monday in December, unless they shall by Law appoint a different Day.]*

Section 5

Each House shall be the Judge of the Elections, Returns and Qualifications of its own Members, and a Majority of each shall constitute a Quorum to do Business; but a smaller Number may adjourn from day to day, and may be authorized to compel the Attendance of absent Members, in such Manner, and under such Penalties as each House may provide.

Each House may determine the Rules of its Proceedings, punish its Members for disorderly Behaviour, and, with the Concurrence of two thirds, expel a Member.

Each House shall keep a Journal of its Proceedings, and from time to time publish the same, excepting such Parts as may in their Judgment require Secrecy; and the Yeas and Nays of the Members of either House on any question shall, at the Desire of one fifth of those Present, be entered on the Journal.

Neither House, during the Session of Congress, shall, without the Consent of the other, adjourn for more than three days, nor to any other Place than that in which the two Houses shall be sitting.

Section 6

The Senators and Representatives shall receive a Compensation for their Services, to be ascertained by Law, and paid out of the Treasury of the United States. They shall in all Cases, except Treason, Felony and Breach of the Peace, be privileged from Arrest during their Attendance at the Session of their respective Houses, and in going to and returning from the same; and for any Speech or Debate in either House, they shall not be questioned in any other Place.

No Senator or Representative shall, during the Time for which he was elected, be appointed to any civil Office under the Authority of the United States, which shall have been created, or the Emoluments whereof shall have been increased during such time; and no Person holding any Office under the United States, shall be a Member of either House during his Continuance in Office.

Section 7

All Bills for raising Revenue shall originate in the House of Representatives; but the Senate may propose or concur with Amendments as on other Bills.

---

*Changed to January 3 by the Twentieth Amendment.

Every Bill which shall have passed the House of Representatives and the Senate, shall, before it become a Law, be presented to the President of the United States: If he approve he shall sign it, but if not he shall return it, with his Objections to that House in which it shall have originated, who shall enter the Objections at large on their Journal, and proceed to reconsider it. If after such Reconsideration two thirds of that House shall agree to pass the Bill, it shall be sent, together with the Objections, to the other House, by which it shall likewise be reconsidered, and if approved by two thirds of that House, it shall become a Law. But in all such Cases the Votes of both Houses shall be determined by yeas and Nays, and the Names of the Persons voting for and against the Bill shall be entered on the Journal of each House respectively. If any Bill shall not be returned by the President within ten Days (Sundays excepted) after it shall have been presented to him, the Same shall be a Law, in like Manner as if he had signed it, unless the Congress by their Adjournment prevent its Return, in which Case it shall not be a Law.

Every Order, Resolution, or Vote to which the Concurrence of the Senate and House of Representatives may be necessary (except on a question of Adjournment) shall be presented to the President of the United States; and before the Same shall take Effect, shall be approved by him, or being disapproved by him, shall be repassed by two thirds of the Senate and House of Representatives, according to the Rules and Limitations prescribed in the Case of a Bill.

Section 8

The Congress shall have Power

To lay and collect Taxes, Duties, Imposts and Excises, to pay the Debts and provide for the common Defence and general Welfare of the United States; but all Duties, Imposts and Excises shall be uniform throughout the United States;

To borrow Money on the credit of the United States;

To regulate Commerce with foreign Nations, and among the several States, and with the Indian Tribes;

To establish an uniform Rule of Naturalization, and uniform Laws on the subject of Bankruptcies throughout the United States;

To coin Money, regulate the Value thereof, and of foreign Coin, and fix the Standard of Weights and Measures;

To provide for the Punishment of counterfeiting the Securities and current Coin of the United States;

To establish Post Offices and post Roads;

To promote the Progress of Science and useful Arts, by securing for limited Times to Authors and Inventors the exclusive Right to their respective Writings and Discoveries;

To constitute Tribunals inferior to the supreme Court;

To define and punish Piracies and Felonies committed on the high Seas, and Offences against the Law of Nations;

To declare War, grant Letters of Marque and Reprisal, and make Rules concerning Captures on Land and Water;

To raise and support Armies, but no Appropriation of Money to that Use shall be for a longer Term than two Years;

To provide and maintain a Navy;

To make Rules for the Government and Regulation of the land and naval Forces;

To provide for calling forth the Militia to execute the Laws of the Union, suppress Insurrections and repel Invasions;

To provide for organizing, arming, and disciplining the Militia, and for governing such Part of them as may be employed in the Service of the United States, reserving to the States respectively, the Appointment of the Officers, and the Authority of training the Militia according to the discipline prescribed by Congress;

To exercise exclusive Legislation in all Cases whatsoever, over such District (not exceeding ten Miles square) as may, by Cession of particular States, and the Acceptance of Congress, become the Seat of the Government of the United States, and to exercise like Authority over all Places purchased by the Consent of the Legislature of the State in which the Same shall be, for the Erection of Forts, Magazines, Arsenals, dock-Yards, and other needful Buildings;—And

To make all Laws which shall be necessary and proper for carrying into Execution the foregoing Powers, and all other Powers vested by this Constitution in the Government of the United States, or in any Department or Officer thereof.

Section 9

The Migration or Importation of such Persons as any of the States now existing shall think proper to admit, shall not be prohibited by the Congress prior to the Year one thousand eight hundred and eight, but a Tax or duty may be imposed on such Importation, not exceeding ten dollars for each Person.

The Privilege of the Writ of Habeas Corpus shall not be suspended, unless when in Cases of Rebellion or Invasion the public Safety may require it.

No Bill of Attainder or ex post facto Law shall be passed.

[No Capitation, or other direct, Tax shall be laid, unless in Proportion to the Census or enumeration herein before directed to be taken.]*

No Tax or Duty shall be laid on Articles exported from any State.

No Preference shall be given by any Regulation of Commerce or Revenue to the Ports of one State over those of another; nor shall Vessels bound to, or from, one State, be obliged to enter, clear, or pay Duties in another.

No Money shall be drawn from the Treasury, but in Consequence of Appropriations made by Law; and a regular Statement and Account of the Receipts and Expenditures of all public Money shall be published from time to time.

No Title of Nobility shall be granted by the United States: And no Person holding any Office of Profit or Trust under them, shall, without the Consent of

---

*Modified by the Sixteenth Amendment.

the Congress, accept of any present, Emolument, Office, or Title, of any kind whatever, from any King, Prince, or foreign State.

Section 10

No State shall enter into any Treaty, Alliance, or Confederation; grant Letters of Marque and Reprisal; coin Money; emit Bills of Credit; make any Thing but gold and silver Coin a Tender in Payment of Debts; pass any Bill of Attainder, ex post facto Law, or Law impairing the Obligation of Contracts, or grant any Title of Nobility.

 No State shall, without the Consent of the Congress, lay any Imposts or Duties on Imports or Exports, except what may be absolutely necessary for executing it's inspection Laws: and the net Produce of all Duties and Imposts, laid by any State on Imports or Exports, shall be for the Use of the Treasury of the United States; and all such Laws shall be subject to the Revision and Control of the Congress.

 No State shall, without the Consent of Congress, lay any Duty of Tonnage, keep Troops, or Ships of War in time of Peace, enter into any Agreement or Compact with another State, or with a foreign Power, or engage in War, unless actually invaded, or in such imminent Danger as will not admit of delay.

Article II

Section 1

The executive Power shall be vested in a President of the United States of America. He shall hold his Office during the Term of four Years, and, together with the Vice President, chosen for the same Term, be elected, as follows:

 Each State shall appoint, in such Manner as the Legislature thereof may direct, a Number of Electors, equal to the whole Number of Senators and Representatives to which the State may be entitled in the Congress: but no Senator or Representative, or Person holding an Office of Trust or Profit under the United States, shall be appointed an Elector.

 [The Electors shall meet in their respective States, and vote by Ballot for two Persons, of whom one at least shall not be an Inhabitant of the same State with themselves. And they shall make a List of all the Persons voted for, and of the Number of Votes for each; which List they shall sign and certify, and transmit sealed to the Seat of the Government of the United States, directed to the President of the Senate. The President of the Senate shall, in the Presence of the Senate and House of Representatives, open all the Certificates, and the Votes shall then be counted. The Person having the greatest Number of Votes shall be the President, if such Number be a Majority of the whole Number of Electors appointed; and if there be more than one who have such Majority, and have an equal Number of Votes, then the House of Representatives shall immediately choose by Ballot one of them for President; and if no Person have a Majority, then from the five highest on the List the said House shall in like Manner choose the President. But in choosing the President, the Votes shall be taken by States, the Representation from each State having one Vote; a quorum for this purpose shall consist of a Member or Members from two thirds of the States, and a Majority of all the States shall be necessary to a Choice. In every Case, after the Choice of the President, the Person having the greatest Number of Votes of the Electors shall be the Vice President. But if there should remain two or more who have equal Votes, the Senate shall choose from them by Ballot the Vice President.]*

The Congress may determine the Time of choosing the Electors, and the Day on which they shall give their Votes; which Day shall be the same throughout the United States.

No Person except a natural born Citizen, or a Citizen of the United States, at the time of the Adoption of this Constitution, shall be eligible to the Office of President; neither shall any Person be eligible to that Office who shall not have attained to the Age of thirty five Years, and been fourteen Years a Resident within the United States.

In Case of the Removal of the President from Office, or of his Death, Resignation, or Inability to discharge the Powers and Duties of the said Office, the Same shall devolve on the Vice President, and the Congress may by Law provide for the Case of Removal, Death, Resignation or Inability, both of the President and Vice President, declaring what Officer shall then act as President, and such Officer shall act accordingly, until the Disability be removed, or a President shall be elected.

The President shall, at stated Times, receive for his Services, a Compensation, which shall neither be increased nor diminished during the Period for which he shall have been elected, and he shall not receive within that Period any other Emolument from the United States, or any of them.

Before he enter on the Execution of his Office, he shall take the following Oath or Affirmation:—"I do solemnly swear (or affirm) that I will faithfully execute the Office of President of the United States, and will to the best of my Ability, preserve, protect and defend the Constitution of the United States."

Section 2

The President shall be Commander in Chief of the Army and Navy of the United States, and of the Militia of the several States, when called into the actual Service of the United States; he may require the Opinion, in writing, of the principal Officer in each of the executive Departments, upon any Subject relating to the Duties of their respective Offices, and he shall have Power to grant Reprieves and Pardons for Offences against the United States, except in Cases of Impeachment.

He shall have Power, by and with the Advice and Consent of the Senate, to make Treaties, provided two thirds of the Senators present concur; and he shall nominate, and by and with the Advice and Consent of the Senate, shall

---

*Changed by the Twelfth and Twentieth Amendments.

appoint Ambassadors, other public Ministers and Consuls, Judges of the supreme Court, and all other Officers of the United States, whose Appointments are not herein otherwise provided for, and which shall be established by Law: but the Congress may by Law vest the Appointment of such inferior Officers, as they think proper, in the President alone, in the Courts of Law, or in the Heads of Departments.

The President shall have Power to fill up all Vacancies that may happen during the Recess of the Senate, by granting Commissions which shall expire at the End of their next Session.

Section 3

He shall from time to time give to the Congress Information of the State of the Union, and recommend to their Consideration such Measures as he shall judge necessary and expedient; he may, on extraordinary Occasions, convene both Houses, or either of them, and in Case of Disagreement between them, with Respect to the Time of Adjournment, he may adjourn them to such Time as he shall think proper; he shall receive Ambassadors and other public Ministers; he shall take Care that the Laws be faithfully executed, and shall Commission all the Officers of the United States.

Section 4

The President, Vice President and all civil Officers of the United States, shall be removed from Office on Impeachment for, and Conviction of, Treason, Bribery, or other high Crimes and Misdemeanors.

Article III

Section 1

The judicial Power of the United States shall be vested in one supreme Court, and in such inferior Courts as the Congress may from time to time ordain and establish. The Judges, both of the supreme and inferior Courts, shall hold their Offices during good Behaviour, and shall, at stated Times, receive for their Services a Compensation, which shall not be diminished during their Continuance in Office.

Section 2

The judicial Power shall extend to all Cases, in Law and Equity, arising under this Constitution, the Laws of the United States, and Treaties made, or which shall be made, under their Authority;—to all Cases affecting Ambassadors, other public Ministers and Consuls;—to all Cases of admiralty and maritime Jurisdiction;—to Controversies to which the United States shall be a Party;—to Controversies between two or more States;—[between a State and Citizens of another State];—between Citizens of different States;—between Citizens of the same State claiming Lands under Grants of different States, [and between a State,] or the Citizens thereof, [and foreign States, Citizens or Subjects].*

In all Cases affecting Ambassadors, other public Ministers and Consuls, and those in which a State shall be Party, the supreme Court shall have original Jurisdiction. In all the other Cases before mentioned, the supreme Court shall have appellate Jurisdiction, both as to Law and Fact, with such Exceptions, and under such Regulations as the Congress shall make.

The Trial of all Crimes, except in Cases of Impeachment, shall be by Jury; and such Trial shall be held in the State where the said Crimes shall have been committed; but when not committed within any State, the Trial shall be at such Place or Places as the Congress may by Law have directed.

Section 3

Treason against the United States, shall consist only in levying War against them, or in adhering to their Enemies, giving them Aid and Comfort. No Person shall be convicted of Treason unless on the Testimony of two Witnesses to the same overt Act, or on Confession in open Court.

The Congress shall have Power to declare the Punishment of Treason, but no Attainder of Treason shall work Corruption of Blood, or Forfeiture except during the Life of the Person attainted.

Article IV

Section 1

Full Faith and Credit shall be given in each State to the public Acts, Records, and judicial Proceedings of every other State. And the Congress may by general Laws prescribe the Manner in which such Acts, Records and Proceedings shall be proved, and the Effect thereof.

Section 2

The Citizens of each State shall be entitled to all Privileges and Immunities of Citizens in the several States.

A Person charged in any State with Treason, Felony, or other Crime, who shall flee from Justice, and be found in another State, shall on Demand of the executive Authority of the State from which he fled, be delivered up, to be removed to the State having Jurisdiction of the Crime.

[No Person held to Service or Labour in one State, under the Laws thereof, escaping into another, shall, in Consequence of any Law or Regulation therein, be discharged from such Service or Labour, but shall be delivered up on Claim of the Party to whom such Service or Labour may be due.]**

---

*Altered by the Twelfth Amendment.
**Repealed by the Thirteenth Amendment.

Section 3

New States may be admitted by the Congress into this Union; but no new State shall be formed or erected within the Jurisdiction of any other State; nor any State be formed by the Junction of two or more States, or Parts of States, without the Consent of the Legislatures of the States concerned as well as of the Congress.

The Congress shall have Power to dispose of and make all needful Rules and Regulations respecting the Territory or other Property belonging to the United States; and nothing in this Constitution shall be so construed as to Prejudice any Claims of the United States, or of any particular State.

Section 4

The United States shall guarantee to every State in this Union a Republican Form of Government, and shall protect each of them against Invasion; and on Application of the Legislature, or of the Executive (when the Legislature cannot be convened), against domestic Violence.

Article V

The Congress, whenever two thirds of both Houses shall deem it necessary, shall propose Amendments to this Constitution, or, on the Application of the Legislatures of two thirds of the several States, shall call a Convention for proposing Amendments, which, in either Case, shall be valid to all Intents and Purposes, as Part of this Constitution, when ratified by the Legislatures of three fourths of the several States, or by Conventions in three fourths thereof, as the one or the other Mode of Ratification may be proposed by the Congress; Provided that no Amendment which may be made prior to the Year One thousand eight hundred and eight shall in any Manner affect the first and fourth Clauses in the Ninth Section of the first Article; and that no State, without its Consent, shall be deprived of its equal Suffrage in the Senate.

Article VI

All Debts contracted and Engagements entered into, before the Adoption of this Constitution, shall be as valid against the United States under this Constitution, as under the Confederation.

This Constitution, and the Laws of the United States which shall be made in Pursuance thereof; and all Treaties made, or which shall be made, under the Authority of the United States, shall be the supreme Law of the Land; and the Judges in every State shall be bound thereby, any Thing in the Constitution or Laws of any State to the Contrary notwithstanding.

The Senators and Representatives before mentioned, and the Members of the several State Legislatures, and all executive and judicial Officers, both of the United States and of the several States, shall be bound by Oath or Affirmation, to support this Constitution; but no religious Test shall ever be required as a Qualification to any Office or public Trust under the United States.

Article VII

The Ratification of the Conventions of nine States, shall be sufficient for the Establishment of this Constitution between the States so ratifying the Same.

The Word, "the," being interlined between the seventh and eighth Lines of the first Page, the Word "Thirty" being partly written on an Erazure in the fifteenth Line of the first Page, The Words "is tried" being interlined between the thirty second and thirty third Lines of the first Page and the Word "the" being interlined between the forty third and forty fourth Lines of the second Page.

Attest William Jackson Secretary

Done in Convention by the Unanimous Consent of the States present the Seventeenth Day of September in the Year of our Lord one thousand seven hundred and Eighty seven and of the Independence of the United States of America the Twelfth In witness whereof We have hereunto subscribed our Names,

G°. WASHINGTON

Presidt and deputy from Virginia

Delaware
Geo: Read
Gunning Bedford
  jun
John Dickinson
Richard Bassett
Jaco: Broom

Maryland
James McHenry
Dan of St Thos.
  Jenifer
Danl. Carroll

Virginia
John Blair
James Madison Jr.

North Carolina
Wm. Blount
Richd. Dobbs Spaight
Hu Williamson

South Carolina
J. Rutledge
Charles Cotesworth
  Pinckney
Charles Pinckney
Pierce Butler

Georgia
William Few
Abr Baldwin

New Hampshire
John Langdon
Nicholas Gilman

Massachusetts
Nathaniel Gorham
Rufus King

Connecticut
Wm. Saml. Johnson
Roger Sherman

New York
Alexander Hamilton

New Jersey
Wil: Livingston
David Brearley
Wm. Paterson
Jona: Dayton

Pennsylvania
B Franklin
Thomas Mifflin
Robt. Morris
Geo. Clymer
Thos. FitzSimons
Jared Ingersoll
James Wilson
Gouv Morris

Articles

In addition to, and Amendment of the Constitution of the United States of America, proposed by Congress, and ratified by the Legislatures of the several States, pursuant to the fifth Article of the original Constitution.

(The first ten amendments to the U.S. Constitution were ratified December 15, 1791, and form what is known as the "Bill of Rights.")

Amendment I

Congress shall make no law respecting an establishment of religion, or prohibiting the free exercise thereof; or abridging the freedom of speech, or of the press; or the right of the people peaceably to assemble, and to petition the Government for a redress of grievances.

Amendment II

A well regulated Militia, being necessary to the security of a free State, the right of the people to keep and bear Arms, shall not be infringed.

Amendment III

No Soldier shall, in time of peace be quartered in any house, without the consent of the Owner, nor in time of war, but in a manner to be prescribed by law.

Amendment IV

The right of the people to be secure in their persons, houses, papers, and effects, against unreasonable searches and seizures, shall not be violated, and no Warrants shall issue, but upon probable cause, supported by Oath or affirmation, and particularly describing the place to be searched, and the persons or things to be seized.

Amendment V

No person shall be held to answer for a capital, or otherwise infamous crime, unless on a presentment or indictment of a Grand Jury, except in cases arising in the land or naval forces, or in the Militia, when in actual service in time of War or public danger; nor shall any person be subject for the same offence to be twice put in jeopardy of life or limb; nor shall be compelled in any criminal case to be a witness against himself, nor be deprived of life, liberty, or property, without due process of law; nor shall private property be taken for public use, without just compensation.

Amendment VI

In all criminal prosecutions, the accused shall enjoy the right to a speedy and public trial, by an impartial jury of the State and district wherein the crime shall have been committed, which district shall have been previously ascertained by law, and to be informed of the nature and cause of the accusation; to be confronted with the witnesses against him; to have compulsory process for obtaining witnesses in his favor, and to have the Assistance of Counsel for his defence.

Amendment VII

In Suits at common law, where the value in controversy shall exceed twenty dollars, the right of trial by jury shall be preserved, and no fact tried by a jury, shall be otherwise re-examined in any Court of the United States, than according to the rules of the common law.

Amendment VIII

Excessive bail shall not be required, nor excessive fines imposed, nor cruel and unusual punishments inflicted.

Amendment IX

The enumeration in the Constitution, of certain rights, shall not be construed to deny or disparage others retained by the people.

Amendment X

The powers not delegated to the United States by the Constitution, nor prohibited by it to the States, are reserved to the States respectively, or to the people.

Amendment XI

Passed by Congress March 4, 1794. Ratified February 7, 1795.

Note: Article III, Section 2, of the Constitution was modified by Amendment XI.

The Judicial power of the United States shall not be construed to extend to any suit in law or equity, commenced or prosecuted against one of the United States by Citizens of another State, or by Citizens or Subjects of any Foreign State.

Amendment XII

Passed by Congress December 9, 1803. Ratified June 15, 1804.

Note: A portion of Article II, Section 1, of the Constitution was superseded by the Twelfth Amendment.

The Electors shall meet in their respective states and vote by ballot for President and Vice-President, one of whom, at least, shall not be an inhabitant of the same state with themselves; they shall name in their ballots the person voted for as President, and in distinct ballots the person voted for as Vice-President, and they shall make distinct lists of all persons voted for as President, and of all persons voted for as Vice-President, and of the number of votes for each, which lists they shall sign and certify, and transmit sealed to the seat of the government of the United States, directed to the President of the Senate;—the President of the Senate shall, in the presence of the Senate and House of Representatives, open all the certificates and the votes shall then be counted;—The person having the greatest number of votes for

President, shall be the President, if such number be a majority of the whole number of Electors appointed; and if no person have such majority, then from the persons having the highest numbers not exceeding three on the list of those voted for as President, the House of Representatives shall choose immediately, by ballot, the President. But in choosing the President, the votes shall be taken by states, the representation from each state having one vote; a quorum for this purpose shall consist of a member or members from two-thirds of the states, and a majority of all the states shall be necessary to a choice. [And if the House of Representatives shall not choose a President whenever the right of choice shall devolve upon them, before the fourth day of March next following, then the Vice-President shall act as President, as in case of the death or other constitutional disability of the President.—]* The person having the greatest number of votes as Vice-President, shall be the Vice-President, if such number be a majority of the whole number of Electors appointed, and if no person have a majority, then from the two highest numbers on the list, the Senate shall choose the Vice-President; a quorum for the purpose shall consist of two-thirds of the whole number of Senators, and a majority of the whole number shall be necessary to a choice. But no person constitutionally ineligible to the office of President shall be eligible to that of Vice-President of the United States.

Amendment XIII

Passed by Congress January 31, 1865. Ratified December 6, 1865.

Note: A portion of Article IV, Section 2, of the Constitution was superseded by the Thirteenth Amendment.

Section 1

Neither slavery nor involuntary servitude, except as a punishment for crime whereof the party shall have been duly convicted, shall exist within the United States, or any place subject to their jurisdiction.

Section 2

Congress shall have power to enforce this article by appropriate legislation.

Amendment XIV

Passed by Congress June 13, 1866. Ratified July 9, 1868.

Note: Article I, Section 2, of the Constitution was modified by Section 2 of the Fourteenth Amendment.

Section 1

All persons born or naturalized in the United States, and subject to the jurisdiction thereof, are citizens of the United States and of the State wherein they reside. No State shall make or enforce any law which shall abridge

*Superseded by Section 3 of the Twentieth Amendment.

the privileges or immunities of citizens of the United States; nor shall any State deprive any person of life, liberty, or property, without due process of law; nor deny to any person within its jurisdiction the equal protection of the laws.

Section 2

Representatives shall be apportioned among the several States according to their respective numbers, counting the whole number of persons in each State, excluding Indians not taxed. But when the right to vote at any election for the choice of electors for President and Vice-President of the United States, Representatives in Congress, the Executive and Judicial officers of a State, or the members of the Legislature thereof, is denied to any of the male inhabitants of such State, being twenty-one years of age,* and citizens of the United States, or in any way abridged, except for participation in rebellion, or other crime, the basis of representation therein shall be reduced in the proportion which the number of such male citizens shall bear to the whole number of male citizens twenty-one years of age in such State.

Section 3

No person shall be a Senator or Representative in Congress, or elector of President and Vice-President, or hold any office, civil or military, under the United States, or under any State, who, having previously taken an oath, as a member of Congress, or as an officer of the United States, or as a member of any State legislature, or as an executive or judicial officer of any State, to support the Constitution of the United States, shall have engaged in insurrection or rebellion against the same, or given aid or comfort to the enemies thereof. But Congress may by a vote of two-thirds of each House, remove such disability.

Section 4

The validity of the public debt of the United States, authorized by law, including debts incurred for payment of pensions and bounties for services in suppressing insurrection or rebellion, shall not be questioned. But neither the United States nor any State shall assume or pay any debt or obligation incurred in aid of insurrection or rebellion against the United States, or any claim for the loss or emancipation of any slave; but all such debts, obligations and claims shall be held illegal and void.

Section 5

The Congress shall have the power to enforce, by appropriate legislation, the provisions of this article.

---

*Changed by Section 1 of the Twenty-sixth Amendment.

Amendment XV

Passed by Congress February 26, 1869. Ratified February 3, 1870.

Section 1

The right of citizens of the United States to vote shall not be denied or abridged by the United States or by any State on account of race, color, or previous condition of servitude.

Section 2

The Congress shall have the power to enforce this article by appropriate legislation.

Amendment XVI

Passed by Congress July 2, 1909. Ratified February 3, 1913.

Note: Article I, Section 9, of the Constitution was modified by Amendment XVI.

The Congress shall have power to lay and collect taxes on incomes, from whatever source derived, without apportionment among the several States, and without regard to any census or enumeration.

Amendment XVII

Passed by Congress May 13, 1912. Ratified April 8, 1913.

Note: Article I, Section 3, of the Constitution was modified by the Seventeenth Amendment.

The Senate of the United States shall be composed of two Senators from each State, elected by the people thereof, for six years; and each Senator shall have one vote. The electors in each State shall have the qualifications requisite for electors of the most numerous branch of the State legislatures.

When vacancies happen in the representation of any State in the Senate, the executive authority of such State shall issue writs of election to fill such vacancies: Provided, That the legislature of any State may empower the executive thereof to make temporary appointments until the people fill the vacancies by election as the legislature may direct.

This amendment shall not be so construed as to affect the election or term of any Senator chosen before it becomes valid as part of the Constitution.

Amendment XVIII

Passed by Congress December 18, 1917. Ratified January 16, 1919. Repealed by Amendment XXI.

Section 1

After one year from the ratification of this article the manufacture, sale, or transportation of intoxicating liquors within, the importation thereof into, or the exportation thereof from the United States and all territory subject to the jurisdiction thereof for beverage purposes is hereby prohibited.

Section 2

The Congress and the several States shall have concurrent power to enforce this article by appropriate legislation.

Section 3

This article shall be inoperative unless it shall have been ratified as an amendment to the Constitution by the legislatures of the several States, as provided in the Constitution, within seven years from the date of the submission hereof to the States by the Congress.

Amendment XIX

Passed by Congress June 4, 1919. Ratified August 18, 1920.

The right of citizens of the United States to vote shall not be denied or abridged by the United States or by any State on account of sex.

Congress shall have power to enforce this article by appropriate legislation.

Amendment XX

Passed by Congress March 2, 1932. Ratified January 23, 1933.

Note: Article I, Section 4, of the Constitution was modified by Section 2 of this amendment. In addition, a portion of the Twelfth Amendment was superseded by Section 3.

Section 1

The terms of the President and the Vice President shall end at noon on the 20th day of January, and the terms of Senators and Representatives at noon on the 3d day of January, of the years in which such terms would have ended if this article had not been ratified; and the terms of their successors shall then begin.

Section 2

The Congress shall assemble at least once in every year, and such meeting shall begin at noon on the 3d day of January, unless they shall by law appoint a different day.

Section 3

If, at the time fixed for the beginning of the term of the President, the President elect shall have died, the Vice President elect shall become President. If a President shall not have been chosen before the time fixed for the beginning of his term, or if the President elect shall have failed to qualify, then the Vice President elect shall act as President until a President shall have qualified; and the Congress may by law provide for the case wherein neither a President elect nor a Vice President shall have qualified, declaring who shall then act as President, or the manner in which one who is to act shall be selected, and such person shall act accordingly until a President or Vice President shall have qualified.

Section 4

The Congress may by law provide for the case of the death of any of the persons from whom the House of Representatives may choose a President whenever the right of choice shall have devolved upon them, and for the case of the death of any of the persons from whom the Senate may choose a Vice President whenever the right of choice shall have devolved upon them.

Section 5

Sections 1 and 2 shall take effect on the 15th day of October following the ratification of this article.

Section 6

This article shall be inoperative unless it shall have been ratified as an amendment to the Constitution by the legislatures of three-fourths of the several States within seven years from the date of its submission.

Amendment XXI

Passed by Congress February 20, 1933. Ratified December 5, 1933.

Section 1

The eighteenth article of amendment to the Constitution of the United States is hereby repealed.

Section 2

The transportation or importation into any State, Territory, or Possession of the United States for delivery or use therein of intoxicating liquors, in violation of the laws thereof, is hereby prohibited.

Section 3

This article shall be inoperative unless it shall have been ratified as an amendment to the Constitution by conventions in the several States, as provided in the Constitution, within seven years from the date of the submission hereof to the States by the Congress.

Amendment XXII

Passed by Congress March 21, 1947. Ratified February 27, 1951.

Section 1

No person shall be elected to the office of the President more than twice, and no person who has held the office of President, or acted as President, for more than two years of a term to which some other person was elected President shall be elected to the office of President more than once. But this Article shall not apply to any person holding the office of President when this Article was proposed by Congress, and shall not prevent any person who may be holding the office of President, or acting as President, during the term within which this Article becomes operative from holding the office of President or acting as President during the remainder of such term.

Section 2

This article shall be inoperative unless it shall have been ratified as an amendment to the Constitution by the legislatures of three-fourths of the several States within seven years from the date of its submission to the States by the Congress.

Amendment XXIII

Passed by Congress June 16, 1960. Ratified March 29, 1961.

Section 1

The District constituting the seat of Government of the United States shall appoint in such manner as Congress may direct:

A number of electors of President and Vice President equal to the whole number of Senators and Representatives in Congress to which the District would be entitled if it were a State, but in no event more than the least populous State; they shall be in addition to those appointed by the States, but they shall be considered, for the purposes of the election of President and Vice President, to be electors appointed by a State; and they shall meet in the District and perform such duties as provided by the twelfth article of amendment.

Section 2

The Congress shall have power to enforce this article by appropriate legislation.

Amendment XXIV

Passed by Congress August 27, 1962. Ratified January 23, 1964.

Section 1

The right of citizens of the United States to vote in any primary or other election for President or Vice President, for electors for President or Vice President, or for Senator or Representative in Congress, shall not be denied or abridged by the United States or any State by reason of failure to pay poll tax or other tax.

Section 2

The Congress shall have power to enforce this article by appropriate legislation.

Amendment XXV

Passed by Congress July 6, 1965. Ratified February 10, 1967.

Note: Article II, Section 1, of the Constitution was affected by the Twenty-Fifth Amendment.

Section 1

In case of the removal of the President from office or of his death or resignation, the Vice President shall become President.

Section 2

Whenever there is a vacancy in the office of the Vice President, the President shall nominate a Vice President who shall take office upon confirmation by a majority vote of both Houses of Congress.

Section 3

Whenever the President transmits to the President pro tempore of the Senate and the Speaker of the House of Representatives his written declaration that he is unable to discharge the powers and duties of his office, and until he transmits to them a written declaration to the contrary, such powers and duties shall be discharged by the Vice President as Acting President.

Section 4

Whenever the Vice President and a majority of either the principal officers of the executive departments or of such other body as Congress may by law provide, transmit to the President pro tempore of the Senate and the Speaker of the House of Representatives their written declaration that the President is unable to discharge the powers and duties of his office, the Vice President shall immediately assume the powers and duties of the office as Acting President.

Thereafter, when the President transmits to the President pro tempore of the Senate and the Speaker of the House of Representatives his written declaration that no inability exists, he shall resume the powers and duties of his office unless the Vice President and a majority of either the principal officers of the executive department or of such other body as Congress may by law provide, transmit within four days to the President pro tempore of the Senate and the Speaker of the House of Representatives their written declaration that the President is unable to discharge the powers and duties of his office. Thereupon Congress shall decide the issue, assembling within forty-eight hours for that purpose if not in session. If the Congress, within twenty-one days after receipt of the latter written declaration, or, if Congress is not in session, within twenty-one days after Congress is required to assemble, determines by two-thirds vote of both Houses that the President is unable to discharge the powers and duties of his office, the Vice President shall continue to discharge the same as Acting President; otherwise, the President shall resume the powers and duties of his office.

Amendment XXVI

Passed by Congress March 23, 1971. Ratified July 1, 1971.

Note: Amendment XIV, Section 2, of the Constitution was modified by Section 1 of the Twenty-Sixth Amendment.

Section 1

The right of citizens of the United States, who are eighteen years of age or older, to vote shall not be denied or abridged by the United States or by any State on account of age.

Section 2

The Congress shall have power to enforce this article by appropriate legislation.

Amendment XXVII

Originally proposed Sept. 25, 1789. Ratified May 7, 1992.

No law, varying the compensation for the services of the Senators and Representatives, shall take effect, until an election of representatives shall have intervened.

APPENDIX III

THE FEDERALIST PAPERS 1, 10, AND 51

By Alexander Hamilton, James Madison, John Jay

The debate over ratifying the Constitution in 1787–1788 was very close, especially in New York. To persuade the people of the state, Hamilton, Madison, and Jay wrote eighty-five newspaper essays arguing for ratification. Three of the most influential, reproduced here, are Federalist Papers 1, 10, and 51.

FEDERALIST No. 1
General Introduction
For the *Independent Journal*. Saturday, October 27, 1787

HAMILTON
To the People of the State of New York:

AFTER an unequivocal experience of the inefficacy of the subsisting federal government, you are called upon to deliberate on a new Constitution for the United States of America. The subject speaks its own importance; comprehending in its consequences nothing less than the existence of the UNION, the safety and welfare of the parts of which it is composed, the fate of an empire in many respects the most interesting in the world. It has been frequently remarked that it seems to have been reserved to the people of this country, by their conduct and example, to decide the important question, whether societies of men are really capable or not of establishing good government from reflection and choice, or whether they are forever destined to depend for their political constitutions on accident and force. If there be any truth in the remark, the crisis at which we are arrived may with propriety be regarded as the era in which that decision is to be made; and a wrong election of the part we shall act may, in this view, deserve to be considered as the general misfortune of mankind.

This idea will add the inducements of philanthropy to those of patriotism, to heighten the solicitude which all considerate and good men must feel for the event. Happy will it be if our choice should be directed by a judicious estimate of our true interests, unperplexed and unbiased by considerations not connected with the public good. But this is a thing more ardently to be wished than seriously to be expected. The plan offered to our deliberations affects too many particular interests, innovates upon too many local institutions, not to involve in its discussion a variety of objects foreign to its merits, and of views, passions and prejudices little favorable to the discovery of truth.

Among the most formidable of the obstacles which the new Constitution will have to encounter may readily be distinguished the obvious interest of a certain class of men in every State to resist all changes which may hazard a diminution of the power, emolument, and consequence of the offices they hold under the State establishments; and the perverted ambition of another class of men, who will either hope to aggrandize themselves by the confusions of their country, or will flatter themselves with fairer prospects of elevation from the subdivision of the empire into several partial confederacies than from its union under one government.

It is not, however, my design to dwell upon observations of this nature. I am well aware that it would be disingenuous to resolve indiscriminately the opposition of any set of men (merely because their situations might subject them to suspicion) into interested or ambitious views. Candor will oblige us to admit that even such men may be actuated by upright intentions; and it cannot be doubted that much of the opposition which has made its appearance, or may hereafter make its appearance, will spring from sources, blameless at least, if not respectable—the honest errors of minds led astray by preconceived jealousies and fears. So numerous indeed and so powerful are the causes which serve to give a false bias to the judgment, that we, upon many occasions, see wise and good men on the wrong as well as on the right side of questions of the first magnitude to society. This circumstance, if duly attended to, would furnish a lesson of moderation to those who are ever so much persuaded of their being in the right in any controversy. And a further reason for caution, in this respect, might be drawn from the reflection that we are not always sure that those who advocate the truth are influenced by purer principles than their antagonists. Ambition, avarice, personal animosity, party opposition, and many other motives not more laudable than these, are apt to operate as well upon those who support as those who oppose the right side of a question. Were there not even these inducements to moderation, nothing could be more ill-judged than that intolerant spirit which has, at all times, characterized political parties. For in politics, as in religion, it is equally absurd to aim at making proselytes by fire and sword. Heresies in either can rarely be cured by persecution.

And yet, however just these sentiments will be allowed to be, we have already sufficient indications that it will happen in this as in all former cases of great national discussion. A torrent of angry and malignant passions will be let loose. To judge from the conduct of the opposite parties, we shall be led to conclude that they will mutually hope to evince the justness of their opinions, and to increase the number of their converts by the loudness of their declamations and the bitterness of their invectives. An enlightened zeal for the energy and efficiency of government will be stigmatized as the offspring of a temper fond of despotic power and hostile to the principles of liberty. An over-scrupulous jealousy of danger to the rights of the people, which is more commonly the fault of the head than of the heart, will be represented as mere pretense and artifice, the stale bait for popularity at the expense of the public good. It will be forgotten, on the one hand, that jealousy is the usual concomitant of love, and that the noble enthusiasm of liberty is apt to be infected with a spirit of narrow and illiberal

distrust. On the other hand, it will be equally forgotten that the vigor of government is essential to the security of liberty; that, in the contemplation of a sound and well-informed judgment, their interest can never be separated; and that a dangerous ambition more often lurks behind the specious mask of zeal for the rights of the people than under the forbidden appearance of zeal for the firmness and efficiency of government. History will teach us that the former has been found a much more certain road to the introduction of despotism than the latter, and that of those men who have overturned the liberties of republics, the greatest number have begun their career by paying an obsequious court to the people; commencing demagogues, and ending tyrants.

In the course of the preceding observations, I have had an eye, my fellow-citizens, to putting you upon your guard against all attempts, from whatever quarter, to influence your decision in a matter of the utmost moment to your welfare, by any impressions other than those which may result from the evidence of truth. You will, no doubt, at the same time, have collected from the general scope of them, that they proceed from a source not unfriendly to the new Constitution. Yes, my countrymen, I own to you that, after having given it an attentive consideration, I am clearly of opinion it is your interest to adopt it. I am convinced that this is the safest course for your liberty, your dignity, and your happiness. I affect not reserves which I do not feel. I will not amuse you with an appearance of deliberation when I have decided. I frankly acknowledge to you my convictions, and I will freely lay before you the reasons on which they are founded. The consciousness of good intentions disdains ambiguity. I shall not, however, multiply professions on this head. My motives must remain in the depository of my own breast. My arguments will be open to all, and may be judged of by all. They shall at least be offered in a spirit which will not disgrace the cause of truth.

I propose, in a series of papers, to discuss the following interesting particulars:

THE UTILITY OF THE UNION TO YOUR POLITICAL PROSPERITY—THE INSUFFICIENCY OF THE PRESENT CONFEDERATION TO

PRESERVE THAT UNION—THE NECESSITY OF A GOVERNMENT AT LEAST EQUALLY ENERGETIC WITH THE ONE PROPOSED, TO THE ATTAINMENT OF THIS OBJECT—THE CONFORMITY OF THE PROPOSED CONSTITUTION TO THE TRUE PRINCIPLES OF REPUBLICAN GOVERNMENT—ITS ANALOGY TO YOUR OWN STATE CONSTITUTION—and lastly, THE ADDITIONAL SECURITY WHICH ITS ADOPTION WILL AFFORD TO THE PRESERVATION OF THAT SPECIES OF GOVERNMENT, TO LIBERTY, AND TO PROPERTY.

In the progress of this discussion I shall endeavor to give a satisfactory answer to all the objections which shall have made their appearance, that may seem to have any claim to your attention.

It may perhaps be thought superfluous to offer arguments to prove the utility of the UNION, a point, no doubt, deeply engraved on the hearts of the great body of the people in every State, and one, which it may be imagined, has no adversaries. But the fact is, that we already hear it whispered in the private circles of those who oppose the new Constitution, that the thirteen States are of too great extent for any general system, and that we must of necessity resort to separate confederacies of distinct portions of the whole. This doctrine will, in all probability, be gradually propagated, till it has votaries enough to countenance an open avowal of it. For nothing can be more evident, to those who are able to take an enlarged view of the subject, than the alternative of an adoption of the new Constitution or a dismemberment of the Union. It will therefore be of use to begin by examining the advantages of that Union, the certain evils, and the probable dangers, to which every State will be exposed from its dissolution. This shall accordingly constitute the subject of my next address.

PUBLIUS

FEDERALIST No. 10
The Same Subject Continued (The Union as a Safeguard Against Domestic Faction and Insurrection)
From the *Daily Advertiser*. Thursday, November 22, 1787.

MADISON
To the People of the State of New York:

AMONG the numerous advantages promised by a well constructed Union, none deserves to be more accurately developed than its tendency to break and control the violence of faction. The friend of popular governments never finds himself so much alarmed for their character and fate, as when he contemplates their propensity to this dangerous vice. He will not fail, therefore, to set a due value on any plan which, without violating the principles to which he is attached, provides a proper cure for it. The instability, injustice, and confusion introduced into the public councils, have, in truth, been the mortal diseases under which popular governments have everywhere perished; as they continue to be the favorite and fruitful topics from which the adversaries to liberty derive their most specious declamations. The valuable improvements made by the American constitutions on the popular models, both ancient and modern, cannot certainly be too much admired; but it would be an unwarrantable partiality, to contend that they have as effectually obviated the danger on this side, as was wished and expected. Complaints are everywhere heard from our most considerate and virtuous citizens, equally the friends of public and private faith, and of public and personal liberty, that our governments are too unstable, that the public good is disregarded in the conflicts of rival parties, and that measures are too often decided, not according to the rules of justice and the rights of the minor party, but by the superior force of an interested and overbearing majority. However anxiously we may wish that these complaints had no foundation, the evidence, of known facts will not permit us to deny that they are in some degree true. It will be found, indeed, on a candid review of our situation, that some of the distresses under which we labor have been erroneously charged on the operation of our governments; but it will be found, at the same time, that other causes will not alone account for many of our heaviest misfortunes; and, particularly, for that prevailing and increasing distrust of public engagements, and alarm for private rights, which are echoed from one end of the continent to the other. These must be chiefly, if not wholly, effects of the unsteadiness and injustice with which a factious spirit has tainted our public administrations.

By a faction, I understand a number of citizens, whether amounting to a majority or a minority of the whole, who are united and actuated by some common impulse of passion, or of interest, adversed to the rights of other citizens, or to the permanent and aggregate interests of the community.

There are two methods of curing the mischiefs of faction: the one, by removing its causes; the other, by controlling its effects.

There are again two methods of removing the causes of faction: the one, by destroying the liberty which is essential to its existence; the other, by giving to every citizen the same opinions, the same passions, and the same interests.

It could never be more truly said than of the first remedy, that it was worse than the disease. Liberty is to faction what air is to fire, an aliment without which it instantly expires. But it could not be less folly to abolish liberty, which is essential to political life, because it nourishes faction, than it would be to wish the annihilation of air, which is essential to animal life, because it imparts to fire its destructive agency.

The second expedient is as impracticable as the first would be unwise. As long as the reason of man continues fallible, and he is at liberty to exercise it, different opinions will be formed. As long as the connection subsists between his reason and his self-love, his opinions and his passions will have a reciprocal influence on each other; and the former will be objects to which the latter will attach themselves. The diversity in the faculties of men, from which the rights of property originate, is not less an insuperable obstacle to a uniformity of interests. The protection of these faculties is the first object of government. From the protection of different and unequal faculties of acquiring property, the possession of different degrees and kinds of property immediately results; and from the influence of these on the sentiments and views of the respective proprietors, ensues a division of the society into different interests and parties.

The latent causes of faction are thus sown in the nature of man; and we see them everywhere brought into different degrees of activity, according to the different circumstances of civil society. A zeal for different opinions concerning religion, concerning government, and many other points, as well of speculation as of practice; an attachment to different leaders ambitiously contending for pre-eminence and power; or to persons of other descriptions whose fortunes have been interesting to the human passions, have, in turn, divided mankind into parties, inflamed them with mutual animosity, and rendered them much more disposed to vex and oppress each other than to co-operate for their common good. So strong is this propensity of mankind to fall into mutual animosities, that where no substantial occasion presents itself, the most frivolous and fanciful distinctions have been sufficient to kindle their unfriendly passions and excite their most violent conflicts. But the most common and durable source of factions has been the various and unequal distribution of property. Those who hold and those who are without property have ever formed distinct interests in society. Those who are creditors, and those who are debtors, fall under a like discrimination. A landed interest, a manufacturing interest, a mercantile interest, a moneyed interest, with many lesser interests, grow up of necessity in civilized nations, and divide them into different classes, actuated by different sentiments and views. The regulation of these various and interfering interests forms the principal task of modern legislation, and involves the spirit of party and faction in the necessary and ordinary operations of the government.

No man is allowed to be a judge in his own cause, because his interest would certainly bias his judgment, and, not improbably, corrupt his integrity. With equal, nay with greater reason, a body of men are unfit to be both judges and parties at the same time; yet what are many of the most important acts of legislation, but so many judicial determinations, not indeed concerning the rights of single persons, but concerning the rights of large bodies of citizens? And what are the different classes of legislators but advocates and parties to the causes which they determine? Is a law proposed concerning private debts? It is a question to which the creditors are parties on one side and the debtors on the other. Justice ought to hold the balance between them. Yet the parties are, and must be, themselves the judges; and the most numerous party, or, in other words, the most powerful faction must be expected to prevail. Shall domestic manufactures be encouraged, and in what degree, by restrictions on foreign manufactures? are questions which would be differently decided by the landed and the manufacturing classes, and probably by neither with a sole regard to justice and the public good. The apportionment of taxes on the various descriptions of property is an act which seems to require the most exact impartiality; yet there is, perhaps, no legislative act in which greater opportunity and temptation are given to a predominant party to trample on the rules of justice. Every shilling with which they overburden the inferior number, is a shilling saved to their own pockets.

It is in vain to say that enlightened statesmen will be able to adjust these clashing interests, and render them all subservient to the public good. Enlightened statesmen will not always be at the helm. Nor, in many cases, can such an adjustment be made at all without taking into view indirect and remote considerations, which will rarely prevail over the immediate interest which one party may find in disregarding the rights of another or the good of the whole.

The inference to which we are brought is, that the CAUSES of faction cannot be removed, and that relief is only to be sought in the means of controlling its EFFECTS.

If a faction consists of less than a majority, relief is supplied by the republican principle, which enables the majority to defeat its sinister views by regular vote. It may clog the administration, it may convulse the society; but it will be unable to execute and mask its violence under the forms of the Constitution. When a majority is included in a faction, the form of popular government, on the other hand, enables it to sacrifice to its ruling passion or interest both the public good and the rights of other citizens. To secure the public good and private rights against the danger of such a faction, and at the same time to preserve the spirit and the form of popular government, is then the great object to which our inquiries are directed. Let me add that it is the great desideratum by which this form of government can be rescued from the opprobrium under which it has so long labored, and be recommended to the esteem and adoption of mankind.

By what means is this object attainable? Evidently by one of two only. Either the existence of the same passion or interest in a majority at the same time must be prevented, or the majority, having such coexistent passion or interest, must be rendered, by their number and local situation, unable to concert and carry into effect schemes of oppression. If the impulse and the opportunity be suffered to coincide, we well know that neither moral nor religious motives can be relied on as an adequate control. They are not found to be such on the injustice and violence of individuals, and lose their efficacy in proportion to the number combined together, that is, in proportion as their efficacy becomes needful.

From this view of the subject it may be concluded that a pure democracy, by which I mean a society consisting of a small number of citizens, who assemble and administer the government in person, can admit of no cure for the mischiefs of faction. A common passion or interest will, in almost every case, be felt by a majority of the whole; a communication and concert result from the form of government itself; and there is nothing to check the inducements to sacrifice the weaker party or an obnoxious individual. Hence it is that such democracies have ever been spectacles of turbulence and contention; have ever been found incompatible with personal security or the rights of property; and have in general been as short in their lives as they have been violent in their deaths. Theoretic politicians, who have patronized this species of government, have erroneously supposed that by reducing mankind to a perfect equality in their political rights, they would, at the same time, be perfectly equalized and assimilated in their possessions, their opinions, and their passions.

A republic, by which I mean a government in which the scheme of representation takes place, opens a different prospect, and promises the cure for which we are seeking. Let us examine the points in which it varies from pure democracy, and we shall comprehend both the nature of the cure and the efficacy which it must derive from the Union.

The two great points of difference between a democracy and a republic are: first, the delegation of the government, in the latter, to a small number of citizens elected by the rest; secondly, the greater number of citizens, and greater sphere of country, over which the latter may be extended.

The effect of the first difference is, on the one hand, to refine and enlarge the public views, by passing them through the medium of a chosen body of citizens, whose wisdom may best discern the true interest of their country, and whose patriotism and love of justice will be least likely to sacrifice it to temporary or partial considerations. Under such a regulation, it may well happen that the public voice, pronounced by the representatives of the people, will be more consonant to the public good than if pronounced by the people themselves, convened for the purpose. On the other hand, the effect may be inverted. Men of factious tempers, of local prejudices, or of sinister designs, may, by intrigue, by corruption, or by other means, first obtain the suffrages, and then betray the interests, of the people. The question resulting is, whether small or extensive republics are more favorable to the election of proper guardians of the public weal; and it is clearly decided in favor of the latter by two obvious considerations:

In the first place, it is to be remarked that, however small the republic may be, the representatives must be raised to a certain number, in order to guard against the cabals of a few; and that, however large it may be, they must be limited to a certain number, in order to guard against the confusion of a multitude. Hence, the number of representatives in the two cases not being in proportion to that of the two constituents, and being proportionally greater in the small republic, it follows that, if the proportion of fit characters be not less in the large than in the small republic, the former will present a greater option, and consequently a greater probability of a fit choice.

In the next place, as each representative will be chosen by a greater number of citizens in the large than in the small republic, it will be more difficult for unworthy candidates to practice with success the vicious arts by which elections are too often carried; and the suffrages of the people being more free, will be more likely to centre in men who possess the most attractive merit and the most diffusive and established characters.

It must be confessed that in this, as in most other cases, there is a mean, on both sides of which inconveniences will be found to lie. By enlarging too much the number of electors, you render the representatives too little acquainted with all their local circumstances and lesser interests; as by reducing it too much, you render him unduly attached to these, and too little fit to comprehend and pursue great and national objects. The federal Constitution forms a happy combination in this respect; the great and aggregate interests being referred to the national, the local and particular to the State legislatures.

The other point of difference is, the greater number of citizens and extent of territory which may be brought within the compass of republican than of democratic government; and it is this circumstance principally which renders factious combinations less to be dreaded in the former than in the latter. The smaller the society, the fewer probably will be the distinct parties and interests composing it; the fewer the distinct parties and interests, the more frequently will a majority be found of the same party; and the smaller the number of individuals composing a majority, and the smaller the compass within which they are placed, the more easily will they concert and execute their plans of oppression. Extend the sphere, and you take in a greater variety of parties and interests; you make it less probable that a majority of the whole will have a common motive to invade the rights of other citizens; or if such a common motive exists, it will be more difficult for all who feel it to discover their own strength, and to act in unison with each other. Besides other impediments, it may be remarked that, where there is a consciousness of unjust or dishonorable purposes, communication is always checked by distrust in proportion to the number whose concurrence is necessary.

Hence, it clearly appears, that the same advantage which a republic has over a democracy, in controlling the effects of faction, is enjoyed by a large over a small republic,—is enjoyed by the Union over the States composing it. Does the advantage consist in the substitution of representatives whose enlightened views and virtuous sentiments render them superior to local prejudices and schemes of injustice? It will not be denied that the representation of the Union will be most likely to possess these requisite endowments. Does it consist in the greater security afforded by a greater variety of parties, against the event of any one party being able to outnumber and oppress the rest? In an equal degree does the increased variety of parties comprised within the Union, increase this security. Does it, in fine, consist in the greater obstacles opposed to the concert and accomplishment of the secret wishes of an unjust and interested majority? Here, again, the extent of the Union gives it the most palpable advantage.

The influence of factious leaders may kindle a flame within their particular States, but will be unable to spread a general conflagration through the other States. A religious sect may degenerate into a political faction in a part of the Confederacy; but the variety of sects dispersed over the entire face of it must secure the national councils against any danger from that source. A rage for paper money, for an abolition of debts, for an equal division of property, or for any other improper or wicked project, will be less apt to pervade the whole body of the Union than a particular member of it; in the same proportion as such a malady is more likely to taint a particular county or district, than an entire State.

In the extent and proper structure of the Union, therefore, we behold a republican remedy for the diseases most incident to republican government. And according to the degree of pleasure and pride we feel in being republicans, ought to be our zeal in cherishing the spirit and supporting the character of Federalists.

PUBLIUS

FEDERALIST No. 51
The Structure of the Government Must Furnish the Proper Checks and Balances Between the Different Departments.

For the *Independent Journal*. Wednesday, February 6, 1788.

MADISON

To the People of the State of New York:

TO WHAT expedient, then, shall we finally resort, for maintaining in practice the necessary partition of power among the several departments, as laid down in the Constitution? The only answer that can be given is, that as all these exterior provisions are found to be inadequate, the defect must be supplied, by so contriving the interior structure of the government as that its several constituent parts may, by their mutual relations, be the means of keeping each other in their proper places. Without presuming to undertake a full development of this important idea, I will hazard a few general observations, which may perhaps place it in a clearer light, and enable us to form a more correct judgment of the principles and structure of the government planned by the convention.

In order to lay a due foundation for that separate and distinct exercise of the different powers of government, which to a certain extent is admitted on all hands to be essential to the preservation of liberty, it is evident that each department should have a will of its own; and consequently should be so constituted that the members of each should have as little agency as possible in the appointment of the members of the others. Were this principle rigorously adhered to, it would require that all the appointments for the supreme executive, legislative, and judiciary magistracies should be drawn from the same fountain of authority, the people, through channels having no communication whatever with one another. Perhaps such a plan of constructing the several departments would be less difficult in practice than it may in contemplation appear. Some difficulties, however, and some additional expense would attend the execution of it. Some deviations, therefore, from the principle must be admitted. In the constitution of the judiciary department in particular, it might be inexpedient to insist rigorously on the principle: first, because peculiar qualifications being essential in the members, the primary consideration ought to be to select that mode of choice which best secures these qualifications; secondly, because the permanent tenure by which the appointments are held in that department, must soon destroy all sense of dependence on the authority conferring them.

It is equally evident, that the members of each department should be as little dependent as possible on those of the others, for the emoluments annexed to their offices. Were the executive magistrate, or the judges, not independent of the legislature in this particular, their independence in every other would be merely nominal.

But the great security against a gradual concentration of the several powers in the same department, consists in giving to those who administer each department the necessary constitutional means and personal motives to resist encroachments of the others. The provision for defense must in this, as in all other cases, be made commensurate to the danger of attack. Ambition must be made to counteract ambition. The interest of the man must be connected with the constitutional rights of the place. It may be a reflection on human nature, that such devices should be necessary to control the abuses of government. But what is government itself, but the greatest of all reflections on human nature? If men were angels, no government would be necessary. If angels were to govern men, neither external nor internal controls on government would be necessary. In framing a government which is to be administered by men over men, the great difficulty lies in this: you must first enable the government to control the governed; and in the next place oblige it to control itself. A dependence on the people is, no doubt, the primary control on the government; but experience has taught mankind the necessity of auxiliary precautions.

This policy of supplying, by opposite and rival interests, the defect of better motives, might be traced through the whole system of human affairs, private as well as public. We see it particularly displayed in all the subordinate distributions of power, where the constant aim is to divide and arrange the several offices in such a manner as that each may be a check on the other—that the private interest of every individual may be a sentinel over the public rights. These inventions of prudence cannot be less requisite in the distribution of the supreme powers of the State.

But it is not possible to give to each department an equal power of self-defense. In republican government, the legislative authority necessarily predominates. The remedy for this inconveniency is to divide the legislature into different branches; and to render them, by different modes of election and different principles of action, as little connected with each other as the nature of their common functions and their common dependence on the society will admit. It may even be necessary to guard against dangerous encroachments by still further precautions. As the weight of the legislative authority requires that it should be thus divided, the weakness of the executive may require, on the other hand, that it should be fortified. An absolute negative on the legislature appears, at first view, to be the natural defense with which the executive magistrate should be armed. But perhaps it would be neither altogether safe nor alone sufficient. On ordinary occasions it might not be exerted with the requisite firmness, and on extraordinary occasions it might be perfidiously abused. May not this defect of an absolute negative be supplied by some qualified connection between this weaker department and the weaker branch of the stronger department, by which the latter may be led to support the constitutional rights of the former, without being too much detached from the rights of its own department?

If the principles on which these observations are founded be just, as I persuade myself they are, and they be applied as a criterion to the several State constitutions, and to the federal Constitution it will be found that if the latter does not perfectly correspond with them, the former are infinitely less able to bear such a test.

There are, moreover, two considerations particularly applicable to the federal system of America, which place that system in a very interesting point of view.

First. In a single republic, all the power surrendered by the people is submitted to the administration of a single government; and the usurpations are guarded against by a division of the government into distinct and separate departments. In the compound republic of America, the power surrendered by the people is first divided between two distinct governments, and then the portion allotted to each subdivided among distinct and separate departments. Hence a double security arises to the rights of the people. The different governments will control each other, at the same time that each will be controlled by itself.

Second. It is of great importance in a republic not only to guard the society against the oppression of its rulers, but to guard one part of the society against the injustice of the other part. Different interests necessarily exist in different classes of citizens. If a majority be united by a common interest, the rights of the minority will be insecure. There are but two methods of providing against this evil: the one by creating a will in the community independent of the majority—that is, of the society itself; the other, by comprehending in the society so many separate descriptions of citizens as will render an unjust combination of a majority of the whole very improbable, if not impracticable. The first method prevails in all governments possessing an hereditary or self-appointed authority. This, at best, is but a precarious security; because a power independent of the society may as well espouse the unjust views of the major, as the rightful interests of the minor party, and may possibly be turned against both parties. The second method will be exemplified in the federal republic of the United States. Whilst all authority in it will be derived from and dependent on the society, the society itself will be broken into so many parts, interests, and classes of citizens, that the rights of individuals, or of the minority, will be in little danger from interested combinations of the majority. In a free government the security for civil rights must be the same as that for religious rights. It consists in the one case in the multiplicity of interests, and in the other in the multiplicity of sects. The degree of security

in both cases will depend on the number of interests and sects; and this may be presumed to depend on the extent of country and number of people comprehended under the same government. This view of the subject must particularly recommend a proper federal system to all the sincere and considerate friends of republican government, since it shows that in exact proportion as the territory of the Union may be formed into more circumscribed Confederacies, or States, oppressive combinations of a majority will be facilitated: the best security, under the republican forms, for the rights of every class of citizens, will be diminished: and consequently the stability and independence of some member of the government, the only other security, must be proportionately increased. Justice is the end of government. It is the end of civil society. It ever has been and ever will be pursued until it be obtained, or until liberty be lost in the pursuit. In a society under the forms of which the stronger faction can readily unite and oppress the weaker, anarchy may as truly be said to reign as in a state of nature, where the weaker individual is not secured against the violence of the stronger; and as, in the latter state, even the stronger individuals are prompted, by the uncertainty of their condition, to submit to a government which may protect the weak as well as themselves; so, in the former state, will the more powerful factions or parties be gradually induced, by a like motive, to wish for a government which will protect all parties, the weaker as well as the more powerful. It can be little doubted that if the State of Rhode Island was separated from the Confederacy and left to itself, the insecurity of rights under the popular form of government within such narrow limits would be displayed by such reiterated oppressions of factious majorities that some power altogether independent of the people would soon be called for by the voice of the very factions whose misrule had proved the necessity of it. In the extended republic of the United States, and among the great variety of interests, parties, and sects which it embraces, a coalition of a majority of the whole society could seldom take place on any other principles than those of justice and the general good; whilst there being thus less danger to a minor from the will of a major party, there must be less pretext, also, to provide for the security of the former, by introducing into the government a will not dependent on the latter, or, in other words, a will independent of the society itself. It is no less certain than it is important, notwithstanding the contrary opinions which have been entertained, that the larger the society, provided it lie within a practical sphere, the more duly capable it will be of self-government. And happily for the REPUBLICAN CAUSE, the practicable sphere may be carried to a very great extent, by a judicious modification and mixture of the FEDERAL PRINCIPLE.

PUBLIUS

Glossary

116th Congress: The Congress elected in November 2018, meeting in 2019–2020. The first Congress met in 1789–1790. Each Congress is elected for two years and numbered consecutively.

527 groups: Organizations that raise and spend unlimited amounts for "issue advocacy."

1963 March on Washington: A massive rally for civil rights that included Martin Luther King's "I Have a Dream" speech.

Abolition: A nineteenth-century movement demanding an immediate and unconditional end to slavery.

Accommodation: The principle that government does not violate the establishment clause as long as it does not confer an advantage to some religions over others. (See "strict separation.")

Advocacy explosion: A vast and relatively swift increase in interest groups active in Washington, DC, beginning in the mid-1960s.

Affirmative action: Direct steps to recruit members of previously underrepresented groups into schools and jobs.

American exceptionalism: The view that the United States is uniquely characterized by a distinct set of ideas such as equality, self-rule, and limited government.

Amicus curiae: A brief submitted by a person or group who is not a direct party to the case.

Approval rating: A measure of public support for a political figure or institution.

Astroturf lobbying: An attempt by interest groups to simulate widespread public engagement on an issue.

Bandwagon effect: When people join a cause because it seems popular or support a candidate who is leading in the polls.

Base voters: Party members who tend to vote loyally for their party's candidates in most elections.

Bicameral: Having two legislative houses or chambers—such as the House and the Senate.

Bill of Rights: The first ten amendments to the Constitution, listing the rights guaranteed to every citizen.

Black power: A slogan that emphasized pride in black heritage and the construction of black institutions to nurture black interests. It often implied racial separation in reaction to white racism.

Block grants: National government funding provided to state and local governments with relatively few restrictions or requirements on spending; programs to block grants introduced a trade-off for state officials: more authority, fewer funds.

Boomerang effect: The discrepancy between candidates' high poll ratings and election performance, caused by supporters' assumption that an easy win means they need not turn out.

Brown v. Board of Education: The landmark Supreme Court case that struck down segregated schools as unconstitutional.

Budget resolution: A joint House–Senate creation that outlines targets for federal spending, revenue levels, and the resultant budget deficit (or surplus) for the coming fiscal year.

Bundling: A form of fundraising in which an individual persuades others to donate large amounts that are then delivered together to a candidate or campaign.

Bureaucratic pathologies: The problems that tend to develop in bureaucratic systems.

Call list: A long list of potential donors who candidates must phone.

Candidate-centered elections: A system in which individual candidates decide run, raise their own money, and design their own strategy—as opposed to party systems, in which political parties play these roles.

Caucus: A local meeting of voters to select candidates to represent a political party in a general election or to choose delegates who select candidates at a convention.

Central clearance: The OMB's authority to review and "clear" (or approve) anything a member of the administration says or does in public.

Central service agencies: The organizations that supply and staff the federal government.

Checks and balances: The principle that each branch of government has the authority to block the other branches, making it more difficult for any one branch or individual to exercise too much power. This system makes passing legislation far more difficult in the United States than in most other democracies.

Chicanismo: A defiant movement expressing pride in Latino origins and culture in the face of discrimination.

Chief of staff: The individual responsible for managing the president's office.

Circuit courts: The second stage of federal courts, which review the trial record of cases decided in district court to ensure they were settled properly.

Civic voluntarism: Citizen participation in public life without government incentives or coercion (speaking at a town meeting vs. paying taxes, for example).

Civil disobedience: Protesting laws one considers unjust by refusing to obey them—and accepting the punishment.

Civil law: Cases that involve disputes between two parties.

Civil liberties: The limits on government that allow people to freely exercise their rights.

Civil rights: The freedom to participate in the full life of the community—to vote, use public facilities, and exercise equal economic opportunity.

Civil Rights Act of 1964: Landmark legislation that forbade discrimination on the basis of race, sex, religion, or national origin.

Civil servants: Members of the permanent executive branch bureaucracy who are employed on the basis of competitive exams and keep their positions regardless of the presidential administration.

Class action: A lawsuit filed on behalf of an entire category of individuals, such as all public housing residents in a state or all female managers in a large company.

Classical republicanism: A democratic ideal, based in ancient Greece and Rome that calls on citizens to participate in public affairs, seek the public interest, shun private gain, and defer to natural leaders.

Clear and present danger: Court doctrine that permits restrictions of free speech if officials believe that the speech will lead to prohibited action such as violence or terrorism.

Clicktivism: Democratic engagement in an online age: point your mouse or scan a QR code, click, and you have donated funds, "liked" a candidate, or (in some states) even cast your vote.

Closed primary: A vote cast by party members to select candidates to represent the party in the general election.

Cloture vote: The Senate's only approved method for halting a filibuster or lifting a legislative hold. If sixty senators—three-fifths of the body, changed in 1975 from the original two-thirds—vote for cloture, the measure can proceed to a vote.

Commerce clause: The Constitutional declaration (in Article 1, Section 8) empowering Congress to regulate commerce with foreign nations, between states, and with Indian tribes.

Committee hearing: A way for committees to gather information and gauge members' support as legislative policymaking gets underway. Hearings usually feature witnesses who submit testimony, make an oral presentation, and answer questions from members of Congress.

Committee markup session: A gathering of a full committee to draft the final version of a bill before the committee votes on it.

Common law: A system of law developed by judges in deciding cases over the centuries.

Compact: A mutual agreement that provides for joint action to achieve defined goals.

Compromise of 1850: A complicated compromise over slavery that permitted territories to vote on whether they would be slave or free and permitted California to enter the Union as a free state. It also included a strict—and hugely controversial—fugitive slave law forcing Northerners to return black men and women into bondage.

Concurrent opinion: A statement that agrees with the majority opinion.

Concurrent powers: Governmental authority shared by national and state governments, such as the power to tax residents.

Confederation: A group of independent states or nations that yield some of their powers to a national government, although each state retains a degree of sovereign authority.

Conference committee: A special House–Senate committee that must reconcile the differences between House and Senate versions of the same bill.

Congressional caucus: A group of House or Senate members who convene regularly to discuss common interests; they may share political outlook, race, gender, or geography.

Conservatives: Americans who believe in reduced government spending, personal responsibility, traditional moral values, secure borders, and a strong national defense. Also known as right or right-wing.

Consolidation: The process whereby a media company grows, acquires other companies, and threatens to dominate the market.

Constitution: A statement of fundamental principles that governs a nation or an organization.

Containment: American Cold War strategy designed to stop the spread of communism.

Continuing resolution (CR): A congressionally approved act required when no national budget has been passed before the start of a new fiscal year. This extends spending at current levels for a prescribed period of time.

Cooperative federalism: Also called marble cake federalism, a system of mingled governing authority, with functions overlapping across national and state governments.

Cost-benefit analysis: A more complex study of the projected costs and benefits associated with a proposed policy.

Cost effectiveness: The projected costs of a proposed policy, as revealed by a relatively simple study.

Covenant: A compact invoking religious or moral authority.

Criminal law: Cases in which someone is charged with breaking the law.

Cycle of nonparticipation: Resistance by political parties to mobilizing disengaged Americans to vote—because their lack of involvement makes their allegiance to one or the other party suspect.

De facto discrimination: More subtle forms of discrimination that exist without a legal basis.

Defendant: The party who is sued in a court case.

De jure discrimination: Discrimination established by laws.

Delegated powers: Powers that Congress passes on to the president.

Delegate representation: Representatives follow the expressed wishes of the voters.

Democracy: A form of government in which the people hold power, either by acting directly or through elected representatives.

Demographic group: People sharing specific characteristics such as age, ethnicity/race, religion, or country of origin.

Devolution: The transfer of authority from the national to the state or local government level.

Diffusion: The spreading of policy ideas from one city or state to others; a process typical of U.S. federalism.

Din: Shorthand for the sheer volume of information and noise generated by online sources; can be a disincentive to participate politically.

Direct action: Participating outside of normal political and social channels through civil disobedience, demonstrations, and even riots.

Discretionary programs: Non-entitlement program spending, subject to the decision ("discretion") of Congress each year.

Disproportionate impact: The effect some policies have of discriminating, even if discrimination is not consciously intended.

Dissent: A statement on behalf of the justices who voted in the minority.

District courts: The first level of federal courts, which actually try the cases. Each decision is based not on a statute but on previous judicial decisions.

Divided government: Periods during which at least one house of Congress is controlled by a party different from the one occupying the White House.

Domestic dependent nation: Special status that grants local sovereignty to tribal nations but does not grant them full sovereignty equivalent to that enjoyed by independent nations.

Double jeopardy: The principle that an individual cannot be tried twice for the same offense.

Dred Scott v. Sandford: A landmark Supreme Court decision holding that black men could not be citizens under the Constitution of the United States. It created a national uproar.

Dual federalism: Also called layer cake federalism, the clear division of governing authority between national and state governments.

Earmark: A legislative item, usually included in spending ("appropriations") bills, that directs Congress to fund a particular item in one House member's district or a senator's state.

Economic equality: A situation in which there are small differences in wealth among citizens.

Electoral activities: Public engagement in the form of voting, running for office, volunteering in a campaign, or otherwise participating in elections.

Electoral bounce: The spike in the polls that follows an event such as a party's national convention.

Electoral College: The system established by the Constitution to elect the president; each state has a group of electors (equal in size to that of its congressional delegation in the House and the Senate); the public in each state votes for electors, who then vote for the president.

Emancipation Proclamation: An executive order issued by President Abraham Lincoln that declared the slaves in all rebel states to be free.

Entitlement program: A government benefit program whose recipients are *entitled* by law to receive payments. Social Security, Medicare, and Medicaid are the three largest.

Equal Employment Opportunity Commission (EEOC): Federal law enforcement agency charged with monitoring compliance with the Civil Rights Act.

Equality: All citizens enjoy the same privileges, status, and rights before the laws.

Equal opportunity: The idea that every American has the same chance to influence politics and achieve economic success.

Equal outcome: The idea that citizens should have roughly equal economic circumstances.

Equal protection of the laws: The landmark phrase in the Fourteenth Amendment that requires equal treatment for all citizens.

Equal Rights Amendment (ERA): An amendment, originally drafted by Alice Paul in 1923, passed by Congress in 1972, and ratified by thirty-five states, that declared: "Equality of rights . . . shall not be denied or abridged . . . on account of sex."

Establishment clause: The First Amendment principle that government may not establish an official religion.

Exclusionary rule: The ruling that evidence obtained in an illegal search may not be introduced in a trial.

Executive agreement: An international agreement made by the president that does not require the approval of the Senate.

Executive Office of the President (EOP): The agencies that help the president manage daily activities.

Executive order: A presidential declaration, with the force of law, that issues instructions to the executive branch without any requirement for congressional action or approval.

Executive privilege: Power claimed by the president to resist requests for authority by Congress, the courts, or the public. Not mentioned in the Constitution but based on the separation of powers.

Expressed powers: Powers the Constitution explicitly grants to the president.

Expressive benefits: Values or deeply held beliefs that inspire individuals to join a public interest group.

Fairness doctrine: Regulation that required media outlets to devote equal time to opposite perspectives.

Fair trade: Trade that emphasizes the inclusion of environmental and labor protections in agreements so that nations do not receive unfair advantages by exploiting workers or harming the environment.

Fake news: The deliberate spread of falsehood or misinformation—often a charge made by politicians facing unfavorable stories.

Federal budget deficit: The gap between revenues received by the national government (primarily through individual income and corporate taxes) and spending on all public programs.

Federalism: Power divided between national and state government. Each has its own sovereignty (independent authority) and its own duties.

Federal poverty line: The annually specified level of income (separately calculated for individuals and families) below which people are considered to live in poverty, and eligible for certain federal benefits. For 2019, the poverty line is set at $25,100 for a family of four.

Federal Regulation of Lobbying Act: The initial U.S. statute spelling out requirements on lobbyists active in Congress, which was passed in 1946.

Fighting words: Expressions inherently likely to provoke violent reactions and not necessarily protected by the First Amendment.

Filibuster: Rule unique to the U.S. Senate that allows any senator to hold the floor indefinitely and thereby delay a vote on a bill to which he or she objects. Ended only when sixty senators vote for cloture.

Final rule: The rule that specifies how a program will actually operate.

First Continental Congress: A convention of delegates from twelve of the thirteen colonies that met in 1774.

Fiscal policy: Taxing and spending policies carried out by government, generally in an effort to affect national economic development.

Fiscal year (FY): In budget calculations, the "new year" beginning October 1 and ending the following September 30. Organized many decades ago for accounting purposes.

Floor: The full chamber, either in the House of Representatives or the Senate. A bill "goes to the floor" for the final debate and vote, usually after approval by one or more committees.

Focusing event: A major happening, often of crisis or disaster proportions, that attracts widespread media attention to an issue.

Framing: The way an issue is defined; every issue has many possible frames, each with a slightly different tilt in describing the problem and highlighting solutions.

Framing effects: The way the wording of a polling question influences a respondent

Freedom: The ability to pursue one's own desires without interference from others.

Freedom of Information Act (FOIA): A 1966 law that facilitates full or partial disclosure of government information and documents.

Freedom Riders: Black and white activists who rode buses together to protest segregation on interstate bus lines.

Free exercise clause: The First Amendment principle that government may not interfere in religious practice.

Free rider problem: A barrier to group or collective action arising because people who do not participate still reap the benefits.

Free trade: Goods and services moving across international boundaries without government interference.

Full faith and credit clause: The constitutional requirement (in Article 4, Section 1) that each state recognizes and upholds laws passed by any other state.

Gerrymander: Redraw an election district in a way that gives the advantage to one party.

Gift ban: A regulation that eliminates (or sharply reduces the permitted dollar amount of) gifts from interest groups to lawmakers.

Going public: Directly addressing the public to win support for oneself or one's ideas.

Grand jury: A jury that does not decide on guilt or innocence but only on whether there is enough evidence for the case to go to trial.

Grand Old Party (GOP): Longstanding nickname for the Republican Party; ironically, bestowed early in the party's history, in the 1870s.

Grand strategy: An overarching vision that defines and guides a nation's foreign policy.

Grants-in-aid: National government funding provided to state and local governments, along with specific instructions about how the funds may be used.

Great Migration: The vast movement of African Americans from the rural South to the urban North between 1910 and the 1960s.

Gross domestic product (GDP): The value of all the goods and services produced in a nation over a year. For 2019, the U.S. GDP is an estimated $21.4 trillion.

Groupthink: The tendency among a small group of decision makers to converge on a shared set of views; can limit creative thinking or solutions to policy problems.

Hate speech: Hostile statements based on someone's personal characteristics, such as race, ethnicity, religion, or sexual orientation.

Hyperpluralism: The collective effect of the vast number of interest groups in slowing the process of American democratic policymaking.

Imperial presidency: A characterization of the American presidency that suggests it is demonstrating imperial traits, and that the republic is morphing into an empire.

Incorporation: The process by which the Supreme Court declares that a right in the Bill of Rights also applies to state governments.

Incumbency advantage: The tendency for members of Congress to win reelection in overwhelming numbers.

Indentured servant: A colonial American settler contracted to work for a fixed period (usually three to seven years) in exchange for food, shelter, and transportation to the New World.

Individualism: The idea that individuals, not the society, are responsible for their own well-being.

Information shortcuts: Cues about candidates and policies drawn from everyday life.

Infotainment: The blurred line between news and entertainment.

Inherent powers: Powers that, although neither specified or implied by the Constitution are necessary for the

President or Congress to fulfil their duties.

Inherent powers of the presidency: Powers assumed by presidents, often during a crisis, on the basis of the constitutional phrase "The executive power shall be vested in the president."

Initiative: A process in which citizens propose new laws or amendments to the state constitution.

Institutions: The organizations, norms, and rules that structure government and public action.

Interest group: An organization whose goal is to influence government.

Intergovernmental lobbying: Attempts by officials in one part of the government to influence their counterparts in another branch, or at a different (state or local) level.

Internationalism: The belief that national interests are best served by actively engaging and working with other nations around the world.

Iron triangle: The cozy relationship in one issue area among interest-group lobbyists, congressional staffers, and executive branch agencies.

Isolationism: The doctrine that a nation should avoid all foreign-policy commitments and alliances and withdraw from world affairs.

Issue advocacy: Organized effort to advance (or block) a proposed public policy change.

Issue campaign: A concerted effort by interest groups to arouse popular support or opposition for a policy issue.

Issue network: Shifting alliances of public and private interest groups, lawmakers, and other stakeholders all focused on the same policy area.

Jim Crow: The system of racial segregation in the U.S. South that lasted from 1890 to 1965, and that was often violently enforced.

Judicial activism: A vigorous or active approach to reviewing the other branches of government.

Judicial restraint: Reluctance to interfere with elected branches, only doing so as a last resort.

Judicial review: The Court's authority to determine whether legislative, executive, and state actions violate the Constitution and overrule those that do.

Judicial rules: Hard-and-fast boundaries between what is lawful and what is not.

Judicial standards: Guiding principles that help governments make judgment calls.

K Street: A major street in downtown Washington, DC, that is home to the headquarters for many lobbying firms and advocacy groups—and thus synonymous with interest-group lobbying.

Legislative hold: An informal way for a senator to object to a bill or other measure reaching the Senate floor. The action effectively halts Senate proceedings on that issue, sometimes for weeks or longer.

Liberalism: A doctrine that views nation–states as benefiting most from mutual cooperation, aided by international organizations.

Liberals: Americans who value cultural diversity, government programs for the needy, public intervention in the economy, and individuals' right to a lifestyle based on their own social and moral positions. Also known as left or left-wing.

Likely voters: Persons identified as probable voters in an upcoming election. Often preferred by polling organizations, but difficult to specify with great accuracy.

Literacy test: A requirement that voters exhibit an ability to read; in reality, a way to restrict black suffrage.

Litigation: The conduct of a lawsuit.

Lobbying coalition: A collection of lobbyists working on related topics or a specific legislative proposal.

Lobbyist: A person who contacts government officials on behalf of a particular cause or issue.

Lochner era: A period from 1905 to 1937, during which the Supreme Court struck down laws (e.g., worker protection or minimum wage laws) that were thought to infringe on economic liberty or the right to contract.

Loud signal: Media stories with very broad coverage and an unambiguous message.

Majority opinion: The official statement of the Supreme Court (or district courts, since they also have multiple justices).

Mandate: Political authority claimed by an election winner as reflecting the approval of the people.

Margin of sampling error: The degree of inaccuracy in any poll, arising from the fact that surveys involve a sample of respondents from a population, rather than every member.

Mass media: Information and entertainment for broad popular audiences including newspapers, magazines, radio, and television.

Material benefits: Items distributed by public interest groups as incentives to sign up or remain a member.

Median: A statistical term for the number in the middle or the case that has an equal number of examples above and below it.

Mediation: A way of resolving disputes without going to court, in which a third party (the mediator) helps two or more sides negotiate a settlement.

Mercantilism: An economic theory according to which government controls foreign trade to maintain prosperity and security.

Midterm elections: National elections held between presidential elections, involving all seats in the House of Representatives, one-third of those in the Senate, 36 governorships, and other positions.

Midterm loss: The president's party loses Congressional seats during the midterm elections. This has occurred in most midterm elections.

Millennials: Americans born between 1983 and 2001. Though very large (some 80 million people) and diverse, millennials tend to share certain characteristics, including political outlook.

Miller test: Three-part test for judging whether a work is obscene (if it has all three, the work loses First Amendment protection).

Miranda warnings: A set of rights that police officers are required to inform suspects of, including the right to remain silent.

Missouri Compromise: An agreement to open southern territories west of the Mississippi to slavery while closing northern territories to slavery.

Monetary policy: Actions of central banks, which in the United States culminate in the Federal Reserve, designed primarily to maximize employment and moderate inflation.

Motor voter law: Passed in 1993, this act enables prospective voters to register when they receive their driver's license.

Multilateralism: A doctrine that emphasizes operating together with other nations to pursue common goals.

Multilateral organization: An international organization of three or more nations organized around a common goal.

Name recognition: An advantage possessed by a well-known political figure, a political celebrity.

National Association for the Advancement of Colored People (NAACP): A civil rights organization formed in 1909 and dedicated to racial equality.

National Organization for Women (NOW): An organization formed in 1966 to take action for women's equality.

Necessary and proper clause: The constitutional declaration (in Article 1, Section 8) that defines Congress's constitutional authority to exercise the "necessary and proper" powers to carry out its designated functions.

Negative campaigning: Running for office by attacking the opponent.

Negative liberty: Freedom from constraints or the interference of others.

New Deal: Broad series of economic programs and reforms introduced between 1933 and 1936 and associated with the Franklin Roosevelt administration.

New federalism: A version of cooperative federalism, but with stronger emphasis on state and local government activity versus national government.

New Jersey Plan: Put forward at the Constitutional Convention by the small states, this plan left most government authority with the state governments.

The New Jim Crow: The idea that mass incarceration of African Americans has the sweeping effects of Jim Crow discrimination laws. The term is the title of a book by Michelle Alexander.

New media: On-demand access to information through digital devices that increasingly feature interactive participation with content.

Nonattitudes: The lack of a stable perspective in response to opinion surveys; answers to questions may be self-contradictory or may display no ideological consistency.

Nonpartisan election: An election in which candidates run as individuals, without any party affiliation. Many towns and cities feature nonpartisan elections.

Open primary: a vote cast by any eligible voter to select candidates to represent the party in the general election.

Open seat: A seat in Congress without an incumbent running for reelection.

Opinion poll: Systematic study of a defined population, analyzing a representative sample's views to draw inferences about the larger public's views. Also termed *survey research*.

Originalism: A principle of legal interpretation that relies on the original meaning of those who wrote the Constitution.

Overhead democracy: A system by which the people elect the president, who, through their appointees, controls the bureaucracy from the top.

Override: The process by which Congress can overcome a presidential veto with a two-thirds vote in both chambers.

Paradox of voting: For most individuals, the cost of voting (acquiring necessary information, traveling to polling site, and waiting in line) outweighs the apparent benefits. Economic theory would predict very low voter turnout, given this analysis.

Partisanship: Taking the side of a party or espousing a viewpoint that reflects a political party's principles or position on an issue.

Party boss: The senior figure in a party machine.

Party caucus: A meeting of all House or Senate members of one or the other main party, usually to discuss political and policy strategies.

Party identification: Strong attachment to one political party, often established at an early age.

Party in government: The portion of a political party's organization that comprises elected officials and candidates for office.

Party in the electorate: The largest (and least organized) component of a political party, drawn from the public at large: registered members and regular supporters.

Party machine: A hierarchical arrangement of party workers, often organized in an urban area to help integrate immigrants and minority groups into the political system. Most active in the late nineteenth and early twentieth centuries.

Party organization: The portion of a political party that includes activists, state/local leaders, and affiliated professionals such as fundraisers and public relations experts.

Party platform: The written statement of a party's core convictions and issue priorities. Generally revised every four years, in time for the national party convention.

Party system: The broad organization of U.S. politics comprising the two main parties, the coalition of supporters backing each, the positions they take on major issues, and each party's electoral achievements.

Path dependence: Social-science term for how policymakers' choices are shaped by institutional "paths" that result from policy choices made in the past.

Pendleton Civil Service Act: The law that shifted American government toward a merit-based public service.

Personal presidency: The idea that the president has a personal link to the public. Made initially possible by twentieth century media.

Plaintiff: The party who brings the action in a lawsuit.

Plessy v. Ferguson: An 1896 Supreme Court case that permitted racial segregation.

Pluralism: An open, participatory style of government in which many different interests are represented.

Policy agenda: The issues that the media covers, the public considers important, and politicians address. Setting the agenda is the first step in political action.

Policy window: A figurative description of the opportunity—often brief, measured in days or weeks rather than years—to pass a bill in Congress or a state legislature.

Political action committee (PAC): An organization of at least fifty people, affiliated with an interest group that is permitted to make contributions to candidates for federal office.

Political appointees: Top officials in the executive agencies, appointed by the president.

Political culture: The orientation of citizens of a state toward politics.

Political elites: Individuals who control significant wealth, status, power, or visibility and consequently have significant influence over public debates.

Political equality: All citizens have the same political rights and opportunities.

Political mobilization: Efforts to encourage people to engage in the public sphere: to vote for a particular candidate (or donate money, work on the campaign, etc.) or to get involved in specific issues.

Political order: The set of institutions, interests, and ideas that shape a political era. Great presidents reconstruct the framework, launching a new order.

Political party: a group that shares political principles and is organized to win elections and hold power.

Political socialization: Education about how the government works and which policies one should support; provided by parents, peers, schools, parties, and other national institutions.

Political voice: Exercising one's public rights, often through speaking out in protest or in favor of some policy change.

Positive liberty: The ability—and provision of basic necessities—to pursue one's goals.

Power elite theory: The view that a small handful of wealthy, influential Americans exercises extensive control over government decisions.

Pragmatism: A principle of legal interpretation based on the idea that the Constitution evolves and that interpretations of the Constitution must be framed in the context of contemporary realities.

Precedent: A judicial decision that offers a guide to similar cases in the future.

Preemption: The invalidation of a U.S. state law that conflicts with federal law.

Preemptive war: The effort to attack hostile powers before they launch attacks. Highly controversial because it sanctions striking first.

President pro tempore: Majority party senator with the longest Senate service.

Primacy: The doctrine asserting that the United States should maintain an unrivaled military.

Priming: Affecting public perceptions of political leaders, candidates, or issues by reporting on topics in ways that either enhance or diminish support.

Principal-agent theory: Details how policymakers (principals) control the actors who work for them (agents)—but who have far more information than they do.

Prior restraint: Legal effort to stop speech before it occurs.

Private contractors: Private companies that contract to provide goods and services for the government.

Progressive federalism: Approach that gives state officials considerable leeway in achieving national programs and goals.

Proportional representation: The allocation of votes or delegates on the basis of the percentage of the vote received; contrasts with the winner-take-all system.

Proposed rule: A draft of administrative regulations published in the *Federal Register* for the purpose of gathering comments from interested parties.

Protectionism: Efforts to protect local business from foreign competition.

Public ownership: A situation in which media outlets are run by the government and paid for by tax dollars.

Public–private partnership: A government program or service provided through the joint efforts of private sector actors (usually businesses) and public officials.

Public watchdog: Media coverage that alerts the public when a problem arises in politics or society.

Push poll: A form of negative campaigning that masquerades as a regular opinion survey. They usually feature unflattering information about an opponent.

Quasi-suspect category: A legal standard that requires governments to have an important state purpose for any legislation that singles out sex or gender. This is not as strong as the suspect category, which requires strict scrutiny.

Racial profiling: A law enforcement practice of singling out people on the basis of physical features such as race or ethnicity.

Random sample: A sample in which everyone in the population (sampling frame) has an equal probability of being selected.

Rational-choice theory: An approach to political behavior that views individuals as rational, decisive actors who know their political interests and seek to act on them.

Realism: A doctrine holding that nation–states seek to amass power to ensure their self-preservation.

Reapportionment: Reorganization of the boundaries of House districts, a process that follows the results of the U.S. census, taken every ten years. District lines are redrawn to ensure rough equality in the number of constituents represented by each House member.

Reconstruction: The failed effort, pursued by Northerners and Southerners, to rebuild the South and establish racial equality after the Civil War.

Referendum: An election in which citizens vote directly on an issue.

Reframing the issue: To redefine the popular perception of an issue.

Regulatory capture: The theory that industries dominate the agencies that regulate them.

Republic: A government in which citizens rule indirectly and make government decisions through their elected representatives.

Reserved powers: The constitutional guarantee (in the Tenth Amendment) that the states retain government authority not explicitly granted to the national government.

Response bias: The tendency of poll respondents to misstate their views frequently to avoid "shameful" opinions that might appear sexist or racist.

Reverse lobbying: Attempts by government officials to influence interest groups on behalf of their preferred policies.

Revolving door: The tendency of many Washington lobbyists to move from government work (e.g., as a Congressional or White House advisor) to lobbying and back again.

Roll-call vote: A congressional vote in which each member's vote is recorded, either by roll call (Senate) or electronically (House).

Rule of four: The requirement that at least four Supreme Court judges must agree to hear a case before it comes before the Court.

Safe district: a district consisting of voters who have historically voted for one party over the other by a large majority.

Sampling frame: A designated group of people from whom a set of poll respondents is randomly selected.

School busing: An effort to integrate public schools by mixing students from different neighborhoods.

Second Continental Congress: A convention of delegates from the thirteen colonies that became the acting national government for the duration of the Revolutionary War.

Section 504: An obscure provision in an obscure rehabilitation act that required all institutions that received federal funds to accommodate people with disabilities.

Security trap: The idea that using military force creates multiple, often unforeseen, problems.

Selective incorporation: The extension of protections from the Bill of Rights to the state governments, one liberty at a time.

Self-rule: The idea that legitimate government flows from the people.

Seneca Falls Convention: The first convention dedicated to women's rights, held in July 1848 in Seneca Falls, NY.

Signing statements: Written presidential declarations commenting on the bill that is being signed into law—often including criticism of one or more provisions.

Social capital: Relations between people that build closer ties of trust and civic engagement, yielding productive benefits for the larger society.

Social democracy: the idea that government policy should ensure that all are comfortably cared for within the context of a capitalist economy.

Social equality: All individuals enjoy the same status in society.

Soft power: The influence a nation exerts through culture and commerce; a contrast to attempted Solidarity benefits: The feeling of shared commitment and purpose experienced by individuals who join a public interest group.

Solidarity benefits: The feeling of shared commitment and purpose experienced by individuals who join a public interest group.

Sound bite: A short audio clip; often refers to a brief excerpt from a politician's speech.

Speaker of the House: The chief administrative officer in the House of Representatives.

Special interest: A pejorative term, often used to designate an interest group whose aims or issue preferences one does not share.

Split-ticket voter: Votes for at least one candidate from each party, dividing his or her ballot between the two (or more) parties.

Spoils system: A system in which government jobs are given out as political favors.

Stare decisis: Deciding cases on the basis of previous rulings or precedents.

Straight-ticket voter: Votes for the same party for all offices on a ballot.

Strategic disengagement: The doctrine that a nation should not interfere in other nations' affairs unless such involvement clearly advances its own interests.

Street-level bureaucrats: Public officials who deal directly with the public.

Strict scrutiny: The standard by which courts judge any legislation that singles out race or ethnicity.

Strict separation: The strict principles articulated in the Lemon test for judging whether a law establishes a religion. (See "accommodation.")

Sunshine laws: Laws that permit the public to watch policymakers in action and to access the records of the proceedings.

Supermajority: An amount higher than a simple majority (50% plus one)—typically, three-fifths or two-thirds of the voters.

Super PACs: Organizations that raise and spend unlimited amounts of money to promote a candidate or publicize a cause. However, they may not directly contribute to a candidate or coordinate with a campaign.

Super Tuesday: The date on the presidential primary calendar when multiple states hold primaries and caucuses.

Supremacy clause: The constitutional declaration (in Article 6, Section 2) that the national government's authority prevails over any conflicting state or local government's claims, provided the power is granted to the federal government.

Symbolic expression: An act, rather than actual speech, used to demonstrate a point of view.

Telecommunications Act of 1996: A major overhaul of communications law that opened the door to far more competition by permitting companies to own outlets in multiple media markets such as radio, television, and magazines, and removing or reducing limits on how many outlets one company can own.

Theory of democratic peace: Theory that strongly democratic nations are less prone to engage in wars with one another.

Time, place, and manner clause: The constitutional clause that delegates control of elections to the state governments.

Trade association: An organized group representing individuals and businesses that belong to the same industry.

Trade deficit: The deficit arising when a nation imports (or buys) more goods from foreign nations than it exports (or sells) to them.

Traditional participation: Engaging in political activities through the formal channels of government and society.

Trustee representation: Representatives do what they regard as being in the best interest of their constituents—even if constituents do not agree.

Unanimous consent: A Senate requirement, applied to most of that body's business, that all senators agree before an action can proceed.

Underdog effect: Sympathy for a candidate behind in the polls, contributing to a higher-than-predicted vote total—and sometimes a surprise election victory.

Unfunded mandate: An obligation imposed on state or local government officials by federal legislation without sufficient federal funding support to cover the costs.

Unicameral: Having a single legislative house or chamber.

Unilateralism: A doctrine that holds that the United States should act independently of other nations. It should decide what is best for itself—not in coordination with partners and allies.

Unitary executive theory: The idea that the Constitution puts the president in charge of executing the laws and that therefore no other branch may limit presidential discretion over executive matters.

Unitary government: A national polity governed as a single unit, with the central government exercising all or most political authority.

Universalistic politics: A government run according to transparent rules, impartially applied.

United Farm Workers (UFW): An influential union representing migrant farm workers in the west.

USA Patriot Act: Legislation that sought to enhance national security, passed in the aftermath of the September 11, 2001, terrorist attacks.

Veto: The constitutional procedure by which a president can prevent enactment of legislation passed by Congress.

Veto power: The presidential power to block an act of Congress by refusing to sign—and returning it to Congress with objections.

Virginia Plan: Madison's plan, embraced by the Constitutional Convention delegates from larger states; this plan strengthened the national government relative to state governments.

Voice vote: A congressional vote in which the presiding officer asks those for and against to say "yea" or "nay," respectively, and announces the result. No record is kept of House or Senate members voting on each side.

Voter turnout: A measure of which proportion of eligible voters actually cast a legitimate ballot in a given election.

War Powers Act: Legislation passed in 1973 to increase congressional involvement in undeclared wars. It requires Congress to approve military action undertaken by the president in no more than 60 days.

Watergate scandal: A failed effort in 1972 by Republican operatives to break into Democratic Party headquarters in the Watergate office complex in Washington, DC. President Nixon tried to cover up the event—eventually causing him to resign from the presidency.

Whistleblower: A federal worker who reports corruption or fraud.

Winner-take-all: The candidate receiving a simple majority (or, among multiple candidates, a plurality) receives all electoral votes or primary delegates. Sometimes called "first-past-the-post."

World Trade Organization (WTO): An international organization that oversees efforts to open markets and promote free trade.

Notes

Chapter 1 Ideas That Shape American Politics

1. Russell A. Burgos, "An N of One: A Political Scientist in Operation Iraqi Freedom," *Perspectives on Politics* 2, no. 3 (2004): 551–56.
2. John Gramlich, "How Countries Around the World View Democracy, Military Rule and Other Political Systems," Pew Research Center, October 30, 2017, http://www.pewresearch.org/fact-tank/2017/10/30/global-views-political-systems/
3. Matt Egan, "Record Inequality: The top 1% controls 38.6% of America's Wealth," *CNN Money*, September 27, 2017, http://money.cnn.com/2017/09/27/news/economy/inequality-record-top-1-percent-wealth/index.html.
4. Pew Research Center, "Most See Inequality Growing, but Partisans Differ over Solutions, January 23, 2014, http://www.people-press.org/2014/01/23/most-see-inequality-growing-but-partisans-differ-over-solutions/.
5. Rasmussen Reports, "Americans Want Christmas, More Religion in Schools," December 15, 2015, http://www.rasmussenreports.com/public_content/lifestyle/holidays/december_2015/americans_want_christmas_more_religion_in_schools.
6. RealClear Politics, "Congressional Job Approval," https://www.realclearpolitics.com/epolls/other/congressional_job_approval-903.html.
7. Harold D. Lasswell, *Politics: Who Gets What, When, and How*, rev. ed. (New York: Smith Books, 1990).
8. Keith Humphreys, "Young People Are Committing much Less Crime. Older People Are Still Behaving As Badly As Before," *Washington Post*, September 7, 2016, http://wapo.st/2FRNCwA; Bradley Depew, "How Millennials Have Disrupted Charitable Giving," *The Balance*, May 29, 2017, http://bit.ly/2dWCoZV;

Malcolm Harris, *Kids These Days: Human Capital and the Making of Millennials* (Boston: Little, Brown, 2017).
9. Simon Schama, *Rough Crossings: Britain, the Slaves, and the American Revolution* (New York: HarperCollins, 2006).
10. Isaiah Berlin, "Two Concepts of Liberty," in *Liberty*, ed. Henry Hardy (Oxford: Oxford University Press, 2002), 166–217.
11. Samuel Huntington, *American Politics: The Promise of Disharmony* (Cambridge, MA: Harvard University Press, 1981).
12. Quoted in James A. Morone, *The Democratic Wish: Popular Participation and the Limits of American Government* (New Haven, CT: Yale University Press, 1998), 54.
13. Thomas Jefferson, "Response to the Citizens of Albemarle," February 12, 1790, in Jefferson, *Writings*, ed. Merrill D. Peterson (New York: Library of America, 2011); First Inaugural Address, March 4, 1801. Jefferson's first inaugural is the best summary of what we now call Jeffersonian democracy.
14. James Madison, *Federalist* no. 10. The quote is from Roger Sherman, recorded in Madison's "Notes of Debates," in *The Federal Convention and the Formation of the Union*, ed. Winston Solberg (Indianapolis, IN: Bobbs Merrill, 1958), 84–85.
15. Michael Kammen, *People of Paradox* (New York: Knopf, 1972), 31.
16. John Kingdon, *America the Unusual* (New York: St. Martin's Press, 1999), 1.
17. Martin Luther King Jr., Speech given at Ohio Northern University, January 11, 1968, http://www.onu.edu/node/28513.
18. Milton Friedman, *Capitalism and Freedom* (Chicago: University of Chicago Press, 1962).

19. The original statement of this theory is by Louis Hartz, *The Liberal Tradition in America* (New York: Harcourt, Brace, and World, 1955). The Theoretical foundations of this view lie in Alexis de Tocqueville, *Democracy in America*, trans. George Lawrence (Garden City, NY: Doubleday, 1969)
20. See Noel Ignatiev, *How the Irish Became White*, 2nd ed. (New York: Routledge, 2009).
21. Franklin quotes taken from *Poor Richard's Almanac*; see http://www.ushistory.org/franklin/quotable/.
22. James Truslow Adams, *The Epic of America* (New York: Taylor & Francis, 1938).
23. Quoted in Jennifer Hochschild, *Facing Up to the American Dream* (Princeton, NJ: Princeton University Press, 1995), vi, 18.
24. Gordon Wood, *The Radicalism of the American Revolution* (New York: Knopf, 1992), 369.
25. Bureau of Labor Statistics, "Measuring Wage Inequality in and Across U.S. Metropolitan Areas, 2003–13," *Monthly Labor Review* (September 2015): 1.
26. Timothy Noah, *The Great Divergence: America's Growing Inequality Crisis and What We Can Do About It* (New York: Bloomsbury, 2012).
27. Roosevelt quoted in James Morone, *Hellfire Nation* (New Haven, CT: Yale University Press, 2004), 347. Tom Krattenmaker, *The Evangelicals You Don't Know: Introducing the Next Generation of Christians* (Lanham, MD: Roman and Littlefield, 2013).
28. Johnson quoted in Morone, *Hellfire Nation*, 427.
29. Pew Research, "Political Typology Reveals Deep Fissures on the Right and Left," October 24, 2017, http://pewrsr.ch/2zzfX6p.
30. Harvard Kennedy School Institute of Politics, "Survey of Young

Americans' Attitudes toward Politics and Public Service 34th Edition, October 31–November 10, 2017," November 2017, http://iop.harvard.edu/sites/default/files/content/docs/171128_Harvard%20IOP_Fall%202017%20Topline.pdf. (The survey is conducted every two years.)

31. Alexis de Tocqueville, *Democracy in America*, trans. George Lawrence (Garden City, NY: Doubleday, 1969), 1:9.

32. Hugh Brogan, *Alexis de Tocqueville: A Life* (New Haven, CT: Yale University Press, 2007), 352.

33. George Gao, "15 Striking Findings from 2015," Pew Research Center, December 22, 2015, http://www.pewresearch.org/fact-tank/2015/12/22/15-striking-findings-from-2015/.

34. See Robert Putnam and David Campbell, *American Grace: How Religion Divides and Unites Us* (New York: Simon & Schuster, 2010); David Masci, "Why Millennials Are Less Religious than Older Americans," Pew Research Center, January 8, 2016, http://pewrsr.ch/1Rymao7.

35. See Putnam and David Campbell, *American Grace: How Religion Divides and Unites Us* (New York: Simon & Schuster, 2010) and David Masci, "Why Millennials Are Less Religious than Older Americans," Pew Research Center, January 8, 2016, http://pewrsr.ch/1Rymao7.

36. Eileen W. Lindner, ed., *Yearbook of American & Canadian Churches* (Washington, DC: National Council of Churches, 2013).

37. Pew Research, Religion and Public Life Project, "Religious Landscape Study," http://religions.pewforum.org/.

38. Pew Charitable Trusts, "Millennials in Adulthood," March 7, 2014, http://www.pewsocialtrends.org/2014/03/07/millennials-in-adulthood/.

39. Clifford Geertz, *The Interpretation of Cultures* (New York: Basic Books, 1973).

40. James A Morone, "Is There an American Political Culture?," in *The Devils We Know: Us and Them in America's Raucous Political Culture*, ed. James Morone (Lawrence: University of Kansas Press, 2014): 1–30

41. Madison, *Federalist* no. 10.

Chapter 2 The Constitution

1. Taylor Branch, *Parting the Waters: America in the King Years 1954–63* (New York: Simon & Schuster, 1989).

2. Edmund Burke, "Speech to the Bristol Electors," in *Representation*, ed. Hannah Pitkin (New York: Atherton Press, 1969), 175–76.

3. See James A Morone, *The Democratic Wish* (New Haven: Yale University Press, 1998), chap. 1

4. Robert Middlekauff, *The Glorious Cause* (New York: Oxford University Press, 1982), 74.

5. Bernard Bailyn, David Brion Davis, David Herbert Donald, John Thomas, Robert Wiebe, and Gordon Wood, *The Great Republic: A History of the American People* (Boston: Little, Brown, 1977), 1:256.

6. Middlekauff, *Glorious Cause*, 223–28, quotation on 226.

7. See David Hackett Fischer, *Washington's Crossing* (New York: Oxford University Press, 2004), 384–85.

8. David Brion Davis, *The Problem of Slavery in the Age of Revolution* (New York: Oxford University Press, 1999).

9. Gordon Wood, *The Creation of the American Republic* (Chapel Hill: University of North Carolina Press, 1969), 404.

10. Rogan Kersh, *Dreams of a More Perfect Union* (Ithaca, NY: Cornell University Press, 2001), 60–67.

11. Quoted in Gordon Wood, *Empire of Liberty* (New York: Oxford University Press, 2009), 14.

12. Richard Beeman, *Plain, Honest Men: The Making of the American Constitution* (New York: Random House, 2009), 3–7.

13. Beeman, *Plain, Honest Men*, 12.

14. Leonard Richards, *Shays's Rebellion: The American Revolution's Final Battle* (Philadelphia: University of Pennsylvania Press, 2002).

15. Beeman, *Plain, Honest Men*, 84.

16. Elbridge Gerry of Massachusetts, quoted in James Madison, "Madison's Notes of Debates," in *The Federal Convention and the Formation of the Union*, ed. Winston Solberg (Indianapolis, IN: Bobbs Merrill, 1958), 84–85.

17. Ibid., 81.

18. Ibid.

19. Ibid., 122 ["swallowed up"]; David Brian Robertson, *The Constitution and America's Destiny* (New York: Cambridge University Press, 2005), 139.

20. Robertson, *The Constitution and America's Destiny*, 140.

21. Francis Fukuyama, "American Political Dysfunction." *The American Interest*. November/December, 2011. http://cf.linnbenton.edu/artcom/social_science/clarkd/upload/American%20Political%20Dysfunction%20Francis%20Fukuyama.pdf

22. John Dickinson, "Notes for a Speech," quoted in Max Farrand's *The Records of the Federal Convention of 1787*, ed. James H. Hutson (New Haven, CT: Yale University Press, 1987), 158.

23. Beeman, *Plain, Honest Men*, 333.

24. Ford in *Congressional Record*, 116 (1970), p. 11913.

25. Herbert Storing, *What the Anti-Federalists Were For: The Political Writings of the Opponents of the Constitution* (Chicago: University of Chicago Press, 1981).

26. Thomas Jefferson, "Letter to Samuel Kercheval, July 12, 1816," in *The Works of Thomas Jefferson*, ed. Paul Leicester Ford (New York: Putnam, 1905), 12:13–14.

27. Robert Dahl, *How Democratic Is the American Constitution?*, 2nd ed. (New Haven, CT: Yale University Press, 2003).

Chapter 3 Federalism and Nationalism

1. Peter Haden, "West Palm Beach Declares Itself 'Welcoming City' For Immigrants," WLRN, March 28, 2017, http://wlrn.org/post/west-palm-beach-declares-itself-welcoming-city-immigrants.

2. Christina Littlefield, "Sanctuary Cities: How Kathryn Steinle's Death Intensified the Immigration Debate," *Los Angeles Times*, July 24, 2015, http://www.latimes.com/local/california/

la-me-immigration-sanctuary-kath-ryn-steinle-20150723-htmlstory.html.

3. David Goodhart, "The Road to Somewhere: The New Tribes Shaping British Politics (London: Penguin UK, 2017).

4. U.S. Census, American Fact Finder Community Facts, Count of Governments (2012), https://factfinder.census.gov/faces/nav/jsf/pages/community_facts.xhtml.

5. U.S. Census, American Fact Finder Community Facts, Federal Government Civilian Employment and Payroll Data (March 2012), https://factfinder.census.gov/faces/tableservices/jsf/pages/productview.xhtml?src=CF.

6. Justin McCarthy, "Americans Still More Trusting in Local Over State Government," Gallup, September 19, 2016, http://news.gallup.com/poll/195656/americans-trusting-local-state-government.aspx; Pew Research Center, "Public Trust in Government: 1958–2017," December 14, 2017, http://www.people-press.org/2017/12/14/public-trust-in-government-1958-2017/.

7. McCarthy, "Americans Still More Trusting."

8. David Brian Robertson, *Federalism and the Making of America* (New York: Routledge, 2012).

9. From Justice Brandeis's dissenting opinion in *New State Ice Co. v. Liebmann*, 285 U.S. 262, 311 (1932).

10. Skocpol, *Protecting Soldiers and Mothers*, 9 (see chap. 1, note 30).

11. James Buchanan and Gordon Tullock, *The Calculus of Consent* (Ann Arbor: University of Michigan Press, 1962), 144.

12. William Berry, Richard Fording, and Russell Hanson, "Reassessing the Race to the Bottom in State Welfare Policy," *Journal of Politics* 65, no. 2 (2003): 327–49.

13. James Morone, *Hellfire Nation: The Politics of Sin in American History* (New Haven, CT: Yale University Press, 2003), part 3.

14. Dirksen quoted in Richard P. Nathan, "Updating Theories of American Federalism," in *Intergovernmental Management for the Twenty-First Century*, ed. Timothy Conlan and Paul Posner (Washington, DC: Brookings Institution Press, 2008), 15.

15. Timothy Conlan and Paul Posner, "American Federalism in an Era of Partisan Polarization: The Intergovernmental Paradox of Obama's New Federalism," *Publius: The Journal of Federalism* 46, no. 3 (2016): 281–307.

16. Quoted in Robert Dreyfuss, "Grover Norquist: 'Field Marshal' of the Bush Plan," *The Nation*, May 14, 2001.

17. *McCulloch v. Maryland*, 17 U.S. 316 (1819).

18. Robert Taylor, Mary-Jo Kline, and Greg L. Lint, eds., *Papers of John Adams* (Cambridge, MA: Harvard University Press, 1980), 3:141.

19. John R. Hibbing and Elizabeth Theiss-Morse, *Stealth Democracy: Americans' Beliefs About How Government Should Work* (New York: Cambridge University Press, 2002).

20. For the classic description of nineteenth-century community activity, see Tocqueville, *Democracy in America* (chap. 1, note 22).

Chapter 4 Civil Liberties

1. Allison Stranger, "Understanding the Angry Mob that Gave Me a Concussion," *New York Times*, March 13, 2017.

2. *Matal v. Tam*, 582 U.S. ___ (2017).

3. Please add text here for the Oliver Wendell Holmes quotation. Schenck v. United States, 249 U.S. 47 (1917).

4. Gallup, "Death Penalty," (2017), http://news.gallup.com/poll/1606/death-penalty.aspx.

5. Death Penalty Information Center, "States with and without the Death Penalty," https://deathpenaltyinfo.org/states-and-without-death-penalty.

6. The cases referred to in the paragraph: *Virginia v. Black* 538 US 343 (2003); *Brown v. Entertainment Merchants Association*, 564 U.S. 786 (2011); *Brandenburg v. Ohio*, 395 U.S. 444 (1969).

7. Shawn Francis Peters, *Judging Jehovah's Witnesses: Religious Persecution and the Dawn of the Rights Revolution* (Lawrence: University Press of Kansas, 2000).

8. The two cases are *Minersville School District v. Gobitis*, 310 U.S. 586 (1940), and *West Virginia State Board of Education v. Barnette*, 319 U.S. 624 (1943).

9. *Barron v. Baltimore*, 32 U.S. 243 (1833).

10. The *Slaughter-House Cases*, 83 U.S. 36 (1873).

11. *Palko v. Connecticut*, 302 U.S. 319 (1937).

12. If you are interested in reading more on any of the cases we discuss, see Corey Brettschneider, ed., *Constitutional Law and American Democracy: Cases and Readings* (New York: Wolters Kluwer, 2012).

13. *Whole Woman's Health v. Hellerstedt*, 579 U.S. ___ 2016.

14. Thomas Jefferson, "Letter to the Danbury Baptist Association," January 1, 1802, https://www.loc.gov/loc/lcib/9806/danpre.html.

15. *Everson v. Board of Education*, 330 U.S. 1 (1947).

16. *Engel v. Vitale*, 370 U.S. 421 (1962).

17. *Lamb's Chapel v. Center Moriches Union Free School District*, 508 U.S. 384 (1993).

18. Perry Grossman and Mark Joseph Stern, "Goodbye, Establishment Clause," *Slate*, June 27, 2017.

19. *Employment Division, Department of Human Resources of Oregon v. Smith*, 494 U.S. 872 (1990).

20. In *Good News Club v. Milford Central School*, 533 U.S. 98 (2001), the Court ruled 6–3 in favor of the club.

21. The decision that explicitly adopted a preferred position for free speech was *Brandenburg v. Ohio*, 395 U.S. 444 (1969), discussed later in this section.

22. John Stuart Mill, a nineteenth-century English political theorist, put it this way: "However true a doctrine may be, if it is not fully, frequently and fearlessly discussed, it will be held as a dead dogma, not a living truth." John Stuart Mill, *On Liberty* (New York: Penguin Classics, 1982), 103. Oliver Wendell Holmes expressed a powerful faith in the marketplace of ideas in his dissent in *Abrams v. United States*, 250 U.S. 616 (1919).

23. *Gitlow v. New York*, 268 U.S. 652 (1925). Gitlow, the socialist author of a left-wing manifesto, was convicted but in the process the courts incorporated free speech.

24. See Rebecca Barrett-Fox, *God Hates: Westboro Baptist Church, American Nationalism, and the Religious Right* (Lawrence: University of Kansas Press, 2016).

25. *Virginia v. Black*, 538 U.S. 343 (2003).

26. *Brandenburg v. Ohio*, 395 U.S. 444 (1969). For a fine discussion, see Harold Sullivan, *Civil Rights and Liberties* (Upper Saddle River, NJ: Pearson Prentice Hall, 2005), chap. 2.

27. *Texas v. Johnson*, 109 S. Ct. 2544 (1989).

28. *United States v. Eichman*, 496 U.S. 310 (1990)

29. Corey Brettschneider, *When the State Speaks, What Should it Say?* (Princeton, NJ: Princeton Univ. Press, 2012).

30. *Chaplinsky v. New Hampshire*, 315 U.S. 568 (1942).

31. *Tinker v. Des Moines Independent Community School District*, 393 U.S. 503 (1969).

32. *Bethel School District No. 403 v. Fraser*, 478 U.S. 675 (1986); *Hazelwood School District v. Kuhlmeier*, 484 U.S 260 (1988).

33. *New York Times Company v. United States*, 403 U.S. 713 (1971).

34. Bob Egelko, "S.F. Judge Dissolves His Wikileaks Injunction," *San Francisco Chronicle*, March 1, 2008, http://www.sfgate.com/bayarea/article/S-F-judge-dissolves-his-Wikileaks-injunction-3226168.php.

35. Catharine MacKinnon, "Pornography, Civil Rights, and Speech," in *Constitutional Law and American Democracy*, ed. Corey Brettschneider (New York: Wolters Kluwer), see note 10, 661–70.

36. *United States v. Williams*, 553 U.S. 285 (2008) upheld a second.

37. Michael M. Grynbaum, "Trump Renews Pledge to "Take a Strong Look" at Libel Laws," *New York Times*, January 11, 2018, B3.

38. Seth Lipsky, *The Citizen's Constitution: An Animated Guide* (New York: Basic Books, 2009), 222.

39. German Lopez, Ryan Mark, and Soo Oh, "After Sandy Hook We Said Never Again," accessed May 18, 2018, *Vox* https://www.vox.com/a/mass-shootings-sandy-hook.

40. Joseph Story, *Commentaries on the Constitution of the United States* (Boston: Hilliard, Gray, 1833), 3:746; Charlton Heston quoted in "Charlton Heston Rips Media," *Chicago Tribune*, September 12, 1997.

41. *District of Columbia v. Heller*, 554 U.S. 570 (2008).

42. Bruce A. Arrigo and Austin Acheson, "Concealed Carry Bans and the American College Campus: A Law, Social Sciences, and Policy Perspective," *Contemporary Justice Review* 19, no. 1 (2016): 120–41, http://dx.doi.org/10.1080/10282580.2015.1101688.

43. Joseph Story, *Commentaries on the Constitution of the United States* (Boston: Hilliard, Gray, 1833), 3:746; Charlton Heston in "Charlton Heston Rips Media," *Chicago Tribune*, September 12, 1997.

44. *United States v. Leon*, 468 U.S. 897 (1984).

45. *Herring v. United States*, 555 U.S. 135 (2009).

46. *Kentucky v. King*, 131 U.S. 865 (2011).

47. *Kentucky v. King*; *Utah v. Strieff*, 579 U.S. ___, 136 S. Ct. 2056 (2016).

48. Linda Monk, *The Words We Live By: Your Annotated Guide to the Constitution* (New York: Hyperion, 2003), 165.

49. *Dickerson v. United States*, 530 U.S. 428 (2000).

50. *Illinois v. Perkins*, 496 U.S. 292 (1990); *New York v. Quarles*, 467 U.S. 649 (1984); *Harris v. New York*, 401 U.S. 222 (1970).

51. Anthony Lewis, *Gideon's Trumpet* (New York: Vintage, 1989).

52. *Missouri v. Frye*, 132 U.S. 55 (2012); Emily Yoffe, "Innocence Is Irrelevant: This is the Age of the Plea Bargain." *The Atlantic Monthly*, September 2017.

53. U.S. Department of Justice, "Access to Justice," http://www.justice.gov/atj/file/788166/download.

54. "New Study Reveals 'Profound and Dramatic Understaffing' of Rhode Island Public Defender System, National Association of Criminal Defense Lawyers website, November 16, 2017, https://www.nacdl.org/Rhode-Island-Project-Release/.

55. The Death Penalty Information Center has put together a useful clearing house of data, https://deathpenaltyinfo.org/race-death-row-inmates-executed-1976?scid=5&did=184.

56. For a list of executions by state and region since 1976, see https://deathpenaltyinfo.org/number-executions-state-and-region-1976.

57. See Frank Baumgartner, Suzanna De Boef and Amber Boydstun, *The Decline of the Death Penalty and the Discovery of Innocence* (New York: Cambridge Univ. Press, 2011). For an updated list of inmates whose crimes have been exonerated by Innocence Project efforts, see http://www.innocenceproject.org/free-innocent/improve-the-law/fact-sheets/dna-exonerations-nationwide.

58. *Kennedy v. Louisiana*, 554 U.S. 407 (2008); *Atkins v. Virginia*, 536 U.S. 304 (2002); *Roper v. Simmons*, 543 U.S. 551 (2005); *Baez v. Rees*, 271 S. W. 3d. 207 affirmed (2007).

59. Charlie Savage, Eileen Sullivan, and Nicholas Fandos, "House Extends Surveillance Law Rejecting Privacy Safeguards," *New York Times*, January 12, 2018, A1.

60. *West Virginia State Board of Education v. Barnette*, 319 U.S. 624 (1943).

Chapter 5 The Struggle for Civil Rights

1. "Unite the Right Torch Rally Ends in Violence at the Rotunda," *The Roanoke Times*, August 11, 2017, http://www.roanoke.com/news/virginia/unite-the-right-torch-rally-ends-in-violence-at-the/article_c009b930-04d2-5ef1-9d0f-e14f6adc80d3.html; Dean Seal, "UVA Removes Black Shroud from Jefferson Statue After Protest," *Richmond Times-Dispatch*, September 13, 2017, http://www.richmond.com/news/virginia/uva-removes-black-shroud-from-jefferson-statue-after-protest/article_7f15d988-cab3-5121-903f-8cf1f1c59952.html; Vernon Freeman Jr., "Marchers and Protesters Clash at 'Unite the Right' Torch Rally at UVA,"

CBS News, August 11, 2017, http://wtvr.com/2017/08/11/marchers-and-protesters-clash-at-unite-the-right-torch-rally-at-uva/; Dahlia Lithwick, "Yes, What About the "Alt-Left"?," *Slate*, August 16, 2017, http://www.slate.com/articles/news_and_politics/politics/2017/08/what_the_alt_left_was_actually_doing_in_charlottes-ville.html.

2. "Unite the Right Torch Rally Ends in Violence at the Rotunda," *The Roanoke Times*, August 11, 2017, http://www.roanoke.com/news/virginia/unite-the-right-torch-rally-ends-in-violence-at-the/article_c009b930-04d2-5ef1-9d0f-e14f6adc80d3.html.

http://www.richmond.com/news/virginia/uva-removes-black-shroud-from-jefferson-statue-after-protest/article_7f15d988-cab3-5121-903f-8cf1f1c59952.html

http://wtvr.com/2017/08/11/marchers-and-protesters-clash-at-unite-the-right-torch-rally-at-uva/

3. Dominique Mosbergen, "Neo-Nazi Site Daily Stormer Praises Trump's Charlottesville Reaction: 'He Loves Us All,'" HuffPost, August 13, 2017, https://www.huffingtonpost.com/entry/neo-nazi-daily-stormer-trump-charlottesville_us_59905c7ee4b08a2472750701; Mary Dejevsky, "Republicans Denounce Bigotry After Trump's Latest Charlottesville Remarks," *The Guardian*, August 15, 2017, https://www.theguardian.com/us-news/2017/aug/15/donald-trump-charlottesville-republicans-react-bigotry.

4. Samuel Huntington, *American Politics: The Promise of Disharmony* (Cambridge, MA: Harvard University Press, 1981).

5. Smith, *Civic Ideals* (see chap. 2, note 3).

6. Roz Edward, "African American Mayors Association statement on President Trump's Transgender Military Ban," Michigan Chronicle, https://michronicleonline.com/2017/07/29/african-american-mayors-association-statement-on-president-trumps-transgender-military-ban-announcement/. See also, the African American Mayors Association, http://ourmayors.org/.

7. U.S. Census 2015 Poverty Report: https://www.census.gov/content/dam/Census/library/publications/2015/demo/p60-252.pdf.

8. Gretchen Livingston and Anna Brown, "Trends and Patterns in Intermarriage," Pew Research Center, May 18, 2017, http://www.pewsocialtrends.org/2017/05/18/1-trends-and-patterns-in-intermarriage/.

9. Jim Norman, "Confidence in Police Back at Historical Average," Gallup, July 10, 2017, http://bit.ly/2FxklGv.

10. *Pierce v. Society of Sisters*, 268 U.S. 510 (1925); *Romer v. Evans*, 517 U.S. 620 (1996).

11. W. E. B. DuBois, *The Souls of Black Folk* (New York: New American Library, 1982), 220.

12. Garry Wills, *Lincoln at Gettysburg* (New York: Simon & Schuster, 1992).

13. C. Vann Woodward, *The Burden of Southern History*, 3rd ed. (Baton Rouge: University of Louisiana Press, 1993), 72.

14. The Civil Rights Cases, 109 U.S. 3 (1883).

15. Richard Valelly, *The Two Reconstructions* (Chicago: University of Chicago Press, 2004), 2.

16. *Plessy v. Ferguson*, 163 U.S. 537 (1896); *Williams v. Mississippi*, 170 U.S. 213 (1898)

17. *Plessy v. Ferguson*, 163 U.S. 537 (1896).

18. Jessie Parkhurst Guzman, *The Negro Yearbook* (Tuskegee, AL: Tuskegee Institute, 1947).

19. Peggy Pascoe, *What Comes Naturally: Miscegenation Law and the Making of Race in America* (New York: Oxford University Press, 2008).

20. Daniel P. Franklin, *Politics and Film: The Political Culture of Film in the United States* (Lanham, MD: Rowman and Littlefield, 2006).

21. *Smith v. Allwright*, 21 U.S. 649 (1944).

22. *Morgan v. Virginia*, 328 U.S. 373 (1946); *Sweatt v. Painter*, 339 U.S. 629 (1950); *McLaurin v. Oklahoma*, 339 U.S. 637 (1950).

23. *Brown v. Board of Education*, 347 U.S. 483 (1954).

24. Taylor Branch, *Parting the Waters* (New York: Simon & Schuster, 1988), 203.

25. *Heart of Atlanta Motel Inc. v. United States*, 379 U.S. 241 (1964); *Katzenbach v. McClung*, 379 U.S. 294 (1964).

26. *Griggs v. Duke Power Co.*, 401 U.S. 424 (1971).

27. *Sheet Metal Workers v. EEOC*, 478 U.S. 421 (1986).

28. *Adarand Construction v. Peña*, 515 U.S. 299 (1995).

29. *University of California v. Bakke*, 438 U.S. 265 (1978).

30. *University of California v. Bakke* (1978); *Fisher v. University of Texas at Austin et al.*, 579 U.S. 14–981 (2016). For a balanced discussion, see Howard Ball, *The Bakke Case* (Lawrence: University of Kansas Press, 2000).

31. Jon Marcus, "Why Men Are the New College Minority," *The Atlantic*, August 8, 2017, https://www.theatlantic.com/education/archive/2017/08/why-men-are-the-new-college-minority/536103/.

32. Abby Kelly Foster, quoted in Morone, *Hellfire Nation*, 166 (see chap. 3, note 7).

33. Ibid.

34. Rebecca Mead, *How the Vote Was Won: Woman Suffrage in the Western United States, 1869–1914.* (New York: NYU Press, 2004).

35. Donald Critchlow, *Phyllis Schlafly and Grassroots Conservatism: A Woman's Crusade* (Princeton, NJ: Princeton University Press, 2005).

36. Sheryl Gay Stolberg, "Obama Signs Equal Pay Legislation," *New York Times*, January 1, 2009.

37. *Wal-Mart Stores Inc. v. Dukes*, 603 F. 3d 571, reversed (2011).

38. Valentina Zarya, "The Share of Female CEOS in the Fortune 500 Dropped by 25% in 2018," *Fortune*, May 21, 2018, http://fortune.com/2018/05/21/women-fortune-500-2018/.

39. Honorable Henry Cabot Lodge, "Lynch Law and Unrestricted Immigration," *North American Review* 152 (1891): 602–12. See Morone, *Hellfire Nation*, chap. 1 (see chap. 3, note 7).

40. Seung Min Kim and Matthew Nussbaum, "White House Doesn't Deny Trump's Shithole Integration Remark," *Politico*, January 12, 2018,

https://www.politico.eu/article/
donald-trump-white-house-doesnt-
deny-trumps-shithole-immigration-
remark/.

41. On immigration history, see
Rogers Smith, *Civic Ideals* (New
Haven, CT: Yale University Press,
1997); Daniel Tichenor, *Dividing
Lines: The Politics of Immigration
Control in America* (Princeton, NJ:
Princeton University Press, 2002);
on shithole countries, Julie Hirshfield
Davis, Sheryl Stolberg, and T. Kaplan,
"Trump Alarms Lawmakers with
Disparaging Words for Haiti and
Africa," *New York Times*, January
11, 2018. https://www.nytimes.
com/2018/01/11/us/politics/trump-
shithole-countries.html

42. Department of Homeland
Security, Office of Immigration
Statistics, "2015 Annual Update,"
August 31, 2015, https://www.dhs.gov/
immigration-data-statistics.

43. Dayana Morales Gomez,
"Undocumented Immigrants Urge
Others to 'Come Out' in Push for
Reform," *Huffington Post*, July 2,
2015, http://www.huffingtonpost.
com/2015/07/02/jose-antonio-vargas-
undocumented_n_7715162.html.

44. Rakesh Kochhar and Richard
Fry, "Wealth Inequality Has Widened
Along Racial, Ethnic Lines Since
End of Great Recession," *Pew
Research Center*, December 12, 2014,
http://www.pewresearch.org/fact-
tank/2014/12/12/racial-wealth-gaps-
great-recession; Roberto A. Ferdman,
"The Great American Hispanic
Wealth Gap," *Washington Post*, July
1, 2014, https://www.washingtonpost.
com/news/wonk/wp/2014/07/01/
hispanics-make-up-more-than-16-of-
the-u-s-population-but-own-less-than-
2-3-of-its-wealth/.

45. Jens Manuel Krogstad, "After
Decades of GOP support, Cubans
Shifting Toward Democratic Party,"
Pew Research Center, June 24,
2014, http://www.pewresearch.org/
fact-tank/2014/06/24/after-decades-
of-gop-support-cubans-shifting-to-
ward-the-democratic-party/.

46. Heather Silber Mohamed,
"Immigration, Protests, and the
Politics of Latino/a Identity" (PhD dis-
sertation, Brown University, 2012).

47. U.S. Census Bureau data, released
June 23, 2016, http://www.census.gov/
newsroom/press-releases/2016/cb16-
107.html.

48. *University of California v. Bakke*,
438 U.S. 265 (1978).

49. Harvard Chan School of Public
Health and the Robert Wood Johnson
Foundation, *Discrimination*,
November, 2017, https://www.npr.org/
assets/news/2017/12/discrimination-
poll-asian-americans.pdf;

Charlotte Brooks, *Alien Neighbors,
Foreign Friends: Asian Americans,
Housing and the Transformation of
Urban California* (Chicago: University
of Chicago Press, 2009), 194; Cindy
I-Fen Cheng, *Citizens of Asian
America: Democracy and Race during
the Cold War* (New York: New York
University Press, 2013).

50. Kristina Campbell, "The 'New
Selma' and the Old Selma: Arizona,
Alabama, and the Immigration Civil
Rights Movement in the Twenty-
First Century," *Journal of American
Ethnic History* 35, no. 3 (Spring 2016);
Anemona Hartocollis, "Does Harvard
Admissions Discriminate?" *New York
Times*, Oct. 15, 2018, https://nyti.
ms/2yj4UjE.

51. Pekka Hämäläinen, *The
Comanche Empire* (New Haven, CT:
Yale University Press, 2008).

52. Ibid.

53. David Masci, Anna Brown, and
Jocelyn Kiley, "5 Facts About Same-
Sex Marriage," Pew Research Center,
June 26, 2017, http://www.pewre-
search.org/fact-tank/2017/06/26/
same-sex-marriage/.

54. Pew Research Center,
"Changing Attitudes on Gay
Marriage," June 26, 2017, http://
www.pewforum.org/fact-sheet/
changing-attitudes-on-gay-marriage/.

55. Alan Feur, "Justice Department
Says Rights Law Does not Protect
Gays," *New York Times*, July 27, 2017.

56. Ibid.; Alan Feuer and Benjamin
Weiser, "Civil Rights Act Protects
Gay Workers, Court Rules," *New York
Times*, February 26 2018, p AI.

57. See Jaime M. Grant, et al.,
*Injustice at Every Turn: A Report of the
National Transgender Discrimination
Survey* (Washington, DC: National
Center for Transgender Equality and

National Gay and Lesbian Task Force,
2011), 2.

58. For a defense of the North
Carolina legislation and cautions about
LGTBTQX rights, see Peter Shuck, "A
Bathroom of One's Own?" *New York
Times*, May 18, 2016; Jane Clark, "The
True Trauma Trigger that the North
Carolina Bathroom Bill is Designed
to Prevent, *National Review*, March
30, 2016; Michael Lipka, "Americans
Are Divided Over Which Public
Bathrooms Transgender People Should
Use," Pew Research Center, October
3, 2016, http://www.pewresearch.org/
fact-tank/2016/10/03/americans-are-
divided-over-which-public-bathrooms-
transgender-people-should-use/; Jason
Hanna, Madison Park, and Eliott C.
McLaughlin, "North Carolina Repeals
Bathroom Bill," CNN, March 30, 2017,
https://www.cnn.com/2017/03/30/pol-
itics/north-carolina-hb2-agreement/
index.html.

59. "'Bathroom Bill' to Cost North
Carolina $3.76 Billion," AP, March 27,
2017, http://cnb.cx/2FILOZm.

60. See Andrew Gelman, *Blue State,
Red State, Rich State, Poor State: Why
Americans Vote the Way They Do*
(Princeton, NJ: Princeton University
Press, 2008).

61. *Shelby County v. Holder*, 557 U.S.
193 (2013).

62. Michelle Alexander, *The New Jim
Crow: Mass Incarceration in the Age of
Color Blindness*, reprint ed. (New York:
New Press, 2012).

63. Marina Sherriff, "Testimony:
Public Hearings on the Rockefeller
Drug Laws, Special Housing Units,
and Transitional Services for Inmates,"
New York Civil Liberties Union,
December 4, 2000, https://www.
nyclu.org/en/publications/testimony-
public-hearings-rockefeller-drug-laws-
special-housing-units-and-0.

Chapter 6 Public Opinion and Political Participation

1. Maureen Dowd, "Don't Harsh Our
Mellow, Dude," *New York Times*, June
4, 2014, A23.

2. Tom Hiddlestone, "Colorado
Topped $1 Billion in Legal Marijuana
Sales," *Fortune*, December 13, 2016,
http://fortune.com/2016/12/13/colo-
rado-billion-legal-marijuana-sales/.

3. Hannah Fingerhut, "Support Steady for Same-Sex Marriage and Acceptance of Homosexuality," Pew Research Center, May 12, 2016, http://pewrsr.ch/2ajmvN7; a 2016 update from Gallup: "In Depth: Topics A to Z: Marriage," http://bit.ly/1iiDKeI.

4. Cary Funk and Brian Kennedy, "The Politics of Climate," Pew Research Center, October 4, 2016, http://www.pewinternet.org/2016/10/04/public-views-on-climate-change-and-climate-scientists/.

5. Coral Davenport and Eric Lipton, "How G.O.P. Leaders Came to View Climate Change as Fake Science," *New York Times*, June 3, 2017, p. A1; Funk, "The Politics of Climate," 2016. For a good overview, see Justin Fox, "97 Percent Consensus on Climate Change? It's Complicated," *Bloomberg View*, June 15, 2017, https://bloom.bg/2takmKz.

6. "Millennials in Adulthood: Chapter 2: Generations and Issues," Pew Research Center, http://www.pewsocialtrends.org/2014/03/07/chapter-2-generations-and-issues/.

7. Why? Because older people vote and politicians are very unlikely to withdraw benefits from highly mobilized voters. Republicans are unlikely to threaten the program because seniors are their most staunch supporters—and are focused on protecting social security; Democrats are not likely to because they consider it an important program. In short, the political support for Social Security is very strong. Despite forty years of repeating that the program will soon collapse (despite no real evidence for that claim) the program enjoys robust support from both parties.

8. Rebecca Blood, *We've Got Blog: How Weblogs Are Changing Our Culture* (Cambridge, MA: Perseus Publishing, 2002).

9. Authors' compilation.

10. Case Foundation, *Millennial Impact Report 2016* (Washington, DC: Case Foundation, 2016).

11. Michael Jackman, ed., *Crown's Book of Political Quotations* (New York: Crown Books, 1982), 181.

12. Mark Losey, "Why I Am a Democrat," DemocraticUnderground.com, accessed July 24, 2011, http://bit.ly/oHsB2C.

13. Orrin Hatch, "Why I Am a Republican," *Ripon Forum* 41, no. 6 (2008): 8.

14. Scott Jaschik, "Professors and Politics: What the Research Says," *Inside Higher Education*, February 27, 2017, http://bit.ly/2mm2igq; Christopher Ingraham, "The Dramatic Shift Among College Professors That's Hurting Student's Education," *The Washington Post*, January 11, 2016, https://www.washingtonpost.com/news/wonk/wp/2016/01/11/the-dramatic-shift-among-college-professors-thats-hurting-students-education/.

15. Drew Desilver, "Partisan Polarization, in Congress and Among Public, Is Greater than Ever," Pew Research Center, July 17, 2013, http://www.pewresearch.org/fact-tank/2013/07/17/partisan-polarization-in-congress-and-among-public-is-greater-than-ever/.

16. Nolan McCarthy, Keith Poole, and Howard Rosenthal, *Polarized America: The Dance of Ideology and Unequal Riches* (Cambridge, MA: MIT Press, 2016). For a summary of the older debate between elites and base, see Morris Fiorina with Samuel Abrams and Jeremy Pope, *Culture War?: The Myth of a Polarized America* (Pearson, 2010); Alan Abramowitz and Kyle Sanders, "Is Polarization a Myth?" *The Journal of Politics* 70, no. 2 (April 2008): 542–55.

17. See Katherine J. Cramer, *The Politics of Resentment: Rural Consciousness in Wisconsin and the Rise of Scott Walker* (Chicago: University of Chicago Press, 2016); David K. Jones, "Health Reform in the South: Re-Tracing Robert F. Kennedy's Steps in Mississippi and Kentucky," *World Medical & Health Policy* 9, no. 2 (2017). For a skeptical view of Frank's book, see Larry Bartels, "What's the Matter with What's the Matter with Kansas," (paper, American Political Science Association, Washington, DC, September 2005), https://www.thenation.com/wp-content/uploads/2015/04/kansas.pdf.

18. Andrew Gelman, *Red State, Blue State, Rich State, Poor State: Why Americans Vote the Way They Do* (Princeton, NJ: Princeton University Press, 2009).

19. John Zaller, *The Nature and Origins of Mass Opinion* (New York: Cambridge University Press, 1992).

20. Bruce Drake, "More Americans Say U.S. Failed to Achieve Its Goals in Iraq," Pew Research Center, June 12, 2014, http://pewrsr.ch/1lsN29q.

21. A good overview is in Spencer Kimball, "2016 Presidential Statewide Polling—A Substandard Performance: A Proposal and Application for Evaluating Preelection Poll Accuracy," *American Behavioral Scientist*, October 12, 2017, https://doi.org/10.1177/0002764217735622.

22. Pew Research Center, "U.S. Survey Research, Questionnaire Design," http://www.pewresearch.org/methodology/u-s-survey-research/questionnaire-design/.

23. Jon Coupal, "Pernicious Push Polls Pervert Politics," *Orange County Register,* May 19, 2018, https://www.ocregister.com/2018/05/19/pernicious-push-polls-pervert-politics/.

24. David O. Sears, "An Ignorant and Easily Duped Electorate?," *Perspectives on Politics* 15, no.1 (2017).

25. Walter Lippmann, *Public Opinion* (New York: Harcourt, Brace, 1922). On the movement to govern through technical expertise, see James A. Morone, *The Democratic Wish: Popular Participation and the Limits of American Government* (New Haven, CT: Yale University Press, 1998), chap. 3.

26. Angus Campbell, Philip E. Converse, Warren E. Miller, and Donald E. Stokes, *The American Voter* (New York: Wiley, 1960).

27. Christopher H. Achen and Larry M. Bartels, *Democracy for Realists: Why Elections Do Not Produce Responsive Government* (Princeton, NJ: Princeton University Press, 2016); Milton Lodge and Charles Taber, *The Rationalizing Voter* (Cambridge: Cambridge University Press, 2013).

28. The classic statement of this position comes from the dean of public opinion research, V. O. Key, *Public Opinion and American Democracy* (New York: Knopf, 1967); Benjamin I. Page and Robert Y. Shapiro, *The Rational Public: Fifty Years of Trends in Americans' Policy Preferences* (Chicago: University of Chicago Press, 1992).

29. James Surowiecki, *The Wisdom of Crowds* (New York: Doubleday, 2004), xii.

30. John F. Harris, *The Survivor: Bill Clinton in the White House* (New York: Random House, 2005), 331.

31. Tocqueville, *Democracy in America*, 1:189–95 (see chap. 1, note 22).

32. Anna Isaac, "The 10 Most Generous Nations in the World," *The Guardian*, November 10, 2015, https://www.theguardian.com/voluntary-sector-network/gallery/2015/nov/10/the-10-most-generous-nations-in-the-world-in-pictures.

33. Jacob Pramuk, "A Record Number of Women Are Running for the House this Year," *CNBC*, April 6, 2018, https://cnb.cx/2GYwgkz.

34. Waleed Aly, "Voting Should Be Mandatory," opinion, *New York Times*, January 19, 2017, https://www.nytimes.com/2017/01/19/opinion/voting-should-be-mandatory.html.

35. Larry M. Bartels, *Unequal Democracy: The Political Economy of the New Gilded Age* (Princeton, NJ: Princeton University Press, 2008).

36. Jens Manuel Krogstad, Antonio Flores, & Mark Hugo Lopez, "Key takeaways about Latino voters in the 2018 midterm elections," Pew Research Center, November 9, 2018, www.pewresearch.org/fact-tank/2018/11/09/how-latinos-voted-in-2018-midterms/.

37. See, e.g., Rob Griffin, Ruy Teixeira, and John Halpin, "Voter Trends in 2016" (November 2017), https://ampr.gs/2s79roN; Jennifer C. Lee and Samuel Kye, "Racialized Assimilation of Asian Americans," *Annual Review of Sociology* 42 (July 2016): 253–73.

38. Donald P. Green and Alan S. Gerber, *Get Out the Vote: How to Increase Voter Turnout*, 2nd ed. (Washington, DC: Brookings Institution Press, 2008).

39. Rogan Kersh, Michael Lamb, and Cameron Silvergate, *Trust, Leadership, and Social Capital Among Millennials*, (forthcoming 2019).

40. Doug McAdam and Karina Kloss, *Deeply Divided: Radical Politics and Social Movements in Post War America* (New York: Oxford University Press, 2014).

41. Suzanne Mettler, *Soldiers to Citizens: the GI Bill and the Making of the Greatest Generation* (New York: Oxford University Press, 2005); Joe Soss, *Unwanted Claims* (Ann Arbor: University of Michigan, 2002).

42. Doug McAdam, *Political Process and the Development of Black Insurgency, 1930–1970*, 2nd ed. (Chicago: University of Chicago Press, 1999).

43. Sidney Verba and Norman Nie, *Voice and Equality* (Chicago: University of Chicago, 1972).

44. John D. Griffin and Michael Keane, "Descriptive Representation and the Composition of African American Turnout," *American Journal of Political Science* 50, no. 4 (2006): 998–1012.

45. See Pew Research, "The Generation Gap in American Politics," March 1, 2018, https://pewrsr.ch/2GTWX6k.

46. Gary C. Jacobson, "The Triumph of Polarized Partisanship in 2016: Donald Trump's Improbable Victory," *Political Science Quarterly* 132, no. 1 (2017): 9–41.

47. John Kenneth Galbraith, *The Culture of Contentment* (New York: Mariner Books, 1993).

48. Theda Skocpol, "Voice and Inequality: The Transformation of American Civic Democracy," *Perspectives on Politics* 2, no. 1 (2004): 14.

49. Yascha Mounk, "Can Liberal Democracy Survive Social Media?" *New York Review of Books* (April 30, 2018), https://bit.ly/2r9Hclz.

50. See Matthew Hindman, *The Myth of Digital Democracy* (Princeton, NJ: Princeton University Press, 2009).

51. See, e.g., Cass R. Sunstein, *#Republic: Divided Democracy in the Age of Social Media* (Princeton, NJ: Princeton University Press, 2018).

52. Frank Konkel, "Pentagon Thwarts 36 Million Breach Attempts Daily," *NextGov*, January 11, 2018, https://bit.ly/2kcWcfg.

53. See Saul Levmore and Martha C. Nussbaum, eds., *The Offensive Internet* (Cambridge, MA: Harvard University Press, 2010). See, for falsehoods, Rhodri Marsden, "Websites Can Create Outrageous Lies Just for Clicks," *Independent*, July 9, 2015, http://www.independent.co.uk/news/science/websites-can-create-outrageous-lies-just-for-clicks-but-why-and-how-is-this-legal-10379088.html.

54. Pew Research Center, "Wide Gender Gap, Growing Educational Divide in Voters' Party Identification" (March 20, 2018), https://pewrsr.ch/2DIaDzc.

55. Pew Charitable Trusts, *Millennials in Adulthood: Detached from Institutions, Networked with Friends* (Washington, DC: Pew Research Center, 2014): 7.

Chapter 7 Media, Technology, and Government

1. Properly speaking, *media* is the plural of *medium*—usually defined as the way we convey something. We use the term *media*—meaning mass communication—as a singular noun in keeping with the way the language is evolving.

2. Nicholas Trübner, *Biographical Guide to American Literature* (London, Trübner & Co., 1859), p. xciii.

3. W. A. Palmer, ed., *Hazell's Annual* (London, 1908), p. 579.

4. Suzanne Kirchoff, "The U.S. Newspaper Industry in Transition," Congressional Research Service Report, September 9, 2010, https://fas.org/sgp/crs/misc/R40700.pdf.

5. Kristen Bialik and Katerina Eva Matsa, "Key Trends in Social and Digital News Media," Pew Research Center, October 4, 2017, https://pewrsr.ch/2fK9az3.

6. Pew Research Center, "Americans' Attitudes About the News Media Deeply Divided Along Partisan Lines," May 9, 2017, https://pewrsr.ch/2JxqvZm.

7. Pew Research Center, "Digital News Fact Sheet," June 6, 2018, updated June 19, 2018, http://www.journalism.org/fact-sheet/digital-news/.

8. Mark Remillard, "Trump Tweets Fake Video of Himself Attacking CNN Logo," *ABC News (kcrg.com)*, July 2, 2017, https://bit.ly/2ME6PEQ.

9. Shanto Iyengar and Donald R. Kinder, *News that Matters: Television and Public Opinion*, 2nd ed. (Chicago: University of Chicago Press, 2010).

10. Norbert J. Michel, "It's Time to Just Kill the Volcker Rule," commentary, *Fortune*, June 4, 2018, https://for.tn/2sHNrOi; Matthew Yglesias, "Republicans Are Sowing the Seeds of

the Next Financial Crisis," *Vox*, May 31, 2018, https://bit.ly/2JoNybV.

11. Emily Flitter and Daniel Rappeport, "Bankers Hate the Volcker Rule. Now, It Could Be Watered Down." *New York Times*, May 22, 2018, https://nyti.ms/2LmlIuX.

12. David Bach and Daniel J. Blake, "Frame or Get Framed," *California Management Review* 58, no. 3 (2016).

13. Reliable historical counts of U.S. newspapers appear in the Inter-University Consortium for Political and Social Research's "United States Newspaper Panel," https://bit.ly/2JpIcxK (accessed June 2018).

14. Lpinto, "NPR Media Bias Update," *Allsides*, (blog) December 13, 2017, https://www.allsides.com/blog/npr-media-bias-update.

15. Samuel Kernell and Laurie L. Rice, "Cable and Partisan Polarization of the President's Audience," *Presidential Studies Quarterly* 41, no. 3 (2011): 693–711.

16. Erik Wemple, "President Trump Is in Constant Contact with Sean Hannity. How Long until He Turns on Him?" *Washington Post*, May 14, 2018, https://wapo.st/2sS8X3V.

17. Markus Prior, "News v. Entertainment: How Increasing Media Choice Widens Gaps in Political Knowledge and Turnout," *American Journal of Political Science* 49, no. 3 (2005): 577–92.

18. "Excerpts from Trump's Interview with *the Times*," *New York Times*, December 28, 2017, https://nyti.ms/2lfHeWH.

19. Doris A. Graber and Johanna Dunaway, *Mass Media and American Politics*, 10th ed. (Washington, DC: CQ Press, 2017), 171.

20. See, e.g., Michael A. DeVito, "From Editors to Algorithms," *Digital Journalism* 5, no. 6 (2017).

21. Brian McNair, *Fake News: Falsehood, Fabrication, and Fantasy in Journalism* (New York: Routledge, 2017).

22. David M.J. Lazer et. al., "The Science of Fake News," *Science* 359, no. 6380 (2018): 1094–96, https://doi:10.1126/science.aao2998.

23. Jeffrey M. Jones and Zacc Ritter, "Americans See More News Bias," Gallup/Knight Foundation, January 17, 2018, https://bit.ly/2mMUfam.

24. "Brat/Melvin MSNBC Interview" *YouTube*, July 15, 2017, https://bit.ly/2l8oLLD.

25. Nik DeCosta-Klipa, "Harvard Study Both Confirms and Refutes Bernie Sanders' Complaints About the Media," *Boston.com*, June 14, 2016, https://bit.ly/2JuILXg.

26. Chris Cillizza, "Just 7 Percent of Journalists Are Republicans," *Washington Post*, May 6, 2014, https://wapo.st/2tiFwXO.

27. Jack Shafer and Tucker Doherty, "The Media Bubble Is Worse than You Think," *Politico Magazine* 4, no. 3 (May/June 2017): 17–20.

28. See the summary in S. Robert Lichter, "Theories of Media Bias," in *The Oxford Handbook of Political Communication*, eds. Kate Kenski and Kathleen Hall Jamieson (New York, Oxford University Press, 2017).

29. Martin Gilens and Craig Hertzman, "Corporate Ownership and News Bias: Newspaper Coverage of the 1996 Telecommunications Act," *Journal of Politics* 62, no. 2 (2000): 369–86; Graham Beattie, Ruben Durante, Brian Knight, and Ananya Sen, "Advertising Spending and Media Bias: Evidence from News Coverage of Car Safety Recalls," NBER Working Paper No. 23940 (October 2017).

30. "Zell speaking on *Last Week Tonight with John Oliver*," *YouTube*, August 7, 2016, https://bit.ly/2M6SK1M.

31. See, e.g., Isaac Chotiner, "Did the Press Create Donald Trump?" *Slate*, March 22, 2016, http://slate.me/22u0KjM.

32. Elaine Tyler May, *Fortress America: How We Embraced Fear and Abandoned Democracy* (New York: Basic Books, 2017).

33. Jones, "Americans See More," (2018).

34. As one example, see Nickesia Stacy Ann Gordon, "Globalization and Cultural Imperialism in Jamaica," *International Journal of Communication* 3 (2009), 307–31, http://ijoc.org/index.php/ijoc/article/download/246/310.

34a. Gary Langer and Benjamin Siu, "Election 2018 exit poll analysis: Voter turnout soars, Democrats take back the House, ABC News projects" *ABC News*, November 7, 2018, abcnews.

go.com/Politics/election-2018-exit-poll-analysis-56-percent-country/story?id=59006586; and Jens Manuel Krogstad and Mark Hugo Lopez, "Hillary Clinton won Latino vote but fell below 2012 support for Obama," *Pew Research Center*, November 29, 2016, www.pewresearch.org/fact-tank/2016/11/29/hillary-clinton-wins-latino-vote-but-falls-below-2012-support-for-obama/.

35. Figures from *Statistia*, "Leading TV Broadcasters in the United Kingdom in 2017 by Audience Share," June 2018, https://bit.ly/2MolRyp.

36. Andrei Markovits, *Uncouth Nation: Why Europeans Dislike America* (Princeton, NJ: Princeton University Press, 2007).

37. Michael Jetter, "The Effect of Media Attention on Terrorism," *Journal of Public Economics* 153 (2017): 53–48.

38. Iyengar, *News that Matters,* 1st ed. (1989).

Chapter 8 Campaigns and Elections

1. For the conventional political science wisdom that Trump (and Sanders almost) shattered: Marty Cohen, David Karol, Hans Noel, and John Zaller, *The Party Decides: Presidential Nominations Before and After Reform* (Chicago: University of Chicago Press, 2008).

2. Ben Schreckinger, "16 Insults that Redefined Acceptable Political Rhetoric," *Politico*, November 6, 2016, https://www.politico.com/story/2016/11/2016-election-best-insults-230794.

3. John Sides and Lynn Vavreck, *The Gamble: Choice and Chance in the 2012 Presidential Election* (Princeton, NJ: Princeton University Press, 2013); William J. Feltus, Kenneth M. Goldstein, and Matthew Dallek, *Inside Campaigns: Elections Through the Eyes of Political Professionals* (New York: Sage, 2017), esp. chap. 2 ("Political Math: How Campaigns Matter").

4. Christopher H. Achen and Larry M. Bartels, *Democracy for Realists: Why Elections do not Produce Responsive Government* (Princeton, NJ: Princeton University Press, 2016).

5. Pew Research Center, "Most Americans Want to Limit Campaign Spending," May 2018, https://pewrsr.ch/2IppJ2Z

6. David Shribman, "In Canada, the Lean Season," *Boston Globe*, May 23, 1997, A3.

7. Christopher Ingraham, "About 100 Million People Couldn't be Bothered to Vote This Year," wonkblog, *Washington Post*, November 12, 2016, https://www.washingtonpost.com/news/wonk/wp/2016/11/12/about-100-million-people-couldnt-be-bothered-to-vote-this-year/?utm_term=.1078b6dbe1a8; Alexander Keyssar, *The Right to Vote* (New York: Basic Books, 2000)

8. *Citizens United v. Federal Election Commission*, 558 U.S. 310 (2010); *McCutcheon v. Federal Election Commission*, 572 U.S. ___ (2014).

9. "Election Overview: 2018 Data," Open Secrets: Center for Responsive Government, https://www.opensecrets.org/overview/index.php?display=T&type=A&cycle=2018; "Election Overview: 2016 Data," Open Secrets: Center for Responsive Government, https://www.opensecrets.org/overview/index.php?display=T&type=A&cycle=2016.

10. "Incumbent Advantage," Open Secrets: Center for Responsive Government, https://www.opensecrets.org/overview/incumbs.php.

11. James Holman, "Mick Mulvaney's Confession Highlights the Corrosive Role of Money in Politics, *The Washington Post*, April 25, 2018, https://www.washingtonpost.com/news/powerpost/paloma/daily-202/2018/04/25/daily-202-mick-mulvaney-s-confession-highlights-the-corrosive-influence-of-money-in-politics/5adfea2230fb043711926869/?utm_term=.e333789d4b43.

12. Richard L. Hansen, *Lobbying, Rent-Seeking, and the Constitution*, Stanford Law Review 64, no. 1 (2012): 191–253; Richard L. Hall and Frank Wayman, *Buying Time: Moneyed Interests and the Mobilization of Bias in Congressional Committees*, American Political Science Review 84, no. 3 (1990): 797–820; Anthony Fowler, Haritz Garro, and Jörg Spenkuch, "When Corporations Donate to Candidates, Are they Buying Influence?," September 5, 2017, https://insight.kellogg.northwestern.edu/author/haritz-garro.

13. Editorial, "How Super PACs Run Campaigns," *New York Times*, April 27, 2015, A18.

14. "Top Individual Contributors." Open Secrets.org. https://www.opensecrets.org/overview/topindivs.php

15. Emily Nussbaum, "The TV That Created Donald Trump," *The New Yorker*, July 31, 2017, www.newyorker.com/magazine/2017/07/31/the-tv-that-created-donald-trump

16. Donald Trump with Tony Schwartz, *The Art of the Deal* (New York: Ballantine Books, 1987), p. 176.

17. Larissa MacFarquhar, "Where the Small-Town American Dream Lives On," *The New Yorker*, November 13, 2017, www.newyorker.com/magazine/2017/11/13/where-the-small-town-american-dream-lives-on.

18. John Sides, Michael Tesler, and Lynn Vavreck, *Identity Crisis: The 2016 Presidential Campaign and the Battle for the Meaning of America* (Princeton, NJ: Princeton University Press, 2018).

19. Political scientists have documented how Russia also has been meddling in former Soviet Union states since 1991 and in Western European countries since 2014—with little success. See Jonathan Masters, "Russia, Trump, and the 2016 U.S. Election, Council on Foreign Relations," *Council on Foreign Relations*, February 26, 2018, https://www.cfr.org/backgrounder/russia-trump-and-2016-us-election.

20. Lucan Ahmad Way and Adam Casey, "Russia Has Been Meddling in Foreign Elections for Decades. Has It Made a Difference?," *Washington Post*, January 8, 2018, https://www.washingtonpost.com/news/monkey-cage/wp/2018/01/05/russia-has-been-meddling-in-foreign-elections-for-decades-has-it-made-a-difference/?noredirect=on&utm_term=.65abad657362.

21. MacFarquhar, *The New Yorker*.

22. Sides, *Identity Crisis* (2018); Matt Barreto, Tyler Reny, and Bryan Wilcox-Archuleta, "Survey Methodology and the Latina/o Vote," *Aztlan: A Journal of Chicano Studies* 42, no. 2 (Fall 2017) 2011–27.

23. Molly O'Toole and Dan De Luce, "The 2016 Election Turned the Politics of Foreign Policy on Its Head: Clinton Is the Hawk This Year," *Foreign Policy*, November 2, 2016 https://foreignpolicy.com/2016/11/02/the-2016-election-turned-the-politics-of-foreign-policy-on-its-head/.

24. Samuel L. Popkin, *The Candidate: What It Takes to Win—and Hold—the White House* (New York: Oxford University Press, 2012); Ashley Parker and David E. Sanger, "Donald Trump Calls on Russia to Find Hillary Clinton's Missing Emails," *New York Times*, July 27, 2016, http://www.nytimes.com/2016/07/28/us/politics/donald-trump-russia-clinton-emails.html?_r=0.

25. Stephen Anslobehere, Jonathan Rodden, and James M Snyder, "The Strength of Issues: Using Multiple Measures to Gauge Preference Stability, Ideological Constraint, and Issue Voting," *American Political Science Review* 102, no. 2 (2008) 215–32.

26. Samuel L. Popkin, *The Candidate: What It Takes to Win—and Hold—the White House* (New York: Oxford University Press, 2012).

27. Ibid.

28. "US Election: The Team Shaping Donald Trump's Campaign," *BBC News*, August 19, 2016, https://www.bbc.com/news/election-us-2016-37108732.

29. Stanley Feldman and Melissa Hermann, "CBS News Exit Polls: How Donald Trump Won the U.S. Presidency," *CBS News*, November 9, 2016, https://foreignpolicy.com/2016/11/02/the-2016-election-turned-the-politics-of-foreign-policy-on-its-head/; "Election 2012: Presidential Exit Poll," *New York Times*, https://www.nytimes.com/elections/2012/results/president/exit-polls.html.

30. National Constitution Center Staff, "A Recent Voting History of the 15 Battleground States," *Constitution Daily*, November 2, 2016, https://constitutioncenter.org/blog/voting-history-of-the-15-battleground-states/; Larry J. Sabato, Kyle Kondik, and Geoffrey Skelley, "The Electoral College: The Only Thing That Matters," *Center for Politics*, March 31, 2016, http://www.centerforpolitics.org/crystalball/articles/the-only-thing-that-matters/.

31. Wendell Cox, "America's Most Urban State," *Newgeography*, March

8, 2016, http://www.newgeography. com/content/005187-america-s-most-urban-states; Emily Schultheis and Julia Boccagno, "Trump v. Clinton: What the Popular Vote in Each State Shows," *CBS News*, December 19, 2016, https://www.cbsnews.com/news/trump-v-clinton-what-the-popular-vote-in-each-state-shows-electoral-college/.

32. For the classic analysis of the bystanders, see E. E. Schattschneider, *The Semisovereign People* (New York: Holt, Reinhardt, and Wilson, 1960).

33. For a good picture of the divide, see Katherine J Cramer, *The Politics of Resentment* (Chicago: University of Chicago Press, 2016); Adrienne LaFrance, "Three Decades of Donald Trump Film and TV Cameos," *The Atlantic*, December 21, 2015, http:// www.theatlantic.com/entertainment/ archive/2015/12/three-decades-of-donald-trump-film-and-tv-cameos/421257/.

34. Robert Mickey, Steven Levitsky, and Lucan Ahmad Way, "Is America Still Safe for Democracy? Why the United States Is in Danger of Backsliding," *Foreign Affairs*, May/June 2017, 20–29, https:// www.foreignaffairs.com/ar-ticles/united-states/2017-04-17/ america-still-safe-democracy.

35. "Cost of Election," Opensecrets: Center for Responsive Government, https://www.opensecrets.org/over-view/cost.php.

36. David Hawkings, "Wealth of Congress: Richer than Ever, but Mostly at the Very Top, *Roll Call*, February 27, 2018, https://www. rollcall.com/news/hawkings/ congress-richer-ever-mostly-top.

37. Peter Applebome, "Personal Cost for 2 Senate Bids: $100 Million," *New York Times*, November 3, 2012, A16.

38. Nathan Burroughs, "The 'Money Primary' and Political Inequality in Congressional Elections," SSRN Working Paper, 2013, http://dx.doi. org/10.2139/ssrn.2251978.

39. On the Frelinghuysen family and other American "dynasties," see Stephen Hess, *America's Political Dynasties: From Adams to Clinton*, 2nd ed. (Washington, DC: Brookings Institution Press, 2016).

40. Jennifer L. Lawless and Richard L. Fox, *It Takes a Candidate: Why Women Don't Run for Office* (New York: Cambridge University Press, 2005).

41. Richard Fenno, *Home Style: House Members in their Districts* (New York: Longman Classics, 2002)

42. Richard F. Fenno, Jr., *Homestyle: House Members in Their Districts* (New York: Longman Classics, 2002).

43. *Shaw v. Reno*, 509 U.S. 630 (1993).

44. Nina Totenberg, "Divided Court Upholds Nearly All of Texas GOP Redistricting Plan," *npr.org*, June 25, 2018, https://www.npr. org/2018/06/25/623327469/divided-supreme-court-upholds-nearly-all-of-texas-gop-redistricting-plan.

45. Richard Lau, Lee Sigelman, and Ivy Brown Rovner, "The Effects of Negative Political Campaigns: A Meta-Analytic Reassessment," *Journal of Politics* 69, no. 4 (November 2007): 1176–1209; Erika Franklin Fowler, Michael Franz, and Travis Ridout, *Political Advertising in the United States* (New York: Westview, 2016).

46. *Arizona State Legislature v. Arizona Independent Redistricting Commission*, 13–1314–576 _US (2015). The four conservative justices voted against the commission.

Chapter 9 Interest Groups and Political Parties

1. Ryan Struyk, "Poll: Views of Democratic Party Hit Lowest Mark in 25 Years," *CNN Politics*, November 7, 2017, https://cnn.it/2mIhymx.

2. Jeffrey Berry and Clyde Wilcox, *The Interest Group Society*, 5th ed. (New York: Routledge, 2008).

3. Transcript, "Washington's Farewell Address of 1796," at https:// bit.ly/2MFEca4.

4. Paul Herrnson, Ronald G. Shaiko, and Clyde Wilcox, *The Interest Group Connection* (Chatham, NJ: Chatham House, 1998), 20.

5. National Rifle Association web-site, home.nra.org.

6. Professor James Thurber, American University.

7. "Annual Lobbying on Health," Open Secrets: Center for Responsive Politics, https://www.opensecrets.org/ lobby/indus.php?id=H&year=2017.

8. Office of Management & Budget, U.S. Federal Budget, 2019.

9. "Year to Date Summary," Open Secrets: Center for Responsive Politics, https://www.opensecrets.org/lobby/ incdec.php.

10. Carolyn M. Proctor, "Here's What D.C. Region's Top Trade Group CEOs Get Paid," *Washington Business Journal*, October 18, 2017, https:// www.bizjournals.com/washington/ news/2017/10/18/heres-what-d-c-regions-top-trade-group-ceos-get.html.

11. For more on how AARP (and other membership groups) wield influence, see Peter Murray, "The Secret of Scale," *Stanford Social Innovation Review* (Fall 2013), http://ssir.org/articles/entry/ the_secret_of_scale.

12. Nitasha Tiku, "Juul's Lobbying Could Send Its Public Image Up in Smoke," *Wired*, July 16, 2018, https:// bit.ly/2O1jgvi.

13. Charles M. Cameron, Cody Gray, Jonathan P. Kastellec, and Jee-Kwang Park, "From Genteel Pluralism to Hyper-Pluralism: Interest Groups and Supreme Court Nominations, 1930–2017" (SSRN working paper, 2018), https://ssrn.com/ abstract=3087987.

14. Alan Shipman, June Edmunds, and Bryan S. Turner, *The New Power Elite: Inequality, Politics, and Greed* (New York: Anthem Press, 2018).

15. Kay Lehman Schlozman, Sidney Verba, and Henry E. Brady, *The Unheavenly Chorus: Unequal Political Voice and the Broken Promise of American Democracy* (Princeton, NJ: Princeton University Press, 2012), chap. 1; Schattschneider, *The Semisovereign People* (1960), 35 (see chap. 8, note 32).

16. Jenavieve Hatch, "Left Out of #MeToo, Strippers Fight for More Rights in the Workplace," *Huffington Post*, January 23, 2018, https://bit. ly/2KMAaLt.

17. See https://www.wearestillin. com; as of summer 2018, more than 2,800 groups and leaders had signed on to this effort.

18. Mancur Olson described the free rider problem more than 50 years ago in his book, *The Logic of Collective Action: Public Goods and the Theory of Groups* (Cambridge MA: Harvard University Press, 1965).

19. Elise Viebeck, "Insurers Tire of 'Frenemy' White House," *The Hill*, March 27, 2014.

20. Catherine Boudreau, "How Congress Killed Efforts to Slash Subsidies For Wealthy Farmers," Politico, Aug. 20, 2018, https://politi.co/2MEPkHw.

21. Mark Peterson, "Congress in the 1990s: From Iron Triangles to Policy Networks," in *The Politics of Health Care Reform*, ed. James Morone and Gary Belkin (Durham, NC: Duke University Press, 1994), 108, 127.

22. Jack L. Walker, Jr., *Mobilizing Interest Groups in America: Patrons, Professions, and Social Movements* (Ann Arbor: University of Michigan Press, 1991).

23. The estimate comes from James Thurber quoted in Marcus E. Howard, "Penalty Against Lobbying Firm Sends Message," *Los Angeles Times*, November 30, 2015.

24. On the shift to lobbying states, see Dante Chinni, "With Gridlock in Washington, Lobbyists Turn to Statehouses," *Wall Street Journal*, January 16, 2016. The Internet Association's "50-State Government Affairs program" is described on the Association website, at https://bit.ly/2ymRWnz.

25. Eric R. Hansen and Virginia Gray, "Interest Group Density and Policy Change in the States" (Paper, Southern Political Science Convention, San Juan, Puerto Rico, January 2016).

26. See Lee Fang, "Where Have All the Lobbyists Gone?" *The Nation*, March 17, 2014.

27. On e-commerce and regulation see Efraim Turban *et. al.*, "E-Commerce: Regulatory, Ethical, and Social Environments," in Turban *et. al.*, eds., *Electronic Commerce 2018* (New York: Springer, 2018).

28. South Dakota v Wayfair, No. 17-494 (2018)

29. One book-length study of interest groups concludes that "the connection between money and influence is subtle." Thomas Holyoke, *Interest Groups and Lobbying: Pursuing Political Interests in America* (Boulder, CO: Westview Press, 2014), 251.

30. Pew Research Center, "Political Partisanship and Animosity in 2016," June 22, 2016, http://pewrsr.ch/28WYkmr; Coral Davenport, "Climate Change Divide Bursts to Forefront of Presidential Campaign,"

New York Times, August 1, 2016, http://nyti.ms/2af8L2W. Pew Research Center, "Why Do People Belong to a Party? Negative Views of the opposing Party are a major factor. March 29, 2018. http://www.pewresearch.org/fact-tank/2018/03/29/why-do-people-belong-to-a-party-negative-views-of-the-opposing-party-are-a-major-factor/

31. Pew Research Center, "Political Partisanship and Animosity in 2016," June 22, 2016, http://pewrsr.ch/28WYkmr; Coral Davenport, "Climate Change Divide Bursts to Forefront of Presidential Campaign," *New York Times*, August 1, 2016, http://nyti.ms/2af8L2W. Pew Research Center, "Why Do People Belong to a Party? Negative Views of the opposing Party are a major factor. March 29, 2018, at https://pewrsr.ch/2J5d4Qs.

32. Bruce Keith, David Magleby, Candice Nelson, Elizabeth Orr, Mark Westlye, and Raymond Wolfinger, *The Myth of the Independent Voter* (Berkeley: Univ. of California Press, 1992).

33. Rachel Weiner, "The Fix: Black voters turned out at higher rate than white voters in 2012 and 2008." *Washington Post* April 29, 2013. https://www.washingtonpost.com/news/the-fix/wp/2013/04/29/black-turnout-was-higher-than-white-turn-out-in-2012-and-2008/?utm_term=.e7e2866b9144

34. See especially Teresa Amato, *Grand Illusion: The Myth of Voter Choice in a Two-Party Tyranny* (New York: New Press, 2009).

35. The Libertarian Party and Green Party Web sites: https://www.lp.org/elected-officials-2/, http://www.gp.org/officeholders.

36. J. David Gillespie, *Challengers to Duopoly: Why Third Parties Matter in Two-Party American Politics* (Columbia: University of South Carolina Press, 2012).

37. *The Mercury and New England Palladium*, Boston MA. January 20, 1801. Page 2. Emphasis original.

38. R. Kent Newmyer, *Supreme Court Justice Joseph Story: Statesman of the Old Republic* (Chapel Hill: University of North Carolina Press, 1985), 158.

39. For a picture of the spoils system, see James A Morone, *The Democratic Wish: Private Power and American Democracy.* (New Haven: Yale Univ. Press, 1998) chap 2.

40. Daniel Walker Howe, *What Hath God Wrought: The Transformation of America, 1815–1848* (New York: Oxford University Press, 2007).

41. If you're going to read just one book on the civil war: James McPherson, "The Battle Cry of Freedom (New York: Oxford University Press, 1988).

42. See W.E.B. DuBois, *Black Reconstruction in America* (New York: Atheneum, 1992) originally published in 1935.

43. Franklin D Roosevelt, 1st inaugural address, March 4, 1933. Washington DC

44. President William Jefferson Clinton, State of the Union Address, January 23, 1996, Washington DC, https://clinton2.nara.gov/WH/New/other/sotu.html (the era of big government os over); President Barack Hussein Obama, Inaugural Address, January 20, 2009, Washington DC, http://bit.ly/1VG1k9q. (promising to end programs that do not work).

45. Frances Lee, Beyond Ideology: Politics, Principle, and Partisans in the U.S. Senate (Chicago: The Univ. of Chicago Press, 2009)

46. See Katherine Tate, *Concordance: Black Lawmaking in the U.S. Congress from Carter to Obama* (Ann Arbor: University of Michigan Press, 2014).

47. John Sides, Michael Tesler and Lynn Vavreck, *Identity Crisis: the 2016 Presidential Campaign and the Battle for the Meaning of America* (Princeton: Princeton University Press, 2018).

48. Alan S. Gerber, Gregory A. Huber, David Doherty, Conor M. Dowling, and Shang E. Ha, "Personality and Political Attitudes: Relationships Across Issue Domains and Political Contexts," *American Political Science Review* 104, no. 1 (2010): 111–33, http://dx.doi.org/10.1017/S0003055410000031.

49. Party identification averages monthly results from Gallup, Jan-June, 2018. https://news.gallup.com/poll/15370/party-affiliation.aspx

50. See Mark Z. Barabak, "Why the Rise of the Independent Voter

is a Political Myth," *Los Angeles Times*, March 1, 2018, https://lat.ms/2NNMD39. See also, Samantha Smith, "5 facts about America's political independents. Pew Research center. July 5, 2016. http://www.pewresearch.org/fact-tank/2016/07/05/5-facts-about-americas-political-independents/

51. Frank D. Bean, "Changing Ethnic and Racial Diversity in the United States," *Population and Development Review* 42, no. 1 (2016): 135–42, 10.1111/j.1728-4457.2016.00113.x.; Rob Griffin, Ruy Teiseira, and Wiiliam Frey, "America's Electoral Future, *Brookings*. April 19, 2018. https://www.brookings.edu/research/americas-electoral-future_2018/; Dante Chini, "Democraphic shifts show 2020 presidential race could be close." April 22, 2018. https://www.nbcnews.com/politics/first-read/demographic-shifts-show-2020-presidential-race-could-be-close-n868146

52. Barbara Norrander, "The Nature of Crossover Voters," in Robert G. Boatright, ed., *Routledge Handbook of Primary Elections* (New York: Routledge, 2018), ch. 6.

53. Marjorie Randon Hershey, *Party Politics in America*, 14th17th ed. (New York: Longman, 2010), 107Routledge, 2017), 108.

54. Pew Research Center, U.S. Politics & Policy, "Partisan Polarization Surges in Bush and Obama Years: Trends in American Values: 1987–2012," June 4, 2012, http://www.people-press.org/2012/06/04/partisan-polarization-surges-in-bush-obama-years/. Pew Research Center, "Government, Regulation, and the Social Safety Net," October 5, 2017. http://www.people-press.org/2017/10/05/2-government-regulation-and-the-social-safety-net/. "When Americans Say They Believe in God, What Do They Mean? April 25, 2018, https://pewrsr.ch/2vFmEqu.

55. Greg Sargent, "A GOP's Remarkable Admission about Trump and Mueller," *The Washington Post*. March 21, 2018. Joseph Lowndes, "White Populism and the Transformation of the Silent Majority," *The Forum* 14, no. 1 (April 2016): 25–37, 10.1515/for-2016-0004.

For the limits of Trumpism in the Republican Party, see Eric Levitz, "Trump has not transformed the Republican Party – Yet." *New York*. June 14, 2018. http://nymag.com/daily/intelligencer/2018/06/trump-has-not-transformed-the-republican-party-yet.html

56. Henry Olsen, "What Happened to the Libertarian Movement. *National Review*. Nov. 20, 2017. https://www.nationalreview.com/2017/11/libertarian-conservatives-influence-republican-party-shrinking/

57. Bradley Thompson, *Neo Conservatism: An Obituary for an Idea* (New York: Taylor & Francis, 2010)

58. Gallup Polls, January 11, 2018. https://news.gallup.com/poll/225074/conservative-lead-ideology-down-single-digits.aspx

59. See James Feigenbaum, Alexander Hertel-Fernandez, and Vanessa Williamson, "Demobilizing Democrats and Labor Unions: Political Effects of Right to Work Laws. *Brookings Institute*. October 4, 2017. Nate Silver, "The Effects of Union Membership on Democratic Voting. *The New York Times*. February 26, 2011. https://fivethirtyeight.blogs.nytimes.com/2011/02/26/the-effects-of-union-membership-on-democratic-voting/

60. David S. Broder, *The Party's Over: The Failure of Politics in America* (New York: Harper & Row, 1972); Martin P. Wattenberg, *The Decline of American Political Parties, 1952–1980* (Cambridge, MA: Harvard University Press, 1985).

61. On rising party polarization and possible responses, see the essays in Nathaniel Persily, ed., *Solutions to Political Polarization in America* (New York: Cambridge University Press, 2015).

62. Cass Sunstein, "Politics and the destructive cycle of hating," *South Florida Sun Sentinel*, May 23, 2018, www.sun-sentinel.com/opinion/fl-op-american-politics-cycle-of-hate-20180522-story.html.

63. Nancy Roman, "Bitter Fruits of Partisanship," *Baltimore Sun*, October 19, 2005.

64. David R. Mayhew, *Divided We Govern: Party Control, Investigations, and Lawmaking, 1946–2002*, 2nd

ed. (New Haven, CT: Yale University Press, 2005).

65. See Thomas E. Mann and Norman J. Ornstein, *It's Even Worse than It Was: How the Americans Constitutional System Collided with the New Politics of Extremism*, 2nd ed. (New York: Basic Books, 2016); Alan I. Abramowitz, *The Disappearing Center: Engaged Citizens, Polarization and American Democracy* (New Haven, CT: Yale University Press, 2010).

66. On the benefits that proportional representation could bring to the United States, see generally Douglas J. Amy, *Real Choices/New Voices: How Proportional Representation Elections Could Revitalize American Democracy* (New York: Columbia University Press, 2002).

67. The term *core commitments* and an extended argument on behalf of stronger parties is in Russell Muirhead, *The Promise of Party in a Polarized Age* (Cambridge, MA: Harvard University Press, 2014).

68. For a good recent study of citizen groups' influence, in this case on behalf of uninsured Americans, see Timothy Callaghan and Lawrence W. Jacobs, "Interest Group Conflict Over Medicaid Expansion," *American Journal of Public Health* 106, no. 2 (2016).

Chapter 10 Congress

1. Ed O'Keefe, "The House Has Voted 54 Times in Four Years on Obamacare," *Washington Post*, March 21, 2014, A18.

2. Quoted in Sheryl Gay Stolberg and Nicholas Fandos, "As Gridlock Deepens in Congress, Only Gloom Is Bipartisan," *New York Times*, January 27, 2018, A1; see also Thomas E. Mann and Norman J. Ornstein, *The Broken Branch: How Congress Is Failing America and How to Get It Back On Track* (New York: Oxford University Press, 2006).

3. Robert A. Caro, *Master of the Senate: The Years of Lyndon Johnson* (New York: Knopf, 2002), 52.

4. This and following figure at "Congress and the Public," Gallup, https://news.gallup.com/poll/1600/congress-public.aspx.

5. This and previous figure available at Congress.gov.

6. For more along this line, see Mark Twain and Charles Dudley Warner, *The Gilded Age* (New York: Oxford University Press, 1996).

7. Frank Bruni, "An Obama Nominee's Crushed Hopes," opinion, *New York Times*, June 6, 2016, http://nyti.ms/2aC1OIG. On the rising use of filibusters and holds more generally, see Gregory Koger, "Partisanship, Filibustering, and Reform in the Senate," in *Party and Procedure in the United States Congress*, 2nd ed., ed. Jacob R. Straus and Matthew E. Glassman (Lanham, MD: Rowman & Littlefield, 2016), chap. 10.

8. Caro, *Master of the Senate*, 9.

9. Sean Theriault, *The Gingrich Senators: The Roots of Partisan Warfare in Congress* (New York: Oxford University Press, 2013).

10. Trump has called several times for the filibuster to end. See, e.g., Chad Pergram, "Trump Amplifying Calls to Ditch the Filibuster as Midterms Near," *Fox News*, July 3, 2018, https://fxn.ws/2NBN8gM.

11. Jane Mansbridge, "Rethinking Representation," *American Political Science Review* 97, no. 4 (2003): 515–28.

12. A thoughtful treatment is in Daniele Caramani, "Will vs. Reason: The Populist and Technocratic Forms of Political Representation," *American Political Science Review* 111 no. 1 (2017), 54–67.

13. Lawrence R. Jacobs and Robert Y. Shapiro, *Politicians Don't Pander: Political Manipulation and the Loss of Democratic Responsiveness* (Chicago: University of Chicago Press, 2000).

14. David R. Mayhew, *Congress: The Electoral Connection*, 2d ed. (New Haven: Yale University Press, 2004); see also, Jamie L. Carson and Jeffery A. Jenkins, "Examining the Electoral Connection Across Time," *Annual Review of Political Science* 14, no. 1 (2011).

15. Nora Kelly, "Are Members of Congress Overpaid?" *The Atlantic*, June 2, 2016, http://theatln.tc/28NLSaE.

16. David E. Price, "Congressional–Executive Balance in an Era of Congressional Dysfunction," *PS: Political Science & Politics* 49, no. 3 (2016): 485–86, http://dx.doi.org/10.1017/S1049096516000755.

17. Linda Greenhouse, "David E. Price; Professor in Congress Is Doing Homework on Theory and Reality," *New York Times*, February 11, 1988.

18. Political scientists also find roll-call votes compelling, in part as a handy data source (hundreds of votes each session, each with a clear yes/no alternative). Despite years of roll-call analyses and associated theories, we are not very good at predicting vote outcomes. Whips and other nose-counters in Congress perform better than academic models.

19. Gail Russell Chaddock, "In Congress, All Roads Lead to a Conference Room," *Christian Science Monitor*, August 4, 2003, https://bit.ly/2LjGv66.

20. Sarah A. Binder, "Where Have All the Conference Committees Gone?," *Brookings Institution*, December 21, 2011, https://www.brookings.edu/opinions/where-have-all-the-conference-committees-gone/.

21. Public Policy Polling, "Congress Losing Out to Zombies, Wall Street, and . . . Hipsters," October 8, 2013, accessed August 1, 2014, http://www.publicpolicypolling.com/main/2013/10/congress-losing-out-to-zombies-wall-street-andhipsters.html.

22. Joanne Freeman, *The Field of Blood: Violence in Congress and the Road to Civil War* (New York: Farrar, Strauss, and Giroux, 2018).

23. Juliet Eilperin, *Fight Club Politics: How Partisanship Is Poisoning the House of Representatives* (Lanham, MD: Rowman & Littlefield, 2007), 13.

24. Barbara Sinclair, *Unorthodox Lawmaking: New Legislative Processes in the U.S. Congress*, 3rd ed. (Washington, DC: CQ Press, 2007), 71.

25. Eilperin, *Fight Club*; Mann and Ornstein, *Broken Branch*; Ken Buck with Bill Blankschaen, *Drain the Swamp: How Washington Corruption Is Worse Than You Think* (Washington, DC: Regnery Publishing, 2017).

26. Danielle M. Thomsen, *Opting Out of Congress: Partisan Polarization and the Decline of Moderate Candidates* (New York: Cambridge University Press, 2017); Jacob S. Hacker and Paul Pierson, *Off Center: The Republican Revolution and the Erosion of American Democracy* (New Haven, CT: Yale University Press, 2006).

27. See, e.g., Patricia A. Kirkland and Justin H. Phillips, "Is Divided Government a Cause of Legislative Delay?" *Quarterly Journal of Political Science* 13, no. 2 (2018): 173–206.

28. David R. Mayhew, *Divided We Govern: Party Control, Lawmaking, and Investigations, 1946–2002*, 2nd ed. (New Haven, CT: Yale University Press, 2005); Keith Krehbiel, *Pivotal Politics: A Theory of U.S. Lawmaking* (Chicago: University of Chicago Press, 1998).

29. Mann and Ornstein, *It's Even Worse Than It Looks*, 110. See also Sarah Binder, *Stalemate: Causes and Consequences of Legislative Gridlock* (Washington, DC: Brookings Institution Press, 2003).

30. John R. Hibbing and Elizabeth Theiss-Morse, *Stealth Democracy: Americans' Beliefs About How Government Should Work* (New York: Cambridge University Press, 2002).

Chapter 11 The Presidency

1. Joseph Ellis, *His Excellency: George Washington* (New York: Random House, 2004), 194–95.

2. See Corey Brettschneider, *The Oath and the Office: A Guide to the Constitution for Future Presidents* (New York: Norton, 2018).

3. The Editorial Board, "Bigoted and Feckless, the Travel Ban Is Pure Trump," opinion, *New York Times*, June 27, 2018, A12, https://www.nytimes.com/2018/06/26/opinion/trump-travel-ban-supreme-court.html.

4. See for example, Julia Glum, "Some Republicans Still Think Obama Was Born in Kenya," *Newsweek*, July 30, 2018 [reporting that 51% believed the so called birther theory] "Trump Supporters Think Obama Is a Muslim Born in Another Country," Another Country, *Public Policy Polling*, September 2015, https://www.publicpolicypolling.com/wp-content/uploads/2017/09/

PPP_Release_National_90115.pdf. For discussion, see Michael Tesler, *Post Racial or Most Racial: Race and Politics in the Obama Era* (Chicago: University of Chicago Press, 2016), 65–68.

5. George Edwards, *Why the Electoral College Is Bad for America* (New Haven: Yale University Press, 2011).

6. For a classic treatment of presidential power, see Richard Neustadt, *Presidential Power and the Modern Presidents: The Politics of Leadership from Roosevelt to Reagan* (New York: The Free Press, 1990).

7. Paul Harris, Kamal Ahmed, and Martin Bright, "Seeing Eye to Eye," *Observer*, November 16, 2003, 1; David Nakamura and Carol D. Leonnig, "Five Myths About Presidential Travel," *Washington Post*, January 23, 2015, http://wapo.st/1SxP5qa; Alexander Ma, "750 Hotel Rooms, a Personal Chef, and the Nuclear Football: Here's Everything Trump Is Bringing on His 4-Day UK Trip, *Business Insider,* July 12, 2018, http://www.businessinsider.com/trump-uk-trip-what-us-president-is-reportedly-bringing-on-4-day-trip-2018-7.

8. Stephen Skowronek, "The Conservative Insurgency and Presidential Power: A Developmental Perspective on the Unitary Executive," *Harvard Law Review* 122 (June, 2009): 2070–103; Steven Calabresi and Kevin Rhodes, "The Structural Constitution: Unitary Executive, Plural Judiciary," *Harvard Law Review* 105 (April 1992): 1153–216.

9. Ashley Parker, "'Imperial Presidency' Becomes a Rallying Cry for Republicans," *New York Times*, March 31, 2014.

10. Frances Fukuyama, *Political Order and Political Decay* (New York: Farrar, Straus, & Giroux) 2015); Arthur Schlesinger, *The Imperial Presidency* (New York: Houghton Mifflin, 1973); Andrew Rudalevige, *The New Imperial Presidency: Renewing Presidential Power after Watergate* (Ann Arbor: The University of Michigan, 2005).

11. Kirk Scharfenberg, "Now It Can Be Told: The Story Behind Campaign'82's Favorite Insult," *Boston Globe*, November 6, 1982.

12. Tocqueville, *Democracy in America*, p. 126 (see chap. 1, note 19).

13. Eric Talbot Jensen, "Future War and the War Powers Resolution," *Emory International Law Review* 29 (2014–2015): 499, https://heinonline.org/HOL/LandingPage?handle=hein.journals/emint29&div=20&id=&page=.

14. For a description of this episode, taken from White House telephone tapes, see David Blumenthal and James Morone, *The Heart of Power: Health and Politics in the Oval Office* (Berkeley: University of California Press, 2009), 142.

15. Dan Bilefsky and Catherine Porter, "Trump's 'Bully Attack' on Trudeau Outrages Canadians," *New York Times*, June 10, 2018, A5; Tom Newton Dunn, "Trump's Brexit Blast: Donald Trump Told Theresa May How to do Brexit 'but She Wrecked It'—and Says the US Trade Deal Is Off," *The Sun*, July 13, 2018, https://www.the-sun.co.uk/news/6766531/trump-may-brexit-us-deal-off/; Christina Maza, "Donald Trump Threw Starburst at Angela Merkel, Said 'Don't Say I Never Give You Anything,'" *Newsweek*, June 20, 2018, https://www.newsweek.com/donald-trump-threw-starburst-candies-angela-merkel-dont-say-i-never-give-you-987178.

16. Ibid.

17. Ewen MacAskill and Pippa Crerar, "Donald Trump tells NATO Allies to Spend 4% of GDP on Defense," *The Guardian*, June 11, 2018, https://www.theguardian.com/world/2018/jul/11/donald-trump-tells-nato-allies-to-spend-4-of-gdp-on-defence.

18. Michael Birnbaum, "As Trump Hammers NATO Allies on Defense Spending, Military Planners Worry about His '2 Percent' Obsession," *Washington Post*, July 10, 2018; Julie Hirschfeld Davis, "Trump Presses NATO on Military Spending, but Signs Its Criticism of Russia," *New York Times*, July 11, 2018.

19. Louis Jacobson, "Has President Trump Signed More Bills than Anyone? No. (His Count Ranks Last)," *Politifact*, December 29, 2017.

20. Leonard White, *The Federalists* (New York: Macmillan, 1942).

21. Kenneth Mayer, *With the Stroke of a Pen: Executive Orders and Presidential Power* (Princeton, NJ: Princeton University Press, 2001).

22. William Howell, Saul Jackman, and Jon Rogowski, *The Wartime President: Executive Influence and the Nationalizing Politics of Threat* (Chicago: The University of Chicago Press, 2013).

23. For a description, see James Morone, *The Democratic Wish* (New Haven, CT: Yale University Press, 1998), 131.

24. Richard Neustadt, *Presidential Power and the Modern Presidents*, rev. ed. (New York: Free Press, 1991).

25. Martha Joynt Kumar, *Managing the President's Message: The White House Communications Operation* (Baltimore: Johns Hopkins University Press) 2010.

26. Samuel Kernell, *Going Public* (Washington, DC: CQ Press, 2007).

27. Lawrence R. Jacobs and Robert Y. Shapiro, *Politicians Don't Pander: Political Manipulation and the Loss of Democratic Responsiveness* (Chicago: University of Chicago Press, 2000).

28. George Edwards, *On Deaf Ears: The Limits of the Bully Pulpit* (New Haven, CT: Yale University Press, 2003).

29. Barbara Hinckley, *Follow the Leader: Opinion Polls and the Modern President* (New York: Basic Books, 1992).

30. Marc Landy and Sidney Milkis, *Presidential Greatness* (Lawrence: University Press of Kansas, 2001).

31. Harry Truman, *Where the Buck Stops*, ed. Margaret Truman (New York: Warner Books, 1989), 371–2; Landy, *Presidential Greatness* (2001).

32. Stephen Skowronek, *The Politics Presidents Make: Leadership from John Adams to Bill Clinton* (Cambridge, MA: Harvard University Press, 1997).

33. Rose McDermott, *Presidential Leadership, Illness, and Decision Making* (New York: Cambridge University Press, 2008).

34. Quoted in Elliot A. Rosen, "'Not Worth a Pitcher of Warm Piss': John Nance Garner as Vice President," in *At the President's Side: The Vice Presidency in the Twentieth Century,* ed. Timothy Walch (Columbia: University of Missouri Press, 2007), 45.

35. Joel K. Goldstein, *The White House Vice Presidency: The Path to Significance, Mondale to Biden* (Lawrence: University Press of Kansas, 2016).

36. Richard J. Ellis, *The Development of the American Presidency* (New York: Routledge, 2012), 284.

37. Joseph Califano, *Governing America: An Insider's Report from the White House and the Cabinet* (New York: Simon & Schuster, 1981), 431; personal interview with the authors, June 15, 2006.

38. For a fine description, see Matthew Dickinson, "The Executive Office of the President: The Paradox of Politicization," in *The Executive Branch,* ed. Joel Aberbach and Mark Peterson (New York: Oxford University Press, 2005), 135–73.

39. Johnson quoted in Blumenthal and Morone, *Heart of Power,* 8.

40. See the excellent treatment in Lauren A. Wright, *On Behalf of the President: Presidential Spouses and White House Communications Strategy Today* (Santa Barbara, CA: Praeger, 2016).

41. Julie Azari and Jennifer Smith, "Unwritten Rules: Informal Institutions in Established Democracies," *Perspectives on Politics* 10, no. 1 (March 2012): 37–55; Brendan Nyhan, "Norms Matter," *Politico,* Sept/Oct 2017, https://www.politico.com/magazine/story/2017/09/05/why-norms-matter-politics-trump-215535

42. Tocqueville, *Democracy in America* (1966), 122 (see chap. 1, note 19).

Chapter 12 Bureaucracy

1. Missouri Department of Health and Senior Services, *Health in Rural Missouri: Biennial Report, 2016–2017,* October 2017, https://bit.ly/2KI9NGf.

2. "Rural America Comes to HRSA," Health Resources Services Administration, accessed March 2018, https://bit.ly/2noP6py.

3. HealthDataUSA, comparison of past/present county data for seven primary Bootheel counties, https://datausa.io/profile/geo/mississippi-county-mo/.

4. Monmouth University Polling Institute, "Public Troubled by 'Deep State,'" March 19, 2018, https://bit.ly/2pvHOlF.

5. Cruz quoted in Stuart Shapiro, "Government Bureaucrats Are People Too," *The Hill,* November 12, 2015, https://bit.ly/1Sm9Khg; President Barack Obama, First Inaugural Address (see chap. 11, note 18).

6. Megan Brenan and Steve Ander, "Republicans Push Government Agency Ratings Up, But Not FBI," *Gallup,* January 2, 2018, https://bit.ly/2uq2fCN.

7. "Branches of the U.S. Government," USA.gov, https://www.usa.gov/independent-agencies.

8. Office of Personnel Management.

9. Paul C. Light, *The True Size of Government* (Washington, DC: Volker Alliance, 2017).

10. William Riordan, *Plunkitt of Tammany Hall: A Series of Very Plain Talks on Very Practical Politics* (New York: Penguin, 1995).

11. What inspired the term *bureaucracy*? The word comes from France where, beginning in the 19th century, executive offices were termed *bureaus.* French officials governed ("-cracy") through these rule-based organizations rather than the whims of a king or ruling family. Though Americans are more apt to use words like *agency* (Central Intelligence Agency) or *department* (Treasury Department), we have a few bureaus as well—the best-known our FBI, the Federal **Bureau** of Investigation.

12. James Sparrow, *Warfare State: World War II Americans and the Age of Big Government* (New York: Oxford University Press, 2012).

13. See Daniel Carpenter, *The Forging of Bureaucratic Autonomy: Reputations, Networks, and Policy Innovation in Executive Agencies* (Princeton, NJ: Princeton University Press, 2001); Morone, *Hellfire Nation* (see chap. 1, note 27).

14. Erika Lee, "The Chinese Exclusion Example: Race, Immigration, and American Gatekeeping, 1882–1924," *Journal of American Ethnic History* 21, no. 3 (2002): 36–62.

15. Max Weber, "Bureaucracy," in *From Max Weber: Essays in Sociology,* ed. H. H. Gerth and C. Wright Mills (New York: Oxford University Press, 1946), 196–98.

16. Jonathan Adler, "Hostile Environment: Trump's EPA is Having a Hard Time in Federal Court," National Review, October 15, 2018, 18-20.

17. *Federal Register,* July 18, 2018, https://bit.ly/2Lx9LSO.

18. Lisa Friedman and Brad Plumer, "EPA Announces Repeal of Major Obama-Era Carbon Rule," *New York Times,* October 10, 2017, A1.

19. Joseph Schoen, "After 500 days, hundreds of white house jobs remain unfilled by the Trump Administration." *CNBC.* June 4, 2018. https://www.cnbc.com/2018/06/04/after-500-days-dozens-of-white-house-jobs-remain-unfilled.html

20. Kelly left DHS after six months to become White House Chief of Staff.

21. See, for example, Laurence J. O'Toole, Jr. and Kenneth J. Meier, "Plus ça Change: Public Management, Personnel Stability, and Organizational Performance." *Journal of Public Administration Research and Theory* 13, no.1 (2003): 43–64; Alexander Bolton, John M. De Figueiredo, and David Lewis, "Elections, Ideology, and Turnover in the U.S. Federal Government," *Academy of Management Proceedings* 2018 no. 1 (2018).

22. Chris Arnold, "Trump Administration's Latest Strike on CFPB: Budget Cuts," *NPR* (Feb. 18, 2018), at https://bit.ly/2vgYak9.

23. Light, "The True Size of Government" (2017), *op. cit.*

24. Truman quoted in Richard Neustadt, *Presidential Power* (New York: Free Press, 1990), 10.

25. Richard Nixon, *RN: Memoirs of Richard Nixon* (New York: Simon & Schuster, 1990), 352.

26. Glenn Thrush and Erica L. Green, "Trump to Propose Government Reorganization, Targeting Safety Net Programs," *New York Times,* June 21, 2018, A17.

27. Anthony Adragna, Alex Guillén, and Emily Holden, "Pruitt Resigns Amid Torrent of Ethics Woes," *Politico,* July 5, 2018, https://bit.ly/2uDAeHV.

28. Michael Lipsky, *Street-Level Bureaucracy: Dilemmas of the Individual in Public Services* (New York: Russell Sage Foundation, 1980).

29. Joe Soss, *Unwanted Claims: The Politics of Participation in the U.S.*

Welfare System (Ann Arbor: University of Michigan Press, 2000).

30. Emily Willingham, "Is the Freedom of Information Act Stifling Intellectual Freedom?" *Forbes*, November 21, 2015, https://bit.ly/2mzCbAE.

31. Al Gore, *Common Sense Government: Works Better and Costs Less* (New York: Random House, 1995); White House, "President Donald J. Trump Is Reforming the Federal Government, Making it More Efficient, Effective, and Accountable," news release, June 21, 2018, https://bit.ly/2yvBAZL.

32. Allison Stanger, *One Nation Under Contract: The Outsourcing of American Power and the Future of Foreign Policy* (New Haven, CT: Yale University Press, 2011).

33. See Bert A. Rockman, "The Melting Down of Government: A Multidecade Perspective," *Governance* 30:1 (2017), 29–35; and Reed Karaim, "Privatizing Government Services," CQ Researcher 27:43 (Dec. 2017), https://bit.ly/2A4Wa3M.

34. Office of Personnel Management, "Full-Time Permanent Age Distributions" (September 2017), https://bit.ly/2OWow3S.

Chapter 13 The Judicial Branch

1. The cases are *Trump v. Hawaii*; *National Institute of Family and Life Advocates v. Becerra*; and *Janus v. American Federation of State, County and Municipal Employees*.

2. Alexander Hamilton, *Federalist* no. 78.

3. The cases are, respectively: *Citizens United* followed by *McCutcheon v. Federal Election Commission* (on money in elections); *Shelby County v. Holder* (striking down key sections of the voting rights act); *Sessions v. Dimaya* (deporting felon), *Husted v. A. Philip Randolph Institute* (Ohio purge).

4. Congressional Research Service, *The Constitution: Analysis and Interpretation*. Prepared for the U.S. Senate, Document No.1129, August 26, 2017, https://www.govinfo.gov/content/pkg/GPO-CONAN-2017/pdf/GPO-CONAN-2017-11.pdf for data for 1789–2017; SCOTUSblog http://www.scotusblog.com/case-files/terms/ot2017/ for data on 2017–2018 term.

5. Tocqueville, *Democracy in America* (1969) 263–70 (chap. 1, note 19).

6. Justin McCarthy, "GOP Approval of Supreme Court Surges, Democrats' Slides," *Gallup*, September 29, 2017, https://news.gallup.com/poll/219974/gop-approval-supreme-court-surges-democrats-slides.aspx.

7. For a full rundown of the complicated selection methods across the country, see Brennan Center for Justice, *Judicial Selection: Significant Figures*, May 8, 2015, https://www.brennancenter.org/rethinking-judicial-selection/significant-figures.

8. John Schwartz, "Effort Begun to End Voting for Judges," *New York Times*, December 23, 2009.

9. The 70% figure from "Negative Views of Supreme Court at Record High, Driven by Republican Dissatisfaction," Pew Research Center, July 29, 2015, http://www.people-press.org/2015/07/29/negative-views-of-supreme-court-at-record-high-driven-by-republican-dissatisfaction/.

10. "Current Judicial Vacancies: Judges and Judgeships," The United States Courts, http://www.uscourts.gov/judges-judgeships/judicial-vacancies/current-judicial-vacancies.

11. In *Boumediene v. Bush* [553 US 723 (2008)] the Supreme Court ruled that prisoners head in Guantánamo have habeas corpus rights (and cannot be held without charges); in *Hamdan v. United States* [696 F.3d 1238 (D.C. Cir. 2012)] the court ruled that military commission trials do not conform to U.S. law. Subsequent legislation tried to respond to the rulings, though their constitutional status remains unclear.

12. Barry J. McMillion, "U.S. Circuit and District Court Judges: Profile of Select Characteristics," *Congressional Research Service,* March 19, 2014, https://www.fas.org/sgp/crs/misc/R43426.pdf; "Trump's Presidency Marks the First Time in 24 Years that the Federal Bench Is less Diverse," June 11, 2018, *The Conversation*, https://theconversation.com/trumps-presidency-marks-the-first-time-in-24-years-that-the-federal-bench-is-becoming-less-diverse-97663.

13. Charlie Savage, "A Judge's View of Judging Is on the Record," *New York Times*, May 14, 2009.

14. Jonathan Kastellec, "Racial Diversity and Judicial Influence on Appellate Courts," *American Journal of Political Science* **57**, no. 1 (2013): 167–83.

15. Adam Cox and Thomas Miles, "Judging the Voting Rights Act," *Columbia Law Review* 108, (2008), University of Chicago Law & Economics, Olin Working Paper No. 337, University of Chicago, Public Law Working Paper No. 159, Second Annual Conference on Empirical Legal Studies Paper, https://ssrn.com/abstract=977271.

16. Nancy Scherer, "Blacks on the Bench," *Political Science Quarterly* 119, no. 4 (2004/2005): 655–75.

17. S. Welsh, M. Combs, and J. Gruhl, "Do Black Judges Make a Difference?," *American Journal of Political Science* 32, no. 1 (1988): 125–36; Christine Boyd, Lee Epstein, and Andrew Martin, "Untangling the Causal Effects of Sex on Judging," *American Journal of Political Science* 54, no. 2 (April 2010): 389–411.

18. Thomas Jefferson, "Letter to Justice Spencer Roane on the Limits of Judicial Review," in *Writings* (New York: Library of America, 1984), 1425–28.

19. Eleventh U.S. Circuit Court of Appeals, Docket No. 05–00530–CV–T–27–TBM (March 25, 2005), 14.

20. *Dred Scott v. Sandford*, 60 U.S. 393 (1857).

21. The case was *Worcester v. Georgia*, 31 U.S. (6 Pet.) 515 (1832).

22. Paul M. Collins Jr., Pamela C. Corley, and Jesse Hamner, "The Influence of Amicus Curiae Briefs on U.S. Supreme Court Opinion Content," *Law and Society Review* 49, no. 4 (December 2015): 917–44, 10.1111/lasr.12166.

23. Adam Liptak, "Are Oral Arguments Worth Arguing About?," *New York Times: Sunday Review*, May 6, 2012.

24. Lee Epstein and Eric Posner, "The Decline of Supreme Court Deference to the President," *University of Pennsylvania Law Review* 166, no. 4 (March 2018): 829–60.

25. Randee Fenner, "Clerking at the Supreme Court," *Stanford Lawyer* 77 (Fall 2007): 7–9.

26. Senate Hrg. 109–158, Hearing Before the Committee on the Judiciary, United States Senate, 109th Congress (September 12, 2005), http://bit.ly/2aLRGSW.

27. See, e.g., Kevin Buckler and Elizabeth L. Gilmore, "Originalism, Pragmatic Conservatism, and Living Document Judicial Philosophies," *American Journal of Criminal Justice* (2016), online first July 28, 2016, 10.1007/s12103-016-9354-6.

28. "Negative Views of Supreme Court at Record High, Driven by Republican Dissatisfaction," Pew Research Center, July 29, 2015, http://www.people-press.org/2015/07/29/negative-views-of-supreme-court-at-record-high-driven-by-republican-dissatisfaction/; in 2012, a Kaiser Family Foundation poll found that 75% of the public "sometimes lets their own ideological vies influence decisions; only 17% thought decisions were based on legal analysis, "Kaiser Health Tracking Poll—January 2012," KFF, January 1, 2012, https://www.kff.org/health-reform/poll-finding/kaiser-health-tracking-poll-january-2012/.

29. Adam Liptak, "In a Polarized Court, Getting the Last Word," *New York Times*, March 8, 2010; for data on the justices' voting patterns and other details, see Lee Epstein, Jeffrey A. Segal, Harold J. Spaeth, and Thomas G. Walker, *Supreme Court Compendium*, 6th ed. (Washington, DC: CQ Press, 2015).

30. Jeffrey R. Lax and Kelly Rader, "Bargaining Power in the Supreme Court: Evidence from Opinion Assignment and Vote Switching," *Journal of Politics* 77, no. 3 (2015): 648–63.

31. Saul Brenner, "Fluidity on the Supreme Court, 1956–1967," *American Journal of Political Science* 90, no. 56 (1996): 90–107.

32. Frederick Schauer, "Incentives, Reputation, and the Inglorious Determinants of Judicial Behavior," *University of Cincinnati Law Review* 68, no. 3 (2000): 615–36.

33. Thomas Keck, "Party, Policy, or Duty: Why Does the Supreme Court Invalidate Federal Statutes?" *American Political Science Review* 101, no. 2 (May 2007): 321ff.

34. *McCulloch v. Maryland*, 17 U.S. (4 Wheat.) 316 (1819).

35. *Dred Scott v. Sandford*, 60 U.S. 393 (1857).

36. Justice Black in *Connecticut General Life Insurance Co. v. Johnson*, 303 U.S. 77 (1938); William O. Douglas, "Stare Decisis," *Columbia Law Review* 49, no. 6 (1949): 735–58.

37. Steven G. Calabresi and James Lindgren, "Term Limits for the Supreme Court: Life Tenure Reconsidered," *Harvard Journal of Law & Public Policy* 29, no. 3 (2009): 769–877.

38. Abraham Lincoln, First Inaugural Address, March 4, 1861; Roy Basler, ed., *The Collected Works of Abraham Lincoln*, Vol. IV (New Brunswick, NJ: Rutgers University Press, 1953): 262–71, quoted at 268; Alexander Hamilton, *Federalist* No. 78; this argument is developed in Ryan Emenaker, "Repairing the Judicial Void: Modifying the Rights-Rescinding Court," PhD dissertation, Political Science Department, Brown University. Providence, RI (2019).

Chapter 14 Domestic and Foreign Policy

1. Jude Clemente, "U.S. Energy Security Begins At Home," *Forbes*, April 15, 2018, https://www.forbes.com/sites/judeclemente/2018/04/15/u-s-energy-security-begins-at-home/.

2. Lisa Friedman, "Trump Moves to Open Nearly All Offshore Waters to Drilling," *New York Times*, January 4, 2018, https://nyti.ms/2lU0SXW.

3. Aaron Hegarty, "Timeline: Immigrant children separated from families at the border," USA Today, June 27, 2018, https://www.usatoday.com/story/news/2018/06/27/immigrant-children-family-separation-border-timeline/734014002/; Ben Gittleson, "Amid pressure from Trump, Mexico says it's dealing with migrant 'caravan'," ABC News, April 3, 2018, https://abcnews.go.com/International/amid-pressure-trump-mexico-dealing-migrant-caravan/story?id=54197928.

4. Human Rights Watch, "Bahrain," *World Report 2018* (2018), https://bit.

ly/2LQDZ3Z; Human Rights Watch, "Cuba," *World Report 2018* (2018), https://www.hrw.org/americas/cuba.

5. "2018 Treaties and Agreements," U.S. State Department, https://www.state.gov/s/l/treaty/tias/c78676.htm.

6. 2018, countryeconomy.com.

7. ibid.

8. Ari Natter and Mark Niquette, "Trump's Gas-Tax Goes Nowhere in Congress," *Bloomberg News*, February 25, 2018, https://bloom.bg/2ol63l4.

9. Deborah Stone, *Policy Paradox: The Art of Political Decision Making*, 3rd ed. (New York: Norton, 2011).

10. Woodrow Wilson, "The Study of Administration," *Political Science Quarterly* 2, no. 2 (1887): 197–222.

11. Rogan Kersh, "Health Reform: The Politics of Implementation," *Journal of Health Politics, Policy, and Law* 36, no. 3 (2011): 613–23.

12. Linda Qiu, "Claims on Rules That Could Use a Little Regulation," *New York Times*, February 24, 2018, A17.

13. Rebecca L. Haffajee, Robert J. MacCoun, and Michelle M. Mello, "Behind Schedule—Reconciling State and Federal Marijuana Policy," *New England Journal of Medicine* 379 (July 11, 2018): 501–504, DOI: 10.1056/NEJMp1804408.

14. On this sequence, see Mark Bovens, Paul't Hart, and Sanneke Kuipers, "The Politics of Policy Evaluation," in *Oxford Handbook of Public Policy*, ed. Michael Moran, Martin Rein, and Robert E. Goodin (New York: Oxford University Press, 2008), 320.

15. Walter I. Trattner, *From Poor Law to Welfare State: A History of Social Welfare in America*, 6th ed. (New York: Free Press, 1998).

16. Pamela Herd, Melissa Favreault, Madonna Harrington Meyer, and Timothy M. Smeeding, "A Targeted Minimum Benefit Plan: A New Proposal to Reduce Poverty among Older Social Security Recipients," *RSF: The Russell Sage Foundation Journal of the Social Sciences* 4, no. 2 (February 2018), 74–90.

17. A good contrast of Republican and Democratic views of fiscal policy, especially of tax cuts, is in Alexander Hertel-Fernandez and Theda Skocpol, "Congress Makes Tax Policy," in Jeffrey A. Jenkins and Eric M. Patashnik, *Congress and Policy Making in the 21st Century* (New York: Cambridge University Press, 2016), 137–160.

18. Ken Thomas and Darlene Superville, "Trump in Ohio Praises Tax Cuts for Growing Economy," *pbs.org*, February 5, 2018, https://to.pbs.org/2shj9oL.

19. Burgess Everett and Sarah Ferris, "Coming Soon: The Fiscal Cliff to End All Fiscal Cliffs," *Politico*, May 8, 2017, https://politi.co/2ncc17s.

20. For a good insider's recap of the crisis and monetary policy responses, see Timothy F. Geithner, *Stress Test: Reflections on Financial Crises* (New York: Random House, 2014), 258–387.

21. Deficit estimates are from the nonpartisan Congressional Budget Office.

22. John Ikenberry, "America's Security Trap," *Democracy: A Journal of Ideas* 1, no. 2 (Fall 2006), http://www.democracyjournal.org/2/6481.php?page=all.

23. See John Tirman, *The Death of Others: The Fate of Civilians in America's Wars* (New York: Oxford University Press, 2012); Philip Bump, "15 Years after the Iraq War Began, the Death Toll Is Still Murky, *Washington Post*, March 20, 2018, https://wapo.st/2Po0oHG; for an analysis of civilian casualty estimates, see the MIT Center for International Studies, "Iraq: The Human Cost," http://web.mit.edu/humancostiraq/.

24. Joseph Nye, *Soft Power: The Means to Success in World Politics* (New York: Public Affairs Books, 2004).

25. This figure excludes military aid. See James McBride, "How Does the US Spend its Foreign Aid?". *Council on Foreign Relations.* https://www.cfr.org/backgrounder/how-does-us-spend-its-foreign-aid

26. Rob Smith, "The World's Biggest Economies in 2018," *World Economic Forum*, April 18, 2018, https://www.weforum.org/agenda/2018/04/the-worlds-biggest-economies-in-2018/.

27. See Charles Mayer, *Among Empires: American Ascendancy and its Predecessors* (Cambridge, MA: Harvard University Press, 2007).

28. Paul Krugman, "How Did Economists Get It So Wrong?," *New York Times Magazine*, September 2, 2009.

29. Yuwa Hedrick-Wong, "China's Japanese Lesson for Fighting Trump's Trade War," *Forbes*, August 5, 2018;

Bob Bryan, "There's No End in Sight for Trump's Trade War with China, Because 'Both Sides Are More Inclined to Elevate Tension than Blink,'" *Business Insider*, August 6, 2018, https://www.businessinsider.com/trump-china-trade-war-tariffs-no-end-2018-8; "The Trade War Is On: Timeline of How We Got Here and What's Next," *Bloomberg News*, July 6, 2018, https://www.bloomberg.com/news/articles/2018-07-06/the-trade-war-is-on-timeline-of-how-we-got-here-and-what-s-next.

30. See the detailed analysis in U.S Energy Information Administration, "The United States Is Projected to Become a Net Energy Exporter in Most AEO2018 Cases," February 2, 2018, https://bit.ly/2HaoJJY.

31. President Woodrow Wilson, "Joint Address to Congress Leading to Declaration of War Against Germany (1917)," April 2, 1917, https://www.ourdocuments.gov/doc_large_image.php?doc=61; Hillary Clinton, *Hard Choices* (New York: Simon & Schuster, 2014), p. 566.

32. On foreign policy and American exceptionalism, see Kalevi Holsti, *Kalevi Holsti: A Pioneer in International Relations Theory, Foreign Policy, Analysis, History of International Order, and Security Studies* (New York: Springer, 2016), chap. 8.

33. For an introduction to American exceptionalism, see Martin Lipsett, *American Exceptionalism: A Double Edged Sword* (New York: Norton, 1996); Godfrey Hodgson, *The Myth of American Exceptionalism* (New Haven, CT: Yale University Press, 2010).

34. See Alex Weisiger and Erik Gartzke, "Debating the Democratic Peace in the International System," *International Organization* 60, no. 3 (2016): 578–85, http://dx.doi.org/10.1093/isq/sqw022.

35. "Tracker: Current U.S Ambassadors." *American Foreign Service Association*. September 13, 2018. http://www.afsa.org/list-ambassadorial-appointments

36. Arthur Vandenberg, *American Foreign Policy (In the Senate)*, January 10, 1945, http://www.senate.gov/artandhistory/history/resources/pdf/VandenbergSpeech.pdf.

37. Hal Brands, "Breaking Down Obama's Grand Strategy," *The National Interest*, June 23, 2014; both Obama quotes are cited here, https://dukespace.lib.duke.edu/dspace/bitstream/handle/10161/8917/Breaking%20Down%20Obama%27s%20Grand%20Strategy%20_%20The%20National%20Interest.pdf?sequence=1

38. Julie Ray, "World's Approval of U.S. Leadership Drops to New Low," Gallup, January 18, 2018, https://news.gallup.com/poll/225761/world-approval-leadership-drops-new-low.aspx?g_source=link_NEWSV9&g_medium=TOPIC&g_campaign=item_&g_content=World%27s%2520Approval%2520of%2520U.S%2520Leadership%2520Drops%2520to%2520New%2520Low.

39. Ken Waltz, "Why Iran Should Get the Bomb," *Foreign Affairs*, July/August 2012; John Mearsheimer, "Here We Go Again," opinion, *New York Times*, May 17, 1998, http://www.nytimes.com/1998/05/17/opinion/here-we-go-again.html.

40. David Sanger, *The Perfect Weapon: War, Sabotage and Fear in the Cyber Age* (New York: Crown, 2018);

Brian Naylor, "Russia Hacked U.S. Power Grid—So What Will the Trump Administration Do About It?" *NPR*, March 23, 2018, https://www.npr.org/2018/03/23/596044821/russia-hacked-u-s-power-grid-so-what-will-the-trump-administration-do-about-it?t=1533679209110; Kate O'Flaherty, "Cyber Warfare: The Threat from Nation States," *Forbes*, May 3, 2018, https://www.forbes.com/sites/kateoflahertyuk/2018/05/03/cyber-warfare-the-threat-from-nation-states/#1e4d145c1c78; "Russian Government Cyber Activity Targeting Energy and Other Critical Infrastructure Sectors," Alert (TA18–074A), US Computer Emergency Readiness Team, March 15, 2018; "Joint US–UK Statement on Malicious Cyber Activity Carried Out by Russian Government," National Cyber Security Centre, April 16, 2018, https://www.ncsc.gov.uk/news/joint-us-uk-statement-malicious-cyber-activity-carried-out-russian-government.

Credits

Photos

About the Authors
p. xviii: Gabby Salazar; p. xviii: WFU/Ken Bennett

Chapter 1
p. 2: Courtesy of the U.S. Air Force. Photo by Staff Sergeant Aaron D. Allmon II; p. 6: MATTES René/hemis.fr via Getty Images; p. 11: Bettman/Getty Images; p 14. REUTERS/Jason Redmond; p. 17: AP Photo/David J. Phillip; p. 20: Win McNamee/Getty Images, Justin Sullivan/Getty Images; p. 21: MPI/Stringer/Getty Images; p. 29: Danny Johnston/ASSOCIATED PRESS, Ian West/PA Archive/PA Images; p. 33: DOONESBURY © 2011 G. B. Trudeau. Reprinted with permission of ANDREWS MCMEEL SYNDICATION. All rights reserved; p. 34: AP Photo/Josh Boak.

Chapter 2
p. 38: Hank Walker/The LIFE Picture Collection/Getty Images; p. 46: Image copyright © The Metropolitan Museum of Art. Image source: Art Resource, NY; p. 50: National Archives and Records Administration NAID 532935; p. 53: George Caleb Bingham, *The County Election*, 1852; p. 56: © Louis Glanzman; p. 62: Original Photographers: McPherson and Oliver; p. 68: SuperStock/Getty Images; p. 70: Sara Krulwich/The New York Times/Redux.

Chapter 3
p. 79: REUTERS/Lucas Jackson TPX IMAGES OF THE DAY; p. 84: Michael Beiriger/Alamy Stock Photo; p. 89: Copyright © Chad Crowe; p. 92: Bettman/Getty Images; p. 94: A 1949 Herblock Cartoon, © The Herb Block Foundation; p. 95: Nick Anderson Editorial Cartoon used with the permission of Nick Anderson, Washington Post Writers Group–Cartoonist Group. All rights reserved; p. 97: ROB KERR/AFP/Getty Images; p. 100: Andrew Harrer/Bloomberg via Getty Images.

Chapter 4
p. 104: Suzi Pratt/FilmMagic/Getty Images; p. 108: Nathan Benn/Corbis via Getty Images; p. 113: © Steve Gates; p. 114: AP Photo/David J. Phillip; p. 117: AP Photo/Harry Cabluck, AP Photo/Harry Cabluck; p. 118: AP Photo/Javier Galeano; p. 120: AP Photo/Alaric Lambert; p. 122: Mark Peterson/Redux, AP Photo/Texas Department of Motor Vehicles; p. 125: Antonio de Moraes Barros Filho/WireImage/Getty Images; p. 128: REUTERS/Jason Miczek; p. 132: Bettman/Getty Images; p. 136: Gina Ferazzi/Los Angeles Times via Getty Images.

Chapter 5
p. 140: Chip Somodevilla/Getty Images; p. 144: Bettman/Getty Images; p. 145: Paula Bronstein/Getty Images; p. 153: Library of Congress, Prints & Photographs Division, Visual Materials from the NAACP Records [LC-USZ62-116927]; p. 154: AP Photo/File; p. 157: AP Photo/Jacquelyn Martin; p. 161: © Aaron Doster–USA TODAY Sports; p. 164: Photo by Adam Jones, PhD/Wikimedia Commons; p. 168: AP Photo/Matt Rourke; p. 170: Fotosearch/Stringer/Getty Images; p. 172: Frontier Forts.

Chapter 6
p. 183: REUTERS/Robert Galbraith/File photo; p. 192: Copyright © 2006 Jake Fuller; p. 197: AP Photo/Charlotte Observer, Diedra Laird; p. 200: Jessica McGowan/Getty Images; p. 201: AP Photo/The Brownsville Herald, Brad Doherty; p. 209: via YouTube; p. 210: AP Photo/Pablo Martinez Monsivais.

Chapter 7
p. 218: Photo by Chip Somodevilla/Getty Images; p. 220: Ronald Reagan Speaks Out Against Socialized Medicine LP Cover (1961), via Facebook; p. 223: via Twitter; p. 224: Photo by Thearon W. Henderson/Getty Images; p. 226: AP Photo; p. 227: Photo by Paul Schutzer/The LIFE Picture Collection/Getty Images; p. 233: iStock.com/welcomia; p. 234: via FoxNews.com; p. 237: AP Photo/Mary Altaffer, File; p. 242: AP Photo/Eddie Adams, File; p. 243: AP Photo/Bebeto Matthews.

Chapter 8
p. 248: AP Photo/Charles Rex Arbogast; p. 258: AP Photo/Mark Lennihan, File; p. 258: AP Photo/Cheryl Senter; p. 262: Bettman/Getty Images; p. 263: Time Life Pictures/National Archives/The LIFE Picture Collection/Getty Images; p. 269: Hulton Archive/Getty Images; p. 270: AP Photo/Mark J. Terrill; p. 274: Bettman/Getty Images.

from the Pew Research Center; p. 190: Created by OUP based on data from the Pew Research Center; p. 212: Created by OUP based on data from the Pew Research Center.

Chapter 12
p. 402: Source: Office of Personnel Management, U.S. Census Bureau; p. 407: Source: U.S. Department of Energy; p. 410: The Office of Management and Budget; p. 412: American Hospital Association; p. 420: Provided by authors, created by OUP.

Chapter 16
p.436: Source: Gallup; p.457: Created by OUP, data from FiveThirtyEight; p.458: Created by OUP, data from Gallup.

Index

Note: Page references followed by a "*t*" indicate table; "*f*" indicate figure, italicized page references indicate photograph